THE CHURCH OF ENGLAND 1815–1948

THE CHURCH OF ENGLAND 1815–1948

A Documentary History

Edited by
R. P. FLINDALL

LONDON **SPCK** 1972

First published in 1972
by S.P.C.K.
Holy Trinity Church
Marylebone Road
London N.W.1

Printed in Great Britain by
Northumberland Press Limited
Gateshead

SBN 281 02618 1

TO

RONALD JOHN WEBB

THE PARISH PRIEST
LITTLE ILFORD
DIOCESE OF CHELMSFORD

CONTENTS

ACKNOWLEDGEMENTS

I am indebted to the staff of the following libraries and institutions for the help they have given me in the preparation of this book:

Sion College Library, London
Lambeth Palace Library, London
The British Museum, London
Great Yarmouth Reference Library
The Borough Archivist, Great Yarmouth
Frank Sayer, the Colman Rye Library, Norwich
Norwich Central Reference Library
U.S.P.G. Library, London
C.M.S. Library, London
Church House Library, London
The Dean and Chapter Library, Norwich
King's College Library, London
S.P.C.K., London

Thanks are due to the following for permission to quote from copyright sources:

Curtis Brown Ltd: *Cosmo Gordon Lang*, by J. G. Lockhart

Jonathan Cape Ltd: *England in the 20th Century, 1914–1963*, by David Thomson

The Church Union: a letter

Clarendon Press: *Letters of Sydney Smith*, by N. C. Smith

Darton, Longman & Todd: *The One-sided Reciprocity*, by Peter Hinchliff

Dean and Chapter of Durham Cathedral: several letters

J. M. Dent & Sons Ltd: *The Memoirs of Sir Thomas Fowell Buxton*

Eyre & Spottiswoode (Publishers) Ltd: *English Historical Documents*, vol. XII, by G. M. Young and W. D. Handcock

Faith Press Ltd: *A. C. Headlam*, by R. C. D. Jasper

The General Synod of the Church of England: extracts from Church Assembly publications

The General Synod of the Church of Ireland: two passion prayers

Earl Halifax: statements from *Conversations at Malines, 1921–5*, original document edited by Lord Halifax

Hodder & Stoughton Ltd: *An Introduction to Canon Law*, by E. W. Kemp; *The Religious Life of London*, by Mudie-Smith

Industrial Christian Fellowship: *Malvern and After*

Longman Group Ltd: *The Proceedings of C.O.P.E.C.*

Longman Group Ltd and David McKay Company, Inc.: *English History in the 19th Century and After*, by G. M. Trevelyan

Macmillan & Co. Ltd: *Kikuyu*, by R. T. Davidson; *Life of A. C. Tait*, by R. T. Davidson and W. Benham

John Murray (Publishers) Ltd: *Life and Correspondence of Arthur Penryn Stanley, D.D.*, by R. E. Prothero and C. C. Bradley

Oxford University Press: *Documents on Christian Unity*, by G. K. A. Bell; *William Temple*, by F. A. Iremonger

Mrs C. Sandiland: *Retrospect of an Unimportant Life*, by H. H. Henson

S.C.M. Press Ltd: *The Church of England, 1900–1965*, by Roger Lloyd

Mrs Frances Temple and the Editor of *Theology*: an article by Archbishop William Temple entitled "Theology Today" (November 1939)

Yorkshire Post

INTRODUCTION

BRITAIN 1815–1948

Peace and War The Congress of Vienna concluded the Napoleonic Wars and British participation in a Europe at war. Apart from distant campaigns in the Crimea, and colonial entanglements in India, the Sudan, and South Africa, Britain was to experience a century of peace. The new century presented a new phenomenon—the world war. From the Treaty of Versailles, which closed the first cosmic conflict, to the invasion of Poland which initiated the second conflagration there was a mere twenty-year interval—two decades of wars and rumours of war. The second half of the twentieth century began in hope with the emergence of the United Nations, marking the beginning of a new experiment in international co-operation.

Reform Radicalism was a child of Revolution. On the European mainland the effects of the French Revolution resulted in the "Year of Revolutions"; the unification of national states; the death of the Austrian Empire; and the collapse of Tsarist Russia. As Europe struggled to find an identity between the two extremes of reaction and revolution, English radicalism, starting from small beginnings, adapted the traditional and flexible national institutions of government and society. Liberty was promoted rather than snatched: the Monarchy, Parliament, Church, municipal corporations, courts, and universities were all reformed rather than abolished. In turn radicalism was replaced by socialism, and this was itself adapted as a British compromise differing from its continental models.

Prosperity Britain's wealth was derived from her agricultural accomplishments and industrial inventiveness. It had grown with the demands of the European war and increased as a colonial empire opened up new markets. The nineteenth century was a time of building, manufacturing, spending, development, and trading, and, as Europe convulsed, the United States of America matured. Towards the end of the century the price of prosperity could be counted: depression, industrial unrest, socialism, war, strikes, unemployment, more war, and nationalization. After the rigours of war-time economies and the disappearance of the uninhibited rich came the experience of an affluent society with its welfare state.

Social Conscience Morality was the virtue of the Age of Victoria and poverty was the unpardonable sin. Morality had been carefully nurtured by the Evangelicals during the Bacchanalian era of the Regency, then under the hand of the Queen and her exemplary Consort it flowered. The conscience of the English gentlefolk, stirred by the fervour of the Radicals, led the battle against slavery, human exploitation, depravity and destitution, plagues and epidemics, intolerance and prejudice. The principle of *laissez-faire* was purported to be scientific, based on the teaching of the Classical Economists and the Manchester School, but its true source was to be found in the popular estimate of the Englishman as honest, dutiful, and conscientious. But the estimate was over-optimistic. Progress and improvement were purchased with slums, lock-outs and unemployment, the scars of mechanized warfare, and the agony of Ireland. *Laissez-faire* died slowly, the Six Acts and Peterloo were mirrored in the *British Gazette*, and the "two nations" were badly mixed rather than integrated in the welfare state. Only slowly was the Poor Law mentality of regarding poverty as sin displaced by the socialist belief in poverty as the shame of a nation.

Liberalism Rationalism was allied to revolution. Tom Paine had preached both. The freedom of the mind led to freedom of inquiry into science, religion, and politics. Any assertion of authority was viewed as a denial of truth as the materialist's mind turned against inherited doctrines which were not empirically verifiable. Paradoxically the rejection of authority led to the setting up of other infallible oracles—Darwin, the Bible, and Free Trade. The sweeping away of the old order with the outbreak of the First World War led to two extremes. There was a longing for the old forms and beliefs bound up with the traditional institutions set against a destructive modernism looking for new creeds and ideologies. This in turn was dwarfed by the birth of the atomic age and the technocratic society where knowledge became synonymous with wealth.

THE CHURCH OF ENGLAND 1815–1948

The Church of England was caught up in the vortex of social change and remained, surprisingly to some, afloat. The Protestant succession had preserved both Church and nation from popery, and the defensive alliance through the eighteenth century had held fast up to the Tory supremacy at the beginning of the nineteenth. Limited religious toleration for dissenters; the enforced silence of Convocation after the Bangorian controversy; and latitudinarianism all helped towards peace and serenity on the ecclesiastical scene. In saying that "The Church, as it now stands, no human power can save", Thomas Arnold mistook the spirit of the Age of Reform The reform of the body politic brought in its wake the reform of the ecclesiastical body resulting in new bishoprics; new churches; new professional standards in the clergy; and the essential corollary of increased discipline.

The historic character of the Church of England forced upon it the roles of custodian to a large number of ancient buildings; guardian of manifold antique offices and sinecures; and recipient of a large revenue. The parochial organization and the unequal distribution of the Church's wealth made it ill equipped to cope with the population growth of the nineteenth century. As a corporation established by law, it was prone to investigation by a reforming Parliament. The establishment of the Ecclesiastical Commission was to assist the English Church in tackling the immense problems brought about by the Industrial Revolution and the fall in the infant mortality rate. It was in keeping with the spirit of the age to assess the significance of the national Church within the social structure, and Parliament undertook this obligation as a matter of mere utility.

It was in protest at the reforming zeal of the Whigs that the Oxford Movement arose with its apologists and revivalists. Thus the relation of Church and State underwent drastic revision, and Parliament was brought face to face with the apostolic ministry, a doctrinal orthodoxy, and a Catholic Church of England. The Evangelicals, who found themselves more and more in conflict with the Catholic movement, were drawn to Erastianism and became the exponents of conservative causes and attitudes.

The Church of England was fortunate in the leaders who engineered the manipulation of the Church by the State, when it was all too easy for a conflict to occur. The eirenic qualities of Howley and the business acumen of Blomfield were recognized by both sides, and to these two, more than to any others, did the reorganization of the Church owe its satisfactory conclusion. The essential weakness of the Victorian approach to the social function of the Church was to view it in terms of buildings, money, and clergy. It might be argued, with some justification, that the legacy of ruinous churches, pluralism, absenteeism, and poor curates, forced these priorities on the leaders of Church and Parliament. Nevertheless, the cost of new churches, the restoration of old churches, the erection of schools, the establishment of diocesan funds, all constituted a failure to grapple with the infidelity of the new working class. The failure became apparent in 1851, was confirmed in 1904, and acknowledged in 1945.

Immediately after the Napoleonic Wars, Parliament was able to accept responsibility for the provision of new churches in populous areas. As legalized dissent made itself felt politically the Government withdrew, leaving the different Churches to promote their own building programmes to the best of their abilities. The Victorian middle class philanthropy, the munificence of the *nouveau riche*, and the moral earnestness of the aristocracy, provided the capital to erect churches, schools, and charitable institutions. The labours of successive bishops of London, for example, to enlarge their diocesan building funds was nothing short of Herculean. However, the provision of buildings and the gradual abolition of pew rents did not provide the panacea for the absence of the working man. The continued existence of the Ecclesiastical Commissioners did mean that the Church's ministers were not so sharply divided into "two nations". Again, the levelling up of clerical incomes and the redistribution of revenue was at a high price. The amputation of a large proportion of the income of cathedral corporations was to stunt their growth, and this proved to be a serious handicap in adapting these institutions to changing needs.

A spiritual revival within the Church of England, marked by the emergence of Methodism, the Evangelical movement, and the Oxford School, reawakened the notion that the Church, although a corporate entity, was fundamentally distinct from other institutions. This awareness, coupled with the Whigs' desire to reform the ancient institutions of the Realm, meant that the principle of church establishment was placed under scrutiny. Although Royal Supremacy was not generally doubted until the Tractarians rocked the boat, its application in spiritual matters was called into question as the decades passed. Gorham, Hampden, the Irish Church, and the Jerusalem bishopric all provoked storms of protest by loyal churchmen against loyal legislators.

The particular form of episcopal nomination by the Crown enjoyed by the Church of England, together with the subsequent confirmation, encouraged a twofold development. On the one hand, the colonial Churches were readily able to redefine episcopacy in an ecclesiastical sense when the legal ties were loosened, whereas on the other, the Established Church continued to respect the system of *congé d'élire*. The history of ecclesiastical government in our period is an attempt to find a satisfactory form of authority within the Church without destroying the connection with the State. The Evangelicals, led by the crusading spirit of Lord Shaftesbury, tended to be Erastian and to look for authority in the legal, the Tractarians vindicated the apostolic ministry and sought it in religious tradition. Between the two was a growing demand for a voice in the State's handling of the Church's affairs, and the revival of Convocation was regarded as the obvious solution. Primarily this demand was a semi-conscious desire for a suitable means of protest against the activity of the secular authorities, but it was to evolve into a desire for a constructive instrument of self-determining ecclesiastical government.

The revival of the Convocations, both of Canterbury and York, revealed the shortcomings of these traditional assemblies for the government of the Church in a new era. Their composition was felt to be too narrow, and the growing recognition that the laity had a right to be heard demanded some means of widening the franchise. In some measure the decreasing use of the courts in religious controversies might be attributed to this constitutional development.

The system of ecclesiastical discipline in the Church of England was established by law, and was of ancient origin. The administration of ecclesiastical law was principally in the hands of the judges and advocates of the Doctors' Commons, and the judges of the Archbishops' Courts were always selected from this association, founded in 1511. Once again changing circumstances had thrown the traditional system into chaos. In 1832 it was calculated that there were 386 ecclesiastical courts in England which dealt with matters of canon law, matrimony, and probate. The Archdeacon's Court had fallen into disuse in the eighteenth century owing to the decrease in the number of disciplinary charges against the laity, and the preference for resorting to the Diocesan Court in the first instance. This latter administered ecclesiastical law within the diocese, and also heard appeals from the Archdeacon's Court, its judge being the Bishop or his Chancellor. From the Diocesan Courts, appeal lay to the Provincial Court of Canterbury, known as the Court of Arches, and to the Provincial Court of York. The final Court of Appeal in causes ecclesiastical was the Court of Delegates set up by 25 Henry VIII, c. 19 to hear appeals which had formerly gone to Rome. A commission of puisne judges and a number of civil lawyers, generally drawn from the advocates of Doctors' Commons, was appointed for each separate case. Leoline Jenkins had, without success, attempted to convert the Commission into a permanent body in the seventeenth century. General dissatisfaction with the many Courts of Peculiars, the lack of continuity in the High Court of Delegates, and the supposed inertia of the

Doctors' Commons, led to Parliamentary investigations and subsequent reform.

The reform of the ecclesiastical system, was, as we have seen, concomitant with the adaptation of most other national institutions with the widening of the franchise. Unfortunately, the zeal of the legislators blinded them to the singular nature of canon law which distinguished it from statute law. The abolition of the Doctors' Commons denied both Church and State a continuing tradition of trained ecclesiastical lawyers. Formerly the abuse of the exercise of appellate jurisdiction of the High Court of Delegates was prevented by the inclusion of advocates from the Doctors' Commons, but the Judicial Committee of the Privy Council, even with episcopal members, was not so immune. The civil judges were hardly competent to interpret the formularies of the Church in such a manner as would commend their decisions to the several parties within the Church. The growing consciousness of the Church of England of having an inherent spiritual authority as distinct from the supremacy of the Crown, led to an antagonism between the law courts and churchmen. This was inflamed by the fierce battles between ritualists and Evangelicals, neologists and conservatives. The question of appellate jurisdiction remained unsolved, the Lincoln judgment evading this particular issue. The principle of authority in doctrine, ritual, and practice, remained undefined since the Church of England was committed neither to an autocratic episcopacy nor to an Erastian bureaucracy.

The relationship between Church and State was rendered more difficult by the Irish question which bedevilled English politics for almost a century. The Anglican Church in Ireland was established by law: its bishops chosen by the Crown; the Book of Common Prayer enforced by statute law; and its councils subjected to Parliament. The rational attack on its temporalities, an act of political expediency, was seen as a prelude to an attack on its English counterpart. What made Keble's *Assize Sermon* important was its realization that Church and State could no longer be viewed as identical. In effect, the disestablishment of the Irish and Welsh Churches was the necessary outcome of the recognition of the existence of nonconformity implicit in the repeal of the Test and Corporation Acts. Parliamentary legislation on ecclesiastical matters had repercussions within the political arena, with hostility between Lords and Commons, Liberals and Conservatives, reaching new heights in the disestablishment Bills.

The Church's willingness to fight the supposed misuse of the Erastian principle was due in part to the fear of all institutions of outside interference, and the mere assumption that the Church could have interests which were not the concern of the State was a sign of the climatic change. A further factor was the rejection by the legislators of the scriptural basis of social morality. The divorce Bills of 1857 and 1920 were introduced into Parliament in the knowledge that churchmen would oppose them as submissions to decadence and irreligion. However, in the event of their becoming Acts of Parliament, the Government was compelled to recognize the conscientious demands of the clergy, and such provision was in itself a denial of the just claims of a Royal Supremacy. Later, the illegal action of the episcopate after the rejection of the Deposited Prayer Book was a further example of the practical denial of the theory of the Royal Supremacy in England. In spite of multifarious commissions on Church and State the question remained unsettled, the apathetic attitude of either side stemming, no doubt, from the retreating Christian influence within society as a whole.

The retreat from Christianity also took place on the academic and intellectual plane. With the decrease in the influence of the Latitudinarians and the rise of the Evangelicals the Church of England was unprepared for the advance of Liberalism, biblical criticism, and the supremacy of the physical sciences. The Evangelical movement had succeeded in bringing to light the ethical implications of Christianity, but in so doing had departed from the tradition of Anglicanism in promoting the Bible to a position above reason and the creeds. The Victorian devotion to Scripture as the infallible oracle of God had important results, since it encouraged a false fundamentalism. Veering between popery and neology the Evangelicals brought the larger proportion of the clergy and laity of the Church of England into collision with both Puseyites and Liberals.

The Puseyites were not unlike the Evangelicals in appealing to tradition in order to erect a bulwark against the advances of liberalism. The difference lay in numbers and identity, the former being a minority associated with the un-English Papists. The conflict between the two was eclipsed by the greater engagement of the Church of England with its own liberal thinkers. The Broad Churchmen had ceased to count as a numerical entity at the end of the eighteenth century, but the nineteenth century saw a small number of brilliant minds working for the reconciliation of Christian verity with scientific surety. Neither the Tractarians nor the Evangelicals could cope with the incursions of literary criticism, and the attempts of the Liberals to compromise met with hostility. When the third generation of Tractarians attempted a reconciliation of the Catholic Faith with modern knowledge it was seen as an act of betrayal. Yet even the *Lux Mundi* essayists were slow and limited in their progress, not daring to subject the New Testament to the radical criticism which had been applied to the Old. Gore and his friends became the most vocal in the attack on the Modernist interpretation of the creeds, becoming rather what Liddon had been a few decades before. The Church of England never completely came to terms with the new rationalism, and the controversies around *Essays and Reviews* and *Lux Mundi* were reflected in those centred on *Foundations* and the Girton Conference.

The situation was further aggravated by the revival of the natural sciences. Not that this was anything new; indeed the eighteenth century had an equal claim with the twentieth to be the century of scientific discovery. What was notable was the self-assurance of the scientific popularizers coming at the moment when the inherited beliefs of the Church were undergoing transformation at the hands of liberal theologians. The empirical evidence of the geologist destroyed the infallible Bible whilst the hypotheses of Darwin and his allies shattered the moral presuppositions of Victorian household religion. Again, it was individuals who searched among the debris of discarded theological assumptions for the essential elements of revealed religion, and it was unfortunate, perhaps, that the most eminent of the reconstructors were Broad Churchmen of doubtful orthodoxy.

The controversies within and without the Church of England led to a deep-seated desire for a definitive statement of belief. This was itself impossible, and even the spectrum of theological opinion which a commission could produce would be found to be dated by succeeding generations. The *Report of the Archbishops' Commission on Doctrine in the Church of England* marked the end of one theological era, and after the Second World War the Church was faced with the atomic age and had no decisive gospel in her hands.

The Industrial Revolution and the Enclosure Movement assisted the break-up of the old communal life of the village and encouraged the migration to the cities with their factories and mills. It was this aspect of the manufacturing and agrarian changes, together with the trading and colonial links with overseas countries, that led to the flood of emigrants from Britain in the nineteenth century. Where the British settled in Australasia, Canada, and South Africa, the religion of the fatherland found a footing. As the nations crossed frontiers and discovered new lands, the chaplains accompanied the traders, soldiers, and convicts, and, in a short while, forged ahead with the pioneers in front of the officials and administrators. The care of the British overseas extended to the care of the natives, and before long the scope of overseas missionary work called for a change in the policy of the British Government. The chaplains were often discouraged, but not always obstructed, from converting the heathen, though their primary duty as salaried ministers was to provide for the needs of the factory and the garrison.

The nineteenth century saw colonial expansion as the extension of the sovereignty of the Crown, and distance, in theory, did not weaken the hold of Parliament over the old or new subject. Parliamentary interest in the colonies increased as time passed, since imperialism had become a Conservative war-cry, and the nation believed it to be beneficial for all mankind to share the fruits of civilization and Christianity. The expansionist policies of other European nations exemplified by the "grab for Africa" did much to stimulate pride in the new overseas possessions. This expansionist interest had a profound effect on the missionary work of the Churches, for churchmen generally came to regard the conversion of the heathen in the overseas dominions as a matter of priority. It was natural to subscribe to the missionary work of the Church abroad, and to neglect the pressing evangelistic problems at home.

The political interests in the colonies had an adverse effect on the Church overseas also. Since the Church of England was formally constituted and governed within the British Isles, it was logical that its representatives should also remain cognizant of the just claims of the Crown when serving beyond the bounds of Britain. The independence of the colonial bishoprics from the control of the Government, especially the Foreign Office, came a little unexpectedly, and it was with surprise that the Church of England found itself the mother of new provinces. The sharp readjustment of the relationship between Parliament and the Anglican Church abroad was due, not only to distance, alien conditions, and the independent spirit of the missionaries, but also to the evolving autonomy of the colonies themselves.

The association of colonialism with mission was not intrinsically good or bad. The energies of the Government furthering trade and prestige provided a vehicle for the Christian gospel, though very often the missionary opened up the way for the Government agents. The prime interest of the colonizer was trade, and the Churches tended to be associated in the minds of native populations with the evils of the white infiltrators. But the Victorian Church did had a social conscience, and the necessary corollary to preaching the gospel in some areas was to fight the slave trade, and occasionally to remind the home Government of its obligations. Furthermore, the mission field was the sphere of operation for men and women of a high calibre, and in spite of the limitations of the thoroughly English missionary, native populations often enjoyed the provision of education, medicine, and instruction, which traders and officials were not always able to give.

A further consequence of the missionary expansion of the Church of England was the end of its period of "splendid isolation", when it became the centre of a network of dioceses and provinces. For many decades the Church of England was to continue to provide leadership, financial support, and guidance for many of these younger Churches. The development of the Lambeth Conference was symptomatic of this state of affairs, and the emergence of the Anglican Communion was to have great repercussions in the strategy of mission and in the movement towards Christian reunion.

The movement towards unity in England was partly brought about by conditions and events outside the British Isles. The long political wrangle between the Established Church and the dissenting bodies had obstructed any fruitful discussion of the theological issues, and even after the social liberation of the nonconformists there was a long period of attack on the privileges of the Church of England in the attempt to put the theoretical equality into practice. It was not until the twentieth century was well under way that attitudes changed enough to allow both sides to discover the religious, rather than the political, points of disagreement. When the scene was finally set for discussion, there followed the long and fluctuating processes of conversations between the Anglican Church and the individual dissenting bodies.

The fact that the Church of England was hampered in its overtures to dissenting bodies by the political history of previous centuries meant that Anglicans found it easier to come to terms with religious bodies outside the British Isles, bodies in that wide circle of acquaintances made by missionary enterprise. Approaches had been made to the Eastern Orthodox before the Tractarians had finally awakened the feeling of catholicity within the Anglican bosom, making Anglicans look sympathetically at the other parts of historic Christendom in other continents. It was the missionary activity of the Church of England abroad which also fostered the change of outlook towards Christians of other Western traditions. Whereas the divisions of Christendom were of historic origin, and the minds of Christians were conditioned to accept denominational barriers in the West, the mission field inherited the divisions but was unable to accept them without question. The growing demand for unity was profoundly encouraged by native churchmen who saw the nature and purpose of the Church in a new light, and Kikuyu exemplified the confrontation between the Western outlook and the missionary mentality. At a later date, the scheme of reunion in South India, Burma, and Ceylon, though thrashed out largely in the theological vernacular of the Europeans, raised the question as to whether or not the Churches in the missionary context could better reflect a true concept of catholicity which had been so decisively distorted by the social changes of Europe. This question could be answered only in practice, and consequently the South Indian scheme was a leap in the dark.

The movement towards reunion passed through many phases, for at no time was the current ideal of the reunited Church totally acceptable to succeeding generations of negotiators. The Lambeth Appeal tended to look at the ideal as an individual entity, but it gradually became apparent that diversity in unity was a necessity, even if it had attendant dangers. The removal of barriers and the growing together of Christian communities so widened the horizons of the dialogue that the inquiry into the form of the Church underwent a radical change. Negotiations between religious bodies, as a rule, could plan only one stage ahead since the ideal was not in focus. As negotiations continued, the theological rifts tended to deepen rather than to disappear, but since the field of theological inquiry was widened also, the result was the pursuit of a common spiritual reality.

From the Anglican viewpoint, the attempts to enter formal negotiations with the largest of the Christian bodies met with failure. By the very nature of the relationship between the two, the debate was centred on the historical matter of the validity of Anglican Orders. The attitude of the Roman Catholic authorities abroad was governed by the attitude of the English hierarchy who had never lost the aggressive disdain of Wiseman and Manning. When approaches were made through the medium of the Belgian hierarchy, it meant ignoring their English counterparts and evading the ultimate issue of the future of English Roman Catholicism. This seemingly unproductive exchange was soon to undergo change when the movement towards unity accelerated after the Second World War.

The ability of Roman Catholicism to retain the allegiance of the Irish working people in Britain threw into sharp relief the estrangement of the English working classes from the English

Church. The rise of Methodism at a time when the spiritual life of the Church was at its lowest ebb drew vast numbers of common people away from the established Church. Nevertheless, the indifference of the eighteenth century to the problems of society was not the basic cause of the developing rift. The divorce lay more in the social changes which led people from the country to the anonymity of urban life. One legacy of the Industrial Revolution was to associate the Church of England with the upper strata of English society, an image it has long sought to efface though the image has long since ceased to be a true representation. The decrease in the number of churchgoers was due mainly to the falling away of the middle classes. For a long time the solid phalanx of merchants, mill-owners, clerks, and professional people formed the backbone of both Church and Chapel, attracted no doubt by the Christian emphasis on moral goodness and honest industry. The falling away of such as these brought the Churches to a clearer recognition of the state of religion in Britain.

The estrangement of the working classes from the Churches was due to the lack of resources in the vast sprawling cities, to the vast social changes which demonstrated the inadequacy of every municipal and government department, and to the limitations of the Anglican social conscience. In the golden age of *laissez-faire* there arose individuals within the Churches who sought social justice on a practical and utilitarian level. It was surprising that the Evangelicals, other-worldly as they were, should concern themselves with the curing of social ills abroad and ignore the matters of the world at home. The strange alliance of churchmen and chartists which occasioned the Christian Socialist movement was an almost unnoticed revolution in the social acclimatization of the Church of England.

The significant thing about the growth of the Christian Socialist movement was its part in transforming the corporate mind of the Church of England. There was a world of difference between the individualism of Stewart Headlam and the departmentalism of the Christian Social Union, but each contributed to the equipping of the Church of England as an active participant in industrial disputes and social practicalities. This concern for social justice always involved the leaders of the Church in the difficult manoeuvre of extricating themselves from party politics and social ideologies. There were always groups within the Church who willingly identified themselves with one party or another, but as a whole there was a reticence to commit the gospel to purely political terms. The independent line taken by the bulk of churchmen on social matters prevented the direct collision between Church and State which was not an uncommon feature of the European scene. This, however, did not prevent certain critics such as Dean Inge from condemning the commitment of the Church's leaders to the working men's cause However, what undergraduates and curates were doing in the 1880s, archbishops were trying in the 1920s.

The period from 1815 to 1948 is a well-defined social and political entity. It began with the Church of England emerging unchanged under the Hanoverian kings as part of the *status quo* safeguarded by the Tories after Waterloo. It ended with the Church of England —two provinces of the Anglican Communion being transformed by the Holy Spirit through the movement of history. Between the two ends the Clapham Sect, the Oxford Apostles, the Christian Socialists, and the disciples of unity all played their part.

THE SELECTION OF DOCUMENTS

The collection of documents is an attempt to allow the subject to speak for itself. However, the very process of selection is to superimpose the ideas and interpretations of the editor on the material at his disposal. Nevertheless, the choice of these documents is made with the intention of faithfully setting forth a representative picture of the Church of England during the period 1815–1948. One safeguard against the errors of commission and omission is to make full use of those well-established texts known to every student through the standard textbooks and primers of ecclesiastical history. This safeguard has been unashamedly employed with the risk of vain repetition. A further safeguard is to quote in full those texts frequently cited either in footnotes or in a fragmentary form by the preponderate number of scholars. For the rest, the editor has felt an obligation to provide such texts as, in his opinion, mirror the subject under discussion and which are not always readily available to the harassed student. It was this last-mentioned character which prompted the idea of such a book.

THE CHOICE OF PERIOD

The historical process is a description of the antecedents, results, causes, conditioning influences, personalities, and events involved in a given moment of time. Although we speak of a period of history as a matter of convenience, we remain aware of the fact that chronological history cannot be readily isolated into watertight compartments. The period of which this collection of documents is a study is an arbitrary choice governed by a confusing number of landmarks. The ends of two wars and the ensuing periods of hopeful social reconstruction are the only justification for the limits that the editor is obliged to set to his work.

THE SCHEME

The texts have been arranged in a general chronological order. They are set out as follows:

1. Title 2. Date 3. Source

4. Introductory note 5. Text 6. Notes

1 THE CHURCH BUILDING ACT 1818

(*Statutes at Large*, 58 Geo. III, c. 45)

The Church Building Society was founded in 1818 to construct and maintain Anglican churches in England and Wales. Donations were received from the King, bishops, deans and chapters, the universities, and city companies.[1] The subject was mentioned in the Prince Regent's speech from the throne. This Act was subsequently passed for the express purpose of providing churches and chapels in the great urban centres. After the Reform Act of 1832 the political influence of the nonconformists made government aid for church building increasingly difficult.[2]

I ... That it shall be lawful for the King's Most Excellent Majesty, by Warrant or Warrants under His Royal Sign Manual, to authorize and empower the Commissioners of His Majesty's Treasury of the United Kingdom of *Great Britain* and *Ireland* now or for the Time being, or any Three or more of them, or the Lord High Treasurer of the United Kingdom of *Great Britain* and *Ireland* for the Time being, to cause or direct any Number of Exchequer Bills to be made out at His Majesty's Exchequer at *Westminster*, not exceeding in the whole the Sum of One Million....[3]

VIII And be it further enacted, That it shall be lawful for His Majesty, by Letters Patent under the Great Seal of the United Kingdom, to nominate, constitute, and appoint such persons as His Majesty shall deem fit to be His Commissioners for carrying into Execution the Purposes of this Act,[4] and to order and direct in such Appointment that any Five or more of such Commissioners may act in the Execution of the Powers of this Act; and such Commission shall continue in force for the Term of Ten Years from the Date of such Letters Patent, unless His Majesty shall think fit sooner to alter or revoke the same.[5]

IX And be it further enacted, That the said Commissioners shall examine into the present State of the Parishes and Extra-Parochial Places in the Metropolis and its Vicinity, and in all other Parts of *England* and *Wales*, so far as conveniently may be, for the Purpose of ascertaining the Parishes and Places in which additional Churches or Chapels for the Performance of Divine Service, according to the Rites of the United Church of *England* and *Ireland* as by Law established, are most required, and the most effectual and proper Means of affording such Accommodation.[6]

XII And be in further enacted, That the said Commissioners shall, as soon after their Appointment as the obtaining necessary Information will allow, draw up certain Rules for their general Proceedings, and shall fix and specify therein the largest Amount of Allowances to be granted for building any Church, and make such other Regulations as the said Commissioners shall deem expedient and necessary to be fixed and known,[7] for the Furtherance of the Purposes of the Act, and from Time to Time, as Occasion may require, shall have Power to alter or vary any such Regulations, and to make any such further or additional Regulations as they may deem expedient; and all such Rules and Regulations shall be laid before His Majesty in Council, who shall have Power to approve or disallow the same.

XIII And be it further enacted, That it shall be lawful for the said Commissioners to make, in His Majesty's Name, out of the Sum so appropriated by this Act, Grants for building, or to cause to be built, Churches or Chapels in such Parishes or Extra-Parochial Places only in which there is a Population of not less than Four thousand Persons, and in which there is not Accommodation in the Churches or Chapels therein for more than One-fourth Part of such Population to attend Divine Service according to the Rites of the United Church of *England* and *Ireland*, or in which there shall appear to the said Commissioners to be One thousand Persons resident more than Four Miles from any such Church or Chapel, and in which the Commissioners shall be satisfied, from the Circumstances of such Parish or Extra-Parochial Place, of the Inability of the Parishioners and Inhabitants thereof to bear any Part of the Charge of such Building in addition to the Charge hereinafter mentioned; and also to make Grants or Loans to assist in building such Churches and Chapels in such other parishes or Places as may contain a like Population, and may equally require further Accommodation for Divine Service, but in which the said Commissioners may deem the Parishioners and Inhabitants thereof capable of bearing a Part of the Expence of erecting such Churches and Chapels, or of repaying the same by Instalments, if advanced by way of Loan.[8]

1 The Church Building Society was largely a product of the Evangelical movement, owing a great deal to Joshua Watson. The Society was constituted on 6 February 1818, and incorporated by Act of Parliament in 1828.

2 Further Church Building Acts include 59 Geo. III, s. 134 (amending

the 1818 Act); 3 Geo. IV, c. 72, 5 Geo. IV, c. 103, 7-8 Geo. IV, c. 72 (all amending previous Acts); 9 Geo. IV, c. 42; 1-2 Wm. IV, c. 38 (patronage); 2-3 Wm. IV, c. 61 (episcopal jurisdiction); 1-2 Vict., c. 107 (patronage); 2-3 Vict., c. 49; 3-4 Vict., c. 60 (assignment and subdivision of districts); 7-8 Vict., c. 56 (marriages); 8-9 Vict., c. 70 (formation of districts); 9-10 Vict., c. 68 (burials); 9-10 Vict., c. 88 (patronage); 11-12 Vict., c. 37 (assignment of districts); 14-15 Vict., c. 97 (patronage and fees); 17-18 Vict., c. 32 (leasehold land); 19-20 Vict., c. 55 (transferring the powers of the Church Building Commissioners to the Ecclesiastical Commissioners).

3 The first *Report* dated 3 February 1821 stated that eighty-five churches had been provided at a cost of £1,068,000. An Act of 1824 voted a further half a million for the same purposes.

4 Commissioners were appointed by Letters Patent in 1818, 1825, and 1845. The first were: Charles Bathurst; Francis Burton; George Cambridge; Lord Colchester; James Cornwallis; the Bishop of Lichfield and Coventry; John Eyre; Lord Grenville; Earl of Hardwicke; Earl of Harrowby; John Headlam; the Bishop of London; the Dean of Westminster; Lord Kenyon; the Bishop of Chester; the Archbishop of Canterbury; the Speaker of the House of Commons; Richard Mant; the Dean of Arches; the Bishop of Winchester; Edmund Outram; Joseph Pott; Sir William Scott; Viscount Sidmouth; the Bishop of Lincoln; Nicholas Vansittart; the Archbishop of York; Joshua Watson; Thomas Whitaker; Francis Wollaston; and Christopher Wordsworth.

5 7-8 Geo. IV, c. 72 extended the Commission's powers to 20 July 1838; 7 Wm. IV and 1 Vict., c. 75 prolonged them a further ten years; 11-12 Vict., c. 71 till 1853; 17-18 Vict., c. 14 till 1856; and 19-20 Vict., c. 55 transferred them to the Ecclesiastical Commission.

6 The bishops were requested to set up diocesan boards to inform the Commissioners on population, church accommodation, and the ability of parishes to raise funds. The Commissioners largely augmented the work of churchmen. For example, in 1836 Blomfield launched a scheme for building fifty churches in the London area. In 1862 Tait was still finding it necessary to meet a shortage of accommodation.

7 Wollaston, Mant, and Watson drew up the *Report*, including the rules, regulations, and procedure. The maximum to be spent on any one building was £20,000 unless special application was made to the Privy Council.

8 Under the Act, the repair of district churches was maintained by a rate levied within the district, the districts remaining liable to rates for parish church repairs for twenty years.

2 THE EVANGELICALS AND SLAVERY, 1821

(*Memoirs of Sir Thomas Fowell Buxton*, p. 59)

The slave trade had been abolished in 1806 but slavery itself continued to exist within the British Empire. Although slavery was a moral issue, it was also an economic one, involving interests at home and abroad. Wilberforce,[1] who had earlier won Pitt over to the cause, obtained Buxton's help in leading the agitation within Parliament.[2] Compromise solutions were advanced, but the agitators demanded the total abolition of slavery. The Bill, finally carried through by E. G. Stanley in 1833, cost the British taxpayer £20 million in compensation to the planters. The anti-slavery campaign has been called the "best known expression of the nascent conscience of the churches".[3]

London, May 24, 1821

My dear Buxton,

It is now more than thirty-three years since, after having given notice in the House of Commons that I should bring forward, for the first time, the question concerning the Slave Trade, it pleased God to visit me with a severe indisposition, by which, indeed, I was so exhausted, that the ablest physician in London of that day declared that I had not stamina to last above a very few weeks. On this I went to Mr Pitt,[4] and begged of him a promise, which he kindly and readily gave me, to take upon himself the conduct of that great cause.

I thank God I am now free from any indisposition; but from my time of life, and much more from the state of my constitution, and my inability to bear inclemencies of weather, and irregularities, which close attendance on the House of Commons often requires, I am reminded, but too intelligibly, of my being in such a state that I ought not to look confidently to my being able to carry through any business of importance in the House of Commons.

Now for many, many years I have been longing to bring forward that great subject, the condition of the negro slaves in our Transatlantic colonies, and the best means of providing for their moral and social improvement, and ultimately for their advancement to the rank of a free peasantry—a cause, this, recommended to me, or rather enforced on me, by every consideration of religion, justice, and humanity.

Under this impression, I have been waiting, with no little solicitude, for a proper time and suitable circumstances of the country, for introducing this great business; and, latterly, for some member of Parliament, who, if I were to retire or to be laid by, would be an eligible leader in this holy enterprise.

I have for some time been viewing you in this connexion; and after what passed last night, I can no longer forbear resorting to you, as I formerly did to Pitt, and earnestly conjuring you to take most seriously into consideration the expediency of your devoting yourself to this *blessed service*, so far as will be consistent with the due discharge of the obligations you have already contracted, and in part so admirably fulfilled, to war against the abuses of our criminal law, both in its structure and its administration.[5] Let me, then, entreat you to form an alliance with me, that may truly be termed holy, and if I should be unable to commence the war (certainly not to be declared this session); and still more, if, when commenced, I should (as certainly would, I fear, be the case) be unable to finish it, do I entreat that you would continue to prosecute it. Your assurance to this effect would give me the greatest pleasure —pleasure is a bad term—let me rather say peace and consolation; for alas, my friend, I feel but too deeply, how little I have been duly assiduous and faithful in employing the talents committed to my stewardship; and in forming a *partnership* of this sort with you, I cannot doubt that I should be doing an act highly pleasing to God, and beneficial to my fellow-creatures. Both my head and heart are quite full to overflowing, but I must conclude. My dear friend, may it please God to bless you, both in your public and private course. If it be His will, may He render you an instrument of extensive usefulness; but above all, may He give you the disposition to say at all times, "Lord, what wouldest Thou have me to do, or to suffer?" looking to Him, through Christ, for wisdom and strength. And while active in business and fervent in spirit upon earth, may you have your conversation in heaven, and your affections set on things above. There may we at last meet, together with all we most love, and spend an eternity of holiness and happiness complete, and unassailable.

Ever affectionately yours,

W. WILBERFORCE[6]

1 Wilberforce, William; *b.* 1759; *educ.* St John's College Cambridge; M.P. for Hull, 1780; travelled on the continent, 1784-5; came under the influence of T. Clarkson and became interested in the slave trade; settled at Clapham, 1797; *Practical View* published, 1797; assisted in the foundation of C.M.S., 1798, and the Bible Society, 1803; resigned, 1825; *d.* 1833.

2 Buxton, Thomas Fowell; *b.* 1786; *educ.* Trinity College, Dublin; entered Truman's Brewery, 1808; became interested in prison reform, 1816; M.P. for Weymouth, 1818; lost his seat, 1837; created baronet, 1840; *d.* 1845.

3 Norman Sykes: *The English Religious Tradition* (1953), p. 71

4 Pitt, William, younger son of the Earl of Chatham; *b.* 1759; called to the bar, 1780; M.P. 1781; Chancellor of the Exchequer, 1782; Prime Minister, 1783; resigned over George III's refusal to grant Catholic Emancipation, 1801; second ministry, 1804–06; *d.* 1806.

5 Buxton had spoken in support of Sir James Mackintosh's Bill for the abrogation of the death penalty in cases of forgery.

6 The Anti-slavery Committee was established in London in 1787, and Wilberforce had introduced motions into the Commons against the slave trade in 1789, 1791, 1795, and 1804. Wilberforce died on 29 July 1833, and the Bill abolishing slavery became law on 28 August.

3 NEWMAN ON THE CHURCH OF ENGLAND, 1866

(Appendix to the French edition of the *Apologia pro Vita Sua*, 1866)

The Church of England in the nineteenth century was divided into several streams of tradition and doctrine. Churchmanship played a large part in the development of the English Church during this era and Newman writes of his own experience of these parties. Oxford University was, in many ways, a microcosm of the Church of England, and Newman's involvement in the ecclesiastical disputes within the university gave him deep insight into the divisive character of the theological movements. Though not an unprejudiced account, this essay conveys the spirit of the age.[1]

APPENDICE

1 NOTES INÉDITES COMPOSÉES PAR LE P. NEWMAN POUR LA TRADUCTION FRANÇAISE

L'ÉGLISE D'ANGLETERRE

Il n'est peut-être aucune institution où les Anglais aient montré leur amour des compromis en matières politiques et sociales d'une manière aussi remarquable que dans l'Église établie. Luther, Calvin et Zwingli, tous ennemis de Rome, étaient également ennemis les uns des autres. D'autres sectes protestantes, les Érastiens, les Puritains et les Arminiens, sont également distinctes et hostiles. Cependant, il n'y a aucune exagération à dire que l'Établissement ecclésiastique anglican est un amalgame de toutes ces variétés de protestantisme, auquel une forte part de catholicisme est mêlée par surcroît. Il est le résultat de l'action successive exercée sur la religion par Henri VIII, les ministres d'Édouard VI, Marie, Élisabeth, les Cavaliers, les Puritains, les Latitudinaires de 1688 et les Méthodistes du xviiie siècle.[2] Il a une hiérarchie venue du moyen âge, richement dotée, élevée par sa position civile, formidable par son influence politique. L'Église établie a conservé les rites, les prières et les symboles de l'ancienne Église. Elle tire ses articles de foi de sources luthériennes et zwingliennes; sa traduction de la Bible sent le calvinisme. Elle peut se vanter d'avoir eu dans son sein, surtout au xviie siècle, une suite de théologiens de grand savoir et fiers de se rapprocher des doctrines et des pratiques de l'Église primitive.[3] En considérant ses docteurs, le grand Bossuet a dit qu'il était impossible que le peuple anglais ne revînt pas un jour à la foi de ses pères; et de Maistre a salué la communion anglicane comme destinée à jouer un grand rôle dans la réconciliation et la réunion de la chrétienté.

Cette Église remarquable a toujours été dans la dépendance la plus étroite du pouvoir civil, et s'en est toujours fait gloire. Elle a toujours vu le pouvoir papal avec crainte, avec ressentiment et avec aversion. Elle n'a jamais gagné le coeur du peuple. En cela, elle s'est montrée, dans tout le cours de son existence, *une* et semblable à elle-même; sous d'autres rapports, ou elle n'a jamais eu d'opinions, ou elle en a constamment changé. Au xvie siècle elle était calviniste; dans la première moitié du xviie, elle était arminienne et quasi-catholique; vers la fin de ce siècle et le commencement de l'autre, elle était latitudinaire. Au milieu du xviiie siècle, elle est décrite par lord Chatham comme ayant "un rituel et un livre de prières papistes, des articles de foi calvinistes et un clergé arminien".

De nos jours elle contient trois partis puissants, dans lesquels revivent les trois principes de religion qui, sous une forme ou sous une autre, apparaissent constamment et depuis le commencement dans son histoire: le principe catholique, le principe protestant et le principe sceptique. Chacun d'eux, il est presque inutile de le dire, est violemment opposé aux deux autres.

Premièrement: le parti apostolique ou *tractarian*, qui va maintenant dans la direction du catholicisme plus loin qu'en aucun temps ou dans aucune manifestation précédente; à ce point qu'en l'étudiant dans ses adhérents les plus avancés, on peut dire qu'il ne diffère en rien du catholicisme, excepté dans la doctrine de la suprématie du pape. Ce parti s'éleva au xviie siècle, à la cour de Jacques Ier et de Charles Ier, il fut presque éteint par les doctrines de Locke et par l'avénement au trône de Guillaume III et de la maison de Hanovre. Mais ses principes furent enseignés et silencieusement transmis, pendant le cours du xviiie siècle, par les *non-jureurs,* secte d'hommes instruits et zélés qui, conservant la succession épiscopale, se détachèrent de l'Église d'Angleterre quand on les somma de prêter serment de fidélité à Guillaume III.[4] De nos jours, on l'a vu revivre et former un parti nombreux et croissant dans l'Église d'Angleterre, au moyen du mouvement commencé par les écrits intitulés: *Tracts for the Times* (et de là nommé *Tractarian*), dont il est souvent question dans ce livre.[5]

Secondement: le parti évangélique, qui fait vivre dans le monde entier toutes les sociétés bibliques et la plupart des associations pour les missions protestantes. On peut faire remonter l'origine de ce parti aux puritains, qui commencèrent à se montrer dans les dernières années du règne de la reine Élisabeth. Il fut presque entièrement jeté hors de l'Église d'Angleterre lors de la restauration de Charles II, en 1660. Il se réfugia parmi les dissidents de cette Église et il se mourait peu à peu, lorsque ses doctrines furent ressuscitées avec une grande vigueur par les célèbres prédicateurs Whitefield et Wesley,[6] pasteurs de l'Église anglicane l'un et l'autre, et fondateurs de la secte puissante des Méthodistes. En même temps qu'elles créaient une secte en dehors de l'Église établie, ces doctrines exercèrent une influence importante au sein de cette Église elle-même, et s'y développèrent peu à peu jusqu'à former le parti évangélique, qui est aujourd'hui de beaucoup la plus puissante des trois écoles que nous nous appliquons à faire connaître.

Troisèmement: le parti libéral, connu dans les siècles qui nous ont précédés sous le nom moins honorable de *latitudinaire*.[7] Il se détacha du parti quasi-catholique, ou parti de la cour, sous le règne de Charles Ier, et fut nourri et répandu par l'introduction en Angleterre des principes de Grotius et des Arminiens de Hollande. Nous avons déjà cité la philosophie de Locke comme ayant agi dans le même sens. Il prit le parti de la Révolution de 1688, et appuya les whigs, Guillaume III et la maison de Hanovre. Le génie de ses principes est contraire à l'extension et au prosélytisme; et, quoiqu'il ait compté dans ses rangs des écrivains remarquables parmi les théologiens anglicans, il n'avait eu que peu de sectateurs, lorsqu'il y a dix ans irrité par le succès des *tractarians*, prenant avantage de la conversion à l'Église romaine de quelques-uns de leurs principaux chefs, et aidé par l'importation de la littérature allemande en Angleterre, ce parti s'est avancé tout à coup sur la scène publique, et s'est propagé parmi les classes éclairées avec une rapidité si étonnante, qu'on est presque autorisé à croire que, dans la génération qui nous suivra, le monde religieux sera partagé entre les déistes et les catholiques. Les principes et les arguments des libéraux ne s'arrêtent même pas au déisme.

Si la communion anglicane se composait uniquement de ces trois partis, elle ne pourrait durer. Elle serait brisée par ses dissensions intérieures. Mais il y a dans son sein un parti plus nombreux de beaucoup que ces trois partis théologiques, qui, créé par la situation légale de l'Église, profitant de ses richesses et des institutions de son culte, est le contre poids et le lien qui maintient l'ensemble. C'est le parti de l'ordre, le parti des Conservateurs, ou, comme on les a appelés jusqu'ici, des *Tories*. Ce n'est par un parti religieux: non qu'il n'ait dans ses rangs un grand nombre d'hommes religieux, main parce que ses principes et ses mots d'ordre sont politiques ou du moins ecclésiastiques plutôt que théologiques. Ses membres ne sont ni *tractarians* ni *évangéliques*, ni *libéraux*; ou, s'ils le sont c'est sous une forme très douce et très inoffensive; car, aux yeux du monde, leur caractère principal est d'être les avocats *d'un Établissement* et de *l'Établissement*, et ils sont plus ardents pour la conservation d'une Église nationale que soucieux des croyances que cette Église nationale professe. Nous avons dit plus haut que le grand principe de l'Église anglicane était sa confiance dans la protection du pouvoir civil et sa docilité à le servir, ce que ses ennemis appellent son *Érastianisme*.[8] Aussi, d'une part, ce respect pour le pouvoir civil est son grand principe, de l'autre, ce principe de l'érastianisme est personnifié dans un parti si nombreux, soit dans le clergé soit parmi les laïques, que c'est à peine si le nom de "parti" peut lui convenir. Il constitute la masse de l'Église. Les membres du clergé spécialement, sur tous les points de l'Angleterre, les évêques, doyens, chapitres, curés, se sont toujours distingués par leur torisme. Au xviie siècle ils professaient le droit divin des rois; depuis ils se sont toujours fait gloire de la doctrine; "Le roi est la tête de l'Église"; et le toast de leurs dîners, "l'Église et le roi", a été leur formule de protestation pour maintenir dans le royaume d'Angleterre la prédominance théorique du spirituel sur le temporel. Ils ont toujours témoigné une aversion extrême pour ce qu'ils appellent le pouvoir usurpé du pape. Leur principal dogme théologique est que la Bible contient toutes les vérités nécessaires, et que tout chrétien est individuellement capable de les y trouver pour son usage. Ils prêchent le Christ comme l'unique médiateur, la Rédemption par sa mort, le renouvellement par son esprit, la nécessité des bonnes oeuvres. Ce grand assemblage d'hommes, véritables représentants de ce bon sens qui rend l'Angleterre si célèbre dans le bien comme dans le mal, regardent pour la plupart avec défiance toute espèce de théologie, toute école théologique, et en particular les trois écoles que nous avons cherché à faire connaître. Au xviie siècle ils combattirent les puritains; à la fin de ce siècle ils combattirent latitudinaires; au milieu du xviiie siècle ils combattirent les méthodistes et ceux du parti évangélique; et de notre temps ils se sont levés énergiquement, d'abord contre les tractarians, et aujourd'hui contre les libéraux.

Ce parti de l'ordre, ou de l'Église établie, a nécessairement beaucoup de subdivisions. Le clergé des campagnes, jouissant d'une grande aisance, en relations intimes avec les seigneurs du voisinage, et toujours bienveillant et charitable, est, par suite de sa position, mais non par l'influence de ses doctrines, très respecté et très aimé des classes inférieures. Mais, parmi les ecclésiastiques qui jouissent de grands revenus et ont peu de chose à faire (comme les membres des chapitres dans les cathédrales), beaucoup, il y a déjà longtemps, sont tombés dans la recherche du bien être personnel. Ceux qui occupaient des positions élevées dans de grandes villes ont été conduits à des habitudes de pompe et de hauteur, et se sont vantés d'une minutieuse orthodoxie qui devenait froide et presque dénuée de vie intérieure. Ces pasteurs indulgents pour eux-mêmes ont reçu dès longtemps le surnom raileur "d'orthodoxes à deux bouteilles" comme si leur plus grand zêle regigieux se manifestait en buvant de vin de Porto à la sante de "l'Église et du roi". Ces pompeux dignitaires de grandes paroisses dans les villes ont été surnommés aussi d'école ou l'Église "*haute et sèche*".[9]

Il nous reste encore à expliquer trois mots, qui sont en opposition les uns avec les autres, et dont l'un ou l'autre trouvera place dans ce livre: *high Church* l'Église haute; *low Church*, l'Église basse; *broad Church*, l'Église large. La dernière de ces dénominations n'offre aucune difficulté: le mot *broad*, large, répond à celui de latitudinaire, et par *l'Église large* on entend le parti Libéral. Mais les dénominations de haute et de basse Église ne peuvent être comprises sans explication.

Le nom de doctrine de la *haute Église* désigne donc l'enseignement qui s'applique à faire ressortir les prérogatives et l'autorité de l'Église; mais non pas tant ses pouvoirs *invisibles*, que ses privilèges et ses dons comme corps *visible*; et comme, dans la religion anglicane, ces privilèges temporels ont toujours dépendu du pouvoir civil, il arrive accidentellement qu'un partisan de la *haute Église* est à peu près un *érastien*, c'est-à-dire un homme qui nie le pouvoir spirituel propre à l'Église, et soutient que l'Église est une des branches du gouvernement civil. Ainsi un calviniste peut être un partisan de la haute Église, comme l'était Whitgift archevêque de Canterbury, sous le règne d'Élisabeth, et comme l'était, au moins dans sa jeunesse Hooker, le maître du Temple.

La *basse Église* est, bien entendu le contraire de la *haute Église*. Si donc le parti de la *haute Église* est le parti de ceux qui tiennent pour l'Église et le roi, "le parti de la *basse Église* est celui qui anathématise cette doctrine érastienne, et considère comme antichrétien de donner à l'État un pouvoir quelconque sur l'Église de Dieu"; c'est ainsi que les puritains et les indépendants préférènt jadis Cromwell au roi Charles. Aujourd'hui, cependant, depuis que les puritains ont cessé d'exister en Angleterre, la dénomination de basse Église a cessé de représenter une idée ecclésiastique et désigne un parti théologique, devenant le synonyme de parti évangélique. En conséquence un changement analogue a eu lieu dans le sens du nom de *haute Église*. Au lieu de désigner uniquement les partisans de "l'Église et du roi", ou *les érastiens*, il arrive à prendre une signification théologique, et à designer le parti semi-catholique. Ainsi, de nos jours, il arrive souvent qu'on donne aux *tractarians* eux-mêmes le nom de partisans de la *haute Église,* quoiqu'ils aient commencé par denoncer l'érastianisme, et qu'à leur origine ils aient été combattus à Oxford avec fureur par le parti de la *haute Église*, ou de l'Église établie.

1 Newman, John Henry; *b.* 1801; *educ.* Ealing and Trinity College, Oxford; Fellow of Oriel, 1822; curate of St Clement, Oxford, 1824; vicar of St Mary, 1828; began *Tracts for the Times*, 1833; withdrew to Littlemore, 1842; joined Church of Rome, 1845; reordained at Rome, 1846; commissioned by Pius IX to institute the Oratory of St Philip Neri in England, 1847; Rector of the Catholic university of Dublin, 1854; created cardinal, 1879; *d.* 1890.

2 Methodism was a name originally applied to the small group centred on Wesley at Oxford in 1729. Whilst still members of the Church of England, John and Charles Wesley came under the influence of the Moravians, while Whitefield adopted Calvinistic views.

3 The desire to return to a primitive pattern of doctrine, worship, and order, was part of the theological movement of the Reformation.

The "Ideal" was sought in the Bible and in the writings of the first five Christian centuries, and classical Anglican thought was grounded in this ideal. The Tractarians sought the catholicism of the Church of England in its retention of the primitive tradition.

4 The Nonjurors were the beneficed clergy who refused in 1689 to take the oath of allegiance to William and Mary. They numbered eight bishops and some 400 priests. In the eighteenth century they were gradually reabsorbed into the established Church where their emphasis on the spiritual nature of the Church and the importance of forms of worship linked them to the Caroline divines on the one hand, and to the Tractarians on the other.

5 Newmanites and Puseyites were the original appellations for Newman and his colleagues. The term Tractarian came into common use for the party as a whole around 1840.

6 Wesley, John; *b.* 1703; *educ.* Charterhouse and Christ Church, Oxford; Fellow and tutor of Lincoln College, 1729; accepted charge of the Georgia mission in 1735; opened a Methodist chapel at Bristol; ordained a minister for his American congregations, 1784; *d.* 1791.

7 The eighteenth-century climate was largely consequential to the latitudinarianism of the seventeenth, and the theological liberalism of the nineteenth century continued the free-thinking tradition within the English Church.

8 Erastus' *Explicatio Gravissimae Quaestionis* was published in London in 1589. The English translation, *The Nullity of Church Censures*, published in 1659, appeared after the initial influence of Erastus came to be felt. Hooker propagated similar views in his *Ecclesiastical Polity* (1594).

9 The term High Church originated in the late seventeenth century and was a hostile nickname, derived from "high-flier" (*Honest Cavalier*, 1680). Low Church referred either to the antithesis of High Church as in Robert South's dedication to Narcissus Boyle, prefixed to the third volume of his *Sermons* (1698), or to churchmen of a liberal attitude, as in *Ne'er a barrel the better herring between Low Church and No Church* (1713). In the nineteenth century Low Church became almost synonymous with Evangelical. Broad Church, according to Jowett, originated with A. H. Clough in 1850.

4 THE TEST AND CORPORATION ACTS 1828

(*Statutes at Large*, 9 Geo. IV, c. 17)

The Corporation Act of 1661 required all members of municipal corporations to receive Holy Communion according to the rite of the Church of England in the year preceding their election to office. The Test Act of 1673 demanded the same of all who held office under the Crown. The repeal of these Acts removed a formal grievance only, since from 1727 an Indemnity Bill had, with four exceptions, been enacted annually by Parliament. The repeal meant the abandonment of the theoretical basis of the establishment that Church and State were identical. Lord John Russell in moving the resolution exemplified the change in outlook, speaking of the evil of "mixing politics with religion".[1]

After the recitation of the Acts 13 Car. II, st. 2, c. I., 25 Car. II, c. 2r., and 16 Geo. II, c. 30, the Act reads:

And whereas it is expedient that so much of the said several Acts of Parliament as imposes the necessity of taking the sacrament of the Lord's Supper according to the rites or usage of the Church of England, for the purposes therein respectively mentioned, should be repealed; be it therefore enacted ... that so much and such parts of the said several Acts ... as require the person or persons in the said Acts respectively described to take or receive the sacrament ... for the several purposes therein expressed ... or as impose upon any such person or persons any penalty, forfeiture, incapacity, or disability whatsoever for or by reason of any neglect or omission to take or receive the said sacrament ... are hereby repealed.[2]

II And whereas the Protestant Episcopal Church of England and Ireland ... and the Protestant Presbyterian Church of Scotland, and the doctrine, discipline, and government thereof, are by the laws of this realm severally established, permanently and inviolably:[3] and whereas it is just and fitting, that on the repeal of such parts of the said Acts as impose the necessity of taking the sacrament of the Lord's Supper according to the rites or usage of the Church of England, as a qualification for office, a declaration to the following effect should be substituted in lieu thereof; be it therefore enacted, that every person who shall hereafter be placed, elected, or chosen in or to the office of Mayor, Alderman,

Recorder, Bailiff, Town Clerk, or common councilman, or in or to any office of Magistracy, or ... employment relating to the government of any city, corporation, borough, or Cinque Port within England and Wales ... shall, within one calendar month ... make and subscribe the declaration following:

"I A.B. do solemnly and sincerely, in the presence of God, profess, testify, and declare, upon the true faith of a Christian, that I will never exercise any power, authority, or influence which I may possess by virtue of the office of —— to injure or weaken the Protestant Church as it is by law established in England, or to disturb the said Church, or the bishops and clergy of the said Church, in the possession of any rights or privileges to which such Church, or the said bishops and clergy, are or may be by law entitled."[4]

1 Lord John Russell, first Earl Russell; *b.* 1792; *educ.*, Edinburgh University; M.P., 1813; Paymaster-general, 1830; Home Secretary and leader in the House of Commons, 1835; Prime Minister, 1846–52, and 1865–66; *d.* 1878.

2 13 Car. II, st. 2, c. 1. Corporation Act; 25 Car. II, c. 2. Test Act; 16 Geo. II, c. 30 The Indemnity Act.

3 Establishment is a particular relationship of Church to State whereby the ecclesiastical machinery is a recognized part of the civil constitution. In England this involves: recognition of the authority of Parliamentary legislation; appointment of bishops and certain other church officers by the Crown; the summoning of Convocations and the enactment of canons by permission of the Crown; and the place of ecclesiastical courts within the framework of the English legal system.

4 Further paragraphs dealt with the manner of making the declaration; officers not required to make it; and the position of persons already in office.

5 CATHOLIC EMANCIPATION, 1829

(*Statutes at Large*, 10 Geo. IV, c. 7)

The Test Act of 1673 required all holders of public office to receive the sacrament of Holy Communion according to the Prayer Book rite, thus excluding Roman Catholics from executive posts. The Act of Union 1800, involving as it did the British Parliament with Irish affairs, did not alleviate the Catholic position. Under the leadership of O'Connell[1] pressure was brought to bear on the Tory administration, and Wellington and Peel,[2] to avoid civil unrest in Ireland, carried the Bill through Parliament in the face of violent opposition. The Act was a further denial of the principle of Church establishment and a further attack on the privileged position of the Church of England.[3]

Whereas by various Acts of Parliament certain restraints and disabilities are imposed on the Roman Catholic subjects of His Majesty, to which other subjects of His Majesty are not liable; and whereas it is expedient that such restraints and disabilities shall be from henceforth discontinued; and whereas by various Acts certain oaths and certain declarations, commonly called the declaration against transubstantiation, and the declaration against transubstantiation and the invocation of Saints and the sacrifice of the Mass, as practised in the Church of Rome, are or may be required to be taken, made, and subscribed by the subjects of His Majesty, as qualifications for sitting and voting in Parliament, and for the enjoyment of certain offices, franchises, and civil rights: be it enacted ... that ... all such parts of the said Acts as require the said declarations, or either of them, to be made or subscribed by any of His Majesty's subjects as a qualification for sitting and voting in Parliament, or for the exercise or enjoyment of any office, franchise or civil right ... are (save as hereinafter provided and excepted) hereby repealed.

II ... From and after the commencement of this Act it shall be lawful for any person professing the Roman Catholic religion, being a Peer, or who shall after the commencement of this Act be returned as a member of the House of Commons,[4] to sit and vote in either House of Parliament respectively, being in all other respects duly qualified to sit and vote therein, upon taking and subscribing the following oath, instead of the oaths of allegiance, supremacy and abjuration.

"I A.B. do sincerely promise and swear, that I will be faithful and bear true allegiance to His Majesty King George IV, and will defend him to the utmost of my power against all conspiracies and attempts whatever, which shall be made against his person, crown, or dignity; and I will do my utmost endeavour to disclose and make known to His Majesty, his heirs and successors, all treasons and traitorous conspiracies which may be formed against him or them: and I do faithfully promise to maintain, support, and defend, to the utmost of my power, the succession of the Crown, which succession ... is and stands limited to the Princess Sophia, Electress of Hanover, and the heirs of her body,[5] being Protestants; hereby utterly renouncing and abjuring any obedience or allegiance unto any other person claiming or pretending a right to the Crown of this realm: and I do further declare, that it is not an article of my faith, and that I do renounce, reject, and abjure the opinion, that Princes excommunicated or deprived by the Pope, or any other authority of the See of Rome, may be deposed or murdered by their subjects, or by any person whatsoever:[6] and I do declare, that I do not believe that the Pope of Rome, or any other foreign Prince, prelate, person, State, or potentate, hath or ought to have any temporal or civil jurisdiction, power, superiority, or pre-eminence, directly or indirectly, within this realm. I do swear, that I will defend to the utmost of my power the settlement of property within this realm, as established by the laws: and I do hereby disclaim, disavow, and solemnly abjure any intention to subvert the present Church Establishment as settled by law within this realm: and I do solemnly swear, that I never will exercise any privilege to which I am or may become entitled, to disturb or weaken the Protestant religion or Protestant Government in the United Kingdom: and I do solemnly, in the presence of God, profess, testify, and declare, that I do make this declaration and every part thereof, in the plain and ordinary sense of the words of this oath, without any evasion, equivocation, or mental reservation whatsoever. So help me God."

X ... It shall be lawful for any of His Majesty's subjects professing the Roman Catholic religion to hold, exercise, and enjoy all civil and military offices and places of trust or profit under His Majesty, his heirs or successors, and to exercise any other franchise or civil right, except as hereinafter excepted, upon taking ... the oath hereinbefore appointed ...

XII ... Nothing herein contained shall extend ... to enable any person or persons professing the Roman Catholic religion to hold or exercise the office of Guardians and Justices of the United

Kingdom, or of Regent of the United Kingdom, under whatever name, style, or title such office may be constituted; nor to enable any person, otherwise than as he is now by law enabled, to hold or enjoy the office of Lord High Chancellor, Lord Keeper or Lord Commissioner of the Great Seal of Great Britain or Ireland or the office of Lord Lieutenant, or Lord Deputy, or other Chief Governor or Governors of Ireland; or His Majesty's High Commissioner to the General Assembly of the Church of Scotland.

XIV ... It shall be lawful for any ... Roman Catholic ... to be a member of any lay body corporate, and to hold any civil office or place of trust or profit therein, and to do any corporate act, or vote in any corporate election or other proceeding, upon taking ... the oath hereby appointed ...

1 O'Connell, Daniel: *b.* 1775; *educ.*, St Omer and Douay; entered Lincoln's Inn, 1794; called to Irish Bar, 1798; campaigned against Act of Union, 1800; founded Catholic Association, 1823; elected M.P. for County Clare, 1828; *d.* 1847.

2 Peel, Sir Robert, 2nd bart.; *b.* 1788; *educ.*, Harrow and Christ Church, Oxford; M.P., 1809; under-secretary for war and colonies, 1810; chief secretary for Ireland, 1812; Home Secretary, 1822 and 1828; Prime Minister, 1834–35, 1841–46; *d.* 1850.

3 Wellington left the Cabinet in April 1827, but agreed, nine months later, to form a government. He remained Prime Minister until November 1830, only accepting the necessity of Catholic Emancipation under strong pressure from Peel.

4 This restriction prevented O'Connell from taking his seat for County Clare without re-election. This gave great offence in Ireland.

5 Sophia; *b.* 1630; married Ernest Augustus, Duke of Brunswick-Lüneburg, later Elector of Hanover; mother of George I.

6 See the Papal Bull *Regnans in excelsis*, 1570 and contemporary English legislation; Bettenson, *Documents of the Christian Church*; Gee and Hardy, *Documents Illustrative of English Church History*.

6 THE JUDICIAL COMMITTEE OF THE PRIVY COUNCIL, 1833

(*Statutes at Large*, 3-4 Will. IV, c. 41)

An Ecclesiastical Courts Commission was appointed on 28 January 1830, and reappointed with five additional members in July of the same year. The Commission included Archbishop Howley and five bishops and was primarily concerned with the efficient working of the ecclesiastical legal system.[1] Under pressure from Brougham[2] the Commission recommended the substitution of the Privy Council for the Court of Delegates for hearing final appeals. The completed *Report* was published in February 1832, and recommended the transfer of the jurisdiction of diocesan courts to provincial courts; the introduction of oral evidence; trial by jury; and the abolition of the provincial court of York. The Act of 1833 modified an earlier one of 1832 in regard to the composition of the Judicial Committee.

Whereas by virtue of an Act passed in a Session of Parliament of the Second and Third Years of the Reign of His present Majesty, intituled *An Act for transferring the Powers of the High Court of Delegates, both in Ecclesiastical and Maritime Causes, to His Majesty in Council,*[3] it was enacted, that from and after the First Day of *February* One thousand eight hundred and thirty-three it should be lawful for every Person who might theretofore, by virtue either of an Act passed in the Twenty-fifth Year of the Reign of King *Henry* the *Eighth*, intituled *The Submission of the Clergy and Restraint of Appeals,*[4] or of an Act passed in the Eighth Year of the Reign of Queen *Elizabeth*, intituled *For the avoiding of tedious Suits in Civil and Marine Causes*, have appealed or made suit to His Majesty in His High Court of Chancery, to appeal or make suit to the King's Majesty, His Heirs or Successors, in Council, within such Time, in such Manner, and subject to such Rules, Orders, and Regulations for the due and more convenient Proceeding, as should seem meet and necessary, and upon such Security, if any, as His Majesty, His Heirs and Successors, should from Time to Time by Order in Council direct: And whereas, by Letters Patent under the Great Seal of *Great Britain*, certain Persons, Members of His Majesty's Privy Council, together with others, being Judges and Barons of His Majesty's Courts of Record at *Westminster*, have been from Time to Time appointed to be His Majesty's Commissioners for receiving, hearing, and determining Appeals from His Majesty's Courts of Admiralty in

Causes of Prize: And whereas, from the Decisions of various Courts of Judicature in the *East Indies*, and in the Plantations, Colonies, and other Dominions of His Majesty Abroad, an Appeal lies to His Majesty in Council: And whereas Matters of Appeal or Petition to His Majesty in Council have usually been heard before a Committee of the whole of His Majesty's Privy Council,[5] who have made a Report to his Majesty in Council, whereupon the final Judgment or Determination hath been given by his Majesty: And whereas it is expedient to make certain Provisions for the more effectual hearing and reporting on Appeals to His Majesty in Council and on other matters and to give such Powers and Jurisdiction to His Majesty in Council as hereinafter mentioned: Be it therefore enacted ... That the President for the Time being of His Majesty's Privy Council, the Lord High Chancellor of *Great Britain* for the Time being, and such of the Members of His Majesty's Privy Council as shall from Time to Time hold any of the Offices following, that is to say, the Office of Lord Keeper or First Lord Commissioner of the Great Seal of *Great Britain*, Lord Chief Justice or Judge of the Court of King's Bench, Master of the Rolls, Vice Chancellor of *England*, Lord Chief Justice or Judge of the Court of Common Pleas, Lord Chief Baron or Baron of the Court of Exchequer, Judge of the Prerogative Court of the Lord Archbishop of *Canterbury*, Judge of the High Court of Admiralty, and Chief Judge of the Court in Bankruptcy, and also all Persons Members of His Majesty's Privy Council who shall have been President thereof or held the Office of Lord Chancellor of *Great Britain*, or shall have held any of the other Offices hereinbefore mentioned, shall form a Committee of His Majesty's said Privy Council, and shall be styled "The Judicial Committee of the Privy Council": Provided nevertheless, that it shall be lawful for His Majesty from Time to Time ... to appoint any Two other Persons, being Privy Councillors, to be Members of the said Committee.[6]

1 Howley, William; *b.* 1766; *educ.*, Winchester and New College, Oxford; Fellow and tutor of New College; canon of Christ Church, 1804; Regius Professor of Divinity, 1809; Bishop of London, 1813; Archbishop of Canterbury, 1828; *d.* 1848.

2 Brougham, Henry Peter, first Baron Brougham and Vaux; *b.* 1778; *educ.*, Edinburgh University; passed advocate, 1800; admitted Lincoln's Inn, 1803; M.P., 1810; Rector of Glasgow University, 1825; Lord Chancellor, 1830; *d.* 1868.

3 2-3 Will. IV, c. 92 (1832). Both the Court of Delegates and the

Judicial Committee of the Privy Council received their jurisdiction from the Crown.

4 25 Henry VIII, c. 19 (1534). See Gee and Hardy, *Documents.*

5 Under the Act of 1832, such bishops and archbishops as were Privy Councillors would be members of the Privy Council hearing such appeals. Under this Act, not only were the episcopal members excluded, but only the Chancellor and the Judge of the Prerogative Court of Canterbury needed to be churchmen.

6 Sir Robert Phillimore, in *The Study of the Civil and Canon Law* (1843), noted the fundamental weakness of the new secular court. "But it can scarcely be denied that the substitution of the Judicial Committee of the Privy Council for the Court of Delegates operated not only unfavourably but unjustly upon our profession. In the latter Court five civilians sat with three Common Law Judges in all cases of appeal: in the new tribunal it may and does sometimes happen that no civilian at all sits, but that four Judges from the Common Law or Chancery determine even upon points of *practice* in the Ecclesiastical courts. It would be a curious sight to behold four civilians sitting in judgment as Court of Appeal upon cases—especially cases of *practice*—from Westminster Hall and Lincoln's Inn; though it would be difficult to say why the injury done would be greater or the injustice more flagrant in the latter than the former case." Quoted in E. W. Kemp, *An Introduction to Canon Law in the Church of England* (1957), p. 74.

7 THE IRISH CHURCH TEMPORALITIES ACT 1833

(*Statutes at Large*, 3-4 Will. IV, c. 37)

The established Church in Ireland comprised twenty-two bishoprics; 1,400 benefices; and served 850,000 Anglicans. The episcopal incomes amounted to £150,000 per annum; those of cathedrals £25,000; and those of parishes to £600,000. In order to remedy the growing resentment of the Roman Catholics the Whigs passed their Irish Church Bill in the face of a storm of protest in England. Archbishop Howley[1] accepted the principle behind the Bill, as did most of the bishops. The Archbishop of Dublin voted for the Bill in the Lords.[2] The "spoilation" of the Irish Church gave rise to the abortive Association of Friends of the Church which drafted a petition to Howley in February 1834,[3] which led to the emergence of the Oxford Movement.

XXXII And whereas His Majesty has been graciously pleased

to signify that He has placed at the Disposal of Parliament His Interest in the Temporalities and Custody thereof of the several Bishopricks and Archbishopricks mentioned in this Act and the Schedule (B) thereto annexed; be it therefore enacted. That the Bishoprick of *Waterford*, now void, shall from and after the passing of this Act, and the other Bishopricks named in the First Column of the Schedule (B)[4] to this Act annexed shall, when and as the same may severally become void, be thenceforth united to and held together with the Bishoprick or Archbishoprick mentioned in conjunction therewith respectively in the Second Column of the said Schedule (B); and that the Archbishops or Bishops of the Archbishopricks or Bishopricks in such Second Column named shall, at such Times respectively as before mentioned, be and become, by virtue of this Act, and without further Grant, Installation, or Ceremony whatsoever, Bishops respectively of the said Bishopricks named in such First Column in conjunction therewith, and shall have and exercise all and every the Ecclesiastical Patronages and Jurisdictions in appointing, collating, and presenting to all and every the Dignities, Rectories, Vicarages, Curacies, Chapelries, or other Offices or Promotions, and all other Jurisdictions whatsoever, by whatever Name called, known, or described, lawfully had, used, exercised, and enjoyed by the respective Bishops of the said Bishopricks in the First Column of the said Schedule (B) named, as also the Right of nominating and appointing to all and every the Offices of Chancellor, Vicar General, Official, Principal Registrar, and all other Ecclesiastical Offices of or belonging or appertaining to such last-mentioned Bishopricks respectively; and His Most Excellent Majesty, His Heirs and Successors, shall at all Times thereafter grant each such Bishoprick in the First column of the said Schedule (B) named, together with the Bishoprick or Archbishoprick to which it may have been united in manner aforesaid, to be held by one and the same Person.

XXXVI Provided nevertheless, and be it enacted, That all and singular the Lands, Tenements, and Hereditaments respectively belonging or in anywise appertaining to the Bishopricks in the First Column of the said Schedule (B) named, together with all and singular the Tithes, Rents, and Emoluments whatsoever to such Bishopricks respectively appertaining or belonging, shall, in the Case of the said Bishoprick of *Waterford*, from and after the passing of this Act, and in the Case of the other Bishopricks in the said Schedule (B) mentioned shall, from and after the Times when such Bishopricks shall become respectively void or united to any other Bishoprick as aforesaid, be and the same are hereby transferred to and vested in the said Ecclesiastical Commissioners and their Successors for ever, subject however to all Leases, Rents, Charges, and Incumbrances now or at the Time of such Transfer legally affecting the same, save and except the annual Tax, Rate, or Assessment by this Act authorized to be imposed and levied; and that all the Rents, Revenues, Issues, Profits, and other Emoluments in any Manner arising or accruing to the said Commissioners and their Successors from or out of any of the said Bishopricks shall be received and applied by such Commissioners and their Successors to, for, and upon the several Trusts, Uses, and Purposes in this Act mentioned, and subject to and under the like Rules and Regulations as are herein declared and expressed of and concerning the said annual Tax vested in and made payable to the said Commissioners and their Successors.[5]

1 The Act of Union 1801 provided the Irish with four spiritual and twenty-four temporal peerages, and one hundred representatives in the Commons. The two episcopal Churches in England and Ireland were to be called "The United Church of England and Ireland", thus making the Archbishop of Canterbury a key figure in the ensuing debate.

2 Whately, Richard; *b.* 1787; *educ.*, Oriel College, Oxford; Fellow of Oriel, 1811; Bampton Lecturer, 1822; rector of Halesworth, 1822; Principal of St Alban Hall, Oxford, 1825; Drummond Professor of Political Economy, 1830; Archbishop of Dublin, 1831; Commissioner of National Education; *d.* 1863.

3 For this see J. W. Burgon, *Lives of Twelve Good Men*, I, pp. 155-60.

4 Column 1: Dromore; Raphoe; Clogher; Elphin; Killala and Achonry; Clonfert and Kilmacduagh; Kildare; Ossory; Waterford and Lismore; Cork and Ross.
Column 2: Down and Connor; Derry (a wealthy see whose income was reduced); Armagh (income also reduced); Kilmore; Tuam (suppressed archbishopric); Killaloe and Kilfenora; Dublin and Glandelagh; Ferns and Leighlin; Cashel (suppressed archbishopric) and Emly; Cloyne.

5 The Tractarian fear was justified, for although an established minority Church was a scandal, the motives behind the passing of the Act were political and economic. Money from suppressed sees, suspended benefices, reduced sees, the sale of tenants' leases, and the income tax on Irish benefices amounted to a calculated £150,000. Of the 2,436 parishes, 18% had no church; and for 1,252 benefices there were 900 incumbents.

8 KEBLE'S ASSIZE SERMON, 1833

(*Sermons, Academical and Occasional* (1848), pp. 127-8, 133-4, 136-8, 142, 145)

"Mr Keble preached the Assize Sermon in the University Pulpit. It was published under the title of 'National Apostasy'. I have ever considered and kept the day, as the start of the religious movement of 1833." It is uncertain as to whether all Newman's contemporaries shared his estimate of Keble's sermon, but certainly it was a signal protest against the alleged spoilation of the Church.[1] The reform of the Church of England undertaken by Parliament was regarded by many churchmen as a sign of the decline of Christian England.

ADVERTISEMENT TO THE FIRST EDITION OF THE SERMON ON NATIONAL APOSTASY

Since the following pages were prepared for the press, the calamity, in anticipation of which they were written, had actually overtaken this portion of the Church of God. The Legislature of England and Ireland, (*the members of which are not even bound to profess belief in the Atonement,*) this body has virtually usurped the commission of those whom our Saviour entrusted with at *least one voice* in making ecclesiastical laws, on matters wholly or partly spiritual. The same Legislature has also ratified, to its full extent, this principle;—that the Apostolical Church in this realm is henceforth only to stand in the eye of the State, as *one sect among many*, depending, for any pre-eminence she may still appear to retain, merely upon the accident of her having a strong party in the country.

It is a moment, surely, full of deep solicitude to all those members of the Church who still believe her authority divine, and the oaths and obligations, by which they are bound to her, undissolved and indissoluble by calculations of human expediency. Their anxiety turns not so much on the consequences, to the State, of what has been done, (*they* are but too evident,) as on the line of conduct which they are bound themselves to pursue. How may they continue their communion with the Church *established*, (hitherto the pride and comfort of their lives,) without any taint of those Erastian Principles on which she is now avowedly to be governed? What answer can we make henceforth to the partisans of the Bishop of Rome, when they taunt us with being a mere Parliamentarian Church? And how, consistently with our present relations to the State, can even the doctrinal purity and integrity of the MOST SACRED ORDER be preserved?

The attention of all who love the Church is most earnestly solicited to these questions. They are such, it will be observed, as cannot be answered by appealing to precedents in English History, because, at most, such could only shew, that the difficulty might have been raised before. It is believed, that there are hundreds, nay thousands of Christians, and that soon there will be tens of thousands, unaffectedly anxious to be rightly guided with regard to these and similar points. And they are mooted thus publicly, for the chance of eliciting, from competent judges, a correct and early opinion.

If, under such trying and delicate circumstances, one could venture to be positive about any thing, it would seem safe to say, that in such measure as it may be thought incumbent on the Church, or on Churchmen, to submit to any profane intrusion, it must at least be their sacred duty, to declare, promulgate, and record, their full conviction, that it *is* intrusion; that they yield to it as they might to any other tyranny, but do from their hearts deprecate and abjure it. This seems the least that can be done: unless we would have our children's children say, "There was once here a glorious Church, but it was betrayed into the hands of Libertines for the real or affected love of a little temporary peace and good order".[2] *July* 22, 1833.

What are the symptoms, by which one may judge most fairly, whether or no a nation, as such, is becoming alienated from God and Christ?

And what are the particular duties of sincere Christians, whose lot is cast by Divine Providence in a time of such dire calamity?

The conduct of the Jews, in asking for a king, may furnish an ample illustration of the first point: the behaviour of Samuel, then and afterwards, supplies as perfect a pattern of the second, as can well be expected from human nature.[3]

I The case is at least possible, of a nation, having for centuries acknowledged, as an essential part of its theory of government, that, as a Christian nation, she is also part of Christ's Church, and bound, in all her legislation and policy, by the fundamental rules of that Church—the case is, I say, conceivable, of a government and people, so constituted, deliberately throwing off the restraint, which in many respects such a principle would impose on them, nay, disavowing the principle itself; and that, on the plea, that other states, as flourishing or more so in regard of wealth and dominion, do well enough without it. Is not this desiring, like the Jews, to have an earthly king over them, when the Lord their God is their King? Is it not saying in other words, "We will be as the heathen, the families of the countries", the aliens to the Church of our Redeemer?...

These, which have been hitherto mentioned as omens and tokens of an Apostate Mind in a nation, have been suggested by the portion itself of sacred history, to which I have ventured to direct your attention. There are one or two more, which the nature of the subject, and the palpable tendency of things around us, will not allow to be passed over.

One of the most alarming, as a symptom, is the growing indifference, in which men indulge themselves, to other men's religious sentiments. Under the guise of charity and toleration we are come almost to this pass; that no difference, in matters of faith, is to disqualify for our approbation and confidence, whether in public or domestic life. Can we conceal it from ourselves, that every year the practice is becoming more common, of trusting men unreservedly in the most delicate and important matters, without one serious inquiry, whether they do not hold principles which make it impossible for them to be loyal to their Creator, Redeemer, and Sanctifier? Are not offices conferred, partnerships formed, intimacies courted,—nay, (what is almost too painful to think of,) do not parents commit their children to be educated, do they not encourage them to intermarry, in houses, on which Apostolical Authority would rather teach them to set a mark, as unfit to be entered by a faithful servant of Christ?[4]

I do not now speak of public measures only or chiefly; many things of that kind may be thought, whether wisely or no, to become from time to time necessary, which are in reality as little desired by those who lend them a seeming concurrence, as they are, in themselves, undesirable. But I speak of the spirit which leads men to exult in every step of that kind; to congratulate one another on the supposed decay of what they call an exclusive system.

Very different are the feelings with which it seems natural for a true Churchman to regard such a state of things, from those which would arise in his mind on witnessing the mere triumph of any given set of adverse opinions, exaggerated or even heretical as he might deem them. He might feel as melancholy,—he could hardly feel so indignant.

But this is not a becoming place, nor are these safe topics, for the indulgence of mere feeling. The point really to be considered is, whether, according to the coolest estimate, the fashionable liberality of this generation be not ascribable, in a great measure, to the same temper which led the Jews voluntarily to set about degrading themselves to a level with the idolatrous Gentiles? And, if it be true any where, that such enactments are forced on the Legislature by public opinion, is APOSTASY too hard a word to describe the temper of that nation? ...

... Should it ever happen (which God avert, but we cannot shut our eyes to the danger) that the Apostolical Church should be forsaken, degraded, nay trampled on and despoiled by the State and people of England, I cannot conceive a kinder wish for her, on the part of her most affectionate and dutiful children, than that she may, consistently, act in the spirit of this most noble sentence; nor a course of conduct more likely to be blessed by a restoration to more than her former efficiency. In speaking of the Church, I mean, of course, the laity, as well as the clergy in their three orders,—the whole body of Christians united, according to the will of Jesus Christ, under the Successors of the Apostles. It may, by God's blessing, be of some use, to shew how, in the case supposed, the example of Samuel might guide her collectively, and each of her children individually, down even to minute details of duty ...

... It is all earnest INTERCESSION with God, grave, respectful, affectionate REMONSTRANCE with the misguided man himself ... On the same principle, come what may, we have ill learned the lessons of our Church, if we permit our patriotism to decay, together with the protecting care of the State. "The powers that be are ordained of God", whether they foster the true Church or no. Submission and order are still duties. They were so in the days of pagan persecution; and the more of loyal and affectionate feeling we endeavour to mingle with our obedience, the better.

After all, the surest way to uphold or restore our endangered Church, will be for each of her anxious children, in his own place and station, to resign himself more thoroughly to his God and Saviour in those duties, public and private, which are not immediately affected by the emergencies of the moment: the daily and hourly duties, I mean, of piety, purity, charity, justice. It will be a consolation understood by every thoughtful Churchman, that let his occupation be, apparently, never so remote from such great interests, it is in his power, by doing all as a Christian, to credit and advance the cause he has most at heart; and what is more, to draw down God's blessing upon it. This ought to be felt, for example, as one motive more to exact punctuality in those duties, personal and official, which the return of an Assize week offers to our practice; one reason more for veracity in witnesses, fairness in pleaders, strict impartiality, self-command, and patience, in those on whom decisions depend; and for an awful sense of God's presence in all. An Apostle once did not disdain to urge good conduct upon his proselytes of lowest condition, upon the ground, that, so doing, they would adorn and recommend the doctrine of God our Saviour.[5] Surely, then, it will be no unworthy principle, if any man be more circumspect in his behaviour, more watchful and fearful of himself, more earnest in his petitions for spiritual aid, from a dread of disparaging the holy name of the English Church, in her hour of peril, by his own personal fault or negligence.[6]

As to those who, either by station or temper, feel themselves most deeply interested, they cannot be too careful in reminding themselves, that one chief danger, in times of change and excitement, arises from their tendency to engross the whole mind. Public concerns, ecclesiastical or civil, will prove indeed ruinous to those, who permit them to occupy all their care and thoughts, neglecting or undervaluing ordinary duties, more especially those of a devotional kind.

These cautions being duly observed, I do not see how any person can devote himself too entirely to the cause of the Apostolical Church in these realms. There may be, as far as he knows, but a very few to sympathize with him. He may have to wait long, and very likely pass out of this world before he sees any abatement in the triumph of disorder and irreligion. But, if he be consistent, he possesses, to the utmost, the personal consolations of a good Christian: and as a true Churchman, he has that encouragement, which no other cause in the world can impart in the same degree: he is calmly, soberly, demonstrably, SURE, that, sooner or later, HIS WILL BE THE WINNING SIDE, and that the victory will be complete, universal, eternal. . . .[7]

1 Pusey's copy of the Assize Sermon survived in his library with its pages uncut. As Faber suggests, this may have been due to his preoccupation with his catalogue of Arabic Mss. See Faber, *Oxford Apostles*, p. 332; Chadwick, *Victorian Church* I, p. 70.

2 It was suggested, as a result of the Hadleigh meeting, that an Association of Friends of the Church be formed. In Newman's mind,

Puritanism in the Church and Liberalism in the world were the two great evils of the day.

3 The sermon was based on the text: "As for me, God forbid that I should sin against the Lord in ceasing to pray for you: but I will teach you the good and the right way" (1 Sam. 12.23).

4 The Hadleigh meeting decided to maintain the doctrine of Apostolical Succession and to defend the integrity of the Prayer Book. Tract 1 by Newman on *Thoughts on the Ministerial Commission Respectfully addressed to the Clergy* (September 1833) reflected the sentiments of the Assize Sermon, concluding with the words, "He that is not with me, is against me, and he that gathereth not with me scattereth abroad".

5 Titus 2.10

6 One notable development was the desire to fulfil the rubrical demands of the Prayer Book, and this in turn gave rise to ritualism among the second generation of Tractarians.

7 Keble, John; *b.* 1792; *educ.*, Corpus Christi College, Oxford, 1806; Fellow of Oriel, 1811; ordained deacon, 1815; priest, 1816; tutor of Oriel, 1817; Professor of Poetry at Oxford, 1831–41; vicar of Hursley, 1836–66; *d.* 1866.

9 ARNOLD ON CHURCH REFORM, 1833

(Thomas Arnold, *Principles of Church Reform* (1883), 2nd edn, pp. 30-3, 55-7, 68-70)

Thomas Arnold[1] wrote his famous pamphlet as a solution to the current difficult position of the Church of England. As an answer to Lord Henley's *Plan for Church Reform*,[2] Arnold found the future of the Church enshrined in the concept of comprehension. The liberal nature of the essay, savouring of concessions to dissenters, was to prevent Arnold from achieving high position in the established Church. His plan was attacked by both Anglicans and dissenters.

... Now, considering that on these great points all Christians are agreed, while they differ on most of them from all who are not Christians, does it seem unreasonable that persons so united in the main principles of man's life, in the objects of their religious affections, and of their hopes for eternity, should be contented to live with one another as members of the same religious society?

But they differ also in many important points, and cannot therefore form one church without seeming to sanction what they respectively believe to be error. Now, setting aside the different opinions on church government, which I shall notice presently, is it true that there are many important points of pure doctrine on which the great majority of Christians in England at this moment are not agreed? The Presbyterians, the Methodists of all denominations,[3] the Independents, the Baptists, the Moravians, can hardly be said to differ on any important point, except as connected with church government, either from one another or from the Establishment. The differences with the Baptists as to the lawfulness of Infant Baptism, may perhaps be thought an exception; but, if I mistake not, one of the highest authorities among the Baptists has expressly maintained the lawfulness of communion with Paedobaptists; and the question is not which practice is the more expedient, but whether Infant Baptism on the one hand, or the refusing it to all who cannot understand its meaning on the other, be either of them errors so fatal as to make it impossible to hold religious communion with those who maintain them.

There remain the Quakers, the Roman Catholics, and the Unitarians, whose differences appear to offer greater difficulty. And undoubtedly, so long as these sects preserve exactly their present character, it would seem impracticable to comprehend them in any national Christian church; the epithet "national" excluding the two former, and the epithet "Christian", rendering alike impossible the admission of the latter. But the harshest and most offensive part of the peculiarities of every sect has always arisen from the opposition of antagonists. Extravagance in one extreme provokes equal extravagance in the other. If, then, instead of devising forms so positive and controversial, as to excite mistrust of their accuracy in the most impartial minds, and a vehement opposition from those whose opinions lean to a different side, we were to make our language general and comprehensive, and content ourselves with protesting against the abuses which may follow from an exclusive view of the question, even when it is in itself substantially true, it is probable that those who differ from us would soon begin to consider the subject in a different temper; and that if truth were the object of both parties, and not victory, truth would in fact be more nearly attained by both. In this respect, the spirit of the Seventeenth Article of the Church of England affords an excellent model, inasmuch as it is intended to be comprehensive and conciliatory, rather than controversial.[4] And the effect to be hoped for from assuming such a tone, would be the bringing reasonable and moderate men to meet us, and to unite with us; there would of course be always some violent spirits, who would maintain their peculiar tenets without modification; but the end of all wise government, whether in temporal matters or in spiritual, is not to satisfy every body, which is impossible, but to make the dissatisfied a powerless minority, by drawing away from them that mass of curable discontent whose support can alone make them dangerous....

... The Church government then would be made more efficient, and at the same time, more popular than it is at present; 1st. By reducing the size of the dioceses:[5] 2nd. By giving the bishop a council consisting of lay members and of clerical, and partly elected by the officers of the respective parishes;[6] which officers should themselves also be lay and clerical, and for the most part elected directly by the inhabitants: 3rd. By the institution of diocesan general assemblies: 4th. By admitting into the Establishment, persons of a class much too poor to support the expense of an university education; but who may be exceedingly useful as ministers, and who do preach at present, but under circumstances which make them necessarily hostile to the National Church, and leave them utterly at liberty to follow their own caprices: 5th. By allowing in many cases the election of ministers, and by giving to the inhabitants of the parish in every case, a greater check over their appointment than they at present enjoy: and 6th. By constituting church officers in every parish, lay as well (as) clerical, who should share with the principal minister in its superintendance; and thus effect generally that good, which in London and elsewhere is now being attempted by individual zeal, in the establishment of district visiting societies. Whilst by rendering the articles far more comprehensive than at present, according to what was said in the earlier part of this sketch, those who are now Dissenting ministers might at once become ministers of the Establishment, and as such, would of course have their share in its government.

It will be observed, that the whole of this scheme supposes an episcopal government, and requires that all ministers should receive episcopal ordination. The Establishment is entitled surely to this concession from the Dissenters, especially when Episcopacy will have been divested of all those points against which their objections have been particularly levelled.[7] Besides, there are many members of the Establishment who believe Episcopacy not expedient only, but absolutely essential to a Christian Church: and their scruples are entitled to quite as much respect as those of the Dissenters....

... Now, considering that some persons would like nothing but the Liturgy, that others, on the contrary, can endure no prayers but such as are extemporaneous,—that many more have a preference for one practice or the other, but not so as to wish to be confined to the exclusive use of it, there seems to be no reason why the National Church should not enjoy a sufficient variety in its ritual, to satisfy the opinions and feelings of all. In a parish where there was but one minister, he might read the Liturgy on Sunday mornings, while on Sunday evenings, and on week days, he might vary the service according to his discretion and the circumstances of the case. But where there were several ministers, as there would be wherever there are now ministers of different denominations, the church might be kept open nearly the whole of the Sunday, and we may hope, during some part at least of every weekday;—the different services being fixed at different hours, and performed by different ministers. And he judges untruly of human nature, who does not see that the peculiarities which men now cling to and even exaggerate, as the badge and mark of their own sect, would then soon sink into their proper insignificance when nothing was to be gained by dwelling on them....

... It may appear to some a point of small importance, but I believe that it would go a long way towards producing a kindly and united feeling amongst all the inhabitants of the parish, that the parish church should, if possible, be the only place of public worship; and that the different services required, should rather be performed at different times in the same spot than at the same time in different places. In this respect, the spirit of the Mosaic law may be most usefully followed, which forbade the multiplication of temples and altars, but fixed on one spot to become endeared and hallowed to the whole people as the scene of their common worship. Besides, the parish church has a sacredness which no other place of worship can boast of, in its antiquity, and in its standing amidst the graves of so many generations of our fathers.[8] It is painful to think that any portion of the people should have ever broken their connection with it; it would be equally delightful to see them again assembled within its walls, without any base compromise of opinion on either side, but because we had learned a better wisdom than to deprive it of its just claim to the affections of all our countrymen, or to exclude any portion of our countrymen from the happiness of loving it as it deserves. Nor is it a light thing in the judgments of those who understand the ennobling effects of a quick perception of what is beautiful and venerable, that some of the most perfect specimens of architecture in existence should no longer be connected, in any man's mind, with the bitterness of sectarian hostility; that none should be forced to associate, with their most solemn and dearest recollections, such utter coarseness and deformity as characterize the great proportion of the Dissenting chapels throughout England.

1 Arnold, Thomas; *b.* 1795; *educ.*, Corpus Christi College, Oxford, 1811; B.A. 1814; Fellow of Oriel, 1815; ordained, 1818; private tutor, 1819; Headmaster of Rugby, 1827; ordained priest, 1828; Regius Professor of Modern History at Oxford, 1841; *d.* 1842.

2 Eden, Robert, Lord Henley; a barrister and a commissioner of bankruptcy. His *Plan of Church Reform* (1832), greatly influenced the Ecclesiastical Commission.

3 Methodist "denominations" included the Methodist New Connexion (1797); Independent Methodists (1805); Primitive Methodists (1810); and the Bible Christians (1815).

4 *Of Predestination and Election.*

5 Henley recommended the erection of a diocese of Windsor from Salisbury; the diocese of Southwell; and that part of Chester diocese should be added to Carlisle.

6 Henley suggested: "That a Commission be appointed to inquire into the best Means of giving Efficiency to the *Convocation*, and to devise a Mode whereby the Attendance of the Bishops in Parliament may be dispensed with, without Danger to the Rights, Liberties and Privileges of the Church of England."

7 Henley advocated: "That no Translation shall ever be made of any Bishop appointed after this Act, being a Lord of Parliament, except to the Sees of Canterbury and York."

8 See the Burial Laws Amendment Act and the Compulsory Church Rate Abolition Act.

10 NEWMAN ON THE *VIA MEDIA*, 1834

(*Tracts for the Times* 38 and 41,
Via Media (*Ad Scholas*), pp. 6, 8-10, 5-6)

Newman wrote to Bowden on 10 August 1834: "I took your hint about Popery immediately, and wrote the Tract called 'Via Media', which appeared the beginning of this month, though I am diffident whether it will answer your aim. I am quite prepared for the charges of both Popery and Pelagianism, nor do I see how to escape them. In my view of the matter, the flood of Puritanism is pouring over the Church, as Liberalism over the world;[1] and any one who believes this and makes a stand will be sure to incur the reputation of those heresies which are the contrary of the fashionable ones." As long as Newman could identify the Church of England with the ideal of the Christian Church in the patristic writers of the first five centuries, the doctrine of the *Via Media* was tenable, but by the time he came to write Tract 90 serious doubts had arisen in his mind.[2]

Laicus Ought you so to speak of the foreign Reformers? To them we owe the Protestant doctrine altogether.

Clericus I like foreign interference, as little from Geneva, as from Rome. Geneva at least never converted a part of England from heathenism, nor could lay claim to patriarchal authority over it. Why could we not be let alone, and suffered to reform ourselves?

Laicus You separate then your creed and cause from that of the Reformed Churches of the Continent?

Clericus Not altogether; but I protest against being brought into that close alliance with them which the world now-a-days would force upon us. The glory of the English Church is, that it has taken the VIA MEDIA, as it has been called.[3] It lies *between* the (so called) Reformers and the Romanists; whereas there are religious circles, and influential too, where it is thought enough to prove an English Clergyman unfaithful to his Church, if he preaches anything at variance with the opinions of the Diet of Augsburg, or the Confessions of the Waldenses.[4] However, since we have been led to speak of the foreign Reformers, I will, if you will listen to me, strengthen my argument by an appeal to them ...

Clericus This is not the first time you have spoken of this supposed system of ours. I will not stop to quarrel with you for calling it *ours*, as if it were not rather the Church's; but explain to me what you consider it to consist in.

Laicus The following are some of its doctrines: that the Church has an existence independent of the State; that the State may not religiously interfere with its internal concerns; that none may engage in ministerial works except such as are episcopally ordained; that the consecration of the Eucharist is especially entrusted to Bishops and Priests. Where do you find these doctrines in the formularies of the Church; that is, so prominently set forth, as to sanction you in urging them at all, or at least so strongly as you used to urge them?[5]

Clericus As to urging them at all, we might be free to urge them even though not mentioned in the Articles; unless indeed the Articles are our rule of faith. Were the Church first set up at the Reformation, then indeed it might be right so to exalt its Articles as to forbid to teach "whatsoever is not read therein, nor may be proved thereby". I cannot consent, I am sure the Reformers did not wish me, to deprive myself of the Church's dowry, the doctrines which the Apostles spoke in Scripture and impressed upon the early Church. I receive the Church as a messenger from CHRIST, rich in treasures old and new, rich with the accumulated wealth of ages.

Laicus Accumulated?

Clericus As you will yourself allow. Our Articles are one portion of that accumulation. Age after age, fresh battles have been fought with heresy, fresh monuments of truth set up. As I will not consent to be deprived of the records of the Reformation, so neither will I part with those of former times. I look upon our Articles as in one sense an addition to the Creeds; and at the same time the Romanists added their Tridentine articles. Theirs I consider unsound; ours as true.[6]

Laicus The Articles have surely an especial claim upon you; you have subscribed them, and are therefore more bound to them, than to other truths, whatever or wherever they be.

Clericus There is a popular confusion on this subject. Our Articles are not a *body of divinity*, but in great measure only protest against certain errors of a certain period of the Church. Now I will preach the whole counsel of GOD, whether set down in the Articles or not. I am bound to the Articles by subscription; but I am bound, more solemnly even than by subscription, by my baptism and by my ordination, to believe and maintain the *whole* Gospel of CHRIST. The grace given at those seasons comes through the Apostles, not through Luther or Calvin, Bucer or Cartwright. You will presently agree with me in this statement ...

Laicus I understand you further to say, that you hold to the Reformers as far as they have spoken out in our formularies, which at the same time you consider as incomplete; that the doctrines which may appear wanting in the Article such as the Apostolical Commission,[7] are the doctrines of the Church Catholic; doctrines, which a member of that Church holds *as such*, prior to subscription; that, moreover, they are quite consistent with our Articles, sometimes are even implied in them, and sometimes clearly contained in the Liturgy, though not in the Articles, as the Apostolical Commission in the Ordination Service; lastly, that we are clearly bound to believe, and all of us do believe, as essential, doctrines which nevertheless are not contained in the Articles, as e.g. the inspiration of Holy Scripture.

Clericus Yes—and further I maintain, that, while I fully concur in the Articles, as far as they go, those who call one Papist, do not acquiesce in the doctrine of the Liturgy.

Laicus This is a subject I especially wish drawn out. You threw out some hints about it the other day, though I cannot say you convinced me. I have misgivings, after all, that our Reformers only *began* their own work. I do not say they saw the tendency and issue of their opinions; but surely, had they lived, and had the opportunity of doing more, they would have given in to much more liberal notions (as they are called) than you are disposed to concede. It is not by producing a rubric, or an insulated passage from the services, that you can destroy this impression. Such instances only show they were inconsistent, which I will grant. Still, is not the genius of our formularies towards a more latitudinarian system than they reach?

Clericus I will cheerfully meet you on the grounds you propose. Let us carefully examine the Liturgy in its separate parts. I think it will decide the point which I contended for the other day, viz. that we are more Protestant than our Reformers.

Laicus What do you mean by Protestant in your present use of the word?

Clericus A number of distinct doctrines are included in the notion of Protestantism: and as to all these, our Church has taken the VIA MEDIA between it and Popery. At present I will use it in the sense most apposite to the topics we have been discussing; viz. as the religion of so-called freedom and independence, as hating superstition, suspicious of forms, jealous of priestcraft, advocating heart worship; characteristics, which admit of a good or a bad interpretation, but which, understood as they are instanced in the majority of persons who are zealous for what is called Protestant doctrine, are (I maintain) very inconsistent with the Liturgy of our Church....

1 See A. R. Vidler, *Essays in Liberality* (S.C.M. Press 1957), Ch. 1.

2 Newman later wrote in the *Apologia*: "A *Via Media* was but a receding from extremes, therefore I had to draw it out into a shape, and a character; before it had claims on our respect, it must first be shown to be one, intelligible, and consistent ... Even if the *Via Media* were ever so positive a religious system, it was not as yet objective and real; it had no original anywhere of which it was the representative. It was at present a paper religion" (p. 147).

3 The conception of the *Via Media* was to be found in such seventeenth-century divines as George Herbert and Simon Patrick. Dean Church maintained that Newman "followed the great Anglican divines in asserting that there was a true authority, varying in degrees, in the historic Church; that on the most fundamental points of religion this authority was trustworthy and supreme; that on many other questions it was clear and weighty, though it could not decide everything". Quoted in Faber, *Oxford Apostles*, p. 324.

4 The *Confession of Augsburg* (1530) was, unlike the *Articles of Religion*, an authoritative doctrinal statement. It was mainly the work of Melanchthon, who considerably revised the original text in 1540. See Kidd, *Documents of the Continental Reformation*, pp. 259-89. The Waldenses had been much publicized in England through the publication of W. S. Gilly's *Narrative of an Excursion to the Mountains of Piedmont and Researches among the Vaudois or Waldenses* (1824).

5 The *Tracts for the Times* were born of the religious implications of the social and political changes between 1829 and 1833. The meeting at Hadleigh Rectory of Rose, Froude, William Palmer, and Perceval, had called for an Association of Friends of the Church. The *Tracts* were the organ of the more militant critics of political liberalism such as Froude, Newman, Pusey, and Keble.

6 When in Rome in 1833, Newman and Froude were told by Wiseman that the Council of Trent barred the way between the Church of England and the Church of Rome. In Tract 90 Newman erroneously argued that the *Articles* only condemned Romish doctrine, not the decrees of the Council of Trent which were published and ratified after the Articles had been drawn up.

7 *Tract 1*, published in September 1833 (*Ad Clerum*) was *Thoughts on the Ministerial Commission Respectfully addressed to the Clergy,*

written by Newman. The following also wrote tracts: Newman (29); Keble (8); Pusey (7); Bowden (5); Thomas Keble (4); Harrison (4); Froude (3); Perceval (3); Williams (3); Palmer, Menzies, Eden, Wilson, Buller, Manning, and Marriott (1). There were reprints from Bishop Wilson (12); Cosin (2); Beveridge (2); Bull (1); and Ussher (1). See: Burgon, *Lives of Twelve Good Men*, vol. 1, appendix D; and Liddon, *Life of Pusey*.

11 THE TITHE COMMUTATION ACT 1836

(*Statutes at Large*, 6-7 Will. IV, c. 71)

The tithe was an integral part of the clerical income, though in many cases it had passed into the hands of lay impropriators with the sale and exchange of church property. Thus in the agricultural risings of 1830 in the South, East, and parts of the Midlands, the rioters demanded a remission of tithes from both clergy and lay landlords. Opposition to the payment of tithe, and disgust at the objectionable methods of collection came largely from dissenters.[1] Many clergy made their own private arrangements for payment to be made in cash instead of kind. The Act set up a Tithe Commission which was to lay an annual report before Parliament.[2]

XVII And be it enacted, That any One or more of the Land Owners or Tithe Owners, whose Interest respectively shall not be less than One Fourth Part of the whole Value of the Lands subject to Tithes, or One Fourth Part of the whole Value of the Tithes of any Parish in *England* or *Wales*, may call a Parochial Meeting of Land Owners and Tithe Owners within the Limits of the Parish, by Notice thereof in Writing under his or their Hand, to be affixed at least Twenty-one Days before such Meeting on the principal outer Door of the Church, or in some public and conspicuous Place within the Limits of the Parish, and to be twice at least during such Twenty-one Days inserted in some newspaper generally circulated within the County in which such Parish is situated, for the Purpose of making an Agreement for the general Commutation of Tithes within the Limits of such Parish; ... and the Land Owners and Tithe Owners who shall be present at any such Meeting called as aforesaid ... may proceed to make and execute a Parochial Agreement for the Payment of an annual Sum by way of Rent-charge, variable as hereinafter provided, instead of the Great and Small Tithes of the Parish collectively,[3] or instead of the Great

Tithes and Small Tithes severally, to the respective Owners thereof in the said Parish; and every Agreement so made and executed, and confirmed in manner hereinafter mentioned, shall be binding on all Persons interested in the Tithes or Lands subject to Tithes of the said Parish.

XIX Provided always, and be it enacted, That the proportional Interest of the Owners of such Lands, or Tithes, so far as relates to their Power to make any such Agreement or provisional Agreement, or to give any Notice to the Comissioners or Assistant Commissioners as hereinafter provided, shall be estimated according to the proportional Sum at which such Lands or Tithes shall be rated to the Relief of the Poor, or, if there shall be no such Rate, according to the Rules by which Property of the same Kind is by Law rateable to the relief of the Poor.

XXVI Provided always, and be it enacted, That in every Case in which any Tithes shall belong to any Ecclesiastical Person in right of any Spiritual Dignity or Benefice, no Agreement for the Commutation of such Tithes made and executed under this Act shall be deemed to be executed by the Owner of such Tithes unless such Consent thereto be given as is hereinafter mentioned; (that is to say), in the Case of an Archbishop or Bishop, the Consent of the Crown signified by the Lord High Treasurer or First Lord Commissioner of the Treasury; and in case of the Incumbent of any other Benefice or Ecclesiastical Dignity, the Consent of the Patron or Person entitled to present to such Benefice or Dignity in case the same were then vacant; and every such Consent shall be given under the Hand of the Person giving the same, and shall be annexed to the Agreement, and taken to be Part of the Execution thereof.[4]

XXXVII And be it enacted, That in every Case in which the Commissioners shall intend making such Award, Notice thereof shall be given in such Manner as to them shall seem fit; and after the Expiration of Twenty-one Days after such Notice shall have been given the Commissioners or some Assistant Commissioner shall, except in the Cases for which Provision is hereinafter made, proceed to ascertain the clear Average Value (after making all just Deductions on account of the Expences of collecting, preparing for Sale, and marketing, where such Tithes have been taken in Kind,) of the Tithes of the said Parish, according to the Average of Seven Years preceding *Christmas* in the Year One Thousand eight hundred and thirty-five: Provided that if during the said Period of Seven Years, or any Part thereof, the said Tithes or any Part thereof shall have been compounded for or demised to the Owner or Occupier of any of the said Lands in consideration of any Rent or Payment instead of Tithes, the Amount of such Composition or Rent or Sum agreed to be paid instead of Tithes shall be taken as the clear Value of the Tithes included in such Composition, Demise, or Agreement during the Time for which the same shall have been made; and the Commissioners or Assistant Commissioner shall award the average annual Value of the said Seven Years so ascertained as the Sum to be taken for calculating the Rent-charge to be paid as a permanent Commutation of the said Tithes: Provided also, that whenever it shall appear to the Commissioners that the Party entitled to any such Rent or Composition shall in any One or more of the said Seven Years have allowed and made any Abatement from the Amount of such Rent or Composition on the ground of the same having in any such Year or Years been higher than the Sum fairly payable by way of Composition for the Tithe, but not otherwise, then and in every such Case such diminished Amount, after making such Abatement as aforesaid, shall be deemed and taken to have been the Sum agreed to be paid for any such Year or Years: Provided also, that in estimating the Value of the said Tithes the Commissioners or Assistant Commissioner shall estimate the same without making any Deduction therefrom on account of any Parliamentary, Parochial, County, and other Rates, Charges, and Assessments to which the said Tithes are liable; and whenever the said Tithes shall have been demised or compounded for on the Principle of the Rent or Composition being paid free from all such Rates, Charges, and Assessments, or any Part thereof, the said Commissioners or Assistant Commissioner shall have regard to that Circumstance, and shall make such Addition on account thereof as shall be an Equivalent.[5]

1 The Quakers were especially vocal in their opposition to tithes as a matter of principle. Since abolition would have meant the compensation of lay impropriators, commutation was the cheapest alternative.

2 There were three commissioners: two nominated by the King and one by the Archbishop of Canterbury.

3 Great tithes included all major crops including wheat and oats. Small tithes included all minor produce such as lambs and poultry. Under the Act of 1891, the payment of rent-charge was the responsibility of the landowner not the tenant.

4 The collection of money was a simpler arrangement than that of

the collection of kind, and therefore involved the clergy in fewer disputes with farmers.

5 The valuation on the market prices of wheat, barley, and oats, was favourable to the clergy while the population was increasing, prices rising, and property highly valued. However, from 1878 till 1901 there was a steady decline in agricultural prosperity which was less advantageous to the clergy.

12 ARCHBISHOP HOWLEY AND THE COPTIC CHURCH, 1842

(B. Harrison, *Christianity in Egypt. Letters and Papers concerning the Coptic Church, 1836–1848* (1883))

The travels of Henry Tattam[1] in the Nitrian desert provided the opportunity for a correspondence between Howley and the leader of the Coptic Church.[2] Although there was no marked development in the relationship between the two Churches, it encouraged a growing interest in the ancient Churches of the East. This aspect of ecumenical interest was continued by the work of such people as John Wordsworth, Bishop Blyth, W. J. Birkbeck, and Bishop Headlam.[3]

Lambeth Palace, August 16, 1842.

WILLIAM LORD ARCHBISHOP OF CANTERBURY, PRIMATE OF ALL ENGLAND AND METROPOLITAN, TO HIS HOLINESS THE PATRIARCH OF CAIRO, GREETING IN THE LORD.

MOST REVEREND PRELATE,

Whereas our well-beloved Presbyter, the Reverend Henry Tattam, a man of eminent piety and learned in Holy Scriptures, is going out to Egypt, under the sanction of the British Government, for the purpose of obtaining manuscripts, and collecting such information as may be of use in promoting the interests of our holy religion, I gladly avail myself of this opportunity of assuring you of the high respect and good-will which are felt by me, and the other rulers of our Church, towards your Holiness and the Churches under your care, and of our desire to render you all the assistance in our power. In proof of this desire on our part, Mr Tattam will exhibit to your Holiness a specimen of the New Testament in the Coptic and Arabic languages, which is now in preparation for the use of your Churches; and he will be happy to receive any suggestions from your Holiness which may render the work more perfect.[4]

I further beg leave most earnestly to commend Mr Tattam to your Holiness' kind consideration, assuring you that any attention which may tend to facilitate the attainment of the objects of his mission will be gratefully acknowledged by me, and by the members of our Church, who unite with me in zeal for the advancement of the Christian religion, and in sentiments of high respect and regard for your Holiness' person and the Church over which you preside.[5]

From your Holiness' brother in Christ,

W. CANTUAR:

Written with my own hand.

1 Tattam, Henry; *b.* 1789; his travels are narrated in Miss Platt, *Journal of a Tour through Egypt, the Peninsula of Sinai, and the Holy Land in 1838, 1839*; became Archdeacon of Bedford, 1845; *d.* 1868.

2 The ancient Egyptian Church became formally Monophysite after the condemnation of Dioscorus in 451, at the Council of Chalcedon.

3 The Copts obtained a measure of freedom of worship with the British occupation of Egypt after 1882. Headlam wrote a report for the Archbishop of Canterbury on the state of the Church in Asia Minor, Egypt, and Greece in 1891, mentioning the Coptic Church.

4 Tattam recovered from the Nitrian desert a number of important Coptic and Syriac manuscripts, including the *Curetonian Syriac.* This version of the Gospels came from the library of the Convent of St Mary Deipara, and was catalogued by William Cureton at the British Museum.

5 The lesser Eastern Churches included the Armenians, Copts, Abyssinians, Jacobites, Assyrians, and the Syrian Orthodox Church in South India. The Patriarch of the Coptic Church is elected by the twelve bishops.

13 GLADSTONE ON THE ROYAL SUPREMACY, 1841

(W. E. Gladstone, *The State in its Relation with the Church* (4th edn, 1841), vol. 2, pp. 27-43)

Gladstone's book was first published in 1838 and was the classic exposition of the theory of Church and State in the nineteenth century. The longevity of his life as a political figure made it possible for him, as an author, to see how the theory worked in practice. The principle of a single state religion which he formerly propounded was found to be untenable in later years, and his erudition and piety served the Church of England well in the developing struggle between the Church and State in England.[1]

28 When two independent bodies enter into reciprocal relations, which neither are such as to fuse into one their distinct personalities, nor are, on the other hand, capable of being determined prospectively by written stipulations, with no other additional provision or reservation than the alternative of a total rupture; it becomes a matter of equal delicacy and importance to constitute a power which may be found generally competent to regulate their joint action according to circumstances as they shall arise, without either being absolutely tied to the limited sphere which a written contract could define, or, on the other hand, hazarding a resort to the extreme measure of dissolving the alliance. That power must be one, and must be paramount. But although paramount, and although mainly deriving its character from one of the two bodies, it does not destroy the independence of the other, because there always remains the ultimate remedy of putting an end to the connection; and the usefulness of the power is of course founded on the assumption that they will be generally in such a degree of harmony, that although there must of necessity be but one fountain of authority for joint administrative purposes arising out of the connection, yet it will express and represent upon the whole the tendencies of both.

29 Now those powers which belong to the Church as a religious society may, of course, be competently administered apart by her spiritual governors, and the analogous proposition holds good with regard to the State; but when the alliance has once been formed, the Church has become an estate of the realm, having certain relations with the other estates, closely united and interwoven with

them, and entailing a necessity, for the well-being of the whole, of some strict uniformity of operation between them. Now it is for the government of these relations from time to time, that an authority is required, neither purely ecclesiastical nor purely civil, inasmuch as the relations themselves are of a compound character. To take an example: if a bishop rejects a candidate for a living[2] upon ecclesiastical grounds, he cannot lawfully be corrected by the State; but if he do it upon arbitrary grounds, or grounds not ecclesiastical, he may; because the accession to the living is not to a spiritual function alone, but to certain civil rights and emoluments along with it. Since then civil and ecclesiastical consequences are thus mixed up together, and both may flow from acts properly ecclesiastical, there arises a necessity for this middle authority, which, having as much sympathy as possible with both bodies, and representing both, shall be more akin to such a kind of jurisdiction than either of them, taken singly, would afford; accordingly the head of the State, invested, according to the Church, with a function of peculiar sacredness, and under the condition that he shall be also personally a member of the Church, is invested with it. He exercises an appellate jurisdiction; he judges not the cause, but the judgment; assuming the grounds which are supplied by ecclesiastical law, and inquiring whether its principles have been fairly applied to the particular subject-matter.

30 In connecting together the Church and the State, it will of course be the dictate of practical prudence to make such arrangements that neither party, within its own peculiar province, shall be needlessly perplexed by the intervention of the other; and the reciprocal confidence which the union of necessity implies will incline each to repose a liberal confidence in the other, and they will freely interchange the care of many collateral interests. There must, however, be regulations provided, which may meet the contingency of possible disagreement between the Church and the State. Let us inquire what considerations are entitled to influence their formation.

31 If, then, in a particular case, it happen that the canons, or the claims, of the Church as established come into collision with the statute or the common law of the realm, in the last issue, it is clear that the former must yield. It will depend upon the intrinsic merits of the principle for which she may be contending, whether she retains her authority in the court of conscience, her final test: it is no part of the law of her earthly condition that her will, even her legitimate and reasonable will, shall always take

practical and bodily effect: whereas this is the absolute condition of the being of the State, that is, of the maintenance of social order on which it depends. The alternative still open to the Church is the resignation of all her peculiar legal privileges. Though her laws be forcibly and unwarrantably resisted, and even overborne, she may remain a Church persuading and admonishing the world; but a State must have compulsory power, to be exercised according to its discretion in the last resort, or the very keystone of civil society is removed.

32 Again: it is the absolute indispensable function of the State, to secure the social machine from stoppage or disruption, by the suppression of all disturbing forces. Hence it claims in every case to supersede of right any power which shall come into collision with its own. On this ground it assumes the prerogative of limiting the action of the Church by its own, the *majestätsrecht des Staates über die Kirche*,[3] and the Church concedes it. Whether the union subsists or not, the State must reserve to itself this authority, to meet the case of necessity. Its acknowledgment by anticipation on the part of the Church does not so much imply actual surrender of any part of her desire, as the common conviction of both parties, that the contingency of collision is both improbable and formidable, and ought by every possible means to be avoided.

33 Of the rigid advocate of Church power I would freely claim the admission, that the State and not the Church is the supreme coercive power on earth, and must therefore finally rule a disputed point in the mixed action of the Church wherever, upon its own responsibility, it may see fit. The Church may not oppose resistance to the law without forgoing the privileges of legal establishment. When she has forgone those privileges she must still obey in all things not sinful, but she has then relieved herself from a particular contract, which she had found to be at variance with her higher and more comprehensive obligations.

34 The argument may even be pushed farther: it may be held that if laws be passed totally incompatible in principle with the distinct spiritual existence of the Church, still she must submit to them until it has become evident that they impair in practice her essential powers. It is a very general rule of Christian kingdoms, that no synod may be held without the permission of the prince.[4] Now it is difficult to conceive anything more demonstratively reasonable, than the claim of the Church to meet in her synods; for it is not pretended by our law, for example, that controversies of faith can be decided anywhere else. It may

therefore be said, that the civil ruler might at all times, according to this prerogative, have prevented synodical assemblies, and it seems that if he had done so, the Church would have been fettered in the exercise of a necessary function. Suppose, again, that the Crown have a *veto* on the appointment of bishops, or have an exclusive right of presenting them for election or consecration, it is clearly invested with a prerogative which may, in its extreme exercise, abolish the power of order, the ministry, the sacraments, and the whole body of the Church. But these are theoretical difficulties; and they can only be used as general objections upon the supposition that power will uniformly be used for objects contrary to those for which it was given, an assumption as false as its direct contradictory would be. They are attended with no real embarrassment, more than such a political principle as, for example, the unlimited power of taxation in the State, which in theory clearly might extend to stripping every subject of his last farthing, and so reducing a people to starvation.[5]

35 The question, therefore, which as practical inquirers we are called to consider is, not whether the law in a particular social relation be such as, if its powers were used in their full extent, would be inconsistent with the Christian liberties of the Church, but whether its spirit and intention, so far as they are really discernible, are, and especially whether its actual exercise has been, such as to prevent her discharging the essential duties committed to her by our Lord, in respect to the maintenance and the propagation of the faith, and the administration of holy ordinances and discipline. In short, we must well consider the conditions of double action, and the limitations it necessarily imposes upon the separate will, as well as the prerogatives which the Church has, even in her best days, recognized as belonging to the prince, before we attempt to decide upon the precise terms of adjustment in particular cases between the secular and the spiritual power.

36 It does not follow from these positions that the Church is left without resort. On the contrary, whether the law may or may not recognize her inherent and organic powers, they may be called into exercise upon sufficient occasion. The doctrine would be monstrous indeed, that the State should monopolize both sides of the alternative; that it should have the constitutional power both of determining the alliance according to its will, and of imposing its indefinite continuance upon a reluctant partner. The connection, then, is one *durante bene placito* of both the contracting parties. And if the conscience of the Church of England should, by its

constituted rulers, require any law, or any meeting to make laws, as essential to its well-being, and such law, or the licence of such meeting, should be permanently refused, it would then be her duty to resign her civil privileges, and act in her free spiritual capacity; a contingency as improbable, we trust, as it would be deplorable, but one which, opening this extreme remedy, testifies to the real, though dormant and reserved, independence of the Church. It must be added, that, although an extreme, it is not a visionary or an impracticable resort, which is here supposed, but one which has been actually realized in our history. Twice partially, (in citing the fact it is quite unnecessary to determine the merits,) in the cases, namely, of Mary, (when, according to Bishop Burnet, three thousand clergy were expelled,) and of the nonjuring bishops: once generally, when no less than eight thousand, as it is stated[6] by writers of the period upon inquiry, were ejected under the Long Parliament and Cromwell. It seems, however, highly probable, that the repetition of such an event would be attended with far more vital struggles than took place upon the first or even on the second of these occasions; and far from a visionary dream, that it might issue in total anarchy.

37 Yet it is evidently within the spiritual competency of the Church. She therefore retains, I will not say universally her actual, but her potential independence—her distinctness of being, and her power of resuming her original and absolute freedom. And it is quite possible, that she may enjoy her internal freedom, while meeting all the conditions of the law. Two wills, like two watches, may be independent while indicating the same hour, and moving at the same rate by virtue of an inward harmony. Such an inward harmony is essentially presumed in any enduring connection of the Church with the State. But at all events, and in the very worst contingency, the parties are independent as two men are independent, who become companions on a journey because they find themselves travelling in the same direction, and who reserve their right to part so soon as the roads, which they respectively intend to follow, shall diverge.

38 There has, however, here been conceded to the State, by way of abstract principle, more than our constitution appears to claim, whether for the sovereign or the legislature. The latter has never asserted an authority of determining heresy, except with the assent of the clergy; and it has settled the Liturgy and Articles on the footing on which they were arranged by the Convocations of 1562 and 1661. Thus the active power of moving the Church in spiritual

matters is not at all arrogated. Again, as to the prerogative of the Crown. Its demand is of a negative character. The sovereign claims under our constitution a *veto* on all canons, and his permission is required for the meeting of Convocation, but he does not claim the right of making by his sole authority any laws for the Church. Indeed a question might, as is said by some, be raised, whether it is or is not competent to the Church of England to meet in synod even without the royal authority, especially when it is considered that this right undoubtedly exists in the provinces of Ireland. The whole of this subject, and the policy which the State ought hereafter to pursue with regard to it, are most important, and require to be fully considered. It is enough here to observe, that if anything has been done of late years in the way either of anomaly or of usurpation, it has been done by the collective legislature in its capacity of political omnipotence; it has been done while the Church organs are in abeyance; it does not bind, or commit the Church, which is not a consenting party, to approbation, but only to obedience. She is only bound to show that in the regal supremacy, as acknowledged by her, which claims a negative upon all Church laws and upon all sentences in mixed matter, there is nothing unscriptural or unecclesiastical; and that in the actual exercise of this or any other State power, there has been nothing which has impaired her essence, whether its particular acts may in every case have been justifiable or not.

39 It is impossible, in point of fact, that any other basis could be adopted than one which gives the State a *veto* on changes in the Church. The Church allies herself with the State in consideration of advantages accorded to her, which are accorded in respect of her peculiar constitution as a Church, and which would cease to be due if she violated that constitution; therefore the State must have the means of observing all her movements, of judging what change is violation, and of interposing the *veto*, which means simply, "If you do so, you must no longer enjoy civil advantages." But the converse argument does not hold as arising from the alliance, that the Church should have a *veto* on projected alterations in the State, because that which she renders to the State, the teaching of obedience, and the promotion of piety and virtue, she owes to it simply as the appointed government of the country, whatever changes its constitution may undergo.

40 This right on the part of the State is no more than analogous to the right of individuals, to be exempted from coercion in forming or modifying their belief. As it is the charge of the individual

from God to determine what conviction shall have sway within the precinct of his own breast, so it is the charge imposed by the same power upon the State to determine what convictions shall prevail within the circle of laws and public institutions. Therefore, when the Church has taken her position within that circle, she must by no means attempt to violate what is a fundamental condition, not indeed only of the welfare of the State, but even of its existence. She went thither in no selfish view, but because duty, and the work entrusted to her care, seemed to conduct her to the post. Of course she must not remain there to the detriment of those interests which she repaired thither to advance and secure.

41 Let us, then, endeavour, by way of summing up this portion of the inquiry, to draw a distinction between the power, the right, and the law, as severally affecting it. First, as respects the power; the civil legislature is, by the first condition of all naturally constituted or tolerable polities, to be socially omnipotent; but as, if it enacted that individuals should sacrifice to idols, they would probably disobey, so the Church would be bound to refuse compliance if an infraction of her divinely established constitution should be attempted. Of course, neither the one case nor the other is stated as a probable contingency; nor is it consistent with the principles of public law, that provisions should be made for any such dilemma.

42 As respects the right, we may or may not think that the Church requires, in this or that particular, a more free and effective organization; but before determining that by not insisting specifically on its being conceded to her, she has forfeited her spiritual character, we should inquire, first, whether anything essential to her constitution has been or is to be violated; and, secondly, whether she has surrendered the right to pass into her state of separate freedom. For example, it is a part of our ecclesiastical law, that if any archbishop or bishop shall refuse, after due notice given, to confirm and consecrate a bishop elect, within a limited time, they and their abettors shall incur a *praemunire*. But the proctor of the dean and chapter must certify the election, in order to the confirmation, and in this point among others, "that the person elected is sufficiently qualified by age, knowledge, learning, orders, sobriety, condition, fidelity to the king, and piety". Of course, the governors of the Church would be bound, by the most absolute obligations of conscience, to incur the civil penalty, rather than confirm or consecrate, should a person ecclesiastically incompetent be presented to them.[7] And the questions which alone

we are here required to consider are, not whether the law be consistent in theory with ecclesiastical freedom, but whether in practice the Church has been debarred from the performance of her essential functions; and if not, then also whether, in the event of her being thus invaded, there be not a remedy in reserve for a contingency so deplorable.

43 As respects the actual law regarding the royal supremacy, we may gather its general principle sufficiently from the doctrine of Blackstone,[8] who sums up the duties of the monarch to his people thus: "To govern according to law; to execute judgment in mercy; and to *maintain* the established religion." And from the coronation oath; in which the promise is, "to *maintain* the laws of God, the true profession of the gospel, and the Protestant reformed religion established by the law": and to "*preserve* unto the bishops and clergy of this realm, and to the churches committed to their charge, all such rights and privileges as by law do or shall appertain unto them, or any of them": terms which imply a power somewhere to change the ecclesiastical laws, but which describe the royal duty as generally a duty of conservation, a duty to "maintain", to "preserve", not to modify or innovate.

44 As respects the appointment of bishops, it is unnecessary to enter into any detailed consideration of this prerogative. It is in a great degree analogous to ordinary lay patronage with respect to the order of the priesthood. It had been long and indisputably in the hands of sovereigns, many centuries before the Reformation. The plea of the war of investitures on the side of the Church was, that a practice had grown up, which seemed to place the spiritual part of the appointment in lay hands. But the crown does not make a bishop; it can merely propose him to be made; and the amount of concession made by the Church is, her consent to a law that no bishop shall be made during the alliance, except such as shall have been designated for that function by the sovereign. Even where (as in Ireland) the canonical election of the bishop by the dean and chapter is not interposed; still it is the consecration, not the appointment, from which, and from which alone, he derives his episcopal character. And though the terms of the law assert simply and without qualification that effect shall be given to nominations, it likewise requires the Church to attest the religious fitness of the party.

45 The office, then, of the sovereign towards the Church in virtue of the ecclesiastical supremacy, seems to consist mainly of the *executive* duty of defending it under the existing laws; the

judicial duty of determining all questions which arise, in mixed subject-matter, out of cases where spiritual and civil right are involved together; and the *negative* duty of permitting the Church to enter, from time to time, upon the consideration of matters of her own internal government, to be subsequently proposed to the great council of the nation, that its members and the crown may have the opportunity of judging how they affect the compact, and that the Church may know, by their assent, that it continues unimpaired; and if, in reference to the anomalies of modern legislation, this shall appear to be theory, let a fair consideration of our whole history declare whether it does not express the ancient practice and the general spirit of the constitution better than a few precedents drawn from periods of indifference or oppression, or both.[9]

46 The recognition of the supremacy has sometimes been made a charge against distinguished members of the Anglican Church, as implying Erastianism. It is, then, singular enough, that its denial should have been one of the charges urged against Archbishop Laud, upon his arraignment for high treason. We are chiefly reproached with it from the quarter of Romanism; but our assailants are probably little aware to how great an extent powers, analogous to and even exceeding such as we recognize, have been exercised by princes in communion with the Papal See.[10]

47 At the same time it should be observed, that the government of England has ever been distinguished, in civil matters, not so much by accuracy of adherence to any dogmatic and determinate theory, as by the skilful use of natural influences, and a general healthiness of tone and harmony of operation, resulting from a happy and providential fusion of elements, rather than from deliberately entertained intention. If this has been the case in our general concerns; if our constitution, as viewed by the crude speculatist, consist of a mass of anomalies, threatening perpetual contradiction and collision; if it has wrought rather by provision for the avoidance of such issues, than for their subsequent remedy; so also it has been with the Church, whose relations with the State had for very many years proceeded rather upon a mutually friendly understanding, than upon precise definitions of rights; and therefore we cannot expect to exhibit a theory which will bear a critical analysis throughout, in this more than in any other department of our national government. Nor are all the proceedings of the Legislature respecting the Church in the present day conceived in a spirit of unfriendliness. On the contrary, in the Session of

1840, it passed an Act for increasing the powers of Bishops against delinquent Clerks, in which, provided the parties consent to such an issue, the Bishop may pronounce sentence, which shall take legal effect without appeal to the Crown.[11] They may, on the other hand, in the exercise of their civil rights as subjects, choose the ordinary method of trial.

1 Gladstone, William Ewart; *b.* 1809; *educ.*, Eton and Christ Church, Oxford; entered Parliament, 1832; under-secretary for war and the colonies, 1835, 1845; vice-president of the Board of Trade, 1841; President, 1843; Chancellor of the Exchequer, 1852–5 and 1859–66; High Commissioner for the Ionian Islands, 1858–9; Prime Minister, 1868–74; 1880–5; 1886; 1892–4; *d.* 1898.

2 See The Gorham Case.

3 F. J. Stahl, *Kirchenverfassung* iii. 1.

4 See The Exeter Diocesan Synod.

5 Gladstone, as Chancellor of the Exchequer, evolved a scheme for the extinction of income tax in 1853. Owing to the Crimean War, the Indian Mutiny, the China and Persia Wars, and the threat of war with France, the programme never took effect.

6 Walker, *Attempt towards recovering an Account of the Numbers and Sufferings of the Clergy* (during the great Rebellion).

7 See The Hereford Bishopric.

8 Sir William Blackstone (1723–80), *Commentaries on the Laws of England,* (1765–9), Book 1, ch. vi.

9 Gladstone adds a note: "Mr Palmer [*On the Church*, part v, ch. vi] gives an enumeration of the powers belonging to the ecclesiastical supremacy."

10 Gladstone cites Count dal Pozzo, *On the Austrian Ecclesiastical Law* (Murray 1827), pp. 22, 23, 55, 81, 101; Palmer, *On the Church*, part i, ch. x, objection xiii.

11 See The Clergy Discipline Act, 1840.

14 REACTION TO THE *TRACTS FOR THE TIMES*, 1838

(Bishop Bagot, *Charge to the Clergy of the Diocese of Oxford, July–August, 1838* in G. M. Young and W. D. Handcock, *English Historical Documents* XII, (1), pp. 344-5).

The *Tracts for the Times* were widely discussed and there was support, as well as opposition, to their contents. Although Bagot's *Charge* showed an awareness of their value, Newman accepted his Bishop's strictures and was prepared to withdraw anything he considered unsound.[1] Newman wrote to Keble: "By doing this I think I set myself right with him. I really cannot go on publishing with this censure upon the *Tracts*. And, if he ordered some to be suppressed, the *example and precedent* [i.e. of episcopal disciplinary action] I am sure would be worth ten times the value of the *Tracts* suppressed. Unless you think this quixotic, I am disposed very much to do it" (Faber, *Oxford Apostles*, p. 364).

I have spoken of increased exertions among us, and of an increasing sense of our Christian responsibilities; and therefore you will probably expect that I should say something of that peculiar development of religious feeling in one part of the Diocese, of which so much has been said, and which has been *supposed* to *tend* immediately to a Revival of several of the Errors of Romanism. In point of fact, I have been continually (though anonymously) appealed to in my official capacity to check breaches both of doctrine and discipline, through the growth of Popery among us.

Now, as regards the latter point, breaches of discipline namely, on points connected with the public services of the Church, I really am unable, after diligent inquiry, to find any thing which can be so interpreted. I am given to understand, that an injudicious attempt was made in one instance, to adopt some forgotten portion of the ancient Clerical dress; but I believe it was speedily abandoned, and do not think it likely we shall hear of a repetion of this, or similar indiscretions. At the same time, so much of what has been objected to, has arisen from minute attention to the Rubric; and I esteem uniformity so highly, (and uniformity never can be obtained without strict attention to the Rubric,) that I confess I would rather follow an antiquated custom (even were it so designated) *with* the Rubric, than be entangled in the modern confusions which ensue from the neglect of it.[2]

With reference to errors *in doctrine*, which have been imputed to the series of publications called the *Tracts for the Times*, it can hardly be expected that, on an occasion like the present, I should enter into, or give a handle to any thing, which might hereafter tend to controversial discussions. Into controversy I will not enter, But, generally speaking, I may say, that in these days of lax and spurious liberality, any thing which tends to recall forgotten truths, is *valuable*:[3] and where these publications have directed men's minds to such important subjects as the union, the discipline, and the authority of the Church, I think they have done good service: but there may be some points in which, perhaps, from ambiguity of expression, or similar causes, it is not impossible, but that evil rather than the intended good, may be produced on minds of a peculiar temperament. I have more fear of the Disciples than of the Teachers.[4] In speaking therefore of the Authors of the Tracts in question, I would say, that I think their desire to restore the ancient discipline of the Church most praiseworthy; I rejoice in their attempts to secure a stricter attention to the Rubrical directions in the Book of Common Prayer; and I heartily approve the spirit which would restore a due observance of the Fasts and Festivals of the Church: *but* I would implore them, by the purity of their intentions, to be cautious, both in their writings and actions, to take heed lest their good be evil spoken of; lest in their exertions to re-establish unity, they unhappily create fresh schism; lest in their admiration of antiquity they revert to practices which heretofore have ended in superstition.[5]

1 Bagot, Richard; *b.* 1782; *educ.*, Rugby and Christ Church, Oxford; Fellow of All Souls, 1804; Dean of Canterbury, 1827–45; Bishop of Oxford, 1829–45; Bishop of Bath and Wells; 1845; *d.* 1854.

2 One of the fundamental tenets of the Tractarians was the catholicity of the Prayer Book which was obscured by the failure to observe its rubrics. The ritual developments later in the century arose largely from this doctrinal standpoint.

3 Newman later defined liberalism in religion as "the doctrine that there is no positive truth in religion, but that one creed is as good as another ... It is inconsistent with any recognition of any religion as true. It teaches that all are to be tolerated, for all are matters of opinion." See Wilfrid Ward, *The Life of John Henry Cardinal Newman*, vol. 2, p. 460.

4 Bagot's views were not unfounded. Articles by Ward, and Frederick Oakeley in the *British Critic*, after the publication of Tract 90, and Ward's *The Ideal of a Christian Church* (1844) proved an acute embarrassment to some older Tractarians.

5 An appended note reads: "As I have been led to suppose that the

above passage has been misunderstood, I take this opportunity of stating that it never was my intention therein to pass any *general censure* on the *Tracts for the Times*. There must always be allowable points of difference in the opinions of good men, and it is only where such opinions are carried into extremes, or are mooted in a spirit which tends to schism, that the interference of those in authority in the Church is called for. The authors of the *Tracts* in question have laid no such painful necessity on me, nor have I to fear that they will ever do so. I have the best reasons for knowing, that they would be the first to submit themselves to that authority, which it has been their constant exertion to uphold and defend. And I feel sure that they will receive my friendly suggestions in the spirit in which I have here offered them" (*E.H.D.* XII (1), p. 345).

15 LORD JOHN RUSSELL ON EDUCATION, 1839

(Letter to Lord Lansdowne; see *E.H.D.* XII (1), pp. 851-4).

The National Society for the Education of the Poor according to the Principles of the Church of England was founded in 1811, and was committed to the teaching of the Prayer Book and the Catechism.[1] The British and Foreign School Society was formed in 1814 under Whig and Dissenting patronage, and was based on undenominational bible teaching.[2] In 1820, Lord Brougham introduced a Bill into Parliament that required all teachers to be Anglicans; that the clergy should control the plan of teaching in schools; that religious teaching should be limited to the Bible; and that no catechism be used. The Bill was dropped because neither side would accept the compromise. Brougham doubted whether anything on a compulsory basis could ever be achieved, but he supported the State grant of £20,000 to the two societies. The desire to make an increased grant led to the formation of a Committee of Council for Education thus involving Parliament in the educational controversy.

Whitehall, 4 February 1839

My Lord,

I have received Her Majesty's Commands to make a communication to your Lordship on a subject of the greatest importance. Her Majesty has observed with deep concern the want of instruction which is still observable among the poorer classes of Her subjects. All the inquiries which have been made show a deficiency in the general Education of the People which is not in accordance with the character of a Civilized and Christian Nation.[3]

The reports of the chaplains of gaols show that to a large number of unfortunate prisoners a knowledge of the fundamental truths of natural and revealed Religion has never been imparted.

It is some consolation to Her Majesty to perceive that of late years the zeal for popular education has increased, that the Established Church has made great efforts to promote the building of schools, and that the National and British and Foreign Schools Societies have actively endeavoured to stimulate the liberality of the benevolent and enlightened friends of general Education.[4]

Still much remains to be done; and among the chief defects yet subsisting may be reckoned the insufficient number of qualified schoolmasters, the imperfect mode of teaching which prevails in perhaps the greater number of the schools, the absence of any sufficient inspection of the schools, and examination of the nature of the instruction given, the want of a Model School which might serve for the example of those societies and committees which anxiously seek to improve their own methods of teaching, and, finally, the neglect of this great subject among the enactments of our voluminous Legislation.

Some of these defects appear to admit of an immediate remedy, and I am directed by Her Majesty to desire, in the first place, that your Lordship, with four other of the Queen's Servants, should form a Board or Committee, for the consideration of all matters affecting the Education of the People.

For the present it is thought advisable that this Board should consist of:

The Lord President of the Council.
The Lord Privy Seal.
The Chancellor of the Exchequer.
The Secretary of State for the Home Department, and
The Master of the Mint.

It is proposed that the Board should be entrusted with the application of any sums which may be voted by Parliament for the purposes of Education in England and Wales.

Among the first objects to which any grant may be applied will be the establishment of a Normal School.

In such a school a body of schoolmasters may be formed, competent to assume the management of similar institutions in all parts of the country. In such a school likewise the best modes of teaching may be introduced, and those who wish to improve the schools of their neighbourhood may have an opportunity of observing their results.[5]

The Board will consider whether it may not be advisable for some years to apply a sum of money annually in aid of the Normal Schools of the National and of the British and Foreign School Societies.

They will likewise determine whether their measures will allow them to afford gratuities to deserving schoolmasters; there is no class of men whose rewards are so disproportionate to their usefulness to the community.

In any Normal or Model School to be established by the Board, four principal objects should be kept in view, *viz.*

1. Religious Instruction.
2. General Instruction.
3. Moral Training.
4. Habits of Industry.

Of these four I need only allude to the first; with respect to Religious Instruction there is, as your Lordship is aware, a wide or apparently wide difference of opinion among those who have been most forward in promoting education.[6]

The National Society, supported by the Established Church, contend that the schoolmaster should be invariably a Churchman; that the Church Catechism should be taught in the school to all scholars; that all should be required to attend Church on Sundays, and that the schools should be in every case under the superintendence of the clergyman of the parish.

The British and Foreign School Society, on the other hand, admit Churchmen and Dissenters equally as schoolmasters, require that the Bible should be taught in their schools, but insist that no Catechism should be admitted.

Others again contend that secular instruction should be the business of the school, and that the ministers of different persuasions should each instruct separately the children of their own followers.

In the midst of these conflicting opinions there is not practically that exclusiveness among the Church Societies, nor that indifference to Religion among those who exclude dogmatic instruction from the school, which their mutual accusations would lead bystanders to suppose.

Much therefore may be effected by a temperate attention to the fair claims of the Established Church, and the religious freedom sanctioned by law.[7]

On this subject I need only say that it is her Majesty's wish that the youth of this kingdom should be religiously brought up, and that the right of conscience should be respected.

Moreover, there is a large class of children who may be fitted to be good members of society without injury or offence to any party—I mean pauper orphans, children deserted by their parents, and the offspring of criminals and their associates.

It is from this class that the thieves and housebreakers of society are continually recruited. It is this class likewise which has filled the workhouses with ignorant and idle inmates.

The Poor Law Commissioners have very properly undertaken to amend the vicious system which has hitherto prevailed, and in the neighbourhood of the metropolis much has been already done under their auspices.[8]

It is in this direction likewise that certain good can be accomplished. It sometimes happens that the training which the child of poor but virtuous parents receives at home, is but ill exchanged for the imperfect or faulty instruction which he receives at school debased by vicious association; but for those whose parents are dead, or who have no home but one of habitual vice, there can be no such danger.

In all such instances, by combining moral training with general instruction, the young may be saved from the temptations to crime, and the whole community receive indisputable benefit.

These and other considerations will, I am persuaded, receive from your Lordship the most careful attention. I need not enter, at present, into any further plans in contemplation for the extension of the blessings of sound and religious education.

I have, &c.

(*signed*) J. RUSSELL

1 Bell, Andrew; *b.* 1753; army chaplain at Madras, 1789; superintended the Madras Male Orphan Asylum; published *An Experiment in Education*, 1797; system adopted at St Botolph, Aldgate, 1798; rector of Swanage, 1801; superintended the work of the National Society which was founded in 1811; *d.* 1832.

2 Lancaster, Joseph; *b.* 1778; naval volunteer; joined Society of Friends; opened a school in Southwark, 1801; published an account of the school, 1803; went to America, 1818; *d.* 1838.

3 The S.P.C.K. had instituted some charity schools after 1699; ancient

grammar schools were supplemented by some similar church foundations; in 1782 Robert Raikes founded the Sunday School movement which was educating a million and a half children by 1834. The *Newcastle Report* on popular education (1861) spoke of the financial sacrifice of local clergy in providing schools, especially in the north of England.

4 In 1813, there were 230 National Schools containing 40,484 pupils; in 1817, 727 schools and 117,000 scholars; 1820, 1,614 schools and 200,000 scholars; in 1830, 3,670 schools and 346,000 scholars. In 1831 there were only 490 British Schools compared with over three thousand National Schools.

5 Both the National and the Lancastrian Schools employed the monitorial system developed independently by Bell and Lancaster, and, though reaching large numbers of the poor, was not conducive to a high standard of education.

6 The later educational controversy was partly due to the Government's failure to take the religious question seriously at this early stage. For churchmen the choice was between a religious education and godlessness: for dissenters it was the choice between freedom of conscience and coercion.

7 The presence of the dissenting influence in Parliament was especially noticeable in the educational conflict which arose after the repeal of the Test and Corporation Acts in 1828.

8 The Poor Law Amendment Act became law in 1834, implementing the Whig philosophy of poverty and its remedy. Frederick Temple became the Principal of Kneller Hall, near Twickenham, in 1850, the training school for teachers in workhouse schools.

16 SYDNEY SMITH AND BISHOP BLOMFIELD, 1840

(*Letters of Sydney Smith* 2, ed. N. C. Smith, pp. 706-10)

The wealth and application of the financial resources of the Church of England were a source of controversy in the immediate period after Waterloo. Sydney Smith, canon of St Paul's,[1] was well known as a commentator on the political events of his day, and his protagonist was the most able bishop in the Church of England at that time. This letter, which appeared in *The Times* on 5 September 1840, is one of Smith's most provocative, as well as being an admirable comment on the internal affairs of the established Church.

A few words more, my dear Lord, before we part, after a controversy of four years:

In reading your speech,[2] I was a good deal amused by your characteristic indignation at the idea of any man, or any body of men, being competent to offer you advice; at the same time I have a sort of indistinct recollection of your name, as defendant in courts of justice, where it appeared, not only to the judges who decided against you, but to your best friends also, that you would have made rather a better figure if you had begged a few contributions of wisdom and temper from those who had any to share: till these cases are erased from our legal reports, it would perhaps be expedient to admit for yourself a small degree of fallibility, and to leave the claim of absolute wisdom to Alderman Wood.[3]

You say that you always consult your archdeacon and rural dean; this I believe to be quite true—but then you generally consult them after the error, and not before. Immediately after this aspernation of all human counsel, I came to the following sentence,—such a sentence as I believe mortal and mitred man never spoke before, and the author of which, as it seems to me, should be loaded with four atmospheres of advice instead of one, and controlled regularly by that number of cathedral councils. In speaking of the 3,000 clergymen who have petitioned against the destruction of the church, you say,

> I could easily get as many to petition upon any subject connected with the church. The mode by which in the present case a great proportion of these signatures have been obtained is as follows: the Archdeacon, who has always great influence with the parochial clergy, and justly so, as visiting them every year, and as being in habits of more familiar intercourse with them than their Bishop, and who is moreover considered by them as acting, in some degree, with the sanction of the Bishop, circulates printed forms of petition against the bill amongst the Rural Deans; the Rural Dean goes with them to the parochial clergy; and he must be a bold or a very well-informed man who refuses to sign a petition so recommended by his immediate ecclesiastical superiors (pp. 6 and 7).

Now I am afraid you will be very angry with me, but for the life of me I cannot discover in this part of your speech any of those marks of unerring and unassistable wisdom—that perfect uselessness of counsellors to the Bishop of London of which you seem to be so intimately convinced; and this, remember, is not a lapse to be forgiven in the fervour of speaking, but a cold printed insult; or what is the plain English of the passage?

> Archdeacons and rural deans are a set of base and time-serving

instruments, whom their superiors can set on for any purpose to abuse their power and influence over the lower clergy, and the lower clergy themselves are either in such a state of intellectual destitution that they cannot comprehend what they sign, or they are so miserably enthralled by their ecclesiastical superiors that they dare not dissent. I could put this depraved machinery in action for any church purpose I wished to carry.

If Lord Melbourne, in the exercise of his caprice, had offered me a bishopric, and I had been fool enough to have accepted it, this insult upon the whole body of the parochial clergy should not have been passed over with the silent impunity with which it was received in the House of Lords. You call me in the speech your facetious friend, and I hasten with gratitude in this letter to denominate you my solemn friend; but you and I must not run into commonplace errors; you must not think me necessarily foolish because I am facetious, nor will I consider you necessarily wise because you are grave; but whether foolish or facetious or what not, I admire and respect you too much not to deplore this passage in your speech; and, in spite of all your horror of being counselled by one of your own canons, I advise you manfully to publish another edition of your speech, and to expunge with the most ample apology this indecent aggression upon the venerable instructors of mankind.

In our future attacks upon the Catholics let us wisely omit our customary sarcasms on their regard for oaths. The only persons who appear to me to understand the doctrine of oaths are the two honest sheriffs whom Lord John put into prison for respecting them.

In the eighth page of your speech you say,

I am continually brought into contact, in the discharge of my official duties, with vast masses of my fellow-creatures living without God in the world. I traverse the streets of this crowded city with deep and solemn thoughts of the spiritual condition of its inhabitants. I pass the magnificent church which crowns the metropolis, and is consecrated to the noblest of objects, the glory of God, and I ask of myself, in what degree it answers that object. I see there a dean and three residentiaries, with incomes amounting in the aggregate to between 10,000*l.* and 12,000*l.* a year. I see, too, connected with the cathedral 29 clergymen, whose offices are all but sinecures, with an annual income of about 12,000*l.* at the present moment, and likely to be very much larger after the lapse of a few years. I proceed a mile or two to the E. and NE., and find myself in the midst of an immense population in the most wretched state of destitution and neglect, artisans,

mechanics, labourers, beggars, thieves, to the number of at least 300,000.

This stroll in the metropolis is extremely well contrived for your Lordship's speech; but suppose, my dear Lord, that instead of going E. and NE., you had turned about, crossed London-bridge, and resolving to make your walk as impartial as possible, had proceeded in a SW. direction, you would soon in that case have perceived a vast palace, containing, not a dean, three residentiaries, and 29 clergymen, but one attenuated prelate with an income enjoyed by himself alone, amounting to 30,000*l.* per annum, twice as great as that of all these confiscated clergymen put together; not one penny of it given up by act of Parliament during his life to that spiritual destitution which he so deeply deplores, and 15,000*l.* per annum secured to his successor: though all the duties of the office might be most effectually performed for one third of the salary.

Having refreshed yourself, my dear Lord, by the contemplation of this beautiful and consistent scene, and recovered a little from those dreadful pictures of spiritual destitution which have been obtruded upon you by the sight of St Paul's, you must continue our religious promenade to the banks of the Thames; but, as the way is long, let us rest ourselves for a few minutes in your palace in St James's-square, no scene certainly of carnal and secular destitution. Having halted for a few minutes in this mansion of humility, we shall now be able to reach your second palace of Fulham, where I think your animal spirits will be restored, and the painful theme of spiritual destitution be for the moment put to sleep. 20,000*l.* per annum to the present possessor increasing in value every hour, not a shilling legally given up during life to "the masses who are living without God", and 10,000*l.* per annum secured to the successor. I know that you are both of you generous and munificent men, but 2,000*l.* or 3,000*l.* subscribed, though much more observed, is much more economical also, than a fixed and legal diminution of an income, now out of all character and proportion, for those who feel the spiritual destitution so deeply. But these feelings upon spiritual destitution, my Lord, are of the most singular description; they seem to be under the most perfect control when bishops are to be provided for, and of irresistible plenitude and power when prebends are to be destroyed; such charity is the charity of my poor dear friend, old Lady C——, who was so powerfully affected (she said) by my sermon, that she borrowed a sovereign of some gentleman in the pew and put it in the plate.

My Lord, you are a very able, honest, and good man, but I pray you, as one of your council,[4] be a little more discreet. You have taught the enemies of the church a fearful lesson, and they are very good scholars. In the midst of your ecclesiastical elegies upon spiritual destitution, take care they do not turn upon you and say, "We can place the bench of Bishops in a position by which their usefulness will be materially increased, and 60,000*l.* per annum be saved for the spiritual destitution of the church."

But, my Lords, the learned counsel and those whom he represents, are grievously mistaken if they imagine that the calm, or rather lull, which now prevails, will be of long continuance, if no effective measures are taken to remove or lessen the anomalies which our Bishops now present, and to make them really conducive to the spiritual instruction of the people. The winds are chained for a season in their cavern; but ere long they will burst forth with redoubled violence, and shipwreck perhaps the vessel of the established church. Bishops may repose a few years longer in their stalls, unshorn of a single item of dignity or revenue; but by and by reform will come upon them as a strong man armed, and will take from them their armour wherein they trusted, and divide the spoils (p. 15).

Your foolish printer has injured the passage by printing it "Deans and Chapters" instead of Bishops.[5]

It is very easy, my Lord, to swing about in the House of Lords, and to be brave five years after the time, and to point out to their Lordships the clear difference between moral and physical fear, and to be nodded to by the Duke of Wellington,[6] but I am not to be paid by such coin. I believe that the old-fashioned orthodox, hand-shaking, bowel-disturbing passion of fear had a good deal to do with the whole reform. You choose to forget it, but I remember the period when the Bishops never remained unpelted; they were pelted going, coming, riding, walking, consecrating, and carousing; the Archbishop of Canterbury,[7] in the town of Canterbury, at the period of his visitation, was only saved from the mob by the dexterity of his coachman. If you were not frightened by all this, I was, and would have given half my preferment to save the rest; but then I was not a Commissioner, and had no great interests committed to my charge. If such had been my lot, I would have looked severely into my own soul. You have laid yourself open to some cruel replies and retorts in various parts of your pamphlet speech; but the law is past, and the subject is at an end.

You are fast hastening on, with the acclamations and gratitude of the Whigs, to Lambeth, and I am hastening, after a life of 70 years, with gout and asthma, to the grave. I am most sincere, therefore, when I say, that in the management of this business you have (in my opinion) made a very serious and fatal mistake: you have shaken the laws of property, and prepared the ruin of the church by lowering the character of its members, and encouraging the aggressions of its enemies. That your error has been the error of an upright, zealous, and honest man, I have not the most remote doubt. I have fought you lustily for four years, but I admire your talents, and respect your character as sincerely as I lament the mistakes into which you have been hurried by the honest and headlong impetuosity of your nature.

I remain, my Lord, your obedient humble servant,

SYDNEY SMITH

1 Smith, Sydney; *b.* 1771; *educ.*, Winchester and New College, Oxford; tutor in Edinburgh; founded the *Edinburgh Review* with Francis Jeffrey and Henry Brougham, 1802; lecturer at the Royal Institution, 1803; incumbent of Foston, Yorkshire; rector of Combe Florey, Somerset; canon of St Paul's, 1831; *d.* 1845.

2 Blomfield had spoken in the Lords on the Dean and Chapter Act. This Act, together with the Established Church Act (1836) and the Pluralities Act (1838) embodied the main proposals of the Ecclesiastical Commission.

3 Alderman Wood, a radical politician, who figured in the Queen's Trial, and described by George IV as that "beast Wood".

4 Traditionally the chapter was the council of the bishop, but since the cathedral foundations were largely of monastic origin they were somewhat apart from the diocesan organization, retaining considerable independence of the bishop.

5 It was the sharp wit epitomized in this sentence that made Smith a far more damaging critic of the Commission than either Manning or Pusey.

6 In 1829 Blomfield had apologized in the Lords for voting against Wellington on Roman Catholic Emancipation, for he "owed a debt of gratitude for his favourable opinion, and for a recommendation to his sovereign for an advancement in the Church".

7 "It was on this occasion that his chaplain complained that someone had thrown a dead cat in his face, only to be met by the Archbishop's cool rejoinder, 'You should think yourself very lucky that it was not a live one'" (J. W. C. Wand, *The Second Reform* (1953), p. 5).

17 THE CLERGY DISCIPLINE ACT 1840

(*Statutes at Large*, 3-4 Vict., c. 86)

The piecemeal overhauling of the judicial system in the nineteenth century affected both the jurisdiction and the procedures of the diocesan courts. This Act was intended to safeguard the position of the bishop, recognizing him as the source of ecclesiastical authority, but by forcing assessors on him interfered with the free exercise of that authority. The Act allowed appeals to be sent up from the consistory court to the Judicial Committee of the Privy Council. An important amendment was included, providing that every archbishop and bishop who was a Privy Councillor might join the Judicial Committee, one such episcopal representative having to be present.

I Repeal of *An Act for Bishops to punish Priests and other Religious Men for dishonest Lives.* 1 Henry 7, c. 4.

(III. The Bishop may issue a Commission of Inquiry.

IV The Commission will ascertain from the parties involved whether there be sufficient *prima facie* Ground for instituting further proceedings.

V The Report of the Commissioners shall be transmitted to the bishop and also filed in the Diocesan Registry.)

VI And be it enacted, That in all Cases where Proceedings shall have been commenced under this Act against any such Clerk it shall be lawful for the Bishop of any Diocese within which such Clerk may hold any Preferment, with the Consent of such Clerk and of the Party complaining, if any, first obtained in Writing, to pronounce, without any further Proceedings, such Sentence as the said Bishop shall think fit, not exceeding the Sentence which might be pronounced in due Course of Law; and all such Sentences shall be good and effectual in Law as if pronounced after a Hearing according to the Provisions of this Act, and may be enforced by the like Means.

(VII If Proceedings are to be instituted the Articles and Depositions are to be filed.

VIII A Copy of the Articles are to be served on the Party accused.

IX The Bishop may require the Party to appear before him.)

XI ... the Bishop shall proceed to hear the Cause, with the Assistance of Three Assessors, to be nominated by the Bishop, One of whom shall be an Advocate who shall have practised not less than Five Years in the Court of the Archbishop of the Province, or a Sergeant at Law, or a Barrister of not less than Seven Years standing, and another shall be the Dean of his Cathedral Church, or of One of his Cathedral Churches, or One of his Archdeacons, or his Chancellor; and upon the Hearing of such Cause the Bishop shall determine the same, and pronounce Sentence thereupon according to the Ecclesiastical Law.[1]

(XII The Sentence of the Bishop to be effectual in Law.

XIII The Bishop may send the Cause to the Court of Appeal of the Province.)

XIV And be it enacted, That in every Case in which, from the Nature of the Offence charged, it shall appear to any Bishop, within whose Diocese the Party accused may hold any Preferment, that great Scandal is likely to arise from the Party accused continuing to perform the Services of the Church while such Charge is under Investigation, or that his Ministration will be useless while such Charge is pending, it shall be lawful for the Bishop to cause a Notice to be served on such Party at the same Time with the Service of a Copy of the Articles aforesaid, or at any Time pending any Proceedings before the Bishop or in any Ecclesiastical Court, inhibiting the said Party from performing any Services of the Church within such Diocese from and after the Expiration of Fourteen Days from the Service of such Notice, and until Sentence shall have been given in the said Cause ...[2]

XVI And be it enacted, That every Archbishop and Bishop of the United Church of *England* and *Ireland*, who now is or at any Time hereafter shall be sworn of Her Majesty's Most Honourable Privy Council, shall be a Member of the Judicial Committee of the Privy Council for the Purposes of every such Appeal as aforesaid; and that no such Appeal shall be heard before the Judicial Committee of the Privy Council unless at least One of such Archbishops or Bishops shall be present at the Hearing thereof: Provided always, that the Archbishop or Bishop who shall have issued the Commission hereinbefore mentioned in any such Case, or who shall have heard any such Case, or who shall have sent any such Case by Letters of Request to the Court of Appeal of the Province, shall not sit as a Member of the Judicial Committee of an Appeal in that Case.[4]

XXV And be it enacted, That nothing in this Act contained shall be construed to affect any Authority over the Clergy of their respective Provinces or Dioceses which the Archbishops or Bishops of *England* and *Wales* may now according to Law exercise personally and without Process in Court; and that nothing herein contained shall extend to *Ireland*.

1 In 1846 there were twenty-six advocates of the Doctors' Commons. The shortage of trained ecclesiastical lawyers became acute as a result of the dissolution of the college by the Court of Probate Act in 1857.

2 The suspension *ab officio* was extended by the Public Worship Regulation Act (1874) as a means of enforcing obedience to the courts. Under section XIV of the present Act the inhibition was specifically to prevent scandal.

3 The two provincial courts were the Court of Arches (Canterbury) under the presidency of the Dean of Arches, and the Chancery Court of York. The two outstanding Deans of Arches in the nineteenth century were Stephen Lushington (1858–67) and Robert Phillimore (1867–75). Under the Public Worship Regulation Act the same judge presides in both provincial courts, and is appointed by the two archbishops with the approval of the Crown.

4 This important amendment was largely withdrawn when the bishops were made assessors under the Judicature Act (1876), thus making the final court of appeal a purely secular body.

18 TRACT 90, 1841

(J. H. Newman, *Remarks on Certain Passages in the Thirty-Nine Articles* (2nd edn, 1841), pp. 1-4, 59-63)

Tract 90 represents Newman's final attempt to justify his position in the Church of England, in the light of his recent studies in the Donatist schism and the Monophysite heresy. Like Froude, Newman had become antipathetic towards the Reformation, and since the Thirty-nine Articles were products of the Reformation, they posed as an obstacle to the Tractarian claim that the Church of England was essentially catholic.[1] Newman interpreted fourteen of the Articles with reference to the supposed teaching of the Church of the first five Christian centuries, when, in fact, his doctrinal norm was rapidly becoming that of the Council of Trent.

It is often urged, and sometimes felt and granted, that there are in the Articles propositions or terms inconsistent with the Catholic faith; or at least, when persons do not go so far as to feel the objections as of force, they are perplexed how best to reply to it, or how most simply to explain the passages on which it is made to rest. The following Tract is drawn up with the view of showing how groundless the objection is, and further of approximating towards the argumentative answer to it, of which most men have an implicit apprehension, though they may have nothing more. That there are real difficulties to a Catholic Christian in the Ecclesiastical position of our Church at this day, no one can deny; but the statements of the Articles are not in the number; and it may be right at the present moment to insist upon this. If in any quarter it is supposed that persons who profess to be disciples of the early Church will silently concur with those of very opposite sentiments in furthering a relaxation of subscriptions, which, it is imagined, are galling to both parties, though for different reasons, and that they will do this against the wish of the great body of the Church, the writer of the following pages would raise one voice, at least, in protest against any such anticipation. Even in such points as he may think the English Church deficient, never can he, without a great alteration of sentiment, be party to forcing the opinion or project of one school upon another. Religious changes, to be beneficial, should be the act of the whole body; they are worth little if they are the mere act of a majority. No good can come of any change which is not heartfelt, a development of feelings springing up freely and calmly within the bosom of the whole body itself. Moreover, a change in theological teaching involves either the commission or the confession of sin; it is either the profession or renunciation of erroneous doctrine, and if it does not succeed in proving the fact of past guilt, it, *ipso facto*, implies present. In other words, every change in religion carries with it its own condemnation, which is not attended by deep repentance. Even supposing then that any changes in contemplation, whatever they were, were good in themselves, they would cease to be good to a Church, in which they were the fruits not of the quiet conviction of all, but of the agitation, or tyranny, or intrigue of a few; nurtured not in mutual love, but in strife and envying; perfected not in humiliation and grief, but in pride, elation, and triumph. Moreover it is a very serious truth, that persons and bodies who put themselves into a disadvantageous state, cannot at their pleasure extricate themselves from it. They are unworthy of it; they are in prison, and CHRIST is the keeper. There is but one way towards a real reformation,[2]—a return to Him in heart and spirit, whose sacred truth they have betrayed; all other methods, however fair they may promise, will prove to be but shadows and failures.

On these grounds, were there no others, the present writer, for one, will be no party to the ordinary political methods by which professed reforms are carried or compassed in this day. We can do nothing well till we act "with one accord"; we can have no accord in action till we agree together in heart; we cannot agree without a supernatural influence; we cannot have a supernatural influence unless we pray for it; we cannot pray acceptably without repentance and confession. Our Church's strength would be irresistible, humanly speaking, were it but at unity with itself: if it remains divided, part against part, we shall see the energy which was meant to subdue the world preying upon itself, according to our SAVIOUR'S express assurance, that such a house "cannot stand". Till we feel this, till we seek one another as brethren, not lightly throwing aside our private opinions, which we seem to feel we have received from above, from an ill-regulated, untrue desire of unity, but returning to each other in heart, and coming together to GOD to do for us what we cannot do for ourselves, no change can be for the better. Till (we) (her children) are stirred up to this religious course, let the Church, (our Mother,) sit still; let (her children) be content to be in bondage; let (us) work in chains; let (us) submit to (our) imperfections as a punishment; let (us) go on teaching (through the medium of indeterminate statements,) and inconsistent precedents, and principles but partially developed. We are not better than our fathers; let us bear to be what Hammond was, or Andrewes, or Hooker; let us not faint under that body of death, which they bore about in patience; nor shrink from the penalty of sins, which they inherited from the age before them.[3]

But these remarks are beyond our present scope, which is merely to show that, while our Prayer Book is acknowledged on all hands to be of Catholic origin, our Articles also, the offspring of an uncatholic age, are, through GOD'S good providence, to say the least, not uncatholic, and may be subscribed by those who aim at being catholic in heart and doctrine.[4] In entering upon the proposed examination, it is only necessary to add, that in several places the writer has found it convenient to express himself in language recently used, which he is willing altogether to make his own. He has distinguished the passages introduced by quotation marks.[5]

9 MASSES

ARTICLE XXXI "The sacrifice (*sacrificia*) of Masses, in the which it was commonly said, that the priests did offer CHRIST for the quick and the dead, to have remission of pain or guilt, were blasphemous fables and dangerous deceits (*perniciosae imposturae*)."

Nothing can show more clearly than this passage that the Articles are not written against the creed of the Roman Church, but against actual existing errors in it, whether taken into its system or not. Here the sacrifice of the *Mass* is not spoken of, in which the special question of doctrine would be introduced; but "the sacrifice of *Masses*", certain observances, for the most part private and solitary, which the writers of the Articles knew to have been in force in time past, and saw before their eyes, and which involved certain opinions and a certain teaching. Accordingly the passage proceeds, "in which it *was commonly said*"; which surely is a strictly historical mode of speaking.

If any testimony is necessary in aid of what is so plain from the wording of the Article itself, it is found in the drift of the following passage from Burnet: [6]

> It were easy from all the rituals of the ancients to shew, that they had none of those ideas that are now in the Roman Church. They had but one altar in a Church, and probably but one in a city: they had but one communion in a day at that altar; so far were they from the many altars in every church, and *the many masses* at every altar, that are now in the Roman Church. They did not know what *solitary masses* were, without a communion. All the liturgies and all the writings of ancients are as express in this matter as is possible. The whole constitution of their worship and discipline shews it. Their worship always concluded with the Eucharist: such as were not capable of it, as the catechumens, and those who were doing public penance for their sins, assisted at the more general parts of the worship; and so much of it was called their mass, because they were dismissed at the conclusion of it. When that was done, then the faithful stayed, and did partake of the Eucharist; and at the conclusion of it they were likewise dismissed, from whence it came to be called the mass of the faithful.
>
> (*Burnet on the XXXIst Article*, p. 482)

These sacrifices are said to be "blasphemous fables and pernicious impostures". Now the "blasphemous fable" is the teaching that there is a sacrifice for sin other than CHRIST'S death, and that masses are that sacrifice. And the "pernicious imposture" is the turning this belief into a means of filthy lucre.

1. That the "blasphemous fable" is the teaching that masses are sacrifices for sin distinct from the sacrifice of CHRIST'S death, is plain from the first sentence of the Article. "The offering of CHRIST *once made*, is that perfect redemption, propitiation, and satisfaction for *all* the sins of the *whole world*, *both original and actual*. And *there is none other* satisfaction for sin, but *that alone*. *Wherefore* the sacrifice of masses, &c." It is observable too that the heading of the Article runs, "Of the one oblation of CHRIST finished upon the Cross," which interprets the *drift* of the statement contained in it about masses.

Our Communion Service shows it also, in which the prayer of consecration commences pointedly with a declaration, which has the fore of a protest, that CHRIST made on the cross, "by His *one* oblation of Himself *once* offered, a *full*, *perfect*, and *sufficient* sacrifice, oblation, and *satisfaction* for the sins of the whole world".

And again in the offering of the sacrifice: "We entirely desire thy fatherly goodness mercifully to accept our sacrifice of praise and thanksgiving, most humbly beseeching Thee to grant that *by the merits and death of Thy* SON JESUS CHRIST, and through faith in his blood, we and all Thy whole Church may obtain *remission of our sins* and all *other benefits* of His passion."

(And in the notice of the celebration: "I purpose, through God's assistance, to administer to all such as shall be religiously and devoutly disposed, the most comfortable Sacrament of the Body and Blood of CHRIST; to be by them received in remembrance of His meritorious Cross and Passion; *whereby alone* we obtain remission of our sins, and are made partakers of the kingdom of Heaven.")

But the popular charge still urged against the Roman system, as introducing in the Mass a second or rather continually recurring atonement, is a sufficient illustration, without further quotations, of this part of the Article.

2. That the "blasphemous and pernicious imposture" is the turning the Mass into a gain, is plain from such passages as the following:

With what earnestness, with what vehement zeal, did our SAVIOUR CHRIST drive the buyers and sellers out of the temple of GOD, and hurled down the tables of the changers of money, and the seats of the dove-sellers, and could not abide that a man should carry a vessel through the temple. He told them, that they had made His

FATHER'S house a den of thieves, partly through their superstition, hypocrisy, false worship, false doctrine, and insatiable covetousness, and partly through contempt, abusing that place with walking and talking, with worldly matters, without all fear of GOD, and due reverence to that place. What dens of thieves the Churches of England have been made by the *blasphemous buying and selling the most precious body and blood of* CHRIST *in the Mass*, as the world was made to believe, at dirges, at months minds, at trentalls,[7] in abbeys and chantries, besides other horrible abuses, (GOD'S holy name be blessed for ever,) which we now see and understand. All these abominations they that supply the room of CHRIST have cleansed and purged the Churches of England of, taking away all such fulsomeness and filthiness, as through blind devotion and ignorance hath crept into the Church these many hundred years. (*On repairing and keeping clean of Churches*, pp. 229, 230.)

Other passages are as follows:

Have not the Christians of late days, and even in our days also, in like manner provoked the displeasure and indignation of ALMIGHTY GOD; partly because they have profaned and defiled their Churches with heathenish and Jewish abuses, with images and idols, with numbers of altars, too superstitiously and intolerably abused, with gross abusing and filthy corrupting of the LORD'S holy Supper, the blessed sacrament of His body and blood, with an infinite number of toys and trifles of their own devices, to make a goodly outward shew, and to deface the homely, simple, and sincere religion of CHRIST JESUS; partly, they resort to the Church like hypocrites, full of all iniquity and sinful life, having a vain and dangerous fancy and persuasion, that if they come to the Church, besprinkle them with holy water, *hear a mass, and be blessed with a chalice*, though they understand not one word of the whole service, nor feel one motion of repentance in their heart, all is well, all is sure? (*On the Place and Time of Prayer*, p. 293.)

Again:

What hath been the cause of this gross idolatry, but the ignorance hereof? What hath been the cause of this *mummish massing*, but the ignorance hereof? Yea, what hath been, and what is at this day the cause of this want of love and charity, but the ignorance hereof? Let us therefore so travel to understand the LORD'S Supper, that we be no cause of the decay of GOD'S worship, of no idolatry, of no *dumb massing*, of no hate and malice; so may we the boldlier have access thither to our comfort. (*Homily concerning the Sacrament*, pp. 377, 378.)

To the same purpose is the following passage from Bishop Bull's Sermons:[8]

It were easy to shew, how the whole frame of religion and doctrine of the Church of Rome, as it is distinguished from that Christianity which we hold in common with them, is evidently designed and contrived *to serve the interest and profit* of them that rule that Church, by the disservices, yea, and ruin of those souls that are under their government ... What can the doctrine of men's playing an aftergame for their salvation in purgatory be designed for, but to enhance *the price of the priests's masses* and dirges for the dead? Why must a *solitary mass, bought for a piece of money*, performed and participated by a priest alone, in a private corner of a church, be, not only against the sense of Scripture and the Primitive Church, but also against common sense and grammar, called a Communion, and be accounted useful to him that buys it, though he himself never received the sacrament, or but once a year; but for this reason, that there is *great gain*, but not godliness at all, in this doctrine? (*Bp Bull's Sermons*, p. 10.)

And Burnet says,

Without going far in tragical expressions, we cannot hold saying what our SAVIOUR said upon another occasion, "My house is a house of prayer, but ye have made it a den of thieves." A trade was set up on this foundation. The world was made to believe, that by the virtue of so many *masses, which were to be purchased by great endowments*, souls were redeemed out of purgatory, and scenes of visions and apparitions, sometimes of the tormented, and sometimes of the delivered souls, were published in all places: which had so wonderful an effect, that in two or three centuries, *endowments* increased to so vast a degree, that if the scandals of the clergy on the one hand, and the statutes of mortmain on the other, had not restrained the profuseness that the world was wrought up to on this account, it is not easy to imagine how far this might have gone; perhaps to an entire subjecting of the temporality to the spirituality. The practices by which this was managed, and the effects that followed on it, we can call by no other name than downright *impostures*; worse than the making or vending false coin: when the world was drawn in by such arts to plain bargains, to *redeem* their own souls, and the souls of their ancestors and posterity, *so many masses were to be said*, and forfeitures were to follow upon their not being said: thus the *masses were really the price* of the lands. (*On Article XXII.*, pp. 303, 304.)

The truth of these representations cannot be better shewn than by extracting the following passage from the Session 22 of the Council of Trent:

Whereas many things appear to have crept in heretofore, whether by the fault of the times or by the neglect and wickedness of men, foreign to the dignity of so great a sacrifice, in order that it may regain its due honour and observance, to the glory of GOD and the edification of His faithful people, the Holy Council decrees, that the bishops, ordinaries of each place, diligently take care and be bound, to forbid and put an end to all those things, which either *avarice*, which is idolatry, or *irreverence*, which is scarcely separable from impiety, or *superstition*, the pretence of true piety, has introduced. And, to say much in a few words, first of all, as to avarice, let them altogether forbid agreements, and bargains of *payment* of whatever kind, and *whatever is given for celebrating new masses*; moreover importunate and mean extortion, rather than petition of alms, and such like practices, which border on simoniacal sin, certainly on *filthy lucre* ... And let them banish from the church those musical practices, *when with the organ or with the chant any thing lascivious or impure is mingled*; also all secular practices, vain and therefore profane conversations, promenadings, bustle, clamour; so that the house of GOD may truly seem and be called the house of prayer. Lastly, lest any opening be given to superstition, let them provide by edict and punishments appointed, that the priests celebrate it at no other than the due hours, nor use rites or ceremonies and prayers in the celebration of masses, other than those which have been approved by the Church, and received on frequent and laudable use. And let them altogether remove from the Church a *set number of certain masses and candles*, which has proceeded rather from *superstitious observance* than from true religion, and teach the people in what consists, and from whom, above all, proceeds the so precious and heavenly fruit of this most holy sacrifice. And let them admonish the same people to come frequently to their parish Churches, at least on Sundays and the greater feasts, &c.

On the whole, then, it is conceived that the Article before us neither speaks against the Mass in itself, nor against its being (an offering, though commemorative,) for the quick and the dead for the remission of sin; (especially since the decree of Trent says, that "the fruits of the Bloody Oblation are through this most abundantly obtained; so far is the latter from detracting in any way from the former"); but against its being viewed, on the one hand, as independent of or distinct from the Sacrifice on the Cross, which is blasphemy; and, on the other, its being directed to the emolument of those to whom it pertains to celebrate it, which is imposture in addition.

One remark may be made in conclusion. It may be objected that the tenor of the above explanations is anti-Protestant, whereas it is notorious that the Articles were drawn up by Protestants, and intended for the establishment of Protestantism; accordingly, that it is an evasion of their meaning to give them any other than a

Protestant drift, possible as it may be to do so grammatically, or in each separate part.

But the answer is simple:

1. In the first place, it is a *duty* which we owe both to the Catholic Church and to our own, to take our reformed confessions in the most Catholic sense they will admit; we have no duties towards their framers. (Nor do we receive the articles from their original framers, but from several successive convocations after their time; in the last instance, from that of 1662.)

2. In giving the Articles a Catholic interpretation, we bring them into harmony with the Book of Common Prayer, an object of the most serious moment in those who have given their assent to both formularies.

3. Whatever be the authority of the (Declaration) prefixed to the Articles, so far as it has any weight at all, it sanctions the mode of interpreting them above given. For its injoining the "literal and grammatical sense", relieves us from the necessity of making the known opinions of their framers, a comment upon their text; and its forbidding any person to "affix any *new* sense to any Article", was promulgated at a time when the leading men of our Church were especially noted for those Catholic views which have been here advocated.[9]

4. It may be remarked, moreover, that such an interpretation is in accordance with the well-known general leaning of Melanchthon, from whose writings our Articles are principally drawn, and whose Catholic tendencies gained for him that same reproach of popery, which has ever been so freely bestowed upon members of our own reformed Church.

"Melanchthon was of opinion," (says Mosheim) "that, for the sake of peace and concord, many things might be given up and tolerated in the Church of Rome, which Luther considered could by no means be endured ... In the class of matters indifferent, this great man and his associates placed many things which had appeared of the highest importance to Luther, and could not of consequence be considered as indifferent by his true disciples. For he regarded as such, the doctrine of justification by faith alone, the necessity of good works to eternal salvation; the number of the sacraments; the jurisdiction claimed by the Pope and the Bishops; extreme unction; the observation of certain religious festivals, and several superstitious rites and ceremonies." (*Cent. XVI*, 3, part. 2, 27, 28.)

5. Further: the Articles are evidently framed on the principle of

leaving open large questions, on which the controversy hinges. They state broadly extreme truths, and are silent about their adjustment. For instance, they say that all necessary faith must be proved from Scripture, but do not say *who* is to prove it. They say that the Church has authority in controversies, they do not say *what* authority. They say that it may enforce nothing beyond Scripture, but do not say *where* the remedy lies when it does. They say that works *before* grace *and* justification are worthless and worse, and that works *after* grace *and* justification are acceptable, but they do not speak at all of works *with* GOD'S aid, *before* justification. They say that men are lawfully called and sent to minister and preach, who are chosen and called by men who have public authority *given* them in the congregation to call and send; but they do not add *by whom* the authority is to be given. They say that councils called *by princes* may err; they do not determine whether councils called *in the name of* CHRIST will err.

(6. The variety of doctrinal views contained in the Homilies, as above shown, views which cannot be brought under Protestantism itself, in its widest comprehension of opinions, is an additional proof, considering the connection of the Articles with the Homilies, that the Articles are not framed on the principle of excluding those who prefer the theology of the early ages to that of the Reformation; or rather let it be considered whether, considering both Homilies and Articles appeal to the Fathers and Catholic antiquity, in interpreting them by these, we are not going to the very authority to which they profess to submit themselves.)

7. Lastly, their framers constructed them in such a way as best to comprehend those who did not go so far in Protestantism as themselves. Anglo-Catholics then are but the successors and representatives of those moderate reformers; and their case has been directly anticipated in the wording of the Articles. It follows that they are not perverting, they are using them, for an express purpose for which among others their authors framed them. The interpretation they take was intended to be admissible; though not that which their authors took themselves. Had it not been provided for, possibly the Articles never would have been accepted by our Church at all. If, then, their framers have gained their side of the compact in effecting the reception of the Articles, let Catholics have theirs too in retaining their own Catholic interpretation of them.

An illustration of this occurs in the history of the 28th Article. In the beginning of Elizabeth's reign a paragraph formed part of it, much like that which is now appended to the Communion

Service, but in which the Real Presence was *denied in words*. It was adopted by the clergy at the first convocation, but not published. Burnet observes on it thus:

When these Articles were at first prepared by the convocation in Queen Elizabeth's reign, this paragraph was made a part of them; for the original subscription by both houses of convocation, yet extant, shews this. But the *design of the government* was at that time much turned *to the drawing over the body of the nation to the Reformation*, in whom the old leaven had gone deep; and no part of it deeper than the belief of the corporeal presence of CHRIST in the Sacrament; therefore it was *thought not expedient to offend* them by so particular a definition in this matter; in which the very word Real Presence was rejected. It might, perhaps, be also suggested, that here a definition was made that went too much upon the principles of natural philosophy; which how true soever, they might not be the proper subject of an article of religion. Therefore it was thought fit to suppress this paragraph; though it was part of the Article that was subscribed, yet it was not published, but the paragraph that follows, "The Body of CHRIST", &c., was put in its stead, and was received and published by the next convocation; which upon the matter was a full explanation of the way of CHRIST'S presence in this Sacrament; that 'He is present in a heavenly and spiritual manner, and that faith is the mean by which He is received". This seemed to be more theological; and it does indeed amount to the same thing. But howsoever we see what was the sense of the first convocation in Queen Elizabeth's reign; it differed in nothing from that in King Edward's time: and therefore though this paragraph is now no part of our Articles, yet we are certain that the clergy at that time did not at all doubt of the truth of it; we are sure it was their opinion; since they subscribed it; though *they did not think* fit to publish it at first; and though it was afterwards changed for another, that was the same in sense. (*Burnet on Article XXVIII*, p. 416.)

What has lately taken place in the political world will afford an illustration in point. A French minister, desirous of war, nevertheless, as a matter of policy, draws up his state papers in such moderate language, that his successor, who is for peace, can act up to them, without compromising his own principles. The world, observing this, has considered it a circumstance for congratulation; as if the former minister, who acted a double part, had been caught in his own snare. It is neither decorous, nor necessary, nor altogether fair, to urge the parallel rigidly; but it will explain what it is here meant to convey. The Protestant Confession was drawn up with the purpose of including Catholics; and Catholics now will not be excluded. What was an economy in the reformers, is a protection to us. What would have been a perplexity to us then, is a perplexity to Protestants now. We could not then have found fault with their words; they cannot now repudiate our meaning.

1 Newman's motives behind the writing of Tract 90 are described in Ch. v of his *Apologia.*

2 In the second Tract (41) on the *Via Media* Newman discussed the need of a "second Reformation" because the Church had, in measure, forgotten its own principles declared in the sixteenth century.

3 Eight years after the Assize Sermon, the protest against Parliamentary interference in ecclesiastical matters continued. Melbourne's choice of R. D. Hampden as Regius Professor of Divinity at Oxford in 1836 increased the ferocity of the Tractarian outcry.

4 This approach to the Articles demonstrating the basic agreement between the Anglican formularies and the Roman Catholic tradition, had been tried by Christopher Davenport (1598–1680) in his *Paraphrastica Expositio Articulorum Confessionis Anglicanae* (1634).

5 Articles discussed were: 6 and 20, 11, 12 and 13, 19, 21, 22, 25, 28, 31, 32, 35, 37.

6 Gilbert Burnet, Bishop of Salisbury (1643–1715), wrote an *Exposition of the XXXIX Articles* (1699). The *Advertisment* to the collected edition of the Tracts of 1839 reads: "The following Tracts were published with the object of contributing something towards the practical revival of doctrines, which, although held by the great divines of our Church, at present have become obsolete with the majority of her members, are withdrawn from public view even by the more learned and orthodox few who still adhere to them."

7 Month's mind: the commemoration of the deceased by the celebration of a mass on a day of the month from the date of death. Trental: a set of thirty masses said on the same day or different days.

8 George Bull, Bishop of St David's (1643–1710), a High Church theologian who was popularized by the Tractarians, Tract 64 being a reprint of one of his works.

9 Subscription to the Articles had been made compulsory for all seeking ordination in 1571. The legal enactment of subscription was one reason why Newman regarded them as legal rather than religious forms.

19 THE LETTER OF THE OXFORD TUTORS, 1841

(Davidson and Benham, *Life of Tait* (1891), 1, pp. 81-2)

Tract 90 appeared in February 1841, and was attacked by Sewell, William Palmer, Golightly, and Robert Lowe, and defended by Pusey, Ward, and Oakeley. A public protest was made by four tutors in a letter drafted by Tait,[1] and the following day printed copies were circulated around Oxford. On 16 March the hebdomadal board declared that Newman had broken the statutes of the University by "reconciling subscription with the adoption of errors which they were designed to counteract". The *Tracts* were brought to an end, and although the decision of the University authorities was not an ecclesiastical judgment, it was seen as a rejection of Newman's religious position, thus ending his usefulness in the Church of England.

To the Editor of the *Tracts for the Times.*

Sir, Our attention having been called to No. 90 in the series of *Tracts for the Times* by Members of the University of Oxford, of which you are the Editor, the impression produced on our minds by its contents is of so painful a character that we feel it our duty to intrude ourselves briefly on your notice. This publication is entitled "Remarks on certain Passages in the Thirty-Nine Articles", and as these Articles are appointed by the Statutes of the University to be the text-book for teachers in their theological teaching, we hope that the situations we hold in our respective Colleges will secure us from the charge of presumption in thus coming forward to address you.

The Tract has, in our apprehension, a highly dangerous tendency, from its suggesting that certain very important errors of the Church of Rome are not condemned by the Articles of the Church of England—for instance, that those Articles do not contain any condemnation of the doctrines:

1. Of Purgatory,
2. Of Pardons,
3. Of the Worshipping and Adoration of Images and Relics,
4. Of the Invocation of Saints,
5. Of the Mass,

as they are taught authoritatively by the Church of Rome, but only of certain absurd practices and opinions which intelligent Romanists repudiate as much as we do. It is intimated, moreover, that the Declaration prefixed to the Articles, so far as it had any weight at all, sanctions this mode of interpreting them, as it is one which takes them in their "literal and grammatical sense", and does not "affix any new sense" to them. The Tract would thus appear to us to have a tendency to mitigate beyond what charity requires, and to the prejudice of the pure truth of the Gospel, the very serious differences which separate the Church of Rome from our own, and to shake the confidence of the less learned members of the Church of England in the Scriptural character of her formularies and teaching.

We readily admit the necessity of allowing that liberty in interpreting the formularies of our Church which has been advocated by many of its most learned Bishops and other eminent divines; but this Tract puts forward new and startling views as to the extent to which that liberty may be carried. For if we are right in our apprehension of the author's meaning, we are at a loss to see what security would remain, were his principles generally recognized, that the most plainly erroneous doctrines and practices of the Church of Rome might not be inculcated in the lecture-rooms of the University, and from the pulpits of our churches.

In conclusion, we venture to call your attention to the impropriety of such questions being treated in an anonymous publication, and to express an earnest hope that you may be authorized to make known the writer's name.[2] Considering how very grave and solemn the whole subject is, we cannot help thinking that both the Church and the University are entitled to ask that some person beside the printer and publisher of the Tract should acknowledge himself responsible for its contents.

We are, sir, your obedient and humble servants,

T. T. CHURTON, M.A.,
Vice-Principal and Tutor of Brasenose College.

H. B. WILSON, B.D.,
Fellow and Senior Tutor of St John's College.[3]

JOHN GRIFFITHS, M.A.,
Sub-Warden and Tutor of Wadham College.

A. C. TAIT, M.A.,
Fellow and Senior Tutor of Balliol College.

Oxford, March 8th, 1841

1 A draft of an individual letter to the Editor of the Tracts was found among Tait's papers after his death. The published protest was almost certainly based on this letter.

2 Golightly informed Bishop Blomfield in March that Newman was the author.

3 H. B. Wilson was to contribute to *Essays and Reviews*, and Tait was to be a member of the Judicial Committee of the Privy Council who passed judgment on Wilson's appeal from the Court of Arches.

20 COLONIALISM AND CHRISTIAN MISSIONS, 1841

(Anthony Grant, *The Past and Prospective Extension of the Gospel by Missions to the Heathen* (1845))

In the Preface to his Bampton Lecture, Grant wrote: "Our colonies are already planted in the midst of them; they are our fellow-subjects; we *must*, as a nation, exercise an untold influence upon them; already the tendency of an unhallowed influence has been witnessed in two fearful results—the extermination of whole races, and a dark scepticism in many of those heathen who have learnt to cast off their native superstitions." As Grant implied, the conversion of the native populations was not the primary concern of missionary societies, though C.M.S. did undertake some evangelistic work as distinct from caring for the British stationed overseas. This Declaration illustrates how closely related the overseas work of the Church of England was to colonial expansion.

At a meeting of Archbishops and Bishops, held at Lambeth, on Tuesday in Whitsun week, 1841, the following DECLARATION was agreed to by all present:

We, the undersigned Archbishops and Bishops of the United Church of England and Ireland, contemplate with deep concern the insufficient provision which has been hitherto made for the spiritual care of the members of our National Church residing in the British Colonies, and in distant parts of the world, especially as it regards the want of a systematic superintendence of the Clergy, and the absence of those ordinances, the administration of which is committed to the episcopal Order. We therefore hold it to be our duty, in compliance with the Resolutions of a Meeting convened by the Archbishop of Canterbury, on the 27th of April last, to undertake the charge of the Fund for the Endowment of additional Bishoprics in the Colonies, and to become responsible for its application.

On due consideration of the relative claims of those Dependencies of the Empire which require our assistance, we are of opinion, that the immediate erection of Bishoprics is much to be desired in the following places:

NEW ZEALAND[1]
THE BRITISH POSSESSIONS IN THE MEDITERRANEAN[2]
NEW BRUNSWICK[3]
CAPE OF GOOD HOPE[4]
VAN DIEMEN'S LAND[5]
CEYLON[6]

When competent provision shall have been made for the endowment of these Bishoprics, regard must be had to the claims of

SIERRA LEONE[7]
BRITISH GUIANA[8]
SOUTH AUSTRALIA[9]
PORT PHILLIP[10]
WESTERN AUSTRALIA[11]
NORTHERN INDIA[12]
SOUTHERN INDIA[13]

In the first instance, we propose that an Episcopal See be established at the seat of Government in New Zealand, offers having been already made which appear to obviate all difficulty as to endowment.

Our next object will be to make a similar provision for the congregations of our own communion, established in the islands of the Mediterranean, and in the countries bordering upon that sea; and it is evident that the position of Malta is such as will render it the most convenient point of communication with them, as well as with the Bishops of the ancient Churches of the East, to whom our Church has been for many centuries known only by name.[14]

We propose, therefore, that a See be fixed at Valetta, the residence of the English Government, and that its jurisdiction extend to all the Clergy of our Church residing within the limits above specified. In this city, through the munificence of Her Majesty the Queen Dowager, a Church is in course of erection, which, when completed, will form a suitable Cathedral.

Our attention will then be directed to the countries named in the foregoing lists, without binding ourselves to the exact order therein followed, or precluding ourselves from granting assistance to any place where means may be found for the earlier endowment of a Bishopric.

In no case shall we proceed without the concurrence of Her Majesty's Government; and we think it expedient to appoint a Standing Committee, consisting of

THE ARCHBISHOP OF CANTERBURY
THE ARCHBISHOP OF YORK
THE ARCHBISHOP OF ARMAGH
THE ARCHBISHOP OF DUBLIN
THE BISHOP OF LONDON
THE BISHOP OF DURHAM
THE BISHOP OF WINCHESTER
THE BISHOP OF LINCOLN
THE BISHOP OF ROCHESTER

with full powers to confer with the Ministers of the Crown, and to arrange measures in concert with them, for the erection of Bishoprics in the places above enumerated.

We appoint as our Treasurers, the Hon. Mr Justice Coleridge,[15] the Venerable Archdeacon Hale, and W. E. Gladstone, Esq. M.P.; and as Honorary Secretary, the Rev. Ernest Hawkins.[16]

For the attainment of these most desirable objects, a sum of money will be required, large as to its actual amount, but small when compared with the means which this country possesses, by the bounty of Divine Providence, for advancing the glory of God and the welfare of mankind. Under a deep feeling of the sacredness and importance of this great work, and in the hope that Almighty God may graciously dispose the hearts of his servants to a corresponding measure of liberality, we earnestly commend it to the good will, the assistance, and the prayers of all the Members of our Church.

W. CANTUAR:	J. ELY
J. G. ARMAGH	E. SARUM:
C. J. LONDON	E. NORWICH
E. DUNELM:	T. HEREFORD
C. WINTON:	J. LICHFIELD
C. BANGOR	C. ST DAVID'S
G. ROCHESTER	P. N. CHICHESTER
F. LLANDAFF	R. DERRY & RAPHOE
J. H. GLOUCESTER & BRISTOL	T. V. SODOR & MAN

We, the undersigned, desire to express our concurrence in the foregoing declaration:

E. EBOR:	W. ST ASAPH
RD. D. DUBLIN	J. LINCOLN
GEO. H. BATH & WELLS	H. CARLISLE

J. B. CHESTER
C. KILDARE
ROBT. P. CLOGHER
J. ELPHIN
R. OSSORY & FERNS
JAMES DROMORE
RD. D. DOWN & CONNOR
S. CORK
R. OXFORD
H. EXETER
C. T. RIPON
G. PETERBOROUGH
H. WORCESTER
GEORGE KILMORE
EDMOND LIMERICK
STEPHEN CASHEL
LUDLOW KILLALOE & CLONFERT
THOMAS TUAM
CHARLES MEATH

1 New Zealand (later Auckland), first bishop, G. A. Selwyn, 1841.

2 Gibraltar, G. Tomlinson, 1842, at the suggestion of the standing committee instead of Malta.

3 Fredericton, J. Medley, 1845. Previous Canadian dioceses formed: Nova Scotia, 1787; Quebec, 1793; Newfoundland, 1832.

4 Cape Town (formerly part of the diocese of Calcutta), Robert Gray, 1847.

5 Tasmania, F. R. Nixon, 1842.

6 Colombo, J. Chapman, 1845.

7 Sierra Leone, E. O. Vidal, 1852.

8 Guiana, W. P. Austin, 1842. Previous West Indian dioceses formed: Jamaica, 1824; Barbados, 1824.

9 Adelaide, A. Short, 1847. Sydney formed 1836.

10 Melbourne, C. Perry, 1847.

11 Perth, M. B. Hale, 1856.

12 Lahore, T. V. French, 1877. Indian dioceses: Calcutta, 1814; Madras, 1835; Bombay, 1837.

13 Travancore and Cochin, J. M. Speechly, 1879.

14 See the incident described in Robert Curzon, *Visits to Monasteries in the Levant* (1955), pp. 275-6; also E. G. W. Bill, *Anglican Initiatives in Christian Unity*, p. 20.

15 Coleridge, John Taylor; *b.* 1790; *educ.* Eton and Corpus Christi College, Oxford; Fellow of Exeter College, 1812; called to the Bar, 1819; Serjeant-at-law and Recorder of Exeter, 1832; Judge of the King's Bench, 1835; Privy Councillor; biographer of Keble; *d.* 1876.

16 Hawkins, Ernest; *b.* 1802; Balliol College, Oxford, 1820; curate of Burwash, Sussex; Fellow of Exeter College, 1831; curate of St George's, Bloomsbury, 1835; under-secretary, S.P.G., 1838; secretary, 1843; prebendary of St Paul's, 1844; minister of the Curzon Chapel, Mayfair, 1850; resigned, 1864; canon of Westminster, 1864; *d.* 1868.

21 THE COLONIAL BISHOPRICS ACT 1841

(*Statutes at Large*, 5 Vict., c. 6)

The overseas work of the Church of England was largely undertaken by the S.P.C.K. (1698); S.P.G. (1701); and C.M.S. (1799). Colonial expansion in India, Australia, and Canada led to a demand for episcopal oversight of the congregations in the colonies. This Act provided the machinery by which new bishops could be consecrated, and the Colonial Bishoprics Fund, supported by Blomfield, Howley, and Ernest Hawkins, financed their work. Problems which were later to confront the colonial Churches arose largely out of the provisions of this Act.[1]

Whereas in and by an Act passed in the Twenty-sixth Year of the Reign of his late Majesty King *George* the Third, intituled *An Act to empower the Archbishop of Canterbury or the Archbishop of York for the Time being to consecrate to the Office of a Bishop Persons being Subjects or Citizens of Countries out of His Majesty's Dominions*,[2] after reciting that "there are divers Persons, Subjects or Citizens of Countries out of his Majesty's Dominions, and inhabiting and residing within the said Countries, who profess the public worship of Almighty God according to the Principles of the Church of *England*, and who, in order to provide a regular Succession of Ministers for the Service of their Church, are desirous of having certain of the Subjects or Citizens of those Countries consecrated Bishops according to the Form of Consecration of the Church of *England*", it is amongst other things enacted, that from and after the passing of the said Act it should and might be lawful to and for the Archbishop of *Canterbury* or for the Archbishop of *York* for the Time being, together with such other Bishops as they should call to their Assistance, to consecrate Persons being Subjects or citizens of Countries out of His Majesty's Dominions Bishops for the Purposes in the said Act mentioned, without the King's Licence for their Election, or the Royal Mandate under the Great Seal for their Confirmation and Consecration, and without requiring them to take the Oaths of Allegiance and Supremacy, and the Oath of due Obedience to the Archbishop for the Time being: And whereas it is expedient to enlarge the Powers given by the said Act; be it therefore enacted by the Queen's most Excellent Majesty, by and with the Advice and Consent of the Lords Spiritual and Temporal, and Commons, in this present Parliament assembled, and by the Authority of the same, That it shall and may be lawful to and for the Archbishop of *Canterbury* or the Archbishop of

York for the Time being, together with such other Bishops as they shall call to their Assistance, to consecrate *British* Subjects, or the Subjects or Citizens of any Foreign Kingdom or State, to be Bishops in any Foreign Country, whether such Foreign Subjects or Citizens be or be not Subjects or Citizens of the Country in which they are to act, and without the Queen's Licence for their Election, or the Royal Mandate under the Great Seal for their Confirmation and Consecration, and without requiring such of them as may be Subjects or Citizens of any Foreign Kingdom or State to take the Oaths of Allegiance and Supremacy, and the Oath of due obedience to the Archbishop for the Time being.

II And be it further enacted, That such Bishop or Bishops so consecrated may exercise, within such Limits as may from Time to Time be assigned for that Purpose in such Foreign Countries by Her Majesty, Spiritual Jurisdiction over the Ministers of *British* Congregations of the United Church of *England* and *Ireland*, and over such other Protestant Congregations as may be desirous of placing themselves under his or their Authority.[3]

III Provided always, That no Person shall be consecrated a Bishop in the Manner herein provided, until the Archbishop of *Canterbury* or the Archbishop of *York* for the Time being shall have first applied for and shall have obtained Her Majesty's Licence, by Warrant under Her Royal Signet and Sign Manual, authorizing and empowering him to perform such Consecration, and expressing the Name of the Person so to be consecrated, nor until the said Archbishop has been fully ascertained of the Sufficiency of such Person in good Learning, of the Soundness of his Faith, and of the Purity of his Manners.[4]

IV Provided always, and be it hereby declared, That no Person consecrated to the Office of a Bishop in the Manner aforesaid, nor any Person deriving his Consecration from or under any Bishop so consecrated, nor any Person admitted to the Order of Deacon or Priest by any Bishop or Bishops so consecrated, or by the Successor or Successors of any Bishop or Bishops so consecrated, shall be thereby enabled to exercise his Office within Her Majesty's Dominions in *England* or *Ireland*, otherwise than according to the Provisions of an Act of the Third and Fourth Years of Her present Majesty, intituled *An Act to make Certain Provisions and Regulations in respect to the Exercise within* England *and* Ireland *of their Office by the Bishops and Clergy of the Protestant Episcopal Church* in Scotland; *and also to extend such Provisions and Regu-*

lations to the Bishops and Clergy of the Protestant Episcopal Church in the United States of America; and also *to make further Regulations in respect to Bishops and Clergy other than those of the United Church of* England *and* Ireland.[5]

1 The overseas work of the Church of England was not, strictly speaking, missionary, being rather the care of English congregations. The East India Company, for example, was firmly against its chaplains being engaged in the evangelization of the native population.

2 26 Geo. III, c. 84.

3 The bishops were issued with Letters Patent defining their jurisdiction, and it was on these that the future controversies were to centre. See the Colenso documents.

4 The first new see was that of New Zealand, founded in 1841, with George Augustus Selwyn as its bishop.

5 3-4 Vict., c. 33.

22 THE JERUSALEM BISHOPRIC, 1841

(*The Jerusalem Bishopric, W. H. Hechler* (1883), pp. 104-12)

The original proposal for a joint bishopric in Jerusalem came from Frederick William IV, King of Prussia, through his special envoy Bunsen. The proposals were accepted by Howley and Blomfield, and a treaty between the two nations was signed on 15 July 1841. Howley introduced a Bill into the Lords which became law on 5 October 1841. Bunsen hoped to introduce episcopacy into the Prussian National Church through the consecration of a Prussian nominee by the English bishops. The venture was bitterly attacked by the Tractarians and warmly approved by Lord Shaftesbury and the Evangelicals.

STATEMENT OF PROCEEDINGS RELATING TO THE ESTABLISHMENT OF A BISHOPRIC OF THE UNITED CHURCH OF ENGLAND AND IRELAND IN JERUSALEM[1]

Published by Authority, London, Dec. 9, 1841.

An Act was passed in the last session of Parliament (5 Victoria cap. 6), empowering the Archbishops of Canterbury and York, assisted by other Bishops, to consecrate British subjects, or the subjects or citizens of any foreign kingdom or state, to be Bishops in any foreign country, and, within certain limits, to exercise spiritual jurisdiction over the ministers of British congregations of the United Church of England and Ireland, and over such other Protestant congregations as may be desirous of placing themselves under the authority of such Bishops.[2]

The Archbishop of Canterbury, having first consulted the Bishops who attended the Convocation in August last, has exercised the power so vested in him, by consecrating the Rev. Michael Solomon Alexander, a Bishop of the United Church of England and Ireland, to reside at Jerusalem, and to perform the duties hereinafter specified. The Bishops assisting at the consecration were those of London, Rochester, and New Zealand.[3] The appointment of a Bishop for Jerusalem was proposed by His Majesty the King of Prussia, who made it the subject of a special mission to the Queen of England, and of a particular communication to the Archbishop of Canterbury. In making this proposal, His Majesty had in view not only the great advantages, to be derived from its adoption, with reference to the conversion of the Jews; but also the spiritual superintendence and care of such of his own subjects as might be disposed to take up their abode in Palestine, and to join themselves to the Church so formed at Jerusalem. There is reason to expect that a considerable number of German as well as English Christians will be attracted to the Holy Land by the influence of strong religious feelings.

In order to obviate the difficulty which might be occasioned by the want of an endowment for the Bishopric, His Majesty undertook to make at once the munificent donation of fifteen thousand pounds towards that object, the annual interest of which, amounting to six hundred pounds, is to be paid yearly in advance, till the capital sum (together with that which is to be raised by subscription for the purpose of completing the Bishop's annual income of twelve hundred pounds), can be advantageously invested in land situate in Palestine.

The immediate objects for which this Bishopric has been founded will appear from the following statement. Its ultimate results cannot be with certainty predicted; but we may reasonably hope that, under the Divine blessing, it may lead the way to an essential unity of discipline, as well as of doctrine, between our own Church and the less perfectly constituted of the Protestant Churches of Europe,[4] and that, too, not by the way of Rome; while it may be the means of establishing relations of amity between the United Church of England and Ireland and the ancient Churches of the East,[5] strengthening them against the encroachments of the See of Rome, and preparing the way for their purification, in some cases from serious errors, in others from those imperfections which now materially impede their efficiency as witnesses and dispensers of Gospel truth and grace. In the meantime, the spectacle of a Church, freed from those errors and imperfections, planted in the Holy City, and holding a pure faith in the unity of the Spirit and in the bond of peace, will naturally attract the notice of the Jewish nation throughout the world; and will centralize, as it were, the desultory efforts which are making for their conversion. It is surely impossible not to recognize the hand of Providence in the remarkable events which have lately happened in the East, opening to Christians, and especially to our own nation (so signal an instrument in bringing those events to pass,[6]), a door for the advancement of the Saviour's kingdom, and for the restoration of God's ancient people to their spiritual birthright.

While the Church of Rome is continually, and at this very moment, labouring to pervert the members of the Eastern Churches, and to bring them under the dominion of the Pope, sparing no arts nor intrigues, hesitating at no misrepresentations, sowing dissension and disorder amongst an ill-informed people, and asserting that jurisdiction over them which the ancient Churches of the East have always strenuously resisted, the two great Protestant Powers of Europe will have planted a Church in the midst of them, the Bishop of which is specially charged not to entrench upon the spiritual rights and liberties of those Churches;[7] but to confine himself to the care of those over whom *they* cannot rightfully claim any jurisdiction; and to maintain with them a friendly intercourse of good offices; assisting them, so far as they may desire such assistance, in the work of Christian education; and presenting to their observation, but not forcing upon their acceptance, the pattern of a Church essentially scriptural in doctrine and apostolical in discipline.

The Bishop of the United Church of England and Ireland at Jerusalem is to be nominated alternately by the Crowns of England and Prussia, the Archbishop having the absolute right of veto, with respect to those nominated by the Prussian Crown.

The Bishop will be subject to the Archbishop of Canterbury as his Metropolitan, until the local circumstances of his Bishopric shall be such as to make it expedient, in the opinion of the Bishops of that United Church, to establish some other relation.

His spiritual jurisdiction will extend over the English clergy and congregations, and over those who may join his Church and place themselves under his Episcopal authority in Palestine, and, for the present, in the rest of Syria, in Chaldea, Egypt, and Abyssinia; such jurisdiction being exercised, as nearly as may be, according to the laws, canons, and customs of the Church of England; the Bishop having power to frame, with the consent of the Metropolitan, particular rules and orders for the peculiar wants of his people. His chief missionary care will be directed to the conversion of the Jews, to their Protection, and to their useful employment.

He will establish and maintain, as far as in him lies, relations of Christian charity with other Churches represented at Jerusalem, and in particular with the orthodox Greek Church; taking special care to convince them, that the Church of England does not wish to disturb, or divide, or interfere with them; but that she is ready, in the spirit of Christian love, to render them such offices of friendship as they may be willing to receive.

A college is to be established at Jerusalem, under the Bishop, whose chaplain will be its first Principal. Its primary object will be, the education of Jewish converts: but the Bishop will be authorized to receive into it Druses and other Gentile converts: and if the funds of the College should be sufficient, Oriental Christians may be admitted: but clerical members of the orthodox Greek Church will be received into the College, only with the express consent of their spiritual superiors, and for a subsidiary purpose. The religious instruction given in the College will be in strict conformity with the doctrines of the United Church of England and Ireland, and under the superintendence and direction of the Bishop.

Congregations, consisting of Protestants of the German tongue, residing within the limits of the Bishop's jurisdiction, and willing to submit to it, will be under the care of German clergymen ordained by him for that purpose; who will officiate in the German language, according to the forms of their national liturgy, compiled from the ancient liturgies, agreeing in all points of doctrine with the liturgy of the English Church, and sanctioned by the Bishop with consent of the Metropolitan, for the special use of those congregations: such liturgy to be used in the German language only. Germans, intended for the charge of such congregations, are to be ordained according to the ritual of the English Church, and to sign the Articles of that Church: and, in order that they may not be disqualified by the laws of Germany from officiating to German congregations, they are, before ordination, to exhibit to the Bishop a certificate of their having subscribed, before some competent authority, the Confession of Augsburg.

The rite of Confirmation will be administered by the Bishop to the catechumens of the German congregations, according to the form used in the English Church.

Subjoined are copies of the Commendatory Letter, addressed by the Archbishop of Canterbury to the Rulers of the Greek Church, and of the same translated into Greek, both of which the newly consecrated Bishop carries with him to the East.[8]

London Dec. 9, 1841.

1 The *Proceedings* were published by authority, this being generally assumed to refer to the Archbishop of Canterbury by the majority of the nineteenth-century historians of the Jerusalem bishopric.

2 See the previous document.

3 I.e. Blomfield, Lord George Murray, and Selwyn, at Lambeth Palace, 7 November 1841.

4 Newman formally protested to the Bishop of Oxford: "Lutheranism and Calvinism are heresies repugnant to Scripture", and that the English Church was admitting heretics into communion without the renunciation of their errors. 11 November 1841.

5 Gobat, who succeeded Alexander, was accused of proselytizing among the Eastern Churches, and as a result the Archbishops of Canterbury, York, Dublin, and Armagh issued a public declaration of confidence in him in 1853.

6 The presence of the British and Prussians in the Middle East was due to the growing weakness of the Turkish Empire and the rise of the Balkan Christian States. Britain and Prussia had signed the Convention of London, together with Austria and Russia, less than a year before the founding of the bishopric.

7 The Roman Catholic threat largely took the form of French political agents in Jerusalem and also the Roman interest in the Holy Places. This latter was to figure as one of the pretexts for the outbreak of the Crimean War.

8 Alexander died in 1845; Samuel Gobat was consecrated in 1846, and died in 1879; Joseph Barclay was consecrated in 1879 and died in 1881. The treaty was dissolved in 1886 and the bishopric reconstituted in 1887 with the consecration of George Popham Blyth.

23 THE HEREFORD BISHOPRIC, 1847

(Henry Christmas, *A Concise History of the Hampden Controversy*)

Hampden's Bampton Lectures, *The Scholastic Philosophy considered in its relation to Christian Theology* (1832), caused a great deal of dismay in academic circles and led to violent opposition on his appointment as Regius Professor of Divinity at Oxford.[1] In 1847, Russell offered him the bishopric of Hereford, and protest was made to Russell from thirteen bishops.[2] The Dean of Hereford notified him that he would refuse to vote for Hampden's election. The strength of Russell's curt reply lay in its implicit recognition of the limitations placed on both clergy and bishops in the established Church in regard to Crown appointments.[3]

THE DEAN OF HEREFORD TO LORD JOHN RUSSELL.

December 22, 1847

MY LORD, I have had the honour to receive your lordship's letter, announcing that you had received my memorial to the Queen, and that you had transmitted it to Sir G. Grey for presentation to her Majesty; and by the same post I also receive the information that Sir G. Grey had laid the same before the Queen, and that "he was to inform me that her Majesty has not been pleased to issue any commands thereupon". Under these circumstances I feel compelled once more to trouble your lordship with a few remarks.

Throughout the correspondence in which I have had the honour to be engaged with your lordship, as well as in the interview which you were pleased to afford me on the subject of the appointment to the see of Hereford, it has been my object frankly and faithfully to declare to you the facts which have come to my knowledge, and the honest conviction of my mind. I desire still to act upon the same principle, and to submit to your lordship finally, and as briefly as possible, the following considerations, upon which I feel constrained to adopt a course which, however I may apprehend it will not be entirely congenial to your lordship's wishes, will, under the circumstances in which I am placed, obtain from your lordship's candour the admission that it is the only course which I could pursue.

I crave your lordship's indulgence whilst I enumerate the special obligations to which I am bound, and I state them in the order of their occurrence.

When matriculated to the University of Oxford, of which I am still a member, the following oath was administered to me, as well as on taking each of my degrees: "Tu dabis fidem ad observandum omnia statuta, privilegia, et consuetudines hujus Universitatis; ita Deus te adjuvet tactis sacrosanctis Christi Evangeliis."

Again—when I was admitted to the sacred orders of priest in the Church of God, a part of my ordination vow was expressed in these words—that I would "banish and drive away all erroneous and strange doctrine contrary to God's word".

Again—when I was inducted, on occasion of the installation to the office which I hold in the cathedral church of Hereford, as I stepped over the threshold of the fabric, the restoration of which, for the due honour of Almighty God, it has been my pride and anxious endeavour to promote, I was required to charge my soul with this responsibility: "Ego, Joannes Merewether, Decanus Herefordensis, ab hâc horâ in antea, fidelis ero huic sacrosanctae Herefordensi ecclesiae, necnon jura, libertates, privilegia, et consuetudines ejusdem, pro viribus observabo et ea manutenebo et defendam pro posse meo; sic me Deus adjuvet, et haec sancta Evangelia."

My lord, I cannot divest my mind of the awful sense of the stringency of those engagements at the present exigency. Let me entreat your lordship's patience whilst I endeavour to explain my apprehension of them.

In my letter of the 1st of December, in reply to the second which your lordship was pleased to address to me—and to which correspondence I trust your lordship will permit me publicly to refer in vindication of my conduct, should need require it—I observed, "In regard to Dr Hampden's tenets, I would abstain from any opinion upon them till I had again fairly and attentively read his writings." That act of justice I have carefully performed, and I will add with an earnest desire to discover grounds upon which, in case of Dr Hampden's ever occupying the high station for which he has been selected by your lordship, my mind might be relieved from all distrust, and I might be enabled as cordially as possible to render that service which the relative duties of diocesan and dean and chapter involve.

It is painful in the extreme to feel obliged to declare that I discover in those writings many *assertions*—not merely references to theories or impressions of others—but *assertions*, which to my calm and deliberate appreciation appear to be heterodoxical, I believe I may say heretical, and very, very much, which is most dangerous, most objectionable, calculated to weaken the hold which the religion we possess as yet obtains, and ought to obtain always, upon the minds of its professors. I feel certain that the perusal of several of these works by any of that class who, "by reason of use" (in cautious examination of such productions) "have not their senses exercised to discern both good and evil", would produce a doubt and distrust in the teaching of our church, in her creeds,—her formularies,—her liturgy; would rob them of the inestimable joy and peace in believing, and be highly detrimental to the spread of true religion.

Such being my conviction, I would ask your lordship how it must affect my conscience in reference to those solemn obligations which I have already detailed? I have sworn that I will observe all the statutes of the University of which I am still a member. The statute of that University touching this matter stands in the following words, at this moment uncancelled, unrepealed: "Quin ab universitate commissum fuerit, S. Theologiae Professori Regio, ut unus sit ex eorum numero a quibus designantur selecti concionatores, secundum Tit. XVI, 58 (Addend. p. 150), necnon ut ejus concilium adhibeatur si quis concionator coram Vice-Cancellario in questionem vocatur, secundum Tit., XVI s. II (Addend. p. 151), quum vero qui nunc Professor est *scriptis suis publici juris factis, ita res theologicas tractaverit, ut in hac parte nullam ejus fiduciam habeat Universitas*; statutum est, quod munerum praedictorum expers sit S. Theologiae Professor Regius, donec aliter Universitati placuerit, ne vero quid detrimenti capiat interea Universitas, Professoris ejusdem vicibus fungantur alii, scilicet, in concionatores selectos designando senior inter Vice-Cancellarii deputatos, vel eo, absente. aut ipsius Vice-Cancellarii locum tenente, proximus ex ordine deputatus (proviso semper quod sacros ordines susceperit) et in consilio de concionibus habendo, Praelector Dominae Margarettae Comitissae Richmondiae." Should I not be guilty of deliberate perjury, if in direct defiance of such a decree I did any act which should place the object of it in such a position as to be not only the judge of the soundness of the theological opinions and preaching of a whole diocese, but of those whom, from time to time, he must admit to cure of souls, and even to the sacred orders of the ministry?

I have sworn, at the most awful moment of my life, that I will "banish and drive away all erroneous and strange doctrines contrary to God's word". It may be replied, that this engagement applies to the ministrations in the care of souls, inherent only in parochial functions; but the statutes of our cathedral church constitute me one of the guardians of the soundness of the doctrine which may be preached in that sacred edifice: "Si quid a quopiam pro concione properatur, quod cum verbo Dei, articulis Religionae, aut Liturgiae Anglicanae consentire non videtur, eâ de re, Decanus atque Residentiarii, quotquot audierunt, Domium Episcopum sine morâ per literas suas monebunt." With what confidence, or what hope of the desired end, should I communicate such a case to a bishop whose own soundness of theological teaching was more than suspected? Should I not be guilty of a breach of my ordination vows if I did not protest against the admission of such a person to such a responsible post, and endeavour to "banish and drive away", by all lawful means, that person of the 18,000 clergy of this land on whom the censure and deprivation of one of the most learned and renowned seminaries of religious teaching in the world is yet in its full operation and effect, one who is already designated thereby as a setter forth of erroneous and strange doctrines.[4] Again, I have sworn to be FAITHFUL to the cathedral church of Hereford. Faithful I could not be, either as to the maintenance of the doctrine, or the discipline of the Church in those respects already alluded to, or the welfare and unity of that Church, either in the cathedral body itself or in the diocese at large, under existing circumstances, if by any act of mine I promoted Dr Hampden's elevation to the episcopal throne of that church and diocese. Faithful I have laboured to be in the restoration and the saving of its material and venerable fabric.[5] Faithful by God's help, I will strive to be, in obtaining for it that oblation of sound and holy doctrine which should ascend, together with the incense of prayer and praise, "in the beauty of holiness", untainted and unalloyed by any tincture of "philosophy and vain deceit, after the tradition of men, after the rudiments of the world, and not after Christ".

But your lordship may reply, there is another oath by which I have bound myself, which I have as yet overlooked: not so, my lord. Of my sentiments on the royal prerogative I have already put your lordship in possession. When I warned you of the consequences of your appointment, of the tendency which it would produce to weaken the existing relations between Church and State, I fully recognized the just prerogative of the Crown; and when I thought I had not sufficiently dwelt upon it, I wrote a second time to make myself distinctly understood.[6]

Nor is it only the sense of legal obligation which would constrain me to a dutiful regard to such observance. Few men have a greater cause to feel their duty in this respect, warmed by the sense of kindness and condescension from those of royal station, than myself. The memory of one who anxiously contemplated the future happiness and *true* glory of his successor, fixed indelibly those sentiments upon my heart. And, if for his sake only, who could to a long course of almost parental kindness, add, in an affecting injunction, the expression of his wishes for my good upon his deathbed, I should never be found forgetful—even although I may never have taken in the present reign the oath of allegiance—of that loyalty and devotion to my Sovereign which is not less a duty of religion than the grateful and constitutional homage of an English heart. Forgive me, my lord, for the reflection on that deathbed injunction, if I say, that had it been observed,—as but for party and political influence it would have been—your lordship, the Church, and the nation, would have been spared this most unhappy trial, the results of which, as I have already again and again foreboded to your lordship, it is impossible to foresee. Nor, under any circumstances, is it likely that the obligation of the oath of allegiance in my person will be infringed upon; its terms are, that "I will be faithful and bear *true* allegiance"; and, accordingly, *the congé d'élire* has these expressions, "requiring and commanding you, by the faith and allegiance by which you stand bound to us, to elect such a person for your bishop and pastor as may *be devoted to God,* and USEFUL *and faithful to us* and *our* KINGDOM". Would it be any proof of fidelity or *true* allegiance, my lord, to elect a person as "MEET TO BE ELECTED" who was the contrary to those requirements? And can it be possible that in the *course of divine service* in the *Chief Sanctuary of Almighty God* in the diocese, however *named* and *recommended*, a person should be "UNANIMOUSLY CHOSEN *and* ELECTED" in the awful falsification of these words, IN THE PRESENCE OF GOD, *against the consciences of the unhappy* electors, simply because the adviser of the Crown (for "the Crown can do no wrong") has in his short-sightedness and ignorance of facts (to say the least), thought fit to name an objectionable person, the one of all the clergy in the land so disqualified; and, when warned of the consequences by the voices of the Primate, of thirteen bishops, and hosts of priests and deacons, clergy and laity by hundreds, of all shades of opinions in the Church, persisted in the reckless determination?

In the words of an eminent writer of our Church, "All power is given unto edification, none to the overthrow and destruction of the Church", *Hooker's Ecclesiastical Polity*, book viii, chap. 7; and the matter is perhaps placed in the true light and position by the learned author of *Vindiciae Ecclesiae Anglicanae*—Francis Mason; the whole of which is well worthy of your lordship's notice. I venture to supply a brief extract, book iv, chap. 13, 1625:

Philodoxus You pretended to treat of Kings electing bishops and conferring of bishoprics, and now you ascribe not the election to Kings, but to the clergy, and claim only nomination for Kings?

Orthodoxus The King's nomination is, with us, a fair beginning to the election. Therefore, when he nominates any person he elects him, and gives, as I may say, the first vote for him.

Philodoxus What kind of elections are those of your deans and chapters? 'Tis certain they can't be called free elections, since nothing is to be done without the King's previous authority.

Orthodoxus The freedom of election doth not exclude the King's sacred authority, but *force and tyranny* only. If any unworthy person should be forced upon them against their will, or the clergy should be constrained to give their voices by force and threatening, such an election cannot be said to be free. But if the King do nominate a worthy person, according to the laws, as our Kings have used to do, and give them authority to choose him, there is no reason why this may not be called a free election; for here is no force or violence used.

Philodoxus But if the King, deceived by *undeserved recommendations*, should happen to propose to the clergy a person unlearned, or of ill morals, or otherwise manifestly unworthy of that function, what's to be done then?

Orthodoxus Our Kings are wont to proceed in these cases maturely and cautiously—I mean with the utmost care and prudence; and hence it comes to pass that the Church of England is at this time in such a flourishing condition.

Philodoxus Since they are but men they are liable to human weakness; and therefore what's to be done, if such a case should happen?

Orthodoxus If the electors could make sufficient proof of such crimes or incapacities, I think it were becoming them *to represent the same to the King, with all due humility, modesty, and duty, humbly* beseeching his Majesty, out of his known clemency, to take care of the interest of the widowed church; and our Princes are so famous for their piety and condescension, that I doubt not that his Majesty would graciously answer their pious petition, and nominate another unexceptionable person, agreeable to all their wishes. Thus a mutual affection would be kept up between the bishop and his church.[7]

Nor is this a mere supposition, but there are instances in the history of this kingdom of such judicious reconsideration of an undesirable appointment. I will cite but one from *Burnet's History of his own Times*, A.D. 1693, vol. iv, p. 209. London 1733:

The state of Ireland leads me to insert here a very particular instance of the Queen's pious care in disposing of bishoprics. Lord Sydney was so far engaged in the interest of a great family in Ireland, that he was too easily wrought on to recommend a branch of it to a vacant See. The representation was made with an undue character of the person; so the Queen granted it. But when she understood that he lay under a very bad character, she wrote a letter in her own hand to Lord Sydney, letting him know what she had heard, and ordered him to call for six Irish bishops, whom she named to him, and to require them to certify to her their opinion of that person. They all agreed that he laboured under an ill fame, and till that examined into they did not think proper to promote him; so that matter was let fall. I do not name the person, for I intend not to leave a blemish on him, but set this down as an example fit to be imitated by Christian Princes.

But, alas! remonstrance seems unheeded, and if our venerable Primate and thirteen bishops have raised their united voice of warning and entreaty to no purpose, it is no marvel that my humble supplication should have pleaded in vain, for time,—for investigation,—for some regard to our consciences,—some consideration for our painful and delicate position.

The time draws near—on Tuesday next the *semblance* of an election is to be exhibited. I ventured to assure your lordship that I could not undertake to say that it would be an unanimous election; I was bold enough to affirm that it would not be unanimous; and I, in my turn, received the intimation and the caution—I will not say *the threat*—that the law must be vindicated. Already have I assured your lordship that the principle on which this painful affair is regarded, is that of the most solemn religious responsibility; thousands regard it in this light. I have already told you, my lord, that the watchword of such is this—"Whether it be right in the sight of God to hearken unto you more than unto God, judge ye." I have anxiously implored your lordship to pause—to avert the blow. I have long since told you the truth. I have endeavoured to prevent, by every means in my power, the commotion which has arisen, and the necessity of the performance of a painful duty. I hoped the *congé d'élire* would not be issued *until a fair inquiry and investigation had been instituted.* A suit has been commenced in the ecclesiastical courts—why not have awaited its issue? When the *congé d'élire* did appear, I at once presumed, humbly but faithfully, though I stood alone, to petition the Crown; and now, when I am officially informed, that "her Majesty has not been pleased to issue any commands thereupon", I feel it to be my bounden duty, after a full and calm deliberation on the whole subject, having counted the cost, but remembering the words of Him whose most unworthy servant I am—"He that loveth house or lands more than me is not worthy of me"—loving my children dearly, and ardently desiring to complete the noble work which I have for seven years laboured to promote, yet not forgetting that there is an "hour of death and a day of judgment", when I trust, through the merits of my Redeemer, to be allowed to look up with hope, that I may be considered by the intercessions of mercy and pity to have been faithful in the hour of trial, to have "fought the good fight, to have kept the faith, to have finished *my* course,"—believing that I risk much, and shall incur your lordship's heavy displeasure, who may, if you will, direct the sword of power against me and mine—being certain that I preclude myself from that which might otherwise have been my lot, and expecting that I shall bring down upon myself the abuse and blame of some—I say, my lord, having fully counted the cost, having weighed *the sense of bounden duty* in the one scale against the consequences in the other, I have come to the deliberate resolve, that on Tuesday next no earthly consideration shall induce me to give my vote in the chapter of Hereford cathedral for Dr Hampden's elevation to the see of Hereford.

I have the honour to be, my lord,
your lordship's faithful humble servant,

JOHN MEREWETHER
Dean of Hereford

LORD JOHN RUSSELL TO THE DEAN OF HEREFORD

Woburn Abbey, Dec. 25.

Sir, I have had the honour to receive your letter of the 22nd instant, in which you intimate to me your intention of violating the law.

I have the honour to be your obedient servant,

J. RUSSELL[8]

1 Hampden, Renn Dickson; *b.* 1793; *educ.*, Oriel College, Oxford; Fellow of Oriel, 1814; Bampton Lecturer, 1832; Principal of St Mary Hall, Oxford, 1833; Regius Professor of Divinity at Oxford, 1836; case of Hampden *v.* Macmullen, 1842; Bishop of Hereford, 1847; *d.* 1868.

2 London (Blomfield), Winchester (Sumner), Lincoln (Kaye), Bangor (Bethell), Carlisle (Percy), Rochester (Murray), Gloucester and Bristol (Monk), Exeter (Phillpotts), Salisbury (Denison), Chichester (Gilbert), Ely (Turton), Oxford (Wilberforce), Bath and Wells (Bagot).

3 It is difficult to account for Russell's choice unless Hampden's liberal views matched Russell's own radical opinions. Wilberforce said of Hampden: "He was not a persecuted man, for he had got

a station higher than he ever dreamed of already; he is not an able, or an active man, or one popular with any party, and unless Lord John Russell wished for an opportunity of shocking the young confidence of the Church in him, I cannot conceive why he should have made it."

4 A statute to exclude Hampden from the boards which inquired into heresy and nominated select preachers was carried in convocation in 1837, and the attempt to repeal it was defeated in 1842.

5 Merewether was dean from 1832 to 1850. The work of restoration was begun under the Cottinghams. After Gilbert Scott's work (1857–63), the cathedral was reopened on 30 June with a sermon delivered by Hampden. Wilberforce said of it: "dull, but thoroughly orthodox" (R. Wilberforce, *Wilberforce*, vol. 3, p. 90).

6 The procedure for the appointment of bishops was laid down by statute in 1534 (25 Hen. VIII, c. 20), and again by the Act of Supremacy (1 Eliz., c. 1) in 1559. The *congé d'eliré* was the royal licence enabling the chapter to elect the person nominated by the Crown. A bill to abolish election was rejected by the House of Commons in 1880.

7 Russell was supported by the Queen, the Prince Consort advocating bishops of liberal views. The Queen was fervently Protestant; intolerant of the Tractarians, and under Albert's guidance she helped free the Establishment of bishops chosen from political motives. The Queen wrote to Russell: "The Bishops behave extremely ill about Dr Hampden, and the Bishop of Exeter is gone so far, in the Queen's opinion, that he might be prosecuted for it, in calling the act settling the supremacy on the Crown a *foul act* and *the Magna Carta of Tyranny*."

8 The election took place after divine service on 28 December. Three residentiary canons and eleven prebendaries voted for Hampden, twelve prebendaries did not appear, and the dean and Canon Huntingford voted against.

24 CHURCH AND CHARTISM, 1848

(*Charles Kingsley*, by his wife (1904), pp. 63-4)

Chartism was an English movement for political reform, which demanded the fulfilment of the People's Charter of 1838.[1] The final agitation, reflecting the general unrest of Europe as a whole, was the public meeting on Kennington Common on 10 April 1848. Two days after the failure of the meeting, Maurice, Ludlow,[2] and Kingsley agreed to publish a cheap journal addressed to working men. At the same time Kingsley's proclamation was being circulated in London.[3] The Christian Social movement, which arose out of the activity of these three, was a reaction against the indifference of the Establishment to social injustice and political inequality.[4]

WORKMEN OF ENGLAND! You say that you are wronged. Many of you are wronged; and many besides yourselves know it. Almost all men who have heads and hearts know it—above all, the working clergy know it.[5] They go into your houses, they see the shameful filth and darkness in which you are forced to live crowded together; they see your children growing up in ignorance and temptation, for want of fit education; they see intelligent and well-read men among you, shut out from a Freeman's just right of voting; and they see too the noble patience and self-control with which you have as yet borne these evils. They see it, and God sees it.

WORKMEN OF ENGLAND! You have more friends than you think for. Friends who expect nothing from you, but who love you, because you are their brothers, and who fear God, and therefore dare not neglect you, His children; men who are drudging and sacrificing themselves to get you your rights; men who know what your rights are, better than you know yourselves, who are trying to get for you something nobler than charters and dozens of Acts of Parliament—more useful than this "fifty thousandth share in a Talker in the National Palaver at Westminster"[6] can give you. You may disbelieve them, insult them—you cannot stop their working for you, beseeching you as you love yourselves, to turn back from the precipice of riot, which ends in the gulf of universal distrust, stagnation, starvation. You think the Charter would make you free —would to God it would! The Charter is not bad; *if the men who use it are not bad*! But will the Charter make you free? Will it free you from slavery to ten-pound bribes? Slavery to beer and gin?[7] Slavery to every spouter who flatters your self-conceit, and stirs up bitterness and headlong rage in you? That, I guess, is real slavery; to be a slave to one's own stomach, one's own pocket, one's own temper. Will the Charter cure *that*? Friends, you want more than Acts of Parliament can give.

Englishmen! Saxons! Workers of the great, cool-headed, strong-handed nation of England, the workshop of the world, the leader of freedom for 700 years, men say you have common-sense! then do not humbug yourselves into meaning "licence", when you cry for "liberty". Who would dare refuse you freedom? for the Almighty God, and Jesus Christ, the poor Man, who died for poor men, will bring it about for you, though all the Mammonites of the earth were against you. A nobler day is dawning for England, a day of freedom, science, industry! But there will be no true freedom without virtue, no true science without religion, no true industry without the fear of God, and love to your fellow-citizens.

Workers of England, be wise, and then you *must* be free, for you will be *fit* to be free.

A WORKING PARSON

1 The Six Points of the Charter were: Universal Suffrage; Vote by Ballot; Annual Parliaments; Payment of M.Ps; Abolition of the Property Qualification; and Equal Electoral Districts.

2 Ludlow, John Malcolm Forbes; *b.* 1821; *educ.*, in France; called to the bar, 1843; *Politics for the People*, 1848; conveyancer, 1843–74; founder of the Working Men's College, 1854; secretary of commission on Friendly and Benefit Societies, 1870; chief registrar for Friendly Societies, 1875–91; C.B. 1887; *d.* 1911.

3 Kingsley, Charles; *b.* 1819; *educ.*, King's College, London, 1836; Magdalene College, Cambridge, 1838; curate of Eversley, 1842; vicar, 1844; Professor of Modern History, Cambridge, 1860; canon of Chester, 1869; canon of Westminster, 1873; *d.* 1875.

4 Chartist agitation turned attention to the plight of the working classes. Thomas Hood's *Song of the Shirt*, Mrs Browning's *Cry of the Children*, Mrs Gaskell's *Mary Barton*, and Kingsley's *Yeast* and *Alton Locke*, were among many works exposing social evil. The Christian Socialists produced *Politics for the People*, *Tracts on Christian Socialism*, *The Christian Socialist*, and *Tracts for Priests and People*.

5 A meeting of these clergy and working men took place on 23 April 1849. Absent from the first meeting, Kingsley attended further meetings in the early summer, and it was at one of these that he declared: "I am a Church of England parson—and a Chartist."

6 The quotation is from Carlyle, and the same sentiments were expressed by George Bernard Shaw in the preface to *The Apple Cart* (1929).

7 Hogarth's *Gin Lane* and Cruikshank's *The Bottle* and *The Drunkard's Children*, did much to influence public opinion. The Churches embraced the temperance cause, the Band of Hope being formed in 1847 and the Church of England Total Abstinence Society in 1862.

25 "PAPAL AGGRESSION", 1850

(*Out of the Flaminian Gate, E.H.D.* XII (1), pp. 364-7)

In 1688 Innocent XI appointed four Vicars Apostolic for England, to serve London, the Midlands, the North, and the West. The revival within the Roman Church in England was due to the Catholic Emancipation Act, Irish immigration, and converts from the Tractarians. The decision was taken in Rome to reconstitute the Roman hierarchy in England. Wiseman's dramatic proclamation led to the charge of "Papal Aggression", and the fact that the Bull had been issued by Pius IX on his restoration to the Vatican by Republican France encouraged the idea that there were political undertones in his actions.[1]

NICHOLAS, BY THE DIVINE MERCY, OF THE HOLY ROMAN CHURCH BY THE TITLE OF ST PUDENTIA CARDINAL PRIEST, ARCHBISHOP OF WESTMINSTER, AND ADMINISTRATOR APOSTOLIC OF THE DIOCESE OF SOUTHWARK:

TO OUR DEARLY BELOVED IN CHRIST, THE CLERGY SECULAR AND REGULAR, AND THE FAITHFUL OF THE SAID ARCHDIOCESE AND DIOCESE:

Health and benediction in the Lord! If this day we greet you under a new title, it is not, dearly beloved, with an altered affection. If in words we seem to divide those who till now have formed, under our rule, a single flock, our heart is as undivided as ever in your regard. For now truly do we feel closely bound to you by new and stronger ties of charity; now do we embrace you in our Lord Jesus Christ with more tender emotions of paternal love; now doth our soul yearn, and our mouth is open to you, though words must fail to express what we feel on being once again permitted to address you. For if our parting was in sorrow, and we durst not hope that we should again face to face behold you, our beloved flock, so much the greater is now our consolation and our joy, when we find ourselves not so much permitted as commissioned to return to you by the supreme ruler of the Church of Christ.

But how can we for one moment indulge in selfish feelings, when, through that loving Father's generous and wise counsels, the greatest of blessings has just been bestowed upon our country, by the restoration of its true Catholic hierarchical government, in communion with the see of Peter?

For on the twenty-ninth day of last month, on the Feast of the Archangel Saint Michael, prince of the heavenly host, his Holiness Pope Pius IX[2] was graciously pleased to issue his Letters Apostolic,[3] under the Fisherman's Ring, conceived in terms of great weight and dignity, wherein he substituted for the eight Apostolic Vicariates heretofore existing, one archiepiscopal or metropolitan and twelve episcopal sees; repealing at the same time, and annulling all dispositions and enactments made for England by the Holy See with reference to its late form of ecclesiastical government.

And by a brief dated the same day his Holiness was further pleased to appoint us, though most unworthy, to the archiepiscopal see of Westminster, established by the above-mentioned Letters Apostolic, giving us at the same time the administration of the episcopal see of Southwark. So that at present, and till such time as the Holy See shall think fit otherwise to provide, we govern, and shall continue to govern, the counties of Middlesex, Hertford, and Essex as ordinary thereof, and those of Surrey, Sussex, Kent, Berkshire, and Hampshire, with the islands annexed, as administrator with ordinary jurisdiction.

Further, we have to announce to you, dearly beloved in Christ, that, as if still further to add solemnity and honour before the Church to this noble act of Apostolic authority, and to give an additional mark of paternal benevolence towards the Catholics of England, his Holiness was pleased to raise us, in the private consistory of Monday, the 30th of September, to the rank of Cardinal Priest of the holy Roman Church. And on the Thursday next ensuing, being the third day of this month of October, in public consistory, he delivered to us the insignia of this dignity, the cardinalitial hat; assigning us afterwards for our title in the private consistory which we attended, the Church of St Pudentiana, in which St Peter is groundedly believed to have enjoyed the hospitality of the noble and partly British family of the Senator Pudens.

In that same consistory we were enabled ourselves to ask for the archiepiscopal Pallium for our new see of Westminster; and this day we have been invested, by the hands of the Supreme Pastor and Pontiff himself, with this badge of metropolitan jurisdiction.

The great work, then, is complete; what you have long desired and prayed for is granted. Your beloved country has received a place among the fair Churches, which, normally constituted, form the splendid aggregate of Catholic Communion; Catholic England has been restored to its orbit in the ecclesiastical firmament, from which its light had long vanished, and begins now anew its course of regularly adjusted action round the centre of unity, the source of jurisdiction, of light and vigour. How wonderfully all this has been brought about, how clearly the hand of God has been shown in every step, we have not now leisure to relate, but we may hope soon to recount to you by word of mouth. In the meantime we will content ourselves with assuring you, that, if the concordant voice of those venerable and most eminent counsellors to whom the Holy See commits the regulation of ecclesiastical affairs in missionary countries, if the overruling of every variety of interests and designs, to the rendering of this measure almost necessary; if the earnest prayers of our holy Pontiff and his most sacred oblation of the divine sacrifice, added to his own deep and earnest reflection, can form to the Catholic heart an earnest of heavenly direction, an assurance that the Spirit of truth, who guides the Church, has here inspired its Supreme Head, we cannot desire stronger or more consoling evidence that this most important measure is from God, has His sanction and blessing, and will consequently prosper.[4]

Then truly is this day to us a day of joy and exaltation of spirit, the crowning day of long hopes, and the opening day of bright prospects. How must Saints of our country, whether Roman or British, Saxon or Norman, look down from their seats of bliss, with beaming glance, upon this new evidence of the faith and Church which led them to glory, sympathizing with those who have faithfully adhered to them through centuries of ill repute for the truth's sake, and now reap the fruit of their patience and long-suffering. And all those blessed martyrs of these latter ages, who have fought the battles of the faith under such discouragement, who mourned, more than over their own fetters or their own pain, over the desolate ways of their own Sion, and the departure of England's religious glory; oh! how must they bless God, who hath again visited his people,—how take part in our joy, as they see the lamp of the temple again enkindled and rebrightening, as they behold the silver links of that chain which has connected their country with the see of Peter in its vicarial government changed into burnished gold; not stronger nor more closely knit; but more beautifully wrought and more brightly arrayed.

And in nothing will it be fairer or brighter than in this, that the glow of more fervent love will be upon it. Whatever our sincere attachment and unflinching devotion to the Holy See till now, there is a new ingredient cast into these feelings; a warmer gratitude, a tenderer affection, a profounder admiration, a boundless and endless sense of obligation, for so new, so great, so sublime a gift, will be added to past sentiments of loyalty and fidelity to the supreme see of Peter. Our venerable Pontiff has shown himself a true shepherd, a true father; and we cannot but express our gratitude to him in our most fervent language, in the language of prayer. For when we raise our voices, as is meet, in loud and fervent thanksgiving to the Almighty, for the precious gifts bestowed upon our portion of Christ's vineyard, we will also implore every choice blessing on him who has been so signally the divine instrument in procuring it. We will pray that his rule over the Church may be prolonged to many years, for its welfare; that health and strength may be preserved to him for the discharge of his arduous duties; that light and grace may be granted to him proportioned to the sublimity of his office; and that consolations, temporal and spiritual, may be poured out upon him abundantly, in compensation for past sorrows and past ingratitude. And of these consolations may one of the most sweet to his paternal heart be the propagation of holy religion in our country, the advancement of his spiritual children there in true piety and devotion, and our ever-increasing affection and attachment to the see of St Peter.

In order, therefore, that our thanksgiving may be made with all becoming solemnity, we hereby enjoin as follows:

1. This our Pastoral Letter shall be publicly read in all the churches and chapels of the archdiocese of Westminster and the diocese of Southwark on the Sunday after its being received.

2. On the following Sunday there shall be in every such church or chapel a solemn Benediction of the Blessed Sacrament, at which shall be sung the *Te Deum*, with the usual versicles and prayers, with the prayer also *Deus omnium Fidelium Pastor et Rector* for the Pope.

3. The collect, *Pro Gratiarum Actione*, for thanksgiving and that for the Pope, shall be recited in the Mass of that day, and for two days following.

4. Where Benediction is never given, the *Te Deum* with its prayers, shall be recited or sung after Mass, and the collects above-named shall be added as enjoined.

And at the same time, earnestly entreating for ourselves also a place in your fervent prayers, we lovingly implore for you, and bestow on you, the blessing of Almighty God, Father, Son, and Holy Ghost. Amen.

Given out of the Flaminian Gate of Rome, this seventh day of October, in the year of our Lord MDCCCL.[5]

(Signed) NICHOLAS
Cardinal Archbishop of Westminster
By command of his Eminence,
FRANCIS SEARLE
Secretary

1 Italian nationalism and the decline of Austria involved the Papacy in the political struggle between States. In Britain, the outburst against the Papacy was not simply of the mob, but reflected the feelings of the nation at large.

2 Pius IX, Giovanni Maria Mastai-Ferretti; *b.* 1792; priest, 1819; papal missioner in Chile, 1823; Archbishop of Spoleto, 1827; Bishop of Imola, 1832; Cardinal, 1840; Pope, 1846; fled to Gaeta, 1848; restored to Rome, 1850; promulgated dogma of the Immaculate Conception, 1854; published *Syllabus Errorum*, convened Vatican Council which defined dogma of Papal Infallibility, 1869–70; deprived of temporal authority by Law of Guarantees, 1871; *d.* 1878.

3 Letters Apostolic: *Universalis Ecclesiae*, 29 September 1850.

4 The imitation of the original mission of Augustine in 597 did little to commend Wiseman to English Roman Catholics. Although this event turned public interest away from the Tractarians for a while, it encouraged the widespread belief that the Tractarians were working for the Roman cause.

5 Wiseman's imprint on the English Roman Catholic Church was to be lasting, and his supercilious attitude towards the Church of England was continued by Manning, though for different reasons. Palmerston commented on the episode: "The thing itself, in truth, is little or nothing and does not justify the irritation. What has goaded the nation is the manner, insolent and ostentatious, in which it has been done" (Marriott, *England Since Waterloo*, p. 161).

26 THE GORHAM CASE, 1850

(*Six Judgments*, pp. 17-18, 22, 37-8)

In determining appeals from the Court of Arches and the Provincial Court of York under the Act of 1833, the Judicial Committee of the Privy Council had to decide on matters arising out of doctrinal disputes. The controversy on the nature of baptism between the Bishop of Exeter and G. C. Gorham was the most notable of such suits. The appeal court's decision safeguarded the position of the Evangelicals within the Church of England, but was also instrumental in driving Manning and others to secede to the Church of Rome. The notion of a secular tribunal being competent to decide in cases of doctrine, especially in an action against a bishop, evoked sharp criticism of the court from many parties within the Church.

This is an appeal by the Reverend *George Cornelius Gorham*[1] against the sentence of the Dean of the Arches Court of *Canterbury* in a proceeding called a *Duplex Querela*,[2] in which the Right Reverend the Lord Bishop of *Exeter*, at the instance of Mr *Gorham*, was called upon to show cause why he had refused to institute Mr *Gorham* to the Vicarage of *Brampford Speke*.

The Judge[3] pronounced that the Bishop had shown sufficient cause for his refusal, and thereupon dismissed him from all further observance of justice in the premises, and, moreover, condemned Mr *Gorham* in costs.

From this sentence Mr *Gorham* appealed to her Majesty in Council. The case was referred by her Majesty to this Committee. It has been fully heard before us; and, by the direction of her Majesty, the hearing was attended by my Lords the Archbishops of *Canterbury* and *York* and the Bishop of *London*, who are members of her Majesty's Privy Council. We have the satisfaction of being authorized to state that the Most Reverend Prelates the Archbishops of *Canterbury* and *York*, after perusing the copies of our judgment, have expressed their approbation thereof. The Right Reverend the Lord Bishop of *London* does not concur therein.

The facts, so far as it is necessary to state them, are as follows:

Mr *Gorham* being Vicar of *St Just in Penwith*, in the Diocese of Exeter, on November 2, 1847, was presented by her Majesty to the Vicarage of *Brampford Speke*, in the same Diocese, and soon afterwards applied to the Lord Bishop of Exeter for admission and institution to the Vicarage.

The Bishop, on November 13, caused Mr *Gorham* to be informed, that his Lordship felt it his duty to ascertain by examination, whether Mr *Gorham* was sound in doctrine before he should be instituted to the Vicarage of *Bramford Speke*.[4]

The examination commenced on December 17, and was continued at very great length for five days in the same month of December, and (after some suspension) for three more days in the following month of March.

The questions proposed by the Bishop related principally to the Sacrament of Baptism, and were very numerous, much varied in form, embracing many points of difficulty, and often referring to the answers given to previous questions.

Mr *Gorham* did not at first object to the nature of the examination; but, during its progress, he at various times remonstrated against the manner in which it was conducted, and the length to which it extended. We are, however, relieved from the necessity of considering whether he could, or could not, lawfully have declined to submit to such a course of examination; because he did, in fact, answer nearly all the questions, and no complaint is made of his not having answered them all.

The examination being concluded, the Bishop refused to institute Mr *Gorham* for the reason (as stated in the notification) that he had, upon examination, found Mr *Gorham* unfit to fill the Vicarage, by reason of his holding doctrines contrary to the true Christian faith, and the doctrines contained in the Articles and Formularies of the United Church of *England* and *Ireland*, and especially in the Book of Common Prayer, administration of the Sacraments, and other rites and ceremonies of the Church, according to the use of the United Church of *England* and *Ireland*.

Adopting this course, the doctrine held by Mr *Gorham* appears to be this: that Baptism is a sacrament generally necessary to salvation, but that the grace of regeneration does not so necessarily accompany the act of Baptism that regeneration invariably takes place in Baptism; that the grace may be granted before, in or after Baptism; that Baptism is an effectual sign of grace, by which God works invisibly in us, but only in such as worthily receive it—in them alone it has a wholesome effect—and that, without reference to the qualification of the recipient, it is not in itself an effectual sign of grace; that infants baptized, and dying before actual sin, are certainly saved; but that in no case is regeneration in Baptism unconditional.

These being, as we collect them, the opinions of Mr *Gorham*, the question which we have to decide is, not whether they are theologically sound or unsound—not whether upon some of the doctrines comprised in the opinions, other opinions opposite to them may or may not be held with equal or even greater reason by other learned and pious Ministers of the Church—but whether these opinions now under our consideration are contrary or repugnant to the doctrines which the Church of *England*, by its Articles, Formularies, and Rubrics, requires to be held by its Ministers, so that upon the ground of these opinions the Appellant can lawfully be excluded from the benefice to which he has been presented....

... We express no opinion on the theological accuracy of these opinions, or any of them. The writers whom we have cited are not always consistent with themselves, nor are the reasons upon which they found their positions always valid; and other writers of great eminence, and worthy of great respect, have expressed very different opinions. But the mere fact that such opinions have been propounded and maintained by persons so eminent, and so much respected, as well as by very many others, appears to us sufficiently to prove that the liberty which was left by the Articles and Formularies has been actually enjoyed and exercised by the members and ministers of the Church of *England*.

The case not requiring it, we have abstained from expressing any opinion of our own upon the theological correctness or error of the doctrine held by Mr *Gorham*, which was discussed before us at such great length and with so much learning. His Honour the Vice-Chancellor *Knight Bruce* dissents from our judgment; but all the other members of the Judicial Committee who were present at the hearing of the case (those who are now present, and Baron *Parke*, who is unavoidably absent on circuit) are unanimously agreed in opinion;[5] and the judgment of their Lordships is, that the doctrine held by Mr *Gorham* is not contrary, or repugnant to the declared doctrine of the Church of England as by Law established, and that Mr *Gorham* ought not, by reason of the doctrine held by him, to have been refused admission to the Vicarage of *Brampford Speke*.

We shall, therefore, humbly report to her Majesty that the sentence pronounced by the learned Judge ought to be reversed, and that it ought to be declared that the Respondent, the Lord Bishop of *Exeter*, has not shown sufficient cause why he did not institute Mr *Gorham* to the said Vicarage.

We shall humbly advise her Majesty to remit the cause with that declaration to the Arches Court of *Canterbury*, to the end that right and justice may there be done in this matter, pursuant to the said declaration.

1 Gorham, George Cornelius; *b.* 1787; *educ.*, Queen's College, Cambridge; B.A., 1808; M.A., 1812; B.D., 1820; ordained by Bishop Dampier of Ely, 1811; instituted to Brampford Speke, 6 August 1851; *d.* 1857.

2 *Duplex Querela*—a process undertaken when a bishop refuses to institute a cleric to a benefice to which he has been presented. Unlike the *Quare Impedit* undertaken by the patron in such cases, the former takes place in an ecclesiastical court.

3 Jenner-Fust, Sir Henry; *b.* 1788; *educ.*, Trinity Hall, Cambridge; LL.B., 1798; LL.D. 1803; called to the Bar, 1800; Fellow of the College of Doctors of Law, 1803; Vicar-General to the Archbishop of Canterbury, 1832; Dean of Arches, 1834; *d.* 1852.

4 It was customary for Phillpotts to examine both curates and incumbents in this fashion. It is noteworthy that Dampier, Bishop of Ely, examined Gorham prior to his ordination and was similarly dissatisfied with his opinions on baptism. See *Church Quarterly Review*, CLXII, no. 345, pp. 447-54.

5 The court which met on 11 December 1849 included the two archbishops and Blomfield, Lord Campbell, Pemberton Leigh, Lord Langdale, Baron Parke, Sir James Knight-Bruce, Dr Lushington, and Lord Lansdowne.

27 CENSUS OF RELIGIOUS WORSHIP, 1851

(*Census of Great Britain* (1851), pp. xxxii-xliii, cxlviii-cxlix, clviii)

Horace Mann was appointed by the Registrar-General to conduct a census of attendance at religious worship, in conjunction with the normal census. The *Report* was not entirely accurate, the cathedrals being scarcely accounted for, and college, workhouse, and school chapels being omitted altogether. Mann's conclusion that 5½ million people in England and Wales were not churchgoers brought home to many the inability of the Churches to cope with the populations of the new cities. He listed among the causes of non-churchgoing: social conditions, popular misconceptions of the motives of the ministers, poverty, and overcrowding.[1]

THE CHURCH OF ENGLAND

The doctrines of the Church of England are embodied in her

Articles and Liturgy: the Book of Common Prayer prescribes her mode of worship; and the Canons of 1603 contain, so far as the clergy are concerned, her code of discipline.

Bishops, Priests, and Deacons are the ministerial orders known to the episcopal establishment of England. In the Bishop lies the power of ordination of inferior ministers, who otherwise have no authority to dispense the sacraments or preach. Deacons, when ordained, may, licensed by the bishop, preach and administer the rite of baptism; Priests by this ceremony are further empowered to administer the Lord's Supper, and to hold a benefice with cure of souls.

Besides these *orders*, there are also several *dignities* sustained by bishops and by priests; as (i) *Archbishops*, each of whom is chief of a certain number of bishops, who are usually ordained by him; (ii) *Deans and Chapters*, who, attached to all cathedrals, are supposed to form the council of the bishop, and to aid him with advice; (iii) *Archdeacons*, who perform a kind of episcopal function in a certain portion of a diocese; (iv) *Rural Deans*, who are assistants to the bishop in a smaller sphere.

These various orders and dignities of the Church have all (except cathedral deans) attached to them peculiar territorial jurisdictions. The theory of the Establishment demands that every clergyman should have his ministrations limited to a specific district or *Parish*; and, when England first became divided into parishes, the number of churches would exactly indicate the number of such parishes,—each parish being just that portion of the country, the inhabitants of which were meant to be accommodated in the newly erected church. In course of years, however, either prompted by the growth of population or by their own capricious piety, proprietors erected and endowed, within the mother-parishes, fresh edifices which were either chapels of ease to the mother church or the centres of new districts, soon allowed by custom to become distinct ecclesiastical divisions known as "chapelries". In this way nearly all the soil of England became parcelled out in ecclesiastical divisions, varying greatly, both in size and population, as might be expected from the isolated and unsystematic efforts out of which they sprung. Of late years, as new churches have been built, some further subdivisions of the larger parishes have been effected by the bishops and commissioners empowered by acts of parliament. The number of ecclesiastical districts and new parishes thus formed was, at the time of the census, 1,255, containing a population of 4,832,491.

In the ancient Saxon period, ten such parishes constituted a

Rural Deanery. The growth, however, of the population, and the increased number of churches, have now altered this proportion, and the rural deaneries are diverse in extent. At present there are 463 such divisions.[2]

Archdeaconries, as territorial divisions, had their origin soon after the Norman Conquest, previous to which archdeacons were but members of cathedral chapters. Several new archdeaconries have been created within recent years, by the Ecclesiastical Commissioners, by virtue of the act of 6 & 7 Wm. IV, c. 77. The total number now is 71.

Bishoprics or *Dioceses* are almost as ancient as the introduction here of Christianity. Of those now extant, all (excepting seven) were formed in Saxon or in British times. The Saxon bishoprics were generally coextensive with the several kingdoms. Of the excepted seven, five were created by Henry the Eighth, out of a portion of the confiscated property of the suppressed religious houses, and the other two (viz. Manchester and Ripon), were created by the Act of 6 & 7 Wm. IV, c. 77. There are two *Archbishoprics* or *Provinces*: Canterbury, comprehending 21 dioceses, and York, comprising the remaining seven. The population of the former in 1851 was 12,785,048; that of the latter 5,285,687.

The discipline of the Church of England is administered by a series of ecclesiastical courts, viz., (i) that of the Bishop; (ii) that of the Archbishop; and (iii) that of the Sovereign, who is, over all, the supreme governor of the Church, and who, as represented by the Privy council, hears and finally decides appeals from all inferior tribunals.

The government of the Church is virtually committed to the sovereign, as its temporal head, and to parliament, as the monarch's council; the Convocation of the clergy, which, in former times, was used to legislate on all ecclesiastical affairs, has not, since 1717, been permitted to deliberate to any purpose. The Crown appoints the archbishops, bishops, and deans, and a considerable portion of the clergy.

Incumbents of parishes are appointed, subject to the approval of the bishop, by *patrons*, who may be either corporate bodies or private persons. Of the 11,728 benefices in England and Wales, 1,144 are in the gift of the crown; 1,853 in that of the bishops; 938 in that of cathedral chapters and other dignitaries; 770 in that of the universities of Oxford and Cambridge, and the colleges of Eton, Winchester, &c.; 931 in that of the ministers of mother-churches; and the residue (6,092) in that of private persons. Incumbents are of three kinds; rectors, vicars, and perpetual curates. Rectors are recipients of *all* the parochial tithes; vicars and perpetual curates are the delegates of the tithe-impropriators, and receive a *portion* only. These appointments are for life. The ordinary curates are appointed each by the incumbent who desires their aid.

The income of the Church of England is derived from the following sources; lands, tithes, church-rates, pew-rents, Easter offerings, and surplice fees (i.e. fees for burials, baptisms, &c.) The distribution of these revenues may be inferred from the state of things in 1831, when it appeared to be as follows:

	£
Bishops	181,631
Deans and chapters	360,095
Parochial clergy	3,251,159
Church-rates	500,000
	4,292,885

In the course of the twenty years which have elapsed since 1831, no fewer than 2,029 new churches have been built, and the value of Church property has much increased; so that, after the considerable addition which must be made to the above amount, in order to obtain an accurate view of the total income of the Church in 1851, it is probable that it will be considerably upwards of 5,000,000*l.* per annum.

The number of beneficed clergy in 1831 was 10,718: the average gross income, therefore, of each would be about 300*l.* per annum. At the same date there were 5,230 curates, the total amount of whose stipends was 424,695*l.*, yielding an average of 81*l.* per annum to each curate. But, as many incumbents possessed more than 300*l.* a year, and some curates more than 81*l.* a year, there must evidently have been some incumbents and curates whose remuneration was below those sums respectively.

For the purpose of raising the stipends of incumbents of the smaller livings, the Governors of Queen Anne's Bounty annually receive the sum of 14,000*l.*, the produce of First Fruits and Tenths; and the Ecclesiastical Commissioners apply to the same object a portion of the surplus proceeds of episcopal and capitular estates.[3]

The progress of the Church of England has, in recent times, been very rapid; and conspicuously so within the twenty years just terminated. Latterly, a sentiment appears to have been strongly prevalent, that the relief of spiritual destitution must not be exclusively devolved upon the State; that Christians in their individual, no less than in their organized, capacity, have duties to discharge in ministering to the land's religious wants. Accordingly, a spirit of benevolence has been increasingly diffused; and private liberality is now displaying fruits, in daily rising churches, almost as abundant as in ancient times—distinguished, also, advantageously, from earlier charity, by being, it may fairly be assumed, the offspring of a more enlightened zeal, proceeding from a wider circle of contributors. The following statistics will exhibit this more clearly:

In 1831, the number of churches and chapels of the Church of England amounted to 11,825. The number in 1851, as returned to the Census Office, was 13,854; exclusive of 223 described as being "not separate buildings", or as "used also for secular purposes"; thus showing an increase, in the course of 20 years, of more than *two thousand* churches. Probably the increase is still larger, really, as it can hardly be expected that the last returns were altogether perfect. The greater portion of this increase is attributable to the self-extending power of the Church,—the State not having, in the twenty years, contributed in aid of private benefactions, more than 511,385*l.* towards the erection of 386 churches. If we assume the average cost of each new edifice to be about 3,000*l.* the total sum expended in this interval (exclusive of considerable sums devoted to the *restoration* of old churches) will be 6,087,000*l.* The chief addition has occurred, as was to be expected and desired, in thickly peopled districts, where the rapid increase of inhabitants has rendered such additional accommodation most essential. Thus, in Cheshire, Lancashire, Middlesex, Surrey, and the West Riding of Yorkshire, the increase of churches has been so much greater than the increase of the population, that the proportion between the accommodation and the number of inhabitants is now considerably more favourable than in 1831.

COUNTY	POPULATION		NO. OF CHURCHES (separate bldgs)		Proportion of Churches to Population	
	1831	1851	1831	1851	1831	1851
					ONE CHURCH TO	
CHESHIRE	334,391	455,725	142	244	2,355	1,868
LANCASHIRE	1,336,854	2,031,236	292	521	4,578	3,899
MIDDLESEX	1,358,330	1,886,576	246	405	5,522	4,658
SURREY	486,434	683,082	159	249	3,059	2,743
YORK (WEST RIDING)	984,609	1,325,495	287	556	3,431	2,384

It is true, indeed, that in the whole of England and Wales collectively the proportion shows no increase, but a decrease—being, in 1831, one church to every 1,175 inhabitants, while in 1851 it was one church to every 1,296; but the latter proportion is not inconsistent with the supposition that, in consequence of better distribution of the churches through the country, the accommodation in reality is greater now than was the case in 1831. But this must be more fully treated in a subsequent part of this Report.

The following view of the periods in which the existing structures were erected, will display, to some extent, the comparative increase in the several decennial intervals of the present century. Of the 14,077 existing churches, chapels, and other buildings belonging to the Church of England, there were built:

Before 1801	9,667
Between 1801 and 1811	55
Between 1811 and 1821	97
Between 1821 and 1831	276
Between 1831 and 1841	667
Between 1841 and 1851	1,197
Dates not mentioned	2,118

This does not, indeed, with strict exactness, show the real number of churches built in each of these decennial intervals; for, possibly, some few, erected formerly, have been replaced by other and larger edifices, which would thus perhaps be mentioned with the later date. The tendency is, therefore, slightly, to augment unduly the numbers in the later, and unduly diminish the numbers in the earlier periods; but this disturbing influence has probably been more than counteracted by the cases where the date has been left unmentioned. The statement, therefore, is perhaps a tolerably fair criterion of the progress of church-building in the nineteenth century. If the preceding estimate be accurate respecting the number of churches built *since* 1831, and if it be assumed, as is most likely, that the greater portion of the 2,118 churches, of which the dates of erection are not specified, were built before 1801, leaving perhaps 60 or 70 built in the period 1801-31; it will follow that, from 1801 to 1831, there must have been above 500 new erections, at a cost, upon the average, of probably 6,000*l*., apiece, being altogether 3,000,000*l*. of which amount, 1,152,044*l*. was paid from parliamentary grants, originated in 1818. Subject to the above-mentioned qualification respecting the dates of churches renovated or enlarged, the whole result of the efforts made in the present century may be represented thus:

PERIODS	NUMBER OF CHURCHES BUILT	ESTIMATED COST		
			CONTRIBUTED BY	
		TOTAL £	PUBLIC FUNDS £	PRIVATE BENEFACTION £
1801 to 1831	500	3,000,000	1,152,044	1,847,956
1831 to 1851	2,029	6,087,000	511,385	5,575,615
1801 to 1851	2,529	9,087,000	1,663,429	7,423,571

Nor has the spirit of activity been satisfied with this astonishing addition to the number of religious edifices. Organized associations for religious objects—almost wholly the productions of the present age—have gained surprising magnitude and influence. Prior to the nineteenth century, only two considerable societies existed for such purposes; viz., the "Society for the Propagation of the Gospel in Foreign Parts", and the "Society for Promoting Christian Knowledge". Since 1801, however, the number and variety of such beneficient associations have greatly and continually increased. The special wants of different classes have called forth almost as many special organizations for their relief; the poor, particularly, as being, either from distaste or from necessity, in general absentees from public worship, are the objects of some dozen different societies, through which, by the aid of laymen and lay scripture-readers, those are reached who otherwise would doubtless never be reclaimed. And, not content with England as the limit of its operations, this abundant charity discovers fields for its development in almost every portion of the world. The following list (B)[4] will indicate the more conspicuous societies connected with the Church *exclusively*. Some other important institutions, in supporting which the Church of England largely shares, are mentioned at page cxvii. From this it will appear that, independently of local effort—of the many District and Parochial Societies for household visitation and for other methods of diffusing moral and religious influence—the Church of England, by its separate centralized exertions, raises above 400,000*l.* per annum for religious objects, out of which 250,000*l.* is applied to foreign missionary operations.

How far these exertions, in conjunction with the usual parochial agencies, are adequate to the position which the Church should occupy with reference to our constantly augmenting population, is a question which remains for our discussion in the second part of this Report.[5]

In the 13,051 returns which furnished information as to sittings, accommodation is stated for 4,922,412 persons. Making an estimate for 1,026 churches, for which no particulars respecting sittings were supplied, it seems that the total accommodation in 14,077 churches was for 5,317,915 persons. The number of *attendants* on the Census-Sunday (after an estimated addition on account of 939 churches, from which no returns of the attendants were received) was as follows: *Morning*, 2,541,244; *Afternoon*, 1,890,764; *Evening*, 860,543.

The summary result of this inquiry with respect to accommodation is, that there are in England and Wales 10,398,013 persons able to be present at one time in buildings for religious worship. Accommodation, therefore, for that number (equal to 58 per cent of the population) is required. The *actual* accommodation in 34,467 churches, chapels, and out-stations is enough for 10,212,563 persons. But this number, after a deduction, on account of ill-proportioned distribution, is reduced to 8,753,279, a provision equal to the wants of only 49 per cent of the community. And further, out of these 8,753,279 sittings, a certain considerable number are rendered *unavailable* by being in churches or chapels which are *closed* throughout some portion of the day when services are usually held. There is therefore wanted an additional supply of 1,644,734 sittings, if the population is to have an extent of accommodation which shall be undoubtedly sufficient. These sittings, too, must be provided *where* they are wanted; i.e. in the *large town districts* of the country,—more especially in London. To furnish this accommodation would probably require the erection of about 2,000 churches and chapels; which, in towns, would be of larger than the average size. This is assuming that all churches and sects may contribute their proportion to the work, and that the contributions of each may be regarded as by just so much diminishing the efforts necessary to be made by other churches. If, as is probable, this supposition be considered not altogether admissible, there will be required a further addition to these 2,000 structures; the extent of which addition must depend upon the views which may be entertained respecting what particular sects should be entirely disregarded.

Of the total existing number of 10,212,563 sittings, the Church of England contributes 5,317,915, and the other churches, together, 4,894,648.

If we inquire what steps are being taken by the Christian church to satisfy this want, there is ample cause for hope in the history of the twenty years just terminated. In that interval the growth of population, which before had far outstripped the expansion of religious institutions, has been less, considerably, than the increase of accommodation,—people having multiplied by 29 per cent, while sittings have increased by 46 per cent; so that the number of sittings to 100 persons, which was only *fifty* in 1831, had risen to *fifty-seven* in 1851. And although this increase has not been confined to one particular church, it will scarcely less perhaps be matter for rejoicing; since, no doubt, the augmentation has occurred in bodies whose exertions cannot fail to have a beneficial influence, whatever the diversities of ecclesiastical polity by which, it may be thought, the value of these benefits in some degree is lessened. Doubtless, this encouraging display of modern zeal and liberality is only part of a continuous effort which—the Christian Church being now completely awakened to her duty—will not be relaxed till every portion of the land and every class of its inhabitants be furnished with at least the *means and opportunities* of worship. The field for future operations is distinctly marked: the *towns*, both from their present actual destitution and from their incessant and prodigious growth, demand almost a concentration of endeavours—the combined exertions of the general Church. Without an inclination for religious worship—certainly without ability to raise religious structures—the inhabitants of crowded districts of populous cities are as differently placed as possible from their surburban neighbours, who, more prosperous in physical condition, possess not only the desire to have, but also the ability to get, an adequate provision for religious culture. New churches, therefore, spring up naturally in those new neighbourhoods in which the middle classes congregate;[5] but, all spontaneous efforts being hopeless in the denser districts peopled by the rank and file of industry, no added churches evidently, can be looked for there, except as the result of missionary labours acting from without.[6] No agency appears more suited to accomplish such a work than that of those societies, possessed by most religious bodies, which collect into one general fund the offerings of the members of each body for church or chapel extension. The Established Church is represented in this way by the Incorporated Society, the Metropolis Churches' Fund, and by several diocesan societies; the Independents, and the Baptists also, each possess their Building Funds; but the support which these societies receive must be enormously increased if any vigorous attempt is to be made to meet and conquer the emergency. Compared with the amount contributed for foreign missionary operations, the support received by organized societies for church and chapel extension here at home appears conspicuously inadequate.[7] The hope may probably be reasonably entertained, that while the contributions to the former work continue undiminished, the disparity between the treatment of the two may speedily disappear.

The most important fact which this investigation as to attendance brings before us is, unquestionably, the alarming number of the non-attendants. Even in the least unfavourable aspect of the figures just presented, and assuming (as no doubt is right) that the 5,288,294 absent every Sunday are not always the same individuals, it must be apparent that a sadly formidable portion of the English people are habitual neglecters of the public ordinances of religion. Nor is it difficult to indicate to what particular class of the community this portion in the main belongs. The middle classes have augmented rather than diminished that devotional sentiment and strictness of attention to religious services by which, for several centuries, they have so eminently been distinguished. With the upper classes, too, the subject of religion has obtained of late a marked degree of notice, and a regular church-attendance is now ranked amongst the recognized proprieties of life. It is to satisfy the wants of these two classes that the number of religious structures has of late years so increased. But while the *labouring* myriads of our country have been multiplying with our multiplied material prosperity, it cannot, it is feared, be stated that a corresponding increase has occurred in the attendance of this class in our religious edifices. More especially in cities and large towns it is observable how absolutely insignificant a portion of the congregations is composed of artisans. They fill, perhaps, in youth, our National, British, and Sunday Schools, and there receive the elements of a religious education; but, no sooner do they mingle in the active world of labour than, subjected to the constant action of opposing influences, they soon become as utter strangers to religious ordinances as the people of a heathen country. From whatever cause, in them or in the manner of their treatment by religious bodies, it is sadly certain that this vast, intelligent, and growingly important section of our countrymen is thoroughly estranged from our religious institutions in their present aspect. Probably, indeed, the prevalence of *infidelity* has been exaggerated, if the word be taken in its popular meaning, as implying some degree of intellectual effort and decision; but, no doubt, a great extent of negative, inert indifference prevails, the practical effects of which are much the same. There is a sect, originated recently, adherents to a system called "Secularism";[8] the principal tenet being that, as the fact of a future life is (in their view) at all events susceptible of *some* degree of doubt, while the fact and the necessities of a present life are matters of direct sensation, it is therefore prudent to attend exclusively to the concerns of that existence which is certain and immediate—not wasting energies required for present duties by a preparation for remote, and merely possible, contingencies. This is the creed which probably with most exactness indicates the faith which, virtually though not professedly, is entertained by the masses of our working population; by the skilled and unskilled labourer alike—by hosts of minor shopkeepers and Sunday traders—and by miserable denizens of courts and crowded alleys. They are *unconscious Secularists*—engrossed by the demands, the trials, or the pleasures of the passing hour, and ignorant or careless of a future. These are never or but seldom seen in our religious congregations; and the melancholy fact is thus impressed upon our notice that the classes which are most in need of the restraints and consolations of religion are the classes which are most without them.

1 The official questionnaire inquired: (i) The number of buildings used for public worship; (ii) the number of sittings provided; (iii) the number of persons present at each of the services held on 30 March 1851.

2 The ancient office of rural dean was restored with practical effect by Kaye, Bishop of Lincoln, Marsh, Bishop of Peterborough, and Blomfield (1844). The last diocese to revive the office of rural dean was Sodor and Man in 1880.

3 The *Report* noted that: 4,700 livings were charged with the payment of first fruits, and 5,000 with yearly tenths. The annual produce of first fruits and tenths is about 14,000*l*. Between 1809 and 1820 Parliament voted eleven grants of 100,000*l*. for the purposes of the corporation. To the end of 1852, the capital appropriated to small livings amounted to 5,027,200*l*. The existing trust capital of the corporation in 1851 was 2,400,000*l*. sterling.

4 The societies and institutions referred to in the text include: Incorporated Society for the Enlargement, Building, and Repairing of Churches and Chapels (1818); Church Extension Fund (1844); Metropolis Churches Fund (1836); C.P.A.S. (1836); Society for Promoting the Employment of Additional Curates in Populous Places (1836); Friends of the Clergy Society (1849); Corporation of the Sons of the Clergy (1678); Society for the Relief of Poor Pious Clergymen (1788); Young Men's Society for Aiding Missions at Home and Abroad (1844); Church of England Scripture Readers'

Association (1844); Prayer Book and Homily Society (1812); British Society for Promoting the Religious Principles of the Reformation (1827); Society for Promoting the Due Observance of the Lord's Day (1831); Thames Church Mission (1844); S.P.C.K. (1698); C.M.S. (1798); S.P.G. (1701); Society for Promoting Christianity amongst the Jews (1809); Loochoo Mission (1845); Colonial Church and School Society (1836); Colonial Bishoprics Fund (1840).

5 The Proprietary Chapel was a feature of the period, where the wealthier classes could listen to the preacher of their choice, supporting the chapel either by subscription or pew rent. Exeter Hall, built in 1830, was the leading unconsecrated centre of London, the Margaret Chapel achieved a notoriety for ritualist practices, and F. W. Robertson completed his ministry at the Trinity Chapel, Brighton.

6 The Salvation Army (1865) and the Church Army (1882) were specifically missionary enterprises in the areas where organized religion failed to meet the needs of the working classes.

7 S.P.G. had an annual income of £83,000; L.M.S. £65,000; the Baptist Missionary Society, £19,000; C.M.S. £120,000. This compared with the Incorporated Society for Church Building, £16,000; the Congregational Chapel Building Society, £3,366; and the Baptist Building Fund, £795.

8 Secularism was promoted by G. J. Holyoake (1817-1906), who founded secular societies in several English towns. Charles Bradlaugh became the president of the London Society in 1858, a post he retained till 1890.

28 THE ECCLESIASTICAL TITLES ACT 1851

(*Statutes at Large*, 14-15 Vict., c. 60)

The passing of this Act was an example of legislation arising out of an outburst of public feeling. Russell wrote to the Bishop of Durham:[1] "There is an assumption of power in all the documents which have come from Rome; a pretension of supremacy over the realm of England, and a claim to sole and undivided sway, which is inconsistent with the Queen's supremacy, with the rights of our bishops and clergy, and with the spiritual independence of the nation, as asserted even in Roman Catholic times. I confess, however, that my alarm is not equal to my indignation." No person was ever prosecuted under the Act's provisions, and there was general agreement when it was quietly repealed by Gladstone in 1871. *E.H.D.* XII (1), p. 368.

Whereas divers of Her Majesty's Roman Catholic subjects have assumed to themselves the Title of Archbishops and Bishops of a pretended Province, and of pretended Sees or Dioceses, within the United Kingdom, under colour of an alleged Authority given to them for that Purpose by certain Briefs, Rescripts, or Letters Apostolical from the See of *Rome*, and particularly by a certain Brief, Rescript, or Letter Apostolical purporting to have been given at *Rome* on the Twenty-ninth of *September* One thousand eight hundred and fifty:[2] and whereas by the Act of the Tenth Year of King *George* the Fourth, Chapter Seven,[3] after reciting that the Protestant Episcopal Church of *England* and *Ireland*, and the Doctrine, Discipline, and Government thereof, and likewise the Protestant Presbyterian Church of *Scotland* ... were by the respective Acts of Union of *England* and *Scotland*, and of *Great Britain* and *Ireland*, established permanently and inviolably, and that the Right and Title of Archbishops to their respective Provinces, of Bishops to their Sees, and of Deans to their Deaneries, as well in *England* as in *Ireland*, had been settled and established by Law, it was enacted, that if any Person after the Commencement of that Act, other than the Person thereunto authorized by Law, should assume or use the Name, Style, or Title of Archbishop of any Province, Bishop of any Bishopric, or Dean of any Deanery, in *England* or *Ireland*, he should for every such Offence forfeit and pay the Sum of One hundred Pounds: And whereas it may be doubted whether the recited Enactment extends to the Assumption of the Title of Archbishop or Bishop of a pretended Province or Diocese, or Archbishop or Bishop of a City, Place, or Territory, or Dean of any pretended Deanery in *England* or *Ireland*, not being the See, Province, or Diocese of any Archbishop or Bishop or Deanery of any Dean recognized by Law; but the Attempt to establish, under colour of Authority from the See of *Rome* or otherwise, such pretended Sees, Provinces, Dioceses, or Deaneries, is illegal and void: And whereas it is expedient to prohibit the Assumption of such Titles in respect of any Places within the United Kingdom: Be it therefore declared and enacted by the Queen's most Excellent Majesty, by and with the Advice and Consent of the Lords Spiritual and Temporal, and Commons, in this present Parliament assembled, and by the Authority of the same, That

I All such Briefs, Rescripts, or Letters Apostolical and all and every the Jurisdiction, Authority, Pre-eminence, or Title conferred or pretended to be conferred thereby, are and shall be and be deemed unlawful and void.

II And be it enacted, That if, after the passing of this Act, any Person shall obtain or cause to be procured from the Bishop or See of *Rome*, or shall publish or put in use within any Part of the United Kingdom, any such Bull, Brief, Rescript, or Letters Apostolical, or any other Instrument or Writing, for the Purpose of constituting such Archbishops or Bishops of such pretended Provinces, Sees, or Dioceses, within the United Kingdom, or if any Person, other than a Person thereunto authorized by Law in respect of an Archbishopric, Bishopric, or Deanery of the United Church of *England* and *Ireland*, assume or use the Name, Style, or Title of Archbishop, Bishop, or Dean of any City, Town, or Place, or of any Territory or District, (under any Designation or Description whatsoever,) in the United Kingdom, whether such City, Town, or Place, or such Territory or District, be or be not the See or the Province, or coextensive with the Province, of any Archbishop, or the See or the Diocese, or coextensive with the Diocese, of any Bishop, or the Seat or Place of the Church of any Dean, or coextensive with any Deanery, of the said United Church, the Person so offending shall for every such Offence forfeit and pay the Sum of One hundred Pounds, to be recovered as Penalties imposed by the recited Act may be recovered under the Provisions thereof, or by Action of Debt at the Suit of any Person in One of Her Majesty's Superior Courts of Law, with the Consent of Her Majesty's Attorney General in *England* and *Ireland*, or Her Majesty's Advocate in *Scotland*, as the Case may be....[4]

1 Maltby, Edward, *b.* 1770; *educ.*, Norwich Grammar School, Winchester, and Pembroke College, Cambridge; B.A., 1972; M.A., 1794; domestic chaplain to the Bishop of Lincoln; prebendary of Lincoln; Preacher at Lincoln's Inn, 1824; Headmaster of Harrow; Bishop of Chichester, 1831; Bishop of Durham, 1836; resigned, 1856; *d.* 1859.

2 See 25, "Papal Aggression", 1850, pp. 116-20 above.

3 See 5, The Catholic Emancipation Act 1829, pp. 29-31 above.

4 Wiseman responded with an *Appeal*, defending the action of the Pope in establishing the Roman Catholic hierarchy. This was published in *The Times* and four other newspapers. This bold step was contributory to making the Act ineffective.

Wiseman, Nicholas; *b.* 1802; Rector of the English College at Rome, 1828; lectured in England, 1835; Bishop of Melipotamus (co-adjutor to Bishop Walsh, and Vicar Apostolic to the Midland District), 1840; Vicar Apostolic to the London District, 1847; Cardinal Archbishop of Westminster, 1850; *d.* 1865.

29 THE EUTHANASIA OF MISSIONS, 1851

(Henry Venn, *The Native Pastorate and Organization of Native Churches.* First Paper, Minute upon the Employment and Ordination of Native Teachers. C.M.S.)

European missionaries tended to import wholesale their western methods, ideas, and practices into their respective areas of operation. An enlightened attitude towards native cultures, thought, and languages was slow in developing, and the entrusting of ecclesiastical oversight to native Christians was not generally acceptable to the Churches. This directive marks a step forward in the official policy of an Anglican missionary society under the leadership of its outstanding secretary, Henry Venn.[1]

GENERAL PRINCIPLES

The advanced state of Missions having rendered it desirable to record the views of the Society upon the employment and ordination of Native teachers, the following particulars are given for the information of its Missionaries:

1 In all questions relating to the settlement of a Native Church in any Mission field, it is important to keep in view the distinction between the office of a *Missionary*, who preaches to the heathen, and instructs inquirers or recent converts, and the office of a *Pastor*, who ministers in holy things to a congregation of Native Christians.

2 Whilst the work of a Missionary may involve for a time the pastoral care of newly baptized converts, it is important that, as soon as settled congregations are formed, such pastoral care should be devolved upon Native Teachers, under the Missionary's superintendence.

3 The Native Teacher who approves himself "apt to teach" is appointed to the office of a *Catechist*. The office of a Catechist has been always recognized in the Church of Christ for evangelistic work, his function being to preach to the heathen, and to minister in congregations of converts until they are provided with a Native Pastor.

4 As a general rule, a Catechist should be presented to the Bishop for ordination only with a view to his becoming Pastor of some specified Native Congregation or district. The cases in which a

Native may be ordained for direct evangelistic work, or while engaged in Missionary education, must be regarded as exceptional.

5 Ordination is the link between the Native Teachers and the Native Church. Native Teachers are to be regarded, after their ordination, as Pastors of the Native Church, rather than as the Agents of a Foreign Society, or of other independent parties. Their social position should be such as is suitable to the circumstances of the Native Church; and their emoluments must be regulated by the ability of the Native Church to furnish the maintenance of their Pastors. Care must therefore be taken to guard Native Teachers from contracting habits of life too far removed from those of their countrymen.

6 The attempts which have been made by this Society to train up Native Missionaries and Pastors by an European education, and in Collegiate establishments, have convinced the Committee, that, under the present circumstances of Missions, Native Missionaries and Pastors may be best obtained by selecting from among the Native Catechists those who have approved themselves faithful and established Christians, as well as "apt to teach", and by giving to such persons a special training in Scriptural studies, in the vernacular language.

7 While any district continues a Missionary district, the Native Pastors located in it are, as a general rule, to be under the superintendence of a Missionary or of some other Minister, appointed by the Society; until, by the Christian progress of the population, the Missionary district may be placed upon a settled ecclesiastical system: it being also understood that the Society is at liberty to transfer a Native Pastor to the office of a Native Missionary, and to place him in the independent charge of a Missionary district if his qualifications have entitled him to that position.

8 It is desirable that all Native Congregations should contribute to a fund for the payment of the salaries of Native Pastors; but that no payment should be made direct from the congregation to the Pastor.

9 To encourage native ordination, the Society will continue to pay a Catechist who may be presented by them for ordination, the same salary which he received as Catechist, as long as the infancy of the Native Church may seem to require it: whatever addition may be requisite for his maintenance as an ordained Pastor must be supplied from local resources, and, if possible, from native

endowments, or the contributions of the Native Church to a general fund for Native Pastors.

10 Regarding the ultimate object of a Mission, viewed under its ecclesiastical aspect, to be the settlement of a Native Church, under Native Pastors,[2] upon a self-supporting system, it should be borne in mind that the progress of a Mission mainly depends upon the training up and the location of Native Pastors; and that, as it has been happily expressed, "the euthanasia of a Mission",[3] takes place when a Missionary, surrounded by well-trained Native Congregations, under Native Pastors, is able to resign all pastoral work into their hands, and gradually to relax his superintendence over the Pastors themselves, till it insensibly ceases; and so the Mission passes into a settled Christian community. Then the Missionary and all Missionary agency should be transferred to "the regions beyond".[4]

1 Venn, Henry, son of John Venn of Clapham; *b.* 1796; *educ.* Queen's College, Cambridge, 1814; Fellow of Queen's College, 1819; ordained 1819; curate of St Dunstan-in-the-West, 1820; lecturer and tutor at Cambridge, 1824; vicar of Drypool, Hull, 1827; vicar of St John's Holloway, 1834; secretary of C.M.S., 1841; prebendary of St Paul's, 1846; *d.* 1873.

2 Venn overcame local opposition from African missionaries, and arranged for the consecration of Samuel Adjai Crowther as bishop "in Western Africa" in 1864. S.P.G. were slower to develop a native ministry and episcopate in the light of Crowther's difficult episcopate which ended with his death in 1892. Roland Allen maintained that "There was no African Church in any real sense of the word. Crowther was really an agent of the Church Missionary Society in Episcopal Orders." (See Bengt Sundkler, *The Christian Ministry in Africa* (1962), ch. 2.)

3 "His Minutes on Corresponding Committees, &c., involving the whole machinery by which the C.M.S. Missions are regulated, all conceived and constructed so as to tend to this *euthanasia*, as Bishop Shirley first happily called it ... (William Knight, *Memoir of the Rev. H. Venn* (1880), p. 277).

4 Africa, where Venn's plans were first put into practice, was slow in receiving a native pastorate—as demonstrated by these figures given in Sundkler, p. 48.

AFRICA SOUTH OF THE SAHARA BUT INCLUDING ETHIOPIA AND ERITREA

	ORDAINED MISSIONARIES	ORDAINED AFRICANS	UNORDAINED	CHRISTIAN COMMUNITY
1900	1,200	408	6,000	560,000
1910	1,300	750	18,700	1,700,000
1925	2,000	1,181	38,126	2,200,000
1938	2,463	4,000	76,000	4,900,000
1949	2,810	3,491	79,600	9,250,000
1957	4,208	5,760	82,433	10,950,000

30 THE EXETER DIOCESAN SYNOD, 1851

(*Hansard*, 2 May 1851)

Bishop Phillpotts[1] summoned the Exeter diocesan synod in response to the Gorham judgment to affirm the doctrine of baptism impugned by the Judicial Committee of the Privy Council. Diocesan synods had little connection with the State historically, and were not affected by the restrictions placed upon Convocations by the Submission of the Clergy.[2] They fell into disuse after the sixteenth century, though occasional examples can be found in the following century. In Parliament, Russell stated the opinion of the Law officers on the legality of such a gathering convened without the Crown's assent.

Sir, the hon. Gentleman having given notice to me, and having given public notice in this House, of the question he intended to put, I thought it necessary to take the opinion of the law officers of the Crown, and to ascertain their views with regard to those Diocesan Synods to which the question of the hon. Gentleman refers. The hon. Member has truly stated that the Bishop of Exeter proposes to call together a certain assembly of the clergy of his diocese, elected after a certain manner, to confer upon subjects to which he adverts in his letter. It does not appear to me that that assembly, although it may be called by the bishop a Synod, bears in any respect the character of a Synod, either in the mode of its assembly, in its constituent parts, or as to the subjects upon which it is to deliberate. In ancient times there were Provincial Synods, with respect to which I need not make any remarks, and there were likewise Diocesan Synods, convened by the bishop, to consider of Church matters once or twice a year. Bishop Gibson,[3] who is a great authority on such subjects, says that such Synods ought to be called together once a year. Now, these Synods continued till the 25th Henry VIII, when an Act was passed which had relation both to the Provincial and Diocesan Synods. With regard to the Provincial Synods, to which the Act chiefly relates, it is stated that they cannot be called together except by the King's writ, and that they cannot issue any decrees or enact any Canons without the consent of the Crown; and that, if they should so do, the persons so offending shall be liable to imprisonment at the pleasure of the Crown. It is obvious that the former part of what I have stated—that such Synods cannot meet without the King's writ—has no relation to diocesan Synods, because they have never at any time been convened by the King's writ, but were always called together by the bishop. With regard to the other point I have mentioned—that the Synods cannot enact any Canons—that certainly may be held to affect Diocesan Synods; but whether it does so or not, it hardly touches upon this question, because the Bishop of Exeter has expressly declared that it is not his intention to propose that the assembly of the clergy he means to call together shall enact any Canons whatever. It appears that the Bishop of Exeter has expressly declared, not only that he does not mean to propose any Canons, but that he would be loth to do anything which could be construed into an act of disobedience or disrespect to the Crown. It is clear, therefore, I think, that whatever purpose the bishop may have in view, it is not the purpose of contravening the Act of the 25th of Henry VIII, commonly called the Act of Submission of the Clergy. Then the question arises whether, the proposed assembly of the clergy not being within the provisions of that Act, there will be anything unlawful in it, supposing it is confined to the objects the bishop has stated, and does not go beyond those objects. My hon. and learned Friends the Attorney and Solicitor General do not think, as far as they have been enabled to form an opinion, that the meeting of that assembly of the clergy will be unlawful. Though it is called a "Synod", it seems to be merely an assumption of the word by the Bishop of Exeter—a very unfortunate assumption, as I think, giving rise to a suspicion that he is going to call together an assembly which is contrary to law, and to proceed to some acts which are forbidden by law. It is, therefore, I think, most unfortunate—to use no harsher term—that the Bishop of Exeter should have called together an assembly to which he gives the name of a Synod, but which is an assembly formed in a different way, and called together for different purposes. The clergy assembled in Synod were either assemblies of the whole of the clergy of a diocese, or of a part of the clergy of a diocese, in places to which they could conveniently resort, or they were sometimes meetings of the deans and chapters to advise the bishops; but the assembly of representative clergy formed in the particular manner proposed by the Bishop of Exeter seems to be entirely unknown to the law of the Church, and completely a device of his own. My hon. Friend [Mr Childers] has also alluded further to the language which has been used by the Bishop of Exeter in his pastoral letter,[4] and especially to his observations upon the Gorham case with respect to the conduct of the Archbishop of Canterbury. Now, with that case I had nothing whatever to do. I had nothing to do with the appointment of the person, or with the subsequent appeal. That appeal was brought finally before the Judicial Committee of the Privy Council, and was there decided according to the law of the land. That question would have been decided by the Court of Delegates some twenty or thirty years ago; but in consequence of some recent alterations in our judicial system, it was now decided by a Court composed of persons of the very highest rank in the law, with the advice—which was especially asked for on this occasion—of the Archbishops of Canterbury and York, and the Bishop of London. The Archbishops of Canterbury and York gave their opinions in consonance with the judgment of the Judicial Committee, and the Bishop of London dissented from their views; but the decision was one made according to the law of the land, to which I conceive every subject of this realm is bound to conform. The Bishop of Exeter has called that judgment in question, and he has apparently convened this assembly or Synod, in order, under cover of declaring an adherence to one of the articles of the Church, and to the doctrine of the Church, which is taken from Scripture, and which is conformable to Scripture, to impugn the decision which has been come to by the Court of Appeal. With respect to that question, of course it remains to be seen what is the language he may use, or what is the proposition he may make, before an opinion is given. With regard to the language the Bishop of Exeter has used relative to the Archbishop of Canterbury, it is well known that the Archbishop of Canterbury is a man of peculiar mildness of character, and of truly Christian forbearance;[5] and I think it is because he is a man of peculiar mildness of character, and of well-known Christian forbearance, that that language has been used. I feel sure, however, that without any interposition of the Government, without any interposition of Parliament, the Archbishop of Canterbury, the chief of the archbishops and bishops of this land, the Primate of all England, will so conduct himself as to merit that veneration which has hitherto been accorded to him, that nothing that may be said or that has been said against him by the Bishop of Exeter can in the least diminish the respect entertained for that most excellent Prelate;[6] and that while he will firmly assert his own opinions, and will firmly maintain those doctrines which he believes to be the true doctrines of his Church, and in conformity with the letter and the spirit of the Scriptures, he will never depart from the character he has acquired, so far as, by the use of unworthy language, or by the interchange of epithets of invective, to diminish in any way the purity and the holiness which belong to his exalted office.[7]

1 Phillpotts, Henry; *b.* 1778; *educ.*, Corpus Christi College, Oxford, Fellow of Magdalen College, Oxford, 1795; rector of Stainton-le-Street, Durham; Dean of Chester, 1828; Bishop of Exeter, 1830; sanctioned the Community of the Sisters of Mercy at Devonport, 1848; *d.* 1869.

2 15 May 1532. In January 1534, the Submission of the Clergy was incorporated into an Act of Parliament, 25 Henry VIII, c. 19.

3 Edmund Gibson; Bishop of London, 1669-1748. The work referred to by Russell was the *Synodus Anglicana*; *or the Constitution and Proceedings of an English Convocation* (1702). A new edition was prepared by Edward Cardwell in 1854.

4 *A Pastoral Letter to the Clergy of the Diocese of Exeter, on the present state of the church* (London 1851).

5 Sumner, John Bird; *b.* 1780; *educ.*, Eton and King's College, Cambridge; Fellow of King's, 1801; assistant master at Eton, 1802; ordained, 1803; canon of Durham; Bishop of Chester, 1828; Archbishop of Canterbury, 1848; *d.* 1862.

6 Phillpotts denounced Sumner as "a favourer and supporter" of heresy, and went on to add: "I cannot, without sin—and by God's grace I will not—hold communion with him, be he who he may, who shall so abuse the high commission which he bears."

7 The Synod met in June and Gorham led fifty clergy in protesting against it.

31 THE REVIVAL OF CONVOCATION, 1851

(*Letters on Church Matters*, by D.C.L. Reprinted from the *Morning Chronicle,* no VII, 1851)

The Convocations were prorogued by Royal Writ during the Bangorian controversy in 1717.[1] The two provincial assemblies were unable to meet to discuss business, and their proceedings were purely formal. A growing demand for the revival of an active convocation was led by Henry Hoare,[2] but the Archbishop of Canterbury was able to claim that a large section of clerical opinion was opposed to it. In 1852 business was again discussed in the Canterbury Convocation, and in the York Convocation in 1861.[3]

LXIX A NEW SESSION OF CONVOCATION

Aug. 30

Sir, Remembering that the 28th of August was the day to which, in the beginning of last February, the Archbishop of Canterbury prorogued the Convocation of his province, I looked with no small interest to your paper of yesterday to see what might have fallen out at the new session of our provincial Synod; and I observed—not, I own, with much surprise—that "his Grace the Archbishop called upon Mr Dyke, the principal registrar of the province of Canterbury, to read the writ of prorogation".

This mockery being terminated, the Metropolitan returned, I suppose, to Lambeth Palace, rejoicing, one may conclude, at having "got over it".

But the Church of England will not so soon get over it. The Church of England knows that her Primate in February prorogued Convocation to a day when he knew that Parliament would be on the moors or the Rhine—and it knows what he has been doing in the meanwhile. Churchmen know his answer to Lord Ashley; they may even recollect the episcopal paper; and they have not forgotten his speech on Lord Redesdale's motion.[4] His letter to Mr Gawthorn is still a novelty.

It may be a rather hard thing to disturb the peace and contentment which are probably reigning in high ecclesiastical quarters of the late escape, by whispering that, although the Jerusalem Chamber is to remain damp and tenantless till February, yet there is a party outside its inhospitable doors which has no great veneration for unrealities, and which respects Archbishop Sumner for all those attributes which he manifests such alacrity to repudiate.[5]

These men, painfully alive to the juggle under which they behold the best interests of the Church wither up, will exclaim—what is the limit, and when will be the end, of all this trifling? The party formerly conspicuous for their endeavours to sap the inner life of the Church were those unhappy persons who, forming a conspicuous portion (for I should be sorry to include all) of what were *then* called High Churchmen, fancied that the barren profession of an attenuated orthodoxy was compensation enough for the omission of all works of love and faith, and who made themselves conspicuous for their zeal in endeavouring too often to combine the maximum of emolument and pomp with the minimum of labour and spirituality. In those days—the days of early Wesleyanism—there were men who, however deficient and erroneous in their theory of the constitution and sacramental aspect of the Christian Church, at least had realized that the object of the Christian religion was to save souls—men like Newton, and Romaine, and Scott. These men were not to be seen in Ministerial saloons—they were not always ready with any excuse to check the budding forth of energy and zeal! and the natural result of their earnestness has been, that, in spite of their short-comings, they won hearts, secured suffrages—and at last their school attained high places, until finally it beholds a leading member of their party upon the throne of Canterbury. Once there, the Low Church Primate, forgetful of the traditions of his own party, and incapable of grasping the import of High Churchmanship in its actual aspect, has subsided into the old do-nothing policy of the men whom his party claims to supplant.

No Convocation, he says—no Synod—no organized endeavours, in other words, to break through the hardened crust of apathy under which the fearful whirlpool of the passions of unchristianized millions is boiling; for then the "prerogative" would have to be called in, and there would be an *imperium in imperio* created. See how we stand. The pupil of these old Evangelicals of the end of the last century playing off the "prerogative" against the voice of conscience and of faith! The, "by Divine Providence, Archbishop of Canterbury, Primate of all England and Metropolitan, *President of the present Provincial Synod or Convocation of the Bishops and Clergy of the Province of Canterbury*", arising in the House of Lords to say that the "*present* Synod or Convocation", of which he is the President, shall be a mockery—in order that the Church of "All England", of which he is the "Primate", may be an establishment, and not an *imperium*—a body constituted without a constitution! The "Protestant" prelate *par excellence*, striving at Papal irresponsibility, and Papal powers of interference with the worship of every Church in the land! These are the portents visible in the Archiepiscopate of Dr Sumner!

While the Archbishop of Canterbury and Mr Dyke are histrionicizing in the Jerusalem Chamber, and making a mummery of a sacred assembly, other men are not so quiet—other men know the value of co-operation, and they proclaim that they know it.

The Archbishop's quondam friends and the Dissenters feel the need which they cannot supply. Foolish and impotent, and a failure in every aspect, practical and religious, as the Evangelical Alliance proves itself, it is *their* best at least—the best and only thing which men, many of them most earnest and zealous, yearning after that counsel, and that unity which they could alone find where they do not look for it—in the Catholic Church of God—can accomplish; and empty and unsatisfactory as will be their retrospect when the session of the Alliance breaks up, they may at least look back and think that they *tried* for something. What has his Grace tried to do, and what had he to look back to as he returned from his *tete à-tête* with Mr Dyke in the Jerusalem Chamber?[6]

Nor has the Evangelical Alliance been the only gathering. Not long since the Mormons—the men who believe that to Joseph Smith a new revelation was given—filled Freemason's Hall. Later, the "New Jerusalem Church"—the men who believe in a new revelation, vouchsafed to the moon-struck Swedenborg—had their synod in this same city, and haughtily invited all men to seek unity and peace within their fold. In the meanwhile the Archbishop has seen Convocation safely stifled by Mr Dyke, and probably went to Addington Park by the next train.[7]

This is the Church of England in the hands of her actual rulers. These are the methods which they adopt to make her safe, and to maintain peace for their palaces and their baronies. To be sure we have an Archbishop who can venture to speak for all his brother prelates but one, and for more than forty-eight out of fifty of the inferior clergy. But we cannot *always* have such good fortune. A mild tyrant makes a State neglectful of constitutional checks, and in the days of his successor, of another temperament, they learn their mistake. Some sleepy diocese leaves all its affairs in the hands of an indolent and indulgent prelate; and all the while some Bishop Lee[8] is treasuring the precedent—some Archbishop Sumner is framing his excuses against a Convocation being an "*imperium*", and against a Church holding "Church principles".

1 Benjamin Hoadly, Bishop of Bangor, preached before George I on 31 March 1717 on "The Nature of the Kingdom or Church of

Christ". In the ensuing controversy a committee of the Lower House of Convocation was appointed to consider the sermon and other writings by Hoadly. In order to prevent the findings going before the Upper House, and a consequent synodical condemnation of Hoadly, the King prorogued Convocation.

2 Henry Hoare, Samuel Wilberforce, Julius Hare, Bishop Monk, and Gladstone were supporters of the revival of Convocation: Sumner, Musgrave, Hampden, Charles Sumner, and Lord John Russell were among the opponents.

3 The steps by which the revival took place may be summarized as follows:

1837	A motion was defeated in the Commons by 24 votes to 19 for its revival.
Feb. 1851	Convocation received a petition from Hoare's meeting on 14 January at the Freemason's Tavern.
July 1851	Lord Redesdale introduced the first formal debate of Convocation by Parliament in the Lords.
Feb. 1852	Convocation received twenty-four petitions in the Upper House, and twenty-seven in the Lower.
Nov. 1852	Both houses of Convocation appointed committees.
Feb. 1855	Convocation sat for three days.
1860	The first new canon was debated; Convocation passing further canons in 1865, 1888, and 1892.

4 Lord Redesdale had also attacked Russell during the Gorham controversy for his Erastian principles.

5 At a new Parliament, the Canterbury Convocation met for opening worship at St Paul's Cathedral where a Latin sermon would be preached; it would then be prorogued for a few days before meeting at Westminster. The revival of Convocation was partly due to the unsettled state of domestic political affairs at the time.

6 The Evangelical Alliance was founded in London in 1846 to "associate and concentrate the strength of enlightened Protestantism against the encroachments of Popery and Puseyism, and to promote the interests of a Scriptural Christianity". The Tractarians were in favour of the revival of Convocation and the Evangelicals generally opposed.

7 Attention was aroused by synods which met in Australia, Toronto, and, of course, Exeter.

8 James Prince Lee, Bishop of the newly founded see of Manchester, 1847.

32 THE DISMISSAL OF PROFESSOR MAURICE, 1853

(*Life of F. D. Maurice*, vol. 2, pp. 190-2)

F. D. Maurice produced his *Theological Essays* as a result of irritations he felt concerning contemporary theology. Originally sermons, the essays were written with the Unitarians in mind, and did not represent Maurice at his most lucid.[2] The final essay on *Eternal Life and Eternal Death* created a storm of protest which led to his dismissal as Professor of Divinity in King's College, London. Maurice refused to equate eternal death with everlasting punishment, the latter being an article of faith of the Evangelical Alliance. The outcome of the controversy was that Maurice, now a popular figure, had the opportunity of founding the Working Men's College and focusing public attention on Christian social teaching.

(Extract from the Minutes of a Special Meeting of the Council of King's College, London, 27 October 1853)

The letter from Dr Jelf[3] to the council dated October 8, enclosing his correspondence with Professor Maurice was read.

The letter from Professor Maurice to the Principal dated October 12, enclosing his answer to the Principal's final letter, was read.[4]

The secretary stated that in a letter to Professor Maurice he had requested him to be in attendance in case the council should wish to see him, and had also asked whether, in the event of the council not wishing to see him, he would desire to have an interview with them. Professor Maurice's reply was read promising to be in attendance, and stating that, although he did not wish to make any formal application to the council for permission to be heard before them, there was one point on which he should perhaps be glad to make a very short explanation.

Professor Maurice being called in explained that having heard complaints of the tone in which he as a professor had addressed the Principal, in his "Answer to the Principal's final letter", he had written that letter as an answer to an indictment, and not as a letter to Dr Jelf; and that if it was thought that there was anything wrong in the tone of that communication, he sincerely apologized for the same and asked the Principal to state what had always been his conduct at King's College.[5]

Dr Jelf cordially accepted Professor Maurice's explanation and bore high testimony to the uniform courteousness of his conduct towards himself, as well as to his unvarying attention to his classes, and zeal for the college.

After long and anxious deliberation the following resolutions were moved and seconded:

The council having taken into consideration an essay lately published by the Reverend Frederick Maurice, Professor of Divinity in King's College, and also a correspondence between the Principal and the professor on the subject of the said essay, and having been informed by Professor Maurice that he does not wish to make any statement in addition to his "Answer to the Principal's final letter", resolve

1 That in their judgment the opinions set forth and the doubts expressed in the said essay, and re-stated in the said answer as to certain points of belief regarding the future punishment of the wicked and the final issues of the day of judgment, are of dangerous tendency, and calculated to unsettle the minds of the theological students of King's College.

2 That the council feel it to be their painful duty to declare that the continuance of Professor Maurice's connection with the college as one of its professors would be seriously detrimental to its usefulness.[6]

3 That the council, while it laments the necessity which constrains them to adopt this resolution, are bound in justice to Professor Maurice to express the sense which they entertain of the zealous and able manner in which he has discharged the duties of the two offices which he has held, and the attachment which he has at all times manifested to the college.

Whereupon the following amendment was moved and seconded:

That the Lord Bishop of London[7] be requested to appoint competent theologians to institute an examination into the question how far the writings of Professor Maurice, or any propositions contained in them, which have been brought under the [notice of the] council,[8] are conformable to or at variance with the three creeds and the formularies of the Church of England, and to make a report thereupon, and that the Lord Bishop be requested to communicate the results of this examination to the council.

The amendment, being put from the chair, was lost upon a division.

The original propositions were then put and carried.

1 Maurice Frederick Denison; *b.* 1805; *educ.*, Trinity College, Cambridge; went to Trinity Hall, 1825; excluded from fellowship and degree; Exeter College, Oxford, 1830; ordained, 1834; curate of Bubbenhall, Warks., chaplain of Guy's Hospital, 1836; Professor of English Literature, K.C.L., 1840; Chaplain at Lincoln's Inn, 1846; Professor of Theology, K.C.L., 1846; founded Working Men's College, 1854; incumbent of St Peter, Vere Street, 1860; Knightbridge Professor of Moral Philosophy at Cambridge, 1866; incumbent of St Edward, Cambridge, 1870; *d.* 1872.

2 Dean Church complained of the "tormenting indistinctness" of the *Theological Essays.*

3 Jelf, Richard William; *b.* 1798; *educ.*, Eton and Christ Church, Oxford; canon of Christ Church, 1830; Principal of K.C.L., 1844–68; *d.* 1871.

It was Jelf's opinion that the conclusions of the offending essay were "very dangerous and unsound".

4 Maurice answered: "I wish certainly that the whole cause should pass into the hands of the council, who I am sure will deal fairly with it . . ."

5 In a letter to Julius Hare, Maurice explained, "I said that if I had seemed to write a theological treatise instead of merely replying to a charge, I did so because the Principal had given that form to his letter."

6 King's College had been founded in 1829 specifically as an alternative to the "godless institution of Gower Street" (London University). A similar incident to this can be found in W. R. Smith's dismissal from his post at the Free Church College, Aberdeen, in 1870.

7 Blomfield had introduced the motion dismissing Maurice and thanking him for his efforts on behalf of the college. Gladstone's amendment found only two other supporters.

8 Frederick Maurice found these words omitted in the copy of the proceedings sent to him.

33 THE DIVORCE ACT 1857

(*Statutes at Large*, 20-21 Vict., c. 85)

A Royal Commission recommended, in 1853, the setting up of a divorce court, thus extending the possibility of divorce to people of limited means. The Bill obtained a second reading in the Lords in both 1854 and 1856, only to be crowded out in the Commons. Introduced again in 1857, it was opposed by Wilberforce in the Lords and by Gladstone in the Commons, and supported by the Archbishop of Canterbury and nine bishops. Clergy who could not uphold a law contrary to their professed belief were duly acknowledged, and no penalty was attached to their refusal to perform such marriage as was sanctioned by the new law.

II As soon as this Act shall come into operation, all Jurisdiction now exerciseable by any Ecclesiastical Court in *England* in respect of Divorces *à Mensâ et Thoro*, Suits of Nullity of Marriage, Suits of Jactitation of Marriage, Suits for Restitution of Conjugal Rights, and in all Causes, Suits, and Matters Matrimonial, shall cease to be so exerciseable, except so far as relates to the granting of Marriage Licences, which may be granted as if this Act had not been passed.

III Any Decree or Order of any Ecclesiastical Court of competent Jurisdiction which shall have been made before this Act comes into operation, in any Cause or Matter Matrimonial, may be enforced or otherwise dealt with by the Court for Divorce and Matrimonial Causes hereinafter mentioned, in the same Way as if it had been originally made by the said Court under this Act.

IV All Suits and Proceedings in Causes and Matters Matrimonial which at the Time when this Act comes into operation shall be pending in any Ecclesiastical Court in *England* shall be transferred to, dealt with, and decided by the said Court for Divorce and Matrimonial Causes as if the same had been originally instituted in the said Court.

VI As soon as this Act shall come into operation, all Jurisdiction now vested in or exerciseable by any Ecclesiastical Court or Person in *England* in respect of Divorces *à Mensâ et Thoro*, Suits of Nullity of Marriage, Suits for Restitution of Conjugal Rights, or Jactitation of Marriage, and in all Causes, Suits, and Matters Matrimonial, except in respect of Marriage Licences, shall belong to and be vested in Her Majesty, and such Jurisdiction, together with the Jurisdiction conferred by this Act, shall be exercised in the Name of Her Majesty in a Court of Record to be called "The Court for Divorce and Matrimonial Causes".

XV All Persons admitted to practise as Advocates or Proctors respectively in any Ecclesiastical Court in *England*, and all Barristers, Attornies, and Solicitors entitled to practise in the Superior Courts at *Westminster*, shall be entitled to practise in the Court of Divorce and Matrimonial Causes; and such Advocates and Barristers shall have the same relative Rank and Precedence which they now have in the Judicial Committee of the Privy Council, unless and until Her Majesty shall otherwise order.[2]

XVI A Sentence of Judicial Separation (which shall have the Effect of a Divorce *à Mensâ et Thoro* under the existing Law, and such other legal Effect as herein mentioned), may be obtained, either by the Husband or the Wife, on the Ground of Adultery, or Cruelty, or Desertion without Cause for Two Years and upwards.[3]

XXII In all Suits and Proceedings, other than Proceedings to dissolve any Marriage, the said Court shall proceed and act and give Relief on Principles and Rules which in the Opinion of the said Court shall be as nearly as may be conformable to the Principles and Rules on which the Ecclesiastical Courts have heretofore acted and given Relief, but subject to the Provisions herein contained and to the Rules and Orders under this Act.

XLVI Subject to such Rules and Regulations as may be established as herein provided, the Witnesses in all Proceedings before the Court where their Attendance can be had shall be sworn and examined orally in open Court: Provided that Parties, except as hereinbefore provided, shall be at liberty to verify their respective Cases in whole or in part by Affidavit, but so that the Deponent in every such Affidavit shall, on the Application of the opposite Party or by Direction of the Court, be subject to be cross-examined by or on behalf of the opposite Party orally in open Court, and after such cross-examination may be re-examined orally in open Court as aforesaid by or on behalf of the Party by whom such Affidavit was filed.[4]

LVII When the Time hereby limited for appealing against any Decree dissolving a Marriage shall have expired, and no Appeal shall have been presented against such Decree, or when any such

Appeal shall have been dismissed, or when in the Result of any Appeal any Marriage shall be declared to be dissolved, but not sooner, it shall be lawful for the respective Parties thereto to marry again, as if the prior Marriage had been dissolved by Death: Provided always, that no Clergyman in Holy Orders of the United Church of *England and Ireland* shall be compelled to solemnize the Marriage of any Person whose former Marriage may have been dissolved on the Ground of his or her Adultery, or shall be liable to any Suit, Penalty, or Censure for solemnizing or refusing to solemnize the Marriage of any such Person.[5]

LVIII Provided always, That when any Minister of any Church or Chapel of the United Church of *England* and *Ireland* shall refuse to perform such Marriage Service between any Persons who but for such Refusal would be entitled to have the same Service performed in such Church or Chapel, such Minister shall permit any other Minister in Holy Orders of the said United Church, entitled to officiate within the Diocese in which such Church or Chapel is situate, to perform such Marriage Service in such Church or Chapel.[6]

1 Divorce *à vinculo*, permitted under the new Act on the grounds of adultery, was contrary to the formularies of the Church of England which maintained the traditional Western principle of the indissolubility of marriage. Western canon law accepted divorce *à Mensâ et Thoro* (judicial separation) on several grounds including adultery.

2 Ecclesiastical lawyers, including Sir Robert Phillimore, were dissatisfied with the existing system of obtaining divorces by private Acts of Parliament. Not only was the procedure costly, on average about £1,000, but it involved enlisting support within Parliament.

3 Only four instances exist of Acts having been passed at the wife's instigation.

4 Queen Victoria disliked the new court because of its public proceedings, which she considered injurious to popular morality.

5 By allowing divorce *à vinculo* for the wife's adultery or for the husband's adultery with aggravating circumstances, the Act distinguished the Statute Law from Ecclesiastical Law. In making this cleavage on a moral issue, the State implied that Church and nation were no longer to be regarded as co-extensive.

6 From 1800 divorces averaged two a year; rising to four in 1850; 1858, 179; 1872, 200; 1875, 300; 1890, 400; 1897, 500; 1901, 600.

34 LIVINGSTONE'S CAMBRIDGE LECTURE, 1857

(*Dr Livingstone's Cambridge Lectures* (1860), pp. 162-8)

Livingstone's lecture in the Senate House, Cambridge, resulted in the formation of the Universities Mission to Central Africa. By 1856, when he returned to England from his travels on the African continent, he was already famous as a missionary and explorer.[1] English missionaries had started work in Mombasa in 1844, but in 1859 the Universities Mission commenced work in the direction of Lake Nyassa, though later moving base to Zanzibar.

... My desire is to open a path to this district, that civilization, commerce, and Christianity might find their way there. I consider that we made a great mistake, when we carried commerce into India, in being ashamed of our Christianity;[2] as a matter of common sense and good policy, it is always best to appear in one's true character. In travelling through Africa, I might have imitated certain Portuguese, and have passed for a chief; but I never attempted anything of the sort, although endeavouring always to keep to the lessons of cleanliness rigidly instilled by my mother long ago; the consequence was that the natives respected me for that quality, though remaining dirty themselves....

... A prospect is now before us of opening Africa for commerce and the Gospel.[3] Providence has been preparing the way, for even before I proceeded to the Central Basin it had been conquered and rendered safe by a chief named Sebituane, and the language of the Bechuanas made the fashionable tongue, and that was one of the languages into which Mr Moffat had translated the Scriptures.[4] Sebituane also discovered Lake Ngami some time previous to my explorations in that part. In going back to that country my object is to open up traffic along the banks of the Zambesi, and also to preach the Gospel.

The natives of Central Africa are very desirous of trading, but their only traffic is at present in slaves, of which the poorer people have an unmitigated horror: it is therefore most desirable to encourage the former principle, and thus open a way for the consumption of free productions, and the introduction of Christianity and commerce.[5] By encouraging the native propensity for trade, the advantage that might be derived in a commercial point of view are incalculable; nor should we lose sight of the inestimable blessings it is in our power to bestow upon the unenlightened African, by giving him the light of Christianity. Those two pioneers of civilization—Christianity and commerce—should ever be inseparable; and Englishmen should be warned by the fruits of neglecting that principle as exemplified in the result of the management of Indian affairs. By trading with Africa, also, we should at length be independent of slave-labour, and thus discountenance practices so obnoxious to every Englishman.

Though the natives are not abolutely anxious to receive the Gospel, they are open to Christian influences. Among the Bechuanas the Gospel was well received. These people think it a crime to shed a tear, but I have seen some of them weep at the recollection of their sins when God had opened their hearts to Christianity and repentance. It is true that missionaries have difficulties to encounter; but what great enterprise was ever accomplished without difficulty? It is deplorable to think that one of the noblest of our missionary societies, the Church Missionary Society, is compelled to send to Germany for missionaries, whilst other societies are amply supplied. Let this stain be wiped off.[6] The sort of men who are wanted for missionaries are such as I see before me; men of education, standing, enterprise, zeal, and piety. It is a mistake to suppose that *any one*, as long as he is pious, will do for this office. Pioneers in every thing should be the ablest and best qualified men, not those of small ability and education. This remark especially applies to the first teachers of Christian truth in regions which may never have before been blest with the name and Gospel of Jesus Christ. In the early ages the monasteries were the schools of Europe, and the monks were not ashamed to hold the plough. The missionaries now take the place of those noble men, and we should not hesitate to give up the small luxuries of life in order to carry knowledge and truth to them that are in darkness. I hope that many of those whom I now address will embrace that honourable career. Education has been given us from above for the purpose of bringing to the benighted the knowledge of a Saviour. If you knew the satisfaction of performing such a duty, as well as the gratitude to God which the missionary must always feel, in being chosen for so noble, so sacred a calling, you would have no hesitation in embracing it.

For my own part, I have never ceased to rejoice that God has appointed me to such an office. People talk of the sacrifice I have made in spending so much of my life in Africa. Can that be called a sacrifice which is simply paid back as a small part of a great debt owing to our God, which we can never repay? Is that a sacrifice which brings its own blest reward in healthful activity, the consciousness of doing good, peace of mind, and a bright hope of a glorious destiny hereafter? Away with the word in such a view, and with such a thought! It is emphatically no sacrifice. Say rather it is a privilege. Anxiety, sickness, suffering, or danger, now and then, with a foregoing of the common conveniences and charities of this life, may make us pause, and cause the spirit to waver, and the soul to sink, but let this only be for a moment. All these are nothing when compared with the glory which shall hereafter be revealed in, and for, us. I never made a sacrifice. Of this we ought not to talk, when we remember the great sacrifice which HE made who left His Father's throne on high to give Himself for us; "Who being the brightness of that Father's glory, and the express image of His person, and upholding all things by the word of His power, when He had by Himself purged our sins, sat down on the right hand of the majesty on high."

English people are treated with respect; and the missionary can earn his living by his gun—a course not open to a country curate. I would rather be a poor missionary than a poor curate.

Then there is the pleasant prospect of returning home and seeing the agreeable faces of his countrywomen again. I suppose I present a pretty contrast to you. At Cairo we met a party of young English people, whose faces were quite a contrast to the skinny, withered ones of those who had spent the latter years of their life in a tropical clime: they were the first rosy cheeks I had seen for sixteen years; you can hardly tell how pleasant it is to see the blooming cheeks of young ladies before me, after an absence of sixteen years from such delightful objects of contemplation. There is also the pleasure of the welcome home, and I heartily thank you for the welcome you have given me on the present occasion; but there is also the hope of the welcome words of our Lord, "Well done, good and faithful servant".

I beg to direct your attention to Africa; I know that in a few years I shall be cut off in that country, which is now open; do not let it be shut again! I go back to Africa to try to make an open path for commerce and Christianity; do you carry out the work which I have begun. I LEAVE IT WITH YOU!

1 Livingstone, David; *b.* 1813; employed in a cotton factory, 1823; self-educated; attended medical classes in Glasgow; joined the London Missionary Society in London, 1838; began work from the Cape of Good Hope, 1840; returned to England, 1856; returned to Africa

in an individual capacity, 1858; returned to England, 1864–5; died at Ilala, May 1873.

2 Chaplains had been appointed under the East India Company in 1614, and, in revising the Charter in 1698, Parliament enacted that the chaplains "should apply themselves to learn the language of the country, the better to enable them to instruct the Gentoos who should be servants of the Company in the Protestant religion". In 1774 Warren Hastings discouraged missionary effort by inhibiting and deporting missionaries. Wilberforce's resolutions supporting missionary work met with Government opposition, and were only included in the Company's Charter in 1813.

3 The exploration of the Dark Continent began between 1795 and 1805 with Mungo Park, and was continued by Livingstone and others. The resources of the land led to the "Scramble for Africa" and the ultimate partitioning of the continent by the major European powers. Livingstone adopted a utilitarian approach to evangelization with an emphasis on education and industry, and the social application of Christianity in underdeveloped lands was to become a feature of later missionary activity.

4 Moffat, Robert; *b.* 1795; attracted to missionary work by Wesleyan influence, 1813; joined London Missionary Society, 1816; arrived at Cape Town, 1817; worked among the Bechuanas, 1821–30; began translation of Luke into Sechwana; returned to England and met Livingstone, 1840; returned to South Africa, 1843; completed translation of the Bible, 1857; remained in South Africa until 1870; *d.* 1883.

5 "It was fortunate that the day of the white man's unlimited power over the black had not come earlier, whilst his only idea of a relation with the aborigines had been the profits of slavery and the slave trade. That bad spirit had not indeed entirely been exorcized among all the white races in their dealings with Africa. But Britain at least made good use in Nigeria and elsewhere of the white man's new power to suppress the slave trade and intertribal massacres" (G. M. Trevelyan, *British History in the Nineteenth Century and After*, pp. 411-12). Britain patrolled the west coast of Africa and made agreements about the right of search with other governments, including France and Spain, in the 1830s. In 1873 the foundation stone of the Anglican cathedral was laid on the site of the former slave market in Zanzibar.

6 The C.M.S. had used Lutheran missionaries in India in the eighteenth century; J. L. Krapf began work in Mombasa in 1844; and, as the influence of the Evangelical movement waned in England, so the number of candidates for overseas work with C.M.S. decreased.

35 THE LIDDELL JUDGMENT, 1857

(*Six Judgments*, pp. 45-6, 47-8, 50-1)

The first of the long series of ritual judgments which the Judicial Committee of the Privy Council was called upon to consider was that of Westerton *v.* Liddell. In his evidence before the Royal Commission on Ecclesiastical Discipline, Archbishop Davidson traced the ritual developments from the Oxford Movement. The new ceremonial practices were a secondary consequence of the Tractarian school, but raised the question of the legality of ancient practices and ecclesiastical ornaments. This judgment was arrived at by a detailed examination of the Prayer Book rubrics, and the Appeal Court's decision, in this suit, gave impetus to the ritual movement.

These cases came before the Court by Appeal from two orders in distinct suits, directing the removal of various articles of Church furniture: in the one case from the District Church, or Chapel, of *St Paul's, Knightsbridge*, and in the other from the Chapel of Ease of *St Barnabas, Pimlico.* Although there is some distinction between the circumstances of the two cases, they involve the same principles; they were included in one argument at this Bar, and will be conveniently disposed of in one judgment.

It appears that the District Church of St *Paul's* was erected by private subscription; that the income by which it is supported is derived from the rent of pews; that Mr *Liddell* is the Incumbent, and Mr *Horne* and Mr *Westerton* the two Churchwardens. The two Churchwardens differed as to the propriety of certain ornaments of the Church, and in Hilary Term, 1855, the suit out of which the present appeal arises was instituted in the Consistory Court of *London*, by Mr *Westerton* against Mr *Horne* and Mr *Liddell*, who are now the Appellants.[1]

The citation called upon the Appellants to show cause why a faculty should not be granted for removing the Altar, or High Altar, and the cloths used for covering the same, together with the wooden cross elevated thereon, and affixed thereto, as well as the candlesticks thereon, together with the Credentia, Preparatory Altar, or Credence Table, used in the said Church or Chapel, and for substituting in lieu and stead thereof a decent and proper table for the administration of the Lord's Supper and Holy Communion, and a decent cloth for the covering thereof.

The answer of the Defendants alleges that the article of Church furniture called in the citation an "Altar" or "High Altar", is in fact, and according to the true and legal interpretation of the 82nd of the Constitutions and Canons of England and Ireland, as by Law established, *mensa congrua et decens*, or a convenient and decent table, such as is required by Law for the celebration of the Holy Communion, and denies that the wooden cross is inconsistent with the Laws, Canons, Customs, and Constitutions of the said Church. In subsequent passages of the answer this Table is always spoken of as the Altar, or Communion Table, and it is alleged that the said Altar, or Communion Table, and the platform on which the same is raised, the wooden cross attached thereto, the gilded candlesticks, and the said side table, or Credence Table, were placed in the same Church as the same now exist, and formed part of the furniture thereof at the time of the consecration of the said Church, and of the furniture thereof, by the Lord Bishop of *London,* on May 30, 1843....

... With respect to the appeal of "*Liddell* and *others* v *Beal*", St *Barnabas* is a chapel of ease within the District Chapelry of St *Paul,* of which the Curates are appointed by Mr *Liddell.* In this case both the Chapelwardens agree with Mr *Liddell* as to the ornaments in question. On January 17, 1855, a monition was issued against them, at the instance of Mr *Beal*, an inhabitant of the District Chapelry of St *Barnabas*, by which they were monished to remove from the said Chapel the roodscreen and brazen gates, together with the cross elevated and fixed on the said screen, and also the stone Altar and cloths now used for covering the same, and the cross ornamented with jewels elevated thereon, and fixed thereto, with the candlesticks and candles placed thereon, and also the marble Credentia, Preparatory Altar, or Credence Table, and to substitute in lieu and stead thereof a decent table for the administration of the Lord's Supper and Holy Communion, and a decent covering thereto, and to set up on the east end of the Chancel of the said Chapel the Ten Commandments, as by the Laws, Canons, Institutions, and Customs of the United Church of *England* and *Ireland* is prescribed....

... The Rubric is in these words: "And here it is to be noted, that such ornaments of the Church, and of the Ministers thereof, at all times of their ministration, shall be retained, and be in use, as were in this Church of *England*, by the authority of Parliament in the second year of the reign of King *Edward* VI."[2]

Dr Lushington[3] was of opinion that, by the true construction of these words, reference must be had to the Act of 2 and 3 *Edward* VI and the Prayer Book, which it established for the purpose of determining what ornaments were thereby sanctioned, but he was perplexed by the difficulty, that although there were words in that Prayer Book, describing the ornaments of the Ministers, there were none which applied to ornaments of the Church, in his understanding of this expression.

Their Lordships, after much consideration, are satisfied that the construction of this Rubric which they suggested at the hearing of the case is its true meaning, and that the word "ornaments" applies, and in this rubric is confined, to those articles the use of which, in the services and ministrations of the Church, is prescribed by the Prayer Book of *Edward* VI.

The term "ornaments" in ecclesiastical law is not confined, as by modern usage, to articles of decoration or embellishment, but it is used in the larger sense of the word *ornamentum*, which, according to the interpretation of *Forcellini's* Dictionary, is used *pro quocumque apparatu seu implemento.* All the several articles used in the performance of the services and rites of the Church are ornaments. Vestments, books, cloths, chalices and patens, are amongst Church ornaments; a long list of them will be found extracted from *Lyndwood*, in Dr *Phillimore's* edition of "*Burn's Ecclesiastical Law*". In modern times organs and bells are held to fall under this denomination.[4]

When reference is had to the First Prayer Book of *Edward* VI with this explanation of the term "ornaments", no difficulty will be found in discovering, amongst the articles of which the use is there enjoined, ornaments of the Church as well as ornaments of the Ministers....

... The Rubric to the Prayer Book of January 1, 1604, adopts the language of the rubric of *Elizabeth.* The rubric to the present Prayer Book adopts the language of the statute of *Elizabeth*; but they all obviously mean the same thing, that the same dresses and the same utensils, or articles, which were used under the first Prayer Book of *Edward* VI may still be used.[5]

1 The two cases of Liddell *v* Westerton and Liddell *v* Beal began in the Consistory Court of London before Lushington in December 1855; went before Sir John Dodson in the Court of Arches in December 1856; and ended up before the Judicial Committee in February 1857. Both the inferior courts decided in Westerton's favour in all points excepting the removal of the candlesticks. The Privy Council upheld all the decisions of the lower courts except for the use of the altar-cloths, credence table, and the cross on the screen, which were deemed to be legal.

2 The ornaments rubric was inserted at the beginning of Morning and Evening Prayer in the 1559 Prayer Book, and retained in a slightly modified form in 1604 and in 1661. The rubric is understood to refer to either:

(i) The first Prayer Book annexed to the Act of Uniformity which passed the Commons on 21 January 1549, and came into force on 9 June 1549, thus authorizing eucharistic vestments. So the decision of the Privy Council in this suit.

(ii) The second year of the reign of Edward VI (28 January 1548 to 27 January 1549), thus including all the pre-Reformation ornaments except those that had been definitely abolished by 1548. This interpretation had been placed before the Judicial Committee in Liddell *v* Westerton.

(iii) The *Advertisements* of 1566, on the grounds that the Act of Uniformity of 1559 contained the words "until other order shall be therein taken", and that such order had been taken in Parker's Advertisements. This restricted interpretation was upheld in the suits of Purchas (1871) and Ridsdale (1877).

3 Lushington, Stephen; *b.* 1782; *educ.*, Christ Church, Oxford; B.A., 1802; M.A., 1806; B.C.L., 1807; D.C.L., 1808; M.P., 1806, supporting Fowell Buxton agitation against the slave trade; Member of the College of Advocates, 1808; Dean of Arches, 1858; resigned, 1867; *d.* 1873.

4 This statement is noteworthy inasmuch that the rule which governed rites and ceremonies could not be extended to articles used in the church.

5 This *obiter dictum*, though not concerned in this suit with eucharistic vestments, encouraged their use. The reversal of this implied sanction did much to discredit the Privy Council as the supreme court in ecclesiastical matters after the Purchas and Ridsdale judgments.

36 LORD SHAFTESBURY'S LIVERPOOL SPEECH, 1858

(*Addresses of the Earl of Shaftesbury and the Hon. W. F. Cowper, delivered in St George's Hall, Liverpool; on Tuesday October the 12th, 1858* ... Liverpool)

The factory system, a product of the Industrial Revolution, was originally untouched by government legislation, and as a result led to the exploitation of the working classes. The failure of the Churches to condemn the lack of principle in the doctrine of *laissez-faire*[1] gave the impression that churchmen were unconcerned with the condition of the artisan classes. Amongst the individual churchmen who decried the evils of the industrial age was George Bull, who was associated with such radicals as Michael Sadler and Richard Oastler.[2] The Earl of Shaftesbury, a leading figure amongst the Evangelicals, led the later campaign against the unrestricted employment of labour in factories and mines.[3]

The Earl of Shaftesbury, amid much cheering, rose and said, My Lords, Ladies, and Gentlemen, I am anxious, as a preliminary, to say a few words upon the peculiar subject that we have before us, because I think that it is liable to misrepresentation. It certainly is liable to be misunderstood, and I know there are many persons—probably many in the town of Liverpool, and certainly a great many in different parts of England—who think that this association, more especially in the particular departments of sanitary arrangements and sanitary provision, is seeking to assume a greater authority than belongs to it; that our object is to promote that to which Englishmen very strongly object, a system of centralization; and that, moreover, we are prepared to assume and utter a language that would savour far more of dictation than of that course which we are determined to pursue—that of inquiry, of research, and of the collection of the experience of all the good, all the wise, and all the intelligent men from all parts of this intelligent community.[4] Now, as for centralization, if we were to centralize our efforts—if we were looking to the constitution of any authority to form a central point, and to direct all the efforts and undertake to guide the energies of the kingdom upon this matter—we should be utterly destroying the great objects we have in view. Unless the whole people take it up as their own especial case, over which they have an especial superintendence, and in which they have an especial interest, the whole of our efforts will be nugatory and vain.

Our object is to excite that interest, to stimulate inquiry, and to collect all the zeal and energy that we can in every district and individual locality, and that each separate locality should be the fountain, the centre, the alpha and the omega, of all the operations that affect that locality. Our object is, that every person, from the highest to the lowest, that every head of a family, that every individual who feels that his health is concerned in this matter, shall be a centre in himself; for sanitary arrangements will never be carried into full effect over the length and breadth of this land, till the head of every family, the head of every domestic establishment, be it of the greatest, or be it of the working man, is fully convinced that there are principles that are essentially necessary to his domestic comfort, his domestic purity, to his physical condition, and to his moral strength. (Hear, hear!) Therefore, so far from seeking centralization, we seek only to make it central in so far as it shall be confined to localities, and in so far as it shall be found the dominant, prevalent, and active principle of every household, and every domestic assemblage. (Hear, hear!)

Then, as for dictation, we do not want here to lay down laws and to declare that such and such results are not to be contradicted, and because they are not to be contradicted they are to be obeyed. Our object is to invite from all quarters the results of experience. Our object is to gather from all who are conversant with this matter, all that they know, all that they can anticipate, all the inferences that they adduce, and to test by general inquiry and by submission of them to as many minds as can be brought to bear upon this great aggregate subject. So far from dictation, we feel that we are now only in the infancy of this science, and that these associations will have the very best effect, in begetting a general interest, in bringing out a vast amount of dormant talent, in exciting a great deal of latent energy, in bringing into the field of inquiry and into the field of operation hundreds, and I may say thousands, who, had it not been for means of this association, would have no beacon to guide their paths, and no centre to which to direct their operations (Hear, hear!)

We wish to beget by these means, to create and to sustain, a true, firm, paramount, and wise public opinion. Public opinion alone will be sufficient to maintain these things. It is not by law, it is not by individual efforts, it is not by the desultory attempts of a few benevolent people, that these results are to be attained—they are to be attained only by constant and vigorous exercise of a wise, benevolent, and instructed public opinion. Let public opinion preside over this as she does over everything else. I mean an instructed, wise, serious, solemn public opinion—let her preside over this, as over everything else, and let her appear as dominant in this matter over the very least as fearing her, and over the greatest as not exempt from her power. Neither do we seek by this association to introduce any new laws.[5] Our object is to inquire how far law is necessary in any of these matters; and law must be resorted to only in cases of admitted necessity. Let law be introduced and brought into action in every instance where the principle is clear; and no one, I think, will gainsay that law must come in to protect the people where it is manifestly impossible that they can protect themselves. (Cheers)

I will just run hastily over a few things that are of paramount interest, to which your attention ought to be directed, to which I hope it will be, and to which I trust you will, at some ensuing gathering, be able to give us full and satisfactory replies. You will find these great matters, which must be brought under sanitary arrangement, will be divided into two great aspects—the physical and moral—they in detail may be considered apart, but they cannot be considered apart as not to be frequently, constantly, nay, perpetually, brought into contact. They act and re-act upon one another in a way quite indivisible; see how it acts in this single instance: A low moral state will bring on intemperance, and with intemperance all that dreadful catalogue of disease and crime that ever follows in the wake of intoxication.

But are there no physical causes that bring on moral evils? Is there any one here in the least degree conversant with the state of our alleys, dwellings, and various localities, who will deny this great undeniable truth, which all experience confirms—for if you go into these frightful places you will see there the causes of moral mischief, and I do verily believe that seven-tenths of it are attributable to that which is the greatest curse of the country—that which destroys their physical and moral existence, cuts through their domestic ties, and reduces them to pauperism, with all its various degradation—habits of drinking and systems of intoxication. (Applause)[6] But those habits of drinking and that system of intoxication are engendered by foul air and the disgusting and depressing influence of the localities in which the people live; by a defective supply of water; by the deleterious and poisonous quality of that water—all combine to drive the people to that immoral curse which we are endeavouring to correct by education, by reformatories, by ten thousand appliances—all of them good, all of them necessary; all of them must be brought to bear, and at the root of it lies this great evil to which I have called your attention. And I ask you to agree with me in what I stated just now, that although a moral and physical evil may in single detail be considered apart, they must, when you come to deal with the question, be regarded as in combination, and in combination producing all those frightful evils which, by God's blessing on our efforts, we will remove—at least to a great degree.

I said I would run through a few points which must be considered because they are of vital importance. They will give rise to deep and solemn thinking; and although there is no time to dwell upon them in detail, as I should have wished to do, I cannot refuse to throw them out for your mature consideration, and for your full and co-operative efforts. I should, indeed, have thought that the valuable document which has just been put out, the statement by Dr Greenough, with a preface by Mr Simon, of the Board of Health, would have been quite sufficient, and that no more would have been required to give force and to point out the necessity of such considerations. Still, as we are collected here, I will bring before you some matters partly in that report and partly from other sources, and submit them for your consideration. I call upon you to consider the effect produced upon the population, morally and physically, by cholera, by fever, by consumption in all its forms. Remember the thousands crippled and enfeebled by it. The number of deaths arising from disease is no measure whatever of its influence upon the population, and no measure whatever of the evils which descend therefrom upon society. Look at the weekly reports of the Registrar-General. We have now become habituated to horrors of the gravest description. When those reports were first published, for a short time the world was aghast, and every man you met asked if they could be true. These reports go on, however,—they are read, they are taken in as matters of course. They come out and are thrown into the waste-paper basket. They appear in *The Times* and other journals, and nobody asks any question about them. It is only on that account the more necessary that an association of this kind should meet from time to time, and impress upon the public at large the deep and lasting evils, the fearful consequences which necessarily flow from neglect and contempt of the great and beneficent laws of nature. (Cheers)

There is another subject to which your attention ought to be drawn. I give no opinion upon it, but it is a matter which can no longer be overlooked. Why is it that we have before us the portentous fact that no less than 60,000 still-born children are produced in this country every year of our lives? I give no opinion on it; I only say that the matter must be looked into, for the fact is manifest, the fact is awful, and the fact demands your most solemn investigation. (Hear, hear!) Again, I say that if you have an interest in the rising generation you should direct your attention to those hospitals which have lately been established, called orthopaedic hospitals, which are established for the purpose of correcting deformities in children, and by surgical processes of the greatest skill and humanity, restoring to them when in tender years, and even when more advanced in life, that perfect straightness of form, and perfect usefulness in their generation. (Hear, hear!) These hospitals reveal an amount of physical degradation and misery that come upon the world which is sufficient to make any thinking man tremble.

Go and look into the records of over-crowded dwellings. Look into the effects of drains, of ill-drained close alleys, of the pestilential localities which are found to be the greatest swarms of all that fills our hospitals with fever, fills our workhouses with paupers, and then bear in mind the great fact that I hope will now be examined into—and I believe the more you examine it the greater illustration you will have of it that crime is now ascertained to be no longer dependent upon poverty or high wages, but that crime is invariably found to be most fertile, most abundant and most constant among ill-drained localities and among closely crowded houses, and in all places where neglect and over-crowding squalor keep festering together. (Cheers) Well, now, I may say, look also to your common lodging-houses. In many places they still retain all their normal evils. Look upon them as hotbeds of vice—as hotbeds of pestilence, and take care that in your survey of the different towns these buildings do not escape your observation.

Again, look—for we are all now considering the present and future generation—look to the effect of over-toil of all kinds upon the young and upon the old. I am not going to say that toil is not the portion of the human race, and I am not going to say that a great deal of toil which has been regarded as unwholesome must also be the portion of many in our complicated state of society.[7] But what I say is this, that when you see these conditions, and regard them as in some respect necessary, direct your attention to ascertain whether the evils of them cannot be mitigated (Hear, hear!) and although you cannot bring them to that state of perfection which you would desire, you will consider whether you cannot be the means of removing much evil and introducing a considerable proportion of good.[8] Then, again, look to the total want of water supply—the total want, in many instances, of a wholesome water supply—in the midst of our dense localities. Look, in consequence, and find no fault with the wretched people who are the victims of that neglect. If you go amongst them and find them covered with dirt so that you cannot distinguish their nakedness from the miserable rags that cover them—if you find them covered with vermin (and I must say I have gone amongst them with my friends, and have returned from amongst them with a considerable household of vermin upon my back) (Laughter) if you go and see these things, do not lay the blame upon them, but lay the blame upon yourselves. You have knowledge, you have the means. They have not the knowledge, they have not the means; and by everything true, by everything holy, you, you are your brother's keeper. (Loud applause)

Well now, again turn your attention to all those deleterious articles of food—turn your attention to the sale of poisons, and to rotten food, and to all those evil things which take place in the midst of dense populations.[9] Why, I know in places where vigilance is not exercised you may find food sold to the poor so poisonous in itself that it is alone sufficient to breed pestilence, to breed only diarrhoea and dysentery, and to decimate the population of a district. Can you wonder, then—I have told you all those physical mischiefs—can you be astonished at the moral evils that flow from them? Go amongst people; hear with your own ears and see with your own eyes what I now state—the utter corruption of language, and of thought, and of practice in all those districts. When I state this I am not speaking in condemnation of those people; for I maintain that the circumstances in which they are are such that these things come upon them almost by inevitable necessity. I will not pass on—I will not dare to speak of many things that cannot be mentioned in any mixed assembly; but you may picture to yourselves what must be the consequences of over-crowded dwellings— I speak not only of health, but where two, three, or four families are living in a crowded house, or in a room, where the sexes are blended—can you wonder at any amount of sin, can you wonder at any amount of vice, can you wonder at anything which we cannot mention in this mixed assembly occurring? You cannot wonder; and if you do wonder, go and inquire for yourselves, and your wonder will cease; for there you will find it clear, unmistakable as any proposition in Euclid. (Applause)

I have already spoken of intoxication and of its degrading qualities; but I must say that there is another very serious and important matter: it is also in reference to the business of one of the departments, to be presided over by my honourable friend and relative, Mr Cowper. I maintain that in this state of things there is an actual impossibility of giving moral education—I maintain that it is positively impossible—I maintain that these classes cannot be taught. You have no means whatever of approaching them; and if you did succeed in bringing their children for a time to the ragged schools and to other institutions, those wretched children go back into those scenes of vice, of infamy, of bestiality (Hear, hear!) and in the midst of all they hear, and all they see, they unlearn in one hour all that has been given to them in the preceding three. (Hear, hear!) That is another proof that all these things must be considered together—that one bears upon the other. (Hear, hear!) Depend upon it your attempts at education will fail; all the best schemes of the training masters, of those who establish the schools, all private and all public efforts, all the activity of the inspectors, all the cogent reports they make upon them—they will fail altogether so long as you have this horrid plague spot in the midst of you, advancing nothing but vice, and violence, and corruption, and ignorance, and everything that is hateful to God and man. (Hear, hear! and cheers.) ...

... We should first, as far as possible, regulate the building of houses, the width and construction of streets. I have seen the greatest possible effect produced by destroying a court as a *cul de sac*, by knocking down the end house and making it a common thoroughfare. You must also erect houses for the people to live in, or go to the adaptation of old houses. All these, as have been seen by proof, have been most effective in their operations. Take for instance the registration of common lodging-houses. There has been no one measure more productive of good results than that. You may now see that although in the whole population of London, where at this moment there are from 50,000 to 60,000 sleeping nightly in the common lodging-houses, there has not been for the last two years one single case of fever engendered in those houses (Hear, hear!) We need not dwell upon the sanitary regulations for the army and barracks—these will be touched upon elswhere; but I think, also, that you must look very attentively to all regulations affecting quarantine, and inquire most minutely whether quarantine is not of itself a grand delusion. (Hear, hear!) And whether the best quarantine is not to be found in the regulations for the cleanliness of ships, in regulations for the cleanliness of towns, in regulations for the cleanliness of the country at large, and whether it is possible by any caution of yours to keep out disease when you yourselves are doing everything you can to engender it. (Hear, hear!)

And amongst your other remedies you must resort to parks and play-grounds. (Loud applause) Not only are they beneficial as open spaces, but they are greatly beneficial as having a moral effect in affording wholesome amusement, relaxation, and pleasure. Depend upon it that the mind must occasionally be amused as well as the body be cared for; and I have often thought there was a good deal of truth in what was said by the well-known Dr Jackson, of Christ Church,[10] who, when asked whether he would not wish to have his college consist of the profoundest and ablest students, replied, "No, I would have no such thing. There must be a certain number of dull men always, to amuse the reading men." (Laughter) Whether you would like to see that carried out in the Queen's College and other places, I cannot say; but of this I am sure, that the principle was correct—and there must be a degree of amusement for all who are engaged in constant work, whether it be of the head, or whether it be of the hand. (Hear, hear!) As the President has suggested to me, the truth is well expressed in the old proverb—"All work and no play makes Jack a dull boy." (Laughter) Don't you press too hard upon your Jack in the chair. (Laughter)[11] Give him fair play, and you will be benefited by his intellect, and his intellect will very often do you a great deal of good if you attend to what he says. Therefore, there is great advantage in reduced hours of labour; there is great advantage in the Saturday half-holiday, and I trust and hope that Liverpool, at least, will not be backward in instituting parks and play-grounds; for not only has she a large population, but I believe I can say without contradiction that the progress of wealth in Liverpool has been the means of depriving the working men of many of their enjoyments by converting the ground used by them for recreation into wharves and docks. If that be the case, do not let wealth be the means of oppression to the working man; but that the greater your wealth and prosperity, the greater is his consideration and more true the dignity of himself and of his household....

... These are some of the evils, of the remedies for which many will be accepted and many rejected; but all ought to be investigated; for, I say it without presumption, the things we state from the platform are founded on experience, and what we propound is no longer matter of experiment. The operation of the Public Health Act showed, in Evesham, that the town might be as healthy as the country; it shows a marvellous reduction of mortality, which is 17 in the thousand, when the mortality of rural districts amounts to 21 in the thousand. It is the same in Coydon; and in Liverpool, I am informed—greatly to your honour, and that adds greatly to your responsibility—that the sanitary arrangements save 3,500 lives a year as compared with former times. Surely that is a matter for deep and solemn consideration, and we are told that the preventible mortality in this country amounts to no less than 90,000 a year. Let us say 40,000; that is four lives an hour. We may be told these things are but in the course of nature, and we ought not to interfere; on such we will turn our backs, we will not listen to such a representation. We may be told these things are costly and require financial effort, and the people are not ready to undertake the expense; but we may safely say that it is disease that is expensive, and it is health that is cheap. There is nothing economical but justice and mercy towards all interests—temporal and spiritual—of all the human race. I have also heard it said that we ought to trust a great deal more to spiritual appliances, and that we ought not to think so much of the perishable body. My answer to that is, that spiritual appliances in the state of things to which I allude are altogether impossible. (Cheers)

Make every effort—push them forward—never desist—lose no moment—but depend upon it that in such a state of things you will in the end be utterly baffled. (Cheers) But when people say we should think more of the soul and less of the body, my answer is, that the same God which made the soul also made the body. It is an inferior work, perhaps, but nevertheless his work, and it must be treated and cared for according to the end for which it was created—fitness for his service. (Hear, hear!) I do maintain that God is worshipped not only by spiritual but by material things. (Hear, Hear! and cheers.) You find it in the records of the Psalms—"Praise Him sun and moon, praise Him all ye stars of light." And this I will maintain, that our great object should be to do all we can to remove the lets and hindrances which stand in the way of such worship and of the body's fitness for His service. (Hear, hear!) If St Paul, calling our bodies the temples of the Holy Ghost, said we ought not to be contaminated by sin, we also say that our bodies, the temple of the Holy Ghost, ought not to be corrupted by preventible disease, ought not to be degraded by filth when it can be avoided, and ought not to be disabled by unnecessary suffering. (Hear, hear! and applause.) Therefore, all that society can do it ought to do to remove the difficulties and impediments, and to do what in us lies to give to every man full, fair, and free opportunity, without let or hindrance, to exercise all his moral, intellectual, physical, and spiritual energies, so that every one may be able to do his duty in that state of life to which it has pleased God to call him. (Loud cheers, amid which Lord Shaftesbury resumed his seat.)

1 *Laissez-faire*—the doctrine of non-interference by Parliament in economic and industrial affairs. This fundamental principle of nineteenth-century Liberalism was derived from the teaching of the classical economists Adam Smith, Malthus, and Ricardo. The Evangelicals realized that legislation was essential to right social ills like the slave trade and human exploitation.

2 Oastler, Richard; *b.* 1789; *educ.*, Moravian school; commission agent; lost his money, 1820; steward to Thomas Cornhill, 1821; addressed the City of London Tavern meeting leading to Shaftesbury's co-operation with the London agitators, 1833; wrote the *White Slavery Letters*, 1835; imprisoned for debt, 1840; edited *The Home*, 1851; *d.* Harrogate, 1861.

3 Shaftesbury, Lord (Anthony Ashley Cooper); *b.* 1801; *educ.*, Harrow and Christ Church, Oxford; Tory M.P., Woodstock, 1826; Commissioner of the Board of Control, 1828; Lord of the Admiralty, 1834; 7th Earl of Shaftesbury, 1851; Chairman of the Sanitary Commission for the Crimea, 1855; Chairman of the Ragged School Union; *d.* 1885. It was Parson Bull who had approached Shaftesbury in 1833 and asked him to present a Ten Hours' Bill into Parliament.

4 This whole question is discussed in Asa Briggs, *Victorian Cities* (1968), ch. 9. Bibliography provided.

5 Local boards of health were created during the cholera outbreak of 1831–3, but these lapsed after the epidemic was over. The Poor Law Commissioners recommended the appointment of medical officers of health, and the promotion of cleanliness as "necessary to the improvement of the moral condition of the population". In 1848 a central board of health was set up, similar to the Poor Law board; in 1854 Parliament altered its character; and in 1858 distributed its duties among the other departments of state. In 1866, an Act compelled local authorities to provide sanitary inspectors, and allowed the central government to insist on the removal of nuisances, the provision of sewers, and a good water supply.

6 The two writings of the period which did much to awaken public opinion were: Friedrich Engels, *The Condition of the Working*

Class in England in 1844, and John Ruskin's *Sesame and Lilies* (1865).

7 See Asa Briggs, *Victorian People* (1955), ch. 5, and E. P. Thompson, *The Making of the English Working Class* (1968), pp. 336-84.

8 The Utilitarian principle, advocated by Jeremy Bentham, was to secure the greatest happiness for the greatest number. Paradoxically, the Utilitarians supported legislation on destitution and health, and opposed Parliamentary control of trade and commerce. "It followed, too, that legislation must have a more positive function in society than Bentham had allowed: it must seek to enable men to exercise their natural capacities, use their talents, and develop their personalities, untrammelled by artificial legal impediments and evil economic conditions. The good society, for Mill, is one of the richest diversity derived from the free interplay of human character and personality; he saw that to attain anything like that society in nineteenth-century Britain a long series of far-reaching reforms would be necessary" (David Thomson, *England in the Nineteenth Century* (1950), p. 49).

9 The first "Co-operative" store, in Toad Lane, Rochdale, was founded in 1844 by a group of twenty-eight working men, *The Rochdale Society of Equitable Pioneers*. The purpose behind the group was to provide pure food at reasonable prices, for the artisan generally had to be satisfied with the inferior goods remaining in the shops at the end of the working day.

10 Jackson was Dean of Christ Church from 1783 to 1809, and did much to promote studies within the college.

11 Lord John Russell was in the chair. The National Society for the Promotion of Social Science attracted many well-known names. Disraeli, facing Liberal attacks at the passing of the Public Health Act in 1876 said: "Well it may be the policy of sewerage to a Liberal Member of Parliament. But to one of the labouring multitude of England, who has found fever always to be one of the inmates of his household—who has, year after year, seen stricken down the children of his loins on whose sympathy and support he has looked with hope and confidence, it is not a policy of sewerage but a question of life and death" (Arthur Bryant, *English Saga* (1943), p. 197).

37 BISHOP WILBERFORCE AND PROFESSOR HUXLEY, 1860

(*Life of Huxley*, pp. 186-7)

The publication of Darwin's *Origin of Species* in 1859 was obscured by the *Essays and Reviews* controversy. At the meeting of the British Association at Oxford, on 30 June 1860, Dr Draper of New York spoke on the *Intellectual Development of Europe considered with reference to the views of Mr Darwin.*[1] In the ensuing discussion Wilberforce made a provocative and uninformed attack on the Darwinian thesis, and the encounter between the Bishop and Huxley was, in many ways, characteristic of the clash between science and religion in the nineteenth century.

The Bishop of Oxford[2] attacked Darwin, at first playfully, but at last in grim earnest. It was known that the Bishop had written an article against Darwin in the last *Quarterly Review*;[3] it was also rumoured that Professor Owen had been staying at Cuddesdon and had primed the Bishop, who was to act as mouthpiece to the great Palaeontologist, who did not himself dare to enter the lists.[4] The Bishop, however, did not show himself master of the facts, and made one serious blunder. A fact which had been much dwelt on as confirmatory of Darwin's idea of variation, was that a sheep had been born shortly before in a flock in the North of England, having an addition of one to the vertebrae of the spine. The Bishop was declaring with rhetorical exaggeration that there was hardly any evidence on Darwin's side. "What have they to bring forward?" he exclaimed, "Some rumoured statement about a long-legged sheep." But he passed on to banter: "I should like to ask Professor Huxley,[5] who is sitting by me, and is about to tear me to pieces when I have sat down, as to his belief in being descended from an ape. Is it on his grandfather's or his grandmother's side that the ape ancestry comes in?" And then taking a graver tone, he asserted, in a solemn peroration, that Darwin's views were contrary to the revelation of God in the Scriptures. Professor Huxley was unwilling to respond: but he was called for, and spoke with his usual incisiveness and with some scorn: "I am here only in the interests of science," he said, "and I have not heard anything which can prejudice the case of my august client." Then after showing how little competent the Bishop was to enter upon the discussion, he touched on the question of Creation. "You say that development drives out the Creator; but you assert that God made you: and yet you know that you yourself were originally a little piece of matter, no bigger than the end of this gold pencil case." Lastly as to the descent from a monkey, he said: "I should feel it no shame to have risen from such an origin; but I should feel it a shame to have sprung from one who prostituted the gifts of culture and eloquence to the service of prejudice and of falsehood."

Account by Canon W. H. Fremantle.[6]

I asserted—and I repeat—that a man has no reason to be ashamed of having an ape for his grandfather. If there were an ancestor whom I should feel shame in recalling it would rather be a *man*—a man of restless and versatile intellect—who, not content with an equivocal[7] success in his own sphere of activity, plunges into scientific questions with which he has no real acquaintance, only to obscure them by an aimless rhetoric, and distract the attention of his hearers from the real point at issue by eloquent digressions and skilled appeals to religious prejudice.

Account by J. R. Green.

1 Darwin, Charles: *b.* 1809; *educ.*, Shrewsbury, Edinburgh, and Christ's College, Cambridge; naturalist on the *Beagle*, 1831–6; settled at Downe, Kent, 1842; *Origin of Species*, 1859; *The Descent of Man*, 1871; *d.* 1882.

2 Wilberforce, Samuel; *b.* 1805; *educ.*, Oriel College, Oxford, 1823; graduated, 1826; deacon, 1828; priest, 1829; rector of Brightstone, 1830–40; chaplain to Prince Consort, 1840; rector of Alverstoke, 1840; Bampton Lecturer, 1840; Archdeacon of Surrey and Canon of Winchester, 1839; Dean of Westminster, 1845; Bishop of Oxford, 1845; founded Cuddesdon Theological College, 1854; Bishop of Winchester, 1869; *d.* 1873.

3 *Quarterly Review*, July 1860. Founded by J. Murray in February 1809, the periodical listed among its contributors: Sir Walter Scott, Canning, Southey, Rogers, Lord Salisbury, and Gladstone.

4 Owen, Richard; *b.* 1804; *educ.*, Lancaster School; conservator of the Hunterian museum; first Hunterian Professor of Comparative Anatomy and Physiology. Owen was a fierce controversialist and was not kindly disposed to Darwin who had anticipated some of his own findings.

5 Huxley, Thomas Henry; *b.* 1825; studied medicine and was appointed surgeon to the *Rattlesnake*, 1846; lecturer in natural history at the Royal School of Mines, 1854; Fellow of the Royal Society, 1851; Hunterian Professor at the Royal College of Surgeons, 1863–9; Fullerian Professor at the Royal Institution, 1863–7; member of the school board for London, 1870; secretary of the Royal Society,

1871; inspector of fisheries, 1881–5; member of ten Royal Commissions, 1862–84; *d.* 1895.

6 Huxley considered Fremantle's account to be "substantially correct", though Green's report of his own speech was rather more accurate.

7 Huxley, however, denied using the word "equivocal".

38 AUBREY MOORE ON DARWIN, 1889

(*Science and the Faith*, pp. 168-70)

The Darwinian school of scientists had rendered obsolete the evidential approach to Christian dogma, which had been associated with William Paley (1743–1805). The advance of contemporary science was met, on the one hand, on untenable theological grounds, as in the case of Wilberforce, or on the other, by the attempt to review the relationship of physical science and religious belief in a dispassionate light. Aubrey Moore,[1] Frederick Temple,[2] R. W. Church,[3] and F. J. Hort[4] were among the churchmen who sought to reconcile science and religion in this way.

EVOLUTION AND CREATION

1. The first difficulty which will probably occur to any one is this: Darwinism offers an explanation of the origin of species. How is this reconcilable with the first article of the Creed, the first sentence of the Bible? A man of average intelligence will not hesitate long here, unless the issue has been confused for him by the one-sided statements of ignorant partisans.[5] For science neither says, nor professes to say, anything about the ultimate origin of things. Mr Darwin says:

I believe that all animals are descended from at most only four or five progenitors, and plants from an equal or lesser number.[6]

All the organic beings which have ever lived on this earth may be descended from some one primordial form.[7]

And he adds:

There is grandeur in this view of life with its several powers having been originally breathed by the Creator into a few forms or into one.[8]

Haeckel, and some other evolutionists, would go farther. They would believe, though all the experimental evidence is at present against such a view, that life ultimately arose from inorganic matter. But even here there is no suggestion as to the ultimate origin of that matter out of which all the world, as we know it, came. In the language of technical theology, evolution deals with secondary (i.e. derivative), but does not touch primary, creation. In Haeckel's less exact way of stating the distinction it deals with "creation of form", but knows nothing about "creation of matter". Of the latter, i.e. original creation, Haeckel says:

This process, if indeed it ever took place, is completely beyond human comprehension, and can therefore never become a subject of scientific inquiry.[9]

Professor Tyndall, speaking of the "evolution hypothesis", says: "It does not solve—it does not profess to solve—the ultimate mystery of this universe. It leaves, in fact, that mystery untouched." Professor Clifford, again, says: "Of the beginning of the universe we know nothing at all."[10] Herbert Spencer, indeed, rejects primary creation, but not on the ground that evolution offers an alternative for it, but because it is "literally unthinkable"; and Professor Huxley seems to argue that, as science knows nothing about it, nothing can be known. But Mr Darwin tells us that "the theory of evolution is quite compatible with the belief in a God"; that when he was collecting facts for the *Origin*, his "belief in what is called a Personal God was as firm as that of Dr Pusey himself;[11] while, even at the time when the *Origin of Species* was published, he "deserved to be called a Theist".[12] Later on he says: "The mystery of the beginning of all things is insoluble by us; and I for one must be content to remain an Agnostic." Yet, three years later (1879), in a private letter, he writes: "In my most extreme fluctuations I have never been an atheist in the sense of denying the existence of God."[13] These quotations, which of course might easily be multiplied, are enough to show that evolution neither is, nor pretends to be, an alternative theory to original creation. An evolutionist, therefore, who denies the fact of creation goes as far beyond the evidence which science offers, as if he had asserted his belief in "the Maker of heaven and earth".

1 Moore, Aubrey Lackington; *b.* 1848; *educ.*, St Paul's School, 1860; Exeter College, Oxford, 1867; B.A., 1871; M.A., 1874; Fellow of St John's College, Oxford, 1872; lecturer and tutor, 1874; rector of Frenchay, 1876; tutor of Keble College, Oxford; contributed to *Lux Mundi*, 1889; *d.* 1890.

2 *The Relations between Religion and Science*, Bampton Lectures, 1884.

3 Church, Richard William; *b.* 1815; *educ.*, Exeter, Redlands, Wadham College, Oxford, 1833; Fellow of Oriel College, Oxford, 1838; deacon, 1839; priest, 1852; rector of Whatley, 1853; Dean of St Paul's, 1871; *d.* 1890.

4 Hort, Fenton John Anthony; *b.* 1828; *educ.*, Rugby and Trinity College, Cambridge; Fellow, 1852; deacon, 1854; priest, 1856; vicar of St Ippolyts (Herts.), 1857–72; Fellow and lecturer of Emmanuel College, 1872–8; member of New Testament revision company, 1870–80; and Apocrypha, 1880–92; Hulsean Professor, 1878–87; Lady Margaret Reader, 1887–92; *d.* 1892.

5 Militant atheism had become fashionable in the 1870s, and was based on a crude materialistic approach to science.

6 *Origin of Species*, p. 424.

7 Ibid., p. 425.

8 Ibid., p. 429.

9 *History of Creation* I, p. 8 (Eng. Trans.).

10 E. B. Tylor's *Researches into the Early History of Mankind* (1865), raised certain issues relating to the origins of religion itself. The evolutionary method was applied to many branches of inquiry, Spencer propounding a concept of evolutionary ethics.

11 Vol. III, p. 236

12 Vol. I, p. 313.

13 Vol. I, p. 304.

39 ESSAYS AND REVIEWS, 1861

(Davidson and Benham, *Life of Tait*, vol. 1, pp. 282-3, 317)

Essays and Reviews, published in 1860, was "an attempt to illustrate the advantage derivable to the cause of religious and moral truth, from a free handling, in a becoming spirit, of subjects peculiarly liable to suffer by the repetition of conventional language and from traditional methods of treatment". The volume was welcomed in the *Westminster Review*, defended by A. P. Stanley[1] in the *Edinburgh Review*, and attacked by Wilberforce in the *Quarterly Review*. An address from a Dorset rural deanery was chosen for its general nature by the bishops, and a remonstrance was drawn up by Wilberforce and issued over the signatures of the Archbishop of Canterbury and several bishops.[2]

Lambeth, February 12, 1861.

Reverend Sir,[3] I have taken the opportunity of meeting many of my Episcopal brethren in London to lay your address before them.

They unanimously agree with me in expressing the pain it has given them that any clergyman of our Church should have published such opinions as those concerning which you have addressed us.[4]

We cannot understand how these opinions can be held consistently with an honest subscription to the formularies of our Church, with many of the fundamental doctrines of which they appear to us essentially at variance.

Whether the language in which these views are expressed is such as to make the publication an act which could be visited in the Ecclesiastical Courts or to justify the Synodical condemnation of the book which contains them, is still under our gravest consideration.[5] But our main hope is our reliance on the blessing of God, in the continued and increasing earnestness with which we trust that we and the clergy of our several dioceses may be enabled to teach and preach that good deposit of sound doctrine which our Church teaches in its fulness, and which we pray that she may, by God's grace, ever set forth as the uncorrupted Gospel of our Lord Jesus Christ. I remain, reverend Sir, your faithful servant,

J. B. CANTUAR:

The consequent synodical condemnation of the book expressed the general feeling of the clergy and bishops. Two essayists were prosecuted before the Dean of Arches; H. B. Wilson by the Reverend James Fendall, and Rowland Williams by the Bishop of Salisbury. The Judicial Committee of the Privy Council upheld the appeal of the two essayists to the dismay of many churchmen. An alliance of churchmen of all schools of thought resulted in the following declaration, drawn up at Oxford, and signed by 11,000 clergymen.[6]

We, the undersigned presbyters and deacons in holy orders of the Church of England and Ireland, hold it to be our bounden duty to the Church of England and Ireland and to the souls of men to declare our firm belief that the Church of England and Ireland, in common with the whole Catholic Church, maintains without reserve or qualification the inspiration and Divine authority of the whole canonical Scriptures, as not only containing, but being, the Word of God, and further teaches, in the words of our blessed Lord, that the "punishment" of the "cursed" equally with the "life" of the "righteous" is everlasting".

Signatures to be sent to the Secretary, Committee-room, 3 St Aldgate's, Oxford.

Names of Committee: C. C. Clarke, D.D., Archdeacon of Oxford; R. L. Cotton, D.D., Provost of Worcester College;[7] G. A. Denison, M.A., Archdeacon of Taunton;[8] W. E. Fremantle, M.A., Rector of Claydon; F. K. Leighton, D.D., Warden of All Soul's College; J. C. Miller, D.D., St Martin's, Birmingham; E. B. Pusey, D.D., Regius Professor of Hebrew.

1 Stanley, Arthur Penrhyn, son of Bishop of Norwich; *b.* 1815; *educ.*, Seaforth, Rugby; Balliol College, Oxford, 1834; Fellow of University College, Oxford, 1838; deacon, 1839; priest, 1843; tutor; secretary of University Commission, 1850; canon of Canterbury, 1851; chaplain to Prince Consort, 1854; Professor of Ecclesiastical History at Oxford, 1856; canon of Christ Church, 1858; Dean of Westminster, 1864; *d.* 1881.

2 The signatories were: Sumner, Longley (York), Tait (London), Villiers (Durham), Sumner (Winchester), Phillpotts (Exeter), Davys (Peterborough), Thirlwall (St David's), Gilbert (Chichester), Lonsdale (Lichfield), Wilberforce (Oxford), Turton (Ely), Short (St Asaph), Prince Lee (Manchester), Hampden (Hereford), Graham (Chester), Ollivant (Llandaff), Auckland (Bath and Wells), Jackson (Lincoln), Baring (Gloucester and Bristol), Hamilton (Salisbury), Bickersteth (Ripon), Pelham (Norwich), Campbell (Bangor), Wigram (Rochester), Waldegrave (Carlisle).

3 The letter was addressed to H. B. Williams, whose name headed the address.

4 The essayists were: Temple, *On the Education of the World*; Rowland Williams, *Bunsen's Biblical Researches*; Baden Powell, *The Study of the Evidences of Christianity*; H. B. Wilson, *The National Church*; C. W. Goodwin, *The Mosaic Cosmogony*; Mark Pattison, *Tendencies of Religious Thought in England, 1688–1750*; Benjamin Jowett, *The Interpretation of Scripture*. It was stated in the preface that each individual was responsible for his own contribution alone.

5 The book was synodically condemned in 1864 as "containing teaching contrary to the doctrine received by the United Church of England and Ireland in common with the whole Catholic Church of Christ". In the Upper House it was carried by 8 votes to 2, and in the Lower House by 39 votes to 19.

6 In December 1862, Lushington condemned Wilson and Williams each on three counts, sentencing them to suspension *ab officio* for one year. The Judicial Committee reversed the sentence on 8 February 1864, the two archbishops dissenting from part of the judgment. Peter Hinchliff comments on the judgment: "... the lord chancellor had specifically declared that the court was bound to interpret the

formularies of the Church in precisely the same way as it would interpret statutes and written instruments. No one could be held guilty until it could be specifically proved that he had contravened some precise provision. In other words canon law was simply to be treated as a branch of English law. It was, in a sense, the final triumph of the secular over the ecclesiastical jurisdiction" (*The One-Sided Reciprocity* (1966), pp. 16-34).

40 COLENSO IN THE COURTS, 1865

As a thoroughgoing Erastian, Bishop Colenso sought vindication for his liberal cause through the English law courts, although theoretically it was a matter for concern for the Anglican Church in South Africa. The judgment of the Privy Council and the Romilly judgment, both involving Colenso, demonstrated the impracticability of the exercise of the Royal Supremacy in ecclesiastical affairs overseas. The action of the South African primate was supported by the bishops of the first Lambeth Conference, and their consolidated opinion characterized the growing sense of unity among the various offshoots of the Church of England.

Judgment of the Lords of the Judicial Committee of the Privy Council upon the Petition of the Lord Bishop of Natal, referred to the Judicial Committee by Her Majesty's Order in Council of the 10th June, 1864; delivered 20th March, 1865.

Present:
Lord Chancellor Lord Cranworth Lord Kingsdown
Dean of the Arches[1] Master of the Rolls

The Bishop of Natal[2] and the Bishop of Capetown[3] (who are the parties to this proceeding) are ecclesiastical persons who have been created Bishops by the Queen, in the exercise of her authority as Sovereign of this realm and Head of the Established Church.

These Bishops were consecrated under mandate from the Queen by the Archbishop of Canterbury, in the manner prescribed by the law of England.

They received and hold their dioceses under grants made by the Crown. Their status, therefore, both ecclesiastical and temporal, must be ascertained and defined by the law of England; and it is plain that their legal existence depends on acts which have no validity or effect, except on the basis of the supremacy of the Crown.[4]

Further, their respective and relative rights and liabilities must be determined by the principles of English law applied to the construction of the grants to them contained in the Letters-Patent; for they are the creatures of English law, and dependent on that law for their existence, rights and attributes.[5]

We must treat the parties before us as standing on this foundation, and on no other.

The Letters-Patent by which Dr Gray was appointed Bishop of Capetown and also Metropolitan, passed the Great Seal on the 8th December, 1853. These Letters-Patent recited, among other things, that it had "been represented to Her Majesty by the Archbishop of Canterbury that the then existing see or diocese of Capetown was of inconvenient extent, and that for the due spiritual care and superintendence of the religious interests of the inhabitants thereof, and for the maintenance of the doctrine and discipline of the United Church of England and Ireland within the Colony of the Cape of Good Hope and its dependencies, and the Island of Saint Helena, it was desirable and expedient that the same should be divided into three (or more) distinct and separate sees or dioceses, to be styled the Bishopric of Capetown, the Bishopric of Grahamstown, and the Bishopric of Natal—the Bishops of the said several Sees of Grahamstown and Natal and their successors to be subject and subordinate to the See of Capetown and to the Bishop thereof and his successors, in the same manner as any Bishop of any see within the Province of Canterbury was under the authority of the Archiepiscopal See of that province and the Archbishop of the same;" and the Letters-Patent contained the following passages:

And we do further will and ordain that the said Right Reverend Father in God, Robert Gray, Bishop of the said See of Capetown, and his successors the Bishops thereof for the time being, shall be and be deemed and taken to be the Metropolitan Bishop in our Colony of the Cape of Good Hope and its dependencies, and our Island of Saint Helena, subject nevertheless to the general superintendence and (super) revision of the Archbishop of Canterbury for the time being, and subordinate to the Archiepiscopal See of the Province of Canterbury: and we will and ordain that the said Bishops of Grahamstown and Natal respectively shall be Suffragan Bishops to the said Bishop of Capetown and his successors. And we will and grant to the said Bishop of Capetown and his successors full power and authority as Metropolitan of the Cape of Good Hope, and of the Island of Saint Helena, to perform all functions peculiar and appropriate to the office of Metropolitan within the limits of the said Sees of Grahamstown and Natal, and to exercise *Metropolitan jurisdiction* over the Bishops of the said Sees and their successors, and over all archdeacons, dignitaries, and all other chaplains, ministers, priests, and deacons in holy orders of the United Church of England and Ireland within the limits of the said dioceses. And we do by these presents give and grant unto the said Bishop of Capetown and his successors full power and authority to visit once in five years, or oftener if occason shall require, as well the said several Bishops and their successors, as all dignitaries and other chaplains, ministers, priests, and deacons in holy orders of the United Church of England and Ireland resident in the said dioceses, for correcting and supplying the defects of the said Bishops and their successors, with all and all manner of visitorial jurisdiction, power, and coercion.

And we do hereby authorize and empower the said Bishop of Capetown and his successors to inhibit during any such visitation of the said dioceses the exercise of all or of such part or parts of the ordinary jurisdiction of the said Bishops or their successors as to him the said Bishop of Capetown or his successors shall seem expedient, and during the time of such visitation to exercise by himself or themselves, or his or their commissaries, such powers, functions and jurisdictions in and over the said dioceses as the Bishops thereof might have exercised if they had not been inhibited from exercising the same.

And we do further ordain and declare that if any person against whom a judgment or decree shall be pronounced by the said Bishops or their successors, or their commissary or commissaries, shall conceive himself to be aggrieved by such sentence, it shall be lawful for such person to appeal to the said Bishop of Capetown or his successors, provided such appeal be entered within fifteen days after such sentence shall have been pronounced.

And we do give and grant to the said Bishop of Capetown and his successors full power and authority finally to decree and determine the said appeals.

And we do further will and ordain that in case any proceedings shall be instituted against any of the said Bishops of Grahamstown and Natal, when placed under the said Metropolitan See of Capetown, such proceedings shall originate and be carried on before the said Bishop of Capetown, whom we hereby authorize and direct to take cognizance of the same....

And if any party shall conceive himself aggrieved by any judgment, decree, or sentence pronounced by the said Bishop of Capetown or his successors, either in case of such review or in any cause originally instituted before the said Bishop or his successors, it shall be lawful for the said party to appeal to the said Archbishop of Canterbury or his successors, who shall finally decide and determine the said appeal.

The Letters-Patent which constituted the See of Natal and appointed the Appellant to that See, were sealed, and bear date on the 23rd November, 1853, fifteen days before the grant of the Letters-Patent to the Bishop of Capetown.

The Letters-Patent creating the See of Natal recited the Patent of September, 1847, which created the original Diocese of Capetown, and appointed Dr Gray the bishop thereof, and that he had since resigned the office of Bishop of Capetown, whereby the said See had become and was then vacant. The Patent also recited that it was expedient and desirable that the said diocese should be divided into three or more distinct and separate dioceses, to be styled the Bishoprics of Capetown, Grahamstown, and Natal, the Bishops of the said several Sees of Grahamstown and Natal to be subject and subordinate to the See of Capetown, and the Bishop thereof and his successors, in the same manner as any Bishop of any See within the Province of Canterbury was under the authority of the Archiepiscopal See of that Province and the Archbishop of the same; and the Letters-Patent proceeded to erect, found, make, ordain, and constitute the district of Natal, to be a distinct and separate Bishop's See and Diocese, to be called the Bishopric of Natal. And after appointing Dr Colenso to be the Bishop of the said See, and granting that the said Bishop of Natal and his successors should be a body corporate, the Letters-Patent contained the following passage:

> And we do further ordain and declare that the said Bishop of Natal and his successors shall be subject and subordinate to the See of Capetown, and to the Bishop thereof and his successors, in the same manner as any Bishop of any See within the Province of Canterbury, in our Kingdom of England, is under the authority of the Archiepiscopal See of that Province, and of the Archbishop of the same: and we do hereby further will and ordain that the said John William Colenso, and every Bishop of Natal, shall, within six months after the date of their respective Letters-Patent, take an oath of due obedience to the Bishop of Capetown for the time being, as his Metropolitan, which oath shall and may be ministered unto him by the said Archbishop, or by any person by him duly appointed or authorized for that purpose.

The Letters-Patent then proceeded to confer on the Bishop of Natal and his successors Episcopal jurisdiction and authority over all rectors, curates, ministers, chaplains, priests, and deacons within the diocese, and directed that, if any party should conceive himself aggrieved by any judgment, decree, or sentence pronounced by the Bishop of Natal or his successors, he should have an appeal to the Bishop of Capetown, who should finally decide and determine the appeal.

Under these Letters-Patent, the Appellant was consecrated on the 30th November, 1853, and he took an oath of canonical obedience to the Metropolitan Bishop of Capetown, which oath was administered to him by the Archbishop of Canterbury, and was in these words:

I, John William Colenso, Doctor in Divinity, appointed Bishop of the See and Diocese of Natal, do profess and promise all due reverence and obedience to the Metropolitan Bishop of Capetown and to his successors, and to the Metropolitan Church of St George, Capetown.

At this time there was not in reality any Metropolitan See of Capetown, or any Bishop thereof in existence.

These several Letters-Patent were not granted in pursuance of any Orders or Order made by Her Majesty in Council, nor were they made by virtue of any statute of the Imperial Parliament, nor were they confirmed by any Act of the Legislature of the Cape of Good Hope or the Legislative Council of Natal.

Previously to these Letters-Patent being granted, the District of Natal had been erected into a distinct and separate Government; and, by Letters-Patent granted by the Crown in 1847, it was ordained that it should have a Legislative Council which should have power to make such laws and ordinances as might be required for the peace, order, and good government of the district. With respect to the Cape of Good Hope, by Letters-Patent dated 23rd May, 1850, it was declared and ordained by Her Majesty that there should be within the Settlement of the Cape of Good Hope a Parliament, which should be holden by the Governor, and should consist of the Governor, a Legislative Council, and a House of Assembly, and that such Parliament should have authority to make laws for the peace, welfare, and good government of the Settlement.

In the year 1863 certain charges of heresy and false doctrine were preferred against the Appellant before the Bishop of Capetown as Metropolitan, and, upon these charges, the Bishop of Capetown, claiming to exercise jurisdiction as Metropolitan, did, on the 16th day of December, 1863, sentence, adjudge, and decree the Appellant, the Bishop of Natal, to be deposed from his office as such Bishop, and to be further prohibited from the exercise of any Divine office within any part of the Metropolitan Province of Capetown.[6] In pronouncing this decree, the Bishop of Capetown claimed to exercise jurisdiction as Metropolitan by virtue of his Letters-Patent, and of the office thereby conferred on him, and as having thereby acquired legal authority to try and condemn the

Appellant; and the Appellant protested against such assumption of jurisdiction.

This sentence and decree of Dr Gray as Metropolitan has been published and promulgated in the Diocese of Natal, and the Clergy of that Diocese have been thereby prohibited from yielding obedience to the Appellant as Bishop of Natal.

In this state of things three principal questions arise, and have been argued before us: First. Were the Letters-Patent of the 8th December, 1853, by which Dr Gray was appointed Metropolitan, and a Metropolitan See or Province was expressed to be created, valid and good in law? Secondly. Supposing the ecclesiastical relation of Metropolitan and Suffragan to have been created, was the grant of coercive authority and jurisdiction expressed by the Letter-Patent to be thereby made to the Metropolitan valid and good in law? Thirdly. Can the oath of canonical obedience taken by the Appellant to the Bishop of Capetown, and his consent to accept his see as part of the Metropolitan Province of Capetown, confer any jurisdiction or authority on the Bishop of Capetown by which this sentence of deprivation of the Bishopric of Natal can be supported?

With respect to the first question, we apprehend it to be clear, upon principle, that after the establishment of an independent Legislature in the Settlements of the Cape of Good Hope and Natal, there was no power in the Crown by virtue of its Prerogative (for these Letters-Patent were not granted under the provisions of any Statute) to establish a Metropolitan See or Province, or to create an Ecclesiastical Corporation whose status, rights, and authority the Colony could be required to recognize.

After a Colony or Settlement has received legislative institutions, the Crown (subject to the special provisions of any Act of Parliament) stands in the same relation to that Colony or Settlement as it does to the United Kingdom.

It may be true that the Crown as legal Head of the Church has a right to command the consecration of a Bishop, but it has no power to assign him any diocese, or give him any sphere of action within the United Kingdom. The United Church of England and Ireland is not a part of the Constitution in any Colonial Settlement, nor can its authorities or those who bear office in it claim to be recognized by the law of the Colony, otherwise than as the members of a voluntary association.

The course which legislation has taken on this subject is a strong proof of the correctness of these conclusions. In the year 1813 it was deemed expedient to establish a Bishopric in the East

Indies (then under the Government of the East India Company), and although the Bishop was appointed and consecrated under the authority of the Crown, yet it was thought necessary to obtain the sanction of the Legislature, and that an Act of Parliament should be passed to give the Bishop legal status and authority. Accordingly, by Statute 53 Geo. III, c. 155, sec. 49, it was enacted that in case it should please His Majesty by his Royal Letters-Patent to erect, found, and constitute one Bishopric for the whole of the British territories in the East Indies and parts therein mentioned, a certain salary should be paid to the Bishop by the East India Company; and by the 51st and 52nd sections it was enacted that such Bishop should not have or use any jurisdiction, or exercise any episcopal functions whatsoever but such as should be limited to him by Letters-Patent, and that it should be lawful for His Majesty by Letters-Patent to grant to such Bishop such ecclesiastical jurisdiction and the exercise of such episcopal functions within the East Indies and parts aforesaid as His Majesty should think it necessary for administering holy ceremonies and for the superintendence and good government of the ministers of the Church Establishment within the East Indies and parts aforesaid. Subsequently, in the year 1833, it was deemed right to found two additional Bishoprics, one at Madras and the other at Bombay, and again an Act of Parliament (3 and 4 Wm. IV, c. 86) was passed, by the 93rd section of which it was enacted in like manner that the Crown should have power to grant to such Bishops within their dioceses ecclesiastical jurisdiction; and it was also enacted and declared that the Bishop of Calcutta should be Metropolitan in India, and should have as such all such jurisdiction as the Crown should by Letters-Patent direct, subject nevertheless to the general superintendence and revision of the Archbishop of Canterbury; and it was provided that the Bishops of Madras and Bombay should be subject to the Bishop of Calcutta as Metropolitan, and should take an oath of canonical obedience to him.

So again when in 1824 a Bishop was appointed in Jamaica by Letters-Patent containing clauses similar to those which are found in the Letters-Patent to the present Appellant, it was thought necessary that the legal status and authority of the Bishop should be confirmed and established by an Act of the Colonial Legislature. The consent of the Crown was given to this Colonial Act, which would have been an improper thing, as an injury to the Crown's prerogative, unless the Law Advisers of the Government had been satisfied that the Colonial Statute was necessary to give full effect to the establishment of the Bishopric.

The conclusion is further confirmed by observing the course of Imperial legislation on the same subject, namely, the creation of new Bishoprics in England.

When four new Bishoprics were constituted by Henry VIII, it appears to have been thought necessary, even by that absolute Monarch, to have recourse to the authority of Parliament, and the Act that was passed (viz. the 31 Henry VIII, cap. 9, which is not found in the ordinary edition) is of a singular character. After referring to the slothful and ungodly life which had been used among all those which bore the name of religious folk, and reciting that it was thought, therefore, unto the King's Highness most expedient and necessary that more Bishoprics, Collegiate and Cathedral Churches, should be established, it was enacted that His Highness should have full power and authority from time to time to declare and nominate by his Letters-Patent or other writing to be made under his Great Seal, such number of Bishops, such number of cities, sees for Bishops, cathedral churches and dioceses by metes and bounds, for the exercise and ministration of their episcopal offices and administration as shall appertain, and to endow them with such possessions after such manner form and condition as to his most excellent wisdom shall be thought necessary and convenient.[7]

This Statute, which was repealed by the 1st and 2nd of Philip and Mary, cap. 8, sec. 18, does not appear to have been revived. It is remarkable as granting power to nominate and appoint new Bishops as well as to create new Sees and dioceses.

So also in recent times the two new Bishoprics of Manchester and Ripon were constituted, and the new Bishops received ecclesiastical jurisdiction, under the authority of an Act of Parliament. It is true that it has been the practice, for many years, to insert in Letters-Patent creating Colonial Bishoprics clauses which purport to confer ecclesiastical jurisdiction; but the forms of such Letters-Patent were probably taken by the official persons who prepared them from the original forms used in the Letters-Patent appointing the East Indian Bishops, without adverting to the fact that such last-mentioned Letters-Patent were granted under the provisions of an Act of Parliament.

We therefore arrive at the conclusion that although in a Crown Colony, properly so called, or in cases where the Letters-Patent are made in pursuance of the authority of an Act of Parliament (such for example as the Act of 6 & 7 Vict., cap. 13), a Bishopric may be constituted and ecclesiastical jurisdiction conferred by the sole authority of the Crown, yet that the Letters-Patent of the Crown will not have any such effect or operation in a Colony or Settlement which is possessed of an independent Legislature.[8]

The subject was considered by the Judicial Committee in the case of Long *v.* the Bishop of Capetown, and we adhere to the principles which are there laid down.

The same reasoning is of course decisive of the second question, whether any jurisdiction was conferred by the Letters-Patent. Let be granted or assumed that the Letters-Patent are sufficient in law to confer on Dr Gray the ecclesiastical status of Metropolitan, and to create between him and the Bishops of Natal and Grahamstown the personal relation of Metropolitan and Suffragan as ecclesiastics, yet it is quite clear that the Crown had no power to confer any jurisdiction or coercive legal authority upon the Metropolitan over the Suffragan Bishops, or over any other person.

It is a settled constitutional principle or rule of law, that although the Crown may by its prerogative establish Courts to proceed according to the Common Law, yet that it cannot create any new Court to administer any other law; and it is laid down by Lord Coke[9] in the 4th Institute that the erection of a new Court with a new jurisdiction cannot be without an Act of Parliament.

It cannot be said that any ecclesiastical tribunal or jurisdiction is required in any Colony or Settlement where there is no Established Church, and in the case of a settled Colony the Ecclesiastical Law of England cannot, for the same reason, be treated as part of the law which the settlers carried with them from the mother country.

So much of the Letters-Patent now in question as attempts to confer any coercive legal jurisdiction is also in violation of the law as declared and established by that part of the Act of the 16 Car. I, c. 11, which remains unrepealed by the 13 Car. II, st. 2, c. 12. It may be useful to state this in detail. By the 16th and 17th sections of the I Eliz., c. 1, entitled "An Act for restoring to the Crown the ancient jurisdiction over the State Ecclesiastical and Spiritual, and abolishing all Foreign Power repugnant to the same", it was enacted that all usurped and foreign power and authority, spiritual and temporal, should for ever be extinguished within the realm, and that such jurisdictions, privileges, superiorities, and pre-eminences, spiritual and ecclesiastical, as by any spiritual or ecclesiastical power or authority had theretofore been or might lawfully be exercised or used for the visitation of the ecclesiastical state and persons, and for reformation, order, and correction of the same, and of all manner of heresies, schisms, abuses, offences, contempts, and enormities, should for ever be united and annexed to the Imperial Crown of this realm. And by the 18th section the Queen was empowered by Letters-Patent to appoint persons to exercise, occupy, use, and execute all manner of spiritual or ecclesiastical jurisdiction within the realms of England and Ireland, or any other the dominions and countries of the Crown.

Under this Statute the High Commission Court was erected, which was abolished by the 16 Car. I, c. 10.

By the Act of the 16 Car. I, c. 11, the 18th section of the 1 Eliz., c. 1, was wholly repealed, and by the 4th section of the same Statute all spiritual and ecclesiastical persons or judges were forbidden under severe penalties to exercise any jurisdiction or coercive legal authority, an enactment which closed all the regular established ecclesiastical tribunals; but by the 13 Car. II, c. 12, the ordinary ecclesiastical jurisdiction and authority, as it existed before the year 1639, was with certain savings restored to the Archbishops and Bishops; and the Act of the 16 Car. I excepting what concerned the High Commission Court or the erection of any such like Court by Commission, was repealed, but with a proviso that nothing should extend or be construed to revive or give force to the enactments contained in the 18th section of the I Eliz., c. 1, which should remain and stand repealed.

There is therefore no power in the Crown to create any new or additional ecclesiastical tribunal or jurisdiction, and the clauses which purport to do so, contained in the Letters-Patent to the Appellant and Respondent, are simply void in law. No Metropolitan or Bishop in any Colony having legislative institutions can, by virtue of the Crown's Letters-Patent alone, (unless granted under an Act of Parliament, or confirmed by a Colonial Statute), exercise any coercive jurisdiction, or hold any Court or Tribunal for that purpose.

Pastoral or spiritual authority may be incidental to the office of Bishop, but all jurisdiction in the Church, where it can be lawfully conferred, must proceed from the Crown, and be exercised as the law directs, and suspension or privation of office is a matter of coercive legal jurisdiction, and not of mere spiritual authority.

If, then, the Bishop of Capetown had no jurisdiction by law, did he obtain any by contract or submission on the part of the Bishop of Natal?

There is nothing on which such an argument can be attempted to be put, unless it be the oath of canonical obedience, taken by the Bishop of Natal to Dr Gray as Metropolitan.

The argument must be, that both parties being aware that the

Bishop of Capetown had no jurisdiction or legal authority as Metropolitan, the Appellant agreed to give it to him by voluntary submission.

But even if the parties intended to enter into any such agreement (of which, however, we find no trace), it was not legally competent to the Bishop of Natal to give, or to the Bishop of Capetown to accept or exercise, any such jurisdiction.

There remains one point to be considered. It was contended before us that if the Bishop of Capetown had no jurisdiction, his judgment was a nullity, and that no appeal could lie from a nullity to Her Majesty in Council.

But that is by no means the consequence of holding that the Respondent had no jurisdiction. The Bishop of Capetown, acting under the authority which the Queen's Letters-Patent purported to give, asserts that he has held a Court of Justice, and that with certain legal forms he has pronounced a judicial sentence, and that by such sentence he has deposed the Bishop of Natal from his office of Bishop and deprived him of his see. He also asserts that the sentence having been published in the Diocese of Natal, the clergy and inhabitants of that diocese are thereby deprived of all Episcopal superintendence. Whether these proceedings have the effect which is attributed to them by the Bishop of Capetown is a question of the greatest importance, and one which we feel bound to decide. We have already shown there was no power to confer any jurisdiction on the Respondent as Metropolitan. The attempt to give Appellate jurisdiction to the Archbishop of Canterbury is equally invalid.

This important question can be decided only by the Sovereign as Head of the Established Church and depositary of the ultimate Appellate jurisdiction.

Before the Reformation, in a dispute of this nature between two independent prelates, an appeal would have lain to the Pope; but all Appellate authority of the Pope over members of the Established Church is by Statute vested in the Crown.

It is the settled prerogative of the Crown to receive Appeals in all colonial causes, and by the 25 Henry VIII, c. 19 (by which the mode of the Appeal to the Crown in Ecclesiastical Causes is directed) it is by the 4th section enacted that "for lack of justice at or in any of the Courts of the Archbishops of this realm, *or in any of the King's dominions*, it shall be lawful to the parties grieved to appeal to the King's Majesty in the Court of Chancery", an enactment which gave rise to the Commission of Delegates, for which this Tribunal is now substituted.

Unless a controversy, such as that which is presented by this Appeal and Petition, fails to be determined by the ultimate jurisdiction of the Crown, it is plain that there would be a denial of justice, and no remedy for great public inconvenience and mischief. It is right to add, although unnecessary, that by the Act 3 and 4 Wm. IV, cap 41, which constituted this Tribunal,[10] Her Majesty has power to refer to the Judicial Committee for hearing or consideration any such matters whatsoever as Her Majesty shall think fit, and this Committee is thereupon to hear or consider the same, and to advise Her Majesty thereon: and that on the 10th June, 1864, it was ordered by Her Majesty in Council that the Petition and Supplemental Petition of the Appellant should be, and the same were, thereby referred to this Committee, to hear the same and report their opinion thereupon to Her Majesty.

Their Lordships therefore will humbly report to Her Majesty their judgment and opinion that the proceedings taken by the Bishop of Capetown, and the judgment or sentence pronounced by him against the Bishop of Natal, are null and void in law.[11]

1 Lushington, Dean of Arches.

2 Colenso, John William; *b.* 1814; *educ.*, St John's College, Cambridge, 2nd Wrangler, 1836; Fellow, 1837; mathematics master at Harrow, 1839; tutor at St John's College, 1842; vicar of Forncett St Mary, Norfolk, 1846; first Bishop of Natal, 1853; revisited England, 1874; *d.* 1883.

3 Gray, Robert, son of Bishop of Bristol; *b.* 1809; *educ.*, Eton and University College, Oxford; ordained 1832; Bishop of Cape Town, 1847; resigned and reappointed, 1853; *d.* 1872.

4 The Judicial Committee was not acting as an ecclesiastical court of appeal in this instance, but was concerned only with the legal constitution of the South African colonies.

5 Under the provisions of 25 Hen. VIII, c. 20, the cathedral chapters receive a licence to elect with a letter missive containing the name of the person they are to elect. After a delay of more than twelve days the Crown appoints by Letters-Patent. As in the case of colonial bishops, where there was no chapter, the Crown appointed directly by Letters-Patent.

6 Colenso had published text-books on arithmetic and algebra and *Ten Weeks in Natal* (1854). The two works which created the storms were: *Preface to "The Pentateuch and Book of Joshua Critically Examined"* (1862–79), and a *Commentary on the Epistle to the Romans* (1861). Both attacked the accepted tenets of the day: the first, the historicity of the Bible, and the second, the doctrine of eternal punishment.

7 In fact, six new diocese were created: Westminster, Bristol, Chester, Gloucester, Oxford, and Peterborough. Westminster diocese was suppressed in 1550.

8 The series of legal decisions involving the colonial Churches brought about a situation described as follows: "The established Church of England cannot exist outside England; therefore bishops in colonies with their own legislatures are bishops without jurisdiction; their authority must rest upon contract or agreement; yet they are capable of holding property in the name of the Church of England and cannot be removed from office; therefore there is a sense in which the Church of England can exist outside England; but a Church which rests its authority entirely on contract and refuses to be bound by the court of appeal of the established Church is not the Church of England, though its bishops are still bishops" Peter Hinchliff, *The One-Sided Reciprocity*, p. 190).

9 Sir Edward Coke (1552–1634); Chief Justice of the Common Pleas in 1606; of the King's Bench in 1613. The *Institutes* (1628–1644), recast, explained, and defended the common law rules.

10 Acts quoted are:
53 Geo. III, c. 155. East India Company Act.
3-4 Will. IV, c. 85 (?) Government of India Act.
31 Hen. VIII, c. 9.
1-2 Philip and Mary, c. 8. 2nd Act of Repeal.
6-7 Vict. c. 13. Settlements on the coast of Africa and the Falkland Islands.
16 Charles I, c. 11, Abolition of the Court of High Commission.
13 Charles II, c. 12, On Ecclesiastical Jurisdiction.
1 Elizabeth, c. 1. Act of Supremacy.
3-4 William IV, c. 41, Judicial Committee of the Privy Council.

11 The Colenso judgment confirmed the judgment in the Long appeal. William Long had refused to obey the summons to Gray's first diocesan synod in 1856. The Attorney General of the colony ruled that there was no legal reason why the clergy should not meet in synod, whereupon Long made a brief appearance. In 1861 Long again disobeyed the summons and Gray cited him to appear before the diocesan tribunal for contumacy. Long was ultimately removed from office, and in dismissing his appeal, the Chief Justice maintained that in accepting a licence from Gray, Long had virtually promised obedience to his bishop. Long appealed to the Privy Council which delivered judgment in June 1863, reversing the Chief Justice's decision.

41 COLENSO AND THE LAMBETH CONFERENCE, 1867

(Davidson, *Five Lambeth Conferences*, pp. 73-5, 55)

Colenso was solemnly excommunicated in 1866, but his immunity from disciplinary action led to the discussion of his orthodoxy at the first Lambeth Conference.[1] The original council was proposed to define orthodoxy as a result of the *Essays and Reviews* controversy and the Colenso affair.

REPORT OF THE COMMITTEE APPOINTED UNDER RESOLUTION VI

By the Resolution of the Lambeth Conference two questions were referred to the Committee:

I How may the Church be delivered from a continuance of the scandal now existing in Natal?
II How may the true faith be maintained?

I On the first question, the Committee recommend that an Address be made to the Colonial Bishoprics Council, calling their attention to the fact that they are paying an annual stipend to a Bishop lying under the imputation of heretical teaching, and praying them to take the best legal opinion as to there being any, and if so what, mode of laying these allegations before some competent court, and if any mode be pointed out, then to proceed accordingly for the removal of this scandal.

The Committee also recommend that the Address to the Colonial Bishoprics Council be prefaced with the following statement:

That, whilst we accept the spiritual validity of the sentence of deposition pronounced by the Metropolitan and Bishops of the South African Church upon Dr Colenso, we consider it of the utmost moment for removing the existing scandal from the English Communion that there should be pronounced by some competent English court such a legal sentence on the errors of the said Dr Colenso as would warrant the Colonial Bishoprics Council in ceasing to pay his stipend, and would justify an appeal to the Crown to cancel his Letters Patent.[2]

II On the second question: "How may the true faith be maintained in Natal?" The Committee submit the following Report:

That they did not consider themselves instructed by the Conference, and therefore did not consider themselves competent, to inquire into the whole case; but that their conclusions are based upon the following facts:

1. That in the year 1863, forty-one Bishops concurred in an Address to Bishop Colenso, urging him to resign his Bishopric.

2. That in the year 1863, some of the Publications of Dr Colenso, viz., *The Pentateuch and Book of Joshua Critically Examined*, Parts I and II, were condemned by the Convocation of the Province of Canterbury.

3. That the Bishop of Capetown, by virtue of his Letters Patent as Metropolitan, might have visited Dr Colenso with summary jurisdiction, and might have taken out of his hands the management of the Diocese of Natal.

4. That the Bishop of Capetown, instead of proceeding summarily, instituted judicial proceedings, having reason to believe himself to be competent to do so.

   That he summoned Dr Colenso before himself and suffragans.
   That Dr Colenso appeared by his proctor.
   That his defence was heard and judged to be insufficient to purge him from the heresy.
   That, after sentence was pronounced, Dr Colenso was offered an appeal to the Archbishop of Canterbury, as provided in the Metropolitan's Letters Patent.[3]

5. That this Act of the African Church was approved

   By the Convocation of Canterbury;
   By the Convocation of York;
   By the General Convention of the Episcopal Church in the United States, in 1865;
   By the Episcopal Synod of the Church in Scotland;
   By the Provincial Synod of the Church in Canada, in the year 1865.

And, finally, the spiritual validity of the sentence of deposition was accepted by *fifty-six* Bishops on the occasion of the Lambeth Conference.

Judging, therefore, that the See is spiritually vacant; and learning, by the evidence brought before them, that there are many members of the Church who are unable to accept the ministrations of Dr Colenso, the Committee deem it to be the duty of the Metropolitan and other Bishops of South Africa to proceed, upon the election of the Clergy and Laity in Natal, to consecrate one to discharge those spiritual functions of which these members of the Church are now in want.

In forwarding their Report to his Grace the Lord Archbishop of Canterbury, as instructed by the Resolution of the Conference, the Committee request his Grace to communicate the same to the adjourned meeting of the Conference, to be holden at Lambeth on the tenth day of the present month.

G.A., NEW ZEALAND, *Convener*[4]

RESOLUTION VII OF THE LAMBETH CONFERENCE

That we who are here present do acquiesce in the Resolution of the Convocation of Canterbury, passed on June 29th, 1866, relating to the Diocese of Natal, to wit:

If it be decided that a new Bishop should be consecrated: As to the proper steps to be taken by the members of the Church in the province of Natal for obtaining a new Bishop, it is the opinion of this House—*first*, that a formal instrument, declaratory of the doctrine and discipline of the Church of South Africa should be prepared, which every Bishop, Priest and Deacon to be appointed to office should be required to subscribe; *secondly*, that a godly and well-learned man should be chosen by the clergy, with the assent of the lay-communicants of the Church, and *thirdly*, that he should be presented for consecration, either to the Archbishop of Canterbury—if the aforesaid instrument should declare the doctrine and discipline of Christ as received by the United Church of England and Ireland—or to the Bishops of the Church of South Africa, according as hereafter may be judged to be most advisable and convenient.[5]

1 The Romilly judgment, 1866, confirmed Colenso in the temporal rights of his see.

2 There were two distinct issues in the Colenso affair: the theological and the constitutional. Pusey pointed out to Tait: "It is his office of Bishop which propagates infidelity. Unbounded toleration to the laity is very different from allowing Bishops and Priests to teach publicly grave errors, destructive of all faith." Colenso's errors fell into three groups: firstly, his toleration of native practices, notably polygamy among kaffir converts; secondly, his treatment of the atonement, everlasting punishment, and the sacraments; thirdly, the scepticism he entertained of the historical trustworthiness of the Pentateuch and Book of Joshua. That his writings arose out of a

pastoral situation is support for the suggestion that he was the greatest missionary of his day, reconciling traditional theology with native culture.

3 Dean Stanley said of Colenso in 1881: "The Bishop of Natal is the one colonial bishop who has translated the Bible into the language of the natives of his diocese. He is the one colonial bishop who, when he believed a native to be wronged, left his diocese, journeyed to London, and never rested till he had procured the reversal of that wrong. He is the one colonial bishop who, as soon as he had done this, returned immediately to his diocese and his work. For these acts he has never received any praise, any encouragement, from this, the oldest of our missionary societies (S.P.G.). For these deeds he will be remembered when you who censure him are dead, buried, and forgotten" (*Life of Dean Stanley*, 2, p. 295).

4 Selwyn, George Augustus; *b.* 1809; *educ.*, Eton and St John's College, Cambridge; deacon, 1833; Bishop in New Zealand (A Tractarian by conviction, he protested against the Erastian implications of his letters-patent), 1841; returned to England, 1867; Bishop of Lichfield, 1868; *d.* 1878.

5 W. J. Butler, vicar of Wantage, was elected by the clergy and laity in 1866, but later withdrew his acceptance of the see. W. K. Macrorie, vicar of Accrington, was chosen in 1868, and finally consecrated Bishop of Pieter Maritzburg in January 1869. In September 1893, A. Hamilton Baynes was consecrated Bishop of Natal, being nominated by Archbishop Benson.

42 THE FIRST LAMBETH CONFERENCE, 1867

(Davidson, *The Five Lambeth Conferences*, pp. 5-7)

The overseas extension of the Church of England led ultimately to the creation of new provinces. It was natural that the new provinces and dioceses should turn to the English Church for leadership. Thus the Provincial Synod of the Canadian Church, in September 1865, unanimously advocated a "General Council of her members gathered from every land", under the auspices of the Archbishop of Canterbury and his province. The Convocation of Canterbury appointed a Committee in May 1866, and Longley[1] issued the following invitation in February 1867.

February 22nd, 1867.
Lambeth Palace,

Right Rev. and Dear Brother, I request your presence at a meeting of the Bishops in visible communion with the United Church of England and Ireland, purposed (GOD willing) to be holden at Lambeth, under my presidency, on the 24th of September next and the three following days.

The circumstances under which I have resolved to issue the present invitation are these: The Metropolitan and Bishops of Canada, last year, addressed to the two Houses of the Convocation of Canterbury the expression of their desire that I should be moved to invite the Bishops of our Indian and Colonial Episcopate to meet myself and the Home Bishops for brotherly communion and conference.

The consequence of that appeal has been that both Houses of the Convocation of my province have addressed to me their dutiful request that I would invite the attendance, not only of our Home and Colonial Bishops, but of all who are avowedly in communion with our Church. The same request was unanimously preferred to me at a numerous gathering of English, Irish, and Colonial Archbishops and Bishops recently assembled at Lambeth; at which—I rejoice to record it—we had the counsel and concurrence of an eminent Bishop of the Church in the United States of America—the Bishop of Illinois.

Moved by these requests, and by the expressed concurrence therein of other members both of the Home and Colonial Episcopate, who could not be present at our meeting, I have now resolved —not, I humbly trust, without the guidance of GOD the Holy Ghost—to grant this grave request, and call together the meeting thus earnestly desired. I greatly hope that you may be able to attend it, and to aid us with your presence and brotherly counsel thereat.

I propose that, at our assembling, we should first solemnly seek the blessing of Almighty GOD on our gathering, by uniting together in the highest act of the Church's worship.[2] After this, brotherly consultations will follow. In these we may consider together many practical questions, the settlement of which would tend to the advancement of the Kingdom of our Lord and Master Jesus Christ, and to the maintenance of greater union in our missionary work, and to increased intercommunion among ourselves.[3]

Such a meeting would not be competent to make declarations or lay down definitions on points of doctrine. But united worship and common counsels would greatly tend to maintain practically the unity of the faith: whilst they would bind us in straiter bonds of peace and brotherly charity.

I shall gladly receive from you a list of any subjects you may wish to suggest to me for consideration and discussion. Should you be unable to attend, and desire to commission any brother Bishop to speak for you, I shall welcome him as your representative in our united deliberations.

But I must once more express my earnest hope that, on this solemn occasion, I may have the great advantage of your personal presence.

And now I commend this proposed meeting to your fervent prayers; and, humbly beseeching the blessing of Almighty GOD on yourself and your diocese, I subscribe myself,

Your faithful brother in the Lord,

C. T. CANTUAR:[4]

1 Longley, Charles Thomas; *b.* 1794; *educ.*, Christ Church, Oxford; taught at Christ Church; Headmaster of Harrow, 1829; first Bishop of Ripon, 1836; Bishop of Durham, 1856; Archbishop of York, 1860; permitted the Convocation of York to meet, 1861; Archbishop of Canterbury, 1862; *d.* 1868.

2 The bishops requested that a service be held in Westminster Abbey, but Dean Stanley was opposed to the idea on several grounds. The concluding service was held in Lambeth Parish Church on Friday 27 September.

3 The three-day conference began on 24 September in the Guard Room of Lambeth Palace. Although the agreed subjects were: Intercommunion between the Churches of the Anglican Communion; the Colonial Churches; and co-operation in Missionary action, the Colenso controversy dominated the later proceedings.

4 The number of bishops present were: 1867, 76; 1878, 100; 1888, 145; 1897, 194; 1908, 242; 1920, 252; 1930, 307; 1948, 329. The English Bishops who, in 1867, were absent on principle were: York (Thomson), Carlisle (Waldegrave), Durham (Baring), Ripon (Bickersteth), Peterborough (Jeune), and Manchester (Prince Lee).

43 THE CLERICAL SUBSCRIPTION ACT 1865

(*Statutes at Large*, 28-29 Vict., c. 122)

The Tractarian movement, German liberalism,[1] and the growing difficulty of reconciling the individual conscience with the recent decisions of the Judicial Committee of the Privy Council, made clerical subscription a pressing issue. It was estimated that each man ordained to a curacy made ten declarations, and an additional four when instituted to a benefice. A Royal Commission, of twenty-seven members, eleven of whom were laymen, unanimously recommended that subscription be reduced to a simpler form. As it was necessary to amend the 36th Canon of 1604, Convocation obtained the necessary leave from the Crown to formulate the alterations.

The following Declaration is hereinafter referred to as the "Declaration of Assent".

I A.B. do solemnly make the following Declaration: I assent to the Thirty-nine Articles of Religion, and to the Book of Common Prayer and of the ordering of Bishops, Priests, and Deacons. I believe the Doctrine of the United Church of England and Ireland, as therein set forth, to be agreeable to the Word of God; and in Public Prayer and Administration of the Sacraments I will use the form in the said Book prescribed, and none other, except so far as shall be ordered by lawful Authority.[2]

4 Every Person about to be ordained Priest or Deacon shall, before Ordination, in the Presence of the Archbishop or Bishop by whom he is about to be ordained, at such Time as he may appoint, make and subscribe the Declaration of Assent, and take and subscribe the Oath of Allegiance and Supremacy according to the Form set forth in the Act of the Session of the Twenty-first and Twenty-second Years of the Reign of Her present Majesty, Chapter Forty-eight.[3]

5 Every Person about to be instituted or collated to any Benefice, or to be licensed to any Perpetual Curacy, Lectureship, or Preachership, shall, before Institution or Collation is made or Licence granted, make and subscribe the Declaration of Assent, and the Declaration against Simony, and take the said Oath of Allegiance[4] and Supremacy, in the Presence of the Archbishop or Bishop by whom he is to be instituted, collated, or licensed, or the Commissary of such Archbishop or Bishop.

7 Every Person instituted or collated to any Benefice with Cure

of Souls, or licensed to a Perpetual Curacy, shall, on the first Lord's Day on which he officiates in the Church of such Benefice or Perpetual Curacy, or on such other Lord's Day as the Ordinary may appoint and allow, publicly and openly, in the Presence of the Congregation there assembled, read the Thirty-nine Articles of Religion, and immediately after reading the same make the said Declaration of Assent, adding, after the words "Articles of Religion", in the said Declaration, the Words "which I have now read before you" ...

10 On all Occasions other than those hereinbefore provided for, on which any Declaration or Subscription with respect to the Thirty-nine Articles or the Book of Common Prayer or the Liturgy is required to be made by any Person in Holy Orders appointed to any Ecclesiastical Dignity, Benefice, or Office, the making and subscribing the Declaration of Assent shall be substituted for the making of any such Declaration or Subscription as aforesaid; and on all Occasions other than those hereinbefore provided, on which any Oath against Simony is required to be taken, the making and subscribing the Declaration against Simony shall be substituted for the taking such Oath.

12 Nothing in this Act contained shall extend to or affect the Oath of canonical Obedience to the Bishop, or the Oath of due Obedience to the Archbishop taken by Bishops on Consecration.

1 The disruptive influence of liberalism was beginning to make itself felt within the Church as a whole, though Newman and the Tractarians had earlier opposed its tendencies. Herbert Marsh had published *The History of Sacred Criticism* in 1809; Pusey wrote to Bishop Maltby in June 1833 on German liberalism (*Theology,* vol. LXI, no. 451, January 1958); and George Eliot had issued her translation of F. D. Strauss' *Leben Jesu* in 1846.

2 Assent replaced formal subscription, but it was not made clear in the Act precisely what assent involved. In a debate in the Lords in 1840, Bishop Stanley spoke of the Church of England as having "a sort of elasticity" which allowed a latitude of interpretation of its articles. It is noteworthy that the previous formula demanding the acknowledgement of "all and every the articles ... being in number nine and thirty" was omitted.

3 21-22 Vict., c. 48. Oath of Allegiance Act, 1858.

4 The Oath of Allegiance replaced the acknowledgement of the sovereign as Supreme Governor which had been required by Canon 36 of 1604. The canon was amended in 1865, the oath being enjoined by the Act of 1868 (31-32 Vict., c. 72), the Promissory Oaths Act.

44 RITUAL PROSECUTION, 1868

(*Six Judgments*, pp. 112-13, 119, 129-30, 160)

In his evidence before the Royal Commission on Ecclesiastical Discipline, Archbishop Davidson spoke of the ritual strife which characterized the period 1866–92, and the formation of church parties for contentious purposes. The Church Association, founded in 1865, maintained the Protestant faith and practice of the Church of England, and between 1865 and 1892 furnished funds for litigation against ritualist clergy. The prosecution of Mackonochie continued from 1867 to 1880 and was undertaken primarily to obtain a decision on disputed points of law.

The case of *Martin* v. *Mackonochie*,[1] commenced before the Bishop of *London*,[2] was under the provisions of the *Clergy Discipline Act*, sent by the Bishop to the Court of the Archbishop of *Canterbury* for trial in the first instance; and, having been fully heard before the Judge of the Arches Court,[3] resulted in a decree made on March 28, 1868.

Mr *Mackonochie*, the Clerk in Holy Orders against whom these proceedings were directed, was charged with four offences against the Laws Ecclesiastical, viz.

First. The elevation during, or after, the Prayer of Consecration, in the Order of the Administration of the Holy Communion, of the Paten and Cup, and the kneeling or prostrating himself before the Consecrated Elements.

Second. Using lighted candles on the Communion Table during the celebration of the Holy Communion, when such candles were not wanted for the purpose of giving light.

Third. Using incense in the celebration of the Holy Communion.

Fourth. Mixing water with the wine used in the administration of the Holy Communion.

The learned Judge of the Arches Court, by his decree, sustained the third and fourth of these charges and admonished Mr *Mackonochie* to abstain for the future from the use of incense, and from mixing water with wine, as pleaded in the Articles. Against this part of the decree there is no appeal.

The second charge, as to lights, was not sustained, the learned Judge holding that it was lawful to place two lighted candles on the Communion Table during the time of the Holy Communion.[4]

Against this the Promoter has appealed.

As to the first charge, Mr *Mackonochie*, while admitting the elevation of the Consecrated Elements at the times and in the manner alleged, pleaded that he had discontinued the practice before the institution of the suit. The learned Judge, therefore, admonished Mr *Mackonochie* not to recur to the practice; but as to the other part of the charge, namely, the kneeling and prostrating himself before the Consecrated Elements, the learned Judge held that if Mr *Mackonochie* had committed any error in that respect, it was one which should not form the subject of a criminal prosecution, but should be referred to the Bishop, in order that he might exercise his discretion thereon.

The Promoter appeals from the latter part of the decision of the learned Judge in this charge, and he also complains in his Appeal that the Defendant was not ordered to pay the costs of the suit.[5] . . .

. . . Their Lordships are of opinion that it is not open to a Minister of the Church, or even to their Lordships in advising her Majesty, as the highest Ecclesiastical Tribunal of Appeal, to draw a distinction in acts which are a departure from, or a violation of, the Rubric, between those which are important and those which appear to be trivial. The object of a Statute of Uniformity is, as its preamble expresses, to produce "an universal agreement in the public worship of Almighty God", an object which would be wholly frustrated if each Minister, on his own view of the relative importance of the details of the Service, were to be at liberty to omit, to add to, or alter any of those details.[6] . . .

. . . By an Order of her Majesty in Council made thereon it was ordered that the decree of the Court below ought to be amended to the extent hereinafter mentioned, the principal cause retained, and therein that, in addition to the matters in which the said *Alexander Heriot Mackonochie* was in the decree appealed from pronounced to have offended, and from which he was thereby monished to abstain for the future, he, the said *Alexander Heriot Mackonochie*, ought to be pronounced to have offended against the Statutes, Laws, Constitutions, and Canons of the Church of *England* by having within the said Church of the new parish of *St Alban's, Holborn*, knelt, or prostrated himself, before the Consecrated Elements during the Prayer of Consecration, and also by having within the said Church used lighted candles on the Communion Table during the celebration of the Holy Communion, at times when such lighted candles were not wanted for the purpose of giving light; and that the said *Alexander Heriot Mackonochie* ought to be admonished to abstain for the future from kneeling, or prostrating himself, before the Consecrated Elements during the Prayer of Consecration, and also from using in the said Church lighted candles on the Communion Table during the celebration of the Holy Communion, at times when such lighted candles were not wanted for the purpose of giving light; and further, that he, the said *Alexander Heriot Mackonochie*, ought to be condemned in the costs incurred on behalf of the said *John Martin*, as well in the Court below as in the Appeal....

The following Order, dated November 25, 1870, was drawn up and issued in pursuance of their Lordships' judgment:

The Lords of the Committee, having maturely deliberated, pronounced that the Reverend *Alexander Heriot Mackonochie*, Clerk, Incumbent, and Perpetual Curate of the new Parish of *Saint Alban's, Holborn*, in the County of *Middlesex*, Diocese of *London*, and Province of *Canterbury*, the Respondent, had not obeyed the Monition, which had been duly served upon him, bearing date January 19, 1869, more especially in not having abstained from the elevation of the Paten during the Prayer of Consecration in the Order of the Administration of the Holy Communion, and from prostrating himself before the Consecrated Elements during the Prayer of Consecration, and their Lordships accordingly ordered that for such his disobedience he, the said Reverend *Alexander Heriot Mackonochie*, be suspended for the space of three months,[7] from and after this day, from the discharge and execution of all the functions of his clerical office—that is to say, from preaching the Word of God, and administering the Sacraments, and performing all other duties of such his clerical office—and their Lordships directed that a Decree of Suspension be issued, suspending him accordingly, and that the same be published by affixing a copy thereof on or near the door of the Church of the said new Parish of *St Alban's*, on Sunday next, November 27, 1870, as also by personally serving it upon the said Reverend *Alexander Heriot Mackonochie*. Their Lordships did further condemn the said Reverend *Alexander Heriot Mackonochie* in the costs incurred by the Appellant in these proceedings.

1 Mackonochie, Alexander Heriot; *b.* 1825; *educ.*, Wadham College, Oxford; B.A. 1848; ordained, 1849; served under W. J. Butler at Wantage, 1852–8; served under C. F. Lowder at St George's-in-the-East, 1858–62; vicar of St Alban's, Holborn, 1862; resigned, 1882; *d.* 1887.

2 Tait, Archibald Campbell; *b.* 1811; *educ.*, Glasgow University, 1827–30; Balliol College, Oxford, 1830; B.A. 1833; Fellow, 1834; tutor, 1835; ordained, 1836; Headmaster of Rugby, 1842; Dean of Carlisle, 1849; Bishop of London, 1856; Archbishop of Canterbury, 1868; *d.* 1882.

3 The case was sent by Letters of Request to the Court of Arches, and heard in December 1867 before Sir Robert Phillimore, the newly appointed Dean of Arches. His judgment was delivered in March 1868.

4 As in all ritual suits, judgments were based on the historical evidence marshalled together by advocates and judges. Phillimore noted, for example, in regard to the second charge, "In 1552, between two and three years after the date of the First Prayer Book, there were in twenty-one counties 1400 churches which possessed each two candlesticks."

5 The payments of costs in these suits was a crushing burden on such clergy as were imprisoned or suspended *ab officio et beneficio.* These costs included the fees for the detection and reporting of the illegalities to the Church Association, besides the usual costs of the legal proceedings. See E. A. Towle, *A. H. Mackonochie: A Memoir* (1890). The recourse to the law courts ultimately weakened support by leading Evangelicals for the Association and its policy.

6 The policy of prosecuting the ritualists was based on a misconception of the nature of ecclesiastical law as a coercive instrument instead of a guiding principle. The confusion of ecclesiastical law with statutory law during this period was largely the cause of this wrong emphasis. The true nature of church law is illustrated by Bishop Gibson's observation of this judgment in the *Appendix* to the *Report* of the Royal Commission on Ecclesiastical Discipline (1906):

"But as a matter of history at all periods practices not enjoined in, and omissions from the requirements of the rubrics have been common, being often not merely acquiesced in, but even approved and sanctioned by Episcopal authority; while every attempt to enforce the strict letter of the law by coercive measures has proved disastrous, and led to a schism in the Church, 'conscience' in each case being pleaded by the recalcitrant party" (iv, pp. 49-57).

Phillimore's judgment on the first charge showed a far greater appreciation of the nature of church law than the judgment of the law lords.

7 In suspending Mackonochie for three months the Appeal Court assumed the power to inflict a purely spiritual penalty of suspension *ab officio et beneficio.* It is noteworthy that the Public Worship Regulation Act (1874) provided for the eventuality of imprisonment for contempt of court.

45 THE IRISH CHURCH ACT 1869

(*Statutes at Large*, 32-33 Vict., c. 42)

Gladstone attempted to settle the Irish question with the Irish Church Act, the Land Act (1881) and the Arrears Act (1882). The passage of this Bill through Parliament was stormy and protracted. It produced a constitutional crisis involving the Queen, for the Lords introduced amendments seeking to improve the financial terms for the Irish Church. It was widely felt that the Bill was a prelude to a general attack on the English Church. The Provincial Synods of the Provinces of Armagh and Dublin resolved in September 1869: "That this Synod deems it its duty to place on record a declaration that it is now called upon not to originate a Constitution for a new Communion, but to repair a sudden breach in one of the most ancient Churches in Christendom."

Whereas it is expedient that the union created by Act of Parliament between the Churches of England and Ireland, as by law established, should be dissolved,[1] and that the Church of Ireland, as so separated, should cease to be established by law, and that after satisfying, so far as possible, upon principles of equality as between the several religious denominations in Ireland, all just and equitable claims, the property of the said Church of Ireland, or the proceeds thereof, should be applied in such manner as Parliament shall hereafter direct[2]:

And whereas Her Majesty has been graciously pleased to signify that she has placed at the disposal of Parliament her interest in the several archbishoprics, bishoprics, benefices, cathedral preferments, and other ecclesiastical dignities and offices in Ireland:

Be it therefore enacted by the Queen's most Excellent Majesty, by and with the advice and consent of the Lords Spiritual and Temporal, and Commons, in this present Parliament assembled, and by the authority of the same, as follows:

2 On and after the first day of January one thousand eight hundred and seventy-one the said union created by Act of Parliament between the Churches of England and Ireland shall be dissolved, and the said Church of Ireland, hereinafter referred to as "the said Church", shall cease to be established by Law.

10 Save as hereinafter mentioned, no person shall, after the passing of this Act, be appointed by Her Majesty or any other person or corporation by virtue of any right of patronage or power

of appointment now existing to any archbishopric, bishopric, benefice, or cathedral preferment in or connected with the said Church.[3]

11 From and after the passing of this Act all property, real and personal, at the date of such passing vested in or belonging to the Ecclesiastical Commissioners for Ireland, is transferred to and vested in the Commissioners appointed under this Act, subject to all tenancies, charges, incumbrances, rights (including tenants rights of renewal), or liabilities affecting the same, and the corporation of the Ecclesiastical Commissioners for Ireland is hereby dissolved.[4]

13 On the said first of January one thousand eight hundred and seventy-one every ecclesiastical corporation in Ireland, whether sole or aggregate, and every cathedral corporation in Ireland, as defined by this Act, shall be dissolved, and on and after that day no archbishop or bishop of the said Church shall be summoned to or be qualified to sit in the House of Lords as such; provided that every present archbishop, bishop, dean, and archdeacon of the said Church shall during his life enjoy the same title and precedence as if this Act had not passed.

19 From and after the passing of this Act there shall be repealed and determined any Act of Parliament, law, or custom whereby the archbishops, bishops, clergy, or laity of the said Church are prohibited from holding assemblies, synods, or conventions, or electing representatives thereto, for the purpose of making rules for the well-being and ordering of the said Church; and nothing in any Act, law, or custom shall prevent the bishops, the clergy, and laity of the said Church, by such representatives, lay and clerical, and to be elected as they the said bishops, clergy, and laity shall appoint, from meeting in general synod or convention, and in such synod or convention framing constitutions and regulations for the general management and good government of the said Church, and property and affairs thereof, and the future representation of the members thereof in diocesan synods, general convention, or otherwise.[5]

21 On and after the first day of January one thousand eight hundred and seventy-one all jurisdiction, whether contentious or otherwise, of all the ecclesiastical, peculiar, exempt, and other courts and persons in Ireland at the time of the passing of this Act having any jurisdiction whatsoever exerciseable in any cause, suit, or matter, matrimonial, spiritual, or ecclesiastical, or in any way connected with or arising out of the ecclesiastical law

of Ireland, shall cease; and on and after the said first day of January one thousand eight hundred and seventy-one the Act of the session of the twenty-seventh and twenty-eighth years of the reign of Her present Majesty, chapter fifty-four,[6] shall be repealed, and on and after the last-mentioned day the ecclesiastical law of Ireland, except in so far as relates to matrimonial causes and matters, shall cease to exist as law.

22 If at any time it be shown to the satisfaction of Her Majesty that the bishops, clergy, and laity of the said Church in Ireland, or the persons who, for the time being, may succeed to the exercise and discharge of the episcopal functions of such bishops, and the clergy and laity in communion with such persons, have appointed any persons or body to represent the said Church, and to hold property for any of the uses or purposes thereof, it shall be lawful for Her Majesty by charter to incorporate such body, with power, notwithstanding the statutes of mortmain, to hold lands to such extent as is in this Act provided, but not further or otherwise.[7]

68 And whereas it is further expedient that the proceeds of the said property should be appropriated mainly to the relief of unavoidable calamity and suffering, yet not so as to cancel or impair the obligations now attached to property under the Acts for the relief of the poor: Be it further enacted, that the said proceeds shall be so applied accordingly in the manner Parliament shall hereafter direct.[8]

1 The Act of Union, 1 January 1801, was intended to secure Catholic Emancipation, but owing to the opposition of George III, it had the reverse effect.

2 The conflict raged around the precise wording of the Preamble, especially in regard to the property of the Irish Church. It was to have read "not for the maintenance of any church or clergy, nor for the teaching of religion, but mainly for the relief of unavoidable calamity and suffering". It was so altered as to permit the surplus to be devoted to concurrent endowment instead of secular purposes. The *Regium Donum* and Maynooth grant also ceased under the Act.

3 The bishops were later elected by the clergy and laity of the diocesan synods, or, in the case of disagreement, by the Bench of Bishops.

4 Gladstone estimated the value of church property to be £16 million. The Bill disposed of £8,650,000 in vested interests and other specified charges, and £7,350,000 was impropriated.

5 The provincial synods of Armagh and Dublin were summoned

in September 1869. The joint synods formed themselves into a Convocation consisting of two Houses. The Lay Assembly met in October, and recommended that a general Convention be summoned. The Convention, comprising the archbishops, bishops, clergy, and laity, met on 15 February 1870, and drew up the constitution of the Irish Church.

6 27-28 Vict., c. 54. Ecclesiastical Courts and Registries (Ireland) Act.

7 The Representative Body, comprising the archbishops, bishops, clerical and lay members, was incorporated on 19 October 1870.

8 The wording of this paragraph was left purposely vague, the original Bill having specified what was to be done with the surplus funds.

46 THE COMPULSORY CHURCH RATE ABOLITION ACT 1868

(*Statutes at Large*, 31-32 Vict., c. 109)

Dissenters were compelled to accept certain remaining social and political disabilities, but they could exercise a refusal to maintain parish churches by refusing to pay the church rate. In 1834 the Whigs proposed to abolish the rate in return for a charge of £250,000 on the land tax, an amount considered too small by churchmen and too large by dissenters.[1] Bills abolishing church rate were frequently introduced into Parliament after 1853. In 1861 a Bill was rejected on the third reading by the Speaker's vote; another Bill to commute them for a rent charge on land was defeated in 1864; and the Lords rejected another Bill in 1867. This Bill was finally passed through the influence of Gladstone.

Whereas Church Rates have for some Years ceased to be made or collected in many Parishes by reason of the Opposition thereto, and in many other Parishes where Church Rates have been made the levying thereof has given rise to Litigation and Ill-feeling:[2]

And whereas it is expedient that the Power to compel Payment of Church Rates by any legal Process should be abolished:

Be it therefore enacted by the Queen's most Excellent Majesty, by and with the Advice and Consent of the Lords Spiritual and Temporal, and Commons, in this present Parliament assembled, and by the Authority of the same, as follows:

1 From and after the passing of this Act no Suit shall be instituted

or Proceeding taken in any Ecclesiastical or other Court, or before any Justice or Magistrate, to enforce or compel the payment of any Church Rate made in any Parish or place in *England* or *Wales*.

2 Where in pursuance of any General or Local Act any Rate may be made and levied which is applicable partly to Ecclesiastical Purposes and partly to other Purposes, such Rate shall be made, levied, and applied for such last-mentioned Purposes only, and so far as it is applicable to such Purposes shall be deemed to be a separate Rate, and not a Church Rate, and shall not be affected by this Act.

Where in pursuance of any Act of Parliament a mixed Fund, arising partly from Rates affected by this Act and partly from other Sources, is directed to be applied to Purposes some of which are Ecclesiastical Purposes, the Portion of such Fund which is derived from such other Sources shall be henceforth primarily applicable to such of the said Purposes as are Ecclesiastical.

8 No Person who makes default in paying the Amount of a Church Rate for which he is rated shall be entitled to inquire into, or object to, or vote in respect of the Expenditure of the Monies arising from such Church Rate; and if the Occupier of any Premises shall make default for One Month after Demand in Payment of any Church Rate for which he is rated, the Owner shall be entitled to pay the same, and shall thereupon be entitled, until the next succeeding Church Rate is made, to stand for all Purposes relating to Church Rates (including the attending at Vestries and voting thereat) in the Place in which such Occupier would have stood.[3]

9 A Body of Trustees may be appointed in any Parish for the Purpose of accepting, by Bequest, Donation, Contract, or otherwise, and of holding, any Contributions which may be given to them for Ecclesiastical Purposes in the Parish....

1 Spring Rice, Chancellor of the Exchequer, advocated the vesting of episcopal and cathedral properties in eleven commissioners, thereby saving £250,000 per annum. The bishops denied Parliament's right to restore revenues to which the Church was legally entitled out of their property.

2 In Veley *v*. Burder, 1837–41, the civil court ruled that churchwardens could not act against the majority of the vestry, as in the case where the majority declared the rate unjust. In Veley *v*. Gosling, 1841–53, the House of Lords declared that a valid rate can only

be made by an actual or constructive majority. As late as 1839, John Thorogood, a Chelmsford shoemaker, was imprisoned for contempt of court in refusing to pay the rate.

3 The Bishop of Oxford (Wilberforce) insisted that none should have a voice in the expenditure of the voluntary rate who did not pay it, and he was opposed by Archbishop Thomson who argued that this would alienate Dissenters who were not hostile to the Church of England.

47 THE ELEMENTARY EDUCATION ACT 1870

(*Statutes at Large*, 33-34 Vict., c. 75)

The granting of aid to voluntary schools involved Parliament in the educational controversy. Of a total of 8,919 schools receiving grant aid in 1870, 6,954 were church foundations. In 1869 the National Educational League was founded in Birmingham by the Radicals, and Forster's Act was influenced by the League's efforts. The new Act provided for a national system of education, accepting, at the same time, the continued existence of voluntary schools. The Radical and Nonconformist dislike of the compromise policy weakened the Liberal Party in the constituencies. The Church of England was equally unhappy, for although unable to find the money for new school buildings, it opposed their provision by the new school boards. Section 14 is the notable *Cowper-Temple* clause.[1]

10 If after the expiration of a time, not exceeding six months, to be limited by the final notice, the Education Department are satisfied that all the public school accommodation required by the final notice to be supplied has not been so supplied, nor is in course of being supplied with due despatch, the Education Department shall cause a school board to be formed for the district as provided in this Act, and shall send a requisition to the school board so formed requiring them to take proceedings forthwith for supplying the public school accommodation mentioned in the requisition, and the school board shall supply the same accordingly.

14 Every school provided by a school board shall be conducted under the control and management of such board in accordance with the following regulations:

(1) The school shall be a public elementary school within the meaning of this Act.
(2) No religious catechism or religious formulary which is distinctive of any particular denomination shall be taught in the school.[2]

74 Every school board may from time to time, with the approval of the Education Department, make byelaws for all or any of the following purposes:

(1) Requiring the parents of children of such age, not less than five years nor more than thirteen years, as may be fixed by the byelaws, to cause such children (unless there is some reasonable excuse) to attend school:
(2) Determining the time during which children are so to attend school; provided that no such byelaw shall prevent the withdrawal of any child from any religious observance or instruction in religious subjects, or shall require any child to attend school on any day exclusively set apart for religious observance by the religious body to which his parent belongs, or shall be contrary to anything contained in any Act for regulating the education of children employed in labour:
(3) Providing for the remission or payment of the whole or any part of the fees of any child where the parent satisfies the school board that he is unable from poverty to pay the same: . . .

97 The conditions required to be fulfilled by an elementary school in order to obtain an annual parliamentary grant shall be those contained in the minutes of the Education Department in force for the time being, and shall amongst other matters provide that after the thirty-first day of March one thousand eight hundred and seventy-one

(1) Such grant shall not be made in respect of any instruction in religious subjects:
(2) Such grant shall not for any year exceed the income of the school for that year which was derived from voluntary contributions, and from school fees, and from any sources other than the parliamentary grant:

but such conditions shall not require that the school shall be in connection with a religious denomination, or that religious instruction shall be given in the school, and shall not give any preference or advantage to any school on the ground that it is or is not provided by a school board: . . .[3]

1 Cowper-Temple, William Francis; *b.* 1811; *educ.*, Eton; Royal Horse Guards, 1827; private secretary to Lord Melbourne, 1835; M.P., 1835; junior lord of the treasury, 1841; Lord of the Admiralty, 1846; under-secretary for home affairs, 1855; president of the board of health, 1855; vice-president of committee of council on education, 1857–8; vice-president of the board of trade, 1859; commissioner of works, 1860–6; created Baron Mount Temple, 1880; *d.* 1888.

2 "The more rapid growth of popular education had been prevented partly by the clash between Church and Dissent, partly by the apathy of the people" (David Thomson, *England in the Nineteenth Century*, p. 135). The National Education League was founded in 1869 by Joseph Chamberlain, R. W. Dale, and others. The supporters of the religious content of education founded a National Education Union. The Act was a compromise which pleased neither party.

3 Forster, William Edward; *b.* 1818; *educ.*, Tottenham Quaker School; entered woollen business, 1836; M.P., 1861; under-secretary for the colonies, 1865–6; vice-president of committee of council for education, 1868–74; chief secretary for Ireland, 1880–2; *d.* 1886.

48 THE PURCHAS CASE, 1871

(*Law Journal Reports, Ecclesiastical Cases*, vol. XL, part 6, new series, pp. 39-48, 50)

The Purchas Judgment[1] condemned many ceremonial practices which had formerly been regarded as legal, thereby making ritualists law-breakers. The dissatisfaction caused by this judgment of the Judicial Committee of the Privy Council was due to its reversal of the implied sanctions in the judgment of Liddell *v.* Westerton. The decision that the Eastward position of the celebrant at Holy Communion was illegal was widely ignored, both Canon Liddon and Canon Gregory at St Paul's officially notifying Bishop Jackson of their refusal to accept this finding.

We find it convenient to adopt the order followed by the learned Dean of the Arches, and to examine first the charge of wearing, and causing to be worn, a chasuble, tunics, or tunicles and albs in the celebration of the Holy Communion.

It is necessary to review shortly the history of the Rubric, usually known as "the Ornaments-Rubric", which governs this question.

The first Prayer Book of King Edward VI (1549), contains the following Rubric at the beginning of the Communion office:

Upon the day and at the time appointed for the ministration of the Holy Communion, the priest, that shall execute the holy ministry, shall put upon him the vesture appointed for that ministration, that is to say, a white alb, plain, with a vestment or cope, and where there may be many priests or deacons, there so many shall be ready to help the priest in the ministration as shall be requisite, and shall have upon them likewise the vestures appointed for their ministry, that is to say, albs with tunicles.

In the second Prayer Book of Edward VI (1552) this was altered, and it was ordered, that the minister

shall use neither alb, vestment, nor cope, but being archbishop or bishop, he shall have and wear a rochet, and being a priest or deacon he shall have and wear a surplice only.

The Prayer Book of Elizabeth (1559) provided, that

the minister at the time of the communion, and at all other times of his administration, shall use such ornaments in the church as were in use by authority of Parliament in the second year of the reign of King Edward VI, according to the Act of Parliament set in the beginning of this book.[2]

This Committee has already decided (Westerton *v.* Liddell), that the words "by authority of Parliament in the second year of the reign of King Edward VI" refer to the first Prayer Book of King Edward VI.

The Act of Parliament set in the beginning of Elizabeth's book is Queen Elizabeth's Act of Uniformity, and the 25th clause of that Act contains a proviso,

that such ornaments of the Church and the ministers thereof shall be retained and be in use, as were in this Church of England by authority of Parliament in the second year of the reign of King Edward VI, and until other order shall be therein taken by the authority of the Queen's Majesty, with the advice of the Commissioners appointed and authorized under the Great Seal of England, for causes Ecclesiastical, or of the Metropolitan of this Realm.

The Prayer Book, therefore, refers to the Act, and the Act clearly contemplated further directions to be given by the Queen, with the advice of Commissioners or of the Metropolitan ...

In the year 1564 appeared the Advertisements of Elizabeth. They make order for the vesture of the minister in these words:

In the ministration of the Holy Communion now in cathedrals and collegiate churches, the principal minister shall wear a cope, with gospeler and epistoler agreeably; and at all other prayers to be said at the said Communion Table to use no copes but surplices. "That every minister, saying any public prayers or ministering the Sacraments or other rites of the Church, shall wear a comely surplice with sleeves, to be provided at the charge of the parish. . . ."

These Advertisements were very actively enforced within a few years of their publication. An inventory of the ornaments of 150 parishes in the Diocese of Lincoln, 1565–1566, has been published by Mr Edward Peacock; and it shews, that the chasubles or vestments and the albs, were systematically defaced, destroyed, or put to other uses, and a precise account was rendered of the mode of their destruction. Proceedings took place under Commissions in Lancashire in 1565 and 1570; in Carlisle in 1573 and following years, when "vestments seem to have disappeared altogether" (Rev. J. Raine, *Vestments*, London, 1866). There is no reason to doubt, that all through the country commissions were issued to enforce the observance of the Advertisements within a few years after they were drawn up. . . .[3]

. . . These, then, are the leading historical facts, with which we have to deal in the difficult task of construing the Rubric of Ornaments. The vestment or cope, alb, and tunicle were ordered by the first Prayer Book of Edward VI. They were abolished by the Prayer Book of 1552, and the surplice was substituted. They were provisionally restored by the statute of Elizabeth, and by her Prayer Book of 1559. But the injunctions and the Advertisements of Elizabeth established a new order within a few years from the passing of the statute, under which chasuble, alb and tunicle disappeared. The canons of 1603–4, adopting anew the reference to the Rubric of Edward VI, sanctioned in express terms all that the Advertisements had done in the matter of the vestments, and ordered the surplice only to be used in parish churches. The revisers of our present Prayer Book in 1662, under another form of words, repeated the reference to the second year of Edward VI, and they did so advisedly, after attention being called to a possibility of a return to the vestments. . . .

Their Lordships think that the defacing and destroying, and converting to profane and other uses of all the vestments now in question, as described in the Lincoln Ms. published by Mr Peacock, shew a determination to remove utterly these ornaments, and not to leave them to be used hereafter when higher Ritual might become possible.

In order to decide the question before the Committee, it seems desirable first to examine the effect of the Church legislation of

1603–4. The 14th Canon orders the use of the Prayer Book without omission or innovation, and the 80th Canon directs that copies of the Prayer Book are to be provided, in its latest revised form, and, by implication, the Ornaments Rubric is thus made binding on the clergy. Canon 24 directs the use of the cope in cathedral and collegiate churches upon principal feast days, "according to the Advertisements for this end, anno 7 Elizabeth". Canon 58 says that

every Minister saying the public prayers, or ministering the Sacraments or other rites of the Church, shall wear a decent or comely surplice with sleeves, to be provided at the charge of the parish.

There is no doubt, that the intention here was not to set up a contradictory rule, by prescribing vestments in the Prayer Book, and a surplice in the Canons, which give authority to the Prayer Book. It could not be intended, in recognizing the legal force of the Advertisements, to bring back the things which the Advertisements had taken away: nor could it be expected, that either the minister or the people should provide vestments in lieu of those, which had been destroyed, and accordingly no direction is given with regard to them. The provisions of the Canons and Prayer Book must be read together, as far as possible; and the Canons upon the vesture of the ministers must be held to be an exposition of and limitation of the Rubric of Ornaments. Such ornaments are to be used as were in use in the second year of Edward VI, limited as to the vestments, by the special provisions of the Canons themselves; and the contemporaneous exposition of universal practice shews, that this was regarded as the meaning of the Canons There does not appear to have been any return to the vestments in any quarter whatever....

But whether this be so or not, their Lordships are of opinion, that as the Canons of 1603–4, which in one part seemed to revive the vestments, and in another to order the surplice for all ministrations, ought to be construed together; so that the Act of Uniformity is to be construed with the two canons on this subject, which it did not repeal, and that the result is, that the cope is to be worn in ministering the Holy Communion on high feast days in cathedrals and collegiate churches, and the surplice in all other ministrations. Their Lordships attach great weight to the abundant evidence, which now exists that from the days of Elizabeth to about 1840, the practice is uniformly in accordance with this view; and is irreconcileable with either of the other views.[4] Through the researches that have been referred to in these remarks, a clear and abundant *expositio contemporanea* has been supplied, which compensates for the scantiness of some other materials for a Judgment.

It is quite true, that neither contrary practice nor disuse can repeal the positive enactment of a statute, but contemporaneous and continuous usage is of the greatest efficacy in law for determining the true construction of obscurely framed documents....

Their Lordships[5] will advise Her Majesty, that the respondent has offended against the Laws Ecclesiastical in wearing the chasuble, alb and tunicle; and that a monition shall issue against the respondent accordingly.

1 John Purchas (1823–72) was vicar of St James' Chapel, Brighton. The original suit had been instituted by Colonel Elphinstone who later died, and was replaced by a retired Indian judge. The suit was undefended, and the taxed costs amounted to £7,661. 18s. 7d.

2 The adverse decision was partly due to the assumption that liturgical documents could be interpreted in the same manner as civil law documents. Because the Prayer Book was annexed to an Act of Parliament, it was assumed "that it should be interpreted precisely like an Act of Parliament—in other words, that its rubrics should be regarded as exhaustive (and therefore prohibiting all practices which they do not specifically command), that they should be logically precise and consistent in every particular, and (above all) that they should be interpreted with little or no reference to the liturgical tradition of which they form part, or to the known views and intentions of their authors" (*Liturgy and Worship* (1954), p. 595).

3 The *Advertisements* were issued in March 1566 by Archbishop Parker, but never received royal sanction. The Privy Council view that the *Advertisements* override the Ornaments Rubric is perverse in view of this; indeed, the re-enactment of the Rubric in 1622 shows the opposite to be true. The critics of the judgment were quick to point out that, though the *Advertisements* were prepared under the Queen's authority, they were issued as a provincial order by the Archbishop on his own authority as metropolitan of the province of Canterbury. In the *Ridsdale Judgment*, 12 May 1877, the same questions were reopened and argued with the same outcome.

4 The chasuble was used at Wilmcote, Warwickshire about 1849, by J. M. Neale at Sackville College, East Grinstead in 1850, at St Ninian's Cathedral, Perth in 1851, and by 1900 in about 1,500 churches in England and Wales.

5 The Judicial Committee consisted of the Lord Chancellor (Lord Hatherly), Archbishop Thomson, Bishop Jackson, and Lord Chelmsford.

49 THE UNIVERSITY TESTS ACT 1871

(*Statutes at Large*, 34-35 Vict., c. 26)

The universities of England were exclusively Anglican establishments before the founding of the University of London in 1827. A petition from sixty members of the Senate of the University of Cambridge in favour of the abolition of religious tests was presented in the Lords by Earl Grey on 21 March 1834. A Royal Commission looked into the state of the universities in 1850, but did not deal with the question of the religious tests. Several petitions were presented after 1862, and Parliamentary bills were also presented without success. The repeal of religious tests became a government issue, and an Act was ultimately carried by Gladstone's ministry, thus removing the last of the privileges of the Church of England as an established body.[1]

Whereas it is expedient that the benefits of the Universities of Oxford, Cambridge, and Durham,[2] and of the colleges and halls now subsisting therein, as places of religion and learning, should be rendered freely accessible to the nation:

And whereas, by means of divers restrictions, tests, and disabilities, many of Her Majesty's subjects are debarred from the full enjoyment of the same:[3]

And whereas it is expedient that such restrictions, tests, and disabilities should be removed, under proper safeguards for the maintenance of religious instruction and worship in the said universities and the colleges and halls now subsisting within the same:

Be it enacted by the Queen's most Excellent Majesty, by and with the advice and consent of the Lords Spiritual and Temporal, and Commons, in this present Parliament assembled, and by the authority of the same, as follows:

3 From and after the passing of this Act, no person shall be required, upon taking or to enable him to take any degree (other than a degree in divinity) within the Universities of Oxford, Cambridge, and Durham, or any of them, or upon exercising or to enable him to exercise any of the rights and privileges which may heretofore have been or may hereafter be exercised by graduates in the said universities or any of them, or in any college subsisting at the time of the passing of this Act in any of the said universities, or upon taking or holding or to enable him to take or hold any office in any of the said universities or any such college as afore-

said, or upon teaching or to enable him to teach within any of the said universities or any such college as aforesaid, or upon opening or to enable him to open a private hall or hostel in any of the said universities for the reception of students,[4] to subscribe any article or formulary of faith, or to make any declaration or take any oath respecting his religious belief or profession, or to conform to any religious observance, or to attend or abstain from attending any form of public worship, or to belong to any specified church, sect, or denomination; nor shall any person be compelled, in any of the said universities or any such college as aforesaid, to attend the public worship of any church, sect, or denomination to which he does not belong: Provided that:

(1) Nothing in this section shall render a layman or a person not a member of the Church of England eligible to any office or capable of exercising any right or privilege in any of the said universities or colleges, which office, right, or privilege, under the authority of any Act of Parliament, or any statute or ordinance of such university or college in force at the time of the passing of this Act, is restricted to persons in holy orders, or shall remove any obligation to enter into holy orders which is by such authority attached to any such office.

(2) Nothing in this section shall open any office (not being an office mentioned in this section) to any person who is not a member of the Church of England, where such office is at the passing of this Act confined to members of the said Church by reason of any such degree as aforesaid being a qualification for holding that office.

4 Nothing in this Act shall interfere with or affect, any further or otherwise than is hereby expressly enacted, the system of religious instruction, worship, and discipline which now is or which may be hereafter lawfully established in the said universities respectively, or in the colleges thereof, or any of them, or the statutes and ordinances of the said universities and colleges respectively relating to such instruction, worship, and discipline.

5 The governing body of every college subsisting at the time of the passing of this Act in any of the said universities shall provide sufficient religious instruction for all members thereof *in statu pupillari* belonging to the Established Church.

6 The Morning and Evening Prayer according to the Order of the Book of Common Prayer shall continue to be used daily as heretofore in the chapel of every college subsisting at the time of

the passing of this Act in any of the said universities; but notwithstanding anything contained in the statute thirteenth and fourteenth Charles the Second chapter four,[5] or in this Act, it shall be lawful for the visitor of any such college, on the request of the governing body thereof to authorize from time to time, in writing, the use on week days only of any abridgment or adaptation of the said Morning and Evening Prayer in the chapel of such college instead of the Order set forth in the Book of Common Prayer.[6]

1 F. D. Maurice, who went to Trinity Hall, Cambridge in 1825, refused to subscribe to the Articles, not being an Anglican, and was thereby excluded from a degree and fellowship.

2 Durham University was founded in 1832 with money provided by the bishop and the Dean and Chapter. The benefactors insisted on its being open only to Anglicans, and there was vigorous opposition from dissenters within Parliament.

3 The universities owed their origin to the existence of churches of secular canons, and were almost wholly clerical and mainly theological. The Reformation saw a waning of the clerical power and large numbers of graduates followed secular callings. "The last half of Victoria's reign was indeed the period when Oxford and Cambridge were most in the public eye . . . The liberal-minded and highly educated governing class of the 'seventies were more nearly affiliated to the Universities than to the declining aristocracy or the rising plutocracy" (Trevelyan, *English Social History*, p. 568). The change in social climate and the utilitarian aspect, rather than religious susceptibility, were the causes of the campaign for the abolition of the religious tests.

4 Nonconformists set up halls at the older universities, but a more significant development was the new provincial universities arising out of the undenominational colleges: Manchester (1851); the Newcastle College of Science (1871); and Leeds, Bristol, Sheffield, Birmingham, Nottingham, Liverpool, Reading, Southampton, Bangor, Cardiff, and Aberystwyth.

5 The Act of Uniformity.

6 The *Shortened Services Act* (The Act of Uniformity Amendment Act), 1872, 35-36 Vict., c. 35, provided for the optional use of abbreviated forms of Mattins and Evensong as additional services in parish churches on holy days and Sundays, and in cathedrals on any day.

50 THE DEATH OF BISHOP PATTESON, 1872

(Minutes of the S.P.G. Standing Committee, Thursday, 18 January 1872)

Patteson[1] was consecrated first Bishop of Melanesia by the New Zealand bishops in Auckland, without Letters-Patent from the Crown. Missionary work in that area was aimed at disturbing the manners and customs of the islanders as little as possible. Patteson protested at the New Zealand General Synod against the activity of "blackbirders", who kidnapped islanders for work on the plantations of Fiji and Queensland. The death of Patteson at the hands of islanders as a reprisal led to the protest by the S.P.G., calling for legislation in the attempt to put down the trade.[2]

Read the proposed draft petition which was adopted as follows:

1 Your Petitioners in conjunction with other Associations and individuals in England, Australia, and New Zealand have for several years past contributed towards the support of Bishop Patteson and the missionaries under him who were engaged both in Norfolk Island and in the Melanesian islands in labour for the conversion and moral and physical improvement of the natives of Melanesia.[3]

2 That the missionaries though almost always favourably received in the Melanesian Islands have yet on a very few occasions met with hostility: and, on 20th September 1871, Bp Patteson was killed by natives at Nukapu off Santa Cruz, and two of his companions died shortly afterwards of wounds received at the same time.

3 That it is on record that Bishop Patteson, and other persons on the spot having the best means of judging, fully expected that such results would follow from the resentment of the Natives excited by the conduct of "traders in labour" who as is alleged decoy Natives on board their ships, confine them by force and transport them to Queensland or the Fiji Islands.

4 That the Queensland Government, by the Polynesian Labourers' Act passed in 1868, endeavoured, not altogether without effect, to prevent kidnapping and other abuses connected with this traffic and generally to regulate it, and that Her Majesty's Government has detached though only on special occasions a ship of war with the same humane intention.[4]

5 That the recent death of Bishop Patteson is a very painful proof

that the measures hitherto adopted are insufficient.

6 Your petitioners therefore pray that your Honourable house after making inquiry into the facts of this traffic will take further steps to relieve Great Britain and other civilized nations from the disgrace entailed by such atrocious acts and to protect the Natives from injuries by which the progress of their moral and physical elevation is grievously impeded.[5]

1 Patteson, John Coleridge; *b.* 1827; *educ.*, Eton and Balliol College, Oxford; ordained, 1853; Fellow of Merton; accompanied G. A. Selwyn to New Zealand, 1855; visited the New Hebrides; consecrated Bishop of Melanesia, 1861; founded college on Norfolk Island for training native boys; killed, 1871.

2 There was a call for legislation in the Queen's Speech and the Pacific Islanders Protection Act was passed. Certain groups of island protectorates were declared in 1893, 1899, and 1900.

3 The death of Patteson evoked a massive response in England, the S.P.G. Memorial fund reaching £7,000. The special day of prayer for overseas missions was not unrelated to this event.

4 The Standing Committee, on Thursday, 11 April 1872, "Agreed with regard to the Pacific Islanders' Protection Bill that the Secretary write to Mr Gladstone and express the opinion of the Standing Committee that it will be necessary that a gunboat should be stationed to enforce the regulations of whatever Bill may be passed."

5 The Melanesian Mission had been accused of slowness in introducing suitable industrial education into the islands.

51 THE REAL PRESENCE, 1872

(*Six Judgments*, pp. 224-5, 232-3, 243-4)

W. J. E. Bennett became vicar of Frome Selwood in 1852, after a stormy ministry at St Paul's, Knightsbridge. The case of Sheppard *v* Bennett was concerned with the doctrinal developments resulting from the Tractarian teaching, especially as regards the *Real Presence* in the Eucharist. As in the Gorham and *Essays and Reviews* judgments, the Judicial Committee of the Privy Council refrained from defining the limits of theological thought in the Church of England. In the similar suit of Ditcher *v* Denison (1854–8), the Privy Council declined to deal with the doctrinal objection, upholding Denison's appeal only on the grounds that the original suit had not been commenced within the prescribed time.

This is an Appeal from the final sentence or decree pronounced by the Dean of the Arches Court of *Canterbury*,[1] on July 23, 1870, and also from two interlocutory orders made by the same Judge, in a cause of the office of the Judge promoted by *Thomas Byard Sheppard*, the Appellant, against the Rev. *William James Early Bennett*, Vicar of the parish of *Frome Selwood*, in the diocese of *Bath* and *Wells*,[2] the Respondent, for having offended against the laws ecclesiastical by having, within two years from the date of the institution of the cause, caused to be printed and published certain works in which he is alleged to have advisedly maintained or affirmed doctrines directly contrary or repugnant to the Articles and Formularies of the United Church of *England* and *Ireland* in relation to the sacrament of the Lord's Supper, such works being entitled respectively "Some Results of the Tractarian Movement of 1833", forming one of the essays contained in a volume entitled *The Church and the World*, edited by the Rev. *Orby Shipley*, Clerk, printed and published in *London* in the year 1867; "A Plea for Toleration in the Church of England, in a Letter addressed to the Rev. *E. B. Pusey*, D.D., Regius Professor of Hebrew, and Canon of *Christ Church, Oxford*", 2nd edition, printed and published in *London* in the year 1867; and "A Plea for Toleration in the Church of England, in a Letter to the Rev. *E. B. Pusey*, D.D., Regius Professor of Hebrew, and Canon of *Christ Church, Oxford*", 3rd edition, printed and published in *London* in the year 1868.

The cause was instituted in the Arches Court of *Canterbury* by virtue of Letters of Request of the late Lord Bishop of *Bath* and *Wells*,[3] in accordance with the provisions of the Act 3rd and 4th of the Queen, cap. 86.[4]

The Respondent was duly cited on July 26, 1869; but no appearance was given to the citation, and in default of appearance articles were filed in accordance with the practice of the Court.

On October 30th, 1869, the Judge, having previously heard counsel on behalf of the Appellant, directed the Articles to be reformed by omitting such parts thereof as charge the Respondent with contravening the 29th Article of Religion, entitled "Of the wicked which eat not the Body of Christ in the use of the Lord's Supper".

From such decree or order a Petition of Appeal was presented, with the permission of the Judge, and the Appeal came before the Judicial Committee of the Privy Council on Mar. 26th, 1870, when the Lords of the Committee, having heard counsel on behalf of the Appellant, agreed to report to Her Majesty their opinion against the Appeal, and that the decree or order appealed from ought to be affirmed, and the cause remitted, with all its incidents, to the Judge of the Court from which the same was appealed.

An Order in Council, confirming the report of the Judicial Committee, was afterwards made....

Dealing only with the 3rd edition of the Respondent's work, and having regard to their former decision, that the charge of contradicting the 29th Article of Religion as to reception of the wicked should be struck out, their Lordships may consider the remaining charges against the Respondent under three heads:

1. *As to the presence of Christ in the Holy Communion.*
2. *As to sacrifice in the Holy Communion.*
3. *As to adoration of Christ present in the Holy Communion.*

The Respondent is charged with maintaining under these three heads the following propositions:

1. That in the sacrament of the Lord's Supper there is an actual presence of the true Body and Blood of our Lord in the consecrated bread and wine, by virtue of and upon the consecration without or external to the communicant, and irrespective of the faith and worthiness of the communicant, and separately from the act of reception by the communicant, and it was contended by counsel under this head that the true Body of Christ meant the natural Body.[5]

2. That the Communion Table is an altar of sacrifice, at which the Priest appears in a sacerdotal position at the celebration of the Holy Communion, and that at such celebration there is a great sacrifice or offering of our Lord by the ministering Priest, in which the mediation of our Lord ascends from the altar to plead for the sins of men.

3. That adoration is due to Christ present upon the altars or Communion Tables of the churches, in the Sacrament, under the form of bread and wine, on the ground that under their veil is the Body and Blood of our Lord.

The several positions so maintained are averred, each and all, to be repugnant to the doctrines of our Church, as set forth in the Articles and Formularies in that behalf specially alleged....

It follows, then, that the Church of *England* has forbidden all acts of adoration to the Sacrament, understanding by that the Consecrated Elements. She has been careful to exclude any act of adoration on the part of the Minister at or after the consecration of the elements and to explain the posture of kneeling prescribed by the Rubric. If the charge against Mr *Bennett* were that he had performed an outward act of adoration on any occasion in the service, the principles laid down in *Martin* v. *Mackonochie*, would apply to this case. Such an act could not be done except in the service, because the Sacrament may not be "reserved".[6] But even if the Respondent's words are a confession of an unlawful act, it is questionable whether such a confession would amount to false doctrine. And it is also fair to remember, in the Respondent's favour, that the judgment in the case of *Martin* v. *Mackonochie*, which established the unlawfulness of introducing acts of adoration, was not delivered until December 23, 1868, after the publication of the words that are now impugned. Some of their Lordships have doubted whether the word "adore", though it seems to point rather to acts of worship, such as are forbidden by the 28th Article, may not be construed to refer to mental adoration, or prayers addressed to Christ present spiritually in the Sacrament, which does not necessarily imply any adoration of the Consecrated Elements or of any corporal or natural presence therein.

Upon the whole, their Lordships, not without doubts and division of opinions, have come to the conclusion that this charge is not so clearly made out as the rules which govern penal proceedings require. Mr *Bennett* is entitled to the benefit of any doubt that may exist. His language has been rash, but as it appears to the majority of their Lordships that his words can be construed so as not to be plainly repugnant to the two passages articled against them, their Lordships will give him the benefit of the doubt that has been raised.

Their Lordships having arrived at the conclusion that they must advise Her Majesty that the Appeal must be dismissed, feel bound to add that there is much in the judgment of the learned Judge in the Court below with which they are unable to concur. The learned Judge has endeavoured to settle by a mass of authorities what is the doctrine of the Church of *England* on the subject of the Holy Communion. It is not the part of the Court of Arches nor of this Committee, to usurp the functions of a synod or council. Happily their duties are much more circumscribed—namely, to ascertain whether certain statements are so far repugnant to, or contradictory of, the language of the Articles and Formularies, construed in their plain meaning, that they should receive judicial condemnation.

1 Sir Robert Phillimore, Dean of the Arches, made a long and carefully reasoned judgment, endeavouring "to settle by a mass of authorities what is the doctrine of the Church of *England* on the subject of the Holy Communion". The rebuke at the conclusion of the Judicial Committee's judgment exemplified the difference between the ecclesiastical and civil law judge. Phillimore, as a trained canonist, knew the functions of his office, and had written in 1843: "Perhaps, if, during the last twenty years, the *Corpus Juris Canonici*, and still more, if the Provincial Constitutions of our country, as given in Lyndewode, had been more thoroughly known and more deeply studied, the Church might have escaped some of those impediments which have been thrown in the way of her discipline and development by Acts of Parliament, framed with the best intentions for the support of her interests" (*The Study of the Civil and Canon Law in its relation to the state, the church, and the universities* (1843), p. 52).

2 It was coincidental that Archdeacon Denison was prosecuted by Ditcher for a course of sermons on this same subject in Wells Cathedral, 1853–4.

3 Lord Auckland, 1854; chaplain to William IV; resigned 1869.

4 The Clergy Discipline Act, 1840.

5 Speaking of the Real Presence, Bennett had written in the earlier edition of his *Plea*: "Who myself adore and teach the people to adore the consecrated Elements, believing Christ to be in them—believing that under their veil is the Sacred Body and Blood of my Lord and Saviour Jesus Christ." This, Phillimore pointed out, was reprehensible language, the amended form, however, was entirely consistent with the teaching of the Church as culled from the mass of authorities. The amended form ran: "Who myself adore and teach the people to adore Christ present in the Sacrament, under the form of Bread and Wine, believing that under their veil is the Sacred Body and Blood of my Lord and Saviour Jesus Christ." Phillimore concluded: "To describe the mode of Presence as Objective, Real, Actual and Spiritual, is certainly not contrary to the law. With respect to the other charges—namely, those relating to Sacrifice and Worship—I pronounced that Mr Bennett has not exceeded the liberty which the law allows."

6 Reservation for the Communion of the Sick was provided by the 1549 Prayer Book, omitted in the 1552 Prayer Book and the English Prayer Book of 1559, but once again included in the Latin version of 1560. The Prayer Book of 1661 retains the regulations of 1559 whereas the Scottish Prayer Book declared the practice to be lawful. J. M. Neale began Continuous Reservation at East Grinstead about 1855; instances are recorded in London during the next decade; and at All Saints, Plymouth, the Reverend R. C. Chase established Permanent Reservation in 1882. To comply with the law, the Reserved Sacrament was often kept in the Clergy houses.

52 THE PUBLIC WORSHIP REGULATION ACT 1874

(*Statutes at Large*, 37-38 Vict., c. 85)

A Royal Commission on Ritual was appointed on 3 June 1867 as a result of the confusion arising from the judgments in ritual cases. This Act was meant to curb irregular ritual practices by disciplinary action, and also to simplify the long and protracted procedure. The Bill was introduced into the Lords by Archbishop Tait, and opposed, though for different reasons, by Shaftesbury and Gladstone. The Bill added to the existing courts by creating a new lay ecclesiastical judge. Monition could be followed by suspension with the possibility of imprisonment for contempt of court, though Tait's success in maintaining the right of the bishop's veto minimized the Erastian nature of the Bill. With the subsequent imprisonment of five clerics between 1878 and 1887, the Act became discredited and ritual prosecutions declined in number.[1]

7 The Archbishop of *Canterbury* and the Archbishop of *York* may, but subject to the approval of Her Majesty to be signified under Her Sign Manual, appoint from time to time a barrister-at-law who has been in actual practice for ten years, or a person who has been a judge of one of the Superior Courts of Law or Equity, or of any court, to which the jurisdiction of any such court has been or may hereafter be transferred by authority of Parliament, to be, during good behaviour, a judge of the Provincial Courts of *Canterbury* and *York*, hereinafter called the judge.

If the said archbishops shall not, within six months after the occurrence of any vacancy in the office, appoint the said judge, Her Majesty may by Letters-Patent appoint some person qualified as aforesaid, to be such judge.[2]

Whensoever a vacancy shall occur in the office of official principal of the Arches Court of *Canterbury*, the judge shall become *ex officio* such official principal, and all proceedings thereafter taken before the judge in relation to matters arising within the province of *Canterbury* shall be deemed to be taken in the Arches Court of *Canterbury*; and whensoever a vacancy shall occur in the office of official principal or auditor of the Chancery Court of *York*, the judge shall become *ex officio* such official principal or auditor, and all proceedings thereafter taken before the judge in relation to matters arising within the province of *York* shall be deemed to be taken in the Chancery Court of *York*; and whensoever a vacancy shall occur in the office of Master of the Faculties to the Archbishop of *Canterbury*, such judge shall become *ex officio* such Master of the Faculties.

Every person appointed to be a judge under this Act shall be a member of the Church of *England*, and shall, before entering on his office, sign the declaration in Schedule (A) to this Act;[3] and if at any time any such judge shall cease to be a member of the Church, his office shall thereupon be vacant.

This section shall come into operation immediately after the passing of this Act.[4]

8 If the archdeacon of the archdeaconry or a churchwarden of the parish, or any three parishioners of the parish, within which archdeaconry or parish any church or burial ground is situate, or for the use of any part of which any burial ground is legally provided, or in case of cathedral or collegiate churches, any three inhabitants of the diocese, being male persons of full age, who have signed and transmitted to the bishop under their hands the declaration contained in Schedule (A) under this Act, and who have, and for one year next before taking any proceeding under this Act have had, their usual place of abode in the diocese within which the cathedral or collegiate church is situated, shall be of opinion,

(1) That in such church any alteration in or addition to the fabric, ornaments, or furniture thereof has been made without lawful authority, or that any decoration forbidden by law has been introduced into such church; or
(2) That the incumbent has within the preceding twelve months used or permitted to be used in such church or burial ground any unlawful ornament of the minister of the church, or neglected to use any prescribed ornament or vesture; or
(3) That the incumbent has within the preceding twelve months failed to observe, or to cause to be observed, the directions contained in the Book of Common Prayer relating to the performance, in such church or burial ground, of the services, rites, and ceremonies ordered by the said book, or has made or permitted to be made any unlawful addition to, alteration of, or omission from, such services, rites, and ceremonies,

such archdeacon, churchwarden, parishioners, or such inhabitants of the diocese, may, if he or they think fit, represent the same to the bishop, by sending to the bishop a form, as contained in Schedule (B) to this Act,[5] duly filled up and signed, and accompanied by a declaration made by him or them under the Act of the fifth and sixth year of King William the Fourth, chapter sixty-two, affirming the truth of the statements contained in the representation: Provided, that no proceedings shall be taken under this Act as regards any alteration in or addition to the fabric of a church if such alteration or addition has been completed five years before the commencement of such proceedings.

9 Unless the bishop shall be of opinion, after considering the whole circumstances of the case, that proceedings should not be taken on the representation —— he shall within twenty-one days after receiving the representation transmit a copy thereof to the person complained of, and shall require such person, and also the person making the representation, to state in writing within twenty-one days whether they are willing to submit to the directions of the bishop touching the matter of the said representation, without appeal; and, if they shall state their willingness to submit to the directions of the bishop without appeal, the bishop shall forthwith proceed to hear the matter of the representation in such manner as he shall think fit, and shall pronounce such judgment and issue such monition (if any) as he may think proper, and no appeal shall lie from such judgment or monition.[6]

Provided, that no judgment so pronounced by the bishop shall be considered as finally deciding any question of law so that it may not be again raised by other parties.

The parties may, at any time after the making of a representation to the bishop, join in stating any questions arising in such proceedings in a special case signed by a barrister-at-law for the opinion of the judge, and the parties after signing and transmitting the same to the bishop may require it to be transmitted to the judge for hearing, and the judge shall hear and determine the question or questions arising thereon, and any judgment pronounced by the bishop shall be in conformity with such determination.

If the person making the representation and the person complained of shall not, within the time aforesaid, state their willingness to submit to the directions of the bishop, the bishop shall forthwith transmit the representation in the mode prescribed by the rules and orders to the archbishop of the province, and the archbishop shall forthwith require the judge to hear the matter of the representation at any place within the diocese or province, or in *London* or *Westminster*....

... In all proceedings before the judge under this Act the evidence shall be given *vivâ voce*, in open court, and upon oath: and the judge shall have the powers of a court of record, and may require and enforce the attendance of witnesses, and the production of evidences, books, or writings, in the like manner as a judge of one of the superior courts of law or equity, or of any court to which the jurisdiction of any such court has been or may hereafter be transferred by authority of Parliament.

Unless the parties shall both agree that the evidence shall be taken down by a shorthand writer, and that a special case shall not be stated, the judge shall state the facts proved before him in the form of a special case, similar to a special case stated under the Common Law Procedure Acts, 1852–1854.

The judge shall pronounce judgment on the matter of the representation, and shall deliver to the parties, on application, and to the bishop, a copy of the special case, if any, and judgment.

The judge shall issue such monition (if any) and make such order as to costs as the judgment shall require.

Upon every judgment of the judge, or monition issued in accordance therewith, an appeal shall lie, in the forms prescribed by rules and orders, to Her Majesty in Council.

The judge may, on application in any case, suspend the execution of such monition pending an appeal, if he shall think fit.

13 Obedience by an incumbent to a monition or order of the bishop or judge, as the case may be, shall be enforced, if necessary, in the manner prescribed by rules and orders, by an order inhibiting the incumbent from performing any service of the church, or otherwise exercising the cure of souls within the diocese for a term not exceeding three months; provided that at the expiration of such term the inhibition shall not be relaxed until the incumbent shall, by writing under his hand, in the form prescribed by the rules and orders, undertake to pay due obedience to such monition or order, or to the part thereof which shall not have been annulled: Provided that if such inhibition shall remain in force for more than three years from the date of the issuing of the monition, or from the final determination of an appeal therefrom, which ever shall last happen, or if a second inhibition in regard to the same monition shall be issued within three years from the relaxation of an inhibition, any benefice or other ecclesiastical preferment held by the incumbent in the parish ... or for the use of which the burial ground is legally provided, in relation to which church or burial ground such monition has been issued as aforesaid, shall thereupon become void, unless the bishop shall, for some special reason stated by him in writing, postpone for a period not exceeding three months the date at which, unless such inhibition be relaxed, such

benefice or other ecclesiastical preferment shall become void as aforesaid; and upon any such avoidance it shall be lawful for the patron ... to appoint, present, collate, or nominate to the same if such incumbent were dead; and the provisions contained in the Act of the first and second year of the reign of Her Majesty, chapter one hundred and six, section fifty-eight, in reference to notice to the patron and as to lapse, shall be applicable to any benefice or other ecclesiastical preferment avoided under this Act; and it shall not be lawful for the patron at any time to appoint, present, collate, or nominate to such benefice or such other ecclesiastical preferment the incumbent by whom the same was avoided under this Act.

18 When a sentence has been pronounced by consent, or any suit or proceeding has been commenced against any incumbent under the Act of the third and fourth year of the reign of Her Majesty, chapter eighty-six, he shall not be liable to proceedings under this Act in respect of the same matter; and no incumbent proceeded against under this Act shall be liable to proceedings under the (Church Discipline Act, 1840), in respect of any matter upon which judgment has been pronounced under this Act.[7]

1 The clergy imprisoned for contumacy were: Arthur Tooth (1877); Pelham Dale (1880); R. W. Enraght (1880); S. F. Green (1881), and J. Bell Cox (1887).

2 The only unqualified ecclesiastical judge, as envisaged by Lord Shaftesbury, to hold the post was Lord Penzance, ex-judge of divorce, who retired in 1899.

3 Schedule (A): "I do hereby solemnly declare that I am a member of the Church of England as by law established."

4 Tait's original plan was to have in each diocese a Board of Assessors, clerical and lay, to whom the bishop should refer complaints and on whose advice he would act. Appeal would be to the archbishop whose judgment should be final. Shaftesbury's clauses were drawn from former Bills he had sought to introduce for the reforming of the ecclesiastical courts.

5 Schedule (B): "To the Right Rev. Father in God, A., by Divine permission Lord Bishop of B. I (We) C.D., Archdeacon of the archdeaconry of ... (*or* a churchwarden *or* three parishioners of the parish of E.,) in your Lordship's diocese, do hereby represent that ... has or have ... (*state the matter to be represented*)."

6 Tait was able to secure the provision of the Bishop's veto in spite of opposition from all quarters. It was estimated that out of twenty-three representations under the provisions of the Act, not less than

seventeen were vetoed. Since the reasons had to be stated publicly, numerous examples could be given of the reticence of bishops to proceed under the terms of the Act. In the matter of the parish of Tedburn St Mary, Bickersteth wrote: "With regard to wafer bread, lighted candles on the holy table in the daytime, and the vestments complained of, I have stated to Mr Tothill that they are, in my judgment, contrary to the laws and usages of the Church of England, and are therefore not only inexpedient, but wrong. I earnestly hope that the rector will yet see it his duty to submit to my admonition as his father in God. But in the present state of the law, I fear that prosecutions in the Courts on such matters of ritual only aggravate the evils they are intended to suppress."

7 Some ritual prosecutions were instituted under the Act of 1840 because the complainant was debarred under the Public Worship Regulation Act.

53 GUILD OF ST MATTHEW, 1890

(Stewart Headlam, *The Guild of St Matthew, An Appeal to Churchmen*, 1890)

The conventional form of ministry to the lower social strata in the latter part of the nineteenth century was generally unsuccessful in gaining their allegiance to the Church. When small groups or individuals sought to reconcile the Church with the labouring classes by unorthodox means they often met with suspicion and hostility. The Guild of St Matthew, founded by Stewart Headlam,[1] was at once religious and political and associated with its work were C. W. Stubbs, later Dean of Ely and Bishop of Truro, Henry Carey Shuttleworth, Vicar of St Nicholas Cole Abbey, and Thomas Hancock.

GUILD OF ST MATTHEW

By manifestation of the Truth commending ourselves to every man's conscience in the sight of God. *2 Cor. 4.2.*

OBJECTS

I To get rid, by every possible means, of the existing prejudices, especially on the part of "Secularists", against the Church—Her Sacraments and Doctrines: and to endeavour "to justify GOD to the people".

II To promote frequent and reverent Worship in the Holy Communion, and a better observance of the teaching of the Church of England as set forth in the Book of Common Prayer.

III To promote the Study of Social and Political Questions in the light of the Incarnation.[2]

RULES

(1) To carry out Object I—*collectively* (e.g. by means of Lectures, Classes, the dissemination of suitable literature, etc.,) and *individually* by personal influence.
(2) To communicate on all the Great Festivals, and at least to be present at a Celebration of the Holy Communion as regularly as possible on Sundays and Holy days.
(3) To meet annually in United Worship on the Feast of ST MATTHEW (Sept. 21st), which day shall be the festival of the Guild.*

* Members at too great a distance from London to attend the Special Festival Services of the Guild, or otherwise bona-fide from doing so, are considered to fulfil this Rule by Communicating for the Intention of the Guild on St Matthew's Day or within the octave.[3]

1 Headlam, Stewart Duckworth; *b.* 1847; *educ.*, Eton and Trinity College, Cambridge, 1865–9; curate of St John's, Drury Lane, 1870; curate of St Matthew, Bethnal Green, 1873; curate of St Thomas, Charterhouse, 1879; refused license by Bishop Jackson, 1881; curate, St Michael, Shoreditch, 1881–4; licensed, 1904; *d.* 1924.

2 Headlam heard Maurice lecture whilst at Cambridge, and was attracted to his theology. The belief in the Fatherhood of God and the Brotherhood of Humanity through the Eternal Sonship of Christ profoundly influenced Headlam.

3 The Guild numbered forty members at its inception on St Peter's Day, 1877; grew to 364 by 1895; and fell to 200 by 1906. Amongst its priest members were Conrad Noel, Percy Dearmer, and Percy Widdrington.

54 DR PUSEY AND CANON FARRAR, 1877

(Farrar, *Eternal Hope* (London 1883), pp. 76-81; Pusey, *What is of Faith as to Everlasting Punishment?* (Oxford 1880), pp. 21-3, 46-7)

F. W. Farrar was a popular preacher and a formative influence on Victorian middle-class culture. He shared Maurice's aversion to the popular exposition of Eternal Punishment, and, in a series of sermons in Westminster Abbey, expounded a belief in Eternal Hope. Pusey and Liddon both attacked Farrar's denial of a material Hell, and the reply was to be the last substantial work to come from the ageing Pusey. Farrar argued, not on an ethical basis, but on the interpretation of certain scriptural passages, and Pusey's reply was an historical justification of the traditional view with reference to Scripture and the patristic writers.[1]

FARRAR:

I am quite content that texts should decide it. Only, *first*, you must go to the inspired original, not to the erroneous translation; and *secondly*, you must take words, and interpret words in their proper and historical significance, not in that sense which makes them connote to you a thousand notions which did not originally belong to them; and *thirdly*, you must not explain away, or read between the lines of the texts which make against the traditional view, while you refuse all limitation of those on the misinterpretation or undue extension of which that view is founded. Now I ask you, my brethren, where would be these popular teachings about hell—the kind of teachings which I have quoted to you and described[2]—if we calmly and deliberately, by substituting the true translations, erased from our English Bibles, as being inadequate or erroneous or disputed renderings, the three words, "damnation", "hell", and "everlasting"?[3] Yet I say, unhesitatingly,—I say, claiming the fullest right to speak on this point,—I say, with the calmest and most unflinching sense of responsibility,—I say, standing here in the sight of God, and of my Saviour, and it may be of the angels and spirits of the dead—that not one of those three expressions ought to stand any longer in our English Bibles, and that, being—in our present acceptation of them—in the notion (that is) which all uneducated persons attach to them—simply *mistranslations*, they most unquestionably will not stand unexplained in the revised version of the Bible if the revisers have understood their duty.[4] The verb "to damn" in the Greek Testament is neither more nor less than the verb "to condemn", and the words translated "damnation" are simply the words which, in the vast majority of instances the same translators have translated, and rightly translated, by "judgment" and "condemnation". The word αἰώνιος, sometimes translated "everlasting", is simply the word which, in its first sense, means *agelong* or *aeonian*; and which is in the Bible itself applied to things which have utterly and long since passed away; and is in its second sense something "spiritual"—something above and beyond time,—as when the knowledge of God is said to be eternal life. So that when, with your futile billions, you foist into this word αἰώνιος the fiction of endless time, you do but give the lie to the mighty oath of that great angel, who set one foot upon the sea, and one upon the land, and with hand uplifted to heaven sware by Him who liveth for ever and ever that "Time should be no more".[5] And finally in the Gospels and Epistles the word rendered Hell is in one place the Greek "Tartarus", borrowed as a name for the prison of evil spirits, not after, but *until*, the resurrection; in five places "Hades", which simply means the world beyond the grave; and in twelve places "Gehenna", which means primarily the Valley of Hinnom outside Jerusalem, in which, after it had been polluted by Moloch-worship, corpses were flung and fires were lit; and is used, secondarily as a metaphor, not of fruitless and hopeless, but—for all at any rate but a small and desperate minority—of that purifying and corrective punishment which, as all of us alike believe, does await impenitent sin both here and beyond the grave.

But, be it solemnly observed, the Jews *to* whom and in whose metaphorical sense, the word was used by our Blessed Lord, never did, either then, or at any period, normally attach to the word Gehenna that meaning of endless torment which we attach to "Hell". To them, and in their style of speech,—and therefore on the lips of our blessed Saviour who addressed it to them, and spake in terms which they would understand—it meant *not* a material and everlasting fire, but an intermediate, a remedial, a metaphorical, a terminable retribution.[6]

PUSEY:

But now before entering into the proofs of the eternity of punishment to those who *will* incur it, let me sum up in one what has been said:

1 Without free-will, man would be inferior to the lower animals, which have a sort of limited freedom of choice.

2 Absolute free-will implies the power of choosing amiss and,

having chosen amiss, to persevere in choosing amiss. It would be self-contradictory, that Almighty God should create a free agent capable of loving Him, without being capable also of rejecting His love.

3 The higher and more complete and pervading the free-will is, the more completely an evil choice will pervade and disorder the whole being.

4 But without free-will we could not freely love God. Freedom is a condition of love.

5 In eternity those who behold Him will know what the bliss is, eternally to love Him. But then that bliss involves the intolerable misery of losing Him through our own evil choice. To lose God and be alienated from Him is in itself Hell, or the vestibule of Hell.

6 But that His creatures may not lose Him, God, when He created all his rational creatures with free-will, created them also in grace, so that they had the full power to choose aright, and could not choose amiss, except by resisting the drawing of God to love Him.

7 The only hindrance to man's salvation is, in any case, the obstinate misuse of that free-will, with which God endowed him, in order that he might freely love Him.

8 God wills that all should be saved, if they *will* it, and to this end gave His Son to die for them, and the Holy Ghost to teach them.

9 The merits of Jesus reach to every soul who wills to be saved, whether in this life they knew Him or knew Him not.

10 God the Holy Ghost visits every soul which God has created, and each soul will be judged as it responded or did not respond to the degree of light which He bestowed on it, not by our maxims, but by the wisdom and love of Almighty God.

11 We know absolutely nothing of the proportion of the saved to the lost or who will be lost; but this we *do* know, that none will be lost, who do not obstinately to the end and in the end refuse God. None will be lost, whom God *can* save, without destroying in them His own gift of free-will.[7]

12 With regard to the *nature* of the sufferings, nothing is matter

of faith. No one doubts that the very special suffering will be the loss of God (*poena damni*): that, being what they are, they know that they were made by God for Himself, and yet, through their own obstinate will, will not have Him. As to "pains of sense", the Church has nowhere laid down as a matter of faith the material character of the worm and the fire, or that they denote more than the gnawing of remorse. Although then it would be very rash to lay down dogmatically, that the "fire" is not to be understood literally, as it has been understood almost universally by Christians, yet no one has a right to urge those representations, from which the imagination so shrinks, as a ground for refusing to believe in hell, since he is left free not to believe them.[8] . . .

But beyond this argument from the "aeonian", that the punishment of the last *need* not be thought to be eternal, Dr Farrar has another, which he calls his "palmary argument", from our Lord's use of the word Gehenna; (that) our Lord can*not* have meant to teach that the sufferings of unrepented sin would be eternal.

We must, he says, understand by "hell" what our Lord meant by Gehenna, and, as used by our Lord, Gehenna did *not* mean endless torment. "In spite of unfair depreciation, I venture to say that, hastily as my book was produced, no modern writer has furnished a fuller contribution from Jewish testimonies to the decision of this important question; and if the position cannot be shaken, how strongly does it tell in favour of Eternal Hope!"[9]

"It surely cannot be denied, that our Blessed Lord, speaking as 'a Jew to Jews among Jews', must have used the words of His day in the sense wherein these words would have been understood by His hearers."

Dr Farrar is mistaken, both in the principle which he lays down, and as to the facts, bearing upon it.

His principle is that, if our Lord used any religious term, already in use among the Jews, He must have used it in the self-same sense, meaning exactly what they meant. But, although, in God's mercy, He took our flesh of the seed of Abraham, He came amongst us to make a new revelation. Then, although He used their language, to engraft His teaching upon their past belief, He had, when need was, to stamp that language anew. This, every one owns that He did as to the terms, "the kingdom of God", "the Messiah", "the being born again", and many others. If then the meaning of a word, already in use among the Jews, is clear from the context of our Lord's words, the question, in what sense the Jews at any time used it among themselves, may be a matter of interest in regard to their history; it has no bearing upon the revelation made by our Lord.

In regard to the facts, Dr Farrar dismisses summarily or overlooks the evidence that the Jews believed in eternal punishment before or at the time of the Coming of our Lord, and called the place of that punishment Gehenna. So that His use of the word Gehenna would, according to Dr Farrar's argument, be one of the proofs (if proof were needed) that He *did* mean to teach the everlastingness of punishment beyond the grave.[10]

1 Farrar, Frederick William; *b.* 1831; *educ.*, King's Colllege, London; Trinity College, Cambridge; housemaster at Harrow, 1855; Headmaster of Marlborough, 1871; canon of Westminster and rector of St Margaret's, 1876; Bampton Lecturer, 1885; Dean of Canterbury, 1895; *d.* 1903.

2 Farrar included among the exponents of the popular teaching on Hell: Tertullian; Minucius Felix; Jonathan Edwards; Pusey; Furniss; Moody; and Spurgeon.

3 Farrar's Bampton Lectures were on *The History of Interpretation*, and were influenced by Coleridge and Maurice. The principle given here reflects Jowett's famous essay in *Essays and Reviews.*

4 Bishop Wilberforce had introduced the revision of the Bible on 10 February 1870, with the express purpose of removing errors in translation. The work of revision began on 30 June 1870; the New Testament was published in May 1881; and the Old Testament in May 1885. In three passages discussed by Farrar in appendixes, the RV uses condemnation for damnation in Mark 14.20; supplies Gehenna as a marginal note for Matt. 23.33; and uses eternal in Matt. 25.46.

5 Rev. 10.7.

6 This same argument is used by Gore in *Lux Mundi* when he argues that Jesus, in using Psalm 110 as a Davidic composition, was addressing the Pharisees *ad hominem* on their assumption that it was Davidic. In so doing, Gore argued that Jesus shared the ordinary knowledge of the educated Jew of his day. Farrar tended to the opposite conclusion, namely that the contemporary use is theologically valid since it was authenticated by our Lord.

7 Pusey considered that Farrar's position was a reaction to his former Calvinism, but if it was due to the influence of Maurice, then "Eternal Hope" was the outcome of an incarnational standpoint.

8 Farrar wrote to Pusey: "Your twelve theses I accept unreservedly. My main divergence from the point of view commonly supposed to be the sole orthodox one, lies in this point—that whereas you and others hold that God may reach many souls, as He reached

the soul of the penitent malefactor, in the hour of death, I have rather believed that the moment of death was not necessarily, and for all, the final irreversible moment of determination respecting the endless years beyond "

9 *Eternal Hope*, p. 81n. See also *Contemporary Review* (June 1878), p. 585; Farrar, *Mercy and Judgment* (1881).

10 Pusey devoted fifty-five pages to Farrar's *palmary argument*; about forty-six of these dealt with the Jewish usage. The Appendix, designed to show that Universalism was condemned at the 5th General Council, consists of 159 pages of patristic evidence.

55 THE BURIAL LAWS AMENDMENT ACT 1880

(*Statutes at Large*, 43-44 Vict., c. 41)

A long-standing grievance of dissenters was that burials had to be performed according to the rites of the Church of England. Several Bills were introduced into Parliament by Sir Morton Peto, a prominent Baptist, and by Osborne Morgan. With immense opposition from members of the established Church, including Bishop Wordsworth, the Liberals carried the Bill by a large majority. Parochial clergy argued that the Bill was a further admission that there was a cleavage between Church and State. However, there was only a comparatively small number of burials according to denominational rites after the passage of the Act, and dissenting opinion was slowly reconciled.

1 After the passing of this Act any relative, friend, or legal representative having the charge of or being responsible for the burial of a deceased person may give forty-eight hours notice in writing, indorsed on the outside "Notice of Burial", to, or leave or cause the same to be left at the usual place of abode of the rector, vicar, or other incumbent, or in his absence the officiating minister in charge of any parish or ecclesiastical district or place, or any person appointed by him to receive such notice, that it is intended that such deceased person shall be buried within the churchyard or graveyard of such parish or ecclesiastical district or place without performance, in the manner prescribed by law, of the service for the burial of the dead according to the rites of the Church of England, and after receiving such notice no rector, vicar, incumbent, or officiating minister shall be liable to any censure or

penalty, ecclesiastical or civil, for permitting any such burial as aforesaid....

6 At any burial under this Act all persons shall have free access to the churchyard or graveyard in which the same shall take place. The burial may take place, at the option of the person so having the charge of or being responsible for the same as aforesaid, either without any religious service, or with such Christian and orderly religious service at the grave, as such person shall think fit; and any person or persons who shall be thereunto invited, or be authorized by the person having the charge of or being responsible for such burial, may conduct such service or take part in any religious act thereat. The words "Christian service" in this section shall include every religious service used by any church, denomination, or person professing to be Christian.[1]

7 All burials under this Act, whether with or without a religious service, shall be conducted in a decent and orderly manner; and every person guilty of any riotous, violent, or indecent behaviour at any burial under this Act, or wilfully obstructing such burial or any such service as aforesaid thereat, or who shall, in any such churchyard or graveyard as aforesaid, deliver any address, not being part of or incidental to a religious service permitted by this Act, and not otherwise permitted by any lawful authority, or who shall, under colour of any religious service or otherwise, in any such churchyard or graveyard, wilfully endeavour to bring into contempt or obloquy the Christian religion, or the belief or worship of any church or denomination of Christians, or the members or any minister of any such church or denomination, or any other person, shall be guilty of a misdemeanor.[2]

12 No minister in holy orders of the Church of England shall be subject to any censure or penalty for officiating with the service prescribed by law for the burial of the dead according to the rites of the said church in any unconsecrated burial ground or cemetery or part of a burial ground or cemetery, or in any building thereon, in any case in which he might have lawfully used the same service, if such burial ground or cemetery ... had been consecrated. The relative, friend, or legal representative having charge of or being responsible for the burial of any deceased person who had a right of interment in any such unconsecrated ground vested in any burial board, or provided under any Act relating to the burial of the dead, shall be entitled, if he think fit, to have such burial performed therein according to the rites of the Church of England

by any minister of the said church who may be willing to perform the same.[3]

13 From and after the passing of this Act, it shall be lawful for any minister in holy orders of the Church of England authorized to perform the burial service, in any case where the office for the burial of the dead according to the rites of the Church of England may not be used, and in any other case at the request of the relative, friend, or legal representative having the charge of or being responsible for the burial of the deceased, to use at the burial such service, consisting of prayers taken from the Book of Common Prayer and portions of Holy Scripture, as may be prescribed or approved of by the Ordinary without being subject to any ecclesiastical or other censure or penalty.

14 Save as is in this Act expressly provided as to ministers of the Church of England, nothing herein contained shall authorize or enable any such minister who shall not have become a declared member of any other Church or denomination, or have executed a deed of relinquishment under the Clerical Disabilities Act, 1870,[4] to do any act which he would not by law have been authorized or enabled to do if this Act had not passed, or to exempt him from any censure or penalty in respect thereof.[5]

1 Only the incumbent and churchwardens had right of access to the parish churchyard. In some places dissenting bodies had their own burial-grounds, which removed this obstacle.

2 Opposition to the Bill came from Radicals who disliked the concessions to the clergy, and also from the clergy who shared Bishop Wordsworth's opinion that it was "an Act for the martyrdom of the National Church under the narcotic influences of chloroform . . ."

3 The increase in population and the growth of the cities led to the establishment of private cemeteries; the growth of burial boards; and the closing and converting of full churchyards. The involvement of the religious aspect with the sanitary problems of the cities made the issue a particularly pressing one.

4 33-34 Vict., c. 91.

5 The Liberation Society, founded in 1844, supported the dissenting cause and used the controversy as a convenient opportunity for attacking the Church of England.

56 THE DEATH OF BISHOP HANNINGTON, 1885

(C.M.S. archives, G.3. A5/0, 1886, 23. Copy of a letter received at Msalala on 28 November from the Reverend R. P. Aske at Buganda, dated 27 October 1885. Received in London, 15 February 1886)

The death of James Hannington[1] awakened a public demand in Britain for the opening up of the African continent. It had demonstrated that amid the persecution and massacre of native converts the European missionaries were not inviolable. The missionary strategy of pioneering the short route to Lake Victoria Nyanza from Mombasa on the coast was a hazardous operation, since the approach from the north through Masrai country was considered by the natives as the route of invasion. The British Government after much hesitation established a Protectorate in Uganda in June 1894.

On Sunday Oct. 25th Mwanga,[2] king of Buganda, despatched an officer named Thakoli (name similar to a Busoga chief; but a different person, a Muganda, a door keeper), to kill Bp Hannington in the face of our assurance that he was an Englishman and our brother. Also a page named Musoke was sent to collect their goods and to bring them here along with their guns. Those responsible with Mwanga are 1. Sekibobo or Katikiro, 2. Pokino (late Kinubugwe) or Kyambalango, 3. Kulugi—with full consent of the other chiefs. It was stated some weeks ago by Engobya at a council—that it would be well to kill us i.e. P. O. Flaherty, A. M. Mackay[3] and myself; for that Luhonge of Ukerewe had killed two Englishmen with impunity. Also in reference to Bp Hannington's preconcerted murder Katikiro made the same statement—What can the English do? Is not Lehonge still there? The messengers sent to murder the Bishop will probably arrive today at the Luba where he is. It is not the *Basoga* but the principal chiefs of Buganda headed by the King who have sent to murder these men.

This statement is written with the strongest supposition that if our Bishop is murdered our deaths will soon follow and with the hope that it may lead to the opening up of Africa to civilization and a stop being put to the gigantic internal slavery which prevails.

Native kings especially of Buganda are the arch slavetraders. Any alliance between a power like England or Germany and a power like Buganda is like a compact between a full grown man and a small child. Deal with the blackman as with a child. Be just with him, keep faith with him, love him: but in the name of God and of humanity and common sense, do not treat him as an equal until by education and civilization he has become such. The party in the rear of the Bishop will also be certainly murdered unless by God's good providence they can be warned. We here are practically prisoners. We dare not go a day's journey from our house without a special messenger from the King. It is doubtful now whether the letters written will not be intercepted.

We heard last Sunday 25th inst: that Bp Hannington was a prisoner at Luba's, his identification was established by the statement of the messengers that he had lost a thumb. We heard that he was in the stocks and ill, taking nothing but milk. We did all in our power to see the King and to urge him to send and countermand his first order. He refused to see us. We waited the whole of Sunday till dark. He bid us come on Monday and he would give a messenger. When we came we brought a letter begging him to tell us about our brother. He put us off saying he would call the French priest Père Lourdel to read it to him refusing to see us.[4] We came away. The F. Priest came down [and] told us he had seen the King, warned him of the folly of murdering a guest and an Englishman. The King answered let Mackay come and write a letter ordering him to go back. Mackay was ill with fever so I took up a letter with all haste to that effect and was soon followed by Mackay on the donkey; but it was all a put off, we had little hope, for we saw they were all playing false with us. Our information is perfectly accurate as it comes from those who are immediately in [the] presence of the King. Repeatedly we have been refused permission to leave this country and every day the position becomes more untenable. The suspicion in the minds of the authorities that we are political agents has never slumbered since the time it was awakened or strengthened by the visit of the Buganda envoys to England under the charge of Missionaries. It is clear that the government is receiving them and in advising Her Majesty to grant them an audience contracted a more than ordinary responsibility towards the mission in Buganda. I can say that Mackay and I have done all we can to disabuse the mind of the people that we are messengers of the English government. Whether if our lives should be temporarily spared it would prove possible to take any steps towards enabling us to leave the country will doubtless meet with consideration in the proper quarter. As we are not openly charged with being enemies we ought to be sent away in a friendly manner with our own goods and more especially with our legally acquired boys.

We have nothing to expect from those in authority but the worst and their determination to kill the Bishop shows that they have come to believe that they may commit such acts with impunity.

We are quietly awaiting the turn which affairs may take, our efforts proving perfectly futile to induce the King to alter his mind, we have decided not to go near the King's enclosure again unless called for. Neither the Bishop nor we are without many warm-hearted sympathizers and earnest prayer is offered from many black lips here as from the lips of Xtians at home. So we are content to leave the issue in our Father's hand. We are going to try and send letters off in secret if possible by the Arab dhow under cover of the French priests whose case we fear is not much brighter than our own—except that the King does not refuse to see them; but if the position was reversed and it were a French Bishop who was at Luba's—he would be just as resolute in refusing to see them.[5]

(not signed)

Buganda, Victoria Nyanza.
Oct. 27th 1885.

1 Hannington, James; *b.* 1847; *educ.*, St Mary's Hall, Oxford, 1868; ordained, 1874; curate of St George, Hurstpierpoint; joined C.M.S., 1882 and went to Zanzibar; returned to England through ill-health, 1883; consecrated first Bishop of Eastern Equatorial Africa, 1884; returned to Mombasa, 1885; martyred October 1885.

2 Mwanga; became king at the age of eighteen on the death of his father Mtesa in 1884. The French, English, Germans, and Arabs sought his support. He was expelled by the Arabs and restored by the Europeans in 1889, and in the war between British and French interests he favoured one then the other. He was finally deported from the British Protectorate.

3 Mackay, Alexander Murdoch; *b.* 1849; studied classics, mathematics, and engineering at Edinburgh; joined C.M.S., 1876; worked in Uganda, 1878; threatened with expulsion by Mwanga in 1884; expelled, 1887; translated the Bible into the Uganda vernacular at Usambiro; *d.* 1890.

4 The arrival of the French Roman Catholic missionaries led to fierce rivalry between the missions. With the establishment of the British Protectorate in 1894 the country was divided into Protestant and Roman Catholic spheres of influence.

5 Hannington was followed briefly by H. P. Parker and then by A. R. Tucker who laid a firm foundation for future missionary activity.

57 ARCHBISHOP BENSON AND THE METROPOLITAN OF KIEV, 1888

(C. R. Davey Biggs, *Russia and Reunion*, pp. 237-9)

The Anglican interest in the Russian Orthodox Church in the early part of the nineteenth century was largely academic. Through the efforts of such individuals as William Palmer[1] there was a growing interest in the Orthodox Churches, and in 1864 the Eastern Churches Association came into being. Following the example of W. J. Birkbeck,[2] contact between the Church of England and the Russian Church was made on notable occasions such as the nine-hundredth anniversary of the conversion of Russia, by Anglican leaders.[3]

EDWARD, BY DIVINE PROVIDENCE ARCHBISHOP OF CANTERBURY, PRIMATE OF ALL ENGLAND, AND METROPOLITAN, TO OUR BROTHER, GREATLY BELOVED IN THE FAITH AND WORSHIP OF THE ALL-HOLY AND UNDIVIDED TRINITY, PLATO, BY DIVINE PROVIDENCE THE MOST REVEREND METROPOLITAN OF KIEV AND GALICIA, GREETING IN THE LORD.

Intelligence having reached Us of the approaching festival at the city of Kiev the Great, We, remembering the commandment of the Blessed Apostle, *χαίρειν μετὰ χαιρόντων*, embrace this opportunity of communicating to your Grace, and through your Grace to the Bishops and clergy and laity of the Church of Russia, Our most sincere sympathy and good will. Great festivals are either religious or national. This celebration which you are holding is, indeed, in the first place, religious; but it is also national in the highest way. It is a thankful recognition before God of the sacred fact that Russia owes all that she has yet attained of power and dignity amongst the nations of Christendom, not merely to the sagacity of her rulers and the inborn strength of her people. You offer your thanksgiving to God because your branch of the Holy Catholic and Apostolic Church, which you reverently link with the name of the Apostle St Andrew, has been coextensive with your nation, and because the Christian faith, through the agency of the illustrious St Vladimir, whose conversion you now commemorate, has illuminated your people through nine long centuries of history. It was our original hope and purpose to have sent a Bishop to Kiev to represent the Church of England at your festival, and We were only prevented from carrying out Our design by the events of the present month. During the whole month of July there is assembled in London under Our presidency the Universal Episcopate of the Anglican Church. That is to say, not only the Bishops of the Church of England itself, but all the Archbishops, Metropolitans and Bishops of the Church of Ireland, Scotland and America, as well as the Bishops of India, and of the British Colonies, with many Missionary Bishops and other Bishops who are in Communion with Us. One hundred and forty of these are now assembled here with Us. This Conference meets once only in ten years, and its assemblies are of great importance to our communion.

We find, therefore, that it would not be fitting for one of their number, who are assembled from all parts of the world, to quit this solemn gathering during its session. Thus We are, much to Our regret and disappointment, compelled to abandon Our intention, and to convey by the present letter Our humble and fraternal congratulations to your Grace, and to the Church in which You worthily bear rule. Our beloved brethren will rejoice in the announcement that We have communicated to You the felicitations and congratulations, and the assurance of prayer, on behalf of your rejoicing multitude, in which We know that all will be of one heart and of one soul.

The Russian and the Anglican Churches have common foes. Alike we have to guard our independence against that Papal aggressiveness which claims to subordinate all the Churches of Christ to the See of Rome. Alike we have to protect our flocks from new and strange doctrines, adverse to that Holy Faith which was handed down to us by the Holy Apostles and Ancient Fathers of the Catholic Church. But the weapons of our warfare are not carnal, and by mutual sympathy that we may be one *ἐν τοῖς δεσμοῖς τοῦ Εὐαγγελίου* we shall encourage each other, and promote the salvation of all men.

Praying, therefore, earnestly in the Spirit for the unity of all men in the Faith of the Gospel, laid down and expounded by the Oecumenical Councils of the Undivided Church of Christ, and in the living knowledge of the Son of God, We remain your Grace's most faithful and devoted servant and Brother in the Lord.

EDW. CANTUAR:

Given at Our Palace of Lambeth in London, and sealed with Our Archiepiscopal Seal on the Western Fourteenth day of July, in the year of Our Salvation, one thousand, eight hundred and eighty-eight.[4]

1 Palmer, William; son of rector of Mixbury, brother of Roundell

Palmer, later Earl of Selborne; *b.* 1811; Fellow of Magdalen College, Oxford, 1832; deacon, 1836; visited Russia, 1840; protested against Jerusalem bishopric; revisited Russia, 1842; joined Church of Rome, 1855; *d.* 1879.

2 W. J. Birkbeck was a Norfolk layman. Brandreth writes: "But Birkbeck's importance was not in what he wrote, but in what he was, one who enthusiastically introduced the two Churches to one another in his own person. He was an expert in Russian affairs, and, until his death in 1916, was the trusted adviser on all such matters of the Anglican episcopate and, on more than one occasion, of the British government" (Rouse and Neill, *A History of the Ecumenical Movement*, p. 281).

3 This greeting was the only one received by the Russian churchmen from a leader of a Western Church.

4 Mandell Creighton, Bishop of Peterborough, represented the Church of England at the coronation of the Tsar in 1896; Archbishop Maclagan visited Russia in 1897; and in that same year Archbishop Antonius of Finland represented the Russian Church at the Diamond Jubilee of Queen Victoria. The Lambeth Conferences of 1888, 1897, and 1908 discussed relations with the Orthodox Churches.

58 CHRISTIAN SOCIAL UNION

The theological outlook of the contributors to *Lux Mundi* led to the founding of the Christian Social Union, with Westcott as President,[1] and Gore and Scott Holland[2] as leaders. The C.S.U. was successful in awakening interest within the Church of England by the publication of writings and the discussion of social questions. By 1910, its peak year, the C.S.U. numbered 6,000 members. Since its concern was the elucidation of a Christian social order, it was unable to embrace the political socialism which was beginning to develop in Britain, and The Christian Socialist League was founded in 1906 to support the new Parliamentary Labour Party.[3]

THE CHRISTIAN SOCIAL UNION—CONSTITUTION

I MEMBERSHIP

(*a*) Any member of the Church of England, or of any body in full communion with her, may become a Member of the Christian Social Union on Election by a Branch of at least twenty-five Members.

(*b*) Election by a Branch shall be understood to mean election by at least two thirds of those present and voting at a meeting of the branch.

(*c*) Members are expected to pray for the well-being of the Union at Holy Communion, more particularly on or about the following days

The Feast of the Epiphany
The Feast of the Ascension
The Feast of St Michael and All Angels.

II OBJECTS

1 To claim for the Christian Law the ultimate authority to rule social practice.
2 To study in common how to apply the moral truths and principles of Christianity to the social and economic difficulties of the present time.
3 To present Christ in practical life as the Living Master and King, the enemy of wrong and selfishness, the power of righteousness and love.

III COUNCIL

(*a*) The Council shall be the governing body of the Union, and shall consist of Delegates elected annually by the various Branches. Each Branch shall be entitled to send one Delegate for every twenty-five members. No Branch shall send more than four Delegates, but each Delegate, or set of Delegates, shall have one vote for every twenty-five Members of the Branch.

(*b*) The Council shall meet at least once a year in the month of November for the election of its Executive, and for other business.

(c) The President and the Secretary of the Executive shall be *ex-officio* Chairman and Secretary of the Council during their term of office.

IV EXECUTIVE

(*a*) The Executive shall consist of the President, two Vice-Presidents, the Treasurer, the Secretary, and ten Members, who shall be elected annually by ballot by the Council and shall be eligible for re-election. Seven members shall form a quorum.

(*b*) The Executive shall have power (i) to call general meetings of the Union, (ii) to issue literature in the name of the Union, (iii) to publish statements expressing the general opinion of the Union, or to organize public meetings, provided that two thirds of the whole Executive approve, and (iv) to perform any other duties delegated to it by the Council.

(*c*) The Executive may at any time summon a meeting of the Council, and must do so on a requisition from three Branches.

V FINANCE

A central fund of the Union shall be formed to meet necessary expenses, including the travelling expenses of members of the Executive, by a contribution levied annually by the Council upon the Branches according to their membership.

VI BRANCHES

(*a*) Branches, though bound by the common objects and conditions of membership, shall be independent of the central Executive in all matters concerning their private action, for which they shall assume the sole responsibility.

(*b*) Every Branch shall send a report of its work for the year to the General Secretary at least one month before the annual meeting of the Council.

(*c*) In regard to their public action Branches are expected to conform to any general rules that may be affirmed by the Council of the Union from time to time.[4]

1 Westcott, Brooke Foss; *b.* 1825; *educ.*, King Edward's School, Birmingham and Trinity College, Cambridge; deacon and priest, 1851; master at Harrow, 1852; canon of Peterborough, 1869; canon of Westminster 1883; Regius Professor of Divinity at Cambridge, 1870; Bishop of Durham, 1890; *d.* 1901.

2 Holland, Henry Scott; *b.* 1847; *educ.*, Eton and Balliol College, Oxford; senior student at Christ Church, 1870; canon of St Paul's, 1884; Regius Professor of Divinity at Oxford, 1910; *d.* 1918.

3 The most able exponent of the C.S.L. was John Neville Figgis; *b.* 1886; *educ.*, St Catherine's College, Cambridge; Wells Theological College, 1894; curate of Kettering, 1894; lecturer at St Catherine's College and chaplain to Pembroke College, 1896; Rector of Marnhull, Dorset, 1902; entered the Community of the Resurrection, 1907; Hulsean lecturer, 1908; *d.* 1919.

4 In 1897, Scott Holland founded and edited *The Commonwealth*, a monthly periodical designed at making popular the teaching of the *Economic Review*. A scathing attack on the clerical preoccupation with social matters is given in W. R. Inge, *Outspoken Essays* (1919), pp. 103-36, entitled: "Bishop Gore and the Church of England".

59 THE CHURCHES IN EAST LONDON, 1889

(Charles Booth, *Life and Labour of People in London*, vol. 1, pp. 119-22)

The object of Booth's inquiry was to demonstrate "the numerical relation which poverty, misery, and depravity bear to regular earnings and comparative comfort, and to describe the general conditions under which each class lives".[1] The social survey which Booth undertook was able to define the place of organized religion in the urban society alongside other institutions. This volume is also notable for its descriptions of the University Settlements[2] and the Salvation Army.[3]

Religion It is difficult to say what part religion takes in the lives of the mass of the people; it is not easy to define religion for this purpose. Comparatively few go to church, but they strike me as very earnest-minded, and not without a religious feeling even when they say, as I have heard a man say (thinking of the evils which surrounded him), "If there is a God, he must be a bad one."

A census of the attendance at church and chapel all over London was taken on October 24th, 1886, and the results were published in the *British Weekly*. The attendance at mission halls was similarly taken on November 27th, 1887, and the figures for our district are appended. The synagogues, of which there are several, were not returned.

Missions, etc. There are at least a hundred agencies of a more or less religious and philanthropic character at work in our district. Most of these are on a small scale, and are local in character, connected with the principal denominations of the parish in which they are carried on. There are, however, a few larger ones, such as the Great Assembly Hall Mission, Mile End Road, which, under the superintendence of Mr F. N. Charrington, is carrying on an extensive work, and draws several thousands of people to its religious services.[4] Harley House, Bow, is the centre of an important evangelical enterprise directed by Mr and Mrs Guinness; and some of the music halls and theatres, as also the Bow and Bromley Institute, are utilized on Sundays for the carrying on of religious work on a large scale. An extensive work is also being carried on in the homes and missions organized by Dr Stephenson at Bonner Road and elsewhere.

Note The generally accepted estimate of Sir Horace Mann is that

58 per cent of the population could, if they chose, attend a place of worship once on Sunday. Deducting from the total population the 50,000 Jews, this would give for our district 498,220 as the possible total of attenders, whereas the actual number, taking together all the services given in the above tables (and assuming that those who attend more than once in the day are balanced by some whose only attendance is at an early morning or extra service) was 202,600, or 23·6 per cent. Applying the same method to the whole of London, the actual number of attenders was 1,171,412, or about 29 per cent.

1 Booth, Charles; *b.* 1840; a shipowner; author of *Labour and Life of the People*, 1889; *Life and Labour of the People in London*, 1891–1903; *d.* 1916.

2 The University Settlements were attempts, by means of residential settlements, to bring university culture into direct contact with the labouring classes. Both Toynbee Hall and Oxford House were to include archbishops, bishops, and statesmen amongst their helpers.

3 The Salvation Army, founded by William Booth in 1865 in East London, was re-formed in 1878. Charles Booth noted that the Salvation Army claimed (Christmas, 1888) 7107 officers, 2587 corps, and 653 outposts, and was established in 33 countries. Charles Booth concluded: "Not by this road (if I am right) will religion be brought to the mass of the English people."

4 The use of unconsecrated buildings as centres for religious worship and teaching was advocated by many leading Evangelicals. Although some Ritualist preachers, such as Father Ignatius, were quite at home in them, they were generally scorned by the High Churchmen.

60 THE JURISDICTION OF THE ARCHBISHOP'S COURT, 1889

(E. S. Roscoe, *The Bishop of Lincoln's Case* (1889), pp. 15-17, 41-2)

Edward King[1] became Bishop of Lincoln in 1885 and was widely revered as a pastor. As a representative of the High Church party complaint was made against him before the Archbishop of Canterbury by the Church Association. Benson[2] was called upon to proceed against his suffragan for a breach of the ecclesiastical law, but first it had to be decided whether the archbishop had the authority to try such a case. On 26 June 1888, he refused to issue a citation. A petition was presented to the Judicial Committee of the Privy Council, and an appeal was allowed on 8 August, and the Archbishop was compelled to issue the citation. King appeared before the Archbishop at Lambeth on 12 February where the Bishops of London, Winchester, Oxford, and Salisbury assisted Benson. The judgment was delivered on 11 May.

The Court has now to give its decision on the protest raised on behalf of the Lord Bishop of Lincoln against the jurisdiction of the Court in this matter.

First, it will be necessary to consider the case stated in the protest; secondly, the authorities and the arguments against and in support of the archiepiscopal jurisdiction; thirdly, to state the conclusion arrived at, and declare the course to be taken upon the decision.

I The protest says:

(i) That the citation issued does not cite the Lord Bishop of Lincoln to appear in any Court or in any proceedings whereof the laws, canons, and constitutions ecclesiastical of this Church and realm and of the Province of Canterbury take cognizance.

(ii) That by the said laws, canons, and constitutions, the Lord Bishop of Lincoln is not bound and ought not to appear before or be tried by the archbishop sitting alone, or to appear before or to be tried by the Vicar-General of the archbishop; and the fact that the archbishop proposes to sit with assessors does not confer a jurisdiction which he would not otherwise have.

(iii) That by the said laws, canons and constitutions, the Lord Bishop of Lincoln as a bishop of the Province of Canterbury ought not to be tried for the offences (if any) with which he is charged in these proceedings, save by the Archbishop of Canterbury together with the other bishops of the province, his comprovincials, assembled either in the Convocation of the said province or otherwise.

(iv) That the charges set forth in the citation are not such charges as by the said laws, canons, and constitutions, the said Lord Bishop of Lincoln is bound, or ought to be tried for before or by any Court of ecclesiastical jurisdiction. The consideration of this fourth point was deferred, without prejudice to his Lordship's position, until the case (in the event of the protest being overruled) should come to be heard on its merits. By the first three articles of the protest, two questions are raised: (*a*) Has the archbishop, either sitting alone or with assessors in the Archiepiscopal Court of his province, jurisdiction? (*b*) Has the archbishop jurisdiction only when sitting together with the other bishops of the province assembled in convocation "or otherwise"? The word "otherwise" is not explained. But the second question (*b*) would not require consideration if the first (*a*) were decided in the affirmative. If it were proved that the archbishop has jurisdiction when sitting in Convocation, this would not in itself prove that he has jurisdiction only when so sitting. It is obvious that such jurisdiction might exist concurrently with a jurisdiction exercised by the archbishop alone or with assessors.

II The arguments in support of the protest and the authorities cited have extended over a wide range. The records of early synods and councils have been much relied upon. As documents ancient, and solemnly accepted, these records deserve all the scholarship and attention with which they have been handled by the learned counsel. Not for this immediate purpose only, but for ourselves always and our beliefs, they have the highest value and weight. It is desirable, therefore, to ascertain, if possible, exactly what kind and amount of support the contention receives from their authority. General impressions are easily created even by raising a contention on such grounds, and then conscientious difficulties gather round those impressions. It is therefore quite worth while to examine in some detail the canons cited, but only for the purpose for which they are cited. The argument which was advanced is very clear and connected.[3] The first canon of the Council of Chalcedon received the canons of "all the holy synods" held before it. The English Church receives the Council of Chalcedon as one of the four general councils.[4] All the canons, therefore, of this and of the earlier synods referred to have become and, if the law has not been altered, are still part of the law of the realm.[5] It is agreed, at the same time, that if the directions contained in ancient canons are ever so clear and definite, they still cannot determine any question of canonical or other law in England unless they have been received and put in use. There is, however, no doubt that in matters of faith and doctrine the decrees of the first four general councils have been so received, as declared in the statute law (25 Hen. 8, c. 13, s. 37; 1 Eliz., c. 1, s. 36). Canons also therein made, when strictly applicable, and when not "contrariant to the law of the Church and realm", have authority....[6]

... The Court has now examined in detail the facts and reasonings which have been submitted to it as ecclesiastical grounds against the validity of its jurisdiction. It desires to express its obligations to the learned counsel on both sides for the learning and lucidity with which they have illustrated the subject and fortified their several contentions. The Court finds that from the most ancient times of the Church the archiepiscopal jurisdiction in the case of suffragans has existed; that in the Church of England it has been from time to time continuously exercised in various forms; that nothing has occurred in the Church to modify that jurisdiction; and that, even if such jurisdiction could be used in Convocation for the trial of a bishop, consistently with the ancient principle that in a synod bishops only could hear such a cause, it nevertheless remains clear that the metropolitan has regularly exercised that jurisdiction both alone and with assessors. The cases came all under one jurisdiction, but in many forms: in synods, episcopal, clerical or mixed, in council, in the Upper House of Convocation, with both Houses, in the Court of Arches, in the Court of Audience[7] (some hold), through the Vicar-General, through arbitrators, with one assessor, with three or four or five assessors, alone *absque consensu cujuslibet Episcopi*, but always, except for some impediment, personally—*ob reverentiam officii* and *ob reverentiam fratris*. Nor is it strange that while the jurisdiction is one, forms should be many and cases few. The question now before us is touching the action of the archbishop, sitting together with comprovincial assessors. There is no form of the exercise of the jurisdiction in this country which has been more examined into and is better attested and confirmed.

III The Court, therefore, although by an entirely different line of inquiry, has arrived at the same conclusion which was arrived at on purely legal principles by the unanimous judgment of the Lord High Chancellor with four judges and five bishops who constituted the Judicial Committee of the Privy Council to advise Her Majesty in August, 1888. The Court decides that it has jurisdiction in this case, and therefore overrules the protest.[8]

1 King, Edward; *b.* 1829; *educ.*, Oriel College, Oxford, 1848; deacon, 1854; priest, 1855; curate of Wheatley, Oxfordshire; chaplain of Cuddesdon Theological College, 1858; Principal and Vicar of Cuddesdon, 1863; Regius Professor of Pastoral Theology and canon of Christ Church, 1873; Bishop of Lincoln, 1885; *d.* 1910.

2 Benson, Edward White; *b.* 1829; *educ.*, King Edward School, Birmingham and Trinity College, Cambridge; assistant master at Rugby, 1852; deacon, 1854; priest, 1856; Master of Wellington College, 1858; Chancellor of Lincoln Cathedral, 1873; first Bishop of Truro, 1877; Archbishop of Canterbury, 1883; *d.* 1896.

3 Sir Walter Phillimore (son of Robert), as Chancellor of the diocese of Lincoln, defended King. The assessors were the Bishops of London (Temple); Rochester (Thorold); Oxford (Stubbs); Salisbury (Wordsworth); and Hereford (Atlay).

4 Article 21 does not specify the number of councils but maintains "they may err, and sometimes have erred, even in things pertaining unto God". Hooker and Andrewes maintained the authority of the first four whereas the *Book of Homilies*, Field, and Hammond accepted the first six.

5 In his *Appendix* to the Royal Commission on the Ecclesiastical Courts' Report in 1883, Stubbs had written: "The laws of the Church of England from the Conquest onwards, were, as before, the customary church law developed by the legal and scientific ability of its administrators, and occasionally improved and added to by the constitutions of successive archbishops, the canons of national councils, and the sentences, or authoritative answers to questions, propounded by the Popes." (To this must be added the *Corpus Juris Canonici* as F. W. Maitland pointed out and Stubbs later acknowledged.) The Archbishop's judgment was based on the historical consideration of canon law and consequently marks a departure from the ninteenth-century tendency to look for both precedent and procedure in statute law. See Kemp: *An Introduction to Canon Law in the Church of England*, (1957), pp. 11-12.

6 1 Eliz., c. 1, *The Act of Supremacy*, 1559. Under section 36, the first four Councils (Nicaea, Constantinople, Ephesus and Chalcedon) and the authority of the canonical Scriptures were the means of adjudicating in matters of heresy.

7 The Court of Audience was formerly the ecclesiastical court of

the Province of Canterbury in which the archbishop exercised his legatine jurisdiction in person. Later, however, he was assisted by Auditors, and finally a single Assessor acted as judge, until at length the court was merged into the Court of Arches in the seventeenth century.

8 The Judicial Committee of the Privy Council was approached by the prosecutors, and judgment was delivered on 3 August. The only precedent for the authority of the court of an archbishop in relation to a suffragan was that of *Lucey* v. *Bishop Watson* (1699). The judgment of the Judicial Committee was: "Their Lordships are of the opinion that the Archbishop has jurisdiction in this case. They are also of opinion that the abstaining by the Archbishop from entertaining the suit is a matter of appeal to Her Majesty; they desire to express no opinion whatever as to whether the Archbishop has, or has not, a discretion whether he will issue a citation; and they will humbly advise Her Majesty to remit the case to the Archbishop to be dealt with according to law."

61 THE LINCOLN JUDGMENT, 1890

(E. S. Roscoe, *The Bishop of Lincoln's Case* (1891), pp. 46-7, 176, 200-2)

The Archbishop delivered his judgment on 21 November 1890. All the assessors concurred in the judgment, apart from one dissentient on one point. The judgment was noteworthy inasmuch as it came to conclusions different from those of the ritual decisions of the Judicial Committee, thus satisfying many churchmen. The Bishop of Lincoln accepted the judgment, and the Judicial Committee confirmed the Archbishop's decision on all points excepting one.

WE EDWARD WHITE by Divine Providence Lord Archbishop of Canterbury Primate of All England and Metropolitan To you THE RIGHT REVEREND FATHER IN CHRIST EDWARD By Divine Permission LORD BISHOP OF LINCOLN All and singular the articles heads and Interrogatories hereunder written touching and concerning your Souls health and the lawful correction of your manners and more especially for having when officiating as Bishop and the principal Celebrant in the administration of the Holy Communion in the Church of St Peter at Gowts in the City of Lincoln and in the Cathedral Church of Lincoln in the month of

December One thousand eight hundred and eighty-seven been party to and taken part in the observance of certain unlawful rites and ceremonies namely the using and permitting to be used lighted candles on the Communion Table during such service as a matter of ceremony and when not wanted for light[1] the mixing of water with the sacramental wine and the consecrating and the administering of the same to the communicants when so mixed openly and ceremoniously making the sign of the Cross during such service the observance of the ceremony of ablution and standing yourself whilst reading the Prayer of Consecration on the west side of the Holy Table with your back to the people in such manner that the communicants could not see you break the bread and take the cup into your hands and for having also been party to the singing of the *Agnus Dei* after you read the Prayer of Consecration and immediately before the reception of the sacramental elements all of which acts observances ceremonies and additions to the said service were in contravention of the ecclesiastical laws of England do by virtue of our office at the voluntary promotion of Ernest de Lacy Read of Cleethorpe in the County and Diocese of Lincoln salesman and auctioneer William Brown of Great Grimsby in the County and Diocese of Lincoln solicitor of the Supreme Court Felix Thomas Wilson of the said Parish of St Peter at Gowts in the City of Lincoln in the same Diocese and John Marshall of the same Parish gardener article and object as follows to wit: ...[2]

... A Court constituted as is the present, having wider duties towards all parties concerned than those of other judges, duties inalienable from that position which makes its members judges, considers itself bound further to observe briefly in relation to this case that,

1. Although religious people whose religious feelings really suffer might rightly feel constrained to come forward as witnesses in such a case, yet it is not decent for religious persons to hire witnesses to intrude on the worship of others for purposes of espial.[3] In expressing this opinion the Court has no intention of criticizing the statements themselves which were in this case given in evidence.

2. The Court has not only felt deeply the incongruity of minute questionings and disputations in great and sacred subjects, but desires to express its sense that time and attention are diverted thereby from the Church's real contest with evil and building up of good, both by those who give and by those who take offence unadvisedly in such matters.[4]

3. The apostolic judgment as to other matters of ritual has a proper reference to these; namely, that things which may necessarily be ruled to be lawful do not for that reason become expedient.

4. Public worship is one of the divine institutions, which are the heritage of the Church, for the fraternal union of mankind.

The Church, therefore, has a right to ask that her congregations may not be divided either by needless pursuance or by exaggerated suspicion of practices not in themselves illegal. Either spirit is in painful contrast to the deep and wide desire which prevails for mutual understanding. The clergy are the natural prompters and fosterers of the divine instinct, "to follow after things which make for peace, and things wherewith one may edify another".

We have given judgment on each article as the several points have been considered. We give no costs....

DECREE

The Lord Archbishop, having heretofore, with the assistance of the said Lord Bishop of London, Lord Bishop of Hereford, Lord Bishop of Rochester, Lord Bishop of Oxford, and Lord Bishop of Salisbury, heard the evidence of the witnesses produced on the part of the promoters and the arguments of counsel on both sides, and having maturely deliberated, by his decree did pronounce and declare:

That the 1st, 2nd, and 16th articles were sufficiently proved.

As to the charge contained in the 3rd article, and the reference thereto in the 13th article, that the promoters had proved that, with the sanction of the Lord Bishop of Lincoln, there were two lighted candles in candlesticks on the holy table, when such lighted candles were not wanted for the purpose of giving light, from before the service for the administration of the Holy Communion began until after it was over, and that this was not contrary to the ecclesiastical laws of England.

As to the charges contained in the 4th article and the references thereto in the 13th and 14th articles, that the promoters had proved that the said Lord Bishop of Lincoln, in the service for the administration of the Holy Communion, and just before the prayer for the Church Militant, caused, permitted, and was a party to, and took part in the mixing of water with the sacramental wine, intended to be used in the administration of the Holy Communion at such service, and subsequently at the said service consecrated the said wine and water so mixed, and administered the said wine and water so mixed to the communicants at such service, and that the mixing of the water with the wine in, and as part of the service, was and is contrary to the ecclesiastical law of England, and that the said Lord Bishop had thereby offended against the ecclesiastical law of England, but that the act of consecrating wine mixed with water before the service, and of administering the same when so mixed to the communicants, would not be offences against the ecclesiastical law of England.

As to the charges contained in the 5th and 10th articles, and the reference thereto in the 15th article, that the promoters had proved that the said Lord Bishop of Lincoln, in the service for the administration of the Holy Communion stood, while reading the prayer of consecration in such service, on the west side of the holy table with his face to the east, and between the people and the holy table, and with his back to the people in such wise that the communicants present when he broke bread and took the cup into his hand could not see him break the bread and take the cup into his hand, that to stand in such wise that the said manual acts would not be visible to the communicants present when conveniently placed, would be unlawful, and that the order of the Holy Communion requires that the manual acts must be performed in such wise as to be visible to the communicants properly placed.

As to the charge contained in the 6th article, and the reference thereto in the 13th article, that the promoters had proved that the said Lord Bishop of Lincoln caused, or permitted, to be sung by the choir before the reception of the elements and immediately after the reading of the prayer of consecration in the service for the administration of the Holy Communion the words "O Lamb of God, that takest away the sins of the world. Have mercy upon us", but that the act of the said Lord Bishop therein was, and is not, contrary to the ecclesiastical law of England.

As to the charges contained in the 7th and 11th articles, and the references thereto in the 13th article, that the promoters had sufficiently proved that the said Lord Bishop of Lincoln, in the service for the administration of the Holy Communion, whilst pronouncing the absolution conspicuously and ceremoniously made with his hand the sign of the cross towards the congregation, and also in like manner, whilst pronouncing the benediction in the same service, made the sign of the cross, and that the act of the said Lord Bishop, on making the sign of the cross whilst pronouncing the absolution and benediction as aforesaid was and is contrary to the ecclesiastical law of England, and that this is an innovation which must be discontinued.

As to the charges contained in the 8th and 12th articles, and the reference thereto in the 13th article, that they were not proved.

As to the charge contained in the 9th article, that the promoters had proved so far only as that the said Lord Bishop of Lincoln during the said service for the administration of the Holy Communion down to the Creed stood or knelt on the west side of the holy table, but that there was no allegation in the articles that the acts charged were unlawful, and that the acts proved would not be unlawful.

And the Lord Archbishop of Canterbury made no order as to the costs of this suit or any part thereof.[5]

1 In the case of *Martin* v. *Mackonochie* altar lights were regarded as illegal. The appeal to the Judicial Committee did not confirm the Archbishop's judgment on this point, but dismissed the appeal on the grounds that the candles had been lighted by the incumbent of the parish and not by the bishop.

2 Article 1: the Bishop of Lincoln is bound to observe the laws, statutes and canons of the realm,
Article 2: bishops are bound to use only the rites and ceremonies as set forth by the Prayer Book,
Article 16: that the Bishop of Lincoln is subject to the jurisdiction of the Archbishop's court.

3 The following entries in the bill of costs presented by the proctors for the Church Association to Mackonochie are instructive. "Attending Mr Pond, instructing him to attend St Alban's on Sunday, July 11 ... Taking his statement and fair copy ... Paid him for his attendance ... Attending Mr Pond, instructing him to attend St Alban's on July 12 and four following days ... Taking his statement and fair copy ... Paid him for his attendance ... (Two guineas for Sunday, one each week-day)." Quoted in S. C. Carpenter, *Church and People*, p. 243.

4 The legal profession did not seem to have fully appreciated, on all occasions, the profound feelings of churchmen regarding the Eucharist and other sacramental forms. The technicalities which obstructed Archbishop Tait in retrieving a consecrated host displayed as evidence in court, are recalled in the *Life*, vol. 2, pp. 263-6.

5 An Evangelical appraisal of the judgment may be found in *The Protestant Dictionary* (1933), ed. C. S. Carter and G. E. Alison Weeks, pp. 377-8.

62 CANON LIDDON AND *LUX MUNDI*, 1889

(Johnstone, *Life and Letters of H. P. Liddon*, pp. 364-6)

Lux Mundi was published in 1889 by a group of Oxford Tractarian scholars. In the religious controversies of the period Tractarian scholarship had always retained a conservative and traditional position, and the adoption of the new critical methods of biblical scholarship in *Lux Mundi* marked the beginning of new Anglo-Catholic outlook. The book's purpose was "to put the Catholic faith into its right relation to modern intellectual and moral problems". Liddon, as a representative of conservative Tractarianism, was distressed by the rationalism which emanated from Pusey House.[1]

TO THE REVEREND CHARLES GORE[2]

3, Amen Court, E.C.,
October 29, 1889.

I am indeed sorry to have been adding to your burden of work when you are so busy. But what I am going to write now needs no answer. You will, I know, do the best you can. No doubt if I had been more observant, or rather less stupid than I am, I should have discovered what you were saying and thinking about the Old Testament. I had thought of you as keenly interested in everything that was said on all sides, but as holding tenaciously to the principles which underlie the trustworthiness of the Sacred Volume.

Of course, I have never heard you lecture, nor had I been present at the other occasions to which you refer. And, as you would know, it does not fall in my way to hear much of what is going on . . .

When you accepted the Principalship of the Pusey Library, I remember your telling me—I thought it had been in conversation—that you could not always agree with Dr Pusey about the Fathers. I believe I replied, that in so wide a field, within the bounds of which so many questions might be raised, anything like absolute agreement was not to be expected, and I instanced Tertullian, whom I knew you to have been reading very carefully, as a writer about whom people might differ widely on a great variety of points without doing any particular mischief. I do not now remember any allusion to the Old Testament. But this may be due to my bad memory; or, if we were talking, to my deafness; or, if you wrote, to a careless way that I have of reading letters imperfectly; or from my turning the subject out of my mind, from thinking at the time that all you meant was that you could not bind yourself to every opinion of Dr Pusey on matters of detail, or to every interpretation of particular passages of Holy Scripture which he has sanctioned....

We are not opposed in *this* sense, that I hold all Criticism to be mischievous, while you hold it to be generally illuminating and useful. For Criticism is an equivocal term, and is applied to very different kinds of Textual or Exegetical work. Dr Pusey, in one sense, was a great critic; in another, Strauss, and Bruno Bauer, and Feuerbach were. What the young "experts", such as Professor Cheyne,[3] mean by Criticism now, is, I suppose, that kind of discussion of doctrines and of documents which treats the individual reason as an absolutely competent and final judge, and which has the most differentiating merit of being independent of Church authority. At least this would be, I fancy, the general sense of the term in that home of modern Criticism, Protestant Germany.[4] Criticism with Dr Pusey was, of course, something very different. It was the bringing all that learning and thought could bring to illustrate the mind of Christian Antiquity which really guided him. All Criticism, I suppose, *really* proceeds on certain principles, preliminary assumptions for the critic to go upon. The question in all cases is, Whence do the preliminary assumptions come? A Catholic critic would say, "From the general sense of the Church".[5] But a modern "psychological" critic (if that is the right word) would say, "From his own notion of the fitness of things, or from the outcome of literature at large". Certainly these *placita* which abound in the new "Old Testament Criticism" do not appear to come from the text itself; they are imposed on it from without. When I saw Dr Döllinger a year ago, we were talking about Wellhausen's *Prolegomena.* I forget how many "assumptions" he told me he had counted, when at last he could stand it no longer, and put the book down.

Now, dearest friend, when you write about recognizing the mythos as an ingredient of the Sacred Scriptures, or about our Lord's references to the Old Testament as *ad hominem* arguments, are you not assuming principles, in the one case out of deference to a supposed analogy of the mental and literary development of Pagan Greece, in the other as an expedient whereby to meet the difficulties which are presented by a modern estimate of the events or texts to which our Lord referred?

But Holy Scripture nowhere suggests that its narratives are mythical; nor does our Lord, in the passages referred to, give a hint that His argument is only *ad hominem.* And Origen and one or two other names, when made the most of, do not go for much against the general *consensus Patrum* on the first point; while I should doubt whether any Father is in favour of the modern view on the second.[6]

But I am writing without books, and may make mistakes. And the questions raised are much too vast to be discussed in a letter. The *immediate* point to be settled—though I fear I understand you to say it *is* settled—is whether all that you have printed should be published. You seem to me to underrate the gravity of publication.

While a man lectures orally, he is relatively uncommitted, he is often swayed by his class, he can retract, or modify, or "efface by silence", without grave difficulty; but if he publishes—*littera impressa manet*—then it is beyond his control for all time. How thankfully would Dr Pusey, in the later years of his life, *not* have published his *Theology of Germany*![7] And is it certain that Bishop Lightfoot has not sometimes wished that he could recall his *Essay on the Christian Ministry*?[8]

And when you think of those who would welcome your publishing the passages in question, is not something to be said for others who love and trust you, and who would be perplexed and distressed by their publication?

Are we not bound, before taking a grave step, to look well on all sides of us, and consider, not only how it would affect those in whom we are immediately interested, but also how it would affect others, who, in the general scheme of Divine Providence, have other, but great claims on our consideration? And might I make one closing suggestion? To wit, whether it would be well to submit the passages in question to a Bishop—say the Bishop of Lincoln, whose Chaplain you are; or the Bishop of Oxford, in whose diocese you are and who is one of our [the Pusey House] Governors; or the Archbishop of Canterbury, as the highest official authority in the Church; or the Bishop of Durham, who combines learning in these subjects with the Episcopal office?[9] If any of them should bid you publish, you would have something to fall back upon in the way of authority; if they should hesitate, you would have a good reason for any inconvenience which delay in publication might cause to your publisher.

For myself, I have no sort of authority, either in Church office or in virtue of special learning. I can only write to you as an old friend, begging you to consider some sides of the matter which you may have overlooked in the pressure of your work, but which cause me much real anxiety.

P.S.—You would, I feel sure, recognize the difference between the claim of any particular intellectual presentation of Truth—however intimately bound up with one's mental history—and that of any certain part of the Catholic Faith. The former *may*, in time, be modified or abandoned, however improbable anything of the sort may seem to us *now*. The latter never, *i.e.*, supposing us to remain in a state of grace.

1 Liddon, Henry Parry; *b*. 1829; *educ*., Christ Church, Oxford; deacon, 1852; priest, 1853; curate of Wantage; vice-principal of Cuddesdon, 1854; vice-principal of St Edmund Hall, 1859; prebendary of Salisbury, 1864; Bampton Lecturer, 1886; canon of St Paul's, 1870; Dean Ireland Professor of Exegesis at Oxford, 1870; visited Döllinger at Munich, 1888; Chancellor of St Paul's, 1886; refused bishopric of St Albans, 1890; *d*. 1890.

2 Gore, Charles; *b*. 1853; *educ*., Harrow and Balliol College, Oxford, 1871; Fellow of Trinity College, Oxford, 1875; Principal of Pusey House, 1884; edited *Lux Mundi*, 1889; Bampton Lecturer, 1891; founded the Community of the Resurrection at Oxford, 1892; vicar of Radley, 1893; canon of Westminster, 1894; Bishop of Worcester, 1902; first Bishop of Birmingham, 1905; Bishop of Oxford, 1911; resigned his see, 1919; *d*. 1932.

3 Cheyne, Thomas Kelly; Oriel Professor of the Interpretation of Scripture at Oxford, 1885–1915. Studied under Ewald at Göttingen in 1862, and had maintained the theory of Pentateuchal sources as early as 1871. He was a visitor to Longworth Rectory where the meetings of Gore's "Holy Party" prepared the ground for the book.

4 Schweitzer's *Von Reimarus zu Wrede* did not appear until 1906 when it brought the Gospels into the centre of the controversy. Gore and his friends were willing to consider the criticism of the Old Testament as advocated by Ewald, Wellhausen, and Duhm, but they withdrew from applying the same critical principles to the New Testament.

5 *Lux Mundi* was specifically an explanation of the Creed by churchmen, owning a corporate responsibility. It was sub-titled "A series of studies in the Religion of the Incarnation", and was a product of the incarnational outlook of contemporary Anglican thought stemming from Maurice and Westcott.

6 Gore had used the patristic writers extensively in his essay on "The Holy Spirit and Inspiration", and though Liddon dealt specifically with Gore's critical conclusions, the real bone of contention at the time was the kenotic view of the person of Christ expounded at the end of the essay. Liddon's Bampton Lectures had been on: *The Divinity of Our Lord and Saviour Jesus Christ*, which had set out the traditional concepts.

7 *An Historical Enquiry into the Probable Causes of the Rationalist Character lately predominant in the Theology of Germany* (Part 1, 1828, Part 2, 1830).

8 The criticism and exegesis of the New Testament was carried forward by the labours of Westcott, Hort, and Lightfoot at Cambridge. The publication of the Greek New Testament by Westcott and Hort in 1881 marked a new era in English textual criticism.

9 Edward King (Lincoln).

William Stubbs had been translated from Chester to Oxford in the same year as the publication of *Lux Mundi*. Pusey House, of which he was governor, was opened in 1884 as a "home of sacred learning and a rallying-point for the Christian faith, and thus it will strengthen all that is dearest to a sincere Christian at what, so far as we can judge, must always be one of the chief centres of the mental life of this country".

E. W. Benson (Canterbury).

Brooke Foss Westcott, who had succeeded J. B. Lightfoot as Bishop of Durham in May 1889.

63 THE CLERGY DISCIPLINE ACT 1892

(*Statutes at Large*, 55-56 Vict., c. 32)

Ecclesiastical discipline relating to the clergy was enforced by statute law in the three main Parliamentary Acts of the nineteenth century. The Church Discipline Act of 1840 provided suspension and deprivation as safeguards against unorthodoxy; the Public Worship Regulation Act of 1874 aimed at enforcing ritual conformity; and the Clergy Discipline Act dealt with the moral conduct of the clergy. Though passed at the height of the ritual controversy it did not attempt to supplement the Act of 1874.

1[1] If either

(*a*) a clergyman is convicted of treason or felony, or is convicted on indictment of a misdemeanour, and on any such conviction is sentenced to imprisonment with hard labour or any greater punishment, or

(*b*) an order under the Acts relating to bastardy is made on a clergyman, or

(*c*) a clergyman is found in a divorce or matrimonial cause to have committed adultery, or
(*d*) an order for judicial separation is made against a clergyman in a divorce or matrimonial cause, or
(*e*) a separation order is made against a clergyman under the Matrimonial Causes Act, 1878;

then, after the date at which the conviction, order, or finding becomes conclusive, the preferment (if any) held by him shall, within twenty-one days, without further trial, be declared by the bishop to be vacant as from the said date, and he shall be incapable, save as in this Act mentioned, of holding preferment.

3[1] The assessors shall be chosen in the prescribed manner from the list of assessors who shall be elected as soon as possible after the commencement of this Act, and every three years afterwards, as follows (that is to say):

(*a*) Three shall be elected from their own number by the members of the cathedral church of the diocese.
(*b*) Four shall be elected from their own number by the beneficed clergy of each archdeaconry in the diocese; and
(*c*) Five shall be elected from the justices of the county by the court of quarter sessions of each county wholly in the diocese, and of such of the counties partly in the diocese as may be prescribed.

6[1] When a clergyman is, under this Act, adjudged guilty

(*a*) regard shall be had in considering the sentence to the interests of the ecclesiastical parish or place concerned, and not to precedents of punishments; and
(*b*) he may be sentenced in every case to deprivation, and if so sentenced shall be incapable, save as in this Act mentioned, of holding preferment; and
(*c*) if he is sentenced to suspension for a term, he shall not, during that term, exercise or perform without leave of the court any right or duty of or incidental or attached to his preferment, nor reside in or within such distance from the house of residence of that preferment as is specified in the sentence, and shall not, at the end of the term, be re-admitted until he has satisfied the court of his good conduct during the term.

8 Where by virtue of this Act, or of any sentence passed in pursuance of this Act, the preferment of a clergyman becomes vacant, and it appears to the bishop of the diocese that such clergyman ought also to be deposed from holy orders, the bishop

may, by sentence and without any further formality, depose him,[1] and the sentence of deposition shall be recorded in the registry of the diocese: Provided always, that such clergyman may appeal against the said sentence within one month from the date thereof to the archbishop of the province, whose decision shall be final.

1 The Ordinary was permitted to depose or degrade by statute law (e.g. 23 Hen. VIII, c. 1, section 6) though the last person to have been deposed under English canon law was Dr Leighton in 1631. Under the provisions of the Act of 1892, deposition is inflicted summarily by pronouncing sentence and without ceremony and formality.

64 ROME AND ANGLICAN ORDERS, 1896

(*Apostolicae curae* (1957), pp. 1-3, 9-13. *Answer of the Archbishops of England to the Apostolic Letter of Pope Leo XIII on English Ordinations* (1957), pp. 23-6, 52-60)

The personal friendship between Lord Halifax[1] and E. F. Portal led to a series of conversations between Anglicans and Roman Catholics in Rome, 1894–6. The Pope appointed a commission to inquire into the validity of Anglican Orders which finished sitting in June 1896. F. W. Puller and T. A. Lacey went to Rome to give any information which might have been required. The encyclical expressed the views of the Roman curia, and was influenced by the hostility of Cardinal Vaughan[2] and the Roman Catholic episcopate in England to the Rome discussions. Archbishop Benson commenced making notes for a reply, but his death in October 1896 left Temple to complete the task. Although Stubbs, Creighton, and Wordsworth were the leading authorities in this inquiry, the official reply appeared over the signatures of the two archbishops, Temple and Maclagan.[3]

LEO, BISHOP, SERVANT OF THE SERVANTS OF GOD
IN PERPETUAL REMEMBRANCE

We have dedicated to the welfare of the noble English nation no small portion of the Apostolic care and charity by which, helped by His grace, We endeavour to fulfil the office and follow in the footsteps of "*the Great Shepherd of the sheep*", Our Lord Jesus Christ. The Letter, which last year We sent to *the English seeking the Kingdom of Christ in the unity of the faith*, is a special witness of Our good will towards England. In it We recalled the memory of the ancient union of her people with Mother Church, and We strove to hasten the day of a happy reconciliation by stirring up men's hearts to offer diligent prayer to God.[4] And, again, more recently, when it seemed good to Us to treat more fully the Unity of the Church in a general Letter, England had not the last place in Our mind, in the hope that Our teaching might both strengthen Catholics and bring the saving light to those divided from Us.

It is pleasing to acknowledge the generous way in which Our zeal and plainness of speech, inspired by no mere human motives, have met the approval of the English people; and this testifies not less to their courtesy than to the solicitude of many for their eternal salvation.

With the same mind and intention We have now determined to turn Our consideration to a matter of no less importance, which is closely connected with the same subject and with Our desires. For already the general belief, confirmed more than once by the action and constant practice of the Church, maintained that when in England, shortly after it was rent from the centre of Christian unity, a new rite for conferring Holy Orders was publicly introduced under Edward VI, the true Sacrament of Orders, as instituted by Christ, lapsed, and with it the hierarchical succession. For some time, however, and in these last years especially, a controversy has sprung up as to whether the Sacred Orders conferred according to the Edwardine Ordinal possessed the nature and effect of a sacrament: those in favour of the absolute validity, or of a doubtful validity, being not only certain Anglican writers, but some few Catholics, chiefly non-English.[5] The consideration of the excellency of the Christian priesthood moved Anglican writers in this matter, desirous as they were that their own people should not lack the twofold power over the Body of Christ. Catholic writers were impelled by a wish to smooth the way for the return of Anglicans to holy unity. Both, indeed, thought that in view of studies brought up to the level of recent research, and of new documents rescued from oblivion, it was not inopportune to re-examine the question by Our authority. And We, not disregarding such desires and opinions, and, above all, obeying the dictates of Apostolic charity, have considered that nothing should be left untried that might in any way tend to preserve souls from injury or procure their advantage.

It has, therefore, pleased Us to graciously permit the cause to be re-examined so that through the extreme care taken in the new examination all doubt, or even shadow of doubt, should be removed for the future. To this end We commissioned a certain number of men noted for their learning and ability, whose opinions in this matter were known to be divergent, to state the grounds of their judgments in writing. We then, having summoned them to Our person, directed them to interchange writings and further to investigate and discuss all that was necessary for a full knowledge of the matter. We were careful also that they should be able to re-examine all documents bearing on this question which were known to exist in the Vatican archives, to search for new ones, and even to have at their disposal all acts relating to this subject which are preserved by the Holy Office—or as it is called the *Supreme* Council—and to consider whatever had up to this time been adduced by learned men on both sides. We ordered them, when prepared in this way, to meet together in special sessions. These to the number of twelve were held under the presidency of one of the Cardinals of the Holy Roman Church, appointed by Ourselves, and all were invited to free discussion. Finally We directed that the acts of these meetings, together with all other documents should be submitted to Our Venerable Brethren, the Cardinals of the same Council, so that when all had studied the whole subject, and discussed it in Our presence, each might give his opinion....

... In the examination of any rite for the effecting and administering of Sacrament, distinction is rightly made between the part which is *ceremonial* and that which is *essential*, usually called the *matter and form*. All know that the Sacraments of the New Law, as sensible and efficient signs of invisible grace, ought both to signify the grace which they effect, and effect the grace which they signify. Although the signification ought to be found in the whole essential rite—that is to say, in the matter and form—it still pertains chiefly to the form; since the matter is the part which is not determined by itself, but which is determined by the form. And this appears still more clearly in the Sacrament of Orders, the matter of which, in so far as We have to consider it in this case, is the imposition of hands, which indeed by itself signifies nothing definite, and is equally used for several Orders and for Confirmation. But the words which until recently were commonly held by Anglicans to constitute the proper form of priestly Ordination, namely, *"Receive the Holy Ghost"*, certainly do not in the least definitely express the Sacred Order of Priesthood, or its grace and power, which is chiefly the power *"of consecrating and of offering the true body and blood of the Lord"* (Council of Trent, Sess. XXIII., *de Sacr. Ord.*,

Can. 1) in that sacrifice which is no *"nude commemoration of the sacrifice offered on the Cross"* (Ibid. Sess. XXII., *de Sacrif. Missae.* Can. 3). This form had indeed afterwards added to it the words *"for the office and work of a priest"*, etc.; but this rather shows that the Anglicans themselves perceived that the first form was defective and inadequate. But even if this addition could give to the form its due signification, it was introduced too late, as a century had already elapsed since the adoption of the Edwardine Ordinal, for, as the Hierarchy had become extinct there remained no power of ordaining. In vain has help been recently sought for the plea of the validity of Orders from the other prayers of the same Ordinal. For, to put aside other reasons which show these to be insufficient for the purpose in the Anglican rite, let this argument suffice for all: from them has been deliberately removed whatever sets forth the dignity and office of the priesthood in the Catholic rite. That form consequently cannot be considered apt or sufficient for the Sacrament which omits what it ought essentially to signify.

The same holds good of Episcopal Consecration. For to the formula *"Receive the Holy Ghost"*, not only were the words *"for the office and work of a bishop"*, etc., added at a later period, but even these, as we shall presently state, must be understood in a sense different to that which they bear in the Catholic rite. Nor is anything gained by quoting the prayer of the preface *"Almighty God"*, since it in like manner has been stripped of the words which denote the *summum sacerdotium.* It is not here relevant to examine whether the Episcopate be a completion of the priesthood or an Order distinct from it, or whether when bestowed, as they say *per saltum,* on one who is not a priest, it has or has not its effect. But the Episcopate undoubtedly by the institution of Christ most truly belongs to the Sacrament of Orders and constitutes the sacerdotium in the highest degree, namely, that which by the teaching of the Holy Fathers and our liturgical customs is called the *summum sacerdotium, sacri ministerii summa.* So it comes to pass that, as the Sacrament of Orders, and the true sacerdotium of Christ were utterly eliminated from the Anglican rite, and hence the sacerdotium is in no wise conferred truly and validly in the Episcopal consecration of the same rite, for the like reason, therefore, the Episcopate can in no wise be truly and validly conferred by it; and this the more so because among the first duties of the Episcopate is that of ordaining ministers for the Holy Eucharist and sacrifice.

For the full and accurate understanding of the Anglican Ordinal, besides what we have noted as to some of its parts, there is nothing more pertinent than to consider carefully the circumstances under which it was composed and publicly authorized. It would be tedious to enter into details, nor is it necessary to do so, as the history of that time is sufficiently eloquent as to the animus of the authors of the Ordinal against the Catholic Church, as to the abettors whom they associated with themselves from the heterodox sects, and as to the end they had in view. Being fully cognisant of the necessary connection between faith and worship, between "*the law of believing and the law of praying*", under a pretext of returning to the primitive form, they corrupted the liturgical order in many ways to suit the errors of the reformers. For this reason in the whole Ordinal not only is there no clear mention of the sacrifice, of consecration, of the sacerdotium, and of the power of consecrating and offering sacrifice, but, as we have just stated, every trace of these things, which had been in such prayers of the Catholic rite as they had not entirely rejected, was deliberately removed and struck out. In this way the native character—or spirit as it is called—of the Ordinal clearly manifests itself Hence if vitiated in its origin, it was wholly insufficient to confer Orders, it was impossible that in the course of time it could become sufficient since no change had taken place. In vain those who, from the time of Charles I, have attempted to hold some kind of sacrifice or of priesthood, have made some additions to the Ordinal. In vain also has been the contention of that small section of the Anglican body formed in recent times, that the said Ordinal can be understood and interpreted in a sound and orthodox sense. Such efforts, We affirm, have been made and are made in vain, and for this reason, that any words in the Anglican Ordinal, as it now is, which lend themselves to ambiguity, cannot be taken in the same sense as they possess in the Catholic rite. For once a new rite has been initiated in which, as we have seen, the Sacrament of Orders is adulterated or denied, and from which all idea of consecration and sacrifice has been rejected, the formula, "*Receive the Holy Ghost*", no longer holds good; because the Spirit is infused into the soul with the grace of the Sacrament, and the words, "*for the office and work of a priest or bishop*", and the like no longer hold good, but remain as words without the reality which Christ instituted.

Several of the more shrewd Anglican interpreters of the Ordinal have perceived the force of this argument, and they openly urge it against those who take the Ordinal in a new sense and vainly attach to the Orders conferred thereby a value and efficacy which they do not possess. By this same argument is refuted the contention of those who think that the prayer "*Almighty God giver of all good things*", which is found at the beginning of the ritual action, might suffice as a legitimate form of Orders, even in the hypothesis that it might be held to be sufficient in a Catholic rite approved by the Church.

With this inherent *defect of form* is joined the *defect of intention*, which is equally essential to the Sacrament. The Church does not judge about the mind or intention in so far as it is something by its nature internal; but in so far as it is manifested externally she is bound to judge concerning it. When anyone has rightly and seriously made use of the due form and the matter requisite for effecting or conferring the Sacrament, he is considered by the very fact to do what the Church does. On this principle rests the doctrine that a Sacrament is truly conferred by the ministry of one who is a heretic or unbaptized, provided the Catholic rite be employed. On the other hand if the rite be changed, with the manifest intention of introducing another rite not approved by the Church and of rejecting what the Church does, and what by the institution of Christ belongs to the nature of the Sacrament, then it is clear that not only is the necessary intention wanting to the Sacrament, but that the intention is adverse to and destructive of the Sacrament.[6]

TO THE WHOLE BODY OF BISHOPS OF THE CATHOLIC CHURCH FROM THE ARCHBISHOPS OF ENGLAND GREETING

I It is the fortune of our office that often, when we would fain write about the common salvation, an occasion arises for debating some controverted question which cannot be postponed to another time. This certainly was recently the case when in the month of September last there suddenly arrived in this country from Rome a letter, already printed and published, which aimed at overthrowing our whole position as a Church. It was upon this letter that our minds were engaged with the attention it demanded when our beloved brother Edward, at that time Archbishop of Canterbury, Primate of all England and Metropolitan, was in God's providence taken from us by sudden death. In his last written words he bequeathed to us the treatment of the question which he was doubtless himself about to treat with the greatest learning and theological grace. It has therefore seemed good to us, the Archbishops and Primates of England, that this answer should be written in order that the truth on this matter might be made known both to our venerable brother Pope Leo XIIIth, in whose name the letter from Rome was issued, and also to all the other bishops of the Christian Church settled throughout the world.

II The duty indeed is a serious one; one which cannot be discharged without a certain deep and strong emotion. But since we firmly believe that we have been truly ordained by the Chief Shepherd to bear a part of His tremendous office in the Catholic Church, we are not at all disturbed by the opinion expressed in that letter. So we approach the task which is of necessity laid upon us "in the spirit of meekness"; and we deem it of greater importance to make plain for all time our doctrine about holy orders and other matters pertaining to them, than to win a victory in controversy over a sister Church of Christ. Still it is necessary that our answer be cast in a controversial form lest it be said by anyone that we have shrunk from the force of the arguments put forward on the other side.[7]

III There was an old controversy, but not a bitter one, with respect to the form and matter of holy orders, which has arisen from the nature of the case, inasmuch as it is impossible to find any tradition on the subject coming from our Lord or His Apostles, except the well-known example of prayer with laying on of hands. But little is to be found bearing on this matter in the decrees of Provincial Councils, and nothing certain or decisive in those of Oecumenical and General Assemblies.

Nor indeed does the Council of Trent, in which our Fathers took no part, touch the subject directly. Its passing remark about the laying on of hands (*session* XIV, *On extreme unction*, chap. III), and its more decided utterance on the force of the words "Receive the Holy Ghost", which it seems to consider the form of Order (*session* XXIII, *On the Sacrament of Order*, *canon IV*), are satisfactory enough to us, and certainly are in no way repugnant to our feelings.

There has been a more recent and a more bitter controversy on the validity of Anglican ordinations, into which theologians on the Roman side have thrown themselves with eagerness, and in doing so have, for the most part, imputed to us various crimes and defects. There are others, and those not the least wise among them, who, with a nobler feeling, have undertaken our defence. But no decision of the Roman pontiffs, fully supported by arguments, has ever before appeared, nor has it been possible for us, while we knew that the practice of reordaining our Priests clearly prevailed (though this practice has not been without exception), to learn on what grounds of defect they were reordained.[8] We knew of the unworthy struggles about Formosus,[9] and the long vacillations about heretical, schismatic and simoniacal ordinations. We had access to the letter of Innocent IIId on the necessity of supplying unction and the Degree of Eugenius IVth for the Armenians; we had the historical documents of the XVIth century, though of these many are unknown even to the present day; we had various decisions of later Popes, Clement XIth and Benedict XIVth, but those of Clement were couched in general terms and therefore uncertain. We had also the Roman Pontifical as reformed from time to time, but, as it now exists, so confusedly arranged as to puzzle rather than enlighten the minds of enquirers. For if any one considers the rite *Of the ordination of a Presbyter*, he sees that the proper laying on of hands stands apart from the utterance of the form. He also cannot tell whether the man, who in the rubrics is called "ordained", has really been ordained, or whether the power, which is given at the end of the office by the words, "Receive the Holy Ghost; whose sins thou shalt have remitted they are remitted unto them, and whose sins thou shalt have retained they are retained", with the laying on of pontifical hands, is a necessary part of the priesthood (as the Council of Trent seems to teach) or not necessary. In like manner if anyone reads through the rite *Of the consecration of an elect as Bishop*, he will nowhere find that he is called "Bishop" in the prayers and benedictions referring to the man to be consecrated, or that "Episcopate" is spoken of in them in regard to him. As far as the prayers are concerned the term "Episcopate" occurs for the first time in the Mass during the consecration. From these documents therefore, so obviously discordant and indefinite, no one, however wise, could extract with certainty what was considered by the Roman Pontiffs to be truly essential and necessary to holy orders.

IV Thus our most venerable brother in his letter dated the 13th of September, which begins with the words *Apostolicae curae*, has approached this question after a manner hitherto unexampled, although the arguments urged by him are sufficiently old. Nor do we desire to deny that in entering upon this controversy he has consulted the interests of the Church and of truth in throwing over the very vain opinion about the necessity of the delivery of the "instruments", which was nevertheless widely accepted by scholastic theologians from the time of St Thomas Aquinas up to that of Benedict XIVth, and even up to the present day. At the same time he has done well in neglecting other errors and fallacies, which for our part also we shall neglect in this reply, and in regard to which we hope that theologians on the Roman side will follow his example and neglect them for the future.

V His whole judgment therefore hinges on two points, namely, on the practice of the Court of Rome and the form of the Anglican rite, to which is attached a third question, not easy to separate from the second, on the intention of our Church. We will answer at once about the former, though it is, in our opinion, of less importance....

XIX What wonder then if our Fathers, wishing to return to the simplicity of the Gospel, eliminated these prayers from a liturgy which was to be read publicly in a modern language? And herein they followed a course which was certainly opposed to that pursued by the Romans. For the Romans, starting from an almost Gospel simplicity, have relieved the austerity of their rites with Gallican embellishments, and have gradually, as time went on, added ceremonies borrowed from the Old Testament in order to emphasize the distinction between people and Priests more and more. That these ceremonies are "contemptible and harmful", or that they are useless at their proper place and time, we do by no means assert—we declare only that they are not necessary. Thus in the XVIth century when our Fathers drew up a liturgy at once for the use of the people and the clergy they went back almost to the Roman starting-point. For both sides alike, their holy Fathers, and ours, whom they call innovators, followed the same most sure leaders, the Lord and His Apostles. Now however, the example of the modern Church of Rome, which is entirely taken up with the offering of sacrifice, is held up to us as the only model for our imitation. And this is done so eagerly by the Pope that he does not hesitate to write that "whatever sets forth the dignity and offices of the priesthood" has been "deliberately removed" from the prayers of our Ordinal.

But we confidently assert that our Ordinal, particularly in this last point, is superior to the Roman Pontifical in various ways, inasmuch as it expresses more clearly and faithfully those things which by Christ's institution belong to the nature of the priesthood and the effect of the Catholic rites used in the Universal Church. And this, in our opinion, can be shown by a comparison of the Pontifical with the Ordinal.

The Roman formulary begins with a presentation made by the Archdeacon and a double address from the Bishop, first to the clergy and people, and then to the candidates for ordination—for there is no public examination in the ordination of a presbyter. Then follows the laying on of the Bishop's hands, and then those of the assistant presbyters, performed without any words; in regard to which obscure rite we have quoted the opinion of Cardinal de

Lugo. Then the three ancient prayers are said, the two short collects, and the longer Benediction which is now said by the Bishop "with his hands extended in front of his breast". This prayer, which is called the "Consecration" in ancient books, is considered by weighty authorities, since the time of Morinus,[10] to be the true "form" of Roman ordination, and doubtless was in old days joined with laying on of hands. Now however "extension of hands" is substituted for laying on of hands, as is the case in Confirmation, while even that gesture is not considered necessary. At any rate, if the old Roman ordinations are valid, directly this prayer has been said the ordination of presbyters is complete in that church even at the present day. For any "form" which has once sufficed for any Sacrament of the Church, and is retained still unaltered and complete, must be supposed to be retained with the same intent as before; nor can it be asserted without a sort of sacrilege that it has lost its virtue, because other things have been silently added after it. In any case the intention of the more recent part of the Roman formulary cannot have been to empty the more ancient part of its proper force; but its object may not improperly be supposed to have been as follows, first that the priests already ordained should be prepared by various rites and ceremonies for the offering of the sacrifice, secondly that they should receive the power to offer it in explicit terms, thirdly that they should begin to exercise the right of the priesthood in the celebration of the Mass, lastly that they should be publicly invested with another priestly power, that of remitting sins. Which opinion is confirmed by the language of the old Pontificals, as for example in the Sarum Pontifical we read "Bless and sanctify these hands *of thy priests*". All therefore that follows after that ancient "form", just like our words added in 1662, is simply not necessary. For those powers above specified can be conveyed either implicitly and by usage, as was the method in ancient times, or at once and explicitly; but the method of conveyance has no relation to the efficacy of ordination.

Our Fathers then, having partly perceived these points, and seeing that the scholastic doctrine concerning the transubstantiation of the bread and wine and the more recent doctrine of the repetition (as was believed) of the sacrifice of the cross in the Mass, were connected by popular feeling with certain of the ceremonies and prayers that followed, asked themselves in what way the whole rite of ordination might not only be brought to greater solidity and purity, but might become more perfect and more noble. And inasmuch as at that time there was nothing known for certain as to the antiquity of the first prayers, but the opinions of learned men assigned all efficacy to the "imperative" forms, they turned their attention to the latter rather than to the former.

With this object therefore in view they first aimed at simplicity, and concentrated the parts of the whole rite as it were on one prominent point so that no one could doubt at what moment the grace and power of the priesthood was given. For such is the force of simplicity that it lifts men's minds towards divine things more than a long series of ceremonies united by however good a meaning. Therefore having placed in the forefront the prayers which declared both the office of the priesthood and its succession from the ministry of the Apostles, they joined the laying on of hands with our Lord's own words. And in this matter they intentionally followed the example of the Apostolic Church, which first "fell to prayer" and then laid on hands and sent forth its ministers, not that of the Roman Church, which uses laying on of hands before the prayers. Secondly when they considered in their own minds the various offices of the priesthood they saw that the Pontifical in common use was defective in two particulars. For whereas the following offices were recounted in the Bishop's address: "It is the duty of a priest to offer, to bless, to preside, to preach, and to baptize" and the like, and mention was made in the old "form" for the presbyterate "of the account which they are to give of the stewardship entrusted to them", nevertheless in the other forms nothing was said except about offering sacrifice and remitting sins, and the forms conveying these powers were separated some distance from one another. Again too they saw that the duties of the pastoral office had but little place in the Pontifical, although the Gospel speaks out fully upon them. For this reason then they especially set before our Priests the pastoral office, which is particularly that of Messenger, Watchman, and Steward of the Lord, in that noble address which the Bishop has to deliver, and in the very serious examination which follows: in words which must be read and weighed and compared with the holy Scriptures, or it is impossible really to know the worth of our Ordinal. On the other hand, as regards the sacraments, in their revision of the "imperative" forms, they gave the first place to our Lord's own words, not merely out of reverence, but because those words were then commonly believed to be the necessary "form". Then they entrusted to our Priests all "the mysteries of the sacraments anciently instituted" (to use the words of our old Sacramentary)[11] and did not exalt one aspect of one of them and neglect the others. Lastly they placed in juxtaposition the form which imprints the character and the form which confers jurisdiction.

And in these and similar matters, which it would take long to recount, they followed without doubt the example of our Lord and His Apostles. . . .

We therefore, taking our stand on Holy Scripture, make reply that in the ordering of Priests we do duly lay down and set forth the stewardship and ministry of the word and Sacraments, the power of remitting and retaining sins, and other functions of the pastoral office, and that in these we do sum up and rehearse all other functions. Indeed the Pope himself is a witness to this, who especially derives the honour of the Pontifical tiara from Christ's triple commendation of His flock to the penitent St Peter. Why then does he suppose that, which he holds so honourable in his own case, to contribute nothing to the dignity and offices of the priesthood in the case of Anglican Priests?

XX Finally, we would have our revered brother in Christ beware lest in expressing this judgment he do injustice not only to us but to other Christians also, and among them to his own predecessors, who surely enjoyed in an equal measure with himself the gift of the Holy Spirit.

For he seems to condemn the Orientals, in company with ourselves, on account of defective intention, who in the *Orthodox Confession* issued about 1640 name only two functions of a sacramental priesthood, that is to say that of absolving sins and of preaching; who in the *Longer Russian Catechism* (Moscow 1839) teach nothing about the sacrifice of the Body and Blood of Christ, and mention among the offices which pertain to Order only those of ministering the Sacraments and feeding the flock. Further, it thus speaks of the three Orders: "The Deacon serves at the Sacraments; the Priest hallows the Sacraments, in dependence on the Bishop; the Bishop not only hallows the Sacraments himself, but has the power also to impart to others by the laying on of his hands the gift and grace to hallow them." The Eastern Church is assuredly at one with us in teaching that the ministry of more than one mystery describes the character of the priesthood better than the offering of a single sacrifice.

This indeed appears in the form used in the Greek Church today in the prayer beginning *"O God who art great in power"*: "Fill this man whom Thou hast chosen to attain the rank of Presbyter, with the gift of Thy Holy Spirit, that he may be worthy blamelessly to assist at Thy Sanctuary, to preach the Gospel of Thy Kingdom, to minister the Word of Thy Truth, to offer Thee spiritual gifts and sacrifices, to renew Thy people by the laver of regeneration", etc. (Habert, *Greek Pontifical* (1643 edn), p. 314).

But let the Romans consider now not once or twice what judgment they will pronounce upon their own Fathers, whose ordinations we have described above. For if the Pope shall by a new decree declare our Fathers of two hundred and fifty years ago wrongly ordained, there is nothing to hinder the inevitable sentence that by the same law all who have been similarly ordained have received no orders. And if our Fathers, who used in 1550 and 1552 forms which as he says are null, were altogether unable to reform them in 1662, his own Fathers come under the self-same law. And if Hippolytus and Victor and Leo and Gelasius and Gregory have some of them said too little in their rites about the priesthood and the high priesthood, and nothing about the power of offering the Sacrifice of the Body and Blood of Christ, the Church of Rome herself has an invalid priesthood, and the reformers of the Sacramentaries, no matter what their names, could do nothing to remedy her rites. "For as the Hierarchy (to use the Pope's words) had become extinct on account of the nullity of the form, there remained no power of ordaining." And if the Ordinal "was wholly insufficient to confer Orders, it was impossible that in the course of time it could become sufficient, since no change has taken place. In vain those who (from the VIth and XIth centuries) have attempted to hold some kind of sacrifice or of priesthood, (and power of remitting and retaining sins), have made some additions to the Ordinal." Thus in overthrowing our orders he overthrows all his own, and pronounces sentence on his own Church. Eugenius IVth indeed brought his Church into great peril of nullity when he taught a new matter and a new form of Order and left the real without a word. For no one knows how many ordinations may have been made, according to his teaching, without any laying on of hands or appropriate form. Pope Leo demands a form unknown to previous Bishops of Rome, and an intention which is defective in the catechisms of the Oriental Church. . . .

1 Wood. Charles Lindley, 2nd Viscount Halifax; *b.* 1839; *educ.*, Eton and Christ Church, Oxford; President of the English Church Union, 1868–1919; 1927–34; *d.* 1934.

2 Vaughan, Herbert; *b.* 1832; priest, 1854; vice-president of St Edmund's College, Ware; toured South America, 1863; founded St Joseph's College, Mill Hill, 1866; owned and edited the *Tablet* in the Ultramontane cause, 1868; Bishop of Salford, 1872; Archbishop of Westminster, 1892; Cardinal, 1893; *d.* 1903.

3 Maclagan, William Dalrymple; *b.* 1826; *educ.*, Edinburgh University; joined Episcopal Church, 1843; Madras cavalry, 1847; Peterhouse, Cambridge, 1852; ordained, 1856; curate of St Saviour's, Paddington; curate of St Stephen's, Marylebone, 1858; organizing secretary of the London Diocesan Church Building Society, 1860; curate in charge, Enfield, 1865; rector of Newington, 1869; vicar of St Mary Abbots, Kensington, 1875; declined bishopric of Calcutta, 1876; Bishop of Lichfield, 1878; Archbishop of York, 1891; resigned, 1908; *d.* 1910.

4 The Apostolic Letter *Ad Anglos* was addressed to "the English seeking the kingdom of Christ in the unity of the faith", but did not take cognizance of the Church of England. Nevertheless it did encourage Halifax and his fellow-participants in the discussions.

5 Among the writings can be included: E. Portal (F. Dalbus), *Les ordinations Anglicanes* (1894); Louis Duchesne in *Bulletin Critique* (15 July 1894); and the letter of Cardinal Bourret to Portal. The sequel to this literary discussion was John Wordsworth's letter to Portal, which was published in 1894. Three years later Wordsworth was to compose the Latin *Responsio*.

6 Benson commented: "This very day the papers tell us of another new defiance of history on the part of that great Church, a new defiance of history which is perfectly in accord with all we knew of Rome before. We could not imagine, we could not reasonably expect, that the present authority of the See of Rome would be asserted in contrariety to so much that has been asserted in that See heretofore. But it may be a lesson of the greatest possible value to those who have been led in quiet years to believe that the Church of Rome has become other than it was" (A. C. Benson, *Benson*, pp. 521-2).

7 The *Responsio* was an important document inasmuch as it categorically stated the official Anglican attitude towards the Christian ministry, and this clarification was of fundamental importance for future ecumenical discussions. An important feature of the *Apostolicae Curae* was the limiting of the question of Anglican Orders to the changes in the Ordinal in the successive Prayer Books. The *Responsio* similarly confined itself to this basic issue.

8 Benson said of the Papal Bull, that "for once Infallibility had ventured to give its reasons".

9 Formosus, Pope from 891–6, refused to accept priests of the Orthodox Church ordained by the Patriarch Photius.

10 John de Lugo (1583–1660), a Spanish Jesuit theologian, widely revered in the Roman Catholic Church of his day, in spite of his independence of mind.

Jean Morin, a convert to Roman Catholicism from Calvinism, rejected the view that the tradition of the instruments (the *Porrectio Instrumentorum*) as was formally expressed in the *Decretum de*

Unione Armeniorum (1439), of Eugenius IV), constituted the matter of Orders, in his *De Sacris Ecclesiae Ordinationibus* (1655).

11 I.e. the Missal of Leofric of Exeter; a Pontifical of Jumièges; and the Sarum Pontifical. The note continues: "This form, which has a certain affinity to those in the Canons of Hippolytus and the Apostolic Constitutions, has an air of great antiquity...." The discussion of the primitive Roman practice was reappraised with the publication of the Verona text by E. Hauler in 1900, and the publication of R. H. Connolly's *The So-called Egyptian Church Order* (1916).

65 LAITY AND CONVOCATION, 1902

(*Chronicle of Convocation* (1902), p. 65)

The Joint Committee of the Convocation of Canterbury, under the chairmanship of the Bishop of Salisbury, published its report on the position of the laity with reference to legislation in matters ecclesiastical, elections of church officers, and judicial functions in the early Church and under the constitution of the Church of England.[1] The Report displayed a depth of learning and included an important section on the period from 1789–1900. Section 1 of chapter v discussed the altered position of the laity in England; and section 2, the position of the laity in other Churches in communion with the Church of England. At the end of the Report were appended the proposed resolutions.[2]

RESOLUTIONS TO BE SUBMITTED TO CONVOCATION

1 That it is desirable that a National Council should be formed fully representing the clergy and laity of the Church of England.

2 That the definition of the powers to be entrusted to this Council, in reference to legislation, of the qualification of electors and of the method of electing and summoning its members, should be determined by a joint meeting of the members of the two Convocations with the Provincial Houses of Laymen, with a view to its receiving statutory authority.

3 That this Council should consist of three Houses, the first that of bishops, the second that of representatives of the clergy, whether official or elected, and the third of elected communicant laymen.

4 That the acceptance of the three Houses, sitting together or

separately, should be necessary in order to constitute an act of the body.

5 Nothing in these Resolutions is intended to interfere with the position of the Convocations as Provincial Synods of the Clergy.

1 The original committee included: Creighton (London); Wordsworth (Salisbury); Kennion (Bath and Wells); Browne (Bristol); Legge (Lichfield); Talbot (Rochester); Bishop Barry (Secretary); the Deans of Salisbury (Webb); Lichfield (Luckock); and Winchester (Stephens); the Archdeacons of Oxford (Bishop of Reading); Ely (Emery); Rochester (Cheetham); and Exeter (Sandford); Canons Hutchings; Moberly; Overton; Sanderson; Worlledge; and Prebendary Villiers. The Committee met on ten occasions.

2 Included also was a memorandum on the constitution of the Ecclesiastical Council of Sweden.

66 BALFOUR'S EDUCATION ACT 1902

(*Chronicle of Convocation* (1902), pp. 150-2)

The Balfour Education Act, produced by R. L. Morant, was the high-water mark of the denominational education controversy. The Act put all schools on the public rate, thereby compelling Nonconformists to contribute towards the upkeep of Anglican schools.[1] In opposing the Act, Free Churchmen overlooked the fact that voluntary schools had long received government grant aid. The real fear was that in "single-school areas" the existing church schools would retain a monopoly, whereas under the existing arrangements the monopoly would come to an end through lack of funds. Passive resistance was threatened by prominent Free Churchmen including John Clifford, whilst Lloyd George[2] attacked the Bill in the Commons.

THE BISHOP OF COVENTRY[3]

... They came then to a much more serious defect which was put forward against the Bill, and that was that Nonconformists would be called upon to support Voluntary Schools by the rates. But Nonconformists already supported Voluntary Schools by their taxes, and where any question of conscience came in by the payment of a tax and a rate it required something that he was afraid was not in a Churchman's view to see the principle. It was threatened that if this Bill became law Nonconformists would not pay the rates, and would thus make a difficulty. He was not afraid of that, because when it came to a matter of conscience the Nonconformist would have first to deduct from his rates all non-educational objects and be ready to pay for those; then deduct the portion taken for technical schools,[4] because there was no question of conscience in that; then he would have further to deduct the portion spent on secondary education; and when he had gone through all these sums, and found the *residuum* which was really due to the support of Voluntary Schools—because he must deduct the portion to the schools provided by the local authority—it would be almost impossible to determine the sum which had gone to Voluntary Schools. But he wanted rather to look at this as a matter of comity between persons warmly and deeply interested in the matter as they understood it. He would treat Nonconformists in the consideration of this matter as those who really desired the good and welfare of the country from the highest point of view and as a matter of religious comity; and, in answer to this religious objection, he would say that, at all events in this measure, Churchmen were asking for nothing that they were not prepared to give. According to the Bill, if it were carried out it would be quite as easy and possible for Nonconformists to have schools supported by rates as it would be for Churchmen. They were told in answer to that that these provisions about fresh schools were quite illusory; that Nonconformists would not be able to obtain sites in villages upon which they could erect schools of their own; and, again, that they had not the money to erect them. But they would be able to go before the local authority and say it was the desire of parents in that place that there should be another school in that district in which they would be free from that intolerance. If that school were given, and Churchmen were willing it should be, Nonconformists should understand that they would not have to provide the money for that school. The local authority would provide it because they were dissatisfied with the kind of religious instruction given in the existing schools. This Bill gave the Nonconformists an enormous weapon against religious intolerance. He thought if that view were fairly put before Nonconformists they would see that what this Bill meant was that Churchmen were giving up the monopoly which they now enjoyed in 9,000 parishes, and in return for that they asked that they might be allowed the rates for the improvement of their schools. The answer to that would be that the result would be to multiply weak schools. He could not see that a small school was necessarily a weak school.

He knew that competition between schools had been one of the very greatest factors in the promotion of education, and he thought one of the influences from which their education was suffering in the past—elementary education in the country at all events—was the absence of some sort of competition as between school and school. The last objection was that the Bill did not give the people who paid for the schools the control of the schools. He could not say that that objection had any weight at all in his mind. What the Bill did was this—it appointed on the management of each school or gave the local authority power to appoint on the management one-third of the managers. Now, that one-third, being appointed by the local authority and in constant touch, must be men of very weak backbone, very little accustomed to town and country parishes, if they found themselves unjustly dominated by the two-thirds, if they could not make such representations as would remove the grievances from which they were suffering. On the other hand, if they were asked to give up half the management, they might inquire why should they pay at all for the support of the schools if more than half of the managers were appointed from outside? It was assumed that they were not making any contribution, but members of that House were sufficient experts to know that they would have to continue to make a very large contribution, and in return for that they deserved to have control of the schools. Further, he asked what would be the consequences of the rejection of this Bill? A continuation of the present system, or rather want of system, for an indefinite period, a continuation of this want of cohesion between primary and secondary education from which too much of our education was suffering, and the whole nation was being kept backward. The postponement of the improvement of secular education until when? Until a Liberal Ministry came in? That was not an answer to it, because at the present time if a Radical Ministry came in it would only come in with the support of the Roman Catholics, and that Ministry would not have a free hand in the question of education. The postponement must be until a Radical Ministry came in which was independent of the Irish vote. He thought they were entitled to say that that day was likely to be a fairly distant date. The Bill was by no means all they wanted. He was sure it would leave very many hardships behind. It would by no means remove all their difficulties, but he believed firmly, and he thought he carried the whole Committee[5] with him in this, that it was a measure of educational progress, and that being so it was the bounden duty of Churchmen to support it to the utmost of their power, and to amend it as far as they could in its progress. For one thing the Church had no worse enemies than ignorance or error, and what they could do in the cause of education they were doing for the welfare of the nation, and, what was higher still, for the glory of God.[6]

1 In 1904 the church schools reached their highest recorded total of 11,874, after which there was a gradual decline in numbers.

2 Lloyd George, David; *b.* 1863; *educ.*, a Welsh village elementary school; articled to a solicitor; qualified as a solicitor, 1884; M.P., 1890; President of the Board of Trade, 1905; Chancellor of the Exchequer, 1908; Minister of Munitions, 1915; Secretary for War, 1916; Prime Minister, 1916; created an earl, 1945; *d.* 1945.

3 Knox, Edmund Arbuthnott; *b.* 1847; *educ.*, St Paul's School and Corpus Christi College, Oxford; deacon, 1870; priest, 1872; Fellow, Tutor, and Dean of Merton College, Oxford; rector of Kibworth Beauchamp, 1884; vicar of Ashton, 1891; Archdeacon of Birmingham, 1894; rector of St Philip's, Birmingham, 1894; Suffragan Bishop of Coventry, 1894; Bishop of Manchester, 1903–21; *d.* 1937.

4 Secondary education was developing under county councils and county boroughs in accordance with the Technical Instruction Act and the school boards of the Elementary Education Acts. Although the Churches had not pioneered secondary education in the way they had elementary education, the religious content was safeguarded by Morant's insistence that the provisions of the Act were to cover both fields of education.

5 The committee comprised: the Prolocutor; the Deans of Norwich, St Asaph, Lincoln, and Chichester; the Archdeacons of Bristol, Essex, Lynn, Birmingham, Berkshire, Exeter, Montgomery, Cornwall, Stafford, Oxford, Worcester, Ely, Kingston-on-Thames, and Bedford; Canons Jelf, Sanderson, Lowe, Savory, Thynne, Quennell, Waller, Gray, Thompson, Childe, and Hankey; Prebendary Ingram; and Mr Harding and Mr Proctor.

6 The Upper House of the Convocation of Canterbury resolved: "This House desires to express a general approval of the Government Education Bill now before Parliament, on the ground that, if it becomes law, it will raise the general standard of education in Elementary Schools, that it will lead to a better co-ordination of educational work in England, that it maintains an undiminished recognition of the claim of religion to enter into the work of National Education, and that it gives hope that Voluntary Schools, freed to some extent from the unequal and increasing burden thrown on them for thirty years, may the better bear their great part in that work for the welfare of the country. The House, however, deprecates very strongly the provision which makes the adoption of Part III permissive and not compulsory, and thinks that it is

undesirable that there should be separate local education authorities for areas so small as those indicated in Part I, Clause I, Paragraph 2. The House is also of opinion that it should be made clear that women may be appointed on the Education Committees, and believes that in some other details the Bill might be improved in the interest of education generally" (*Chronicle of Convocation* (1902), p. 222).

67 REPRESENTATIVE CHURCH COUNCIL, 1903

(*Chronicle of Convocation*. 1904)

As the revived Convocations pursued their courses in the latter part of the nineteenth century, the question of the position of the laity in the government of the Church of England came to the fore. The proposal for a National Church Council had been widely discussed in both provinces and in the two houses of laymen. Under the guidance of the Bishop of Salisbury[1] a meeting of the members of Convocations sitting in Committee, and of the houses of laymen, met in July 1903. In spite of the unconstitutional existence of the new body, it marked a development towards the National Assembly.[2]

THE REPRESENTATIVE CHURCH COUNCIL

The following are the Resolutions passed at the Joint Meeting on July 9th and 10th, 1903.

1. That it is desirable to make provision for the calling together of a Representative Council consisting of clergy and laity of the Provinces of Canterbury and York.

2. That the question of obtaining legal constitution and authority for such a Council be reserved for consideration until after the Council has, upon a voluntary basis, come into working order.

3. That such steps shall be taken as may prove to be necessary for the reform of the two Convocations, and for their sitting together from time to time as one body.

4. That, with a view to providing the lay element in the proposed Council, it is desirable that the Archbishops should continue to summon Houses of Laymen, pending any future legislation on the subject.[3]

5. That this Council shall be divided into three Houses: the first consisting of the members of the Upper Houses of the Convocations of Canterbury and York; the second of the Lower Houses of the said Convocations; the third of the members of the Houses of Laymen of the two Provinces; and that acceptance by each of the three Houses, sitting together or separately, shall be necessary in order to constitute an act of the whole body, provided that in no case shall there be any interference with the powers and functions of each of the three Houses.

6. That the initial franchise of lay electors shall be exercised in each ecclesiastical parish or district by those persons of the male sex (possessing such house-holding, or other vestry qualification in the parish or district as may be defined by the Committee to be hereafter appointed) who declare themselves in writing, at the time of voting, to be lay members of the Church of England, and of no other religious communion, and are not legally and actually excluded from communion, and by such other persons residing in the parish or district as are lay communicants of the Church of England, of the male sex, and of full age.[4]

7. That representatives elected by the lay electors shall be of the male sex and of full age, and shall be communicants.

8. That a Committee of Bishops, Clergy, and Laity be appointed by the two Archbishops to prepare a scheme in further detail to give effect to the foregoing Resolutions, and to report to the Convocations and to the Houses of Laymen.

The following Committee was appointed by the two Archbishops under Resolution 8, and drew up the appended Scheme.

The Bishop (*Ryle*) of Winchester (*Chairman*)
The Bishop (*Boyd-Carpenter*) of Ripon
The Bishop (*Wordsworth*) of Salisbury
Bishop Barry
The Dean (*Wace*) of Canterbury
The Archdeacon (*Watkins*) of Durham
Sir L. T. Dibdin, K.C., Dean of Arches
Sir Edward Russell
Chancellor P. V. Smith

Scheme to give effect to the Resolutions passed at the Joint Meeting on July 9th and 10th, 1903.

1 The body to be called together in pursuance of Resolution 1

shall be called "The Representative Church Council".

2 The Council may be summoned by the two Archbishops at such time and place as they shall think fit. The Archbishops shall be joint Presidents. The Archbishop of Canterbury, or in his absence the Archbishop of York, or in his absence the Bishop next in precedence present and willing to act, shall be Chairman of meetings of the Council.

3 The agenda for the first meeting of the Council shall be settled by the two Archbishops.

4 The Council shall at their first meeting make provision for the establishment of regulations and bye-laws for the conduct of their business and procedure, and until the establishment of such regulations and bye-laws, and subject to them when established, the business and procedure at any meeting of the Council shall be regulated by the Chairman thereof.

5 The Houses of Laymen for the time being shall constitute the Third House mentioned in the 5th Resolution. The 6th Resolution shall everywhere come into operation at as early a date as possible. The householding or other vestry qualifications in an ecclesiastical parish or district mentioned in that Resolution shall be the qualification of ownership or occupation giving a title to vote at a vestry thereof if the parish or district is an ancient parish, or which would give such title if it were an ancient parish.

NOTE I It would be outside the province of this Committee to make further recommendations as to the method of election of the Houses of Laymen. But they desire to point out that the matter requires to be speedily dealt with. What seems to be now needed is that the Houses of Laymen and the two Archbishops should arrange one uniform scheme for the election of members of those Houses, so that the method may be the same in every diocese of both provinces. It is to be noted that the Resolutions of the Joint Committee do not deal with the Constitution of the Houses of Laymen, except with regard to the qualifications of lay members of the Council and of the electors of such lay members. As the Houses of Laymen are to constitute the Lay House in the Council the Resolutions, in fact, define what in future must be the qualifications of the members of the Houses of Laymen and of the electors of members. But while the Resolutions to this extent inevitably interfere with the constitution of the Houses of Laymen, in all other respects their constitution is a matter which must be decided by the Houses of Laymen themselves and the Archbishops by whose will they exist.

NOTE II The persons qualified under these words to vote in an ecclesiastical parish or district will be those who occupy houses, lands, or other tenements therein, in respect of which rates are paid (either by owner or occupier).

This statement is substantially complete but does not cover certain exceptional cases.

1 Wordsworth, John, son of Bishop of Lincoln; *b.* 1843; *educ.*, Winchester and New College, Oxford; Fellow of Brasenose, 1867; prebendary of Lincoln, 1870; Bampton Lecturer, 1881; Oriel Professor of the Interpretation of Scripture, 1883; Bishop of Salisbury, 1885; *d.* 1911.

2 In the past, delay had been caused by the necessity of the two Convocations having to sit separately, the archbishops having no authority to summon a national synod without the consent of the Crown. Joint meetings could only be held informally (as in 1896 and 1899), and a Bill enabling them to sit together was rejected by Parliament in 1901.

3 In 1885 both Houses of the Convocation of Canterbury agreed on a scheme for the constitution of a House of Laymen. The Canterbury House of Laymen first met in 1886, and that of York in 1892.

4 There was considerable discussion as to whether the basis of lay franchise should be Holy Communion, Confirmation, or Baptism. This was to become a real issue in the setting up of the Church Assembly.

68 THE CHURCH IN A LARGE CITY, 1904

(Richard Mudie-Smith, *The Religious Life of London*, pp. 281-2)

The problem of equipping the Church of England to cope with its mission to urban centres was not solved by the increased number of church buildings. The slums, poverty, and illiteracy in the towns widened the cultural gap between the organized Churches and the working classes, though efforts by individuals[1] and small groups to integrate the two met with varied success. The findings of this survey reinforced the facts of the 1851 census that churchgoing was not an integral part of the life of the artisan class.[2]

When the *British Weekly* Census was taken, the Church of England in London had a great preponderance over all forms of Nonconformity put together. The most startling feature of the *Daily News* Census is the decrease of worshippers in the Established Church. The *Guardian*, commenting on Dr Robertson Nicoll's figures as given in the paper he read in July 1902 at Sion College, says: "If his calculations are correct, the outcome is, that, while the population of the London area has increased by some 500,000 during the last seventeen years, there has, nevertheless, been a decrease of something like 150,000 in the attendances. This decrease is almost confined to the Church of England, for whereas Nonconformity shows a falling off from 369,000 to 363,000 (in round numbers) the Church attendances have diminished from 535,000 to 396,000, excluding mission-halls. In other words, religious worship generally has not kept pace with population, and in the Church of England there are only three worshippers in 1902–3 for every four who were found there in 1886. The figures which concern the Church are so remarkable that we hope that they will form the subject of a special inquiry by the authorities of the dioceses of London and Rochester.[3] The Wesleyan Methodist Conference, we notice, has appointed a Committee to inquire into the statistics affecting Wesleyan Methodism, and a joint committee might well be appointed by the Bishops to whom the spiritual oversight of the metropolis is entrusted.

The number of worshippers at the Anglican churches for the morning and evening services realized in 1886 the total of 535,715, exclusive of missions. The *Daily News* gives a total of 396,196, excluding missions. The decline of nearly 140,000 in the Anglican figures would of itself account for the total decrease which has taken place in the last sixteen years. In 1886 the number of Nonconformist worshippers at the two services, excluding missions, and the Salvation Army, was 369,349, the Church of England having thus a majority over all Nonconformists of about 165,000. The *Daily News* Census gives the total Nonconformist figures, excluding missions and the Salvation Army, as 363,882. The Free Churches, as Dr Nicoll has pointed out, have not quite held their ground, but they have held it so nearly that the numerical distance between them and the Church of England has almost disappeared. The *Daily News* estimates that the Church of England and her missions number 429,822 worshippers, while the Nonconformist Churches and their missions, including the Salvation Army, which has a total attendance of 22,402, number 416,977. For one Church of

England worshipper there is practically another Nonconformist worshipper.

1 Notably, Barnett, Samuel Augustus; *b.* 1844; *educ.*, Wadham College, Oxford; deacon, 1867; founded Charity Organization Society, 1869; vicar of St Jude, Whitechapel, 1873–94; first Warden of Toynbee Hall, 1884–96; canon of Westminster, 1906; *d.* 1913.

2 The *British Weekly* Census was held on Sunday, 24 October 1886, when about 1,500 churches and chapels were visited. The *Daily News* Census extended from November 1902 to November 1903, and 2,688 places of worship, including sixty-two synagogues, were visited.

3 The diocese of Southwark, formed in 1905, and the diocese of Chelmsford, founded in 1913, both covered parts of London which were densely populated.

69 ROYAL LETTERS OF BUSINESS, 1906

(*Chronicle of Convocation* (1906), pp. 330-46)

The ritual controversies resulted in agitation both within the Church of England and within Parliament. The Prayer Book was enforced by statute law and the existence of ritual lawlessness proved to be a matter of concern at a time when Parliament was generally antipathetic towards the Church of England. With the findings of the Royal Commission on Ecclesiastical Discipline, the archbishops requested that steps be taken to revise the form of the Church's worship. It was the desire to uphold legality within the Church that made the task of Prayer Book revision so difficult in the future.

EDWARD R. & I

EDWARD THE SEVENTH, by the Grace of God of the United Kingdom of Great Britain and Ireland and of the British Dominions beyond the Seas, King, Defender of the Faith, To Our Right Trusty and Right Entirely Beloved Councillor RANDALL THOMAS, Archbishop of Canterbury, Knight Grand Cross of Our Royal Victorian Order, Primate of All England and Metropolitan,[1] to the Right Reverend the Bishops, the Very Reverend the Deans, the Venerable the Archdeacons, and to the Reverend the Proctors representing the Cathedral and Collegiate Chapters and Clergy of the Province of Canterbury Greeting!

Whereas our Commissioners appointed to inquire into the alleged prevalence of breaches or neglect of the law relating to the conduct of Divine Service in the Church of England have submitted to Us their Report:[2]

And whereas We deem it expedient that certain recommendations of Our said Commissioners should be by you discussed:

Our will and pleasure therefore is and We do hereby authorize you the said Randall Thomas, Archbishop of Canterbury, President of the said Convocation, and the Bishops of your said Province, and the Deans of the Cathedral Churches, and also the Archdeacons and the Proctors representing the Chapters and Colleges, and the whole Clergy of every Diocese of your said Province, that you do debate, consider, consult, and agree upon the following points, matters, and things contained in the recommendations of the said Report, *videlicet* the desirability and the form and contents of a new rubric regulating the ornaments (that is to say, the vesture) of the ministers of the church at the times of their ministrations, and also of any modifications of the existing law relating to the conduct of Divine Service and to the ornaments and fittings of churches; and, after mature debate, consideration, consultation, and agreement that you do present to Us a Report or Reports thereon in writing.[3]

Given at Our Court at Sandringham the tenth day of November, 1906, in the sixth year of Our Reign.

(Signed) H. J. GLADSTONE

1 Davidson, Randall Thomas; *b.* 1848; *educ.*, Harrow and Trinity College, Oxford; deacon, 1874; curate of Dartford, Kent; chaplain to Archbishop Tait, 1878; Dean of Windsor, 1883; Bishop of Rochester, 1891; Bishop of Winchester, 1895; Archbishop of Canterbury, 1903; resigned 1928; *d.* 1930.

2 See following document (70).

3 The Convocations of York and Canterbury made their answer in April 1920, the former dissenting from the latter in respect of the revised eucharistic canon. With the existence of the new Church Assembly it was no longer left with the Crown or with Parliament to decide what steps should next be taken.

70 ROYAL COMMISSION ON ECCLESIASTICAL DISCIPLINE, 1906

(*Report*, vol. 4, pp. 75-9)

A. J. Balfour appointed a commission of ten members to "inquire into the alleged prevalence of breaches or neglect of the law relating to the conduct of Divine Service in the Church of England and to the ornaments and fittings of churches; and to consider the existing powers and procedure applicable to such irregularities", on 23 April 1904. 118 meetings were held, 164 witnesses examined, including twenty bishops, various scholars, and church societies. Evidence was sent to diocesan bishops for their comments, together with questions relating to the use of vestments, and canonical obedience. A unanimous report was presented on 21 June 1906 which summarized the evidence and made certain recommendations.

CONCLUSION

Our consideration of the evidence laid before us has led us to two main conclusions. First, the law of public worship in the Church of England is too narrow for the religious life of the present generation. It needlessly condemns much which a great section of Church people, including many of her most devoted members, value; and modern thought and feeling are characterized by a care for ceremonial, a sense of dignity in worship, and an appreciation of the continuity of the Church, which were not similarly felt at the time when the law took its present shape. In an age which has witnessed an extraordinary revival of spiritual life and activity, the Church has had to work under regulations fitted for a different condition of things, without that power of self-adjustment which is inherent in the conception of a living Church, and is, as a matter of fact, possessed by the Established Church of Scotland. The result has inevitably been that ancient rubrics have been strained in the desire to find in them meanings which it has been judicially held they cannot bear; while, on the other hand, the construction placed on them in accordance with legal rules has sometimes appeared forced and unnatural. With an adequate power of self-adjustment, we might reasonably expect that revision of the strict letter of the law would be undertaken with such due regard for the living mind of the Church as would secure the obedience of many, now dissatisfied, who desire to be loyal, and would justify the Church as a whole, in insisting on the obedience of all.

Secondly, the machinery for discipline has broken down. The means of enforcing the law in the Ecclesiastical Courts, even in matters which touch the Church's faith and teaching, are defective and in some respects unsuitable. They have been tried and have often failed; and probably on that account they have been too much neglected. Although attempts to deal administratively with ritual irregularity have been made, they have been unsuccessful, in some cases on account of the lack of firmness of those who made them, but also largely because, in regard to the rites and ceremonies of public worship, the law gives no right or power to discriminate between small and great matters.

It is important that the law should be reformed, that it should admit of reasonable elasticity, and that the means of enforcing it should be improved; but, above all, it is necessary that it should be obeyed. That a section of clergymen should, with however good intentions, conspicuously disobey the law, and continue to do so with impunity, is not only an offence against public order, but also a scandal to religion and a cause of weakness to the Church of England. It is not our duty to assign responsibility for the past; we have indicated our opinion that it lies in large measure with the law itself. But with regard to the future we desire to state with distinctness our conviction that, if it should be thought well to adopt the recommendations we make in this report, one essential condition of their successful operation will be, that obedience to the law so altered shall be required and, if necessary, enforced, by those who bear rule in the Church of England.

RECOMMENDATIONS

We desire to state that those of our recommendations which will require legislation are framed as a complete scheme and must be considered mutually dependent.

We recommend that

1 The practices to which we have referred in paragraphs 397 and 398 of our Report, as being plainly significant of teaching repugnant to the doctrine of the Church of England and certainly illegal, should be promptly made to cease by the exercise of the authority belonging to the Bishops and, if necessary, by proceedings in the Ecclesiastical Courts.

2 Letters of Business should be issued to the Convocations with instructions: (*a*) to consider the preparation of a new rubric regulating the ornaments (that is to say, the vesture) of the ministers of

the Church, at the times of their ministrations, with a view to its enactment by Parliament; and (*b*) to frame, with a view to their enactment by Parliament, such modifications in the existing law relating to the conduct of Divine Service and to the ornaments and fittings of churches as may tend to secure the greater elasticity which a reasonable recognition of the comprehensiveness of the Church of England and of its present needs seems to demand.

It would be most desirable for the early dealing with these important subjects that the Convocations should sit together, and we assume that they would take counsel with the Houses of Laymen.[1]

3 In regard to the sanction to be given for the use of additional and special services, collects, and hymns, the law should be so amended as to give wider scope for the exercise of a regulative authority. This authority should be exercised within prescribed limits by the Archbishops and Bishops of both Provinces acting together for the sanction and regulation of additional and special services and collects in accordance with the teaching of the Holy Scriptures and the Book of Common Prayer, and for the forbidding of the use of hymns or anthems not in accordance with such teaching.[2]

The administrative discretion of individual Bishops within the several dioceses should be used in conformity with such sanction and regulation.

4 Bishops should be invested with power to refuse the institution or admission of a presentee into a benefice who has not previously satisfied the Bishop of the diocese of his willingness to obey the law as to the conduct of Divine Service and as to the ornaments and fittings of churches, and to submit to directions given by the Bishop in accordance with Recommendation 3.

5 The recommendation of the Ecclesiastical Courts Commission in 1883 as to the constitution of the Diocesan and Provincial Courts and of the Court of Final Appeal should be carried into effect with one modification, namely to substitute for the recommendation of the Ecclesiastical Courts Commission quoted in paragraph 368 of our Report, the following:

Where, in an appeal before the Final Court which involves charges of heresy or breach of ritual, any question touching the doctrine or use of the Church of England shall be in controversy, which question is not in the opinion of the Court governed by the plain language of documents having the force of Acts of Parliament, and involves the doctrine or use of the Church of England proper to be applied to the facts found by the Court, such questions shall be referred to an assembly of the Archbishops and Bishops of both Provinces, who shall be entitled to call in such advice as they may think fit; and the opinion of the majority of such assembly of the Archbishops and Bishops with regard to any question so submitted to them shall be binding on the Court for the purposes of the said appeal.

6 In all cases in which a sentence of an Ecclesiastical Court passed on an incumbent in a suit brought under the Church Discipline Act, 1840, is wilfully disobeyed, power should be given to the Court whose sentence is thus disobeyed, by an order made on a summary application, the Court being satisfied of such wilful disobedience, to declare the benefice of such incumbent vacant; and no such incumbent should be eligible for appointment to any other benefice or to receive a licence as a curate or preacher, until he has satisfied the Archbishop of the province that he will not offend in like manner in future.

7 The Episcopal veto in respect of any suit under the Church Discipline Act, 1840, should be abolished; but it should be open to the Court in which any such suit is brought to stay proceedings therein (subject to appeal) on the ground that the suit is frivolous or vexatious. It should also be in the power of the Court in its discretion, at any stage of the proceedings, to require security for costs to be given by the promoter of a suit.

The Public Worship Regulation Act, 1874, should be repealed.

8 A Bishop should have power at any time, by an order or monition made by himself or by his Chancellor, after due opportunity to be heard on the matter has been given to the incumbent and churchwardens and any other persons whom the Bishop or his Chancellor (as the case may be) may direct, to order the removal of ornaments, objects of decoration, or fittings placed in a church, as to which ornaments, objects, or fittings no faculty has been obtained, and to provide for the disposal of such ornaments, objects, or fittings when removed. A Bishop should have a *locus standi* in his Consistory Court in all faculty cases affecting the ornaments, objects of decoration, or fittings of churches in his diocese.

9 Episcopal and Archidiaconal visitations and Rural Dean's inspections of churches should be more effectively employed as the regular and official means of keeping the Bishop informed with

regard to the conduct of Divine Service in, and the ornaments, objects of decoration, and fittings of, the churches in his diocese.[3] Articles of inquiry in visitation should be framed with a view to elicit this information from the churchwardens. Greater strictness should be used in seeing that such articles are answered, and that any action is taken which the answers may require. Directions in accordance with law given by a Bishop or Archdeacon in visitation as to the conduct of Divine Service and as to the ornaments, objects of decoration, and fittings of churches should be enforceable against incumbents and churchwardens by means of a summary application to the Consistory Court of the diocese. Any order thus made should be subject to appeal to the Provincial Court.

10 For the purposes of effective supervision and administration, it is desirable that many dioceses should be subdivided; and that a general Act providing machinery for the creation of new dioceses by Order in Council should be passed so as to prevent the necessity of the enactment of a separate statute on the formation of each new diocese.[4]

1 The Letters of Business were issued to Convocations on 10 November 1906, initiating the process of Prayer Book revision culminating in the controversy of 1928.

2 The Act of Uniformity Amendment Act (the Shortened Services Act 1872, 35-36 Vict., c. 35) permitted additional services on special occasions, if approved by the Ordinary and entirely derived from holy Scripture and the Prayer Book.

3 The office of Rural Dean was revived under Bishop Kaye of Lincoln and Bishop Marsh of Peterborough in the 1830s. Blomfield created rural deans in London in 1844, and his example was followed by Sumner at Winchester and Stanley at Norwich. The last diocese to revive the office was Sodor and Man in 1880.

4 The creation of new bishoprics required an Act of Parliament followed by an Order in Council. Since 1914 the following dioceses have been created: Chelmsford, Sheffield, Ipswich and St Edmundsbury, 1914; Coventry, 1918; Bradford, 1920; Leicester and Blackburn, 1926; Derby, Guildford, and Portsmouth, 1927. The difficulties in creating new sees is described in Bell, *Davidson*, pp. 644-6, and a criticism of the policy of creating new sees is set out in Henson, *Retrospect*, vol. 2, pp. 94-6.

71 BISHOP GORE AND CANON HENSON, 1909

(Extract from the Bishop's Act Book, Birmingham Diocesan Registry)

The conflict between Charles Gore and Hensley Henson was a clash between two schools of thought. Gore was a High Churchman with a deep concern for the inherent authority of the episcopal office, whereas Henson was a representative of the latitudinarian school having a great respect for the rights of the establishment. In opposition to Gore, Henson maintained that the clergy "*are governed by the Law and only by the Bishops within the limits which the Law prescribes*".[1]

INHIBITION

The Reverend Canon Herbert Hensley Henson, D.D.

1909 March 26
The Bishop this day issued the following inhibition:

To the Reverend Herbert Hensley Henson, D.D., Canon of Westminster and Rector of St Margaret's Westminster

WHEREAS it has been represented to us that you the Reverend Canon Herbert Hensley Henson are publicly announced to preach in connection with a certain first anniversary in an Institute called the Digbeth Institute[2] situate in the parish of St Gabriel's in the City and Diocese of Birmingham being a parish wherein you have no cure of souls AND WHEREAS the Reverend Walter H. Carris, Vicar of the said parish, has protested and refused his consent thereto and has communicated to us his said protest and refusal of consent NOW WE CHARLES by Divine Permission Bishop of the said Diocese of Birmingham having regard to the rights of the Vicar of the said parish and in exercise of the powers inherent in us in that behalf do hereby inhibit you the said Reverend Canon Hensley Henson from preaching or officiating within the limits of the said parish.[3]

GIVEN under our hand and seal this twenty-sixth day of March in the year of our Lord One thousand nine hundred and nine.

C. BIRMINGHAM

1 An inhibition, though an episcopal order, was governed by the provisions of the Church Discipline Act (1840) and the Clergy Discipline Act (1892) after judicial inquiry. In this singular incident,

Henson "had hoped that the issue (of cardinal importance in its bearing on the relation of the Church of England to the non-Episcopal Churches) would have been finally determined in a friendly action by the proper Court" (Henson, *Retrospect of an Unimportant Life*, vol. 1, pp. 92-6).

2 The Digbeth Institute was maintained by the Carr's Lane Congregational Church in a poor district of Birmingham. The minister was Dr J. H. Jowett.

3 One of the reasons why Gore did not institute legal proceedings against Henson for defying the inhibition was the possibility of an appeal to the Judicial Committee of the Privy Council, the authority of which, in spiritual matters, he refused to acknowledge. Prestige says of the inhibition: "It is a historic document. The fact of its reception and of the recipient's disobedience marks a definite stage in the breakdown of episcopal control over the actions of the clergy" (Henson, *Retrospect*, vol. 1, p. 95).

72 KIKUYU, 1913

(Kikuyu, Box 1, Davidson Papers, Lambeth Palace, 30 September 1913)

At a missionary conference of Protestant Churches in British East Africa in June 1913, a *Proposed Scheme of Federation of Missionary Societies working in British East Africa* was issued. There was no explicit mention of episcopacy in the scheme, and it was proposed that members of any of the Churches had the right to receive Communion in any of the others. The Bishop of Zanzibar[1] condemned the action of the two Anglican bishops in giving Communion to members of non-episcopal Churches at the concluding service, as well as their acceptance of the proposals. The controversy, which was largely conducted in England, rallied the Anglo-Catholics around Weston. The Archbishop of Canterbury refused a trial of the two bishops, but summoned the Consultative Committee of the Lambeth Conference to meet in June 1914.

To the Most Reverend Father in God Randall, by Divine Providence Lord Archbishop of Canterbury and Metropolitan, Greeting in the Lord.

Whereas the *Ecclesia Anglicana* claims to be and in fact is within the Body of the Holy Catholic Church of Christ,

And whereas the Holy Catholic Church everywhere maintains and confesses the Creed commonly called that of Saint Athanasius;

and teaches the doctrine of the Real Presence of Our Lord's Body and Blood in the Holy Communion consecrated by a priest of her own Ministry; and holds and uses the Rites of Confirmation and Absolution as means of Grace; and acknowledges herself to be essentially based upon the Apostolic Ministry of Bishops, the successors of the Apostles; and uses everywhere the custom of baptizing Infants;

And whereas, in a document entitled "Proposed Scheme of Federation of Missionary Societies working in British East Africa", published by Leader, Nairobi, and Mombasa, June 1913, it is clearly implied and taught that in so confessing, teaching, and using the Catholic Church has gone beyond the revelation committed to her;

And whereas in the same document it is agreed to found a new Church for East Africa in which the Rites of Confirmation and Absolution will not be used, from which the Creed of St Athanasius is excluded, and in which Infant Baptism will be optional;

And whereas in the same document it is announced that all parties consenting thereto shall combine to establish a new Ministry of four new orders to the exclusion of the Catholic and Apostolic Episcopal Ministry;

And whereas in the same document it is clearly taught that the Holy Communion consecrated by a priest of the Catholic Church in no way differs from Communion administered by a minister of a protestant body;

And whereas in the same document it is laid down that one and the same doctrine is sufficient for a candidate for baptism in the Church and for a candidate for the baptism of Christ as explained by any protestant body included in the proposed Federation; and that one and the same course of doctrine is sufficient for a candidate for the ministry of the Catholic Church and for a candidate for the ministry of any protestant body in the proposed Federation;

And whereas this document bears the signature of the Right Reverend Father in God, John Jameson, Lord Bishop of Uganda[2] as Chairman of the Conference whose belief and teaching it expresses; and also the signature of the Right Reverend Father in God, William, Lord Bishop of Mombasa[3] as representing the Church Missionary Society; and also the name of George W. Wright, a Priest licensed by the said Lord Bishop of Mombasa, as Secretary of the Conference;

And whereas on the closing day of the Conference, June 21st 1913, the Holy Communion was celebrated in a Presbyterian Church at Kikuyu, British East Africa, by the aforesaid Right

Reverend William, Lord Bishop of Mombasa, in the presence of the said Right Reverend John Jameson, Lord Bishop of Uganda, the Sacrament being given to many members of protestant bodies whose very existence is hostile to Christ's Holy Church;

And whereas African Christians of the dioceses of Mombasa and Uganda have been entirely misled and deceived as to the true teaching of the Catholic Church as represented by the *Ecclesia Anglicana* through the words and acts of the aforesaid Bishops of Mombasa and Uganda;

And whereas the Diocese of Zanzibar and East Africa is so situated that whatever is taught by the Bishops of Mombasa and Uganda is known and repeated, and is able to be quoted as being the doctrine of the *Ecclesia Anglicana*, and therefore of the Catholic Church;

And whereas Christians of the diocese of Zanzibar and East Africa are continually travelling in the dioceses of Mombasa and Uganda, and are easily moved to wonder at these contradictions of the Catholic Faith, to their distress and possible loss;

And whereas it is of the first importance that an authoritative statement be made to the Church people of the dioceses of Mombasa, Uganda, and Zanzibar, in which these teachings and actions of the aforesaid Bishops of Mombasa and Uganda may be declared contrary to the faith of the Catholic Church and to her practices, and may be utterly repudiated and forbidden; lest the witness of the Church be falsified and a multitude perish from the Way of Truth;[4]

Therefore, We, Frank, by Divine Permission Lord Bishop of Zanzibar and East Africa do by these presents accuse and charge the Right Reverend Father in God William, Lord Bishop of Mombasa, and the Right Reverend Father in God John Jameson, Lord Bishop of Uganda, with the grievous faults of propagating heresy and committing schism;

And We do hereby most humbly implore Your Grace to obtain from them for publication in East Africa and Zanzibar a complete and categorical recantation of the errors which they have taught in word and action;

Or failing that, We do hereby request Your Grace to appoint us a day and place in which, comformably with Catholic precedent, We may appear before You and not less than twelve of Your Grace's comprovincial Bishops[5] sitting with Your Grace as Judges of this cause, and to permit us there and then to meet the aforesaid Lord Bishop of Mombasa and Lord Bishop of Uganda, and in open Assembly to allow us to make and sustain our charges and accusations against them;[6]

In all that We have set forth We have been mindful of Your Grace's pre-eminent position and Our own unworthiness: yet none the less have We felt Our own personal responsibility to Our Lord Jesus Christ for any the least acquiescence in such a state of confusion as now obtains in East Africa through the action and teaching of which we complain.

And inasmuch as the scandal caused by this heresy and schism is both grave and widespread, and is in no way to be done away merely by the suppression of the proposed Federation.

We do most earnestly, and after much earnest prayer, beg Your Grace to order the Assembly as early in the New Year as is consistent with the gravity of the issues involved, if so be no speedy recantation shall have been made.

Given under Our hand and seal, in Our Cathedral City of Zanzibar, on this thirtieth day of September in the Year of Our Lord one thousand nine hundred and thirteen, and of Our Consecration the fifth.

FRANK ZANZIBAR

The Consultative Body met at Lambeth on 27 July 1914 and continued its meetings to the 31 July. It examined the papers and pamphlets relating to the controversy, and also interviewed the Bishops of Mombasa, Uganda, and Zanzibar. Its Report was unanimous, and was submitted in writing to the Archbishop of Canterbury. Davidson made his formal reply to the Bishop of Zanzibar at Easter 1915, and, in the context of the war, the controversy was put aside (Davidson, *Kikuyu* (1915), pp. 42-7, Appendix B).

Your Grace has addressed to us two questions concerning the recent Missionary Conference at Kikuyu in East Africa. We have thought it best to give our answer to these questions in the form of the following statement.

I

In replying to your Grace's first question with regard to the "Proposed Scheme of Federation of Missionary Societies", we clearly recognize that the Scheme was not drawn up with a view to immediate publication: that it was intended to be merely tentative: and that it was meant to serve as a series of proposals to be submitted for consideration to the recognized authorities of all the bodies concerned, and in particular by the Bishops of Mombasa and Uganda to the Archbishop of Canterbury in view of his metropolitan relation to them.

The Scheme is thus to be regarded as a stage in negotiations still incomplete, rather than as an arrangement that has been definitely adopted. Accordingly, in many cases, the terms used in the Scheme have not taken matured and settled form.

Bearing this in mind, the Central Consultative Body heartily appreciate the fact that the main object of the Kikuyu Conference, namely, the promotion of a brotherly spirit, and the adoption of practical steps towards unity, is wholly desirable. The Conference laid emphasis before the natives of Africa and in the face of Islam, upon what unites rather than upon what separates bodies of Christians. It endeavoured to secure a clear understanding as to the mutual relations of Churches or Societies in the field, and working agreements on certain points. The attempt to bring to a common standard rules relating to probation and discipline, admirably serves the main object, and is in itself of great moral and religious value.

All this, with the mutual consideration involved, and with the united testimony borne to the faith which is enshrined in the Apostles' and Nicene Creeds, plainly makes for unity; and it is by such methods and by such a temper, more, perhaps, than by formal organization, that the conditions may be realized in which the end of our efforts and our prayers—a genuine African Church—will be shaped by the Holy Spirit of God according to His Will.

But the proposal of "Federation" evidently goes much further than such particular agreements as those of which we have just been speaking. It opens manifold questions. It is of a constitutional or semi-constitutional character. For "Federation" has, word and thing, political associations, and federal authority often is, or increasingly becomes, dominant over the federated units. Declarations of "autonomy" do not sufficiently meet this difficulty.

It is probable that the arrangements proposed are largely due to the special circumstances and conditions of particular dioceses. But the effect of the proposals may be far-reaching.

Plainly, for example, it is not without its bearing on the characteristic position of the Anglican Communion and on the harmony of the different convictions which by the goodness of God and the power of His Spirit have been held together within it.

Further, what is done in one part of our Church, though it may there have been intended only to meet local needs, is likely to be followed in other places, and even to become the starting point for further movement in the same direction.

It therefore appears to us that such a constitutional scheme is quite distinctly the kind of change, or step in advance, which ought not to be made by a diocese or group of dioceses without opportunity given to the whole Communion, through the Lambeth Conference, to advise upon it, at least in its main principles.

This recommendation of reference to the Lambeth Conference does not in any way mean that we suggest the postponement of the whole matter for four years. The parties who met at Kikuyu have formulated a number of suggestions for common action. Many, probably most, of these can be carried out by the method of mutual agreement. They tend to unity without any compromise of independence.

There are, however, some proposals in the Scheme, which require the most anxious consideration:

1. It is proposed in the Scheme that "all recognized as ministers in their own Churches shall be welcome as visitors to preach in other federated Churches". We see no essential difficulty in inviting a minister or lay person not of our own Communion to address our people, provided that the Bishop inviting him or authorizing the invitation is satisfied as to his qualifications. We concur in the Bishop of Uganda's statement that "such an invitation would obviously be purely voluntary, and neither could nor would be claimed as a right". But the terms of the proposal to which we have called attention do not seem to us sufficiently to safeguard this principle.

2. A graver question is that which arises as to the admission to Holy Communion in Anglican Churches of Communicants belonging to other denominations.

The principles accepted by the Church of England as bearing on admission to Holy Communion (apart from the moral conditions laid down in the formularies of the Church) start, it need hardly be said, from the presupposition that the candidate for admission is a baptized person.

Further, it is the undoubted rule of the Church of England that those who are to be admitted to the Holy Communion must have been "Confirmed", or be "ready and desirous to be confirmed".

In strictness this forbids admission to the Holy Communion till the requirements of the Church have been complied with; and here it should not be forgotten that the Church regards Confirmation not merely as a condition of admission to Holy Communion, but as an apostolic means of grace by which the life of the baptized is strengthened for Christian service through the Holy Spirit

On the other hand, the lack of Confirmation cannot be held, as the lack of Baptism must be held, to render a person incapable, so far as man can judge, of sacramental communion.

The evidence is abundant to show that exceptions to the rule have been allowed in special cases by many Bishops of weight and learning and of diverse theological positions, in all parts of the Anglican Communion.

But this relaxation has been a matter of episcopal discretion exercised expressly in view of special circumstances, and therefore, in our view, has not compromised the Church's witness to her principles.

Few rubrics, moreover, are so rigid as to admit of no exception; nor can the rubric in this case be so interpreted as to prevent the admission to occasional communion of individuals who from peculiar circumstances are deprived of the ministrations of the Churches to which they belong.

This seems to be eminently a matter in which the administrative and pastoral discretion of the Bishop may well be exercised, especially, though not exclusively, in the mission field.

3. It appears to be implied in the proposed Scheme that members of our own Church resident in districts assigned to the care of a non-episcopal mission would communicate in the churches of that mission. This seems to us to be a question on an altogether different level from that with which we have just been dealing. It needs separate treatment, and it is one upon which our advice is expressly asked.

We are not here called upon to consider individual cases. We are confronted by definite proposals, to which two Bishops of our Communion have been parties, for arrangements of a general character between different religious bodies. In these it seems to be implied that members of our Church would be encouraged or even expected to communicate in non-episcopal Churches.

We are bound to say that we cannot regard any such arrangements as consistent with the principles of the Church of England. In saying this we associate ourselves with the words used, though in a different order, by the Committee of the last Lambeth Conference on "Reunion and Intercommunion": "It is no part of our duty, and therefore not our desire, to pronounce negatively upon the value in God's sight of the ministry in other Communions. But Anglican Churchmen must contend for a valid ministry as they understand it, and regard themselves as absolutely bound to stipulate for this for themselves."[7]

II

We go on to deal with your Grace's second question. The Communion Service at the end of the Conference at Kikuyu does not come within the scope of the considerations which we have previously advanced about exceptional cases of admission to Holy Communion. For there was on that occasion no such necessity as we were then contemplating. It was an act of a different nature, unpremeditated, and prompted by an impulse of a deeply Christian kind. We desire to abstain from any expression of judgment about it. We can well believe that for the purity of its motive, and for the love that was in it, it was acceptable to Him to whom it was offered, and whom its participants united to adore.

But after saying this, we are bound to add that any attempt to treat it as a precedent, or to encourage habitual action of the kind, must be held to be inconsistent with principles accepted by the Church of England. It would be a very serious alteration of the terms of communion, made not by any deliberate and corporate resolution of the Church, but by the sporadic action of individuals. However well intended, it would be subversive of Church order. It would perplex the minds and distress the consciences of multitudes of loyal Churchmen. So far from promoting unity, it would in our judgment, rather imperil the measure of unity which we now possess, and the prospects of the fuller unity for which we pray. Inspired by the laudable motive of charity towards those from whom we are unhappily separated, it would be grievously hurtful to charity among ourselves.[8]

In the advice which we have given to your Grace, we have had chiefly in view the case of Native Converts in the Mission Field, but we see no reason, for the purposes of our reply, to distinguish between them and European Christians living among them.

COSMO EBOR:
J. B. ARMAGH
E. JAMAICA, Archbishop of the West Indies
S. P. RUPERTSLAND, Primate of all Canada
WALTER J. F. ROBBERDS, Bishop of Brechin, Primus
EDW: WINTON
R. S. COPLESTON, Bishop
FREDERIC WALLIS, Bishop
H. E. RYLE, Bishop
A. EXON:
HY. GIBRALTAR

1 Weston, Frank; *b.* 1871; *educ.*, Dulwich College and Trinity College, Oxford; curate of Trinity College Mission, 1894; curate of St Matthew, Westminster, 1896; chaplain at St Andrew's College, Zanzibar, 1898; Warden of St Mark's Theological College, 1899; Principal of St Andrew's Training College, Kuingani, 1901; Chancellor of Zanzibar Cathedral, 1904; Bishop of Zanzibar, 1908; *d.* 1924.

2 Willis, John Jameson; *b.* 1872; *educ.*, Haileybury College, Pembroke College, Ridley Hall, Cambridge; curate of Great Yarmouth, 1895; C.M.S. missionary in Ankole, 1900; Entebbe, 1902; Kavirondo, 1905; Archdeacon of Kavirondo, 1909; Bishop of Uganda, 1912; Assistant Bishop of Leicester, 1935; retired, 1949; *d.* 1954.

3 Peel, William George; *b.* 1854; C.M.S. Theological College, Islington; ordained, 1879; curate of Trowbridge, 1879; Rugby Fox Master of C.M.S. College, Masulipatam, 1880; C.M.S. secretary, Madras, 1888 and 1892; C.M.S. secretary, W. India, 1892; Bishop of Mombasa, 1899; *d.* 1916.

4 Weston was distressed over the consequences of the theological uncertainty in the mission field caused by such writings as *Foundations*, the volume he considered to be the most damaging expression of the liberal principle.

5 The bishops of missionary dioceses were under the direct jurisdiction of the See of Canterbury and could not, therefore, be summoned before an episcopal court of the Province of Canterbury.

6 Gore expressed his doubts as to what Weston's accusation of heresy and schism really meant. Weston himself was bent on raising the issues involved in the proposed Federation in such a manner that they could not be overlooked.

7 Henson summed up the conflict in the following question: "Was the Church of England really so plainly committed to the exclusive episcopalianism which the Tractarians had taught, that religious fellowship with non-episcopalian Churches was inadmissible?" Henson, *Retrospect*, vol. 1, p. 161. Lang, on the other hand, described it as the conflict between "two great principles, each in itself high and noble".

8 Of this second section of the answer, it was said at the time: "The Commission comes to the conclusion that the Service at Kikuyu was eminently pleasing to God, and must on no account be repeated" (attributed to Ronald Knox).

73 THE WELSH CHURCH ACT 1914

(*Statutes at Large*, 4-5 Geo. V, c. 91)

Church disestablishment had figured in the Newcastle programme of 1891 when the new radical strength of the Liberal Party attacked the ecclesiastical establishment in Scotland and Wales. Unsuccessful Bills were introduced by the Liberals in 1895 and 1909, both strongly opposed in the House of Lords. The provisions of the present Bill were introduced into Parliament in April 1912, and, with the removal of the House of Lords' power of permanent veto, became law in 1914. The Act did not come into force until after the war, when the Act of 1919 proved to be more beneficial to the Welsh Church.[1]

An Act to terminate the establishment of the Church of England in Wales and Monmouthshire, and to make provision in respect of the Temporalities thereof, and for other purposes in connection with the matters aforesaid.

(18th September 1914)

Be it enacted by the King's most Excellent Majesty, by and with the advice and consent of the Commons, in this present Parliament assembled, in accordance with the provisions of the Parliament Act, 1911, and by authority of the same, as follows:

DISESTABLISHMENT AND VESTING AND DISTRIBUTION OF PROPERTY

DISESTABLISHMENT

1

On the day after the expiration of six months, or such extended period as His Majesty shall fix by Order in Council, not being more than twelve months, after the passing of this Act, (in this Act referred to as the date of disestablishment), the Church of England, so far as it extends to and exists in Wales and Monmouthshire (in this Act referred to as the Church in Wales), shall cease to be established by law, and, save as by this Act provided, no person shall, after the passing of this Act, be appointed or nominated by His Majesty or any person, by virtue of any existing right of patronage, to any ecclesiastical office in the Church in Wales.

2

(1) On the date of disestablishment every cathedral and ecclesiastical corporation in the Church in Wales, whether sole or aggregate, shall be dissolved.

(2) On and after the date of disestablishment no bishop of the Church in Wales shall as such be summoned to or be qualified to sit or vote as a Lord of Parliament; but save as aforesaid every person who is at the passing of this Act a bishop, dean, canon, or archdeacon of or the holder of any ecclesiastical office in the Church in Wales, shall during his life enjoy the same title and precedence as if this Act had not passed.[2]

(3) Writs of summons shall be issued to bishops not disqualified by this enactment for sitting in the House of Lords as if the bishops so disqualified had vacated their sees.

(4) On and after the date of disestablishment no person shall be disqualified or liable to any penalty for sitting or voting in the House of Commons by reason of having been ordained to the office of priest or deacon if the ecclesiastical office he holds is an ecclesiastical office in the Church in Wales, or, if he does not hold any ecclesiastical office, if the last ecclesiastical office which he held was an ecclesiastical office in the Church in Wales.

3

(1) As from the date of disestablishment ecclesiastical courts and persons in Wales and Monmouthshire shall cease to exercise any jurisdiction, and the ecclesiastical law of the Church in Wales shall cease to exist as law.

(2) As from the same date the then existing ecclesiastical law and the then existing articles, doctrines, rites, rules, discipline, and ordinances of the Church of England shall, with and subject to such modification or alteration, if any, as after the passing of this Act may be duly made therein, according to the constitution and regulations for the time being of the Church in Wales, be binding on the members for the time being of the Church in Wales in the same manner as if they had mutually agreed to be so bound and shall be capable of being enforced in the temporal courts in relation to any property which by virtue of this Act is held on behalf of the said Church or any members thereof, in the same manner and to the same extent as if such property had been expressly assured upon trust to be held on

behalf of persons who should be so bound:

Provided that no alteration in the articles, doctrines, rites, or, save so far as may be rendered necessary by the passing of this Act, in the formularies of the Church in Wales, shall be so far binding on any ecclesiastical person having any existing interest save by this Act, as to deprive him of that interest, if he, within one month after the making of the alteration, signifies in writing to the representative body hereinafter mentioned his dissent therefrom.

(3) The said constitution and regulations of the Church in Wales may, notwithstanding anything in this section, provide for the establishment for the Church in Wales of ecclesiastical courts, and, if the Archbishop of Canterbury consents, for appeals from any of the courts so established being heard and determined by the provincial court of the Archbishop, and the Archbishop may, with the approval of His Majesty in Council, give such consent, but no such courts shall exercise any coercive jurisdiction and no appeal shall lie from any such court to His Majesty in Council.[3]

(4) The power of making by such constitution and regulations alterations and modifications in ecclesiastical law shall include the power of altering and modifying such law so far as it is embodied in the Church Discipline Act, 1840, the Public Worship Regulation Act, 1874, the Clergy Discipline Act, 1892 or the Ecclesiastical Dilapidations Acts, 1871 and 1872, or any other Act of Parliament.

(5) As from the date of disestablishment the bishops and clergy of the Church in Wales shall cease to be members of or be represented in the Houses of Convocation of the Province of Canterbury, but nothing in this Act shall affect the powers of those Houses so far as they relate to matters outside Wales and Monmouthshire.

VESTING OF PROPERTY

4

(1) As from the date of disestablishment there shall, save as by this section provided, vest in the Welsh Commissioners hereinafter mentioned

(*a*) all property vested in the Ecclesiastical Commissioners or Queen Anne's Bounty, which is ascertained as hereinafter mentioned to be Welsh ecclesiastical property; and[4] (*b*) all property not so vested, and not consisting of charges on the common fund of the Ecclesiastical Commissioners, which, at the passing of this Act, belongs to or is appropriated to the use of any ecclesiastical office or cathedral corporation in the Church in Wales, or the holder of any such office as such; subject, in the case of all such property, to all tenancies, charges, and incumbrances, and to all rights and interests saved by this Act, affecting the property.

(2) All plate, furniture, and other moveable chattels belonging to any church affected by this Act, or used in connection with the celebration of Divine worship therein, not being the property of a private individual, shall vest in the representative body hereinafter mentioned if and when incorporated.

Provided that if such a body is not incorporated at the date of disestablishment all such moveable chattels as aforesaid shall, until the incorporation of such a body, remain vested in the same persons and be applicable to the same purposes as before the date of disestablishment.[5]

DISTRIBUTION OF PROPERTY

8

(1) Subject to the provisions of this Act, the Welsh Commissioners shall by order transfer the property vested in them by this Act, as follows:

(*a*) they shall transfer to the representative body

(i) all churches;

(ii) all ecclesiastical residences, together with any moveable chattels held and enjoyed with or as incident to the occupation of any such residence, by the incumbent for the time being of the office to which the residence is attached;

(iii) all funds or endowments specially allocated to the repair, restoration, or improvement of the fabric of any such church or ecclesiastical residence;

(iv) all property which consists of or is the produce of or is or has been derived from grants made by Queen Anne's Bounty out of moneys provided by Parliament;

(v) all property which consists of or is the produce of or is or has been derived from grants made by Queen Anne's Bounty out of the Royal Bounty Fund;

(vi) all private benefactions;

(vii) if so requested by the representative body, any glebe or other land, not comprised within any of the above-mentioned categories and not being a burial ground; subject to the payment by the representative body to the Welsh Commissioners of a sum equal to the value thereof, such value to be determined in default of agreement by arbitration, regard being had to the tenancies, charges, incumbrances, interests, and rights subject to which the land is transferred to the representative body;

(viii) if so requested by the representative body, any burial grounds which before the date of disestablishment have been closed under or in pursuance of the provisions of any Act of Parliament or of any Order in Council made thereunder;

(*b*) (*burial grounds* ...)

(*c*) of the property not so tranferred to the representative body they shall transfer any tithe rentcharge which was formerly appropriated to the use of any parochial benefice to the council of the county in which the land out of which the tithe rentcharge issues is situate:

Provided that where such land is not situate in Wales or Monmouthshire they shall transfer the tithe rentcharge to the council of such county in Wales and Monmouthshire as the Welsh Commissioners think fit;

(*d*) of the property not so transferred to the representative body they shall transfer any other property which was formerly appropriated to the use of any parochial benefice (including the money paid under this section by the representative body in respect of glebes) to the council of the county in which the ecclesiastical parish to the use of which the property was so appropriated is situate:

Provided that if such ecclesiastical parish is situate in more than one county the property shall be transferred to such one or more of those councils or be divided between them as the Welsh Commissioners may think fit;

(*e*) they shall transfer all other property vested in them to the University of Wales.

(2) Save as otherwise provided by this Act, all property transferred under this section shall be held subject to all existing public and private rights with respect thereto, and all tenancies, charges, and incumbrances which may at the date of transfer

be subsisting therein, and in the case of all such property, except tithe rentcharge transferred to a county council, to the existing interests of all persons who at the passing of this Act hold ecclesiastical offices in the Church in Wales, and in the case of such tithe rentcharge to the obligation to make such provision as is hereinafter mentioned in lieu of such existing interests.

(3) Where property of any such class as aforesaid has before the date of disestablishment been sold, redeemed, or otherwise converted, or where any moneys are at that date held upon trust to be applied in the building purchase or repair of, or to make good dilapidations in, property of any such class as aforesaid, the proceeds of sale, redemption, or other conversion, and such moneys as aforesaid or the securities in which such proceeds or moneys are for the time being invested, shall be dealt with in like manner as if they were property of that class.

CONSTITUTION OF THE REPRESENTATIVE BODY

13

(1) Nothing in any Act, law, or custom shall prevent the bishops, clergy, and laity of the Church in Wales from holding synods or electing representatives thereto, or from framing, either by themselves or by their representatives elected in such manner as they think fit, constitutions and regulations for the general management and good government of the Church in Wales and the property and affairs thereof, whether as a whole or according to dioceses, and the future representation of members thereof in a general synod or in diocesan synods, or otherwise.[6]

(2) If at any time it is shown to the satisfaction of His Majesty the King that the said bishops, clergy, and laity have appointed any persons to represent them, and hold property for any of their uses and purposes, His Majesty in Council may by charter incorporate such persons (in this Act referred to as the representative body), with power to hold land without licence in mortmain.

APPLICATION OF RESIDUE

19

(1) Subject to the provisions of this Act, the property vested in the Welsh Commissioners by this Act, other than the property

transferred to the representative body and burial grounds, shall be applied as follows:

(*a*) The property formerly appropriated to the use of parochial benefices and transferred to a county council shall be applied, in accordance with one or more schemes made by that council either alone or jointly with any other such council and approved by the Secretary of State, to any charitable or eleemosynary purpose of local or general utility, including the aiding of poor scholars;

(*b*) All other property to which this section relates shall be applied in the first instance towards payment of the expenses of carrying this Act into execution (exclusive of any expenses incurred in the administration of any scheme made by a county council) and subject thereto, shall be applied by the University of Wales by way of the appropriation or payment either of capital or annual sums, or partly in one such way and partly in the other, for the benefit of the University and the following institutions, that is to say, the University College of Wales, Aberystwyth, the University College of North Wales, The University College of South Wales and Monmouthshire, (the University College of Swansea) and the National Library of Wales, so, however, that the ultimate share of each such university college shall be three-sixteenths, and of the National Library of Wales one-eighth, of the total amount so distributable, and that in applying its share each such university college shall have regard to the needs of poor scholars.

(2) In framing schemes under this section as to the application of property formerly appropriated to the use of parochial benefices, due regard shall be had to the wants and circumstances of the parish in which the property is situate or from which it is or has been derived, and of the parish comprising the ecclesiastical parish to which any such property was attached, and generally to the circumstances of each particular case.

(3) A scheme made under this section may be amended or revoked by a scheme made and confirmed in like manner as the original scheme.

(4) Every scheme made and confirmed under this section shall be laid before both Houses of Parliament as soon as may be after it is confirmed, and shall have effect as if enacted in this Act.[7]

1 A Royal Commission was appointed in 1907 and reported in 1910. A Bill was introduced in the Commons in April 1912; a second reading was carried in May; and by February 1913 had passed through all its necessary stages. It was rejected in the Lords on 13 February. Introduced a second time into the Commons it reached the Lords in July only to be rejected again. It was introduced a third time in April 1914 into the Commons and passed. The Act was finally passed under the provisions of the Parliament Act (1911) in spite of Archbishop Davidson's opposition.

2 The four Welsh dioceses in the Province of Canterbury were: St David's (John Owen); St Asaph (A. G. Edwards, later archbishop); Bangor (W. H. Williams); and Llandaff (J. P. Hughes). The sees of Monmouth, and Swansea and Brecon, were created in 1921 and 1923 respectively.

3 The Suspensory Act postponed the operation of the Act during the duration of the war. The four Welsh bishops were finally released from their Oaths of Due Obedience to the Archbishop of Canterbury as Metropolitan as from 31 March 1920. The Supreme Court of the Province of Wales consists of the Archbishops of Canterbury, York, Armagh, and Dublin, and the Primus of the Episcopal Church of Scotland.

4 The Welsh Church's income from endowments in 1910 was £268,558. Ancient endowments (prior to 1662) which were no longer to be paid to the Welsh Church amounted to around £102,000 a year.

5 The Representative Body of the Church in Wales was incorporated by Royal Charter on 24 April 1919.

6 The first meeting of the Governing Body was held in London in January 1918. It made the following resolution: "The Governing Body does hereby accept the Articles, Doctrinal Statements, Rites, and Ceremonies, and save in so far as they may be necessarily varied by the Welsh Church Act, 1914, the formularies of the Church of England as accepted by that Church, and set forth in or appended to the Book of Common Prayer of the Church of England." The new province was inaugurated at St Asaph on 1 June 1920.

7 Whereas the Lords had succeeded in obtaining better financial terms for the Irish Church in 1869, they were unable to prevent the more unfavourable terms of the financial arrangements of the Welsh Church Act. It is noteworthy that the Church of Ireland was a minority Church and that the Church in Wales was the largest single body in the land. It was estimated that there were 193,081 Churchmen; 175,147 Congregationalists; 170,617 Calvinistic Methodists; 143,835 Baptists; 40,811 Wesleyans; 64,000 Roman Catholics; and 19,870 of other denominations in Wales.

74 THE NATIONAL MISSION

The National Mission of Repentance and Hope was an organized attempt on the part of the Church of England to take advantage of the upheaval occasioned by the war. Archbishop Davidson appointed a committee in the autumn of 1915 to discuss the opportunities confronting the Church in war-time, and the recommendation was that a Mission of witness be held in 1916. In spite of the official support of the episcopate in the conducting of the Mission, there was considerable scepticism among the clergy, the most discerning critic being Hensley Henson.

(*The Evangelistic Work of the Church.* Report of the Archbishops' Third Committee of Inquiry (1918), p. 9)

This Report belongs to a series: it is one of five. They have the same historic origin, and that origin should be steadily in the thoughts of those who read them.

Two years ago, in this grave crisis of our nation's history, after much thought and prayer, we called the people of England to a National Mission of Repentance and Hope.[1]

First, during 1916, came the preparation of the Church itself. In every Diocese and Parish we sought fresh guidance of the Holy Spirit to reveal to us our own failures, both as individuals and as members of the Church and nation. Then followed, in every corner of the land, the Mission-call to corporate repentance and to hope in Christ as the living answer to our needs. The call told: not, of course, universally, but very widely. We found that people were ready to face familiar facts afresh: that a new spirit was breathing upon dry bones: that we must, and could, be up and doing. As we appraised the outcome of the Mission-call five subjects in the life of Church and nation stood out with obvious claim for our rehandling. The character and manner of our teaching: our worship: our evangelistic work: the discovery of removable hindrances to the Church's efficiency: the bearing of the Gospel message on the industrial problems of today.

Five Committees of our best and strongest were accordingly appointed to deal with these, and 1917 was given to the task. Let no one regard as a disappointing thing the pause which that deliberation involved. It may prove, by its results, to have been the most fruitful time of all.

And now in 1918 the five Reports are in our hands. They are not official documents, but whether we accept the conclusions or not they have the high authority which belongs to the opinions of specially qualified men and women who have devoted long months to their elaboration. The roadway to right knowledge and effective action is now open. It is a roadway which is offered not to those only who approach it as churchmen and churchwomen, but to the English people as a whole. It is the most important stage of the National Mission. With all earnestness I invite, for these Reports, the study and thought of men and women of good will. We shall not all agree about the various recommendations. We want critics as well as advocates. Let there be quiet reading of all that they contain. Let there be meetings large and small. Let there be sermons and addresses and study circles, that we may perceive and know what things we ought to do, and that together, as the needs of our day demand, we may "go forward". "It is not a vain thing for us: it is our life."

Lent 1918. RANDALL CANTUAR:

FIRST FRUITS OF THE NATIONAL MISSION

With the conclusion of the delivery of the message the movement which produced the National Mission entered upon a very vital stage. In the light of that experience the Church has set itself seriously to consider how to amend its ways. Five Committees of Inquiry have been at work, and now present their Reports to the Archbishop. But already diocesan efforts at reconstruction have begun. There has been an increase in the number of diocesan evangelistic councils. In several cases bands of mission clergy have been either re-established or inaugurated, and in some centres the Committee of the National Mission has become a permanent evangelistic council for the district, while many plans are being formulated locally. In nearly all the dioceses such evangelistic efforts as the Pilgrimage of Prayer or itinerant missions of clergy have been planned for the future, and in some places parochial missions and teaching missions are to be held for the purpose of deepening the effect that was made at the time of the delivery of the message. Deanery evangelistic councils have been formed in some places, and in one diocese training lectures for young evangelists have been held, and have proved most valuable.

With regard to mission work overseas, almost the first outcome of the National Mission was the planning of a great missionary convention in London. This had to be given up, owing to war restrictions on travelling, but careful plans have been made for similar efforts in some dioceses. There is more thought today about the great commission of the Church than there has been for years. The value of all this to evangelistic work at home cannot fail to be considerable.

No class in the community has derived more benefit from the National Mission than the clergy themselves. Its demands have brought home to them the responsibility of their position. Many have realized their own and the Church's failure to commend Christianity to the nation, and have heard the call to fresh consecration in their own lives. As a result of their experience in retreat, and of sharing in the delivery of the message, either as mesengers or as parish priests, many have gone forward in their ministry with renewed hope, and some in the joy of having discovered gifts of which they were before unconscious.

Fellowship between men of different points of view has widened their sympathy and strengthened their faith. Clergy and laity who represent different schools of thought or who have been separated from one another for other reasons, have been knit together in new fellowship as they have met for prayer and conference, and have discovered the power of common purpose and united action.[2]

We find that the desire for fellowship among the members of the Church has also been strengthened. The plan of group study and prayer which has been so widely adopted has had a remarkable effect on many congregations. People have learned to know one another as they never did before; shyness in speaking about spiritual things has been broken down. A great hope for the future lies in this simple method of fellowship.

A striking feature of the movement has been the amount of directly evangelistic work done by the laity. Though there is still that spirit among the clergy which speaks of "making use of the laity", a spirit which has been one of the main causes that has in the past kept many of the laity from being "made use of", on the whole co-operation between clergy and laity is increasing in the Church, to the benefit of all, and in dealing with common problems they are being drawn closer together.[3]

Further, the Church has been in some degree aroused to a new consideration of its own aims and possibilities in relation to the national life. Church reform is increasingly seen as a matter of vital urgency by many who have never before realized its intimate connection with evangelistic work. A new interest is growing in questions relating to labour and social reconstruction, and their spiritual importance is being better understood. The National Mission has already done much to produce in the Church conditions which are wholly favourable to the extension of evangelistic work, and the Church in consequence of the movement is better able to bear its part in the great task of the evangelization of England.

(Henson,[4] *Retrospect* 1, pp. 177-80).

The project of a "National Mission", organized and directed by the entire episcopate, under the supreme authority of the two Archbishops, was planned, officially adopted, and very widely welcomed. The elaborateness of the preparations, the scale of the spiritual campaign, and the frank acknowledgement that the familiar version of the Christian Message had largely ceased to wake response from modern audiences, aroused large expectations, and also in some quarters suggested many misgivings. In my own mind, the misgivings outweighed the expectations. It seemed to me that the Church of England was too inwardly divided to make effective corporate appeal to the Nation; that the nature and extent of the indispensable re-statement of the Christian Message, were still too little realized by English churchmen; and that, if a "National Mission" were actually undertaken, its temper and method would almost inevitably be determined by the professed and professional missioners, who were little likely to be either able or willing to alter their accustomed procedure. I thought that the "new wine" of the re-stated Christian Message could not be safely entrusted to the "old wine-skins" of uninformed and often unsympathetic veterans, who would naturally, but none the less disastrously, prefer the "old mumpsimus" which had become endeared to them by so many experiences. Moreover, I did not think that the nation, absorbed by the efforts, and distracted by the anxieties and excitements of war, could be reasonably expected to give audience to a religious appeal, however well considered, well informed, and honestly delivered. Accordingly I found myself once more carried into the unfortunate and invidious position of a dissenter from the official policy of the hierarchy....

... It implies no inability to appreciate the attractive personality and admirable evangelistic zeal of the late Bishop of London [Dr Ingram[5]] to maintain that he was peculiarly unfitted, both by temperament and by habit, to direct a mission which was designed to break with convention, and take account of an unprecedented situation. For he was not only temperamentally unable to understand the actual problem, but he had been himself a most successful example of the conventional type of missioner.

When I was Vicar of Barking, I had been able to observe, with admiration, not wholly unmixed with envy, the sympathy and skill which marked his conduct of a mission in that parish; and, indeed, I think, if anybody could have revitalized the conventional type of mission, it would have been Dr Ingram; but the task was beyond his power. If this National Mission were to succeed, it could not follow a method which was confessedly becoming obsolete. On October 6th, 1916, I find that I wrote in my Journal depressingly:

> If religious revival is to take place, I suspect that it will come from outside the Church, not from inside. This much-trumpeted "National Mission" appears to become more utterly conventional every day. Those who are running about the country, exhorting little companies of puzzled women, have no vision of any larger teaching than that which has passed on their lips for years, and is now admittedly powerless. A dervish-like fervour cannot be maintained, and is not really illuminating or morally helpful....

... The National Mission was in my belief a failure. This was not, of course, the universal view, but, so far as I could discover it was the general opinion. The Archbishop himself thought otherwise. "It altered the whole attitude of the laity in the diocese of Canterbury towards me", he said to me when we were discussing the subject. That was a judgment which it was obviously impossible for me either to appreciate or to challenge. The Archbishop's opinion cannot be lightly regarded, and it was not unsupported, yet I continue to think that he was mistaken, and I am sure that he did not express the prevailing view. It cannot, indeed, be supposed that a religious venture undertaken with the highest object, carried through with faith and effort, and supported by a great volume of enthusiasm, would be wholly without effect, but I cannot observe or discover any lasting improvement in the religious situation. The churches are still confronted with the perturbing problem of popular indifference. They are still embarrassed and perplexed by the apparent inability of their spiritual appeal to rouse in their hearers the interest and response which had formerly been observed. The "slump in religion" which the National Mission was designed to arrest has continued. Indeed, we have not even yet experienced its worst expressions.

1 The Committee reported on "The Spiritual Call to the Nation and the Church—what is being done by the War and what should be done". The chairman was Armitage Robinson, the members included Temple, Frere, Burroughs, Joyce, Peter Green, and Storr.

2 This optimism was ill-founded as the Prayer Book controversy and the Modernist debate were later to demonstrate.

3 In 1883 Temple had disclaimed proposals for special activities in evangelizing the large urban masses. He concluded: "Now I am convinced that what is wanted is not special action, but greater labour in following out the line on which the Church usually works."

4 Henson, Herbert Hensley; *b.* 1863; *educ.*, Oxford; Fellow of All Souls, 1884; vicar of Barking, 1888; chaplain of St Mary's Hospital, Ilford, 1895; rector of St Margaret, Westminster, 1900; Dean of Durham, 1912; Bishop of Hereford, 1918; Bishop of Durham, 1920–39; *d.* 1947.

5 Winnington-Ingram, Arthur Foley; *b.* 1858; *educ.*, Marlborough and Keble College, Oxford; private tutor, 1881; curate of St Mary, Shrewsbury, 1884; private chaplain to the Bishop of Lichfield, 1885; Head of Oxford House, Bethnal Green, chaplain to the Archbishop of York and Bishop of St Albans, 1889; rector of Bethnal Green, 1895; rural dean of Spitalfields, 1896; Bishop of Stepney and Canon of St Paul's, 1897; Bishop of London, 1901–39; *d.* 1946.

75 THE MILITARY SERVICE ACT 1916

(*Statutes at Large*, 5-6 Geo. V, c. 104)

Among the problems thrown up by the Great War was the increasing demand for men in the several theatres of war, and conscription of all males of certain age groups, regardless of their personal opinions and beliefs, was the consequence. The three major problems confronting the Church of England were: the position of the clergy; the demand for service chaplains; and conscientious objectors. Both Davidson and Lang advocated that the clergy should be non-combatant but should have the opportunity of enlisting as chaplains.[1]

Be it enacted by the King's most Excellent Majesty, by and with the advice and consent of the Lords Spiritual and Temporal, and Commons, in this present Parliament assembled, and by the authority of the same, as follows:

1

(1) Every male British subject who

(*a*) on the fifteenth day of August nineteen hundred and fifteen, was ordinarily resident in Great Britain, and had attained the age of eighteen years and had not attained the age of forty-one years; and

(*b*) on the second day of November nineteen hundred and fifteen was unmarried or was a widower without any child dependent on him;

shall, unless he either is within the exceptions set out in the First Schedule to this Act,[2] or has attained the age of forty-one years before the appointed date, be deemed as from the appointed date to have been duly enlisted in His Majesty's regular forces for general service with the colours or in the reserve for the period of the war, and to have been forthwith transferred to the reserve.

2

(1) An application may be made at any time before the appointed date to the Local Tribunal established under this Act by or in respect of any man for the issue to him of a certificate of exemption from the provisions of this Act

(*a*) on the ground that it is expedient in the national interests that he should, instead of being employed in military service, be engaged in other work in which he is habitually engaged or, in which he wishes to be engaged, or if he is being educated or trained for any work, that he should continue to be so educated or trained; or

(*b*) on the ground that serious hardship would ensue, if the man were called up for Army Service, owing to exceptional financial or business obligations or domestic position; or[3]

(*c*) on the ground of ill-health or infirmity; or

(*d*) on the ground of a conscientious objection to the undertaking of combatant service;[4]

and the Local Tribunal, if they consider the grounds of the application established, shall grant such a certificate.[5]

1 It was not the suggestion of the Archbishops that the clergy be exempted from general conscription, though, when a draft Bill in 1918 did include the clergy, they opposed it. The 37th *Article*

maintains the Christian duty to bear arms though the canon law of the Church of England forbids the clergy to do so. (Bell, *Davidson*, p. 775n.)

2 The First Schedule exceptions included "Men in holy orders or regular ministers of any religious denomination". The total number of clergy of the Church of England commissioned as chaplains was 3,030; killed or died on active service, 88. See Evelyn Waugh, *Ronald Knox* (1962), pp. 111–39. The selection and control of chaplains lay in the hands of:

Smith, John Taylor; *b.* 1860; deacon, 1885; priest, 1886; curate of St Paul, Penge; canon of St George's Cathedral, Freetown, 1890; Bishop of Sierra Leone, 1897; Chaplain-General to the Forces, 1901; retired 1925; *d.* 1938.

Gwynne, Llewellyn Henry; *b.* 1863; St. John's Hall, Highbury; curate of St Chad's, Derby, 1886; curate of St Andrew, Nottingham, 1889; Vicar of Emmanuel, Nottingham, 1892; missionary in Khartoum, 1899; Archdeacon of the Sudan, 1905; Bishop of Khartoum, 1908; Forces chaplain in France, August 1914; Deputy Chaplain-General in France, 1915; Bishop of Egypt and the Sudan, 1920; Bishop in Egypt, 1945; resigned, 1946; *d.* 1957.

3 In October 1914 the bishops pressed for official recognition of the needs of unmarried mothers, a class of dependendants then neglected.

4 Henson preferred conscription to recruitment on a voluntary basis, on the grounds that it was generally assumed that the only reason for not enlisting was cowardice. Although the Anglican Church was not committed to pacifism, the bishops became actively concerned with the plight of conscientious objectors.

5 The attitude of the Church of England towards specific problems of war-time policy largely remained a matter of individual initiative. Most bishops, including Gore, accepted the morality of Britain's part in the war, but their criticisms of the national mood increased as the war progressed. Reprisals, war-hate, misleading official statements, the post-war election campaign, and the Treaty of Versailles were all attacked to some degree. Henson spoke of the unpopularity of the bishops as a class, and this was no doubt due to their often unpopular views during the war years, and also to the post-war disillusionment.

76 THE CREDAL CONTROVERSY, 1918

(Bell, *Davidson*, pp. 859-62)

The nomination of Henson to the bishopric of Hereford in 1917 was the first episcopal appointment made by Lloyd George. Henson was well known as a popular preacher and a prolific writer, but whose doctrinal position was strongly suspect to Gore and other High Church theologians. In the bitter controversy over miracle and subscription to the Creeds, Gore and his sympathizers would not allow of a symbolic interpretation of the credal statements on the virgin birth and the resurrection. Henson, primarily a historian, was an injudicious writer on behalf of the liberal cause.

GORE TO DAVIDSON.

Cuddesdon, Wheatley, Oxon.
Jan. 3rd, 1918

I am compelled, under an overwhelming sense of responsibility, to address to you a solemn protest against the nomination of Dr Hensley Henson, Dean of Durham, to the bishopric of Hereford. I am not taking this action because of anything which he has said about the ministry of the Church, or any other matter of Church polity or policy, with regard to which he and I have publicly differed in the past, for in respect of these things his views are shared substantially by many Evangelical and other members of the Church, with whom I am quite conscientiously able to live in unity of fellowship. I am driven to act as I am doing solely because his expressed beliefs touching the fundamental matters of faith seem to me incompatible with the sincere profession of the Creeds.[1]

In more than one book he has argued that, though a man has been led to believe that our Lord was not born of a virgin mother, he should still be free to exercise his ministry in the Church and to recite the services of the Church in which the miracle is unmistakably and repeatedly affirmed: and even if he believe that "no miracles accompanied His entrance into, or presence in, or departure from the world" he should still hold this "freedom" to make public profession to the contrary.[2]

But may I think that the Dean is simply pleading for freedom for others? I am led reluctantly to conclude that I cannot. His treatment of the Virgin Birth seems to me incompatible with personal belief in its occurrence.[3] Again, he expressly repudiates belief in the "nature-miracles"[4] recorded in the Gospels as wrought by our Lord. He writes explicitly, "From the standpoint of historical science they must be held to be incredible."[5] But the birth of a virgin mother, and the bodily resurrection of our Lord—that His body did not "see corruption" but was raised again the third day to a new and wonderful life—are similar "nature-miracles" ascribed in the Gospels to the same power and Spirit of the Father as the miracles upon nature worked by our Lord during His ministry. I can conceive no rational ground for repudiating the latter as incredible and believing the former. The Dean himself seems incidentally to include both classes of miracles in the same category.[6] He does indeed confidently and constantly affirm the truth of the Resurrection of Christ; but he seems to me by "resurrection" to mean no more than personal survival.[7] He repudiates again and again any insistence upon the "empty tomb", and declares it to have no significance.[8] But the empty tomb was an absolutely necessary condition of any such resurrection as the New Testament postulates. If the tomb was not empty, Christ was not, in the New Testament sense, risen again. On the whole I am led irresistibly to the conclusion that, though he nowhere explicitly expresses in so many words his personal disbelief in the physical miracles affirmed in the Creeds, he does in fact regard them as incredible.

I am amazed by what seems to me the one-sidedness and unsatisfactoriness of the Dean of Durham's presentation of the evidence. But that is not my point at present. Again, I am amazed at the naive confidence with which he assumes that the theological ideas of the Creed and the New Testament, to which he gives noble expression, can survive unimpaired when the miraculous facts have been repudiated—an assumption which the history of recent criticism in Europe generally seems to me to negative. But that again is not my point at present. I am now concerned only with the conditions on which a man can sincerely profess the Creeds and exercise his ministry in the Church of England. And here I will recall the terms of a solemn declaration which the Bishops of our Province recently affirmed:

Inasmuch as there is reason to believe that the minds of many members of the Church of England are perplexed and disquieted at the present time in regard to certain questions of Faith (and of Church order), the Bishops of the Upper House of the Province of Canterbury feel it to be their duty to put forth the following resolutions:

1 We call attention to the resolution which was passed in this House on May 10, 1905, as follows:

> That this House is resolved to maintain unimpaired the Catholic Faith in the Holy Trinity and the Incarnation as contained in the

Apostles' and Nicene Creeds, and in the Quicunque Vult, and regards the Faith there presented, both in statements of doctrine and in statements of fact, as the necessary basis on which the teaching of the Church reposes.

We further desire to direct attention afresh to the following resolution which was unanimously agreed to by the Bishops of the Anglican Communion attending the Lambeth Conference of 1908:

The Conference, in view of tendencies widely shown in the writings of the present day, hereby places on record its conviction that the historical facts stated in the Creeds are an essential part of the Faith of the Church.

2 These resolutions we desire solemnly to re-affirm, and in accordance therewith we express our deliberate judgment that the denial of any of the historical facts stated in the Creeds goes beyond the limits of legitimate interpretation, and gravely imperils that sincerity of profession which is plainly incumbent on the ministers of the Word and Sacraments. At the same time, recognizing that our generation is called to face new problems raised by historical criticism, we are anxious not to lay unnecessary burdens upon consciences, nor unduly to limit freedom of thought and enquiry whether among clergy or among laity. We desire, therefore, to lay stress on the need of considerateness in dealing with that which is tentative and provisional in the thought and work of earnest and reverent students.

Of course if, in order to be affected by this declaration, a man must explicitly and in so many words have denied the particular miraculous facts recorded in the Creeds, the Dean of Durham is not affected by it. But then I think the declaration is nugatory. A man can express a negative intention without any such express verbal denial. I think the declaration must be supposed to take into account the whole effect of a man's language. And taking this into account, apart from any fresh declaration of his belief which he may think fit to make, I can only draw the conclusion that the Dean's language falls outside the limits of "legitimate interpretation" of the statements of the Creeds which according to our declaration must be observed by the clergy and, most of all, I suppose, by the bishops. As things stand, that is, judging only from his published writings, if Dr Henson were to take his place among the bishops, I think three results would follow:

1 It would be impossible to deny that the Bishops—not all of them individually, but the bishops as a body—are prepared to admit to the episcopate, and therefore to the other orders of the ministry, one who does not believe in the miracles of the Creed,

supposing he unfeignedly believes (as Dr Henson does) in the doctrine of the person of Christ. And this, it appears to me, is to abandon the standing ground of the Catholic Church from the beginning, which has insisted on holding together the ideas and the miraculous facts. I do not mean that the action of the bishops would commit the Church of England. I think the mind of the Church of England would be opposed to their action. But I think it would commit the bishops corporately.

2 An atmosphere of suspicion will increasingly attach itself in the mind of the nation to the most solemn public assertions of the clergy, in the matter of religion, just at the time when we are constantly hearing that the awful experiences of the war have forced us back upon realities.

3 An effective (though not, I think, a legitimate) excuse will be afforded to all officers of the Church to treat their solemn declarations on other subjects as "scraps of paper".[9] Any discipline on the basis of official declarations will become more and more difficult; and the authority of the episcopate will be quite undermined.

In order that such disastrous consequences may be avoided, I feel myself constrained to intreat your Grace and my brother bishops, in the event of the Dean of Durham being elected to the see of Hereford by the chapter, to refuse him consecration.

I need not say with what profound sorrow I have written this protest and appeal. Dr Henson and I have always been friends, and, though we have often differed in public, I believe no angry word has ever passed between us or marred our friendship: and I believe him to be personally among the most honourable and courageous of men. Nevertheless I have been obliged to write it.

With the humble prayer that God will cleanse and defend the distracted part of the Church to which we belong and will guide your Grace and the Bishops with the spirit of wisdom.[10]

It was assumed by many informed people that Henson's position was identical with that of the Modernists.[11] Sanday's intervention confirmed this belief[12] and Dean Inge noted in his diary concerning the inhibition of J. M. Thompson, "Henson is very indignant and wants to fight".[13] After the Girton Conference in 1921, Henson moved further away from the Modernist position and was accused by Inge of being "unstable as water". This memorandum, made informally to Archbishop Davidson in a private interview at Lambeth, shows clearly that, whereas Henson supported the liberal cause, he did not accept, as a consequence, modernist conclusions.

(Bell, *Davidson*, p. 872)

HENSON TO DAVIDSON

I repeat and accept the words of the Creed *ex animo*. I use them without any sense of incongruity, and with no desire to change them. With me it is a question of emphasis. I desire that the emphasis of the Apostolic teaching should be preserved in the teaching of the Church. No man who believes in the Incarnation could postulate for Our Saviour an ordinary Birth. I believe that in the Birth of Jesus Christ, Whom I worship, as in the fullest sense Divine, there was special action of the Holy Spirit. But when in the Creed I affirm, as I readily do, the traditional belief of the Church in the Birth of Jesus Christ without a human father, I am bound to add that the belief in the Incarnation may be consistent now, as it was consistent in Apostolic days, with other notions or explanations of the mode of what happened therein. I have never seen any satisfying alternative to the dogma of the Virgin Birth.[14]

(Bell, *Davidson*, pp. 875-8)

DAVIDSON TO GORE

Lambeth Palace
16 January 1918

You need no assurance from me as to the grave and sedulous care with which I have weighed all that you say in your published letter of Protest respecting the Crown's nomination of Dr Hensley Henson to the See of Hereford.

I have, as you know, always maintained that in the last resort a large measure of responsibility must belong to the Ecclesiastical authorities, and especially to the Archbishop of the Province, in regard to the filling of a vacant See by the consecration thereto of a priest duly nominated by the Crown. It is therefore appropriate that you should write to me as you have written on a matter about which you feel so strongly. No constitutional rule or usage can force the Archbishop to the solemn act of Consecration, if he be prepared, by resignation or otherwise, to abide the consequences of declaring himself *in foro conscientiae* unable to proceed. I should be deliberately prepared to take that course if I found myself called upon at any time to consecrate to the Episcopate a man who, in my judgment, is clearly unworthy of that Office or false to the Christian Faith as taught by the Church of England.

Dr Hensley Henson has now, on the nomination of the Crown, been duly elected by the Chapter of Hereford. I have personal knowledge of the care taken by some at least of the prebendaries who voted for him to satisfy themselves as to his teaching, and I am informed that of the nineteen members of the Chapter who took part in the proceedings, all but four voted in his favour. I do not say that the fact of his formal election finally disposes of all question as to his consecration: I mention it because it is an important step in the procedure. I have now, by the help of GOD, to exercise my own responsibility to the best of my power.

You call upon me to refuse consecration to Dr Henson. You rest your protest simply on his published writings. These extend over many years, during which he has held positions of considerable importance in the Church of England, and has there been liable to formal proceedings in case of heresy or false teaching. To the best of my belief, no such accusation has ever been formulated against him in such manner as to enable it to be authoritatively tested.

During the last few weeks I have read with care most of Dr Henson's published books, and since receiving your Protest I have re-read with close attention all the passages to which your Protest refers. Taking them, as in fairness they must be taken, with their full context, I find opinions expressed with which I definitely disagree: I find in some pages a want of balance, and a crudity of abrupt statement, which may give satisfaction or even help to certain minds or temperaments, but must inevitably be painful and possibly even dangerous to others: I find what seem to me to be almost irreconcilable inconsistencies: I find much that seems to me to need explanation, qualification or re-statement. But the result of my consideration of the whole matter—and it has not been slight or hurried—is that, neither in Dr Henson's books nor in the careful communications which have taken place between him and myself on the subject, have I found anything which, when it is fairly weighed in its true setting, I can regard as inconsistent with the belief which he firmly asserts in the facts and doctrines of the Faith as set forth in the Creeds. Some of the collections of isolated extracts from his writings, as sent to me by correspondents, are even more than usually unfair. And, as you say in your letter, "he gives noble expression" to what you have called "the Theological ideas of the Creed and the New Testament".

We are familiar with the danger, common in ecclesiastical controversy, that a critic, taking his opponent's premises, may base on them what seems to him to be an obvious conclusion, and then describe, or perhaps denounce, that conclusion as the opinion of the man whom he is criticizing, when, as a matter of fact, whether logically or illogically, the writer commits himself to no such opinion. This danger is very real in the case of a writer so exuberant as Dr Henson. It is a satisfaction to me to note your explicit statement that the "denial" which you attribute to him, is your inference from what he has written and is not found in the words themselves.

I am bold to say that no fair-minded man can read consecutively a series of Dr Henson's sermons without feeling that we have in him a brilliant and powerful teacher of the Christian faith, who regards the Incarnation of the Son of God as the central fact of human history, who accepts without qualification the Divinity of our Blessed Lord, and who brings these supreme realities to bear with persuasive force upon the daily problems and perplexities of human life. That he has also a singular power of effectively presenting the Gospel message to the hearts of a congregation of quite ordinary and untheological people, is a fact of which I have personal knowledge and experience.

You have legitimately directed attention to a Resolution which was adopted *nemine contradicente* by the Bishops of the Province of Canterbury on April 30, 1914, in reply to certain Memorials which had been presented to us. I do not myself find in that Resolution, interpreted either literally as it stands, or in the light of the ample and weighty debate which introduced it, anything which leads me, as one of those who voted for it, to feel that I should be acting inconsistently in proceeding in due course to the consecration of Dr Henson.[15]

I am acting, in a difficult matter, with a sense of high and sacred responsibility towards God and man, after giving weight to the theological, the ecclesiastical, the constitutional, the practical, and the personal issues involved.

I think it right to add that, while my conclusion is, in all the circumstances, clear, I do not regard without appreciation and even sympathy the anxieties to which expression has been given by yourself, and by others who have, in a less formal and responsible way, addressed me. Yet I believe that, under the good Hand of God, the outcome of these anxious days will be to his glory, and to the well being of the Church of His Son, Jesus Christ our Lord.

Every controversy must be decided on its own merits, and, in such a connection, precedents and analogies are dangerous, but it cannot be quite out of place that I should add a brief reference to some historical precedents within our own life-time. You are familiar with the remarkable Chapter written by Dean Church at the very close of his life, in which he looks back upon the Hampden controversies of half a century before, and in language of characteristic force and moderation shows how easily in such controversies unfairness may be shown and serious misunderstandings may arise. "A manifold and varied experience", he says, "has taught most of us some lessons against impatience and violent measures."[16]

Not dissimilarly, in the course of a Debate in which I was myself concerned, in the Lower House of Canterbury Convocation on February 4th 1891, Archdeacon Denison, the protagonist in the denunciation of *Essays and Reviews* thirty years before, and in the subsequent and consequent opposition to Dr Temple's consecration to the See of Exeter,[17] confessed that he would not, after the lapse of years, endorse the protest which he had himself drawn up and presented to Convocation in 1861.[18]

That incident occurred in the Convocation Debate upon the volume called *Lux Mundi*. It is my unhesitating belief that, if the life of the great teacher and divine, Henry Parry Liddon, had been, to our great gain, prolonged for twenty or even ten years, his view of that volume would have been very different from what it was when he wrote of it, in the last year of his life, as a book with "a materialistic and Pelagianizing tone, the writers [of which] seem to think it a gain when they can prune away or economize the supernatural".[19] To myself, as one who owes much to that volume, those words seem almost incredibly unfair.

I thank you, as an old and tried friend, for having written to me so frankly in this grave matter. May God the Holy Spirit guide us both in discharging to the best of our power the great trust which He has laid upon us.[20]

1 Gore's sacerdotalism and Henson's latitudinarianism placed them in different camps, but the former's High Church contention was that the bishop maintained the standard of orthodoxy required by the formularies of the Church.

2 Henson had taken it upon himself to uphold freedom of inquiry. Gore, on the other hand, had already made his position clear in the matter of the Reverend C. E. Beeby who had claimed the right to hold a benefice and, at the same time, to deny the Virgin Birth. *The Creed in the Pulpit* (1912), pp. xivff.

3 *Sincerity and Subscription* (1903), pp. 43ff.; *The Creed*, &c., pp. xxiv, 18-22, 49.

4 Physical miracles which the "normal" order of nature cannot account for; Dr Henson distinguished such "nature-miracles" from

the miracles of healing which he thinks may "be fairly called normal".

5 *The Creed*, &c., pp. 88-9.

6 *The Creed*, &c., pp. 90-1 (at the bottom).

7 For example, he speaks of Christ returning to the Church in "the fullness" or "plenitude of personal life" (p. 211). But he speaks also of all the dead as "persisting in the plenitude of individual being".

8 *The Creed*, &c., pp. 199, 208, 211.

9 A reference to the Treaty of London (April 1839) which guaranteed Belgium as "an independent and perpetually neutral state", which was referred to as a "scrap of paper" by the German Chancellor when the treaty was broken in 1914.

10 The protest was sent to Lambeth on 3 January and published in *The Times* on 10 January.

11 The term *modernist* was applied originally to members of the Roman Catholic Church condemned by Pius X in the encyclical *Pascendi gregis*, 8 September 1907. English Modernism owed a great deal to Liberal Protestantism, and was in some respects the descendant of the old Broad Church party.

12 Sanday, William; *b*. 1843; *educ*., Repton; Balliol and Corpus Christi Colleges, Oxford; Principal of Hatfield Hall, Durham, 1876; Dean Ireland Professor of Exegesis, Oxford, 1882; Lady Margaret Professor of Divinity, 1895; Bampton Lecturer, 1893; *d*. 1920.

13 In 1911, Bishop Talbot of Winchester withdrew the licence of J. M. Thompson, Fellow and Dean of Divinity at Magdalen College, on account of his book *Miracles in the New Testament* (1911). In *The Creed in the Pulpit*, Henson criticized both Talbot and Gore, the latter having refused Thompson permission to officiate in the Diocese of Oxford.

14 Henson's memorandum was for the benefit of the Archbishop in dealing with the controversialists. Davidson's attitude towards a defined orthodoxy in this debate is characteristic of the man.

15 Henson wrote of Davidson with regard to the Prayer Book controversy: "The life-long habit of 'getting round' difficulties, instead of facing them, hardly prepares a man for the handling of a crisis" (Henson, *Retrospect*, vol. 2, p. 183). The same may be said of Davidson's handling of the doctrinal crisis. The resolution of the Bishops in 1914 was never formally set aside.

16 Dean Church, *The Oxford Movement, 1833-1845*, ch. ix.

17 Temple, Frederick; *b*. 1821; *educ*., Balliol College, Oxford, 1839; B.A., 1842; deacon, 1845; priest, 1846; Headmaster of Rugby, 1858; *Essays and Reviews*, 1860; Bishop of Exeter, 1869; Bampton Lecturer, 1884; Bishop of London, 1885; Archbishop of Canterbury, 1897; *d*. 1902.

18 *Chronicle of Convocation*, 4 February 1891 pp. 60, 109.

19 Letter to Lord Halifax, 19 February 1890; *Liddon*, p. 372.

20 Henson refused to clarify his position publicly but reassured the Archbishop privately, and by writing an agreed answer to *The Times* (18 January) to a letter from the Archbishop placated Gore. The Archbishop's letter to Gore was published in the same newspaper on 18 January 1918.

77 THE LIFE AND LIBERTY MOVEMENT

The difficulties in the relationship between Church and State implicit in the Establishment, led to a growing demand for the "liberation" of the Church. The continual demand for the disestablishment of the Church of England, the National Mission, and the Church Reform League were all responsible for the changing climate of opinion. The movement held its first conference on 29 March 1917 at the Vicarage of St Martin-in-the-Fields. Temple was the group's most able advocate and many influential names figured amongst its adherents.[1]

(Iremonger, *Temple*, pp. 227-8)

To the Editor of *The Times*, 20 June 1917

Sir,

Amid the ruins of the old world, the new world is already being born. In the ideas of reconstruction now being formed there is hope of a new and better era. The Church has felt, and to some extent imparted, the new impulse in the National Mission. It has in altogether new ways realized its responsibilities and its impotence at the present time to discharge them.... A vigorous forward movement just now may revive waning enthusiasm and hopes, retain for the service of the Church the eager souls who now doubtfully watch it, and, by combining these together, exert such pressure on the official bodies as may result in real reform.[2]

But as soon as we consider the changes that are needed to make the Church a living force in the nation, we find ourselves hampered at every turn by an antiquated machinery which we are powerless to change except by a series of Acts of Parliament. Everyone sees that the House of Commons is a highly unsuitable place for the settlement of questions affecting the Church's life and work; and even if it were suitable in its composition it has no time. Whatever else may be thought of the scheme suggested by the Archbishop's Committee on Church and State, it has at least this advantage, that under its provisions it would be necessary to find time to stop legislation for Church reform from taking effect, instead of its being necessary, as it is now, to find time to pass it.

If the Church is to have new life, even if it is to maintain the life which it has, it must have liberty. Those who are promoting this Movement are convinced that we must win for the Church full power to control its own life, even at the cost, if necessary, of disestablishment and of whatever consequences that may possibly involve.

It is proposed to hold a meeting at Queen's Hall on the evening of Monday, July 16, when these principles will be enforced and support for them enlisted.... We propose to do whatever can be done by constitutional channels; we wish to arouse the Church to a sense of its vital need, and to call on all who love it to demand for it the liberty which is essential to its life. We believe that the leaders of the Church are ready to advance along the path of progress if they are assured of an earnest and widespread desire to go forward. But with them or without them we are constrained by love of our Church and country to raise the standard of advance and call to it those who share our anxiety and our hope.

Yours faithfully,

LOUISE CREIGHTON
A. A. DAVID
A. MANSBRIDGE
J. B. SEATON
A. L. SMITH
W. TEMPLE, Chairman
A. P. CHARLES
F. A. IREMONGER
H. R. L. SHEPPARD, Hon. secretaries

Although the meeting was not widely advertised it was well attended. The speakers include Temple,[3] Maude Royden,[4] Walter Carey,[5] Harry Blackburne,[6] and Dick Sheppard.[7] Henson's famous account of the meeting is described by Iremonger as "an account written by the only person (of the two thousand present) who voted against the resolution —an account, moreover, marred by distortions and coloured by prejudice, and utterly at variance with every other contemporary record" (Iremonger, *Temple*, p. 233).

(Bell, *Davidson*, pp. 963-4)

HENSON TO ARCHBISHOP DAVIDSON

The Athenaeum, Pall Mall, S.W.
July 17th, 1917

It occurs to me that you might care to have a record of the impression which last night's meeting of the "Life and Liberty" agitators made on an unsympathetic but never deliberately unfair observer. So far as numbers went, it was a good meeting; indeed, there was an overflow. The audience was three parts composed of women, and the remaining part was mainly made up of youngish parsons. Socially, I conjectured that the meeting consisted of upper middle-class people, who form the congregations of West-end churches. There was no trace of the working classes perceptible. The ecclesiastical type of the audience was, perhaps, disclosed by the circumstance that, when the Apostles' Creed was repeated, the crowded platform *seemed* to make the Sign of the Cross unanimously. I was quite startled by so unusual a phenomenon. This petty incident was significant because ordinary English Churchmen are not accustomed to the practice of signing themselves with the Cross. The Headmasters seem to be deep in the movement. David of Rugby read prayers, and the Headmasters of Eton and Harrow were on the platform. Of course family reasons may have led the latter rather than personal conviction: but this display of pedagogues set me thinking. The academic, the feminist, the Socialist, the clericalist—these are not the constituents of an ecclesiastical policy which is likely to be tolerant, or virile, or just, or large. Temple's speech was well phrased and well delivered. He has an admirable voice, and, though his manner is a little too dogmatic and professional, he is in the succession of orators. There was not much stuff in the speech, perhaps because he had "said his say" in a pamphlet which had been distributed in the seats: but he made it very plain that the "Life and Liberty" Movement intends the *present* Parliament to pass the requisite legislation, either to grant autonomy, or to disestablish. The duration of the war was spoken of as an "accepted hour", in which the Church of England must "find salvation" or for ever fall! None of the other speakers were adequate. Miss Maude Royden was confused, incoherent, and when intelligible, irrelevant. "Father" Carey adopted a jocose manner, unworthy of the occasion, and seemed to blame the Church for the defects of the individual clergy. A returned chaplain in khaki assured us that great numbers of officers and men were eagerly longing for the prompt and drastic handling of the Church: and Mr "Dick" Sheppard concluded with an ecstatic appeal for enthusiasm. *Voilà tout!* I cannot say that the meeting seemed to me in any marked degree enthusiastic. Partly this may have been due to the great predominance of women: but mostly, I suspect, it arose from the fact that neither the Catholic, nor the national note was sounded, but only the "denominational", and you can't get up much enthusiasm over sectarianizing a national Church. I do not doubt that both the E.C.U. and the Church Defence Institution could get together more enthusiastic meetings. The Bishop of Oxford's name was greeted with applause, but then the meeting was "Gore's crowd".[8]

I held up my hand against a resolution that said what my experience for thirty years past proves to me is untrue, that the present conditions of the Church's life constitute "AN INTOLERABLE HINDRANCE TO HER SPIRITUAL WORK".[9] No clergyman who speaks the truth can really say *that* of his personal knowledge. But I will not embark on a discussion where I only designed a description.[10]

1 Temple, William, 2nd son of Frederick Temple; *b.* 1881; *educ.*, Rugby and Balliol College, Oxford; Fellow and lecturer of Queen's College, Oxford, 1904; deacon, 1908; priest, 1909; Headmaster of Repton, 1910; contributed to *Foundations*, 1912; rector of St James, Piccadilly, 1914–17; canon of Westminster, 1919; Bishop of Manchester, 1921; Archbishop of York, 1929; Archbishop of Canterbury, 1942; *d.* 1944.

2 The aim was stated in an early circular: "The Life and Liberty Movement aims at securing for the Church without delay Liberty in the sense of full power to control its own life and organization. It does this in the belief that a unique opportunity is before the Church, which existing conditions prevent it from claiming to the full. The rising tide of Life within the Church demands Liberty, because Liberty is indispensable to the fullness of Life and its practical expression. It must no longer be necessary to wait for the convenience of Parliament before adaptations can be made and reforms effected" (Iremonger, *Temple*, p. 224).

3 Temple described three possible roads of advance in the pamphlet *Life and Liberty* as: trying to get reforms under the existing Constitution; disestablishment; and the scheme proposed by the *Report of the Archbishops' Committee on Church and State*, whereby the Church would have the power to legislate on all matters affecting the Church subject to Parliamentary veto.

4 Maude Royden (later Royden-Shaw); an advocate of the place

of women workers in the Church, member of the Life and Liberty Council.

5 Walter Carey; Bishop of Bloemfontein, 1921–34.

6 H. W. Blackburne; Assistant Chaplain-General in France; Dean of Bristol.

7 H. R. L. Sheppard; vicar of St Martin-in-the-Fields, 1914–27; canon of St Paul's; Dean of Canterbury.

8 Gore had edited *Essays on Church Reform* (1898), which had sought for: the end of the sale of advowsons; the end of the traditional forms of church establishment in England; the means by which the laity could prevent improper appointments to benefices and secure the removal of unsatisfactory clergy; and the protection of the clergy from wealthy parishioners.

9 The resolution ran: "That whereas the present conditions under which the Church lives and works constitute an intolerable hindrance to its spiritual activity, this Meeting instructs the Council, as a first step, to approach the Archbishops, in order to urge upon them that they should ascertain without delay, and make known to the Church at large, whether and on what terms Parliament is prepared to give freedom to the Church in the sense of full power to manage its own life, that so it may the better fulfil its duty to God and to the nation and its mission to the world" (Iremonger, *Temple*, p. 233).

10 Davidson refused to be carried along by popular opinion, but a Grand Committee of the Representative Church Council was appointed in November 1917, under the chairmanship of Bishop Ryle, and was commissioned to produce a report which was published a year later.

78 THE ADDRESS TO THE KING, 1919

(*The Law of the Parish Church*, pp. 115-19)

Sir Lewis Dibdin,[1] speaking of the *Report of the Archbishops' Committee on Church and State* (1917), said: "We want not only to end the mischievous paralysis of legislation from which the Church has suffered now for many years, but also that its law-making should be in more suitable hands than those of an always reluctant and often hostile House of Commons." The difficulty confronting the Church in setting up a new legislative assembly was in obtaining Parliamentary sanction without appearing to accept a form of church-government imposed by the State. The constitution of the National Assembly was settled by the Representative Church Council, adopted by Convocations, and presented as an appendix to the Address to the Sovereign. Thus Parliament granted recognition to the new body without being primarily responsible for it.

ADDRESS FROM THE CONVOCATION OF CANTERBURY[2]

MAY IT PLEASE YOUR MAJESTY,

We, Your Majesty's loyal and faithful subjects, the Archbishops, Bishops, and Clergy of the Province of Canterbury in Convocation assembled, approach Your Majesty with the dutiful assurance of our devotion to Your Throne and Person.

We desire to lay before your Majesty a recommendation agreed to by both Houses of this Convocation on the 8th day of May, 1919, that, subject to the control and authority of Your Majesty and of the two Houses of Parliament, powers in regard to legislation touching matters concerning the Church of England shall be conferred on the National Assembly of the Church of England constituted in the manner set forth in the Appendix attached to this Address.

We pray, as in duty bound, that the blessing of Almighty God our Heavenly Father, through our Lord Jesus Christ, may rest upon your Majesty.

9th May 1919

RANDALL CANTUAR
HERBERT E. RYLE (Bp)[3]
Prolocutor of the Lower House
of the Convocation of Canterbury

APPENDIX

CONSTITUTION OF THE NATIONAL ASSEMBLY OF THE CHURCH OF ENGLAND

1 There shall be a National Assembly of the Church of England (hereinafter called "the Assembly") to deliberate on all matters concerning the Church of England and to make provision in respect thereof.

2 The Assembly shall consist of three Houses: The House of Bishops, the House of Clergy, and the House of Laity.

3 *House of Bishops* The House of Bishops shall consist of the

members for the time being of the Upper Houses of the Convocations of Canterbury and York.

4 *House of Clergy* The House of Clergy shall consist of the members for the time being of the Lower Houses of the Convocations of Canterbury and York.

5 The members of the Houses of Bishops and Clergy shall continue to be members of the Assembly after the dissolution of the Convocations until the new Convocations come into being.[4]

6 *House of Laity* The House of Laity shall consist of representatives of the Laity of the Provinces of Canterbury and York elected in accordance with the provisions of the Schedule to this Constitution. There shall be an election to the House of Laity every five years at such time as the Assembly appoints, or in the absence of such appointment, as the Archbishops of Canterbury and York direct.

7 *Meetings of the Assembly* The Assembly shall meet in session at least once a year, and at such times and places as the Assembly provides, or in the absence of such provision as the Archbishops of Canterbury and York direct.

8 *Chairman* The Archbishop of Canterbury, or in his absence the Archbishop of York, or in his absence the Bishop next in precedence and willing to act, shall be chairman of meetings of the Assembly and of the House of Bishops when sitting separately or with another House.

9 The House of Clergy and the House of Laity shall each elect a chairman to preside over them. When they sit together they shall elect a chairman for the occasion.

10 *Voting* Nothing (except what relates only to the conduct of business) shall be deemed to be finally passed by the Assembly which has not received the assent of a majority of the members present and voting of each of the three Houses sitting together or separately; and accordingly at sittings of the Assembly, or of any two Houses:

(*a*) Any motion relating solely to the course of business or any procedure shall be determined by a show of hands.

(*b*) Any other motion may be similarly determined unless any ten members present demand a division by Houses, in which case the motion shall be lost unless it is carried by a majority of the members of each House present and voting.

11 *Legislative Committee* The Assembly shall appoint a "Legislative Committee" including members of all three Houses, to whom all measures which it is desired should pass into law shall be referred. The Legislative Committee shall thereupon take such action as may be authorized by statute in order that such measure may become law.[5]

12 *Standing Orders* The Assembly may make, revoke, or alter standing orders, consistent with this Constitution, for the conduct of elections, and for the meetings, procedure, and business of the Assembly, and for joint sittings of any two Houses.

13 Subject to this Constitution and to any standing orders from time to time made by the Assembly with reference thereto, the business and procedure at any meeting of the Assembly, or of any two Houses sitting together, or of any House sitting separately, shall be regulated by the Chairman thereof.

14 *Functions of the Assembly* The functions of the Assembly shall be as follows:

(*a*) The Assembly shall be free to discuss any proposal concerning the Church of England and to make provision in respect thereof, and where such provision requires Parliamentary sanction the authority of Parliament shall be sought in such manner as may be prescribed by statute:

Provided that any measure touching doctrinal formulae or the services or ceremonies of the Church of England or the administration of the Sacraments or sacred rites thereof shall be debated and voted upon by each of the three Houses sitting separately, and shall then be either accepted or rejected by the Assembly in the terms in which it is finally proposed by the House of Bishops.

(*b*) The Assembly or any of the three Houses thereof may debate and formulate its judgment by resolution upon any matter concerning the Church of England or otherwise of religious or public interest:

Provided that it does not belong to the functions of the Assembly to issue any statement purporting to define the doctrine of the Church of England on any question of theology, and no such statement shall be issued by the Assembly.

15 Nothing in this Constitution shall be deemed to diminish or derogate from any of the powers belonging to the Convocations of the Provinces of Canterbury and York or of any House thereof;

nor shall the Assembly exercise any power or perform any function distinctively belonging to the Bishops in right of their episcopal office.

16 Any question concerning the interpretation of this Constitution shall be referred to the Archbishops of Canterbury and York and by them decided.

17 In the event of the Assembly receiving statutory powers in regard to legislation, it shall, before entering on any other legislative business, make further provision for the self government of the Church by passing through the Assembly measures

(*a*) declaring that the Convocations of Canterbury and York have power, by canon lawfully passed and promulged, to amend the Constitution of the Lower Houses thereof;
(*b*) conferring upon the Parochial Church Councils constituted under the Schedule to this Constitution such powers as the Assembly may determine.

1 Dibdin, Lewis Tonna; *b.* 1852; *educ.*, St. John's College, Cambridge, 1869; graduated, 1874; called to the Bar, 1876; Chancellor of Rochester (1866), Exeter (1888), and Durham (1891); Dean of Arches, 1903; Master of the Faculties; official principal of the Chancery Court of York; Vicar-General of the Province of Canterbury, 1925; resigned, 1934; *d.* 1938.

2 An identical address was presented by the Convocation of York, and signed "Cosmo Ebor: *President*; and W. Foxley Norris, *Prolocutor*".

3 Ryle, Herbert Edward, son of Bishop of Liverpool, 1880–1900; *b.* 1856; *educ.*, Eton and King's College, Cambridge, 1875; Fellow of King's College, 1881; deacon, 1882; priest, 1883; Principal of St David's, Lampeter, 1886; Hulsean Professor of Divinity at Cambridge, 1887; President of Queen's College, Cambridge, 1896; Bishop of Exeter, 1901; Bishop of Winchester, 1903; chairman of the Archbishop of Canterbury's commission on Anglo-Swedish relations, 1909; Dean of Westminster, 1911; chairman of the "Grand Committee" of the Representative Church Council; Prolocutor of the Lower House of Canterbury Convocation, 1919; *d.* 1925.

4 Since Convocation is dissolved with Parliament the election of proctors must take place after the dissolution of each Convocation. The constitution provides for the Assembly to continue without the loss of two of its Houses for any length of time.

5 The Church of England Assembly (Powers) Act 1920.

79 THE ENABLING ACT, 1919

(*Statutes at Large*, 9-10 Geo. V, c. 76)

The passing of this Act was an immediate result of the activities of the Life and Liberty movement. In the removal of certain legal disabilities which had hindered the work of the Church of England, the Act generally followed the recommendations of the *Report on the Relations of Church and State* (1916). Although the National Assembly has tended to be cumbersome in its relations with both Parliament and the Diocesan Conferences, it has successfully maintained the connection between Church and State in legislative matters.[1]

1

DEFINITIONS

(1) "The National Assembly of the Church of England" (hereinafter called "the Church Assembly") means the Assembly constituted in accordance with the Constitution set forth in the Appendix to the Addresses presented to His Majesty by the Convocations of Canterbury and York on the tenth day of May nineteen hundred and nineteen, and laid before both Houses of Parliament;
(2) "The Constitution" means the Constitution of the Church Assembly set forth in the Appendix to the Addresses presented by the Convocations of Canterbury and York to His Majesty as aforesaid;
(3) "The Legislative Committee" means the Legislative Committee of the Church Assembly appointed in accordance with the provisions of the Constitution;
(4) "The Ecclesiastical Committee" means the Committee established as provided in section two of this Act;
(5) "Measure" means a legislative measure intended to receive the Royal Assent and to have effect as an Act of Parliament in accordance with the provisions of this Act.

2

ESTABLISHMENT OF AN ECCLESIASTICAL COMMITTEE

(1) There shall be a Committee of members of both Houses of Parliament styled "The Ecclesiastical Committee".
(2) The Ecclesiastical Committee shall consist of fifteen members

of the House of Lords nominated by the Lord Chancellor, and fifteen members of the House of Commons nominated by the Speaker of the House of Commons, to be appointed on the passing of this Act to serve for the duration of the present Parliament and thereafter to be appointed at the commencement of each Parliament to serve for the duration of that Parliament.

Any casual vacancy occurring by the reason of the death, resignation, or incapacity of a member of the Ecclesiastical Committee shall be filled by the nomination of a member by the Lord Chancellor or the Speaker of the House of Commons, as the case may be.

(3) The powers and duties of the Ecclesiastical Committee may be exercised and discharged by any twelve members thereof, and the Committee shall be entitled to sit and to transact business whether Parliament be sitting or not, and notwithstanding a vacancy in the membership of the Committee. Subject to the provisions of this Act, the Ecclesiastical Committee may regulate its own procedure.

3

MEASURES PASSED BY CHURCH ASSEMBLY TO BE SUBMITTED TO ECCLESIASTICAL COMMITTEE

(1) Every measure passed by the Church Assembly shall be submitted by the Legislative Committee to the Ecclesiastical Committee, together with such comments and explanations as the Legislative Committee may deem it expedient or be directed by the Church Assembly to add.

(2) The Ecclesiastical Committee shall thereupon consider the measure so submitted to it, and may, at any time during such consideration, either of its own motion or at the request of the Legislative Committee, invite the Legislative Committee to a conference to discuss the provisions thereof, and thereupon a conference of the two committees shall be held accordingly.

(3) After considering the measure, the Ecclesiastical Committee shall draft a report thereon to Parliament stating the nature and legal effect of the measure and its views as to the expediency thereof, especially with relation to the constitutional rights of all His Majesty's subjects.

(4) The Ecclesiastical Committee shall communicate its report in draft to the Legislative Commiteee, but shall not present it to Parliament until the Legislative Committee signify its desire that it should be so presented.

(5) At any time before the presentation of the report to Parliament the Legislative Committee may, either on its own motion or by direction of the Church Assembly, withdraw a measure from further consideration by the Ecclesiastical Committee; but the Legislative Committee shall have no power to vary a measure of the Church Assembly either before or after conference with the Ecclesiastical Committee.

(6) A measure may relate to any matter concerning the Church of England, and may extend to the amendment or repeal in whole or in part of any Act of Parliament, including this Act:[2]

Provided that a measure shall not make any alteration in the composition or powers or duties of the Ecclesiastical Committee, or in the procedure in Parliament prescribed by section four of this Act.[3]

(7) No proceedings of the Church Assembly in relation to a measure shall be invalidated by any vacancy in the membership of the Church Assembly or by any defect in the qualification or election of any member thereof.

4

PROCEDURE ON MEASURES REPORTED ON BY THE ECCLESIASTICAL COMMITTEE

When the Ecclesiastical Committee shall have reported to Parliament on any measure submitted by the Legislative Committee, the report, together with the text of such measure, shall be laid before both Houses of Parliament forthwith, if Parliament be then sitting, or, if not, then immediately after the next meeting of Parliament, and thereupon, on a resolution being passed by each House of Parliament directing that such measure in the form laid before Parliament should be presented to His Majesty, such measure shall be presented to His Majesty, and shall have the force and effect of an Act of Parliament on the Royal Assent being signified thereto in the same manner as to Acts of Parliament:[4]

Provided that if, upon a measure being laid before Parliament, the Chairman of Committees of the House of Lords and the Chairman of Ways and Means in the House of Commons acting in consultation shall be of opinion that the measure deals with two or more different subjects which might be more properly divided, they may, by joint agreement, divide the measure into two or more separate measures accordingly, and thereupon this section shall have effect as if each of the measures resulting from such division had been laid before Parliament as a separate measure.

5

SHORT TITLE

This Act may be cited as the Church of England Assembly (Powers) Act, 1919.

1 Davidson moved the second reading of the Bill in the Lords on 3 June 1919; the committee stage was fixed for 10 July; and the third reading carried on 21 July. In the Commons the second reading was carried on 7 November; the third on 5 December; the Lords accepted the amendments on 15 December; and the Bill received the Royal Assent on 23 December.

2 The first Church Assembly Measure was the Convocations of the Clergy Measure (1920), which declared that the Convocations of Canterbury and York had the power to make canons for amending the constitution of their two lower Houses.

3 In effect the Act prevented the setting aside of ecclesiastical business in Parliament through the increasing pressure of work. A footnote in Dix, *The Shape of the Liturgy* (1954), p. 714, n. 2, is instructive on this point.

4 There were two amendments of importance: one in the Commons and one in the Lords. In the Commons the proposed Ecclesiastical Committee of the Privy Council was replaced by the Ecclesiastical Committee of both Houses of Parliament. In the Lords an amendment by the Lord Chancellor provided that only "on address from each House of Parliament asking that such Measure should be presented to His Majesty, such Measure shall be presented to His Majesty, and shall have the force and effect of an Act of Parliament on the Royal Assent being signified thereto". It was originally proposed that: "If the Ecclesiastical Committee shall have advised His Majesty to give His Royal Assent to the measure, then, unless within forty days either House of Parliament shall direct to the contrary, such measure shall be presented to His Majesty, and shall have the force and effect of an Act of Parliament on the Royal Assent being signified thereto."

80 THE WELSH CHURCH TEMPORALITIES ACT 1919

(*Statutes at Large*, 9-10 Geo. V, c. 65)

The future of the Welsh Church remained unsettled throughout the war, and thus an opportunity was afforded for a reconsideration of the provisions of the original Act. Although disestablishment was still fiercely opposed, it was realized that the proposed Bill was more generous to the Welsh Church than the original Act. Although the ecclesiastical questions, such as the relationship of the Church in Wales to the Church of England, were readily settled, the poverty of the Welsh Church became an accepted fact.[1]

An Act to continue in office the Welsh Commissioners appointed under the Welsh Church Act, 1914, to postpone the date of disestablishment, and to make further provision with respect to the temporalities of, and marriages in, the Church in Wales.

(19 August 1919)

Be it enacted by the King's most Excellent Majesty, by and with the advice and consent of the Lords Spiritual and Temporal, and Commons, in this present Parliament assembled, and by the authority of the same, as follows:

1

(1) His Majesty in Council may, from time to time, on the application of the Welsh Commissioners appointed under the Welsh Church Act, 1914, suspend the dissolution of the said Commissioners and, subject to revision by the Treasury of the salaries of the said Commissioners and the remuneration and number of their officers, continue their powers for such time as His Majesty thinks fit.

(2) Notwithstanding anything in the Welsh Church Act, 1914, the expenses of carrying that Act into execution, including the salaries and remuneration of the Commissioners and their staff, shall be apportioned between the property to be transferred to the University of Wales and the several county councils in

proportion to the value of the property to be so transferred to them respectively.

2

The date of disestablishment of the Church in Wales shall, notwithstanding anything in the Welsh Church Act, 1914, or the Suspensory Act, 1914, or any order made thereunder, be, for the purposes of this Act and of the first-mentioned Act, the thirty-first day of March, nineteen hundred and twenty.

3

(1) Section eighteen of the Welsh Church Act, 1914, shall have effect as if the representative body had signified by notice in writing to the Welsh Commissioners that they have adopted the scheme of commutation set for in that Act; and in paragraph (*b*) of the said section the expression "the existing interests of holders of ecclesiastical offices in the Church in Wales" means and shall be deemed always to have meant existing interests of persons who, at the time of the passing of the Welsh Church Act, 1914, were holders of ecclesiastical offices in the Church in Wales.

(2) There shall be paid out of moneys provided by Parliament to the Welsh Commissioners a sum of one million pounds to be applied by them towards the payment of the sum due to the representative body under the said scheme of commutation.

(3) The annual income derived from property mentioned in paragraph 4 of the Fourth Schedule to the Welsh Church Act, 1914, shall, as respects tithe rentcharge, be taken to be the amount of tithe rentcharge according to the septennial average computed at the date of disestablishment as if the Tithe Act, 1918, had not passed, after making the deductions specified in the said paragraph.

(4) The annual income derived from property mentioned in paragraph 2 of the Fifth Schedule to the Welsh Church Act, 1914, shall, as respects tithe rentcharge, be the amount of tithe rentcharge computed in accordance with the Tithe Act, 1918, after making the deductions specified in the said paragraph.[2]

(5) If the Welsh Commissioners shall not have paid to the representative body, within six months after the date of commutation, the aggregate value of the existing interests of holders of ecclesiastical offices in the Church of Wales, as ascertained in

the manner provided by the Fourth Schedule to the Welsh Church Act, 1914, and this Act, they shall pay interest on any amount unpaid at the rate of five and a half per centum per annum until such payment.

(6) Where, on the first day of January, nineteen hundred and thirteen, any ecclesiastical office in the Church in Wales, was vacant, the person appointed to hold that office next after that date shall, for the purposes of paragraph 1 of the Fourth Schedule to the Welsh Church Act, 1914, be treated as if he had been the holder of that office on that date.

4

(1) The Welsh Commissioners may postpone the transfer under the Welsh Church Act, 1914, of any property vested in them to any person or body of persons, whether corporate or unincorporate, other than the representative body, and such person or body of persons shall not be bound to accept the transfer of any such property until the Secretary of State so directs; and so long as any tithe rentcharge which was previously attached to a benefice remains vested in the Welsh Commissioners, the Welsh Commissioners shall be deemed to be the owners of a tithe rentcharge attached to a benefice for the purposes of the Tithe Rentcharge (Rates) Act, 1889.

(2) If the Welsh Commissioners so agree with the representative body, it shall be lawful for the Welsh Commissioners to buy and for the representative body to sell to them any of the tithe rentcharge transferred to the representative body under the Welsh Church Act, 1914, at a price to be ascertained by the same method as that prescribed by the Tithe Act, 1918, for the payment of compensation for the redemption of tithe rentcharge; and the Welsh Commissioners may determine out of what part of the funds vested in them the purchase money payable for any such tithe rentcharge is to be paid and the tithe rentcharge when purchased shall be dealt with by the Welsh Commissioners in like manner as if it had been derived from the same source as the purchase money:

Provided that, if the tithe rentcharge at the time of sale is subject to any existing interest, it shall be discharged from that interest, and the representative body shall be liable to pay to the person entitled to the existing interest, so long as that interest would have continued, an annuity equal to the annual value of his interest therein ascertained in manner provided by the Fifth Schedule to the Welsh Church Act, 1914, and this Act.

(3) There shall be included in the property which the Welsh Commissioners are required by subsection 1 of section eight of the Welsh Church Act, 1914, to transfer to the representative body any tithe rentcharge derived from sources other than endowments of any ecclesiastical office or cathedral corporation in the Church in Wales, and not being Welsh ecclesiastical property, which has been appropriated since the year sixteen hundred and sixty two to benefices in Wales and Monmouthshire.[3]

5

(1) It shall be lawful for the Ecclesiastical Commissioners by agreement with the representative body, instead of charging their common fund with the payment of the perpetual annuity mentioned in proviso (*c*) to section six of the Welsh Church Act, 1914, to pay to the representative body out of any capital money belonging to them (including money invested under section six of the New Parishes Act, 1843), not being Welsh ecclesiastical property, a capital sum not exceeding such amount as may in the opinion of the Ecclesiastical Commissioners be the capitalized value of such annuity, and any charge upon the said common fund made in respect of such annuity before the date of disestablishment shall, upon payment to the representative body of a capital sum in lieu thereof, cease to have effect.[4]

Notwithstanding the limitation imposed by proviso (*d*) of section six of the Welsh Church Act, 1914, upon the sum which the Ecclesiastical Commissioners may pay in any year to the representative body, it shall be lawful for the Ecclesiastical Commissioners with the consent of the representative body to pay to that body a sum in excess of the said limitation, upon condition that no further payment shall be made by the Ecclesiastical Commissioners under the powers granted to them by that proviso.

Parts I and III of the Schedule to the Welsh Church Act, 1914 (which define the property which may be transferred by the Ecclesiastical Commissioners to the representative body) shall have effect as if the words "date of disestablishment" were therein substituted for the words "passing of this Act".[5]

1 The Representative Body of the Church in Wales was sanctioned by the Welsh Church Act, 1914; incorporated by Royal Charter, 1919; and created by the Cardiff Convention in 1917. Its functions were to be financial and administrative: to hold the property transferred by the Welsh Church Commission; to manage the income arising from the diocesan quotas; to pay stipends and pensions; maintain parsonages; and provide for the training of ordinands.

2 Among the benefits of this Act was the allowance of £30,000 from the commutation of vested interests of tithe.

3 Under the 1914 Act the Welsh Church was to lose £102,000 a year, but under the 1919 Act this was reduced to £48,000, thus restoring £54,000 a year of the lost property. This was largely due to the allowance of £22,500 for the lapsed vested interests of incumbents who had vacated their benefices between September 1914 and the date of disestablishment.

4 The Ecclesiastical Commissioners were empowered to make compensation for the loss of capital and other augmentation grants which would have been made to the Welsh Church but for the passing of the 1914 Act. Davidson signified his approval of the Bill to Bonar Law and Lloyd George partly on the grounds of its financial provisions.

5 The Bill was opposed by Lord Salisbury and Lord Robert Cecil, and two amendments were introduced in the Lords which returned disused graveyards to the Church, and made the withdrawal of the Welsh dioceses from Convocation optional. The amendments were withdrawn and the Bill carried.

81 CHURCH ASSEMBLY AND CONVOCATION

The Enabling Act was based on the representative principle and the development of parochial church councils and diocesan conferences were natural consequences of the Act. The House of Clergy was not representative, the *ex officio* members, deans, archdeacons, and representatives of Chapters, outnumbering the elected members. The Convocations of the Clergy Measure 1920 provided that the elected element is always a majority, thus extending the democratic principle to the second House.

(Church Assembly Publications, vol. 1, N.A. 7)

NATIONAL ASSEMBLY OF THE CHURCH OF ENGLAND

REPORT OF THE COMMITTEE ON THE REFORM OF CONVOCATION

MEMBERS

The Dean of Westminster (Chairman)
The Bishop of Ely
The Bishop of Manchester
The Bishop of Gloucester
The Dean of York
The Archdeacon of Dorset
The Archdeacon of Leicester
The Reverend Dr Kidd
The Reverend Dr Sparrow Simpson
The Reverend Dr Frere
Sir Samuel Hoare, Bart, M.P.
Chancellor North
The Lord Parmoor
The Lord Phillimore
The Marquis of Salisbury

The Committee were appointed by the Assembly with the following terms of reference:

To consider and report upon a measure declaring that the Convocations of Canterbury and York have power, by Canon lawfully passed and promulged, to amend the constitution of the Lower Houses thereof; and also to put their recommendations into the form of a draft measure.

They recommend the following draft measure for the approval of the National Assembly:

MEASURE PROPOSED TO BE PASSED BY THE NATIONAL ASSEMBLY OF THE CHURCH OF ENGLAND DECLARING THE POWER OF EACH OF THE CONVOCATIONS OF CANTERBURY AND YORK TO AMEND THE CONSTITUTION OF THE LOWER HOUSE THEREOF

Whereas by the Constitution of the National Assembly of the Church of England as defined in the Church of England Assembly (Powers) Act, 1919, it is provided that the said Assembly shall, before entering on any other legislative business, make further provision for the self-government of the Church by passing through the Assembly (*inter alia*) a measure declaring that the Convocations of Canterbury and York have power by Canon lawfully passed and promulged to amend the constitution of the Lower Houses thereof.[1]

1 It is hereby declared that the Convocation of each of the said Provinces has power, with His Majesty's Royal Assent and Licence, to make, promulge and execute Canons for the amendment of the constitution of the Lower House thereof.[2]
2 This Measure may be cited as "The Convocations of the Clergy Measure 1920".[3]

Signed on behalf of the Committee
HERBERT E. RYLE, Bishop
October 21st, 1920 *Chairman.*

1 In the Lower House of the Convocation of Canterbury there were formerly 99 *ex officio* members, 25 Proctors for Chapters, 54 Proctors for the Clergy; in that of the Convocation of York: 31 *ex officio* members, 8 Proctors for Chapters, 49 Proctors for the Clergy. The total number of members for both Lower Houses of Convocation were, after the passing of the canon, 126 *ex officio* members, 211 elected members, and 5 university representatives.

2 The Constitution laid down that "Nothing in this Constitution shall be deemed to diminish or derogate from any of the powers belonging to the Convocations of the Provinces of Canterbury and York or of any House thereof." The Church Assembly, therefore, was not empowered to draw up new canons for the Church.

3 The measure was approved by the Church Assembly on 16 November 1920 and received the Royal Assent on 23 December. The Convocations then passed canons *de Representatione Cleri in Inferiore Domo Convocationis*, which received Royal Assent and Licence on 14 April 1921.

(*The Official Year Book of the Church of England* (1942), pp. 190-201)

CANTERBURY

1. The Dean of every Cathedral Church in the Province and the Deans of the two Collegiate Churches of St Peter in Westminster, and of St George, Windsor; or if the Dean of any such Cathedral or Collegiate Church be unwilling or unable to act, then one Proctor elected by the Dean and Chapter; or when there is no Dean, then one Proctor elected by the Chapter from among the members of the said Chapter; also the Provost of Eton, provided he be in Priest's Orders in the Church of England;

2. The two Archdeacons in each Diocese who are senior by date of appointment as Archdeacon in such Diocese, or if either of them be unwilling or unable to act, then the Archdeacon who is next in seniority of appointment;

3. Proctors for the Clergy who shall be elected in the manner following in such proportion to the number of electors as shall from time to time be determined by Convocation, provided that no Diocese shall have less than three Proctors:

(*a*) The electoral areas shall be:
- (i) The several Dioceses in the Province.
- (ii) The Universities in the Province:
  - (*a*) The University of Oxford,
  - (*b*) The University of Cambridge,
  - (*c*) The University of London,
  - (*d*) Other Universities in the Province acting together for this purpose:[1]

  Provided always that it shall be competent for the Archbishop of the Province, after consultation with the Prolocutor of the Lower House of the Convocation, to postpone or suspend the operation of this area should the number of electors appear to them to be insufficient for representation as a separate electoral area.

(*b*) The electors shall be:
- (i) Where the Diocese is the area, all clergymen beneficed in the Diocese, or licensed under seal by the Bishop of the Diocese, or holding office in the Cathedral Church, or in the above-mentioned Collegiate Churches, provided that they be not *ex-officio* members of Convocation, and that no one shall be entitled to vote in more than one Diocese.
- (ii) Where a University, or group of Universities, is the area, all clergymen of the Church of England whose names are entered on an electoral roll kept in accordance with rules made from time to time by Convocation:

  Provided that no one shall be entitled to vote in more than one such electoral area.

(*c*) All clergymen in the Church of England who have been admitted to Priest's Orders shall be eligible for election.

(*d*) The mode of voting shall be such as may from time to time be determined by Convocation.

YORK

1. The Dean of every Cathedral Church in the Province, or if the

Dean of any such Cathedral Church shall be unwilling or unable to act, then one Proctor elected by the Dean and Chapter from among the members of the said Chapter;

2. The Archdeacon of every Archdeaconry within the Province, save that when there are more than two Archdeacons in a Diocese, only the two Archdeacons who are senior by date of appointment shall be cited, and that when either of the said Archdeacons is unwilling or unable to act, then the Archdeacon who is next to him in seniority of appointment shall be cited in his place;

3. Proctors for the Clergy, who shall be elected in the manner following:

(i) The electoral area shall be the Diocese, but it shall be competent for the Archbishop of the Province on the petition of the electors in the Diocese to direct the formation of electoral areas within that Diocese and to assign to each area from the number allowed to the whole Diocese a number of Proctors proportioned to the number of electors within the area.

(ii) The Diocese of Sodor and Man shall be entitled to one Proctor for the Clergy, but no other Diocese shall be represented by less than three Proctors. Subject to this provision the number of Proctors in every Diocese shall be in such proportion to the number of electors as shall be from time to time determined by Convocation with the approval of the Archbishop of the Province.

(iii) The electors shall be:

(*a*) All Clergy beneficed in the Diocese.

(*b*) All Priests and Deacons who being unbeneficed hold the Bishop's Licence to officiate in the Diocese and are resident therein.

Provided that no one be entitled to vote in more than one Diocese: that only Priests who have a right to vote in a Diocese shall be eligible as Proctors of that Diocese: that a Proctor ceasing to hold a benefice or a licence in the Diocese for which he was returned shall *ipso facto* vacate his seat in Convocation: and that the method of voting in every Diocese shall be decided from time to time by the Bishop of the Diocese, subject to the approval of the Archbishop.

1 Paragraph 3 of the Canterbury canon was amended in 1936 to provide for the university representation.

82 THE MATRIMONIAL CAUSES BILL 1920

(*Hansard,* Lords (10 March 1920))

The Divorce Act of 1857 had not produced any alteration in the canon law of the Church of England, consequently the law of the realm and the church law existed side by side differing in point of principle. The Matrimonial Causes Bill was introduced into the Lords by Lord Buckmaster and supported by Lord Birkenhead. Although it passed its second and third readings, it was not taken up in the Commons. Lang's speech is notable, not for its advocacy of the Church of England's traditional teaching, but for its awareness of the social problems involved in the five additional grounds for divorce.[1]

Now I come to the main portion of this Bill—it is contained in Clause 8—the provision of five additional grounds of divorce in this country. I think the House would listen with respect to the speech delivered by the Noble Lord who has moved that the Bill be read this day six months. It was an indication (though I think it was really not needed) of the depth and intensity of religious conviction which forms the background of our discussion here. It is quite unnecessary to remind your Lordships that while you may seem to be endeavouring to heal the wounds of a large number of persons to whom matrimony has been a curse and not a blessing, you may be doing deep injury to the profoundest convictions of a vast multitude of the citizens of this country, for the views that were expressed by the noble Lord are not confined to the members of his communion. They are, I believe, shared by at any rate a great multitude of those of my own, and certainly by large numbers of the Nonconformists of this country.[2]

I ought to say at once that I thankfully recognize the place given to conscientious conviction in the Bill—in Clause 34—as regards the clergy of the Church of England. That clause is an improvement upon a similar section in the Act of 1857, inasmuch as the Act of 1857 gave this measure of relief to the clergy only in the case of what is called the "innocent party", whereas this Bill gives that relief in every case where a person's marriage has been dissolved and where one of the parties is still living. But I venture to think, especially if this Bill were to become law, that it would be necessary to extend this provision for the relief of conscience, and to extend it to the use of the parish church. Since the Act of 1857 the State has provided a complete system of civil marriage. There is therefore no hardship in asking that those who desire to be married after having obtained divorce, upon grounds which I venture to think can hardly be described as consonant with Christian tradition, should be married in the civil registry.[3] Moreover, you have to consider in this matter, not only the conscience of the clergyman but the conscience of many of his parishioners, and of the laity of the communion to which he belongs. And once again I suggest that it is conferring no public advantage to allow in the parish churches of the country the repetition of what must necessarily be somewhat of a mockery, when persons rehearse to one another as before God a solemn vow that they will be faithful, for richer or poorer, for better or worse, till death parts them, when one of the parties has already made, in the same solemn circumstances, the same declaration to someone who is still living.

I ought to say, I think, in candour that to me personally the conception of marriage as dissoluble only by death, which has been so impressively sustained by the Christian Church, especially in the West, during all these centuries, is the conception which answers to the mind and teaching of its divine Founder and Head. The allegiance which any man owes to Him as the Supreme Guide of human life and conduct must necessarily determine his attitude to divorce. But I recognize that the existing law avails itself of a possible exception, authorized by Christ Himself. There is, as all your Lordships are aware, an account of His words, early, authentic, not I think the most authentic, which permits this exception. The existing law has availed itself of that exception and it has to be recognized, but I do not think anyone could maintain that the proposals which are contained in this Bill are consistent with any interpretation of the words of Christ, if they are regarded as still binding upon the Christian conscience.

While I have said this quite candidly, however, it seems to me clear that circumstances might arise in which it might not be possible for the State to impose Christian standards by law on all its subjects, many of whom would not accept the authority upon which those standards rest. After all, I admit that civil legislation cannot permanently sustain itself upon a level which the public opinion of the community is unable to reach. Therefore it is not upon the ground of religious authority, but upon the ground of public welfare, that I wish this afternoon to discuss this matter. I have stated my own belief, but I hope, and I think, I am able sincerely to discuss the matter also from the point of view of its bearing on the welfare of the people as a whole. The principle upon which the existing law rests, rightly or wrongly—we are not called upon to decide that matter—is that marriage in this country is to be regarded as a lifelong contract which can only be dissolved by adultery. It is needless to dwell upon the reasons which mark that offence as constituting a breach in the marriage tie wholly unique in its character. It means the wilful transfer to another person of that physical union which has been universally regarded as the sign of the completion of marriage. The question is whether this House is prepared to take the lead in recommending that other causes of divorce should be added to the only one which at present exists.[4]

The noble and learned Lord spoke with feeling and eloquence about the hardships which the existing law often imposes. I need not assure him that no one in this House feels the force of those hardships more than I do. A man would have a heart of steel who did not realize the pathos and pity of these cases. I will not labour the old adage that "hard cases make bad laws". I admit that hardships may occur so complete that they compel legislation. But in thinking of the weight which ought to be attached to these impressive cases of hardship I would ask your Lordships to bear three considerations in mind. The first is: Are we to impose any limit to the claims of our sympathy? The principle, so far as I could gather it, of my colleagues in the majority on the Royal Commission[5] appears to be that causes ought to be regarded as sufficient for justifying divorce which were recognized as leading to the break-up of married life, or, in the words which the noble and learned Lord quoted, "which frustrate the objects for which marriage was formed". But where will that principle lead? Words may be as cruel as blows; studied indifference and neglect may be harder to bear than bouts of drunkenness or the tragedy of insanity. How can it be said that the functions of married life can be adequately fulfilled if the wife has a deaf and dumb or paralysed husband? The discovery that love has ceased between a man and his wife must bring bitter and enduring pain. All these things in a real sense frustrate the objects for which the marriage was begun. Multitudes of people gave evidence before the Commission pressing upon us that no limit should be placed on the claims of sympathy, and that the only way of dealing justly with the hardships was to permit divorce by mutual consent. One witness frankly said that divorce should occur wherever there was a serious desire on the part of either of the parties not to live with the other. If the law is to follow the sympathy inevitably aroused by such cases as those to which Lord Buckmaster referred, I do not see how we can resist this conclusion, and I am equally sure that it is not a conclusion to which your Lordships would desire to bring the marriage laws of this country.

In the second place, through the door which you open for cases appealing to sympathy and pity others will enter who are entitled to neither. A little carefully concealed collusion will be sufficient to get them through. We have the example of the United States of America.[6] The number of divorces there is double what it is in any other country except Japan, where it is one in six. It cannot be doubted that the immense number of divorces in the United States is due not to the number of real hardships, to the number of cruel husbands or malicious wives, but to the fact that through the door opened for cases of desertion and cruelty multitudes of other people easily walk into a termination of the life they no longer desire.[7]

Then I also ask your Lordships to remember that the pressure of emotion caused by these individual cases of hardships must be balanced by care for the general welfare. The whole basis of any marriage law is, of course, that the making and breaking of the marriage contract is a matter which concerns the whole community and is not merely a private transaction which concerns the individuals themselves. The aim, I presume, of our marriage law, as of all marriage laws, ought to make it lifelong in its obligation. The as stable as possible, and to make it lifelong in its obligations. The stability of the institution of marriage is therefore of more importance than the relief of individuals. Hitherto in this country the law has been supported in its efforts by public opinion. And why? Because the conception conveyed in the old familiar words, "For better, for worse, for richer, for poorer, until death us do part", has become part of the common conscience of the community. They are familiar still to 61 per cent. of the marriages that take place in this country, and they impart a conception of marriage as not primarily a mutual arrangement for happiness but an obligation of lifelong and faithful service. I suggest that it is taking a very strong step for the Legislature to disturb the strength of that common conscience upon which its own desire to maintain the strength of the institution of matrimony so largely depends.[8]

1 Lang, Cosmo Gordon; *b.* 1864; *educ.*, Glasgow University, 1878; Balliol College, Oxford, 1882; Fellow of All Souls, 1888; Cuddesdon, 1889; ordained, 1890; curate at Leeds Parish Church, 1890; Dean of Divinity at Magdalen College, Oxford, 1894; vicar of St Mary, Oxford, 1894; vicar of Portsea, 1896; Bishop of Stepney, 1901; Archbishop of York, 1908; Archbishop of Canterbury, 1928; resigned, 1942; *d.* 1945.

2 As Lords Spiritual the Bishops were virtually the spokesmen for all

Christian opinion in the Lords, though Nonconformist strength in the Commons was always able to act as a corrective.

3 Lord John Russell introduced the necessary legislation for civil marriage in 1836 (6-7 Will. IV, c. 85).

4 The proposed new grounds were: desertion for three years; cruelty; incurable insanity after five years confinement; habitual drunkenness found incurable after three years from the first order of separation; and imprisonment under a commuted death sentence.

5 Asquith wished to exclude church leaders from the Commission set up in 1909, but he gave way under pressure from Davidson. The minority Report was signed by Sir William Anson, Sir Lewis Dibdin, and Lang.

6 It was ironical that Lang was called upon to intervene during the Abdication Crisis which involved a divorce suit.

7 Lang spoke of the war as causing "an enormous number of marriages" contracted "with very great recklessness and disregard of responsibilities". In 1912, when the Commission reported, there were 1,168 petitions; in 1917, 1,720; in 1918, 2,709; and in 1919, 5,789.

8 The relationship between Church and State during this period, though subject to considerable strain, did remain unimpaired. The growing independence of the Church's leaders is exemplified by Lang when he maintained: "A Christian society should be at liberty to give or withhold its own religious sanction to marriages to which the State reluctantly, but under pressure of social facts, feels compelled to give its civil consent."

83 THE LAMBETH APPEAL, 1920

(Bell, *Documents on Christian Unity*, 1, pp. 1-5)

During the Lambeth Conference a group of younger bishops met in the Lollards' Tower and included the Bishops of Bombay (Palmer), Pretoria (Talbot), and Pennsylvania (Rhinelander). At a meeting in the garden of Lambeth Palace on 18 July 1920 it was decided that the various drafts and resolutions be transposed into an Appeal.[1] The Appeal was greatly influenced by Lang, though its final form was largely due to Palmer. Prefaced by an encyclical letter and followed by a series of resolutions dealing with some of the questions likely to arise from the contents, it put forward practical suggestions for the realization of organic unity.[2]

FROM THE BISHOPS ASSEMBLED IN THE LAMBETH CONFERENCE OF 1920

We, Archbishops, Bishops Metropolitan, and other Bishops of the Holy Catholic Church in full communion with the Church of England, in Conference assembled, realizing the responsibility which rests upon us at this time and sensible of the sympathy and the prayers of many, both within and without our own Communion, make this appeal to all Christian people.

We acknowledge all those who believe in our Lord Jesus Christ, and have been baptized into the name of the Holy Trinity, as sharing with us membership in the universal Church of Christ which is His body. We believe that the Holy Spirit has called us in a very solemn and special manner to associate ourselves in penitence and prayer with all those who deplore the divisions of Christian people, and are inspired by the vision and hope of a visible unity of the whole Church.

I We believe that God wills fellowship. By God's own act this fellowship was made in and through Jesus Christ, and its life in His Spirit. We believe that it is God's purpose to manifest this fellowship, so far as this world is concerned, in an outward, visible, and united society, holding one faith, having its own recognized officers, using God-given means of grace, and inspiring all its members to the world-wide service of the Kingdom of God. This is what we mean by the Catholic Church.[3]

II This united fellowship is not visible in the world today. On the one hand there are other ancient episcopal communions in East and West, to whom ours is bound by many ties of common faith and tradition. On the other hand there are the great non-episcopal Communions, standing for rich elements of truth, liberty and life which might otherwise have been obscured or neglected. With them we are closely linked by many affinities, racial, historical and spiritual. We cherish the earnest hope that all these Communions, and our own, may be led by the Spirit into the unity of the Faith and of the knowledge of the Son of God. But in fact we are all organized in different groups, each one keeping to itself gifts that rightly belong to the whole fellowship, and tending to live its own life apart from the rest.

III The causes of division lie deep in the past, and are by no means simply or wholly blameworthy. Yet none can doubt that self-will, ambition, and lack of charity among Christians have been principal factors in the mingled process, and that these, together with blindness to the sin of disunion, are still mainly responsible for the breaches of Christendom. We acknowledge this condition of broken fellowship to be contrary to God's will, and we desire frankly to confess our share in the guilt of thus crippling the Body of Christ and hindering the activity of His Spirit.

IV The times call us to a new outlook and new measures.[4] The Faith cannot be adequately apprehended and the battle of the Kingdom cannot be worthily fought while the body is divided, and is thus unable to grow up into the fullness of the life of Christ. The time has come, we believe, for all the separated groups of Christians to agree in forgetting the things which are behind and reaching out towards the goal of a reunited Catholic Church. The removal of the barriers which have arisen between them will only be brought about by a new comradeship of those whose faces are definitely set this way.

The vision which rises before us is that of a Church, genuinely Catholic, loyal to all Truth, and gathering into its fellowship all "who profess and call themselves Christians", within whose visible unity all the treasures of faith and order, bequeathed as a heritage by the past to the present, shall be possessed in common, and made serviceable to the whole Body of Christ. Within this unity Christian Communions now separated from one another would retain much that has long been distinctive in their methods of worship and service. It is through a rich diversity of life and devotion that the unity of the whole fellowship will be fulfilled.[5]

V This means an adventure of good will and still more of faith, for nothing less is required than a new discovery of the creative resources of God. To this adventure we are convinced that God is now calling all the members of His Church.

VI We believe that the visible unity of the Church will be found to involve the whole-hearted acceptance of:

The Holy Scriptures, as the record of God's revelation of Himself to man, and as being the rule and ultimate standard of faith; and the Creed commonly called Nicene, as the sufficient statement of the Christian faith, and either it or the Apostles' Creed as the Baptismal confession of belief:

The divinely instituted sacraments of Baptism and the Holy Communion, as expressing for all the corporate life of the whole fellowship in and with Christ:

A ministry acknowledged by every part of the Church as possessing not only the inward call of the Spirit, but also the commission of Christ and the authority of the whole body.[6]

VII May we not reasonably claim that the Episcopate is the one means of providing such a ministry? It is not that we call in question for a moment the spiritual reality of the ministries of those Communions which do not possess the Episcopate. On the contrary, we thankfully acknowledge that these ministries have been manifestly blessed and owned by the Holy Spirit as effective means of grace. But we submit that considerations alike of history and of present experience justify the claim which we make on behalf of the Episcopate. Moreover, we would urge that it is now and will prove to be in the future the best instrument for maintaining the unity and continuity of the Church. But we greatly desire that the office of a Bishop should be everywhere exercised in a representative and constitutional manner, and more truly express all that ought to be involved for the life of the Christian Family in the title of Father-in-God. Nay more, we eagerly look forward to the day when through its acceptance in a united Church we may all share in that grace which is pledged to the members of the whole body in the apostolic rite of the laying on of hands, and in the joy and fellowship of a Eucharist in which as one Family we may together, without any doubtfulness of mind, offer to the one Lord our worship and service.[7]

VIII We believe that for all the truly equitable approach to union is by way of mutual deference to one another's consciences. To this end, we who send forth this appeal would say that if the authorities of other Communions should so desire, we are persuaded that, terms of union having been otherwise satisfactorily adjusted, Bishops and clergy of our Communion would willingly accept from these authorities a form of commission or recognition, which would commend our ministry to their congregations, as having its place in the one family life.

It is not in our power to know how far this suggestion may be acceptable to those to whom we can offer it. We can only say that we offer it in all sincerity as a token of our longing that all ministries of grace, theirs and ours, shall be available for the service of our Lord in a united Church.

It is our hope that the same motive would lead ministers who have not received it to accept a commission through episcopal ordination, as obtaining for them a ministry throughout the whole fellowship.

In so acting no one of us could possibly be taken to repudiate his past ministry. God forbid that any man should repudiate a past experience rich in spiritual blessings for himself and others. Nor would any of us be dishonouring the Holy Spirit of God, whose call led us all to our several ministries, and whose power enabled us to perform them. We shall be publicly and formally seeking additional recognition of a new call to wider service in a reunited Church, and imploring for ourselves God's grace and strength to fulfil the same.

IX The spiritual leadership of the Catholic Church in days to come, for which the world is manifestly waiting, depends upon the readiness with which each group is prepared to make sacrifices for the sake of a common fellowship, a common ministry, and a common service to the world.

We place this ideal first and foremost before ourselves and our own people. We call upon them to make the effort to meet the demands of a new age with a new outlook. To all other Christian people whom our words may reach we make the same appeal. We do not ask that any one Communion should consent to be absorbed in another. We do ask that all should unite in a new and great endeavour to recover and to manifest to the world the unity of the Body of Christ for which He prayed.[8]

1 The Appeal was meant to be reciprocal and did succeed in initiating discussions at home and abroad.

2 The conception of a united Church was basically different from a federation of Churches as envisaged by the Kikuyu conference. From the outset it was asked whether the notion of a united Church was the true goal of the ecumenical movement.

3 The question of the nature of the Church was discussed at some depth by Anglican theologians in the years between the two wars. Under the influence of the ecumenical movement, among other things, Gore, Headlam, Darwell Stone, Quick, and Temple contributed to the debate.

4 Henson commented: "All agreed in saying that unless recognition of non-episcopal ministries and intercommunion were conceded, all hope of negotiations with the non-episcopal churches must be given up. In Australia, Canada, and China there was a strong tendency towards union, and, unless the Anglican Church made haste to associate itself therewith, it would lose all chance of leadership in the recovery of unity, and would compel the creation of a Protestant Federation, from which Anglicanism would be thrust out" (Henson, *Retrospect*, vol. 2, pp. 11-12).

5 The replies to the Appeal included the following among things distinctive of the Christian Communions: the position and function of lay preachers as in Methodism; the presbyteral order; and the congregational order.

6 Paragraph VI contains the essentials for a reunited Church from the standpoint of the Lambeth Quadrilateral of 1888. The Quadrilateral was a revision of the four Articles accepted at the General Convention of the Protestant Episcopal Church at Chicago in 1886.

7 A further difference from the "Kikuyu" approach towards unity was in regarding the common sharing of the Eucharist as the end, rather than the means, to reunion.

8 A joint conference at Lambeth Palace between Anglican and Free Church representatives was held in January, March, and April 1922. A report of the committee under the chairmanship of Lang was approved on 24 May 1922. The Appeal also occasioned a renewed series of conversations with Roman Catholic representatives at Malines. By Christmas, 1923, Davidson was able to write to the archbishops and metropolitans of the Anglican Communion giving them an unofficial summary of the position since the issuing of the Appeal.

84 THE CHURCH OF SWEDEN, 1920

(Bell, *Documents on Christian Unity* 1, pp. 10-11)

The Church of England's isolation from continental Protestantism was brought to an end by the appointment of a commission by Archbishop Davidson under the chairmanship of Bishop Ryle in 1909. The Commission visited Sweden and, after conferring with a Swedish committee, published a report in 1911. On the basis of this report two resolutions were passed by the Lambeth Conference.[1] Although the Swedish Church maintained the historic episcopal succession, only a limited measure of intercommunion could be recommended since the Swedish Church maintained complete fellowship with the non-episcopal Lutheran Churches.[2]

24 The Conference welcomes the Report of the Commission appointed after the last Conference entitled, "The Church of England and the Church of Sweden", and, accepting the conclusions there maintained on the succession of the Bishops of the Church of Sweden and the conception of priesthood set forth in its standards, recommends that members of that Church, qualified to

receive the Sacrament in their own Church, should be admitted to Holy Communion in ours. It also recommends that on suitable occasions permission should be given to Swedish ecclesiastics to give addresses in our churches.

If the authorities of any province of the Anglican Communion find local irregularities in the order or practice of the Church of Sweden outside that country, they may legitimately, within their own region, postpone any such action as is recommended in this Resolution until they are satisfied that these irregularities have been removed.[3]

25 We recommend further that in the event of an invitation being extended to an Anglican Bishop or Bishops to take part in the consecration of a Swedish Bishop, the invitation should, if possible, be accepted, subject to the approval of the Metropolitan. We also recommend that, in the first instance, as an evident token of the restoration of closer relations between the two Churches, if possible more than one of our Bishops should take part in the Consecration.[4]

1 The Lambeth Conference was a purely advisory gathering and did not frame legislative acts which were binding on individual provinces.

2 Henson wrote: "Allowing fully for the saving factor of episcopacy, the fact that the Church of Sweden is a Lutheran church is the salient feature in this whole incident" (Henson, *Retrospect*, vol. 2, pp. 39-40). Whereas the Jerusalem Bishopric had envisaged the growing together of the Anglican and a Lutheran national Church, it did so as a missionary venture: it did not attempt to bring the Churches together in a permanent relationship at home as these proposals did.

3 The irregularities in question were the lack of bishops in the missions of the Swedish Church in South India and South Africa.

4 Henson (Durham) and Woods (Peterborough) took part in the consecration of the Bishops of Västerås and Visby in Uppsala Cathedral on 19 September 1920. The Bishop of Härnösand took part in the consecration of the Bishop of Dover in Canterbury Cathedral on 1 November 1927.

85 INTERNATIONAL MISSIONARY COUNCIL, 1920

(S.P.G. Letter Book, Kenneth Maclennan to Bishop King (21 October 1920), C.L.R./Home 3; *also* Minutes of the Standing Committee)

The idea of an International Missionary Council arose out of the commissions of the Edinburgh World Missionary Conference in 1910.[1] Representatives of missionary Churches, excepting the Roman Catholic, had discussed the common problems facing the Churches in the mission field. The Lambeth Conference in 1908 had maintained that it "could not but believe that the Foreign Mission Field is likely to react upon the Church at home by teaching a truer proportion, widening the outlook and strengthening the spiritual vision". The acceptance of the proposed I.M.C. by the larger Anglican missionary societies marked a new era in the international outlook of the Church of England.

Dear Bishop King,[2]

By the direction of the Standing Committee we have sent to you (per separate parcel) for submission to your Committee the proposals (of which a print is enclosed) for the formation of an international missionary committee, drawn up by the conference which met at Crans, near Geneva, last June.

You will perhaps remember that among the duties assigned to the Continuation Committee by the World Missionary Conference, 1910, was "to confer with the Societies and boards as to the best method of working towards the formation of such a permanent international missionary committee as is suggested by the commissions of the conference, and by various missionary bodies apart from the conference". The Continuation Committee was never able to carry these instructions into effect, but ten years after the conference in Edinburgh an international missionary conference has been able to formulate proposals to submit to the missionary societies.[3]

The Standing Committee have approved of these proposals. They are of opinion that if there is to be missionary co-operation at all on any adequate scale, it must of necessity be international, since in the mission field neighbouring missions are as often of different as of the same nationality.

In regard to cost, the budget for an international committee was approved by the Conference of Missionary Societies at its meeting at Swanwick last June and has been included in the budget already submitted to the missionary societies.

Your attention is called to the fact that all the provisions in the proposed constitution are to be interpreted as subject to Clause 1(1) which lays down that the Committee shall be established on the basis "that the only bodies entitled to determine missionary policy are the missionary societies and boards and the churches in the mission field".[4]

In Clause 1(8) it is stated that "the conclusions of the committee shall be reported to the national missionary organizations for their approval". It is of course understood that this approval will be given by the national missionary organizations such as the Standing Committee only when they are confident that they have the support of the Boards which they represent.

The Standing Committee desire to know:

First, whether your Society approves generally of the formation of an international missionary committee on the general lines proposed; and

Secondly, whether you have any suggestions to make in regard to the details of the proposed constitution, which after consideration by the Standing Committee may, if they meet with general approval, be submitted by the British representatives at the first meeting of the international missionary committee which is expected to take place in 1921.[5]

We are,
Yours faithfully,
KENNETH MACLENNAN.

1 The Conference was attended by 1,200 people representing the Churches of Asia, Africa, North America, Great Britain, and Europe and some 160 Missionary Societies and Boards. The chairman was John R. Mott; Talbot, Frere, Scott Holland, and Gore shared in the preparatory commissions; and Davidson addressed the Conference. The S.P.G. was not officially represented and made no reference to it in its *Report* for 1910.

2 King, George Lanchester; *b.* 1860; *educ.*, Clare College, Cambridge; curate of Tudhoe Grange, Durham, 1884; curate of Holy Trinity, Gateshead, 1889; curate of St Mary, South Shields, 1890; vicar, 1894; Bishop of Madagascar, 1899; secretary, S.P.G., 1919; canon of Rochester, 1923; *d.* 1941.

3 The secretary of the Continuation Committee was J. H. Oldham. The intervention of the war years made possible a gradual change

in the attitude of certain of the missionary societies, including the S.P.G., due in part, to the increasing influence of the "younger churches".

4 The Conference of Missionary Societies in Great Britain and Ireland was formed in 1912, arising out of the World Missionary Conference. Its members were later to include: C.M.S., S.P.G., C.E.Z.M.S., U.M.C.A., S.P.C.K., Church Mission to Jews, Jerusalem and the East Mission, South American Missionary Society, and the Representative Council of the Episcopal Church in Scotland

5 The S.P.G. answered: "Agreed to approve of the formation of the proposed Committee if assurance be given that the Missionary Societies of other branches of the Catholic Church, beside the Anglican, have received or will receive similar invitations to join."

86 MODERNISM 1921

(*Chronicle of Convocation* (1922), p. 238)

A Conference of Modern Churchmen was held at Girton College, Cambridge, in August 1921. The subject of the Conference was "Christ and the Creeds", and among the speakers were Foakes Jackson, R. G. Parsons, M. G. Glazebrook, H. D. A. Major[1] and Hastings Rashdall.[2] The Bishop of Gloucester[3] presented a petition in the Upper House of the Convocation of Canterbury on behalf of the English Church Union, which was instrumental in influencing Archbishop Davidson to set up a doctrinal commission. The Girton Conference was the high-water mark of the influence of the Modernist movement within the Church of England.

To his Grace the Most Reverend the Metropolitan and the Right Reverend the Lord Bishop of the Province of Canterbury in Synod assembled. The Petition of the undersigned the President[4] and Members of the Council of the English Church Union: Humbly sheweth: That a book entitled *The Modern Churchman*, Volume II, Nos. 5 and 6, was published at Oxford by Basil Blackwell in the month of September A.D. 1921. That the said book, a copy of which is sent herewith, consists of a number of papers written by various persons, most of whom are clergymen of the Church of England, being papers read at a Meeting or Conference held at Girton College, in the Parish of Girton in the Diocese of Ely in the summer of 1921, together with an introduction: That the said book contains teaching that is contradictory to the Faith—to wit: (i) The doctrine of the unique and distinctive character of the Being of God is denied: (ii) The doctrine of the Incarnation as taught in the Creeds and in Holy Scripture is repudiated: (iii) The idea that a divine character was infused into a human person is substituted for the scriptural doctrine that "The Word was made Flesh": (iv) The authority of the Creed of the whole Catholic Church of Christ is repudiated: (v) A desire is expressed either to abolish Creeds or to formulate new in place of the existing Creeds. Your Petitioners submit that such teaching is entirely subversive of the Christian Faith and the Christian Religion and therefore calls for authoritative condemnation. Your Petitioners therefore most earnestly pray your Venerable House to take the doctrinal teaching contained in the said book into consideration and to pass judgment upon it. And your Petitioners as in duty bound will ever pray.[5]

1 H. D. A. Major, founder of *The Modern Churchman*, was Principal of Ripon Hall, Oxford, 1919–1948.

2 Rashdall, Hastings; *b.* 1858; *educ.*, Harrow, 1871; New College, Oxford, 1877; taught at St David's Lampeter, 1883 and at University College, Durham, 1884; Fellow of Hertford College, Oxford, 1888; tutor and chaplain of Balliol; tutor of New College, 1895; canon of Hereford, 1909; Bampton Lecturer, 1914; Dean of Carlisle, 1917; *d.* 1924.

3 Gibson, Edgar Charles Sumner; *b.* 1848; *educ.*, Charterhouse and Trinity College, Oxford; chaplain of Wells Theological College, 1871; vice-principal, 1875; Principal of Leeds Clergy School, 1876; Principal of Wells, 1880; lecturer on Pastoral Theology at Cambridge, 1893; vicar of Leeds, 1895; Bishop of Gloucester, 1905; resigned 1922; *d.* 1924.

4 The English Church Union, formed in 1859, was at first greatly involved in the ritual prosecutions, but, as these diminished in number, so it became more active in doctrinal and moral controversies.

5 The Bishops resolved: "This House declares its conviction that adhesion to the teaching of the Catholic Church, as set forth in the Nicene Creed—and in particular concerning the eternal pre-existence of the Son of God, his true Godhead and his Incarnation—is essential to the life of the Church, and calls attention to the fact that the Church commissions as its ministers those who have solemnly expressed such adhesion."

87 DOCTRINAL COMMISSION, 1922

(Bell, *Davidson*, pp. 1149-50)

The Anglo-Catholic Congress of 1920 put forward a demand for a defined statement of belief. The Anglo-Catholic leaders saw in Modernism a threat to the status of the historic facts of the Creeds in the faith of the Church of England. A group of younger theologians propounded a scheme for a doctrinal commission of all schools of thought within the Church of England, but they sought an authoritative statement of the common mind of the Church of England rather than a mere corporate view. Bishop Burge approached the Archbishop in August 1921, and an official memorial was presented to him in January 1922. In spite of misgivings a commission was appointed, holding its first meeting at University College, Oxford, in September 1923.

DAVIDSON TO BURGE.

Lambeth Palace, S.E.,
December 28, 1922.

In pursuance of my letter of September 8 and of your subsequent letter of November 29, I write on behalf of the Archbishop of York and myself to say that it is our wish to nominate those whose names I append hereto to act as a Commission with the following Reference

> To consider the nature and grounds of Christian Doctrine with a view to demonstrating the extent of existing agreement within the Church of England and with a view to investigating how far it is possible to remove or diminish existing differences.

We note and approve your proposal that the Report of the Commission should not be an authoritative statement, but that it should, when prepared, be laid before the Bishops for them to consider what further action (if any) should be taken.

LIST OF THOSE SUGGESTED AS MEMBERS OF THE COMMISSION ON CHRISTIAN DOCTRINE.

The Bishop of Oxford[1]
The Bishop of Manchester[2]
The Dean of Bristol[3]
The Reverend F. R. Barry[4]
The Reverend Prebendary E. J. Bicknell[5]

The Reverend J. M. Creed[6]
The Reverend Canon J. R. Darbyshire[7]
The Reverend C. W. Emmet[8]
The Reverend H. B. Gooding[9]
The Reverend L. W. Grensted[10]
The Reverend W. L. Knox[11]
The Reverend Professor W. R. Matthews[12]
Professor W. Moberly[13]
The Reverend J. K. Mozley[14]
The Reverend Canon O. C. Quick[15]
The Reverend A. E. J. Rawlinson[16]
The Reverend E. G. Selwyn[17]
The Reverend C. J. Shebbeare[18]
W. Spens, Esq.[19]
The Reverend Canon V. F. Storr[20]
The Reverend Canon H. B. Streeter[21]
Professor A. E. Taylor[22]
The Reverend L. S. Thornton[23]
Professor C. C. J. Webb[24]
The Reverend Canon H. Albert Wilson[25]

1 Burge, Robert Murray; chairman until his death in 1925.

2 Temple, William, later chairman; contributed to *Foundations*; philosopher.

3 Burroughs, Edward; later Bishop of Ripon.

4 Barry, Frank Russell; Principal of Knutsford Ordination Test School; later canon of Westminster; Bishop of Southwell; New Testament scholar.

5 Bicknell, Edward John; vice-principal of Cuddesdon; later Professor of New Testament Exegesis, London; contributor to *Essays Catholic and Critical.*

6 Creed, John Martin; later Ely Professor of Divinity at Cambridge; contributor to *Mysterium Christi.*

7 Darbyshire, John Russell; Ridley Hall, Cambridge; later Bishop of Glasgow and Galloway.

8 Emmet, C. W.; Ripon Hall; author of *Conscience, Creeds, and Criticism.*

9 Gooding, H. B.; Principal of Wycliffe Hall.

10 Grensted, Laurence William; later Nolloth Professor of the Philosophy of the Christian Religion at Oxford.

11 Knox, Wilfred, O.G.S.; contributor to *Essays Catholic and Critical.*

12 Matthews, Walter Robert; lecturer in Philosophy; Professor of Philosophy of Religion, King's College, London; later Dean of St Paul's.

13 Moberly, W. H.; this name was absent from the original list but was included in the published letter; contributor to *Foundations.*

14 Mozley, John Kenneth; later canon of St Paul's; contributor to *Essays Catholic and Critical.*

15 Quick, Oliver Chase; canon of Newcastle; later Regius Professor of Divinity at Oxford.

16 Rawlinson, Alfred Edward John; student and tutor at Christ Church, Oxford; later Bishop of Derby; contributor to *Foundations*; *Essays Catholic and Critical.*
17 Selwyn, Edward Gordon; rector of Redhill, Havant; later Dean of Winchester; editor, *Essays Catholic and Critical*; editor, *Theology.*
18 Shebbeare, C. J.; rector of Stanhope; introduced Karl Barth to the British reading public.
19 Spens, Will; later Master of Corpus Christi College, Cambridge; contributor to *Essays Catholic and Critical.*
20 Storr, Vernon; canon of Westminster; author of *Liberal Evangelicalism.*
21 Streeter, Burnett Hillman; later canon of Hereford; editor, *Foundations*; supporter of the Modern Churchmen's Union.
22 Taylor, Alfred Edward; Professor of Moral Philosophy at St Andrews; contributor to *Essays Catholic and Critical.*
23 Thornton, Lionel, C.R.; contributor to *Essays Catholic and Critical.*
24 Webb, Clement C. J.; Oriel Professor of the Philosophy of the Christian Religion at Oxford.
25 Wilson, Henry Albert; rector of Cheltenham; later Bishop of Chelmsford.

88 THE ORTHODOX CHURCHES AND ANGLICAN ORDERS, 1922

(Bell, *Documents on Christian Unity* 1, pp. 94-7)

Conversations between the Orthodox and Anglican Churches were held in 1874–5. In 1897 the Lambeth Conference sent Bishop Wordsworth to deliver the resolutions on Christian Unity to the Orthodox Patriarchs. In 1919 Davidson appointed an Eastern Churches Committee under Charles Gore, and a delegation from Constantinople conferred with this committee. One of the Eastern delegates, Professor Kommenos of Halki, made a careful study of Anglican orders, publishing his conclusions in the first volume of his *Contribution towards Reunion.*[1] The Patriarch of Constantinople informed the Archbishop that the Holy Synod had accepted the validity of Anglican orders, and in the following year the same decision was made by the synods of Jerusalem and Cyprus. Davidson judiciously took note of the communication insisting that it was an acknowledgment of what Anglicans had always known to be true.

FROM THE OECUMENICAL PATRIARCH TO THE PRESIDENTS OF THE PARTICULAR EASTERN ORTHODOX CHURCHES.

The Most Holy Church of Constantinople, kindled from the beginning with zeal for universal union, and always keeping in mind the Lord's words prayed by Him to his heavenly Father just before His Saving Passion, has always followed with keen interest every movement in the separated Churches, and has examined with care and study their every and any expression of faith which might point towards a *rapprochment* with Orthodoxy. Further, it has concluded with real joy that amongst them the Church, which has manifested the most lively desire to remove the obstacles towards a *rapprochment*, and, indeed, to full union with the Orthodox Church, is the Episcopal Anglican Church, which herself, having first received the light of Christianity from the East, has never ceased to remember the East, and to account as an important end a sincere *rapprochment* towards a full union in Christ Jesus with the Orthodox in the East.[2]

Therefore the great Church of Christ (now) under our presidency, necessarily honouring the readiness of this Church in former periods, and especially in the last twenty years, entered into many sincere brotherly relations with it, and recently established a special committee, with instructions to report upon the still existing points of difference on the basis of a scientific inquiry, and on the method of their removal, with a view to accomplishing a full union of the two Churches in the same Orthodox Christian spirit.

Perceiving in its labour that on an important question—namely, the validity of Anglican ordinations—the Holy Orthodox Church had not yet officially delivered any opinion either as a whole or through any of the particular Holy Synods, although there have been many discussions on the matter from time to time among her theologians, and that an authoritative investigation and canonical solution of this important question would greatly facilitate the desired union by removing one of the more serious obstacles that oppose the goal of reunion which is sought on either side, and is dear to God, the Committee brought under the judgement of our Holy Synod a special report scientifically treating the above-named question. Our Holy Synod studied this report of the Committee in repeated sessions, and took note:

1 That the ordination of Matthew Parker as Archbishop of Canterbury by four bishops is a fact established by history.

2 That in this ordination and those subsequent to it there are

found in their fullness those orthodox and indispensable visible and sensible elements of valid episcopal ordination—namely, the laying on of hands and the *Epiklesis* of the All-Holy Spirit, and also the purpose to transmit the *charisma* of the Episcopal ministry.

3 That the Orthodox theologians who have scientifically examined the question have almost unanimously come to the same conclusions, and have declared themselves as accepting the validity of Anglican ordinations.

4 That the practice in the Church affords no indication that the Orthodox Church has ever officially treated the validity of Anglican Orders as in doubt in such a way as would point to the reordination of the Anglican clergy being regarded as required in the case of the union of the two Churches.

5 That expressing this general mind of the Orthodox Church the Most Holy Patriarchs at different periods and other Hierarchs of the East, when writing to the Archbishops of the Anglican Church, have been used to address them as "Most Reverend Brother in Christ", this giving them a brotherly salutation.

Our Holy Synod, therefore, came to an opinion accepting the validity of the Anglican priesthood, and has determined that its conclusion should be announced to the other Holy Orthodox Churches, in order that opportunity might be given them also to express their opinion, so that through the decisions of the parts the mind of the whole Orthodox world on this important question might be known.[3]

Accordingly, writing to your well-beloved (Beatitude) and informing you of the considerations which, in this question, prevail with us, we have no doubt that your (Beatitude) also investigating this question with your Holy Synod, will be pleased to communicate the result of your consideration to us, with a view to a further improvement of our relations in regard to union with the Anglican Church, in the good hope that the Heavenly Ruler of the Church will supply that which is lacking through His all-strengthening grace, and will guide all who believe in Him to a full knowledge of the truth and to full union, that there may be formed of them one flock under a Chief Shepherd—the true Shepherd of the sheep, our Lord Jesus Christ, to whom be the glory for ever. Amen.[4]

1 Archbishop Benson, being asked by the Metropolitan of Kiev to state the conditions for unity between the two Churches sent him

four books: Stubbs, *Episcopal Succession in England*; Courayer, *Validity of English Orders*; Haddan, *Apostolic Succession*; and Bailey, *Ordinationum Ecclesiae Anglicanae Defensio*.

2 The origins of the Romano–British Church must necessarily remain obscure, but the evidence suggests that the Celtic Church originated with Christians in Gaul and Ireland who had connections with the East rather than with Rome.

3 The Churches of Constantinople, Jerusalem, and Cyprus concluded that Anglican Orders had the same validity as those of the Roman Catholic, Old Catholic, and Armenian Churches. The Church of Alexandria followed suit in 1930, and the Rumanian Church in 1935.

4 The Anglican and Eastern Orthodox Churches Union was founded in 1906 to promote the work of reunion between the two Churches. The Fellowship of St Alban and St Sergius was founded in 1928 to promote understanding between the two, receiving its impetus from the Russian exiles in Paris and London.

89 MALINES, 1923

The Malines conversations were revived by the impetus given by the Lambeth Appeal. The first meeting was in December 1921 and included Lord Halifax, Armitage Robinson,[1] Walter Frere,[2] Cardinal Mercier, Mgr van Roey, and Portal among the participants. In November 1922 Pius XI authorized Cardinal Gasparri to inform Mercier that "the Holy See approves and encourages such conversations, and prays God with all its heart to bless them". A second meeting in March 1923 discussed practical measures for regulating the position of the Church of England within the Roman Communion. A third meeting included Gore, Kidd,[3] Batiffol, and Hemmer, and on Davidson's suggestion discussed the position of Peter in relation to the other apostles and the position of the Pope in relation to the episcopate.

(Bell, *Davidson*, pp. 1262-4)

THE FRENCH STATEMENT, MARCH 1923.

Cette fois, la question examinée par nous revient à ces termes: Suppose que l'assentiment des esprits soit accompli sur le terrain doctrinal, dans quelles conditions pourrait s'opérer l'union de l'Église Anglicane à l'Église Romaine?

La préoccupation dominante de l'Église Anglicane est de garder, dans la mesure du possible, son organisation et sa hiérarchie actuelles, son rite, sa discipline.

Puisqu'il s'agit non d'un retour de personnalités isolées a l'Église de Rome, mais d'un retour collectif, cette préoccupation est tout naturelle.

Il est naturel que l'Archevêque de Cantorbéry, considéré par les évêques, par le clergé, par les fidèles de l'Église Anglicane, comme leur chef, soit considéré aussi comme devant continuer à leur égard l'exercice de son autorité.

Moyennant cet exercice, les rites et la discipline seraient suffisamment maintenus. L'entrée en masse dans le giron de l'Église Romaine serait ainsi facilitée. Certaines mesures, d'ailleurs, pourraient avoir un caractère temporaire.

Alors, la question fondamentale qui se pose paraît être la suivante:

Le Saint-Siège approuverait—il que l'Archevêque de Cantorbéry, acceptant la suprématie spirituelle du Souverain Pontife et le cérémonial jugé par lui nécessaire à la validité de la consécration de l'Archevêque, fût reconnu comme le Primat de l'Église Anglicane rattachée à Rome?

Le Saint-Siège consentirait-il à accorder à l'Archevêque de Cantorbéry et aux autres métropolitains le pallium comme symbole de leur juridiction sur leurs provinces respectives?

Permettrait-il à l'Archevêque de Cantorbéry d'appliquer aux autres évêques Anglicans le ceremonial de validation accepté par l'Archevêque?

Permettrait-il enfin à chaque Métropolitain de confirmer et de consacrer à l'avenir les évêques de sa province?

Tante que cette question primordiale n'aura pas été résolue, il nous serait malaisé de poursuivre nos négociations. Si elle était résolue affirmativement, la voie serait aplanie qui pourrait nous conduire a l'examen de questions ultérieures d'application.

We accept the above for submission to the respective authorities.[4]

HALIFAX	+D. -J. CARD. MERCIER
J. ARMITAGE ROBINSON	E. VAN ROEY, vic. gen.
WALTER HOWARD FRERE, C.R.	F. PORTAL. p.d.l.M.

(Bell, *Davidson*, pp. 1263-4)

THE ENGLISH STATEMENT, MARCH 1923

The Anglican representatives being in hearty agreement with the statement drawn up by His Eminence desire on their part to sum up the position in the following terms.

As a result of the recent conversations at Malines it was agreed by those who were present that, supposing the doctrinal differences now existing between the two Churches could be satisfactorily explained or removed, and further supposing the difficulty regarding Anglican Orders were surmounted on the lines indicated in the Lambeth Appeal, then the following suggestions would form a basis of practical action for the reunion of the two Churches.

1 The acknowledgement of the position of the Papal See as the centre and head on earth of the Catholic Church, from which guidance should be looked for, in general, and especially in grave matters affecting the welfare of the Church as a whole.[5]

2 The acknowledgement of the Anglican Communion as a body linked with the Papal See in virtue of the recognition of the jurisdiction of the Archbishop of Canterbury and other Metropolitans by the gift of the Pallium.[6]

3 Under the discipline of the English Church would fall the determination of all such questions as:
The English rite and its use in the vernacular,
Communion in both kinds,
Marriage of the clergy.

4 The position of the existing Roman Catholic Hierarchy in England with their Churches and congregations would, for the present, at any rate, remain unaltered. They would be exempt from the jurisdiction of Canterbury, and, as at present, directly depend on the Holy See.

Accepté pour être soumis aux autorités respectives[7]

+D. -J. CARD. MERCIER
Arch. de Malines
E. VAN ROEY, vic. gén.
F. PORTAL, p.d.l.M.

HALIFAX
J. ARMITAGE ROBINSON
WALTER HOWARD FRERE, C.R.

(Bell, *Davidson*, pp. 1268-73)

MERCIER TO DAVIDSON, 11 APRIL 1923

Your kind letter of 24th March has reached me safely, but a ten days' absence from Malines has prevented me from replying to it immediately.[8]

Please accept my thanks for it and find herewith the reflections which it has suggested to me.

It is very gratifying to me to learn that the Archbishop of York and yourself have taken note of the memoranda which your three delegates have brought back from Malines; that you have both given them a sympathetic reception; and that you both wish for the continuation of the conferences inaugurated at Malines.

Since the first conference, in December 1921, it has seemed to us that we ought at once to concentrate our attention on the fundamental question of the primacy of the Roman Pontiff.

Lord Halifax, who suggested to me this meeting at Malines, and his two companions, were in agreement with my Vicar-General, with the Abbé Portal, and with myself on this point.

But then, when, this year, there came to us, from Dean Robinson and his two colleagues, the memorandum for discussion in the course of our second conference, I was surprised to see that the projected conversation deviated from the original doctrinal point of view, and invited us to consider questions of a rather more practical and "administrative" kind.

Since our sole desire was to comply with the appeal of the loyal and generous souls who had of their own accord come to meet us, we felt that we ought, without making any objections, to agree to the proposition which was put before us. Also, these administrative questions, perhaps of secondary importance, ought none the less, sooner or later, to be submitted to the examination of the authorities and, in addition, the memorandum of the Dean of Wells contained the formal declaration that the solutions which should be given now to these disciplinary questions, would not be put into practice until the day when agreement should be reached in the realm of doctrine.[9]

That is to say, my dear Lord, that I share your opinion and that of the Archbishop of York, when you shew yourselves anxious to bring back the conversation to what we call with you "the large doctrinal matters which underlie the whole".

I believe, nevertheless, that I am voicing the deep desire of all the members of the Conference in expressing to you here a wish:

Since, as a matter of fact, "administrative" questions have formed, at the request of your delegates, the object of our second conference, and the two groups face to face have pledged in the examination of these questions their responsibility at the same time personal and collective, would you not feel yourself able to let us know your opinion and that of your colleague of York on the conclusions to which our conference has come, and which are to be found recorded in the report of the meeting, and in the two memoranda which your delegates have had the honour of placing in your hands?

You will agree, in fact, my dear Lord, that if we were able to reciprocate to the two Archbishops of Canterbury and York the compliment which they have had the kindness to address to us with gratitude "for the clearness with which we have set forth the position taken by ourself and by those with whom we act" the two groups engaged in the conference would take up their task again with more assurance and on firmer ground.

Having said that, in all frankness and in the interest of the cause in which we are collaborating, I come readily to the "fundamental" question of the position accorded to the Sovereign Pontiff in the Roman Catholic Church.

The logical train of our conferences, as well as the mutual duties of loyalty on the part of the members who meet there, oblige us to take up again this examination of the primacy of the Bishop of Rome, successor of Peter, defined as a dogma of the catholic faith by the Vatican Council.

Our third conference, which like you I hope may be soon and, to a certain extent, enlarged, will assume then the task of studying this doctrine more thoroughly, and will apply itself, in accordance with your desire, to making more precise its significance.

Meanwhile, I make it my personal duty to tell you what I believe to be the Roman Catholic doctrine on the special point about which you wish to question me.

You ask me if the Primacy accorded to the Sovereign Pontiff signifies or entails this consequence, that alone, by divine right, the Pope is the Vicar of Christ on earth, in this sense that from him alone derives, directly or indirectly, all legitimate power to exercise validly a ministry in the Church: "If the term 'primacy' is understood as implying that the Pope holds *jure divino* the unique and solemn position of sole Vicar of Christ on earth, from whom as Vicar of Christ must come directly or indirectly the right to administer validly within the Church."

Certainly, the Pontiff of Rome is, in a special sense, the Vicar of Christ on earth, and the piety of the faithful is accustomed to bestow on him this title by choice.[10] But Saint Paul states that all the apostles are the ministers of Christ: *Sic nos existimet homo ut ministros Christi.* The Roman Liturgy, in the Preface to the Mass for Apostles, calls all the apostles the "Vicars" put in charge by the eternal Shepherd of the pastoral direction of his work: *Gregem tuum, pastor aeterne, non deseras, sed per beatos apostolos tuos continua protectione custodias: ut iisdem rectoribus gubernetur, quos operis tui Vicarios eidem contulisti praeesse pastores.* Still more, of the simple priest in the exercise of his ministry, we say readily that he is the representative of Christ, "another Christ", *sacerdos, alter Christus.* If he did not occupy the place of Christ, *vices gerens Christi, Vicarius Christi,* how could he truthfully say of the Body and of the Blood of our Saviour: *Hoc est Corpus meum: hic est calix Sanguinis mei*; how could he, in remitting sins, which God alone can absolve, say: "Ego te absolvo", "*I* absolve thee"?

The ordinary application of the title "Vicar of Christ" to the Sovereign Pontiff does not involve therefore as a consequence, that *alone* the Bishop of Rome possesses powers coming direct from Christ.

The powers of the Bishop refer for one part to the Body, real, historical, of our Lord Jesus Christ—"Power of Order"—for the other part, to his mystical Body—"Power of jurisdiction".

The power of "Order", power of consecrating the Body and Blood of our Saviour in the Holy Eucharist, power of conferring on someone else the fulness of the priesthood, including in that the ability to transmit it with a view to perpetuating the Christian life in the Church, was given by Christ to all his apostles. It belongs fully to the bishops, their successors, inalienably; no human authority whatever could break its validity.

Is it not well known, for example, that the Church of Rome recognises the persisting validity of the Orders and Sacraments in the Eastern Orthodox Church, which, nevertheless, has been separated for a thousand years from the Roman Primacy?

The power of "jurisdiction", power of ruling the Church, the mystical body of Christ, belongs by divine right to the episcopate, that is to say to the bishops, successors of the apostles, in union with the Sovereign Pontiff.

The episcopate, regarded as the whole institution of government, is of divine right and it would not be in the power of the Bishop of Rome to abolish it.

The power of "jurisdiction" devolved upon each bishop is also of divine right; it is ordinary and immediate within the limits of the diocese assigned to the bishop by the Sovereign Pontiff.

The peace and the unity of the Christian Society demand, in fact, that at the head of the government of the Church there should be a supreme authority, itself ordinary and immediate, over the whole Church, over the faithful and their pastors;[11] to this supreme authority belongs the prerogative of assigning to each bishop the portion of the Christian flock which he is called to rule in union with the Pontiff of Rome and under his authority.

The bishop's power of jurisdiction over his flock is of divine right, but when the theologians ask how this divine origin ought to be interpreted, their counsels are divided.

One party holds that this power of jurisdiction comes immediately from God, like the power of "Order". According to this conception, the Pope nominates the bishop, assigns to him his subjects, but the jurisdiction over these subjects comes from God, without human intermediary. This opinion, in the words of Benedict XIV, has on its side solid arguments, *validis fulcitur argumentis.*

But, he adds, to this opinion is opposed another, according to which the jurisdiction comes from Christ, as principal source, but is granted to the bishop through the intermediary of the Roman Pontiff. According to this conception, episcopal consecration gives to the bishop the qualification for jurisdiction, but the actual complete jurisdiction is dependent on the mandate of the Sovereign Pontiff.

This opinion, says Benedict XIV, seems to have on its side better arguments of reason and authority: *rationi et auctoritati conformior videtur sententia.*[12]

No further decision, which commands universal assent, has settled the controversy.

Neither does the *Codex juris canonici* edited by Pope Benedict XV, the word of which is law in the Catholic Church, settle it. It sums up in these words the general doctrine of the Roman Church concerning the episcopate: *"Episcopi sunt apostolorum successores atque ex divina institutione peculiaribus ecclesiis praeficiuntur quas cum potestate ordinaria regunt sub auctoritate Romani Pontificis".*[13]

This universal authority of the Sovereign Pontiff, say the Fathers of the Vatican Council, ought not to be considered by the bishops as a menace or a danger. It is, on the contrary, for the authority of the bishop over against his flock, a support, a strength, a protection. *"Tantum abest, ut haec Summi Pontificus potestas officiat ordinariae ac immediatae illi episcopalis jurisdictionis potestati, qua Episcopi, qui positi a Spiritu Sancto in Apostolorum locum successerunt, tanquam veri pastores assignatas sibi greges, singuli singulos, pascunt et regunt, ut eadem a supremo et universali Pastore asseratur, roboretur et vindicetur."*[14]

More than once, in the course of my episcopal career, my experience has confirmed the truth of this conciliar declaration.

But this is not the time for me to enlarge on this subject. I must confine myself to replying briefly to the question about which your valued letter has engaged for the moment my attention. The conference which we shall, shortly, please God, have occasion to resume, will have to examine more closely the question which surpasses all the others in importance both christian and social, of the Primacy of the Pope.

I hope that you will not think it unfitting that in bringing to a close these lines, I should express to you the feeling which is prompted in my heart by my love for our Saviour Jesus Christ, my love for His Church: We are engaged in collaborating for the re-establishment of peace in the world by the drawing together of the souls baptized in the same sheep-fold, under the crook of the same shepherd, *ut fiat unum ovile et unus pastor!* Let us pray with all our heart unceasingly for one another for the realization of this great ideal of unity for which Christ prayed and suffered and gave His life. Let us quicken ourselves with Christian power and with the spirit of charity, in order that among us all may be fulfilled the prayer of our holy Liturgy: *Ut et ea quae agenda sunt videant et ad agenda quae viderint, convalescant.*

Please accept, my dear Lord, and convey to your revered colleague, the Archbishop of York, the assurances of my respectful esteem and of my religious zeal.

P.S. Allow me to make you a present of a Pastoral letter relating to the Encyclical *Ubi Arcano Dei* of His Holiness Pope Pius XI, and an attempted translation of this weighty document.

(Bell, *Davidson*, pp. 1273-6)

DAVIDSON TO MERCIER, 15 MAY 1923

I owe apologies to Your Eminence for delay in replying further to your very important letter, dated 11th April, for which I briefly thanked you on April 13th. During these weeks my work has been even exceptionally onerous, and it has been difficult to find time for other than urgent correspondence.

I have now considered with great care all that Your Eminence was good enough to write in the letter of 11th April, and I have had opportunity also of taking counsel with the Archbishop of York, as well as with the Dean of Wells.

In the light of your letter and of these conversations, I desire to assure Your Eminence that we perfectly understand how it was that in the two Conferences at Malines the course of proceeding was followed which you have described to me. After recounting the order of proceeding, Your Eminence asks "Ne jugeriez-vous pas pouvoir nous faire connaître votre appréciation et celle de votre collègue de York sur les conclusions auxquelles notre conférence a abouti et qui se trouve consignées dans le procès-verbal de la réunion et dans les deux memorandums que vos délégués ont eu l'honneur de déposer en vos mains?" The difficulty we find in expressing an opinion about these conclusions is this:

The administrative suggestions are not only hypothetical in themselves (depending as they do on the condition that some measure of general agreement should first have been reached upon the large doctrinal question we have referred to), but the actual suggestions as they stand can only be interpreted aright if we know what the words imply; and this knowledge we cannot have until the preliminary discussions have resulted in some positive statement. To take an example of what I mean, an example which I select because it is obvious and simple, I find in the Memorandum drawn up by the Roman Catholic Members of the Conference the following suggestion for consideration:

> Le Saint Siège consentirait-il à accorder à l'Archevêque de Cantorbéry et aux autres Métropolitains le pallium comme symbole de leur juridiction sur leurs provinces respectives?

It is impossible to express an opinion upon this suggestion without a clear knowledge of what is meant or implied by the giving of the pallium. I should feel it to be impossible to express even provisional assent to such a suggestion until it has been made clear:

(i) Whether the Act of the Holy See in giving the pallium as a symbol of jurisdiction did or did not imply that the recipient was recognized as being already the holder of Valid Orders, and,

(ii) Whether the Act of the Archbishop in receiving the pallium did or did not imply an acceptance of the doctrine that his jurisdiction must, if it is to be valid, be conferred by the Pope.[15] It is of course obvious that these questions would require careful discussion, involving the consideration of large problems, both doctrinal and historical. In this connection, I note with the utmost interest the opinion expressed by Your Eminence:

La conférence que nous aurons, s'il plaît à Dieu, bientôt, l'occasion de reprendre, aura à examiner de plus près la question, qui prime toutes les autres en importance chrétienne et sociale, de la Primauté du Pape.

Your Eminence has been good enough to set out with admirable clearness in the same letter the distinction which must be borne in mind between Questions of Order and Questions of Jurisdiction. And I have purposely taken as an example of my difficulty one question only, a question belonging to the subject of jurisdiction. There are of course very many other large and far-reaching problems belonging to every branch of the subject, and it would, I hope, be possible to deal with some of these when the Conferences are resumed.

My point today is simply to make clear to Your Eminence why it is that I cannot at present meet the desire which you express when you say "Ne jugeriez-vous pas pouvoir nous faire connaître votre appréciation ... sur les conclusions, etc."[16]

It has probably been an excellent thing to set forth examples in the form of suggestions, as to some of the practical and administrative details which might hereafter emerge if the greater matters had received solution, and I find no difficulty in saying that if upon the large preliminary questions both of Order and Jurisdiction a really satisfactory agreement had been reached, the actual process of outward arrangement suggested in the signed paper might well form the subject of friendly and hopeful consideration. To make such a statement, however, at this juncture, would seem to me to have little significance while the underlying questions of a fundamental character remain quite unsolved. Your Eminence has explained to me that on some of those great questions there are different, and it would seem rival, theories of interpretation which have a place, more or less authoritative, within the Church of Rome, and, if the discussions go forward, as I hope they may, in further Conferences, it would be of supreme interest to us to understand whether both sets of opinion are now permissible among you and may be taught without breach of loyalty. But all this lies in the future, and I am not asking Your Eminence for an answer to such enquiry. I thank Your Eminence for the generous readiness with which you have been willing, notwithstanding the responsibilities of your great office, to write and speak with so much freedom upon the solemn and difficult points of controversy which have emerged during the discussions. My sole desire at this moment is to make it clear that there must be further discussion upon the great question underlying the series of suggestions formulated at Malines, and that until preliminary elucidation has been given to it I am not in a position to say more than I have said.

In again thanking Your Eminence for your unwearied kindness in this grave matter, I desire to express my concurrence in what you have said as to the advantage of some addition, when the Conference is resumed, to the number of those who take part in it. I should like to invite Bishop Gore[17] or another of our leading theologians to associate himself with the Dean of Wells and with Dr Frere, and I hope I am not mistaken in thinking that this would be welcomed by Your Eminence.

It is, I think, obvious that no advantage would arise from our making public at present anything which has passed in the conversations at Malines. Such partial and fragmentary statements as would alone be possible, would, I think, inevitably lead to misunderstanding. If I find it to be desirable to make a brief reference in general terms to the fact of our having taken advantage of your gracious invitation to Malines, I would venture to submit beforehand to Your Eminence a copy of anything which I propose to say.[18]

1 Robinson, Joseph Armitage; *b.* 1858; *educ.*, Liverpool; Christ's College, Cambridge; ordained, 1881; Fellow of Christ's, 1881; domestic chaplain to J. B. Lightfoot, 1883; curate of St Mary the Great, 1885; vicar of All Saints, 1888; Norris-Hulse Professor of Divinity at Cambridge, 1893; prebend of Wells, 1894; rector of St Margaret's and canon of Westminster, 1899; Dean of Westminster, 1902; Dean of Wells, 1911; resigned, 1933; *d.* 1933.

2 Frere, Walter Howard; *b.* 1863; *educ.*, Charterhouse and Trinity College, Cambridge; Wells theological college; ordained 1887; curate of St Dunstan, Stepney; joined the Community of the Resurrection, Mirfield, 1892; Superior, 1902–13, 1916–22; Bishop of Truro, 1923; resigned, 1935; *d.* 1938.

3 Kidd, Beresford James; *b.* 1864; *educ.*, Christ's Hospital and Keble College, Oxford; ordained, 1887; curate of St Philip and St James, Oxford, 1887; chaplain of Pembroke College, Oxford, 1894; vicar of St Paul, Oxford, 1904; Warden of Keble College, 1920; Prolocutor of Canterbury Convocation, 1932; *d.* 1948.

4 The conversations were in no way official though they were recognized by the authorities on either side. The weaknesses of the conversations were that the Anglican party was not truly representative of the Church of England, and that the English Roman Catholic Church did not participate.

5 The decree on Papal Infallibility (1870) maintained: "That the Roman Pontiff, when he speaks *ex cathedra* (that is, when—

fulfilling the office of Pastor and Teacher of all Christians—on his supreme Apostolical authority, he defines a doctrine concerning faith or morals to be held by the Universal Church), through the divine assistance promised in blessed Peter, is endowed with that infallibility, with which the Divine Redeemer has willed that His Church—in defining doctrine concerning faith or morals—should be equipped." See: Bettenson, *Documents of the Christian Church*, p. 382.

6 Originally the pallium had no connection with the See of Rome, but after the ninth century metropolitans were required to petition for it. The granting of the pallium to archbishops in the Roman Catholic Church symbolizes participation in the authority of the Pope, and their jurisdiction may not be exercised until the petition has been made and granted.

7 In the original text of the French statement these words were in the handwriting of Viscount Halifax. In the original of the English statement, the handwriting was that of Cardinal Mercier.

8 In his letter of 24 March, Davidson had written: "I do not doubt that Your Eminence will agree with me in thinking that, after all, the really fundamental question of the position of the Sovereign Pontiff of the Roman Catholic Church must be candidly faced before further progress can be made" (Bell, *Davidson*, pp. 1267-8).

9 It is interesting to note that the Church of England itself was seeking an agreed doctrinal basis in the setting up of the doctrinal commission, and the Roman Church had not yet recovered from the influence of Modernism which was associated with Loisy and other French theologians.

10 Prior to the tenth century it was not uncommon to find bishops using the title "Vicar of Christ" of themselves. The title was assumed by the Pope in the eighth century and it later superseded the more ancient title of "Vicar of St Peter".

11 "Si quis dixerit Romanum Pontificem ... non habere plenam et supremam potestatem jurisdictionis in universam Ecclesiam ... aut hanc ejus postestatem non esse ordinariam et immediatam sive in omnes ac singulas ecclesias, sive in omnes et singulos pastores et fideles, anathema sit" (*Conc. Vat.*, Sess. IV, Cap. III).

12 *De Synodo diocesana*, Lib. I, Cap. IV, n. 2.

13 *Titul. VIII*, Cap. I, de Episcopis, Can. 329.

14 *Conc. Vat.*, Sess. III, Cap. III.

15 The standpoint of the *Articles* is expressed in XXXVII, and, in spite of the changed historical circumstances, it found full support amongst many of the clergy and laity still. Davidson noted in a memorandum: "... it ought to be made clear on the Anglican side, beyond possibility of doubt, that the great principles upon which the Reformation turned are our principles still, whatever

faults or failures there may have been on either side in the controversies of the sixteenth century." Bell, *Davidson*, p. 1279.

16 Davidson was anxious that the conversations did not receive premature publicity, the Prayer Book controversy and the Anglo-Catholic Congress both making a general discussion inopportune.

17 Gore had written *Roman Catholic Claims*, an Anglo-Catholic answer to a book by a seceded Anglican named Rivington, whilst at Pusey House. Gore's own views were discussed by Dom John Chapman in his book, *Bishop Gore and the Catholic Claims* (1905). Gore had doubts as to accepting the Archbishop's invitation since he felt that the "concessiveness of our delegation to Malines, apparently at the first conference and certainly at the second, seems to be more disastrous and perilous the more I think of it".

18 Mercier had spoken of "la grande reserve des deux archvêques de Cantorbéry et d'York" after the first conversation, and with the death of Mercier and Portal in 1926 there was insufficient impetus on either side for the meetings to continue.

90 C.O.P.E.C., 1924

(*Proceedings of C.O.P.E.C.*)

William Temple believed that the Conference on Politics, Economics, and Citizenship was the outcome of an S.C.M. conference at Matlock in 1909. The Matlock conference had discussed "Christianity and Social Problems", and had reached three unanimous conclusions: that churchmen were generally ignorant of the elements of social problems; that education must precede conviction; and that some organization was necessary to prepare books for social studies. The idea of the Birmingham conference was first mooted when Temple was canon of Westminster and was supported at an International Conference of Social Service Unions. Four years were allowed for study; twelve interdenominational commissions were appointed; and reports were produced by these commissions.

The following members were appointed to act as a Reference Committee for the Conference: Rt Rev. Bishop Hamilton Baynes, Rev. Henry Carter, Rev. T. E. Clarke, Rev. Gwilym Davies, Miss Gardner,[1] Rev. Dr A. E. Garvie, Rev. Dr A. H. Gray, Mr Fred Hughes, Rt Rev. the Lord Bishop of Lichfield,[2] Rev. Professor Lofthouse, Ven. Archdeacon Macmillan, Rt Rev. the Lord Bishop of Manchester, Rev. Hugh Martin, Rev. A. S. Mellor, Rev. Dr Harry Miller, Mrs George Morgan, Rev. Canon Newsom, Mr A. R.

Pelly, Mr George Peverett, Rev. Dr C. E. Raven,[3] Rev. Will. Reason, Rev. J. L. Roberts, Rev. Dr Ivor Robertson, Miss H. A. Spence, Rev. Malcolm Spencer, Rev. E. B. Storr, Rev. Dr David Watson, Mr H. G. Wood,[4] and Rev. Canon E. S. Woods.[5]

The Rt Rev. the Bishop of Manchester gave his address as Chairman of the Conference.

Three features seem to give our gathering its peculiar significance. These are: 1. the scope of the Conference; 2. its representative character; 3. its spiritual basis and aim.

1. *The Scope of the Conference* Many Conferences have been held on the various subjects we are to consider, but those subjects have been usually considered in separation from each other. That makes possible a thoroughness of discussion which is impossible here; but it also involves a real falsification of the issues. Human life is too completely one for consideration of any one aspect in isolation to be really satisfactory. Attention has often been concentrated, for example, on the problems of industry; but the reforms advocated are often dependent for feasibility on parallel reforms in education and international relations, as well as in many other departments of life. There was a clear need, therefore, for such a survey of the whole field as is attempted in this Conference and in the Reports presented to it. But we must also mark the limitations of such an enterprise. Our discussions cannot be detailed, and unless there is almost universal agreement among us, we cannot usefully pledge ourselves to resolutions which can only carry weight if they rest on such detailed discussion. On the other hand, an abundance of detailed inquiry and discussion lies behind the Reports of our Commissions, so that when we are at all generally agreed in support of their recommendations, we can say so with a clear conscience and with genuine determination to act on what we say.

2. *The Representative Character of the Conference* A main feature of this Conference is that all kinds of Christian people have united in the preparation for it. That is not new in itself, but it is the biggest manifestation of such unity hitherto. In the years just before the war Christians of all denominations were coming increasingly together, and in 1910 the Interdenominational Conference of Social Service Unions was founded under the presidency of the then Bishop of Birmingham, Dr Gore. It was at a meeting of that Interdenominational Conference held shortly after Peace had been declared that the project of this Conference was launched.

A little later the issue by the Anglican Bishops of the Lambeth Appeal gave a great impetus to the cause of Christian unity. Our gathering here is not an effort to unite Christian people in social witness so much as an expression and result of their growing sense of unity.

It is a matter of profound regret to all of us that the Roman Catholic Church has felt unable to be in any way officially represented here. I wish to express our warm thanks to those members of that great Church who have helped us in the work of the Commissions, both for the valuable aid which they brought and for the cordiality of their co-operation; and we are glad to have with us some who are attending the Conference not as representatives but as individuals.

But this Conference is also, as I have said, representative of a great movement within the Church which is, I am convinced, a movement of the Holy Ghost. Christians had, with few exceptions, lost the vision of the Kingdom of God as claiming the allegiance of all nations and authority over all departments of life. In the middle of the nineteenth century the reassertion of that claim was vigorously made, and has been more and more widely proclaimed ever since. In many utterances of high authority it has been pressed upon the conscience of the Church. I will mention only three: the noble encyclical of Pope Leo XIII;[6] the Report of the Archbishops' Fifth Committee of Inquiry entitled "Christianity and Industrial Problems"; and the Report of the American Interdenominational Committee, "Christianity and Industrial Reconstruction". Moreover, our Conference is itself the British preparation for the Universal Conference on the Life and Work of the Church. With the steadily growing sense that Machiavellian statecraft is bankrupt there is an increasing readiness to give heed to the claim of Jesus Christ that He is the Way, the Truth and the Life. We represent here today the convergence of a spiritual movement in the Church prompted by loyalty and hope, and a spiritual movement in the world prompted by disillusion and despair. Our opportunity is overwhelmingly great; so also is our responsibility.

3. *The Spiritual Basis and Aim of the Conference* Just because the opportunity and responsibility are so great we are thrown back upon God Himself. What is it that we have, above all else, to do? The main thing is that we ourselves should be led to a real repentance—that is, a change of outlook such that we cease to look at life as men tend to look at it, and learn to look at it as God sees it. It is not enough to hail Jesus as our King, as

St Peter did at Caesarea Philippi, if we go on, as he did, to rebel against the principle of His Kingship. Very apposite to many of our schemes for the Kingdom are the words of that terrible rebuke, "Get thee behind me, Satan, for thou thinkest not God's thoughts but men's thoughts". True repentance is precisely that we think not men's thoughts but God's thoughts. If, by the power of the Holy Ghost upon us, amongst us, and within us, we are brought to such a repentance, we shall scatter over the country when the week ends with a revitalized Gospel—the same Gospel, come to new life in us and for us; and in regional conferences and local conferences we shall help others to find what we have found here.

Our aim then is not to join in debate or listen to debate. Our aim is to hear God speak. We know that a great deal in our life is defiant of His Will. We bear on our hearts the burden of unemployment,[7] and in our consciences the challenge which tells us that where such things happen God's Kingdom is not yet come on earth as it is in heaven. We cannot forget the anxiety about international peace or the misery of multitudes in consequence of the war and its results. We remember those who have fallen into crime or are victims of lust, and we know that we have some share of the guilt of their degradation. All these things will be the theme of our discussion; we shall be facing realities and in no way seeking an escape in religion from the ugly facts of life. We are here at all only because these facts are a declaration that our life is based on unchristian principles. But our aim in relation to all these things is, through the contributions of various speakers and perhaps through the very clash of their opinions, to hear God speak. In this effort all must help. Those who speak will speak as in God's presence; those who listen will listen in dependence on God.

There is no limit to what God may do through us this week and in all that follows from it. But whatever is done must be done by Him. Our aim is that, in famous words, we may "be to the Eternal Goodness what a man's hand is to a man". Our task is beyond man's strength, but with God all things are possible. Let us stand in silence.

(Report: *The Social Function of the Church*, pp. 52-3)

Recommendations We may now attempt the difficult task of

briefly stating some principles of guidance on this difficult question. Let us again make it clear that we are alluding not to independent action on the part of individual Christians or groups of Christians, but to official action taken by the Church corporately or through its accredited leaders. In speaking of "The Church" we include corporate action taken not only by the denominations acting together (as in the Temperance Council), but by any given denomination.

1. The primary business of the Church is to inspire, to supply the highest motive power, to take care that God is not forgotten, especially not forgotten by those who ought as Christians to judge all things in the Christian light, and to allow no field of collective action whatsoever to be excluded from the rule of Christian principles.

2. The Church is sometimes justified in pronouncing judgment on questions of acute controversy, e.g. industrial disputes. But it is necessary that the facts should be clear and the moral issue unmistakable.

3. A Christian preacher, as representing the Church and not himself only, will hesitate to express judgment from his point of vantage in the pulpit on matters where good men may legitimately hold different opinions. If he does give such judgments, he should make it clear that he speaks only upon his own authority and should provide subsequent opportunity for question and discussion.

4. It is, however, the duty of the Church to narrow the scope of these exceptions more and more by assisting its members and ministers to know far more of the facts of social life and of the underlying relations and maladjustments from which disputes and troubles spring, and far more of the judgments which instructed Christian consciences are reaching with regard to them.

5. We need hardly add that it is a grievous thing for any denomination to use political weapons more readily when its own institutional rights and wrongs are concerned than where the rights and wrongs at stake are those of the poor and oppressed.

6. Where Christians differ and there is no indisputably Christian conclusion as to the Christian course in a political issue, it may often be the duty of the Church to bring the representatives of opposing views together, to see if their differences cannot be removed by mutual exchange of knowledge and opinion in an atmosphere of Christian trust and sympathy.

7. Christian people should be a united force in the endeavour to carry as much as possible of the spirit of Christ into the methods of political action and government (both central and local).

8. The most powerful impact which the Church can make on politics and industry is by the strong and unmistakable witness of its own Christ-ordered life corporately and among its members. The ideal is that the Church should be as soul to the nation.

(Report: *Industry and Property*, pp. 153-7)

In the discussions and often the controversies of the present day individual and collective ownership are frequently put into mutual opposition. According to the point of view, one is considered to be a good thing in itself and the other bad. There is, however, no ground in the nature of things for this, and the exaltation of either into a fetish merely obscures the true issues and delays a helpful solution of the troubles which are so pressing today.[8]

As a matter of fact, both exist in our own civilization and both have existed together as far back as can be traced. It is true that, as has been said, the development both of what we call individual personality and of individual property belongs to the development of civilization, and it is also true that the whole worth of life is found in personality. But it must be observed that while personality is centred in individuals, it is insuperably associated with the development of social life and all the associations and intercourse which flow from it. It is from the enhanced social life which civilization brings, with its new groupings which always replace the old, that the richness of personality is derived. In it especially the moral and spiritual life finds both its conditions and its fulfilment. Apart from the society of which he is a member the individual is a poor and powerless person.

Responsibility is the characteristic of the moral personality, and in practice this must be both individual and collective. For there are some duties which cannot be performed by the community for the individual and some that can only be discharged corporately. In so far as property is concerned, these responsibilities are inseparable from ownership in some form, and therefore we find that, despite exclusive theories, individuals, corporate associations, villages, townships, counties and the nation itself hold their appropriate properties and are compelled to do so for the due fulfilment of their functions.

Nor are the two exclusive of each other so that they merely exist side by side. The community is compelled to delegate the active functions of ownership to certain individuals, and, as has been seen in Section A, all individual rights depend ultimately on the sanction of the community, which prescribes, conditions, limits and enforces those rights. Further, the values of different kinds of property are derived from both individual and social activities.

It seems quite possible, therefore, for the community and the individual to be in partnership rather than in opposition, even as concerns ownership of the same things. For there are different functions of ownership and different degrees, not merely in theory but in actual practice. There are rights of use without rights of sale or other disposition; rights to receive portions of the produce without the right to control the working; rights for a fixed term or for natural life or with power to hand on to someone else; rights vested in a single individual and rights exercised and enjoyed in common with others.

It is forgetfulness of this which seems to lead to considerable confusion of thought. Criticism of method of administration is supposed to be valid criticism of ownership itself, as when the national ownership of some monopoly is identified with centralized administration from an office in Whitehall which had its origin in quite other needs. There is really no reason why a great industry should not be given self-control, with responsibility to citizen owners instead of to shareholders, if that were found on sufficient grounds to be desirable. On the other hand, criticism of private ownership of business which are practically monopolies does not necessarily mean an objection to the personal enterprise which makes experiments and justifies its handling of the property concerned by the public service rendered.

If, as is maintained by many, the development of personality is bound up with personal ownership of property, the fact already quoted, that according to Inland Revenue experience five-sixths of the people have no more than £100 worth at most, shows convincingly that our modern society, which has made it almost a religion to favour individual ownership against collective, has somehow missed its own way, and the problem is how to make individual "enterprise" a reality for the many instead of for the few. The argument that the high positions of wealth and power are open to all who can take them contains the same fallacy as the saying attributed to Napoleon, that every soldier of his had a possible Field-Marshal's baton in his knapsack. "Anybody" is not the same thing as "everybody".

Since a system so emphatically based upon a theory of individual ownership has left the vast majority without much ownership to speak of, and stress upon individual freedom has resulted in a tremendous regimentation of men and pressure into social strata and industrial types, it is at least worth seriously considering whether there are not collective responsibilities of ownership which are necessary to bring true opportunities of individuation to the majority. At any rate the individual use of the roads is freer because of collective ownership, and is only endangered when the community fails to exercise the control, which is one of the responsibilities of that ownership, upon those individuals who use their superior powers of speed to the hurt of others. It is possible that this is not an extraordinary exception but a typical example.

What appears to be greatly needed is the laying aside of prejudice and the repetition of catch phrases that there may be a clearer recognition of the powers and responsibilities that really belong to individuals, to groups and to the community as a whole, so that the various kinds of ownership rights may be distributed accordingly. The doctrine of stewardship as applied to property, wholly admirable in itself, presupposes for its working out that the right person is acting as steward.[9]

1 Gardner, Lucy; secretary of the Collegium which met in St George's Square as a direct result of the Matlock Conference.

2 Kempthorne, John Augustine; Bishop of Lichfield, 1913–37; later to play a prominent part in the discussions for a settlement of the mining dispute in 1926.

3 Raven, Charles Earle; *b.* 1885; *educ.*, Gonville and Caius College, Cambridge; deacon, 1909; priest, 1910; assistant master, Tonbridge School, 1915; chaplain to the Forces, 1917; Donnellan Lecturer, Trinity College, Dublin, 1919; Dean, Fellow, and lecturer of Emmanuel College, Cambridge, 1909–20; rector of Bletchingley, 1920; Lady Margaret Professor, Cambridge, 1925; Chancellor of Liverpool Cathedral, 1931; canon of Ely, 1932; Regius Professor of Divinity, Cambridge, 1932; Warden of Madingley Hall, 1950–4 *d.* 1965.

4 The development of a theoretical basis of Christian social action was the notable thing in this era, Temple's *Christianity and Social Order* (1942) being the most concise expression of the Church's position.

5 Woods, Edward Sydney; Bishop of Lichfield, 1937–53; associated with the Life and Liberty movement.

6 *Rerum Novarum*, the encyclical issued on 15 May 1891 by Leo XIII on *De Conditione Opificum*.

7 "No Government of the twenties found a way of reducing the figure of the registered unemployed below the one-million mark. Among various reasons for this failure was the reliance of the British economy upon an international trade which had not recovered from its war-time disorganization and which, from the beginning of 1929 until 1934, steadily shrank in amount and in value. This shrinkage was in part due to deliberate policies—to tariffs which obstructed trade, to financial policies which hampered exports. It was, even more, the result of a general *malaise* of the economy of the world" (David Thomson, *England in the Twentieth Century*, p. 130). Temple led a Committee which published, in 1938, a Report entitled *Men Without Work*.

8 Syndicalism had some following in Britain between 1911 and 1914 seeking to secure ownership of industry by workers through "direct action". In the Emergency Powers Act 1920, a royal proclamation could empower the government to make provision for food, water, fuel, light, and means of locomotion, in the event of widespread industrial action.

9 The British political scene did not wholly accept the basic tenets of European socialism, and the arrival of a Marxist government in Russia compelled British Socialists to take a stand for or against Marxist principles. Advocates of both Marxism and radical Socialism could be found amongst certain of the Anglo-Catholic clergy. The right of private ownership had been vindicated in the *Rerum Novarum* in the face of militant socialism in the industrial centres of western Europe.

91 THE GENERAL STRIKE, 1926

(Bell, *Davidson*, p. 1308)

The General Strike was an unparalleled event in British history arising out of a dispute in the mining industry. Agreement could not be reached between the miners and the owners and a coal stoppage took place on 30 April; a state of emergency was proclaimed on 1 May; and the General Council of the Trades Union Congress ordered a General Strike on 3 May.[1] Davidson arranged to make an Appeal on the radio, the form of which was approved by the President of the Free Church Council and Cardinal Bourne. Permission to broadcast was suddenly withdrawn but the Appeal was published in *The Times*[2] though refused a place in the *British Gazette*.

THE CRISIS

APPEAL FROM THE CHURCHES

After full conference with leaders of the Christian Churches in this country the Archbishop of Canterbury desires to make public the following expression of considered opinion:

Representatives of the Christian Churches in England are convinced that a real settlement will only be achieved in a spirit of fellowship and co-operation for the common good, and not as a result of war. Realizing that the longer the present struggle persists the greater will be the suffering and loss, they earnestly request that all the parties concerned in this dispute will agree to resume negotiations undeterred by obstacles which have been created by the events of the last few days. If it should seem to be incumbent on us to suggest a definite line of approach, we would submit, as the basis of a possible Concordat, a return to the *status quo* of Friday last. We cannot but believe in the possibility of a successful issue. Our proposal should be interpreted as involving simultaneously and concurrently

(1) The cancellation on the part of the T.U.C. of the General Strike;[3]
(2) Renewal by the Government of its offer of assistance to the Coal industry for a short definite period;[4]
(3) The withdrawal on the part of the mine owners of the new wages scales recently issued.

7 May 1926[5]

1 The miners, threatened by wage cuts, asked the T.U.C. to conform to a resolution supporting the miners carried at the 1925 Congress, by which all major industries would stop work. "Lord Birkenhead wrote: 'It would be possible to say without exaggeration of the miners' leaders that they were the stupidest men in England, if we had not frequent occasion to meet the owners.' On this remark, the comment of Mr L. S. Amery was: 'He omitted the prior claim of the Government itself, whose financial policy was so largely responsible for creating the situation in which both sides found themselves, and whose inhibitions and internal divisions forbade the obvious remedies that might have eased it' " (Thomson, *England in the Twentieth Century*, pp. 110-11).

2 The Government monopoly of the information services, including the radio, weakened the tight control necessary to make the strike successful. Churchill's role as editor of the *British Gazette* was

performed in a cavalier and non-placatory manner. The refusal to allow the broadcast was the decision of J. W. C. Reith, the Director-General of the B.B.C., who felt that it would "run counter to his tacit arrangement with the Government about such things".

3 In the original draft (1) was placed at the end, but on the suggestion of Ramsay MacDonald the withdrawal of the strike became (1) instead of (3). Baldwin disapproved of the words "simultaneously and concurrently", adhering to his declaration that the complete withdrawal of the strike must precede negotiations.

4 A breakdown in the mining industry had only been averted in 1925 by the Government paying a temporary subsidy. Baldwin commented that the perpetual trouble with the coal industry had been the past readiness of Governments to intervene; and that the industry had been taught to expect public money whenever it howled and that he was determined to end that. A loan was suggested to meet the Prime Minister's refusal of a subsidy.

5 Inge wrote in his diary: "A miserable time. In the words of the Government 'an organized attempt is being made to ruin the country and wreck the State'. Voluntary help frustated the conspiracy, and after nine days the general strike was called off. The Bishops have come out of it very badly, bleating for a compromise while the nation was fighting for its life. Cardinal Bourne won golden opinions by saying what our Bishops were too cowardly to say: 'This strike is a sin against God. Catholics must support the Government' " (W. R. Inge, *Diary of a Dean* (1949), p. 111.)

92 PRAYER BOOK REVISION, 1928

(Church Assembly, *Report of Proceedings*, Vol. IX, No. 2, pp. 115-6)

The revision of the Book of Common Prayer came to an end when the Prayer Book measure was introduced into Parliament. It was passed in the Lords but rejected in the Commons in December 1927; re-introduced into the Commons in June 1928 it was again rejected. Withstanding the demands of those churchmen who would act in defiance of Parliament the Bishops agreed unanimously on a statement which was to be made to Church Assembly by the Archbishop of Canterbury. The action of the Commons in rejecting the Prayer Book measure was constitutionally justified but it nevertheless called into question the right of the Church of England to be the determinant of its own faith and doctrine. Garbett later commented: "It is clearly unsuitable that a Parliament in which Churchmen are in a minority should debate and decide on the manner in which the Church should worship God and administer the Sacraments"[1] (Smyth, *Garbett*, p. 405).

At first sight one might deem it a disastrous one, deplorable both in its incidence and in its possible consequences. It was perfectly legal. Those who voted on either side were exercising a right conferred on them by the Enabling Act; an Act passed by Parliament at the request of the Church which had framed that Act. But the House of Commons in thus exercising its unquestionably legal power departed, lamentably as it seems to me, from the reasonable spirit in which alone the balanced relationship of Church and State in England can be satisfactorily and harmoniously carried on. While claiming to appraise what can be called Church opinion, it deliberately traversed the declared desire of the Church's official and representative bodies—Bishops, Clergy, and Laity.[2] It declined to respect the wishes of the solid central body of Church opinion duly expressed and recorded both centrally and locally throughout the land, and allowed itself, on the contrary, to be influenced by the representations of the strange combination of vehement opposite groups or factions of Churchmen united in their resolve to get the Measure and the Book defeated.[3]

The vote, however, has been given, and, whatever the intention or sentiment of those who voted, the implications and incidental consequences are serious and may be far-reaching. For that reason I must say something more. On this point I am able to tell you that I have been in touch during the last week with the whole body of diocesan bishops (save two, the Bishops of Bath and Wells and of Sodor and Man[4] who were unavoidably absent), and that, although the actual words are my own, I am allowed to add that what I am now about to say has their concurrence:

It is a fundamental principle that the Church—that is, the Bishops together with the Clergy and the Laity—must in the last resort, when its mind has been fully ascertained, retain its inalienable right, in loyalty to our Lord and Saviour Jesus Christ, to formulate its Faith in Him and to arrange the expression of that Holy Faith in its forms of worship.

I venture to believe that no one can challenge that principle as a principle however loyal he be to the true relation which that principle bears in a Christian land, and ours is a Christian land, to the recognized constitutional rights of the State or nation as such. I do not regard that principle of our fundamental loyalty to Christ and its full expression as in the least inconsistent with, or traversed by, the national position which the life-history of England has, thank God, accorded to our Church and has steadily maintained under all the changes of Parliamentary conditions. But whatever may have been the intentions of those who voted, the recent decision has troubled many consciences and has raised anxious questions.

It is our firm hope that, when the facts have been quietly considered, some strong and capable committee of statesmen and Churchmen may be appointed to weigh afresh the provisions of the existing law in order to see whether any readjustment is required for the maintenance, in the conditions of our own age, of the principle which we have here and now reasserted.

I ask you to observe that in the asseveration which I have made, and in the firm hope associated with it, I can claim the concurrence, of the whole—please note that it is now the whole—Diocesan Episcopate of England. Such concurrence is surely significant.[5]

(*Acts of the Convocation of Canterbury and York*, pp. 63-4)

The worship of God is in every generation a primary concern of the Church. For many years the Church of England has been engaged in an endeavour to amend the existing laws of public worship so as to make fuller provision for the spiritual needs of the Church and to bring order into the variety of usage which has become prevalent. This endeavour has for the present failed. It is impossible and undesirable to bring back the conduct of public worship strictly within the limits of the Prayer Book of 1662. Accordingly the bishops, having failed to secure the statutory sanction which was desired and sought, are compelled in the present difficult situation to fulfil by administrative action their responsibility for the regulation of public worship.

On September 29th, 1928, the bishops announced that they intended to consult the clergy and laity of their dioceses. These consultations have now been held in almost every diocese, and in view of the information gained and desires expressed, the bishops hereby resolve that in the exercise of their administrative discretion they will in their respective dioceses consider the circumstances and needs of parishes severally, and give counsel and directions. In these directions the bishops will conform to the principles which they have already laid down, namely:

1. That during the present emergency and until further order be taken the bishops, having in view the fact that the Convocations of Canterbury and York gave their assent to the proposals for deviations from and additions to the Book of 1662, as set forth in the

Book of 1928, being laid before the National Assembly of the Church of England for Final Approval, and that the National Assembly voted Final Approval to these proposals, cannot regard as inconsistent with loyalty to the principles of the Church of England the use of such additions or deviations as fall within the limits of these proposals. For the same reason they must regard as inconsistent with Church order the use of any other deviations from or additions to the Forms and Orders contained in the Book of 1662.[6]

2. That accordingly the bishops, in the exercise of *that* legal or administrative discretion, *which belongs to each bishop in his own diocese*, will be guided by the proposals set forth in the Book of 1928, and will endeavour to secure that practices which are consistent neither with the Book of 1662 nor with the Book of 1928 shall cease.

Further,

3. That the bishops, in the exercise of their authority, will only permit the ordinary use of any of the Forms and Order contained in the Book of 1928 if they are satisfied that such use would have the goodwill of the people as represented in the parochial church council, and that in the case of the Occasional Offices the consent of the parties concerned will always be obtained.[7]

1 Garbett, Cyril Forster; *b.* 1875; *educ.*, Keble College, Oxford; Cuddeston; 1898; ordained, 1899; curate of St Mary, Portsea; vicar of Portsea, 1909; Bishop of Southwark, 1919; Bishop of Winchester, 1932; Archbishop of York, 1942; *d.* 1955.

2 There was some justification for those Members of Parliament who believed they were better equipped to recognize the mind of the Church of England than the Bishops. The fact that a large minority of Churchmen consistently maintained the right to differ from the prescribed government of the Church in doctrinal and ritual matters weakened the Church's claim to autocracy.

3 The Deposited Book was attacked by the Anglo-Catholics led by Darwell Stone, and by the Evangelicals led by Sir William Joynson Hicks, the Bishop of Norwich, and Sir Thomas Inskip. In the Church Assembly (July 5-6 1927) the Prayer Book measure was approved after the following voting:

Bishops	*for*	34	*against*	4
Clergy	*for*	253	*against*	37
Laity	*for*	230	*against*	92
Total	*for*	517	*against*	133

4 Bath and Wells (Wynne-Willson) and the recently consecrated Bishop of Sodor and Man (William Stanton Jones).

5 The four opposing bishops: Norwich (Bertram Pollock); Birmingham (E. W. Barnes); Worcester (E. H. Pearce); and Exeter (R. E. W. G. Cecil) nevertheless supported the Church of England's claim to be the sole arbiter of its own faith and doctrine.

6 The "present emergency" continued indefinitely without coercive action by Parliament or undue licence within the Church.

7 An almost identical resolution was passed by the Convocation of York.

93 THE AGREEMENT OF BONN, 1931

(*Acts of Convocations*, p. 125)

At the Bonn conferences of 1874–5 representatives of the Orthodox, Old Catholic,[1] and Anglican Churches met under the leadership of Döllinger.[2] The Lambeth Conference of 1878 showed some interest in the Old Catholic Church, though hostility was later aroused by the consecration of a bishop for work among the Old Catholics in England in 1908. A conference on intercommunion and interconsecration was held at Bonn in 1931 at which agreement was reached. The resolution of both the Convocations marked the first instance of formal relations between the Church of England and a European Church.

That this House approves of the following statements agreed on between the representatives of the Old Catholic Churches and the Churches of the Anglican Communion at a Conference held at Bonn on July 2nd, 1931:[3]

1 Each Communion recognizes the catholicity and independence of the other, and maintains its own.
2 Each Communion agrees to admit members of the other Communion to participate in the Sacraments.[4]
3 Intercommunion does not require from either Communion the acceptance of all doctrinal opinion, sacramental devotion, or liturgical practice characteristic of the other, but implies that each believes the other to hold all the essentials of the Christian Faith.

And this House agrees to the establishment of Intercommunion between the Church of England and the Old Catholics on these terms.

1 The Old Catholic Church was a fusion of German, Austrian, and Swiss Churchmen who refused to accept the Vatican decrees on Papal Infallibility (1870); with the Church of Utrecht which had separated from Rome in 1724. The doctrinal basis of the Old Catholic Church was the Declaration of Utrecht made in 1889.

2 Döllinger, John Joseph Ignatius; *b.* 1799; ordained, 1822; Professor of Church History at Aschaffenburg, 1826; Professor of Church History at Munich, 1826; published the *Letters of Janus* (1869), and *Letters of Quirinus* (1869–70); excommunicated by the Archbishop of Munich, 1871; President of the Bavarian Royal Academy of Sciences, 1873; *d.* 1890.

3 The Anglican party was of eight members under the leadership of Bishop A. C. Headlam, and included N. P. Williams and G. F. Graham-Brown representing the Anglo-Catholics and the Evangelicals respectively. Clause 3 was largely the work of these two delegates.

4 The Old Catholic Church had recognized the validity of Anglican Orders in 1925. An Old Catholic bishop took part in the consecration of Graham-Brown as Bishop in Jerusalem in 1932, and in 1937 Headlam and the Bishop of Fulham took part in the consecration of the Archbishop of Utrecht.

94 MISSIONARY RESPONSIBILITY, 1933

(*With One Accord* (1935), pp. 106-14)

The overseas work of the Church of England had been largely undertaken by the missionary societies, and in order to co-ordinate their efforts the Missionary Council of the Church Assembly came into being in 1921. The Council, under the chairmanship of Archbishop St Clair Donaldson,[1] was successor to the two provincial Boards of Missions set up in 1884 and the Central Board of Missions established in 1908. The function of the Missionary Council "should certainly include a survey of the whole field comprising the work done by all Christian bodies, so as to present the position to the Church at home, and to stir up zeal and to direct efforts for the extension of the Kingdom of our Lord throughout the world ..." (N.A. 26). The Unified Statement resulted from a resolution adopted at a meeting of overseas bishops held at Chichester in June 1930.[2]

The United Statement is a Budget—the clearest available statement to the Church of England of its responsibilities to the Church overseas in the year 1933. This Budget calls for a minimum of £1,047,588.

What is it in the situation of the Church overseas in 1933 which justifies this appeal to the Church in England in this time of financial pressure?

The answer to this question is contained in the surveys which accompany the Budget, and in the answers of the bishops overseas to the Missionary Council questionnaire on which the surveys are based. There is remarkable agreement amongst the bishops as to the main features of the 1933 situation in the mission field. Writing from every corner of the earth they urge the same considerations on the Church at home.

I THEY SHOW US A CHURCH IN THE MIDST OF THE GRAVEST DIFFICULTIES

1 *An Unparalleled Financial Crisis*

The appeal for 1933 is made in the midst of universal and unexampled depression. In post-war Europe, though there was financial crash in nation after nation, in some countries there was remarkable prosperity. Today not one nation is prosperous and the greatest financial experts declare themselves baffled by the complications of modern monetary and currency questions. The economic situation of the missionary world is likewise without parallel. After the war, the Churches of England and America carried the burden of the Missionary Societies of the Continent of Europe. When bad times came, England looked, only too readily perhaps, to prosperous America.[3]

Today no nation can hand its burden to another. Missionary Societies and Boards of Missions are everywhere in difficulties, and in every land were forced last year to retrench. The income of the Missionary Societies in North America in 1930 fell by 6½ per cent; this was followed by another serious fall in 1931. In England the corresponding income in 1931 diminished only by 3 per cent, a token of the steady and determined giving of the missionary constituency. Nevertheless, the S.P.G. in 1931 had to reduce its grants by 7½ per cent; the U.M.C.A. in 1932 by 10 per cent. The C.M.S. in 1933–34 is making reductions of £36,000; and the C.E.Z.M.S. in 1931–32 reduced maintenance grants by 10 per cent, and missionaries' allowances by 5 per cent.[4]

But reduction of grants from home is only the beginning of the cumulative pressure of financial difficulties on the Church overseas. Our Church in non-Christian lands has drawn supplies from other lands than England. The Dominions, generous, but hard-hit, cannot do what they have done; nor can the United States. The failure of the wheat crop in Canada checks the flow of Canadian support to the Diocese of Honan in China and to the Diocese of Mid-Japan. The lowered price of wool in Australia and New Zealand reduces support of missions in Central Tanganyika, China, and the missionary Dioceses of New Guinea, Melanesia, and Polynesia.

Reduced grants, due to our own severe financial depression, reach lands where depression is even more severe. Every area tells of acute poverty and widespread unemployment. One flourishing industry after another has collapsed: cocoa in West Africa; rubber and tin in Malaya; copper mines in Northern Rhodesia, and with them the collieries in Southern Rhodesia. Paralysis of shipping follows the collapse of industry. South Africa, Canada, and Japan add a tale of bad harvests. And on the top of all this has come natural disaster after disaster, each bringing starvation and disease in its train; hurricanes in the West Indies and Japan; earthquakes in New Zealand; in China the most appalling floods in recorded history. On the Canadian Church has fallen the unnatural disaster of a ruinous defalcation.

Finally, lowered grants from home may be further reduced by exchange. In South Africa, while on the gold standard, all gifts from the Church in England were reduced by 30 per cent before reaching the Church of the Province. Exchange in Honduras automatically reduces all clergy stipends by 33 per cent. Money remitted to Canada loses over 20 per cent on the way. Loss on exchange alone forces diocese after diocese to choose between reducing the pay of workers or reducing their numbers.

2 *Great and Imminent Dangers*

A wave of materialism is sweeping round the world, to all human seeming, irresistible. The scientific education of the west, so eagerly welcomed today in the east, with all the glorious enlightenment and development it brings, disintegrates the beliefs by which man has lived, and the social ties and customs which have bound him to his neighbour. On every established idea and institution, modern man inscribes a huge question mark. The drive and pressure of modern industrialism which are penetrating even the forests of Central Africa and the plains of Central Asia, make men everywhere dependent on, and preoccupied with, material things.

At home, the Church has talked, perhaps too glibly, in pulpit or on platform of "the menace of secularism"; though even in England we can catch more than a glimpse of its meaning. But to the Church overseas these things are grim realities, enemies with which it is at grips. East and west in Africa all reports show us the African stepping suddenly out of primitive tribal life into the modern industrial world, and, if the Christian mission fails him, inevitably turning to Islam or falling into the practical materialism of the modern industrial worker. At the other end of the scale, the educated Jew of today, detached from his religious past, is seen too often as an apostle of materialism amongst the nations. This unconscious and almost universal secularization of outlook is the most difficult enemy the Church has to fight. It is an atmosphere penetrating every gap in the Church's armour, and testing every form of missionary endeavour.

But the Church has a new danger to face in land after land—determined and hostile attack. From Soviet Russia, a definitely anti-religious communism is pushing west into Europe and America, east into Persia, India, China, and Japan. It is an economic theory, definitely harnessed to disbelief in God. It is a religious irreligion. Communism of the type the Church faces today in China and Japan has a gospel of its own, powerfully attractive in a suffering, poverty-stricken world. It has a passionate sense of mission and is carrying on its campaign at the Church's base in Christian lands as well as launching an offensive against its front line in non-Christian lands. Such a conscious, avowed, organized attack against religion in general and Christianity in particular is something new in history.

Equally deliberate in some lands in its determined hostility to Christianity is another form of social and political faith-nationalism. But the nationalist attack on Christianity, unlike communism, is often bound up with some form of national religion—with Islam in Persia and Egypt, with Buddhism in Ceylon, while the struggle for communal rights in India is allied with a revival both of Hinduism and Islam.

PARALYSING UNCERTAINTIES

Uncertainty is a more searching test of faith than any clear seen danger. To this test the Church overseas is brought at every point. In India, the one thing certain about the future is that it will bring new problems to the Church. Government grants for chaplaincies and for Christian education, already reduced on grounds of economy, are likely to be still further diminished under the coming political regime, whatever it may be; the future of the Anglo-Indian community and of the work of the Church on its behalf is obscure and troubled.

In China and Persia, government regulations are making the future of mission colleges and schools exceedingly uncertain, while throughout China, continuity of work, security of property, and even the personal safety of the missionary are at the mercy of change of government, civil war, and banditry. Friction between Jew and Arab in the Near East and between Chinese and Japanese in the Far East threatens the peace of the world. The innumerable uncertainties as to the outcome of the Disarmament Conference, the World Economic Conference, and the Round Table Conference affect the missionary world no less than the political.

But far more devastating is the universal financial uncertainty. Calculations for the future can be made on announced reductions of grants this year, but will these reductions be the last? Can the Church at home make good its promises? What will the state of exchange be next year? Has the turn come or is there worse ahead? All this uncertainty produces a fatal result on the Church overseas —paralysis of statesmanship. Every missionary now has need to be a statesman. But what field is there for the statesmen's gifts today?

The Missionary Council, in November 1931, asked the bishops for statements about their plans for the immediate future, hoping to relate the appeal from overseas to a well-thought-out plan for each area. But as the months passed financial uncertainties increased and it became more and more difficult to present the 1933 appeal in terms of plans for advance. Some bishops, indeed, in response to the questionnaire put forward plans for future developments, though, to quote one of them, such plans have become "rather wistful hopes". But others gently hint it is mockery to ask about their future plans, seeing that these must chiefly be concerned with cancelling their past ones. In the words of the Bishop of Pretoria, "Those who are hanging by their eyelids over precipices are apt to be lacking in plans".[5]

H. G. Wells, speaking last November on the developments of modern transport, pleads for government departments of foresight to deal with its problems. In the missionary world departments of foresight are already in existence, provided by the International Missionary Council.[6] Its Commission on Higher Education for India, under the chairmanship of the Master of Balliol,[7] has given the Church a carefully thought-out, far-reaching plan for the future of Christian colleges in India. Its Department of Social and Industrial Research has sent a commission to investigate the effect of modern labour conditions on the tribal life of the African. It has given us plans whereby the Church may deal in statesmanlike fashion with the economic, agricultural, and educational problems resulting from the employment of mixed multitudes of tribesmen in the copper mines of Northern Rhodesia. But what use are departments of foresight to the Church overseas, if it is financially impossible to act on their recommendations?

II YET A CHURCH FILLED WITH UNCONQUERABLE HOPE

Against all these odds, the bishops are full of courage and hope. Nowhere in their answers is there a trace of defeatism, and only in two or three can discouragement be discerned. With little or nothing in outward circumstances to justify hope, ultimate victory is assumed. There is a sense of boundless opportunity. At home there is in some quarters fear and depression, but not overseas. This is due to no easy optimism, for the bishops are clear enough about the dangers and perplexities of the situation.

The ground of their courage and hope is the fact of the young Church which God is calling into being—in India, China, Japan, Persia, and Africa. They are far from blind to its weaknesses and speak frankly enough, now about its moral defects, now about its lack of spiritual and intellectual development. They see and feel the storms which are sweeping round it, but they know that "the gates of hell cannot prevail against it". As we see the Church through their eyes, we shall share their belief that in spite of all danger and perplexity the future is secure. What manner of Church is it in which they dare to place such trust?

A Church Witnessing under its Own Leaders

In the seven years since the World Call the number of Asiatic and African bishops has increased from four to thirteen. In many fields there has been a corresponding increase in the native ministry. Most of these leaders are men with an evangelistic message, and nothing is more characteristic of the younger Churches today than definite movements of witness. If every European missionary were withdrawn the witness of the Church would continue.

Under the leadership of Toyohiko Kagawa, the Kingdom of God Movement in Japan aims at preaching a gospel which will touch all sides of Japanese life, and at so increasing and building up the membership of the Church that it may become a real power in the land. The Five Year Movement in China, with Dr Cheng Ching Yi as its leader, has a similar aim for China. In India the movement amongst the outcaste villagers has given such witness to the power of Christ, that a caste movement towards Christianity has begun, and in the Diocese of Dornakal alone, under the first Indian bishop, it has brought in 21,000 converts in five years.[8]

In the islands of the Pacific a Melanesian Brotherhood is committed to pioneer evangelism; in the West Indies and in South Africa much of the work of the Church is carried on by unpaid catechists; in Persia young converts from Islam are giving courageous witness even at the risk of martyrdom.

This practical realization of the Lambeth ideal of the Church as a fellowship of witness is significant to the whole Church of Christ. The Mission of Fellowship from India to England last autumn was a milestone in the history of the Church. Their word was with power for they brought from India a message from a Church whose witness is bearing fruit. The sight of the power of God at work overseas is, in the words of the Archbishop of Canterbury, "a powerful tonic to the discouraged and fearful at home".

Moving forward in Self-Support

This Statement is the first attempt to show to what extent the dioceses and provinces which still ask aid from the Church at home are supporting themselves. The results set forth in the Statistical Tables for 1931 give ground for confident thanksgiving.

The Churches in Australia and Canada, hard pressed as they are, ask nothing in 1933 except for the means to meet a definite need in a definite area directly created by recent immigration from England. Even in Qu'Appelle, one of the prairie dioceses of Canada where distress is most acute, the Church gives to its own work three-and-a-half times what it receives from England and from Eastern Canada. In Australia, even in the hard-hit Diocese of Bunbury, the proportion of self-support to gifts from England is as five to one.

In non-Christian lands where much of the work is still in the pioneer stage of evangelism, where the Christian communities are small and their normal condition is often desperate poverty, the proportion of self-help cannot yet be so great as in the Dominions. Nevertheless even in China it is as one to six; in Japan as one to two; in South India as two to three; in the Niger as thirteen to four. These figures, though sufficiently remarkable, nevertheless underestimate the gifts of the Church, as many local contributions, for example to the building of churches, do not appear in the returns. Moreover, we are reminded again and again that the giving of the Church in these lands cannot be reckoned in money only, but consists largely of gifts of produce or of voluntary labour.

So much is it now a missionary commonplace that the young Churches should support themselves, and so eager are they in many lands to do it, that a caution is necessary. Several bishops in the Far East, in India and in Africa, remind us that concentration on self-support may obscure even more important issues, and that the desperate struggle to support the local Churches and pastors has, in some districts, checked forward moves in evangelism. We must beware of such facile expression of confidence in the younger Churches as shall mean that we seek a way out of our own financial difficulties by withdrawing help from them before they are ready to stand alone.

Steadily Taking Over its Own Burdens

From country after country comes evidence that the Church overseas is determined at the earliest possible moment to accept the responsibilities of independence. The Church of India, Burma, and Ceylon is sacrificing government stipends that it may be free to order its own life. The Church in China sees good in its financial troubles because of the growing sense of responsibility in the Chinese Church. The Church on the prairies of Canada with splendid courage has undertaken, by the self-sacrifice of its own members, to repair the heavy blow under which it lies almost crippled. This spirit of independence and the steady growth of self-support cannot but engender confidence in the Church of England, as it comes to realize that the Church overseas is not content to be a continuous and unending drain upon the Church at home.

Yet it is manifest that without large help from the Church in England it cannot for many years to come cope with the tremendous demands which are made upon it. There are mighty tasks ahead. Even in lands where missions have been long established the Church is still surrounded by overwhelming millions who have yet to be evangelized. Fresh horizons in untouched districts are opening before it—fresh calls for evangelism summon it to work beyond its strength. Without the help of workers and funds from the Church in England many open doors must long remain unentered.

There are special fields too—higher education, hospital work, and literature—which will long demand the resources and experience of the Church in the west. The great institutions built up by the Missionary Societies in many lands have greater service than ever to render, but their maintenance and development are far beyond the resources of the young Church.

1 Donaldson, St Clair George Alfred; *b.* 1863; *educ.*, Eton and Trinity College, Cambridge; Wells Theological College; deacon, 1888; curate, St Andrew, Bethnal Green; resident chaplain to Archbishop Benson; priest, 1889; Eton Mission, Hackney Wick, 1891; rector and rural dean of Hornsey, 1901; Bishop of Brisbane, 1904; first Archbishop of Brisbane, 1905; Bishop of Salisbury, 1921; Chairman of the Missionary Council, 1921; *d.* 1935.

2 The Resolution read: "There should be a single and authoritative statement of the estimated diocesan or provincial needs each year, showing what each diocese (or province) hopes to do for itself, and what it expects to receive from the Home Church through Societies and Associations. And this Conference requests the Missionary Council of the Church Assembly, after consultation with all concerned, to issue such statement to the Church."

3 The "World Slump" of 1929–34 affected agriculture, finance, and industry. A fever of speculation in the U.S.A. led to the withdrawal of funds from Europe and the Wall Street Crash of October 1929. The general effect of the depression was to increase economic planning and to encourage political nationalist movements as alternatives to communism.

4 The Missionary Societies whose average annual overseas missionary income from England exceeded £25,000 were: S.P.C.K., S.P.G., C.M.S., The British and Foreign Bible Society, Church Mission to the Jews, Colonial and Continental Church Society, Missions to Seamen, U.M.C.A., Church of England Zenana Missionary Society, and the Bible Churchmen's Missionary Society.

5 Neville Talbot, 1920–33.

6 Scattered references to the achievements of the International Missionary Council occur in Ruth Rouse and Stephen Neill, *A History of the Ecumenical Movement, 1517–1948* (1967). This Report makes little mention of the growing co-operation and movement towards reunion in the missionary field.

7 Dr A. D. Lindsay, later Lord Lindsay.

8 Azariah, V. S.; *b.* 1874; a secretary of Y.M.C.A.; secretary of National Missionary Society of India, 1905; Bishop of Dornakal, 1912–44; Chairman of the National Christian Council of India; *d.* 1945.

95 THE CHURCH OF FINLAND, 1935

(*Acts of Convocations*, pp. 126-7)

Bishop Headlam[1] had visited the Church of Finland in 1927 and established a relationship which was reinforced after the succeeding Lambeth Conference. A conference in 1933 suggested that "economic intercommunion should be established between the two Churches, by which the spiritual efficacy of Finnish Orders would be recognized on condition that they would be regularized when the opportunity arose.[2] The York Convocation accepted the Report but the Lower House of the Canterbury Convocation pressed for a further examination of the Finnish practice, the Anglo-Catholic wing being powerful enough to delay a large measure of intercommunion between the two Churches.

BY BOTH HOUSES

(B) Having learnt from the Archbishop of Turku (Abo) that he has authority, after consultation with the Conference of bishops of the Church of Finland and with the agreement of its Church Assembly, to seek closer relations with the Church of England in response to the Archbishop of Canterbury's invitation (conveyed in pursuance of Resolution 38 of the Lambeth Conference, 1930) this House welcomes the approaches thus made, and expresses the hope that in due course complete intercommunion, based on a common episcopal ministry, may be achieved.[3]

Further, and as a means towards such a complete unity, this House, noting that the Episcopal Ordination of Presbyters is the regular practice of the Church of Finland, and assuming that the bishops of the Church will take steps to put the practice of the Church of Finland beyond doubt—[4]

BY THE UPPER HOUSE

approves the following recommendations:

That if the Archbishop of Canterbury be invited by the Archbishop of Turku (Abo) to appoint a bishop to take part in the consecration of a bishop in the Church of Finland, he may commission a bishop for such a purpose; and in the same way, if the Archbishop of Canterbury shall invite the Archbishop of Turku (Abo) to take part in the consecration of a bishop in the Church of England, it is hoped that he will be willing to commission a bishop for such a purpose.

That members of the Church of Finland may be admitted to

Communion in the Church of England, provided that they are at that time admissible to Communion in their own Church.[5]

BY THE LOWER HOUSE

(B) . . . is of opinion:

That if the Archbishop of Turku (Abo) shall invite the Archbishop of Canterbury to appoint a bishop to take part in the consecration of a bishop in the Church of Finland, he may commission a bishop for such purpose.

That members of the Church of Finland may be admitted to Communion in the Church of England in accordance with the terms of Resolution 2 (*a*) on the Unity of the Church communicated by the Upper House of this House on 4th June, 1931.

1 Headlam, Arthur Cayley; *b.* 1862; *educ.*, Winchester and New College, Oxford; priest, 1889; Fellow of All Souls, 1885; rector of Welwyn, 1896; Professor of Dogmatic Theology, King's College, London, 1903; Regius Professor of Divinity at Oxford, 1918; Bampton Lecturer, 1920; Bishop of Gloucester, 1923–45; *d.* 1947.

2 The National Church of Finland was a Lutheran body which had maintained episcopal succession until 1884 when all three sees became vacant simultaneously. Under a canon of 1870 a new archbishop of Turku was consecrated by the Dean of Abo, since the Russian authorities prevented episcopal consecration from other Churches.

3 The Finnish Church hoped to recover the historic succession at the hands of Swedish bishops, and this was accomplished after some years.

4 Finnish Church Law permitted presbyteral ordination if a bishop was not available, and though such ordinations were infrequent, it was felt that a change in this existing law would be difficult to obtain.

5 The Finnish practice differed from the Anglican inasmuch as the laying on of hands was included in the rite of Baptism, and confirmation was not regarded as a necessary sacrament. Anglo-Catholic opinion within the Church of England insisted that this matter be discussed even though it was not an integral part of the Lambeth Quadrilateral.

96 ABDICATION, 1936

The constitutional crisis arising out of the desire of King Edward VIII to marry an American whose two previous marriages had ended in divorce, involved Lang as Archbishop of Canterbury. The matter was brought into public notice by the Bishop of Bradford's address at his Diocesan Conference.[1] Under the guidance of Lang the Church of England made little attempt to force a decision on the Prime Minister,[2] but acted as a channel of opinion. Criticism of the Church's attitude came largely from a section of public opinion who were unsympathetic to the moral issues involved in relation to the King as the supreme governor of the Church.

(*Yorkshire Post*)

Leeds, Wednesday Dec. 2, 1936

THE KING AND HIS PEOPLE

The Bishop of Bradford said yesterday that the benefit to be derived by the people from the King's Coronation would depend in the first instance on "the faith, prayer and self-dedication of the King himself". Referring to the moral and spiritual side of that self-dedication, the Bishop said the King would abundantly need Divine grace if he were to do his duty faithfully, and he added: "We hope that he is aware of his need. Some of us wish that he gave more positive signs of such awareness."

Dr Blunt must have had good reason for so pointed a remark. Most people by this time, are aware that a great deal of rumour regarding the King has been published of late in the more sensational American newspapers.[3] It is proper to treat with contempt mere gossip such as is frequently associated with the names of European royal persons. The Bishop of Bradford would certainly not have condescended to recognize it. But certain statements which have appeared in reputable United States' journals, and even, we believe, in some Dominion newspapers, cannot be treated with quite so much indifference. They are too circumstantial and have plainly a foundation in fact. For this reason, an increasing number of responsible people is led to fear lest the King may not yet have perceived how complete in our day must be that self-dedication of which Dr Blunt spoke if the Coronation is to bring a blessing to all the peoples of the Empire, and is not, on the contrary, to prove a stumbling-block.

When King Edward succeeded King George "the well-beloved", the nation acclaimed him with the glad conviction that he would indeed, as he himself promised, follow in his father's footsteps. Deep disappointment must necessarily result if, instead of this continuity of example, there should develop a dispute between the King and his Ministers such as must almost inevitably raise a constitutional issue of the gravest character.[4] There is no man or woman in any rank of life who has not some conception of the very high demands which are made on the King-Emperor, demands which many men might well shun. But the demands carry with them today the greatest opportunity, perhaps, that could be given to any one man. The King, by manifesting his own grave sense of responsibility, can do more than any other man to ensure that his subjects likewise will be of one mind to walk warily in very dangerous days.[5]

(*The Archbishop's Broadcast Speech*, Sunday, 13 December;[6] Lockhart, *Lang*, pp. 405-6)

... Seldom, if ever, has any British Sovereign come to the Throne with greater natural gifts for his kingship. Seldom, if ever, has any Sovereign been welcomed by a more enthusiastic loyalty. From God he had received a high and sacred trust. Yet by his own will he has abdicated—he has surrendered the trust. With characteristic frankness he has told us his motive. It was a craving for private happiness. Strange and sad it must be that for such a motive, however strongly it pressed upon his heart, he should have disappointed hopes so high and abandoned a trust so great. Even more strange and sad it is that he should have sought his happiness in a manner inconsistent with the Christian principles of marriage, and within a social circle whose standards and ways of life are alien to all the best instincts and traditions of his people. Let those who belong to this circle know that today they stand rebuked by the judgment of the nation which had loved King Edward. I have shrunk from saying these words. But I have felt compelled for the sake of sincerity and truth to say them.

Yet for one who has known him since his childhood, who has felt his charm and admired his gifts, these words cannot be the last. How can we forget the high hopes and promise of his youth; his most genuine care for the poor, the suffering, the unemployed; his years of eager service both at home and across the seas? It is the remembrance of these things that wrings from our hearts the cry, "The pity of it, O, the pity of it!" To the infinite mercy and the protecting care of God we commit him now, wherever he may be....

1 Blunt, Alfred Walter Frank; *b.* 1879; *educ.*, Marlborough and Exeter College, Oxford; assistant master at Wellington College, 1902, Fellow and Classical Lecturer, Exeter College, 1902; curate of Carrington, Nottingham, 1907; vicar of Carrington, 1909; vicar of St Weburgh, Derby, 1917; Bishop of Bradford, 1931; resigned, 1955; *d.* 1957.

2 Baldwin, Stanley; *b.* 1867; *educ.*, Harrow and Trinity College, Cambridge; Conservative M.P. for Bewdley, 1908; joint financial secretary to the Treasury, 1917; President of the Board of Trade, 1921; Chancellor of the Exchequer, 1922; Prime Minister in succession to Bonar Law, 1923; Prime Minister 1924; Lord President of the Council in the National Government, 1931; Prime Minister, 1935; resigned, 1937; created Earl of Bewdley, 1937; *d.* 1947.

3 Henson commented on the divorce proceedings in America as having been obtained "in circumstances of such unusual character as made the suggestion of collusion inevitable" (*Retrospect*, vol. 2, p. 378). There was an agreed silence in the British press about the King's attachment to Mrs Simpson and Blunt's speech broke that silence: *The Times*, *Daily Mail*, and *News Chronicle* taking the matter up.

4 David Thomson writes: "Baldwin's oratorical skill lay in adroitly confusing and smothering the issue, while giving every impression of clarifying it. When, for once, he chose not to abdicate responsibility but to display and deploy his full resources of ingenuity, agility, and relentlessness, it was another who had to abdicate. It was only a month since he had made his 'appalling frankness' speech, confessing an incapacity to change public opinion" (*England in the Twentieth Century*, p. 167).

5 Blunt was not referring to the King's moral conduct but to his irregular churchgoing. Nevertheless, the criticism of the King was a significant and uncharacteristic action for an Anglican bishop.

6 The Abdication Bill was passed by both Houses of Parliament on 11 December, and that same evening the King himself broadcast from Windsor Castle.

97 DOCTRINE IN THE CHURCH OF ENGLAND, 1938

(*Report of the Archbishops' Commission*, pp. 4-7, 16-18)

The Doctrinal Commission was a long time in preparing its Report which set out the various theological viewpoints within the Church of England. Although it arose directly from the controversies of the 1920s, the dogmatic assumptions of Modernism were conspicuously absent. The Prolegomena on the Sources and Authority of Christian Doctrine, was followed by sections on the Doctrines of God and of Redemption; the Church and the Sacraments; and Eschatology. In the Report the Chairman, (Temple) recognized the changed theological climate since the inception of the Commission.

Readers of the Report who wish to estimate its significance accurately must keep in mind the limitation of scope implied in the circumstances of the Commission's appointment. It was not appointed in order to survey the whole field of theology and produce a systematic treatise in which the space allotted to any subject would bear some appreciable relation to the inherent importance of that subject. The Commission was appointed because the tensions between different schools of thought in the Church of England were imperilling its unity and impairing its effectiveness. Consequently those subjects (on the whole) receive most attention in the Report which are at this time, or have been during the period of the Commission's labours, occasions of controversy within the Church of England or sources of confusion in Anglican practice.[1]

These are not the same as those which cause most concern to Continental theologians. If any such honour us by reading this Report they will be startled to find so little said about the Fall; about Freedom, Election, and Predestination; about Justification by Faith; about the Order of Creation and the Order of Redemption; about the possibility of Natural Theology.[2] They will be filled with astonishment at the brevity of our treatment of Divine Grace under that title. Our reply that almost the whole of our Report is concerned with Divine Grace in its various manifestations would do little to diminish their bewilderment.

That is one illustration of the difference of habit in theological thought as this has developed under the different conditions prevalent in our own country and on the Continent.[3] This difference has many causes; among these may be the constant stream of Platonism which Dr Inge claims to have been a special characteristic of

English thought;[4] but certainly we must reckon among the special determinants of English theology the fact that our Reformation Fathers appealed so largely to the authority of Patristic, and especially Greek Patristic, writings. They were at one with the Continental Reformers in their indebtedness to St Augustine; but to a greater extent they paid regard also to the works of Origen, Athanasius, Basil, and the two Gregories. In these the distinctive doctrines of St Augustine, which he developed in his controversy with Pelagianism, are (naturally) not to be found. The heirs of Luther's Augustinianism are apt to accuse English Christianity as a whole of Pelagianism; and it must be admitted that we have a perpetual tendency in that direction. As I regard Pelagianism as of all heresies spiritually the most pernicious, I share in some degree the Continental anxiety concerning our habitual inclination towards it. Yet I am glad that we have not been lastingly subjected to the distinctively Augustinian doctrine of the Fall, but can balance this with the very different doctrine of some of the Greek Fathers.

In recent times the great influence of Westcott[5] and of the *Lux Mundi* school has strengthened the dependence of Anglican theology upon the Greek as contrasted with the Latin Fathers. In the result there is found to be a closer relationship in theology between the Orthodox Churches of the East and the Church of England than between the former and either Rome on the one hand or Wittenberg or Geneva on the other.

Our Report must be read in the context of the thought of our time and with regard to its constant changes. Even during the period of our labours great fluctuations of mental habit have been apparent in the spheres of secular science and philosophy. An astonished public has been made aware that some leading students of physics consider that the knowledge gained by their studies is schematic only and not a knowledge of Reality. In the political world the ideas of freedom and fellowship are passing through readjustment and revaluation. And in our own sphere, that of Theology, the work of such writers as Karl Barth in Europe and Reinhold Niebuhr in America has set many problems in a new perspective. It has not been our task to comment on these variations in the intellectual atmosphere; but if what is either preached or written is to be understood, its expression must be adapted to the minds which may hear or read. Our task has been, so far as we were able, to discuss the unchanging truths of the Christian revelation, and the various interpretations of these current in the Church of England, in such a way as to be intelligible to those of our contemporaries who have some acquaintance with theology.

But it has always been our desire to set forth the truth of the Everlasting Gospel unchanged in substance. Indeed, we believe that its permanence amidst the welter of modern theories, which seem to succeed each other with kaleidoscopic inconsequence, may be one of its chief means of drawing to itself the attention of a bewildered generation.

Our aim, however, is not specifically to commend the doctrine of the Church, but to examine the differences of interpretation current in the Church of England and to elucidate the relations of these one to another. If in so doing we have commended to any perplexed minds the Gospel itself or have removed obstacles to belief, we are thankful that our work should have this result. But that is a different function from ours, and, doubtless, a higher. Our function, allotted to us by those who called us into existence as a Commission, is what we have described. This accounts for, and as we hope justifies, the rather detached and academic quality of our work. There is in the Church of England a rich treasury of spiritual experience, a living tradition of personal devotion and freely moving thought. The same is true of every one of the schools of thought within it. The examination of these, and discussion of their interrelations, cannot have the vitality and richness characteristic of the traditions themselves which are thus discussed. The fault of detachment, if any regard it so, is inseparable from the particular service which we were asked to render[6] ...

... As I review in thought the result of our fourteen years of labour, I am conscious of a certain transition of interest in our minds, as in the minds of theologians all over the world. We were appointed at a time when theologians were engaged in taking up the prosecution of the task which the war had compelled them to lay aside. Their problems were still predominantly set by the interest of "pre-war" thought. In our country the influence of Westcott reinforced by that of the *Lux Mundi* school had led to the development of a theology of the Incarnation rather than a theology of Redemption. The distinction is, of course, not absolute or clean-cut, but the tip of the balance makes a vast difference not only in presentation but in direction of attention and estimate of relative values. A theology of the Incarnation tends to be a Christocentric metaphysic. And in all ages there is need for the fresh elaboration of such a scheme of thought or map of life as seen in the light of the revelation in Christ. A theology of Redemption (though, of course, Redemption has its great place in the former) tends rather to sound the prophetic note; it is more ready to admit that much in this evil world is irrational and strictly unintelligible; and it looks to the coming of the Kingdom as a necessary preliminary to the full comprehension of much that now is.

If the security of the nineteenth century, already shattered in Europe, finally crumbles away in our country, we shall be pressed more and more towards a theology of Redemption. In this we shall be coming closer to the New Testament. We have been learning again how impotent man is to save himself, how deep and pervasive is that corruption which theologians call Original Sin. Man needs above all else to be saved from himself. This must be the work of Divine Grace.

If we began our work again today, its perspectives would be different. But it is not our function to pioneer. We may call the thinkers and teachers of the Church of England to renewed devotion of their labour to the themes of Redemption, Justification, and Conversion. It is there that, in my own judgment at least, our need lies now and will lie in the future. To put the matter in another way: theology in the half-century that ended with the war was such as is prompted by and promotes a ministry mainly pastoral; we need and must work out for our own time a theology such as is prompted by and promotes a ministry at least as much evangelistic as pastoral.

As that work proceeds new problems will arise and new divisions cutting across all existing party cleavages. Then our successors in another doctrinal commission may attempt the reconciling work that in our own field was committed to us. We have tried to discharge our own commission faithfully, and commend our work to God with the prayer that He will render ineffectual whatever in our work is due to our blindness or prejudice, and prosper with His blessing whatever has been directed by His Spirit, so that the result of our labours may be the peace of His Church.[7]

October 1, 1937 WILLIAM EBOR:

1 In spite of the repeated warnings about the nature and purpose of the report it was fiercely attacked in Convocations. The nature of the report was neither what its original promoters intended nor what Convocations desired.

2 The new currents of theological thought were seen most clearly in the revival of the classical Reformation theologies; the neo-Calvinistic movement associated with Karl Barth; the newly developed biblical theology; and the problems arising out of Christian reunion.

3 "Particular theological stresses and tendencies have gained their significance, not, usually, as the expressions of the teaching of an individual scholar, but as characteristic of a group which saw in them the dogmatic emphasis that cohered with its whole conception of Christian life, thought, and devotion. Theological movement in England has been continually involved in controversies that have ranged far afield, and raised questions which have, at least apparently, concerned themselves not so much with whether such and such opinions were true, but whether they ought to be held and taught in the Church of England" (Mozley, *Some Tendencies in British Theology*, p. 100).

4 Inge, William Ralph, *b.* 1860; *educ.*, Eton, 1874; King's College, Cambridge, 1879; B.A. 1882; Fellow of Hertford College, Oxford, 1889; Bampton Lecturer, 1899; vicar of All Saints, Knightsbridge, 1905; Lady Margaret Professor of Divinity, Cambridge, 1907; Dean of St Paul's, 1911–34; Gifford Lecturer, 1918; *d.* 1954.

5 The incarnational bias of Anglican theology was derived largely from Maurice and Westcott.

6 Davidson asked Burge whether an unofficial inquiry like that of *Lux Mundi* was preferable to a commission, but Burge pointed out that the former was the work of men of one school, whereas he had proposed a commission of men of all schools of thought.

7 The Commission first met at University College, Oxford in September 1923; then it met for a week a year with the exceptions of 1934, 1935, 1936, when it met for two weeks. From 1925 onwards, three groups, formed on a geographical basis, met separately at least twice a year.

98 OUTLOOK FOR THEOLOGY, 1939

(*Theology* (November 1939), pp. 326-33)

THEOLOGY TODAY

It is probable that the outbreak of war will prove to have intensified a sense of divergence between older and younger theologians which, in the latter, was already acute. It is extremely important to recognize the fact of this divergence, and to do what may be possible to mitigate a tension which, in some form, may be inevitable and even wholesome. If the divergence is unrecognized, or if no attempts are made to reach mutual understanding, its results may be a loss of spiritual fellowship, and a lack of balance in both parties.

As a contribution to the "appeasement" which is desirable I am moved to attempt my own diagnosis of the situation, and to offer my own theological confession and *apologia*. I hope this may lead others, especially of the younger theologians, to do the same. Thus, in the interchange which takes place, we may be brought to a greater measure of mutual appreciation. I am sure the older, among whom I regretfully take my place, have a great deal to learn from the younger; I also think the younger are in danger of losing much, and partly spoiling their own contribution, if they so far fail to appreciate their immediate predecessors as to ignore their aim and totally repudiate their method.[1]

No generalization about the older group would be just to all, and I propose to be shamelessly egoistic, because I am likely to avoid misrepresenting myself and might easily misrepresent others.

Some of our younger friends feel that we who reached our conclusions and settled our methods of thought in the first decade of this century have gone up a blind-alley and are now content to settle down at the end of it. But so far as we had any measure of success in our aim, we must refuse that account of our work. For a blind-alley is a road that leads nowhere, and our road led us and some others to Christ. The difficulty which many of the younger generation find about it is not that it leads nowhere, but that it starts from a place where they are not standing and to which they cannot get. I am reminded of the undergraduate who said to me in 1911 or 1912, after listening to Bishop Gore: "I could see that his mind was an awfully jolly merry-go-round, but it never stopped where I was so that I could get on."

My contemporaries grew up in a stable world. Of course, it was not a Christian world in any adequate sense of the words. But it professed Christianity; it was so far sincere in this that it was troubled at any suggestion that it ignored Christian standards of conduct; and in fact its own ostensible standards were to a great extent a Christian heritage. The great Victorian Agnostics had thought it would be possible to retain Christian ethics while discarding Christian doctrine; and (which is more important) they wished to retain Christian ethics and took it for granted that all men of goodwill wished it also. On the ethical side we could assume acceptance of Christian principles.

Along with this went a most un-Christian belief in automatic progress, which was an inheritance from the Rationalists of the eighteenth century. Christian principles provided the standard of life; education and scientific discovery would of themselves produce increasing conformity to that standard. Evil, therefore, was regarded as a survival from a passing age. There was no need for redemption, nor even for God except as the "tendency that makes for righteousness".[2]

That situation constituted our problem. We had to do what we could to persuade people possessed of that outlook to believe that they needed a saviour, and that God is something more than a diffused essence of amiability. We had to do this in face of evidence that already the fabric of life was insecure, though only the more alert were sensitive to that evidence. There was a great industrial upheaval planned for the autumn of 1914—almost a general strike. During the previous summer, in May or early June, I consulted Bishop Gore about some action in view of it; he replied that he had no hope of doing anything useful because on the one side it was too late to check the upheaval, on the other it was impossible to make the hitherto secure classes attend to their peril; and anyhow we all deserved the judgment that was coming. (It came from without, not from within; but it came.)

We were involved in a sex-war which was already a public nuisance and was developing into a menace. We were on the brink of civil war in Ireland. And nowhere was there enough good sense or goodwill to provide a hope of that give-and-take which was needed for a solution. And the root of this obstinacy was the habit of security. No one would believe that any great evil could threaten society as we knew it. There are still multitudes of people for whom, in spite of all to disturb them, the Victorian or Edwardian outlook is axiomatic. Consequently, the theology arising from and addressed to that outlook still has its appeal and value.

It is futile to utter proclamations or denunciations to such a frame of mind. Moreover, we were of necessity infected by it. We saw, as folk who desired to think like Christians, a little further into the meaning of our world than those who sought no illumination from that faith. We had to lead as many as we could to see life in that light of the knowledge of God, which we had ourselves received. We tried, so to speak, to make a map of the world as seen from the standpoint of Christian faith.

In my own case the preparation for this enterprise was more philosophical than theological. The teacher who most influenced me was Edward Caird.[3] The books to which I owed most in the forming of my general outlook were *The World and the Individual* by Royce, and Bernard Bosanquet's[4] two volumes of Gifford Lectures—*The Principle of Individuality and Value* and *The Value and Destiny of the Individual.* I never accepted Bosanquet's ultimate position, and at one time my main concern was to discover what was my point of divergence from one who carried me so far with him.[5] All the time there was in the background the pervasive and increasing influence of Plato—especially of the *Republic, Phaedrus, Theaetetus* and *Sophist.*

With such an aim and such an approach I was concerned to lead a few members of a generation which accepted one large part of the Christian heritage to enter also on the rest. In the Preface to *Christus Veritas* I spoke of the contemporary intellectual atmosphere as "dominated by a philosophy which leaves no room for a specific Incarnation".

> This philosophy [I went on] is not materialist or atheist; it is both spiritual and theistic; but the idea of God which it reaches is such as to preclude His ever doing anything in particular in any other sense than that in which He does everything in general. *I believe that a very slight touch to the intellectual balance may make the scales incline the other way.* Part of the trouble is that theologians have left the field of most general inquiry too largely to non-theological philosophers; they have tended to write either history or detailed discussion of particular doctrines. *What is needed is the exposition of the Christian idea of God, life and the world, or, in other words, a Christo-centric metaphysics.*

The two sentences which I have italicized seem very remote today. The estimate expressed in the earlier was probably mistaken in 1924, when that sentence was written; it has no relevance to the situation today. The later sentence expresses what I believe to be a permanent need and the supreme task of theology; but it is a task of which we now see the impracticability in anything less than many generations.

In the Preface to *Doctrine in the Church of England* I tried to indicate a sense of the new needs. After mentioning that under the influence of Westcott and Gore most Anglican theology was centred upon the Incarnation, I said:

A theology of the Incarnation tends to be a Christo-centric metaphysic. And in all ages there is need for the fresh elaboration of such a scheme of thought or map of life as seen in the light of the revelation in Christ. A theology of Redemption (though, of course, Redemption has its great place in the former) tends rather to sound the prophetic note; it is more ready to admit that much in this evil world is irrational and strictly unintelligible; and it looks to the coming of the Kingdom as a necessary preliminary to the understanding of much that now is. If the security of the nineteenth century, already (1937) shattered in Europe, finally crumbles away in our own country, we shall be pressed more and more towards a theology of Redemption. In this we shall be coming closer to the New Testament.

Now we turn to the world in which the younger theologians have formed their habits of thought. Christian standards of conduct are challenged as radically as Christian doctrine. Men and women come to maturity with no sense that there is a place for them somewhere in a society resting on secure principles which it regards as Christian. There may be no discoverable place for them at all. Society rests on no ascertainable principles, but is rather in its structure an accidental resultant of blind forces, which are in process of undermining what they have produced. The Christian view of life is not only relegated to the background as unnecessary, but openly repudiated by adherents of a philosophy which is far more obviously effective than Christianity; for if a young man becomes a Communist or Fascist he is told very plainly what to think and do, whereas the Church leaves him with nothing but principles so general as to afford no actual guidance. Meanwhile, the world has been fumbling about with a League of Nations, till its drift to another war became evident, though statesmen declared that this would be the end of civilization.

When the older theologians offer to men fashioned by such influences a Christian map of the world, these rightly refuse to listen. The world today is one of which no Christian map can be made. It must be changed by Christ into something very unlike itself before a Christian map of it is possible. We used to believe in the sovereignty of the God of love a great deal too light-heartedly. I have much more understanding now than I had in 1906 or thereabouts (when he said it) of Bishop Gore's passionate outburst at a meeting of the Synthetic Society: "If it were not for the miracles, and supremely the Resurrection, I should see no more reason for supposing that God is revealed in Jesus Christ than that He is revealed in Nero."

There is a new task for theologians today. We cannot come to the men of today saying: "You will find that all your experience fits together in a harmonious system if you will only look at it in the illumination of the Gospel." We may still hope that one day they will look back at their experience and see that all of it falls within the purpose of the God of Righteous Love. But that kind of theology belongs to the Kingdom which is to come. Our task with this world is not to explain it but to convert it. Its need can be met, not by the discovery of its own immanent principle in signal manifestation through Jesus Christ, but only by the shattering impact upon its self-sufficiency and arrogance of the Son of God crucified, risen and ascended, pouring forth that explosive and disruptive energy which is the Holy Ghost. He is the source of fellowship and all true fellowship comes from Him. But in order to fashion true fellowship in such a world as this, and out of such men and women as we are, He must first break up sham fellowships with which we have been deluding ourselves. Christ said that the effect of His coming would be to set men at variance. We must expect the movement of His Spirit among us to produce sharper divisions as well as deeper unity.

All this still falls formally, I think, within the formulations which we reached in the pre-war days, and which were indeed only a rephrasing of traditional Christian positions. In *Mens Creatrix* (1916) and *Christus Veritas* (1924) I argued that evil, *when overcome*, is justified, and that no justification for any one instance of evil is possible until that evil is overcome. I still think that this formally covers the ground. But to the new generation the approach, the tone, the emphasis seem all to be wrong—so wrong that they cannot even be interested in the question whether the formula is valid. War—nothing less—overshadows life. We have to maintain our faith in God under the shadow and shock of war. Facile generalizations are an affront. We must start from the fearful tension between the doctrine of the Love of God and the actual facts of daily experience. When we have eliminated war, it will be time to discuss whether its monstrous evil can then be seen as a "constituent element of the absolute good" (*Christus Veritas*, p. 254). Till then we had better get on with the job of eliminating it by the power of the Gospel, which we must present, not as the clue to a universal synthesis, but as the source of world-transformation.

Partly for this reason, and still more because of the convergence of all lines of New Testament scholarship upon the central place of the Ecclesia in the Apostolic experience and teaching, theologians of today are more concerned than we were in 1910 or 1920 about the theological status of the Church. The Church is part of its own Creed. To be in Christ is to be in the Church—and *vice versa.* Hence there is a new appreciation of the importance of the Church for faith itself. In the midst of this world where it appears that the devil's claim is valid—"it hath been delivered unto me, and to whomsoever I will I give it"—the individual Christian is helpless except as a member of the Body, the Church. So the Church, alike as ground and object of faith, and as the agent of the Kingdom endowed even now with its powers, has a new prominence in the minds of thoughtful Christians. We did not fail a quarter of a century ago to insist on the necessity and claim of the Church. But this was secondary and derivative; now it is primary and basic.

Theology today, as I think, has two main tasks. They are one at the root, and those engaged on each should be concerned also for the other. But they are very different. First there is the thinking out afresh what are the standards of life to which a society must aim at conforming if it is to be in any sense a Christian society. We lack, and desperately need, an ethic of collective action. What is the duty of a Christian managing-director or of a Christian trade union secretary in an industrial dispute? Neither may act in his own name alone. All the perspectives are different from those of individual relationships. But we offer no guidance whatever. And in the modern world half the decisions that men have to take are on behalf of some collective unit. This problem appears in its acutest form in the pacifist controversy.[6]

In all this field, effective action is possible only if Christians (*a*) are ready to co-operate with non-Christians who share their aim, (*b*) are able to present what they believe on Christian grounds to be right as commendable also on general grounds of reason. Here is a field for the utmost co-operative effort in thought and action. The two great Papal Encyclicals *Rerum Novarum* and *Quadragesimo Anno*, and such writings as those of Maritain,[6] set us an example from the Roman Catholic side. Those of us who, in comparison, are handicapped by inability to accept the Thomist scheme as an assured starting-point, though having nothing which is really so complete and thorough to put in its place, must do our best, even if for a time it makes poor showing beside the achievement of our colleagues. Perhaps one main task is to become clear precisely where and why we dissent from the Thomist basis, and see whether the whole structure may not be susceptible of modification in the light of our different or additional principles. But whether in that way or in some other, we must labour for the rebirth of Christendom.

Behind and beneath all this is the need to recover our apprehension of the Gospel alike in its essence and in its impact upon ourselves and the world. We have to face this tormented world, not as offering a means to its coherence in thought and its harmony in practice, but as challenging it in the name and power of Christ crucified and risen. We shall not try to "make sense" of everything; we shall openly proclaim that most things as they are have no sense in them at all. We shall not say that a Christian philosophy embraces all experience in a coherent and comprehensive scheme; we shall declare that in the Gospel there is offered to men deliverance from a system of things—"the world"—which deserves the destruction which is coming upon it, a deliverance offered to all so that "the world" itself may receive it if it will. We proclaim, not general progress, but salvation to them that believe.

Here at once two problems confront us. First, what is the relation between that Order of Redemption which the Christian enters by faith and the Order of Creation to which he belongs as a man? Here is the pacifist problem again. Is there a Natural Order which is from God, as Catholic tradition holds? Or is there only Natural Disorder, the fruit of sin, from which Christ delivers us, as continental Protestantism has held? And if the latter view be adopted, does the deliverance take effect in this life or only in the life to come?

Secondly, what is that Gospel which we are to proclaim? Or, if we like to put it otherwise, what is the content of Revelation? Are there revealed truths, which can be formulated in propositions? Or is Revelation (as I am led to think) always given in Events? If that is so, there are truths about Revelation, but not actually revealed truths.

We must dig the foundations deeper than we did in pre-war years, or in the inter-war years when we developed our pre-war thoughts. And we must be content with less imposing structures. One day theology will take up again its larger and serener task and offer to a new Christendom its Christian map of life, its Christocentric metaphysic. But that day can hardly dawn while any who are now already concerned with theology are still alive. The task that claims our labour now is far less alluring to one of my own temperament and upbringing, yet there can be no doubt that in theology as in life we shall be rather enriched than impoverished, even though we are concerned to light beacons in the darkness rather than to illuminate the world, if we are more completely dominated in thought and aspiration by the redeeming acts of God in Jesus Christ.

WILLIAM EBOR:

1 J. K. Mozley (*Tendencies in British Theology*, p. 95) lists the following nine books among the works written by Anglicans which were important in the field of philosophical theology: Temple, *Mens Creatrix* (1917); *Christus Veritas* (1924); *Nature, Man and God* (1934); W. R. Matthews, *God in Christian Thought and Experience* (1930); *Essays in Construction* (1933); *The Purpose of God* (1935); O. C. Quick, *The Ground of Faith and the Chaos of Thought* (1931); *The Christian Sacraments* (1927); *Doctrines of the Creed* (1938).

2 Roger Lloyd wrote: "The attitude towards life of men like Thomas Huxley and Lowes Dickinson, Professor Bury and Hastings Rashdall, Bishop Percival of Hereford and T. R. Glover was not likely to be ignoble. It might indeed be mistaken through excess of optimism, as the passage of time has proved it to be. But Liberalism's prestige was enormous, and in its heyday, the period of Asquith's administration, its optimism did not seem unreasonable" (*The Church of England: 1919–1939*, p. 256).

3 Caird, Edward; *b.* 1835; *educ.*, Greenock Academy, Glasgow and St Andrews Universities, Balliol College, Oxford; Fellow and tutor of Merton College; Professor of Moral Philosophy at Glasgow, 1866; Master of Balliol College, 1893; Gifford Lecturer; *d.* 1908.

4 Bosanquet, Bernard; *b.* 1848; *educ.*, Balliol College, Oxford; Fellow of University College, 1870; Professor of Moral Philosophy at St Andrews 1903–8; *d.* 1923.

5 "With F. H. Bradley (1846–1924), Bernard Bosanquet (1848–1923) and J. McT. E. McTaggart (1866–1925) the Hegelian influence intensifies and in regard to religion all three writers assume positions away from the general current even of liberal theological thinking. To conceptualize the Absolute they found it necessary to sacrifice one after another of the convictions which personal idealists took to be fundamental" (B. M. G. Reardon, *Religious Thoughts in the Nineteenth Century*, p. 354).

6 Dick Sheppard founded the Peace Pledge Union in October 1934, and within a year 80,000 pledged themselves on postcards not to fight in the event of war.

99 MALVERN CONFERENCE, 1942

(*Malvern and After*, pp. 2-3)

The Malvern Conference was a purely Anglican gathering under the presidency of William Temple which met to discuss the social action of the Church of England after the war. The purpose of the conference was "to consider from the Anglican point of view what are the fundamental facts which are directly relevant to the ordering of the new society that is quite evidently emerging, and how Christian thought can be shaped to play a leading part in the reconstruction after the war is over". Sir Richard Acland's[1] claim that common ownership was a matter of fundamental Christian principle became the main issue, and Temple's draft on private ownership had to be revised before it was adopted without dissentient vote.

Res. 14. God Himself is the Sovereign of all human life; all men are His children, and ought to be brothers of one another; through Christ the Redeemer they can become what they ought to be.

There can be no advance towards a more Christian way of life except through a wider and fuller acceptance of this faith, and through the adoption, by individuals, of the way of living which it implies.

There is no structural organisation of society which can bring about the coming of the Kingdom of God on earth, since it is a gift of God, and since all systems can be perverted by the selfishness of man. Therefore, the Church as such can never commit itself to any proposed change in the structure of society as being a self-sufficient means of salvation.[2]

But the Church can point to those features of our existing society which, while they can never prevent individual men and women from becoming Christian, are contrary to divine justice, and act as stumbling blocks, making it harder for men to live Christian lives.

Res. 15 In our present situation we believe that the maintenance of that part of the structure of our society by which the ultimate ownership of the principal industrial resources of the community can be vested in the hands of private owners may be such a stumbling block.[3] On the one hand it may deprive the poorest members of the community of the essentials of life. On the other, while these resources can be so owned, men will strive for their ownership for themselves. As a consequence, a way of life founded on the supremacy of the economic motive will remain, which is contrary to God's plan for mankind.[4]

For one or both of these reasons, the time has come for Christians to proclaim the need for striving towards a form of society in which, while the essential value of the individual human personality is preserved, the continuance of these abuses will be no longer possible.

Members of the Church of England, clergy and laity alike, cannot take part in this work unless they are ready to advocate and bring about a complete change in the internal financial position of the Church of England.

1 Acland, Richard Thomas Dyke; *b.* 1906; *educ.*, Rugby and Balliol College, Oxford; M.P., Barnstaple, 1935–45; M.P., Gravesend, 1947–55; Second Church Estates Commissioner, 1950–1.

2 Henson commented in 1944: "It is everywhere agreed that the prevailing current of opinion within Western civilization is towards the reorganization of society on the principle of socialism, or (the same thing though rather more logically conceived) Communism. Does it not follow, therefore, that the Christian Church will move in the same direction, and by doing so will both strengthen the current and make it more unmanageable? For the Church will inoculate economic and political movements with all the fire of its own zeal, and the uncompromising logic of its own conviction" (*Retrospect*, vol. 3, pp. 276-7).

3 Temple deprecated the use of "may be", and preferred "is" in this sentence. Nevertheless "ultimate" in the same sentence was a word to be stressed emphatically.

4 Collective ownership derived its political importance from the experience of two wars and a series of industrial disputes. The coal mining industry and the railways had long been particularly vexed in the matter of industrial relationships, and it was hardly surprising that they were high on the socialist list of priorities for nationalization.

100 BUTLER'S EDUCATION ACT 1944

(*Statutes at Large*, 7-8 Geo. VI, c. 31)

The changed climate of Anglican and Free Church relations in Britain made possible the wide acceptance of the 1944 Education Act. The Bill had a strong advocate in Temple; among its opponents was Headlam who saw in it "a monopoly of education" by the State and the virtual disappearance of church schools. On the one hand, Temple saw the new regulations maintaining the dual system by improving school buildings, and on the other, Headlam believed they would prevent it by putting greater pressure on the Church's financial means. The Bill, which became law on 3 August 1944, provided for an undenominational system of religion in county schools.

MAINTAINANCE OF VOLUNTARY SCHOOLS

15

(3)*a* The following expenses shall be payable by the managers or governors of the school, that is to say, the expenses of discharging any liability incurred by them or on their behalf or by or on behalf of any former managers or governors of the school or any trustees thereof (in connection with the provision of premises or equipment for the purposes of the school); any expenses incurred in effecting such alterations to the school buildings as may be required by the local education authority for the purpose of securing that the school premises should conform to the prescribed standards, and any expenses incurred in effecting repairs to the school buildings not being repairs which are excluded from their responsibility by the following paragraph.[1]

(4) If at any time the managers or governors of an aided school or a special agreement school are unable or unwilling to carry out their obligations under paragraph (*a*) of the last foregoing subsection, it shall be their duty to apply to the Minister for an order revoking the order by virtue of which the school is an aided school or a special agreement school, and upon such an application being made to him the Minister shall revoke the order.[2]

RELIGIOUS EDUCATION IN COUNTY AND VOLUNTARY SCHOOLS

25

(1) Subject to the provisions of this section, the school day in

every county school and in every voluntary school shall begin with collective worship on the part of all pupils in attendance at the school, and the arrangements made therefor shall provide for a single act of worship attended by all such pupils unless, in the opinion of the local education authority or, in the case of a voluntary school, of the managers or governors thereof, the school premises are such as to make it impracticable to assemble them for that purpose.

(2) Subject to the provisions of this section, religious instruction shall be given in every county school and in every voluntary school.

(3) It shall not be required, as a condition of any pupil attending any county school or any voluntary school, that he shall attend or abstain from attending any Sunday school or any place of religious worship.

(4) If the parent of any pupil in attendance at any county school or any voluntary school requests that he be wholly or partly excused from attendance at religious worship in the school, or from attendance at religious instruction in the school, or from attendance at both religious worship and religious instruction in the school, then, until the request is withdrawn, the pupils shall be excused from such attendance accordingly.

(5) Where any pupil has been wholly or partly excused from attendance at religious worship or instruction in any school in accordance with the provisions of this section, and the local education authority are satisfied:

(*a*) that the parent of the pupil desires him to receive religious instruction of a kind which is not provided in the school during the periods during which he is excused from such attendance;
(*b*) that the pupil cannot with reasonable convenience be sent to another county or voluntary school where religious instruction of the kind desired by the parent is provided; and
(*c*) that arrangements have been made for him to receive religious instruction during school hours elsewhere,

the pupil may be withdrawn from the school during such periods as are reasonably necessary for the purpose of enabling him to receive religious instruction in accordance with the arrangements:

Provided that the pupil shall not be so withdrawn unless the local education authority are satisfied that the arrangements are such as will not interfere with the attendance of the pupil at school on any day except at the beginning or end of the school session on that day.

26

Subject as hereinafter provided, the collective worship required by subsection (1) of the last foregoing section shall not, in any county school, be distinctive of any particular religious denomination, and the religious instruction given to any pupils in attendance at a county school in conformity with the requirements of subsection (2) of the said section shall be given in accordance with an agreed syllabus adopted for the school or for those pupils and shall not include any catechism or formulary which is distinctive of any particular religious denomination ...

(6) Subject to any arrangements made under subsection (1) of this section,[3] the religious instruction given to the pupils in attendance at a controlled school shall be given in accordance with an agreed syllabus adopted for the school or for those pupils.[4]

1 Substitution was made in 9-10 Geo. VI, c. 50, ss. 4(2), 14, sch. 2, Pt II. Headlam estimated that the diocese of Gloucester would need to raise £1,350,000 to comply with the terms of the Act. Two random notes occur in biographies of the period: "Many parishes came to realize the value of their Church schools, and worked together to save them while there was still time" (R. P. Stacy Waddy, *Philip Lloyd, Missionary and Bishop* (1954), p. 142); and "The implementing of the 1944 Education Bill at the cessation of the war made it necessary to deal with the question of Church schools; of them the Archbishop said: 'Many are certain to disappear in the near future', but he saw, as time went on, the necessity of saving all that could be salvaged, and the last time he chaired a meeting was at the Diocesan Council of Education on October 1, 1955. Here he made it clear that the diocese must do its utmost to keep the schools scheduled to be kept. It was, however, somewhat late in the day and very few schools, comparatively speaking will benefit from this intervention" (The Prioress of Whitby, *Archbishop Garbett* (1957), pp. 55-6).

2 Ext. 9-10 Geo. VI, c. 50, s. 2, (5).

3 Provision was made for parents to request religious instruction in accordance with the provisions of a trust deed relating to the school, not exceeding two periods a week.

4 Under Schedule 5, a conference for the drawing up of an agreed syllabus was to include: local religious representatives, representatives of the Church of England, teachers, and the local authority.

101 ARCHBISHOP FISHER'S CAMBRIDGE SERMON, 1946

(G. F. Fisher, *A Step Forward in Church Relations* (1946))

As an outcome of the Lambeth Appeal, discussions between Anglicans and the Free Churches in Britain led to the publication of an *Outline of a Reunion Scheme* in 1938. The Second World War prevented any further development in the bringing together of the different bodies. In a sermon preached before the University of Cambridge on 3 November 1946 the Archbishop of Canterbury opened the way for renewed discussion. The sermon outlined three reasons why "constitutional" schemes of reunion were difficult to effect, and suggested the possibility of the Free Churches taking episcopacy into their systems of church government.[1]

I am the Door: by me if any man enter in, he shall be saved and shall go in and out, and find pasture. The thief cometh not but for to steal and to kill and to destroy: I am come that they might have life and that they might have it more abundantly.

John 10.9-10

This parable "of the Sheep, the Shepherd, and the Brigands" echoes all the main themes of the Christian Gospel. Our Lord is the Door, through whom we men can know God in His true Fatherhood: He is the one Saviour who calls men to follow Him, calls them individually and by name: those who hear His call and obey it, not only enter through Him but possess His life. He is the Shepherd as well as the Door. And in Him they become one flock with one Shepherd who has given His life for the sheep.

That is our Lord's divine answer to human need. That is what all Christians find in Him.

It is of matters relating to the unity of the Church that I wish to speak: and therefore I have put first the unity which already exists before speaking of that which does not. In every main Christian denomination are found in abundance those who have entered by the one Door, have found the one Saviour and draw from Him their life. Of all such Christ is the Shepherd and all such belong to His flock; but they are in different folds, fenced off from one another by barriers, some trivial enough, some reaching up (as it would seem) to heaven itself, which the long course of the Church's history has erected.

So while in each fold the followers of our Lord draw their life from Him, that divine life does not freely circulate between the folds in the life-giving operations of worship to Him who is the Head of the Church and of sacramental fellowship between His members. In the temporal sphere, in the historical Church, the circulation of the Church's life-blood is impaired or blocked: and thereby of necessity its work and witness are enfeebled. Even though many of the divisions had their historical justification and their consicentious cause, even though God has used them to preserve this part or that of the riches of Christ from being lost, to our Lord and to His people they are a scandal and a rock of offence to be removed, that the life of His Church may be more abundant.

The imperfections of the Church caused these disunities and every denomination has its imperfections still. But at last the minds of Christians are turned earnestly towards recognizing in one another the manifest signs of the faith and life of Christ and towards praying that the many may again become visibly one in the Holy Catholic Church of Christ.

It has been the great achievement of the past two generations, of the ecumenical movement, of Lambeth Conferences and of countless faithful souls, to focus attention upon that which all denominations hold in common and receive from Christ, their one Shepherd. Rome alone remains officially unwilling to acknowledge other folds under the one Shepherd or even to join in prayer with them.[2] Between all the others there is an interchange of fellowship and prayer and thought and a searching to overthrow the barriers between them. On the theology of Redemption and Grace, of the Scriptures, the Creeds, the Sacraments, even of the Church itself, there are no barriers that reach up to heaven.

It is round the theology of the ministry that the tensions most exist: some would regard the ministry of the Church as solely derived from and subject to the will of the Church, the Spirit-bearing Body, while others regard it as the original gift of Christ to His Church to be preserved in unbroken succession: and the synthesis of these not necessarily contradictory views has not yet been found.

But there are all sorts of other barriers, not of theology but of habit which, when it comes to living together, have a great importance and which because they are matters of habit widely diffused and long valued are not readily amenable to change. Each denomination has its own idiom of worship within the framework of the Christian verities, its own idiom of thought and speech, of procedure and government, of family life. Two neighbouring households may be friendly and yet not at ease at the prospect of living in one household. And the inertia in the minds of many people of many denominations as regards steps to unity is due less to theological reasons than to dislike of a merging of domestic habits.

In what I go on to say, I am thinking simply of the situation in Britain. There have been years of conversations between the Church of England, the Church of Scotland, and the Free Churches. There has been great growth in understanding: there have been sketches of a united church, outlines of reunion schemes. Then came the war and put an end to that period.

How shall we begin again? I sense a certain reluctance to begin at all.

A distinguished theologian has recently expressed the opinion that all schemes of reunion should be postponed until further study, theological thinking and prayer in all Christian communions have led them to a recovered apprehension of the integrity and balance of Christian truth, alike in the sphere of faith and in that order, based on a renewed understanding of the Scriptures of the Old and New Testaments and of the witness of Christian antiquity.

That is to suggest that nothing should be done until the theologians have begun all over again and reached agreed conclusions. The past does not suggest that such theological unanimity will come in any forseeable future. But meanwhile there is the life, the life of Christ, visible in every denomination: and its circulation impaired or blocked. There is the one Shepherd, and the separated folds. In the history of the Church the divine life creates, and the theology is controlled by, the life as much as the life is controlled by the theology.[3]

I believe the difficulty of beginning again lies elsewhere. Schemes of reunion have generally been what I will call constitutional. They posit between two or more denominations an agreed constitution by acceptance of which they become one. Its articles must be such as to satisfy and to bind the negotiating parties. They must contain all that each negotiating party specially values and omit anything which it stubbornly resists: they must be non-committal where there is unresolved difference of opinion: they must set out an organization and a method of government: with this new constitution in their hands the negotiating denominations are to lose their formerly separate identities and become a "new Province of the Universal Church", unsure at its birth what will be its relations to other Christian communions and whether former affiliations of the uniting bodies will be impaired or not. I think that reluctance is caused partly by fear of that loss of identity which is a precious thing to those concerned, partly by fear of compromises, the full implications of which cannot be foreseen, partly by fear of unfamiliar forms of government, and all the time by fear of a written constitution. It is designed to help denominations to "grow together" in the unity of the life of Christ. But a constitution is an artificial thing and may imperil the life it seeks to promote.[4]

In this country I think there are three special reasons which make the constitutional method the most difficult of all ways to reunion.

In the first place the Church of England is an established Church; it has a very complicated legal nexus with the State, which enters deeply into its machinery of government.

The Free Churches would certainly not accept the establishment as it is. And while they might agree that a reunited church could valuably retain some measure of State connection, the process of extricating the Church of England from what it was not desired to retain and of accomplishing its transference to a newly devised constitution would be a work of even greater magnitude and difficulty than the scheme of reunion itself.

Secondly, its position in the Anglican Communion requires that the Church of England should not confuse its own identity. It is the nodal point of that Communion. It is one thing for four dioceses in India to go out of the Anglican Communion into a province with a constitution of its own and a position within the Catholic Church still to win. But for the Church of England to go out of the Anglican Communion would disrupt that Communion itself, by depriving it of its nodal point. The Church of England by the nature of the case can only move along with its fellow-churches in every part of the world. It cannot submit itself to any constitution convenient for these islands unless it is one which in principle its related churches can adopt for themselves. The time may come when in the service of the unity of the Church, the Anglican Churches can cease to exist as a distinct group. But that time is not yet in sight for us and the Free Churches might well say the same for their own groups.

Thirdly, there are tensions within the Church of England itself which are not resolved: it has its own problem of recovering its own spiritual authority over itself and of re-ordering its own life. As I believe, the Church of England is being called and led to resettle its own inner life in loyalty to the tradition and the task which God has entrusted to it. But when it is thus engaged in a delicate task, it is unwise at the same time to involve it in questions of constitutional affiliation to other denominations. We need to have, as I believe we are getting, a surer hold upon our own tradition before it can be offered to, or accepted by, others as their own.

If then procedure by constitutional reunion is so beset by difficulties, is there any other way of advance? Any other means by which we can get towards that free circulation of the life of Christ between the folds of His flock?

There is a suggestion which I should like in all humility to make to my brethren of other denominations. We do not desire a federation: that does not restore the circulation. As I have suggested the road is not yet open, we are not yet ready for organic or constitutional union. But there can be a process of assimilation, of growing alike. What we need is that while the folds remain distinct, there should be a movement towards a free and unfettered exchange of life in worship and sacrament between them as there is already of prayer and thought and Christian fellowship—in short that they should grow towards that full communion with one another, which already in their separation they have with Christ.

The Church of England is in full communion with the Old Catholics on the Continent: and its relations with the Orthodox Churches on the one hand, and with the Churches of Sweden and Finland on the other, already approach, if they do not yet reach, full communion. My longing is, not yet that we should be *united* with other churches in this country, but that we should grow to *full communion* with them.

As I have said and as negotiations have shown, no insuperable barrier to that remains until we come to questions of the ministry and government of the Church. Full communion between churches means not that they are identical in all ways, but that there is no barrier to exchange of their ministers and ministries. Every Church's ministry is effective as a means by which the life of Christ reaches His people. Every Church's ministry is defective because it is prevented from operating in all folds of His flock. For full communion between churches there is needed a ministry mutually acknowledged by all as possessing not only the inward call of the Spirit but also the authority which each church in consequence requires.

At the Lausanne Conference of Churches in 1927, it was said that in view of the place which the Episcopate, the Council of Presbyters, and the Congregation of the Faithful, respectively had in the constitution of the early Church, in view of the fact that these three elements are each today and have been for centuries accepted by great communions in Christendom, and that they are each believed by many to be essential to the good order of the Church, "We recognize that these several elements must all ... have an appropriate place in the order of life of a reunited Church."[5]

Every constitutional scheme has proceeded on those lines. The non-episcopal churches have accepted the principle that episcopacy must exist along with the other elements in a reunited Church. For reasons obvious enough in Church history, they fear what may be made of episcopacy. But they accept the fact of it. If they do so for a reunited Church, why not also and earlier for the process of assimilation, as a step towards full communion?

It may be said that in a reunited Church they could guard themselves in the constitution against abuses of episcopacy. But they could do so far more effectively by taking it into their own system. The Church of England has not yet found the finally satisfying use of episcopacy in practice: nor certainly has the Church of Rome. If non-episcopal churches agree that it must come into the picture, could they not take it and try it out on their own ground first?

It is not of course quite as simple as all that. There are requirements and functions which Catholic tradition attaches to the office of a bishop in the Church of God, which, if our aim is assimilation and full communion, must be safeguarded. Negotiators in the past have been able to agree upon them, and could with hope inquire into them further, if our non-episcopal brethren were able to contemplate the step I suggest.

As it seems to me, it is an easier step for them to contemplate than that involved in a union of churches: and if achieved, it would immensely carry us forward towards full communion, without the fearful complexities and upheavals of a constitutional union. In such a giving and receiving of episcopacy, there would be a mutual removal of a barrier between the folds.

Nor would any fresh barriers be raised, such as may be by a constitutional scheme. For no previously existing affiliations would be impaired. The Church of England can be in communion with the Church of Sweden which in its turn is in communion with the Church of Norway, although as yet the Church of England is not in communion with the Church of Norway. That may be illogical, but it is the way of Christian life and love. William Temple used to quote Fr Kelly as saying that we must not regard the churches as we regard a row of separate boxes, but as rays of coloured lights shading into one another.

In putting forward this suggestion, I am presupposing that

between the churches which concerned themselves with it there would be found to be agreement upon the essential principles of the Church, the Scriptures, the Creeds, the Sacraments and of the Ministry itself as "a gift of God through Christ to His Church, essential to its being and well-being, perpetually authorized and made effective through Christ and His Spirit" (Lausanne, Report 5): and I believe that presupposition to be reasonable. Differences of interpretation are not such as to forbid communion and indeed are to be found within each body.

If then non-episcopal churches could thus take episcopacy into their systems, I hope that the step would not stand alone. I should hope that in preparation for it, along the lines of recent Canadian proposals, each communion, episcopal and non-episcopal, should contribute the whole of its separate ministry to so many of the ministers of the other as were willing to receive it. By that means there would be assimilation at work from the start at the presbyteral level as well as at the episcopal level.[6]

I love the Church of England, as the Presbyterian and the Methodist love their churches. It is, I think, not possible yet nor desirable that any church should merge its identity in a newly constituted union. What I desire is that I should be able freely to enter their churches and they mine in the sacraments of the Lord and in full fellowship of worship, that His life may freely circulate between us. Cannot we grow to full communion with each other before we start to write a constitution? Have we the wisdom, the humility, the love and the spirit of Christ sufficient for such a venture as I have suggested? If there were agreement on it, I would thankfully receive at the hands of others their commission in their accustomed form and in the same way confer our own; that is the mutual exchange of love and enrichment to which Lambeth 1920 called us.[7]

1 Fisher, Geoffrey Francis; *b.* 1887; *educ.*, Exeter College, Oxford; B.A. 1910; deacon, 1912; priest, 1913; assistant chaplain of Marlborough College, 1912; Headmaster of Repton, 1914; Bishop of Chester, 1932; Bishop of London, 1939; Archbishop of Canterbury, 1945; resigned, 1960.

2 Fisher visited Pope John XXIII in Rome in 1960. The Archbishop's part in the drawing of the Roman Church into the ecumenical movement is described in Bill, *Anglican Initiatives*, pp. 94-104, where Cardinal Bea is quoted as saying: "It was Dr Fisher who sensed the change of atmosphere; pointed it out; realized the obligations entailed and took the necessary steps to bring the public to a greater

awareness of the new atmosphere and to foster their interest" (p. 104).

3 A joint conference was set up to examine the implications of the Archbishop's proposals, and in 1950 produced a report entitled *Church Relations in England*. See, Rouse and Neill, *A History of the Ecumenical Movement* (1953), pp. 484-6.

4 Fisher later wrote: "I became Archbishop just as the war ended, and I wanted to do what I could to bring about in England a renewal of the inter-Church discussions which had been everywhere halted by the war, and if possible a renewal on more promising lines. It happened that just at that time I read the outline of a scheme for uniting the Anglican and Presbyterian Churches in the United States. Like the English outline to which I referred just now, it covered all the requirements for a unified Church in meticulous detail. As it seemed to me it put the two Churches into a strait jacket with no elbow room at all. At the same time I heard something of a scheme in Canada which seemed to suggest that in outlying districts in the far North if there was a Methodist minister but no Anglican priest, the Anglican Church should ordain the minister so that he could serve both Churches. The one scheme seemed to be too strait laced and the other too lax. I had always kept in my mind the Bonn Agreement of 1931 made between the Church of England (and later almost all other Anglican Provinces) and the Old Catholic Churches of the Continent. This agreement had seemed to me to be a model of Christian wisdom and grace, and now seemed to me to provide the way forward which was needed. It was thus that I was led to preach my Cambridge Sermon of November 1946 which did serve to set things moving again" (*A Survey of Church Relations* (1967), pp. 11-12).

5 The first "Faith and Order" conference held under the leadership of Bishop Charles Brent and attended by delegates of all major denominations excepting the Roman Catholic and Russian Orthodox churches.

6 In both Australia and Canada schemes were put forward for an enlarged commission whereby separate ministries were to be united in the person of individual ministers by a wider commissioning through a Mutual Formula.

7 "For a long time the sermon achieved only its immediate purpose of getting the discussions started again ... How much is owed to the Cambridge sermon preached in 1946 it is hardly possible even to guess, but it did take the movement out of the deep freeze and got inter-Church discussions started again. There is surely a connection between the sermon and the new proposals for communion and finally organic unity between the Methodist Church and the Church of England. It had been one of the most effective of modern sermons" (Lloyd, *The Church of England: 1900–1965*, p. 470).

102 THE CHURCH OF SOUTH INDIA, 1944

The *Scheme for Church Union* for South India was, in many ways, a test case for the Church of England. The *Scheme* envisaged the uniting of episcopal, congregational, and presbyterian elements into a single church order. The *Scheme* received cautious approval from the Lambeth Conferences of 1920 and 1930, the Lambeth *Report* noting "a complete agreement between the uniting Churches on certain points of doctrine and practice is not expected to be reached before inauguration of the union". There were many opinions expressed within the Church of England reflecting the different theological standpoints. Many critics, especially among Anglo-Catholics, saw it as a denial of the Church's Catholic principles in regard to the historic episcopate, the sacraments, and the creeds. Since much of the overseas work of the Church of England had been undertaken and superintended by the missionary societies, it was to be expected that they should be called upon to express their views, though their opinion in no way bound the official judgement of the government of the Church of England.[1]

(G. F. Cranswick and M. A. C. Warren, *A Vital Issue: Church Union in South India* (2nd edn, London n.d.), pp. 6-13)

NEGOTIATIONS FOR UNION

Bearing in mind this very brief outline of the situation it is not surprising that the pressure for union should come from Indians themselves. In 1919 thirty-three men met at Tranquebar in South India, the place where in 1706 the first Lutheran missionaries landed. Of that number thirty-one were Indians, one was an American, and one an Englishman. They were members of the Anglican Church and the South India United Church, which had been formed in 1906 when Presbyterians, Congregationalists, and Lutherans joined together. A few months later the Bishops of our Church in India welcomed the findings of this group of thirty-three men and expressed their sympathy for a new approach being made towards union. After ten years of prayer and careful work a first draft of a union plan was published in 1929. Further discussions by a joint committee took place. These meetings were characterized by an experience of deep spiritual unity and by a vivid sense that those present were being led by the Holy Spirit throughout all their deliberations, in which differences were frankly faced. After a further twelve years of work the final and definitive form of a Scheme for Union was published at the end of 1941.

This Scheme has been approved by the Methodist Conference in this country as well as by the Provincial Synod of that Church in South India. Five out of eight of the Councils of the South India United Church have already given their approval. The remaining three Councils which comprise more than half the membership of that Church have still to come to a decision. The General Assembly of the S.I.U.C., which is the final authority in such matters, will be meeting in September 1943.

The Episcopal Synod of the Anglican Communion in India, known as the Church of India, Burma, and Ceylon, has commended the Scheme for consideration by the Diocesan Councils. These are now, or will shortly be meeting. The General Council of the Church of India, Burma, and Ceylon has been summoned to meet in January 1944, when it will have to decide against or in favour of union. If agreement to unite is secured from the three uniting Churches, it is hoped that arrangements for the inauguration of union will proceed immediately.

The Scheme is a great adventure of faith and courage, and expresses a real willingness on the part of all those joining in to make their own full contribution to the United Church, and to welcome the contribution of others which perhaps they have not understood or appreciated before. It will be the first union between Episcopal and Free Churches that has taken place. The Mar Thoma Church of Travancore did not feel able to join in the negotiations when they considered the matter in the early years of these negotiations because they felt that their first duty was to regain union with their mother Jacobite Church. Progress in this is slow, mainly because of the Jacobites being preoccupied and divided over the question of their relation to the Patriarchate of Antioch. So the Roman and Jacobite Churches are not involved in the South India Scheme, nor are the Lutherans (American and Continental) or the Baptists (American and Canadian), who make up practically all the other non-Roman Christians in South India.

AN OUTLINE OF THE SCHEME

Of the three Churches seeking union one, the Anglican, is an episcopally-ordered Church, and its worship, rites, and ceremonies are governed by the Book of Common Prayer; one, the South India United Church, generally speaking follows the Presbyterian model of order and worship combined with that of the Congregational Church. This body lays special stress on the importance of each congregation as representing the Church of Christ in that area. The third is the Methodist Church which, while it has much in common with the Anglican Church from which it took its origin, has developed a greater freedom in its worship and use of lay people in the conduct of services and in administration.

These three Churches comprise over one million adherents, of which nearly half are Anglicans and of these the greater number owe their spiritual heritage to the C.M.S.

At the outset it should be remembered that the Scheme was drawn up to meet the particular circumstances of the Churches in South India. They recognize that three scriptural elements, the Episcopal, Presbyterian, and Congregational, must be conserved and have their place in the order of life of the United Church. Each Church will bring its own contribution to the whole which will not be an absorption of any one by any other.

All the essential features of the Scheme are set out in a Draft Basis of Union (Part I) which is enlarged and amplified in the Governing Principles and Constitution of the Church of South India (Part II). The joint committee representing the three uniting Churches recognized that the first essential in any negotiations for union must always be agreement on fundamental matters. They were conscious of the danger of classing as fundamental things which while true in themselves may not be the whole truth, or may even be of secondary importance. It was also seen that matters which are really of primary importance may be omitted. The late Bishop Waller[2] who was a member of the joint committee has written: "Most divisions are caused either by reaction from an exaggerated principle or by over-emphasis of a neglected truth. The foundations of union have to be wide but there cannot be a lasting union without definite truth as its foundation."

1. THE FAITH OF THE CHURCH

The most important point in union is the Faith. It might be taken as a foregone conclusion that three Christian Churches would agree on what the Faith is. While this may be true it is vitally important for the Church to have a statement of the Faith which would not only be a safeguard against the possible errors of a young Church in heathen surroundings but also a definite assurance to all the world that the fundamental Christianity of the Church is not to be questioned.

The faith of the Church of South India therefore is based on "the Holy Scriptures of the Old and New Testaments as containing all things necessary to salvation and as the supreme and decisive standard of faith". The uniting Churches also "accept the Apostles' Creed and the Creed commonly called the Nicene, as witnessing to and safeguarding that faith; and they thankfully acknowledge that same faith to be continuously confirmed by the Holy Spirit in the experience of the Church of Christ".

2. THE SACRAMENTS

The Sacraments of Baptism and the Supper of the Lord are accepted as "means of grace through which God works in us", and the belief is expressed "that while the mercy of God to all mankind cannot be limited, there is in the teaching of Christ the plain command that men should follow His appointed way of salvation by a definite act of reception into the family of God and by continued acts of fellowship with Him in that family, and that this teaching is made explicit in the two Sacraments which He has given us". "The Sacraments will be observed with unfailing use of Christ's words of institution and of the elements ordained by Him." It is affirmed that: "Baptized children are members of the Church, and share in the privileges and obligations of membership so far as they are capable of doing so." It is also stated that: "It is a rule of order in the Church of South India that the celebration of the Holy Communion shall be entrusted only to those who have by ordination received authority thereto."

3. THE MINISTRY

It is not surprising that in this first attempt to reunite Episcopal with Free Churches the question of the ministry was found to be a difficult one. The uniting Churches believe that it is the will of God "that there should be a ministry accepted and fully effective throughout the world-wide Church". At the present there is no ministry which is universally recognized. This fact cannot be too strongly emphasized. Anglican orders are not accepted by Rome, and other Episcopal Churches still have their doubts about them, or hesitate to come into full intercommunion with us. There is no doubt that the blessing of God has rested on the ministries of each of the uniting Churches. Therefore: "They acknowledge each other's ministries to be real ministries of the Word and Sacraments, and thankfully recognize the spiritual efficacy of sacraments and other ministrations which God has so clearly blessed."

Two of these Churches have one order of ministry only. Their ministers in addition to being ordained to the ministry of the Word and Sacraments have also, in a body, authority to ordain, and to them is given the chief voice in matters of discipline such as admission to or exclusion from Communion. It is a matter of profound thankfulness that for the sake of union members of these

Churches have accepted the historic Episcopate in a constitutional form as part of the Basis of Union. There are differing views and beliefs about apostolic succession even in our own Church and there is no official Anglican theory of Episcopacy. Whatever differences there may be, however, the uniting Churches are agreed that "as Episcopacy has been accepted in the Church from early times, it may be in this sense fitly be called historic, and that it is needed for the shepherding and extension of the Church in South India".[3]

A bishop is described as "the chief pastor and father in God". He is "as shepherd, not as lord either in act or title". His functions are defined in the Constitution and are described as including pastoral oversight, teaching, supervision of public worship, ordination of ministers, and oversight of discipline. Bishops are to be elected by the diocese and the authorities of the whole Church, thus following the Anglican custom in countries outside England.

Members of the second order are to be known as presbyters. It is interesting to remember that the word priest in our Prayer Book is derived from the N.T. word presbyter through the Anglo-Saxon *preost* (Lightfoot, *Philippians*, p. 244). Presbyters are dispensers of God's Word and Sacraments; they declare His message of pardon to penitent sinners; they are to share with the bishops and lay members in the government of the Church and in administration of discipline. They shall be ordained by the laying on of hands of the bishop and other presbyters.

The functions of deacons, the third order, shall include assisting the presbyter in the Holy Communion and in other services of the Church; administering of baptism; ministering in the temporalities of the Church. "The ministry of the diaconate may be undertaken for life by persons who have been accepted for this ministry by the diocesan authorities and have received due training."

There is a chapter in the Constitution dealing with the ministry of the laity, which is a special feature of the Scheme. It begins by saying: "To the whole Church and to every member of it belongs the duty and privilege of spreading the good news of the kingdom of God and the message of salvation through Jesus Christ. The Church of South India therefore welcomes and will as far as possible provide for the exercise of lay persons, both men and women, of such gifts of prophecy, evangelization, teaching, healing and administration as God bestows upon them. . . ." This ministry of the laity may be performed by men and women who, in response to God's call, devote their whole time to it, and for whose support the Church must therefore in general make provision. Further, it is stated that voluntary work should be undertaken by men and women who, while following their ordinary calling in life, also engage in the work of the Church. Such work may include one or more of the following: assisting in Pastoral Work, Evangelism, Preaching, Caring for Youth, Administration, and Social Service. "It is desirable that lay persons who are appointed to any office in the Church should be set apart at a service in which they are reminded of the nature and importance of their office, and prayer is offered that they may receive the Holy Spirit to equip them for their work and make them faithful in the discharge of their responsibilities."

4. THE CONGREGATION

Each congregation, locally representing the one holy, catholic and apostolic Church, "shall, with its pastor, be responsible for watching over its members, for keeping its life and doctrine pure, for ordering its worship, and for the proclaiming of the Gospel to those outside the Church".

Freedom for every pastor and congregation to determine their own forms of public worship extends to everything, subject only to any provisions in the Constitution or in synodical regulations with regard to ordinations and consecrations and to the essential elements of services such as Baptism, Holy Communion, and Marriage.

It is clear from this that what is contemplated is comprehension not limitation. Members of the united Church while firmly holding the fundamentals of the Faith will be allowed wide freedom of opinion in all other matters and wide freedom of action in the case of difference of practice. Such freedom, however, must be consistent with the general framework of the Church as one organized body. By such means it is believed that a new enrichment of the life of the united Church will result. It is recognized that "the act of union will initiate a process of growing together into one life and of advance towards complete spiritual unity". To quote Bishop Waller the principle is laid down "that no forms of worship now in use should be forbidden, and provided that the bare minimum requirements for the celebration of the sacraments should never be omitted. The whole problem of the development of worship in ways suitable to the country and people must be necessarily worked out in India as it was in Greece, in Western Europe, and in England. At the same time all the obligations undertaken by the Anglican Church to its European congregations are to be solemnly taken over in the united Church, so the continuation of the Prayer

Book services, guaranteed under the Indian Church Act rules, remains secure."

Rather than by attempting to safeguard such wide freedom by rules and regulations it has been wisely decided that assurances shall be given and received in a spirit of confidence and love. "The Church of South India therefore pledges itself that it will at all times be careful not to allow any overriding of conscience either by Church authorities or by majorities, and will not in any of its administrative acts knowingly transgress the long-established traditions of any of the Churches from which it has been formed. Neither forms of worship or ritual, nor a ministry, to which they have not been accustomed, or to which they conscientiously object, will be imposed upon any congregation; and no arrangements with regard to these matters will knowingly be made, either generally or in particular cases, which would either offend the conscientious convictions of persons directly concerned, or which would hinder the development of complete unity within the Church or imperil its progress towards union with other Churches."

5. INITIAL MEMBERSHIP AND MINISTRY

It is laid down that "all persons who at the time of the union are communicant members of any of the uniting Churches in the area of the union shall have the privileges and responsibilities of communicant members of the united Church, and as such shall be at liberty to receive communion in any of its churches", also "that all the ministers working in those Churches in the area of the union at the time of the inauguration of the union shall be accepted as constituting the initial ministry of the united Church". Ministers or missionaries of any Church whose missions have founded the several parts of the uniting Church may be received as ministers of the united Church, without necessity of episcopal ordination provided they are willing to give the same assent to the Governing Principles of the united Church and the same promise to accept its Constitution as will be required from persons to be ordained or employed for the first time in that Church.

It is expected that this arrangement will continue for thirty years. It must be frankly admitted that during this period there will be a "dual ministry". But it is very important to remember that it will be a ministry that is accepted and duly recognized by all in the area, and that after union all new ministers will be episcopally ordained. Moreover, on the completion of the interim period "it is the intention and expectation of the Church of South India that eventually every minister exercising a permanent ministry in it will be an episcopally ordained minister".[4]

This then in very brief outline is the proposed plan of Union. It directly concerns the four Anglican dioceses of Madras, Dornakal, Tinnevelly, and Travancore. There are of course rules and regulations for the organization of the Church into Pastorate Committees, Diocesan Councils, and a Synod. This body shall consist of all bishops of the Church, with presbyters and laymen representing each diocese. "The Synod is the supreme governing and legislative body of the Church of South India, and the final authority in all matters pertaining to the Church."[5]

(Church Union, *Open Letter to the Bishops of the Anglican Communion* (1944))

In the first place, we desire to call attention to the misleading assurances which are frequently given both in this country and in India to the effect that a real agreement has been reached in the South Indian Scheme upon fundamentals of Faith and Order, e.g. the Episcopal Synod in India passed a resolution at their meeting in February 1942, in which they said:

> This Synod has received with much thankfulness the seventh edition[6] of the Scheme for union in South India. It rejoices in the large measure of agreement which has been reached by the negotiating bodies in fundamentals of Faith and Order.

If the text of the Scheme be carefully studied, it will be seen that such agreement as is expressed by the acceptance of the Historic Episcopate, Episcopal Ordination, the Sacraments of Baptism and Holy Communion, the Apostles' and Nicene Creeds and Synodical Government is only made possible by the deliberate refusal to define the sense in which these terms are used, or the nature of the acceptance given to them. Indeed, it will be found in one instance after another that those with whom the Anglicans have been negotiating have, in consistency with their own beliefs, protected themselves from the acceptance of these fundamentals in any adequately Catholic sense, and from any reference to the authority of the Catholic Church which alone can make them fundamental. In support of this statement, we would make a few brief observations....

(The letter then deals with the following topics: the Historic Episcopate, Episcopal Ordination, the Sacraments, the Creeds, and Synodical Government.)

Episcopal Ordination is treated in the same way, but here not only is all definition excluded, but both in statement and in the practice constitutionally ordered, the indisputable implication is that the Church of South India places the non-episcopal ministries of the uniting bodies on an equal status with the apostolic ministry of the Church. The following quotations are offered in support of this statement:

The uniting Churches recognize, however, that God has bestowed His grace with undistinguishing regard through all their ministries in His use of them for His work of enlightening the world, converting sinners and perfecting saints. They acknowledge each other's ministries to be real ministries of the Word and Sacraments, and thankfully recognize the spiritual efficacy of sacraments and other ministration which God has so clearly blessed.

It has in experience been found best that one minister should lead the worship of the Church, and pronounce the words of consecration in the service of Holy Communion. From very early times it has been the custom of the Church that those only should exercise this function who have received full and solemn commission from the Church to do so. This commission has ordinarily been given by Laying on of hands in ordination. The only indispensable conditions for the ministration of the grace of God are the unchangeable promise of God Himself and the gathering together of God's elect people in the power of the Holy Ghost.

After union certain exceptional arrangements will continue until permanent arrangements can be made by the united Church. The Synod of the united Church will have full authority to make what provision is needed for the administration of the Sacraments in all its congregations.

We understand that this might involve the continuation of the permission to two Congregationalist laymen to celebrate the Holy Communion. In any case, the vagueness of this note, in a matter so strongly at issue between Anglicans and Congregationalists, is greatly to be deplored.

The acceptance of this provision [episcopal ordination] does not involve any judgment upon the validity or regularity of any other form of the ministry, and the fact that other Churches do not follow the rule of Episcopal Ordination shall not in itself preclude the united Church from holding relations of communion with them.

The Scheme provides that the ministers of those bodies with which the Anglicans are uniting will continue to minister in the Church of South India and will be fully authorized to do so without episcopal ordination. It also especially provides that, whatever changes may be made in the Constitution of the Church after thirty years (such changes might take the form of the abandonment of episcopal ordination), the rights of these ministers and apparently of visiting ministers from the parent bodies to exercise their ministry in the Church of South India without episcopal ordination shall be safeguarded. Those Anglicans who were formerly communicants of the dioceses of Madras, Travancore, Tinnivelly, and Dornakal, though not obliged to receive from non-episcopally ordained ministers, are urged to do so for the sake of unity:

> One essential element of the attainment of such complete unity is that all the members of the united Church should be willing and able to receive Communion equally in all its Churches, and it is the resolve of the uniting Churches to do all in their power to that end.

Our Anglican negotiators endeavoured by every means in their power to secure a more satisfactory basis of agreement on the question of the ministry. They were fully aware of the grave difficulty which these provisions would occasion. Attempts were made to induce the uniting bodies to accept the suggestion of the Lambeth Conference in 1920 for mutual ordinations so that all ministers would be assured of an ordination all would recognize, but this was completely rejected. Attempts were made then to find precedents in the early Church for Lay Celebration (this we may suppose was intended for Anglican consumption only), then the dispensing power of the Church was invoked and the purely Eastern theory of Economy, but all these attempts were equally unavailing. It only remained for the Anglicans to accept in their Basis of Union the firm requirement of the other negotiators for an equal status for all ministries, episcopal or non-episcopal. Thus it has come to pass that the Church of India will be compelled to consent to that which is in direct contradiction of its own formularies:

> It is evident unto all men diligently reading Holy Scripture and ancient authors, that from the Apostles' time there have been these orders of ministers in Christ's Church ... and therefore to the intent that these orders may be continued and reverently used and esteemed in the Church of England no man shall be accounted or taken to be a lawful Bishop, Priest or Deacon in the Church of England, or suffered to execute any of the said functions except he be called, tried, examined and admitted thereto according to the form hereafter following, or hath had formerly Episcopal Consecration or Ordination. (Preface to Ordinal, Book of Common Prayer. This is the Ordinal used in the Church of the Province.)

To no person except a Bishop or Priest is it committed or allowed to celebrate the Holy Communion (Declaration 5, Constitution of the Church of India, Burma and Ceylon).

If after this we turn to pages 21 and 22, where the provisions for intercommunion and intercelebration with other Christian bodies are summarized, we find how far this departure from the standard of the Church extends. Indeed, we find ourselves involved in such a tangle of relationships that we cannot avoid the impression that all idea of fundamental principle has been abandoned, and that we have here simply the Protestant conception of groups of completely independent Churches owning no allegiance except to such regulations as they draw up for themselves.

Members of the united Church ... shall not forgo any rights with regard to intercommunion which they possessed before the union. It is hoped that all the Churches with which the united Church has relations of communion and fellowship will be willing to receive them to Communion as visitors. Ministers of the united Church shall not forgo any rights with regard to intercommunion and intercelebration which they possessed before the union. They shall be at liberty to exercise any ministry in a Church outside the area of the union which they were entitled to exercise before the union. They shall be at liberty to minister and to celebrate Holy Communion in any church of a Church with which any of the uniting Churches enjoys relations of fellowship if they are invited to do so. Any communicant member of any Church which is in fellowship with any of the uniting Churches will be at liberty to communicate in any church of the united Church. Any minister of any Church which is in fellowship with any of the uniting Churches will be free as a visitor to minister or to celebrate in any church of the united Church if he is invited to do so....

It is sad to think that the Church of Pusey, Keble, Church, Liddon, Newbolt, Stubbs, Swete, Hort, Lightfoot, Scott Holland, should become a party to such a scheme. We are obliged reluctantly to say that it remains for those who give consent to this Scheme to clear themselves from the charge of consenting to an act of schism....

The final form of the *Scheme of Church Union* was approved by the Joint Committee of the Indian Churches. The Metropolitan of India sought advice on the position of the Anglicans involved in the scheme from the consultative body of the Lambeth Conference and the metropolitans of the Anglican Communion.[7]

(*Acts of Convocation*, pp. 133-6)

Lambeth Palace, S.E.
January 31 1944

My Dear Metropolitan,[8]

With this letter I am sending the formal reply to the questions which you sent me in your letter dated 4th February, 1943. It is inevitably formal in character. But the feeling among the bishops and clergy in Convocation was very far from formal. The Lower House expressed both its regret that, should the union be inaugurated, the four dioceses concerned would cease, at any rate for a time, to be constituent parts of the Anglican Communion, and also its deep appreciation of the spirit of devotion to the cause of unity which has animated them. I need not say that I share both of those feelings to the full.

The Lower House also expressed the wish that I should recall all concerned to the *Appeal to All Christian People* issued by the Lambeth Conference of 1920. I understand that they had in mind especially the requirement of assured agreement in matters of faith, and the proposal that "a ministry acknowledged by every part of the Church" should be secured by means of a mutual commission. You probably know that anxiety has been expressed in this country with regard to the former point, though I think this has been due to misunderstanding; and the adoption of the latter would, no doubt, make acceptance of the Scheme easier for Anglicans, provided that the form of commission were satisfactory.

We have based our reply on the advice given to the various provinces of the Anglican Communion by the Lambeth Conference of 1930, and we actually quote a passage of several lines from the Encyclical Letter issued by that Conference. In the quotation will be found the words—referring to the united Church —"its bishops will be received as bishops". As this statement is not repeated in the numbered paragraphs setting out the lines of administrative action which the bishops will follow, I think it worth while to say here that it is obviously accepted, for without it the whole structure of our reply would lack coherence.

The Upper House, after settling the contents of the formal reply, asked me to convey to you and through you to our brothers, the bishops of the Church of India, Burma, and Ceylon, our affectionate sympathy in the special burden of responsibility which they have to carry, both in regard to the whole situation in India and in relation to the subject-matter of this correspondence, our thankfulness for the eager desire to attain unity manifested by the Christians of South India, and our prayer that they may be guided by the Holy Spirit to fulfil that desire in such a way as may most promote the glory of God and the true welfare of His Church.

I enclose also a copy of the address with which I closed the discussion of the matter in the Upper House; I am, of course, alone responsible for this, but the bishops associated themselves cordially with the spirit of it.

With deep personal regard and affection,

I am,

Yours very sincerely,

(Signed) WILLIAM CANTUAR:

Lambeth Palace, S.E.

My Dear Metropolitan,

I duly received your letter in which you put to me, as Metropolitan of the Province of Canterbury, two questions concerning the action of this province in the event of the inauguration of a united Church of South India in accordance with the Proposed Scheme of Church Union as this is presented in the seventh edition of that Scheme. You asked me whether this province would

(*a*) break off communion with the Church of India, Burma and Ceylon;

and/or

(*b*) refuse to be in communion with the Church in South India.

I have put these questions before the diocesan bishops of the Province of Canterbury in the Upper House of Convocation, and they in turn sought the counsel of the Lower House. You will, of course, understand that our concern was to answer your questions, and to consider the Scheme itself only so far as seemed necessary to that purpose. What I am now conveying to you is therefore not to be regarded as a formal Act of Convocation registering approval or disapproval of the Scheme. You will also understand that our answer must be regarded as liable to review if need arises, since it is not yet known what will be the future course either of the proposed United Church or of the relations between it and the Church of India, Burma, and Ceylon. With this understanding I proceed in what follows to express the common mind of the bishops, who have approved the contents of this statement after receiving a reply from the Lower House to the request for its comment and counsel.

(*a*) As regards the first of the two questions to which we are asked to reply our answer is quite simple: the answer is No. The Church of India, Burma, and Ceylon will, if the Scheme of Union in South India takes effect, lose four of its dioceses; apart from this it will remain unaltered. The Church of India, Burma, and Ceylon is, according to the practice of the Anglican Communion, responsible for deciding, in accordance with the doctrine of the Church and with its knowledge of the special conditions in the area concerned, whether or not to give its sanction to the Scheme.

(*b*) The second question cannot be quite so simply answered. When the Lambeth Conference in 1930 expressed its "strong desire that, as soon as the negotiations are successfully completed, the venture should be made and the union inaugurated" (Resolution 40c) it also approved the following description of the resulting situation:

The united Church in India will not itself be an Anglican Church; it will be a distinct province of the Universal Church. It will have a very real intercommunion with the Churches of the Anglican Communion, though for a time that intercommunion will be limited in certain directions by their rules. Its bishops will be received as bishops by these Churches. Its episcopally ordained ministers—a continually increasing number—will be entitled under the usual rules to administer the Communion in the Churches of the Anglican Communion. Its communicants will be entitled to communicate with the Churches of the Anglican Communion, except in cases forbidden by the rules of those Churches. On the other hand no right to minister in the Churches of that Communion will be acquired by those ministers who have not been episcopally ordained (Encyclical Letter, p. 27).[9]

In accordance with that anticipation, and provided that the Scheme as finally adopted does not differ, in any point affecting the relation of the Church of England to the Church of South India, from that which is contained in the Seventh Edition of the Scheme, I am conveying the common mind of the bishops of the Province of Canterbury as finally expressed after considering the comments and counsel of the clergy of the province as represented by the Lower House of Convocation, when I say that their administrative action will follow these lines:

1. Subject to such rules and customs as are accepted in respect of all communicants in the province, a communicant member of the united Church would be admissible to Communion in the Churches of the province;

2. An episcopally ordained minister of the united Church would be qualified to receive the Licence or Permission of a bishop to officiate, subject, when they apply, to the provisions of the Colonial

Clergy Act, and to such rules and customs as are accepted in respect of all ministers in the province; thus, for example, if he applied for and received such Licence or Permission it would be on the understanding that he should not officiate in non-Anglican Churches except in such ways—e.g., preaching by special invitation on particular occasions—as are permissible or customary for priests or deacons of the Church of England.

3. A minister of the united Church who has not received episcopal ordination would not be qualified to receive a Licence or Permission to officiate in the province, except in such manner as is permitted under the regulations governing the Interchange of Preachers and set out in an Act of Convocation agreed to by both Houses in May 1943, of which I enclose a copy.

4. No censure would attach to any member, ordained or unordained, of this province who may be in South India or go thither, if he communicates with the united Church or takes work of any kind in it.

I hope that I have made clear what the position would be. The united Church would not be a province of the Anglican Communion, and there would not at this stage be unrestricted intercommunion between it and this province, but there would be such intercommunion between clergy and laity of the united Church and those of this province as I have stated.

These provisions represent certain restrictions upon full communion, that is to say, upon complete interchangeability of Ministers and complete mutual admissibility to Communion. We reiterate the hope expressed by the Committee of the Lambeth Conference of 1930 on the Unity of the Church, "that when the unification within the united Church, contemplated in the Proposed Scheme, is complete, full communion in that sense will be secured between the united Church and "the Church in this province".[10]

Yours very sincerely,

January 21st, 1944. (Signed) WILLIAM CANTUAR:

1 The General Committee of the C.M.S. resolved on October 20, 1942:

In view of the fact that the scheme of Church Union in South India in its definitive form is now before the councils of the participating Churches, and that the time for decision is imminent:

The Committee of the Church Missionary Society reaffirm their conviction that this development of the life of the Church in India is in full accord with the principles and policy which have guided the Society throughout its history.

They are convinced that the Scheme will further the cause of unity in the Church throughout the world which they believe to be according to the will of God.

They are satisfied that the Scheme adequately safeguards the witness of the Church to the Apostolic Faith, and at the same time secures due order without involving an unreasonable loss of freedom.

Bearing in mind that it is intended and expected that after thirty years the Church will be episcopally ordered throughout, they consider that the provisional arrangements during the interim period are satisfactory.

The venture of faith demanded by the Scheme is approved to their conscience by the conviction that the challenge is not from men but from God.

They, therefore, most thankfully and confidently commend the Scheme to the attention of the missionaries of the Society in India and elsewhere, to the attention of those Christians in India who have been associated with our Missions, and to the attention of all members of the Society in this country, praying that God may soon bring to fulfilment this movement towards closer union which has so manifestly been guided by the Holy Spirit.

2 Bishop of Madras, 1923–41.

3 The Anglican view of episcopacy is ably debated in Norman Sykes, *Old Priest and New Presbyter* (1956), and A. L. Peck, *Anglicanism and Episcopacy* (1958).

4 Stephen Neill comments: "This meant that, during the period of unification, there would be three types of minister in the Church—those ordained after the union, those episcopally ordained before union, and those non-episcopally ordained before union. This was bound to involve certain inconveniences and abnormalities. But the plan was perfectly honest, in recognizing both the consequences of four centuries of division and the desire for union, and in pointing forward to a time in which that union could be perfectly attained" (Rouse and Neill, *A History of the Ecumenical Movement*, p. 474). See also Jasper, *Headlam*, ch. 17.

5 The Scheme in its final draft was approved by the Church of India, Burma, and Ceylon in January 1945 in spite of attempts to postpone a decision until after the next Lambeth Conference. The formation of the Church of South India took place on 27 September 1947.

6 The main events leading up to the formation of the Church of South India were:

March 1920: first meeting of the Joint Committee.

1929: First appearance of the *Scheme of Church Union in South India.*
1930: Lambeth Conference.
1941: Scheme in its final form was approved by the joint committee.
28-29 January 1943: Synod of the Methodist Church in South India agreed to enter into union.
January 1945: the Church of India adopted the Scheme.
September 1946: the South India United Church General Assembly accepted the Scheme.

7 It was the Church Union who requested the Indian Metropolitan to ask these questions, and the request was supported by the Bishops of Colombo (Horsley) and Nagpur (Hardy). Temple consulted the Upper House and that in turn sought the advice of the Lower House; some leading figures including Kirk, Bishop of Oxford, considered the consultations inadequate. Garbett, however, gave a reply from the full synod of the York Convocation.

8 Westcott, Foss, son of Bishop of Durham; *b.* 1863; *educ.*, Cheltenham College and Peterhouse, Cambridge; ordained 1886; curate of St Peter, Bishopwearmouth; joined S.P.G. mission, Cawnpore, 1889; Bishop of Chota Nagpore, 1905; Bishop of Calcutta and Metropolitan, 1919–45; *d.* 1949.

9 The resolutions of the 1948 Lambeth Conference respecting the Church of South India are numbers 52 and 53 which state:

52 We

(*a*) endorse generally the paragraphs in the Report of our Committee on Unity which refer to South India;
(*b*) give thanks to God for the measure of unity locally achieved by the inauguration of the Church of South India, and pledge ourselves to pray and work for its development into an ever more perfect fulfilment of the will of God for His Church; and we
(*c*) look forward hopefully and with longing to the day when there shall be full communion between the Church of South India and the Churches of the Anglican Communion.

53 The Conference expresses the hope that, so soon as it may appear to the authorities of the Church of South India to be expedient to take up the matter, such provisions of the Constitution of that Church and such statements contained therein as are known to have given rise either to uncertainty or to grave anxiety in the minds of many, may be reconsidered with a view to their amendment. The Conference would call special attention to the six points specified in the Report of its Committee on Unity.

10 The Church of South India was divided into fourteen dioceses: the five Anglican bishops were re-elected to continue their functions;

and nine new bishops, Indian and European, were consecrated on the day of inauguration. The diocesan bishops numbered eight Europeans and six Indians; seven former Anglican and seven former Free Churchmen.

103 WORLD COUNCIL OF CHURCHES, 1940

The World Council of Churches was the consequence of the fusion of two ecumenical movements, "Life and Work" and "Faith and Order". The two important stages in the formation of a World Council were the meeting at Bishopthorpe in 1933 when Temple called together a group of ten officers of ecumenical bodies; and the meeting of thirty-five leaders at Westfield College, Hampstead, in July 1937.[1] The Oxford and Edinburgh Conferences opened the way for the formation of the World Council but, within the Church of England, Temple was opposed by Headlam in his promoting of the Council.[2]

(Jasper, *Headlam*, pp. 276-8)

BISHOP OF GLOUCESTER TO THE ARCHBISHOP OF CANTERBURY

I am afraid I look upon the proposal (for a World Church Council) with extreme suspicion, and a good deal of bitterness has been created. I first heard about it from Bishop Perry, who was very angry at what had happened at the Oxford Conference. He complained and many other people have complained to me, that they were summoned at 4.30 to discuss the proposal, and there was interpolated before it a motion, which again many people objected to, by the Bishop of Chichester about the German Church.[3] The result of which was that the proposal for the World Council was carried without any proper debate. Exactly the same thing happened at Edinburgh. We were summoned at 8.30 to discuss the proposal, but before it came on there were interpolated a large number of purely formal resolutions which lasted till nearly 10. At 10 o'clock I had arranged to go, thinking that the debate was over, and I was not able to stay any longer, and the matter was closured after a very short debate. A good many people thought that this was by design.... I don't know anything about that, but, at any rate, great irritation was caused among the minority. When the matter came on again I had the greatest difficulty in getting the amendment inserted stating that some members of the Conference objected to the proposal. As far as I can make out, the whole of the delegation of the Episcopal Church of America are opposed to it, all the Orthodox with the exception of the Bishop of Thyateira, about half or rather more of the Anglican delegation, and a good many scattered people, whom I cannot identify, who talked to me about it. The reasons that we object to it are:

1. That it associates us too closely with the Life and Work Movement, which has been continually involved in political matters and controversy, and is largely influenced by the passion for identifying Christianity with Socialism. There is no doubt that the Conference at Edinburgh has suffered a considerable amount by the Conference at Oxford.

2. We think that such a Council, with which it is proposed to associate a sort of bureau at Geneva, may have very dangerous tendencies. The habit of passing resolutions about political matters seems to us very dangerous, and it will be even more futile and quite as provocative as the League of Nations.

3. It seems to be part of a movement for substituting a Federation of the Churches in the place of a united Catholic Church, and may tend to produce a lower ideal.[4]

At any rate, I suppose as a punishment for our action, the Archbishop of Dublin, Bishop Palmer, Dr Macdonald, Canon Douglas and I were all turned out of the Continuation Committee, which, as we were the people who had worked the hardest for the movement, we naturally resented. That has been remedied, but they have still kept out Dr Gavin, who is quite the ablest of the American theologians. Throughout it seemed to some of us that the Conference was in danger of getting into the hands of the Student Christian Movement and of the American Protestant Churches, who, for the most part, seem to take no interest in theological questions at all. I think the representatives of the American Episcopal Church were very much disgruntled altogether, as the Conference had really emanated from them, and they found themselves with very little voice in anything.

I have written to you very frankly because I think it is desirable that these reactions ought to be known to you. Of course, I am quite definitely putting forward my own view of things, and you might very likely hear different opinions from other people, but still I think this point of view ought to be put before you.[5]

(*Church Assembly: Report of Proceedings* (1940), pp. 31-4)

THE ARCHBISHOP OF YORK:

said that the history of the proposal was set out sufficiently in the Explanatory Memorandum which had been circulated together with the Constitution. It sprang out of the Life and Work movement and the Faith and Order movement, and also out of the fact of their both holding World Conferences in the same year, 1937, and in the same country. It had been carried in both these World Conferences by very large majorities.

It would be hard to say that there was any one main motive behind the proposal to set up that Council. The movement came from a number of different angles. The Church from which the pressure had first been exerted was the Church of Sweden, a Church of predominantly Lutheran tradition. The motive which had always been predominant was that the growing fellowship of Christians drawn from different countries and Churches should have some symbol before the world.

It might be hard for those who had not had contact with world movements such as Life and Work, Faith and Order, or the International Missionary Council, to appreciate the degree and depth of the sense of intimate spiritual fellowship which had grown up among all those who had any share in those movements. It had been felt that there ought to be some normal channel, through which that great current of Christian fellowship should flow. In addition to that, there had been the experience within the two movements themselves, the Life and Work movement and the Faith and Order movement. They had been to a more considerable extent getting on to one another's ground, and more particularly the Life and Work movement had been finding itself increasingly impelled to take up theological ground. It had been felt very inconvenient, and uneconomic, for them to conduct their operations through separate offices and officers.

That brought in the question of the financing of the movement. The Faith and Order movement had in fact kept its head above water in two ways. The first was that its Theological Secretary, Dr Hodgson, had most generously undertaken the whole work of the office without any remuneration at all, until the period of the Edinburgh Conference in 1937. It would have been quite unreasonable to ask him to continue it. Over and above that, he (the speaker) had been personally raising some £400 a year to keep the funds going, but was at the end of his resources. He was convinced that contributing bodies such as the Assembly were more ready to contribute to a single body for those ecumenical purposes than to a number of separate funds, and that it would be far easier to finance and staff those movements adequately if they were working under one council which represented the whole of that international activity of the Church.

Upon one feature of the whole movement he would lay emphasis, the intense interest in the movement taken by the younger Churches, such as the Churches of China, of Japan and of India.

It would be proposed not to vote upon the subject that day, but to leave it over until after the war, on the ground that many Churches could not at the present time be interesting themselves in the question. But the World Council would come into existence only when its own assembly was first summoned, and everything done before then was provisional only. It was hoped to go as far as possible in having something ready to call together as soon as the state of the world made that practicable, as a demonstration to the world of the widest possible fellowship of Christians overlapping all national boundaries, and even national enmities.

The question to be decided was not whether there should be a World Council of Churches. There would be a World Council of Churches; fifty-nine Churches had already given their adherence, including five Churches of the Anglican Communion. The Protestant Episcopal Church of America had not yet had an opportunity of answering the invitation; but its Standing Committee had intimated its approval.

He would now turn to the difficulties and the objections which would be brought forward against his proposal. Everyone who cared for the ecumenical movement and the Faith and Order movement in particular would always be under the most profound obligation to the Bishop of Gloucester for his untiring labours. It was therefor a profound sorrow that the Bishop was unable to agree about that Council. The Bishop had set out some of his points of objection in a memorandum and said first of all that such a Council meant the substitution of a federation of Churches for Christian reunion as the aim of the ecumenical movement. But federation meant, in one way or another, a superior body which acted for its subordinates without any special commission from them or which could override them; and it was expressly laid down in the constitution of the Council that neither of those things could happen. Therefore the formation of the Council did not seem to point towards a federal solution.

The Bishop of Gloucester then suggested that the result would be the organization of Christendom into two camps, Roman and non-Roman. But the Council was not being organized on an anti-Roman basis. When the constitution of the World Council had been completed by the conference at Utrecht, to which the Assembly had authorized the appointment of delegates, it had immediately been communicated to the Vatican, with the statement that if the Church of Rome desired to participate, there would be the most hearty welcome. There had been a most courteous reply, but it had been intimated that it was better to go on side by side. He did not see why it should be thought that there would be any kind of opposition or resistance at those points.

Perhaps the chief point in the Bishop of Gloucester's memorandum was his fear that the World Council would issue pronouncements. Evidently if leaders of the Christian Church from all over the world were assembled from time to time they would make known their mind upon the subjects which they debated. Those utterances might be found to carry very great weight; on the other hand, they might be found to have very little. He hoped that those dealing with any controversial issue, and anything political, would be extremely rare, and that the main topics to be discussed would be such as that chosen for the first meeting of the assembly, whenever it might be convened, namely Evangelism.

The Bishop of Gloucester, speaking of the Provisional Committee, said that that body had been set up, "with what authority I know not". There was no mystery. It had been set up by the authority first of all of the Utrecht Conference and then approved by the governing body of the Life and Work movement and by the continuation committee of the Faith and Order movement.

The basis of the constitution was that which had long been familiar in the Faith and Order movement and which was contained in the invitation to Churches throughout the world to join in that movement: Churches which accepted the Lord Jesus Christ as God and Saviour. That was not a creed at all. Such a brief formula could not be regarded as a theological statement. It was an indication that the basis of the movement was the acceptance of the doctrines of the Incarnation and the Atonement.

The constitution gave 60 representatives to Great Britain and Eire, and with 60 representatives allotted to those countries it should be possible to secure really adequate and fair representation. His motion did not ask the Standing Committee to appoint, but to consider how the appointments should be made if the Assembly decided to accept.

Although he wished that the Council could have represented a still wider unity, an all-embracing unity of Christians, yet, that being for the moment out of the question, might not the Assembly take a step which enabled it to share in the largest actual demonstration of spiritual fellowship among Christian peoples which circumstances made possible, at a time when the witness of that unity was wanted more than ever in the face of a world torn by war.

In 1938 the Constitution of the proposed World Council of Churches, an Explanatory Memorandum drawn up by Temple, and a letter of invitation signed by the members of the Committee of Fourteen were sent out. The World Council of Churches was brought into formal existence by a resolution of its first Assembly held at Amsterdam from August 22 to September 4 1948.[6] In the Church Assembly in February 1938 Temple introduced a motion to appoint representatives to attend a provisional Conference in May 1939 to consider a draft constitution. The Assembly passed a resolution proposed by Temple on 11 June 1940: "That this Assembly welcomes the establishment of the World Council of Churches constituted in accordance with the scheme submitted to the Assembly and accepts the invitation to be represented."

(*Official Year Book of the Church of England* (1949), p. 182)

1412 On the motion of the *Bishop of Chichester* the resolution passed at the Summer Session, 1940 (1046 (2)), directing the Standing Committee to appoint representatives to the World Council of Churches was rescinded and it was resolved:

That of the twenty principal delegates representing the Church of England at the First Assembly of the World Council of Churches, and the twenty alternates, ten principal delegates and ten alternates shall be elected by the Church Assembly from amongst its own members; and ten principal delegates and ten alternates shall be nominated by the Archbishops of Canterbury and York; all of whom shall serve for a period of five years from the date of their election or nomination.

That five of the principal delegates and five of the alternates in each of the above two categories shall be lay persons.[7]

1 The Westfield meeting adopted this proposal: "That, with a view to facilitating the more effective action of the Christian Church in the

modern world, the movements known as 'Life and Work' and 'Faith and Order' should be more closely related in a body representative of the Churches and caring for the interests of each movement." See Rouse and Neill, *A History of the Ecumenical Movement, 1517–1948.*

2 Iremonger wrote: "The more far-seeing leaders in all countries knew that the moment had now come when the seal might be set on all the preparatory work of the last thirty years. From every point of view—whether of efficiency, expense, practical convenience, or the concentration of spiritual strength—it was desirable that a single body should be set up in which all the organizations working for Church unity could be merged, and so present to the world a united front of Christian thought and effort. 'Overlapping,' Temple declared, 'and even collision are increasing'" (Iremonger, *Temple,* p. 410). Lockhart adds: "... it was he who there inspired and promoted the design which brought the various streams of the Ecumenical Movement into the broad river of a World Council of Churches" (Lockhart, *Lang,* p. 367).

3 Bell, George Kennedy Allen; *b.* 1883; *educ.*, Christ Church, Oxford; ordained, 1907; curate of Leeds, 1907; lecturer and tutor of Christ Church, Oxford, 1910; resident chaplain to Davidson, 1912–24; lecturer in pastoral theology, Cambridge, 1926; Dean of Canterbury, 1924; Bishop of Chichester, 1929; resigned, 1957; *d.* 1958.

4 Temple stated in the Explanatory Memorandum: "It is not a federation as commonly understood, and its Assembly and Central Committee will have no constitutional authority whatever over its constituent churches. Any authority that it may have will consist of the weight it carries with the churches by its wisdom" See *Proceedings of Church Assembly.*

5 Headlam was *par excellance* the ecumenical theologian of the Church of England. Beginning with a work on *The Teaching of the Russian Church* in 1897, he wrote on a variety of subjects including *The Lambeth Conference and the Union of Churches* (1908), *Kikuyu* (1914), *The Russian and English Churches* (1916), *Eastern Christianity* (1919), the Bampton Lectures on *The Doctrine of the Church and Christian Reunion* (1920), *The Serbian Church* (1926), *The Lausanne Conference and the Orthodox Eastern Church* (1927), the *South Indian Reunion Scheme* (1935), *Christian Unity and Freedom* (1938).

6 John R. Mott became Honorary President; and the six Presidents were Dr Marc Boegner, the Archbishop of Canterbury, Dr T. C. Chao, Archbishop Germanos, Bishop G. Bromley Oxnam, and Archbishop Eidem. In the year of its inception it was composed of 142 constituent Churches which included every province of the Anglican Community.

7 Roger Lloyd commented: "From the very beginning of the Council

ten years before, the Anglican Communion had steadfastly supported it. Many Anglicans went to Amsterdam. They had to find their right place in an assembly dominated financially by the Americans, and theologically by the famous protestant divines of continental Europe, such as Karl Barth, Hendrik Kraemer of the Netherlands, and the Czech communist Josef Hromadka. The Anglican delegation could offer no names of comparable prestige, and the chief contribution they made by their presence was the shielding of the movement from the reproaches often levelled against it, that it was no better than a pan-protestant movement on a large scale. The Anglicans were known to be heart and soul in it because they believed that it would work towards the knitting together of the Body of Christ by helping to create the conditions of an organic union between all Churches" (*The Church of England*, p. 489).

104 TOWARDS THE CONVERSION OF ENGLAND, 1945

(*Towards the Conversion of England*, pp. 9-15)

This Report, like the National Mission a generation before, was an attempt to provide a pastoral policy after the upheaval of war-time. It was an attempt to "survey the whole problem of modern evangelism with special reference to the spiritual needs and prevailing intellectual outlook of the non-worshipping members of the community". It ran through eight editions in eight months and was widely discussed throughout the Church of England.[1] Henson concluded that "this Report is offensively conventional, and will gain acceptance from none but those who do not know, or will not accept, the facts of the religious situation in England" (*Retrospect*, vol. 3, p. 323). The value of the Report lay in its diagnosis of the religious state of England.

The reinforcement of Humanism[2] has been occasioned by the stupendous advance of science and invention during the present century, the Age of Progress. If in Mid-Victorian times it could be said that "science has made God unnecessary", how much more reason have we to be dazzled by the power that has come into our hands? To form, however, a true estimate of the effect of scientific advance upon our generation, there are three further factors, resulting from it, that demand serious attention.

1. INCREASING URBANIZATION

First, there is the revolutionary change in the distribution of population, as between country and town. A century ago, in 1840 (almost, that is, within living memory), only a quarter of England's fifteen millions lived in towns of over twenty thousand inhabitants. In 1881, seventeen and a half, out of twenty-six millions, of the population were living in towns. By 1891 the proportion had increased to twenty-one millions of the population, out of twenty-nine millions; and the drift to the towns has steadily continued ever since. Thus, increasingly, the masses of our people have migrated from the influence of nature to be absorbed in the materialism of urban surroundings.

The effect of this, more particularly in the impressionable years of childhood and youth, has been profound. In 1843 George Borrow wrote that he had "always found in the dispositions of the children of the fields a more determined tendency to religion and piety than amongst the inhabitants of towns and cities"; for "they are less acquainted with work of men's hands than with those of God". For this reason many today believe that religious revival will come from the countryside. But while in Borrow's day three English children out of every four were born in rural areas, the proportion today is more than reversed.[3]

Youthful imagination now receives its stimulus from the shop window, the newspaper placard, the cinema and cinema poster. Much that passes today for art and literature has, on the whole, proved a corrupter of youth. The most popular art, that of the cinema, with its immense influence, is almost totally devoid of any Christian background. The cinema "has shown an apparently pleasant world of unbridled desire, of love crudely sentimental or fleshly, of vast possessions, of ruthless acquisition, of reckless violence, of incredible kindliness; a maelstrom of excitement played upon by the glamour of false emotionalism". The road to speedy and spectacular riches for film magnates has been to popularize and beglamour a distorted picture of the most degenerate aspects of a materialistic age; and an erotic film industry has been allowed to be the chief single influence to which the young have been subjected during their formative years.

2. SECULAR EDUCATION

The second factor is the one-sided character of the education of the past generation, and its increasingly secular outlook. The general community is, indeed, far more widely instructed than any previous generation. But the whole trend of modern education has been increasingly towards the sciences, to the exclusion of the humanities or the liberal arts. Indeed, the preponderance of higher education is on the lines of applied science. This fact has an important bearing upon the evangelistic task of the Church. It is true that the general outlook of scientists today is more congruous to the Christian view of life than perhaps ever before: but a scientific education, of necessity, inculcates a mental habit which does not predispose to a Christian view of life. It is an axiom of scientific training that nothing must be taken on trust. It upholds (and rightly within its own sphere) a sceptical temper towards all hypotheses which have not been tested on a factual basis, and cannot be demonstrated as true with mathematical certainty. Further, and more far-reaching in its moulding of mental habit, science trains its votaries to look for the *How*, and to disregard the *Why*; to concentrate on *means* and to ignore *purpose*. Homo thus ceases to be *Sapiens* and becomes *Sciens*.

Experience proves what we could only expect—namely, that an overweighted scientific education tends to produce a mentality which inevitably finds it hard to appreciate the importance which the Christian lays upon faith as a primary necessity, or his insistence that it is "purpose" and not "mechanism" which is of first importance. The cumulative result of modern education is, thus, to reinforce the humanistic view of life, if only by making it harder for man to understand and to accept the Christian faith.

Religious education, meanwhile, has steadily receded into the background, despite promising efforts to check an ebbing tide. It is true that the public schools "have preserved for English education a belief ... in the essential part to be played by religion in education". It is true also, that Church schools, though diminishing in number, have kept the same principle alive in national education. And it is true that in Council schools there have always been found many good Christian teachers who have sincerely and devotedly tried to train children in the Christian way of life. But they have laboured under grave disadvantages and been hampered by many restrictions. It cannot be said that the national system has allowed Christian teaching to take its proper place as the unifying factor in education, co-ordinating all learning, inculcating a sense of responsibility, revealing the meaning and purpose of life. Indeed, the whole country was so shocked at the amount of the sheer pagan ignorance among the youthful products of elementary and secondary schools which evacuation disclosed, that the long and persistent efforts of Christian educationists have received recognition in the Education Act, 1944. We welcome the place in education that religious instruction and worship has thereby been given. More particularly we rejoice that, although these were more or less customary in most schools before the Act, they are now a matter of statutory obligation in all schools, and are thus accorded that recognized position of importance which should ensure their efficient and effective operation.

If we have to confess that education has become increasingly secular, scepticism has increasingly characterized educational technique. The individualism of the last century fostered the ideal of the completely undogmatic teacher, who thus (often unconsciously) inculcated an all-embracing scepticism in unreflecting youth. The notion was fostered that everyone was entitled to his own truth, and that (in the last resort) one belief was probably no truer than another. The consequence is only too apparent in the prevailing intellectual outlook. In the sphere of wisdom, the young cannot be expected to rediscover for themselves, unaided, those moral and spiritual truths which have been proved over and over again by the accumulated experience of past generations. The agnostic vacuum has inevitably been filled, and the refusal to teach children dogmatic religion has, in fact, amounted to teaching them the paramount importance of the economic appetites which so obviously dominate the world outside their schools.

It has, also, been forgotten that true Christian education is far more than to teach a certain subject at a certain time. It is a particular kind of education in all subjects and at all times—not only in the classroom. In other words, Christian education means schools with every activity pervaded by religion. But from at least the last quarter of the nineteenth century onwards, our national system of education has ruled that the young should contrast their childish memories of mother's knee religion with their knowledge of science or politics acquired at an adult level.

The cumulative effect has been that masses of our young people have lost a whole dimension of life—the spiritual dimension. They seem neither to be conscious of being spirit, nor to possess the faculty for apprehending the realms of the spirit.

3. MECHANIZED THINKING

The third factor in the reinforcement of Humanism is the appearance of the mechanistic mind. If scientific discovery and invention gave birth to the Industrial Revolution, the Industrial Revolution has, in turn, given birth to the Machine Age and has manufactured a mechanically minded nation. In an article, *The Perils of a purely Scientific Education*, the late Dr William Temple foretold that such an education must produce a generation adept in dealing with things, indifferently qualified to deal with people, and incapable of dealing with ideals. Today we are in a position to realize the truth of his warning. There is a large section of our people, whom it would be more accurate to describe as *mechanically*, rather than *scientifically*, educated. They may be highly trained and skilled mechanics. Within narrow limits their brains work keenly and quickly. They think clearly and originally about problems concerned with their craft; and many of them teach mechanics admirably. And yet great numbers, even of the most able among them, are incapable of reasoning or thinking clearly on abstract subjects, such as politics or religion. Professor T. E. Jessop, after an exceptionally wide experience with the Forces, and speaking as a psychologist, has diagnosed their mentality as definitely lacking in the necessary apperception for apprehending abstract ideas: "It is not that they won't; it is that they can't!" Here, obviously, is a new factor in the present situation, and one of primary importance.

THE MODERN EXPOSURE OF HUMANISM

We turn from the reinforcement which the humanist view of life has received in our times, to the shock which it has recently sustained. It is the shock of shattering disillusionment. The trust in human progress (evidenced in the last war by the high hopes we entertained of a better social order) has been pulverized by the brutal logic of events. Instead of man being "the master of things", he finds himself their slave—the serf of the very civilization that he has created, and the powerless victim of mechanical laws of his own devising. It is not man who has been set free, but the blind materialistic forces he has unleashed. The machine has taken charge of its directors and reduced the common people to mere cogs in its wheels.

In industry, irresponsible centres of economic power—international in their scope—exercise a virtual tyranny over the lives of masses of men. Between the two wars what economists (in their failure to make sense of the runaway process) termed cycles of fluctuation and financial blizzards, occasioned the macabre misery of starvation in the midst of plenty, and condemned honest workmen to an awful sense of insecurity. At that time unemployment produced a settled apathy (political and social as well as religious) among multitudes of the most alert and self-respecting sections of the community. It had to be witnessed to be believed. Then too, the soullessness of the present industrial system, with its huge combines, has opened the door to evil forces which have infected its structure. For example, the only forms of employment to many men and women are such as deprive them of that sense of vocation and public service which is their birthright.

In politics, the ordinary citizen feels he has no real say in the government of the country and is restive lest bureaucracy should break up his home life.

These are the days of Great Society in which social techniques have increasingly concentrated power in the hands of the few, and discouraged enterprise and creative individuality on the part of the many. The Englishman, with his innate independence of character, can never be happy to become a cipher among undifferentiated millions, living on the top of each other, in a mechanized community. To this situation is due, more than is realized, the present-day collapse of morals. The need for self-expression has been so frustrated that it finds its easiest outlet in sex-indulgence.

Finally, the outbreak of a second World War, after an uneasy truce of twenty-one years' duration, brought home to man how irrational is human nature, as well as the failure of the weapon of political power to "ring in the thousand years of peace". It confronted him, instead, with the hellish might of scientific invention when turned, almost exclusively, to the work of destruction.[4]

1 Garbett reported that: "The parochial church council recently held six meetings, without the vicar, discussing the report on Evangelisation. At their last meeting they passed a resolution saying that in their deliberate opinion there was no need for evangelisation in England!" (Smyth, *Garbett*, p. 354).

2 Popular or scientific humanism, in contrast to renaissance humanism, was based on the nineteenth-century notion that religion and material existence were directly opposed.

3 Nineteenth-century local records relating to rural areas do not support the assumption that country people were more disposed to religion than the townsmen. The break-up of the small community and the uprooting of families in the migration to the towns had more to do with non-churchgoing than the actual material surroundings.

4 The Commission was appointed by the Archbishops after the November session of the Church Assembly in 1944. Its members included: the Bishop of Rochester (Chavasse), the Bishop of Chelms-

ford (Wilson), Canon Bloomer (later Bishop of Carlisle), H. G. Herklots, Roger Lloyd, Mervyn Stockwood (later Bishop of Southwark), and Oliver Tomkins (later Bishop of Bristol).

105 CHURCH COMMISSIONERS, 1948

(*Church Assembly Measures*, C.A. 794A)

The Church Commissioners Measure (10 and 11 Geo. 6, No. 2), appointed a new corporation to "promote the more efficient and economical administration of the resources of the Church of England". The Measure received the Royal Assent on 2 April 1947, and on 1 April 1948 Queen Anne's Bounty and the Ecclesiastical Commissioners were amalgamated.[1]

SCHEDULE I

CONSTITUTION OF THE COMMISSIONERS[2]

1 The Commissioners shall be:

the Archbishops of Canterbury and York and the diocesan bishops of the Provinces of Canterbury and York;
the three church estates commissioners;
five deans appointed by the Church Assembly, three from the Province of Canterbury and two from the Province of York;
ten other clerks in Holy Orders appointed by the Church Assembly;
ten laymen appointed by the Church Assembly;
four laymen nominated by His Majesty, and four persons nominated by the Archbishop of Canterbury: provided that at least two of the eight Commissioners so nominated shall be, or shall have been, of counsel to His Majesty;
The Lord Chancellor, The Lord President of the Council, the First Lord of the Treasury, the Chancellor of the Exchequer, and the Secretary of State for the Home Department;
the Speaker of the House of Commons;
the Lord Chief Justice, the Master of the Rolls, the Attorney-General, and the Solicitor-General;
The Lord Mayor and two aldermen of the City of London and the Lord Mayor of the City of York; and
one representative from each of the universities of Oxford and Cambridge, being either the Vice-Chancellor or a person

nominated by him to serve during his own term of office.

2 Commissioners appointed by the Church Assembly (who need not be members thereof) shall be appointed for five years in such manner as the Assembly may from time to time determine.

Commissioners nominated by the Archbishop of Canterbury shall be nominated for such number of years as he may from time to time determine.

The two aldermen of the City of London shall be appointed by the court of aldermen thereof either for one year or for such number of years not exceeding five as the court may from time to time determine.

In this paragraph the expression "year" means a period of twelve months commencing on the first day of April.

Any such Commissioner as is referred to in this paragraph shall be eligible for re-appointment or re-nomination.

3 In the event of delay in the appointment or nomination of a successor any such Commissioner as is referred to in the last preceding paragraph shall, notwithstanding the expiration of the period for which he was appointed or nominated, continue to hold office until a successor is appointed or nominated.

4 A person shall be disqualified from being a Commissioner so long as he is a salaried official of any central or diocesan body in the Church of England.

5 If an appointed Commissioner who was qualified for appointment by virtue of being a dean, a clerk in Holy Orders, or a layman appointed by the Church Assembly, ceases to be so qualified, he shall thereby vacate his membership.

6 Every lay Commissioner not being a Commissioner in right of office shall, before otherwise acting in connection with the business of the Commissioners, declare in writing before an officer of the Commissioners that he is a member of the Church of England.

SCHEDULE II

CONSTITUTION OF THE BOARD OF GOVERNORS

1 The Board shall consist of the following persons:
the Archbishops of Canterbury and York;
the three church estates commissioners;
twenty-two other Commissioners appointed by the Commissioners, and

such other Commissioners, if any, as may be co-opted in accordance with the provisions of this Schedule.

2 Of the twenty-two members to be appointed by the Commissioners six shall be diocesan bishops, two shall be deans, six shall be other clerks in Holy Orders, and eight shall be laymen, of whom six shall be chosen from those appointed by the Church Assembly.

3 At the inaugural general meeting of the Commissioners twenty-two members shall be appointed in the proportions laid down in the preceding paragraph and of the members so appointed one-half shall hold office for six years and the remainder for three years. Thereafter, in every third year eleven members shall be appointed at the annual general meeting of the Commissioners to fill the places of members retiring in that year.

4 The period of office of an appointed member shall run from the day following the annual general meeting at which he is appointed to the close of the day on which his successor is appointed.

A member appointed at the inaugural general meeting shall enter upon his office forthwith, but the date for his retirement shall be calculated as if he had been appointed at the first annual general meeting of the Commissioners.

5 The eleven original members to hold office for six years shall be three bishops, one dean, three other clerks, three of the laymen appointed by the Church Assembly, and one of the laymen not so appointed.

6 As between members in any category, those to hold office for six years shall be those receiving most votes:

Provided that if

(*a*) in any category there is no contest; or
(*b*) in a category where there is a contest, a selection must be made between two or more members whose votes were equal;

any necessary selection shall be made by lot.

For the purposes of this paragraph, lots shall be drawn by such persons and in such manner as the Chairman may direct.

7 The Board may from time to time co-opt as additional members of the Board not more than three persons being Commissioners at the date of co-optation.

Such co-optation may be for any period not extending beyond the next triennial election of members of the Board.

8 If a member of the Board who was qualified for membership by virtue of being a diocesan bishop, a dean, a clerk in Holy Orders, or a layman appointed by the Church Assembly, ceases to be so qualified, he shall thereby vacate his membership.

SCHEDULE III

THE ECCLESIASTICAL COMMISSIONERS ACT, 1850

Sections 8 and 9, as adapted

8 It shall be the duty of the Estates and Finance Committee, or any three of them, of whom two or more shall be Church Estates Commissioners, to consider all matters in any way relating or incidental to the sale, purchase, exchange, letting, or management, by or on behalf of the Commissioners, of any lands, tithes, or hereditaments, and to devise such measures touching the same as shall appear to such committee to be most expedient; and such committee, or any three of them, of whom two or more shall be Church Estates Commissioners, shall have full power and authority subject to such general rules as shall have been made by the Board of Governors of the Commissioners, to do and execute any act, including the affixing of the common seal to any scheme or other instrument within the power of the Commissioners, in respect of the sale, purchase, exchange, letting, or management, of any lands, tithes, or hereditaments:

Provided always, that no such act shall be done or executed by the Commissioners otherwise than by the said Estates and Finance Committee, nor by such committee unless with the concurrence of two at least of the Church Estates Commissioners.

9 At all meetings of the Estates and Finance Committee the first Church Estates Commisioner shall preside, or, if he is absent, the other Church Estates Commissioner appointed by His Majesty or the Church Estates Commissioner appointed by the archbishop, shall be chairman at alternate meetings; and in case of an equality of votes the chairman shall have a second or casting vote.

THE ECCLESIASTICAL COMMISSIONERS ACT, 1866

Section 2, as adapted

All acts which the Estates and Finance Committee of the Commissioners are authorized by law to do and execute or to complete may be done and executed or completed by any two members of such Committee being Church Estates Commissioners.[3]

1 The administrative functions of the new body included: ecclesiastical reorganization; formation of new parishes; alteration of parochial and deanery boundaries; union of benefices; conveyance of sites for churches and houses; fixing of tables of parochial fees; transfers and exchanges of patronage, sales and purchases of glebe; securing of gifts of property, and the regulation of capitular accounts.

2 The Ecclesiastical Commissioners comprised: the two archbishops, forty bishops, five cabinet ministers, two judges, three deans, and twelve eminent laymen. The Governors of the Queen Anne's Bounty included: the archbishops, diocesan bishops, and *ex officio* ecclesiastical and lay persons.

3 The final accounts of Queen Anne's Bounty and the Ecclesiastical Commissioners were kept open until 31 March 1948. The first A.G.M. of the Commissioners was held in July 1948 to adopt these final accounts. The amounts of surplus income to meet existing and new needs in the financial year to 31 March 1949 were:

	£
From Queen Anne's Bounty	203,744
From Ecclesiastical Commissioners	943,202
	£1,146,946

APPENDIX

REIGNING BRITISH MONARCHS

George III	1760–1820
George IV	1820–1830
William IV	1830–1837
Victoria	1837–1901
Edward VII	1901–1910
George V	1910–1936
Edward VIII	1936–Abdicated
George VI	1936–1952

ARCHBISHOPS

CANTERBURY	YORK
Charles Manners Sutton 1805–1828	Vernon Harcourt 1807–1847
William Howley 1828–1848	Thomas Musgrave 1847–1860
John Bird Sumner 1848–1862	Charles Longley 1860–1862
Charles Longley 1862–1868	William Thomson 1862–1890
Archibald Campbell Tait 1868–1882	William Connor Magee 1891
Edward White Benson 1883–1896	William Maclagan 1891–1908
Frederick Temple 1896–1902	Cosmo Gordon Lang 1910–1928
Randall Thomas Davidson 1903–1928	William Temple 1929–1942
Cosmo Gordon Lang 1928–1942	Cyril Forster Garbett 1942–1955
William Temple 1942–1944	
Geoffrey Francis Fisher 1946–1961	

MINISTRIES

Tory	June 1812	Lord Liverpool
Tory	April 1827	George Canning
Tory	Sept. 1827	Lord Goderich
Tory	Jan. 1828	Duke of Wellington
Whig	Nov. 1830	Lord Grey
Whig	July 1834	Lord Melbourne
Conservative	Dec. 1834	Sir Robert Peel
Whig	April 1835	Lord Melbourne
Conservative	Sept. 1841	Sir Robert Peel
Whig	July 1846	Lord John Russell
Conservative	Feb. 1852	Lord Derby
Coalition	Dec. 1852	Lord Aberdeen
Whig	Feb. 1855	Lord Palmerston
Conservative	Feb. 1858	Lord Derby
Whig-Liberal	June 1859	Lord Palmerston
Whig-Liberal	Oct. 1865	Lord John Russell
Conservative	June 1866	Lord Derby
Conservative	Feb. 1868	Disraeli
Liberal	Dec. 1868	Gladstone
Conservative	Feb. 1874	Disraeli
Liberal	April 1880	Gladstone
Conservative	June 1885	Lord Salisbury
Liberal	Feb. 1886	Gladstone
Conservative	Aug. 1886	Lord Salisbury
Liberal	Aug. 1892	Gladstone
Liberal	March 1894	Lord Rosebury
Conservative	June 1895	Lord Salisbury
Conservative	July 1902	A. J. Balfour
Liberal	Dec. 1905	Henry Campbell-Bannerman
Liberal	April 1908	H. H. Asquith
Coalition	May 1915	H. H. Asquith
Coalition	Dec. 1916	Lloyd George
Conservative	Oct. 1922	Bonar Law Stanley Baldwin
Labour	Jan. 1924	Ramsay MacDonald
Conservative	Nov. 1924	Stanley Baldwin
Labour	June 1929	Ramsay MacDonald
National	Aug. 1931	Ramsay MacDonald
National	June 1935	Stanley Baldwin Neville Chamberlain

SOURCES

Anglican Orders, London 1957.

Archbishop of York's Conference, 1941, *Malvern and After*. Report of the Committee of Industrialists and Economists with Theologians on those parts of the Malvern Report, especially sections 19 to 25, on which further comments were desired by the Malvern Conference, Westminster 1942.

Arnold, Thomas, *Principles of Church Reform*. 2nd edn. London 1833.

Bell, G. K. A., *Documents on Christian Unity*, vol. 1. London 1924.

— *Randall Davidson*, London 1952.

Biggs, C. R. D., *Russia and Reunion. A translation of Wilbois' "L'Avenir de l'Eglise Russe"*.... 1908.

Birmingham, The Act Book of the Bishop of (Birmingham Diocesan Registry).

Booth, Charles, *Life and Labour of People in London*. 1892–7.

Brooke, William G., *Six Judgments ... in Ecclesiastical Cases, 1850–1872. With an historical introduction ... edited by W. G. Brooke*. London 1872.

Buxton, Charles, *Memoirs of Sir Thomas Fowell Buxton, Baronet. With selections from his correspondence. Edited by his son, C. Buxton*. London 1925.

Census of Great Britain, 1851. Religious Worship. London 1853.

Christian Social Union, Constitution of (British Museum).

Christmas, Henry, *A Concise History of the Hampden Controversy, from the period of its commencement in 1832 to the present time. With all the documents that have been published, and a brief examination of the "Bampton Lectures" for 1832 and of the "Observations on dissent"*. London 1848.

Chronicle of the Convocation of Canterbury.

Church Assembly Measures.

Church Assembly Publications.

Church Assembly, *Report of Proceedings*.

Church Assembly Report, *With One Accord*. London 1933.

Church Missionary Society (Archives).

Church Union, *Open Letter to the Bishops of the Anglican Communion*. London 1944.

C.O.P.E.C., *Proceedings of C.O.P.E.C*. London 1924.

Cranswick, G. F. and Warren, M. A. C., *A Vital Issue. Church Union in South India*. 2nd edn. London n.d.

Davidson, Randall Thomas, *The Five Lambeth Conferences*. London 1920. *Kikuyu*. London 1915.

Davidson, Randall Thomas and Benham, William, *Life of Archibald Campbell Tait, Archbishop of Canterbury*. 2 vols. London 1891.

Davidson Papers (Lambeth Palace).

D. C. L., *Letters on Church Matters*. Reprinted from the *Morning Chronicle*, No. VII. 1851 (Sion College).

Doctrine in the Church of England. Report of the Archbishops' Commission on Christian Doctrine. London 1938.

The Evangelistic Work of the Church. The National Mission. The Archbishops' Third Committee of Inquiry. London 1918.

Farrar, Frederic William, *Eternal Hope*. London 1883.

Fisher, Geoffrey Francis, *A Step Forward in Church Relations*. London 1946.

Gladstone, William Ewart, *The State in its Relations with the Church*. 2 vols. 4th edn. London 1841.

Grant, Anthony, *The Past and Prospective Extension of the Gospel by Missions to the Heathen*. London 1844.

Hansard, *Parliamentary Debates*.

Headlam, Stewart, *The Guild of St Matthew. An Appeal to Churchmen*. London 1890 (British Museum)

Hechler, William Henry, *The Jerusalem Bishopric. Documents, with translations, chiefly derived from "Das Evangelische Bisthum in Jerusalem"*. London 1883.

Henson, Herbert Hensley, *Retrospect of an Unimportant Life*. 3 vols. London 1942–50.

Howley, William, *Christianity in Egypt. Letters and Papers concerning the Coptic Church ... during the primacy of Archbishop Howley, 1836–1848*. 1883.

Huxley, L., *Life and Letters of Thomas Henry Huxley. By his son L. Huxley*. 2 vols. London 1900.

Iremonger, Frederic Athelwold, *William Temple, Archbishop of Canterbury. His Life and Letters*. London 1948.

Jasper, Ronald C. D., *Arthur Cayley Headlam. The Life and Letters of a Bishop*. London 1960.

Johnston, John Octavius, *Life and Letters of Henry Parry Liddon*. London 1904.

Keble, John, *Sermons, Academical and Occasional*. Oxford 1848.

Kingsley, Frances E., *Charles Kingsley: his letters and memories of his life. Edited by his wife*. London 1904.

Livingstone, David, *Dr Livingstone's Cambridge Lectures, together with a prefatory letter by Professor Sedgwick. Edited with introduction, life of Dr Livingstone, notes and appendix by W. Monk*. 2nd edn. Cambridge 1860.

Lockhart, John Gilbert, *Cosmo Gordon Lang*. London 1949.

Maurice, J. F., *The Life of Frederick Denison Maurice, chiefly told in his own letters. Edited by his son, F. Maurice.* 2 vols. London 1884.

Moore, Aubrey Lackington, *Science and the Faith. Essays on apologetic subjects, with an introduction.* London 1889.

Newman, John Henry, *Apologia Pro Vita Sua.* French edn. 1866 (British Museum).

Official Year Book of the Church of England, The. London 1942, 1949.

Pusey, Edward Bouverie, *What is of Faith as to Everlasting Punishment? In Reply to Dr Farrar's Challenge in his "Eternal Hope".* Oxford 1880.

Roscoe, E. S., *The Bishop of Lincoln's Case.* London 1889, 1891.

Royal Commission on Ecclesiastical Discipline, Report of. 1906.

Shaftesbury, Earl of, *Addresses of the Earl of Shaftesbury and the hon. W. F. Cowper, delivered in St George's Hall, Liverpool; on Tuesday October the 12th, 1858* ... Liverpool 1858.

Smethurst, A. F., Wilson, H. R., and Riley, H., *Acts of the Convocation of Canterbury and York.* Enlarged edn. London 1961.

Smith, Nowell C., *The Letters of Sydney Smith.* 2 vols. London 1953.

Smith, Richard Mudie, *The Religious Life of London. Edited by R. Mudie Smith.* London 1904.

Society for the Propagation of the Gospel (Archives).

Statutes at Large.

Tracts for the Times. Oxford 1833–41.

Theology. November 1939. London.

Towards the Conversion of England. London 1945.

Venn, Henry, *The Native Pastorate and Organization of Native Churches. First Paper. Minute upon the Employment and Ordination of Native Teachers, C.M.S.* London 1851.

Yorkshire Post. December 1936.

Young, G. M. and Handcock, W. D., *English Historical Documents, 1833–1874.* vol. xii (1). London 1956.

INDEX OF NAMES

INDEX OF SUBJECTS